C++ Programmer's Guide

VERSION 5.0

Borland®
C++

Borland International, Inc., 100 Borland Way
P.O. Box 660001, Scotts Valley, CA 95067-0001

1E0R0196   WBC1350WW21771
9697989900-9 8 7 6 5 4 3 2 1
D2
ISBN 0-672-30923-8

Contents

Chapter 3
C++ specifics   105

Chapter 39
Turning an application into an OLE automation server   563

Chapter 40
Turning an application into an OLE automation controller   585

Introduction

Borland C++ is a powerful, professional programming tool for creating and maintaining DOS, Win16, and Win32 applications. Borland C++ supports both the C and C++ langugages with its integrated development environment and command-line tools.

How this book is organized

This book is divided into the following parts:

- **Part I, "Programming with Borland C++"** describes the implementation and extensions to the C and C++ programming languages. It provides you with programming information on C++ streams, container classes, persistent streams, inline assembly, and ANSI implementation details.

- **Part II, "Borland C++ DOS programmer's guide,"** provides information you might need to develop 16-bit applications that are targeted to run under DOS.

- **Part III, "Borland C++ class libraries guide,"** is a programmer's guide to using Borland's implementation of container classes, iostreams classes, persistent streams classes, and mathematical classes.

- **Part IV, "Standard class libraries guide,"** documents the Rogue Wave Software, Inc., implementation of the Standard C++ Library.

- **Part V, "ObjectComponents programmer's guide,"** describes how to create different kinds of programs using ObjectComponents, a set of classes for creating OLE 2 applications in C++.

- **Part VI, "Visual Database Tools developer's guide,"** explains how to use Visual Database Tools to build database applications using C++.

- **Part VII, "Borland Windows Custom Controls guide,"** explains how to use the Borland custom dialog class to change the appearance of your dialog window depending on the target display device. It also presents design considerations for custom dialog boxes.

- **Appendix A, "What is OLE?,"** discusses support for OLE in Borland C++.

Typefaces and icons used in this book

This book uses the following special fonts:

Monospace	This type represents text that you type or text as it appears onscreen.
Italics	These are used to emphasize and introduce words, and to indicate variable names (identifiers), function names, class names, and structure names.
Bold	This type indicates reserved keywords words, format specifiers, and command-line options.
Keycap	This type represents a particular key you should press on your keyboard. For example, "Press *Del* to erase the character."
Key1+Key2	This indicates a command that requires you to press *Key1* with *Key2*. For example, *Shift+a* (although not a command) indicates the uppercase letter "A."
ALL CAPS	This type represents disk directories, file names, and application names. (However, header file names are presented in lowercase to be consistent with how these files are usually written in source code.)
Menu | Choice	This represents menu commands. Rather than use the phrase "choose the Save command from the File menu," Borland manuals use the convention "choose File | Save."
Note	This icon indicates material that you should take special notice of.

Programming with Borland C++

Part I contains materials for the advanced programmer. If you already know how to program well (whether in C, C++, or another language), this manual is for you. It describes the implementation and extensions to the C and C++ programming languages. It is a language reference, and provides you with programming information on C++ streams, container classes, persistent streams, inline assembly, and ANSI implementation details.

How this part is organized

Chapters 1–5 describe the C and C++ languages as implemented in Borland C++. Together they provide a formal language definition, reference, and syntax for both the C++ and C aspects of Borland C++. These chapters do not provide a language tutorial. We use a modified Backus-Naur form notation to indicate syntax, supplemented where necessary by brief explanations and program examples. The chapters are organized in this manner:

- **Chapter 1, "Lexical elements,"** shows how the lexical tokens for Borland C++ are categorized. It covers the different categories of word-like units, known as *tokens*, recognized by a language.

- **Chapter 2, "Language structure,"** explains how to use the elements of Borland C++. It details the legal ways in which tokens can be grouped together to form expressions, statements, and other significant units.

- **Chapter 3, "C++ specifics,"** covers those aspects specific to C++.

- **Chapter 4, "Exception handling,"** describes the exception-handling mechanisms available to C and C++ programs.

- **Chapter 5, "Programming for portability,"** explains the basics of programming under Windows. See Part II, "Borland C++ DOS guide" for information on DOS programming.

- **Chapter 6, "Using dynamic-link libraries,"** explains dynamic-link libraries and dynamic linking.

- **Chapter 7, "Using inline assembly,"** explains how to embed assembly language instructions within your C/C++ code.

- **Chapter 8, "Header files summary,"** explains how to use precompiled headers to greatly speed up compilation times.

- **Chapter 9, "Using EasyWin,"** explains how to compile standard DOS applications that use traditional "TTY style" input and output so they run as Windows programs.

- **Chapter 10, "Math,"** covers floating-point issues. Much of the information regarding math operations is specific to DOS applications.

- **Chapter 11, "16-bit memory management,"** explains what memory models are, how to choose one, and why you would (or wouldn't) want to use a particular memory model.

- **Chapter 12, "ANSI implementation-specific standards,"** describes those aspects of the ANSI C standard that have been left loosely defined or undefined by ANSI. This chapter tells how Borland C++ operates in respect to each of these aspects.

Borland C++ is a full implementation of AT&T's C++ version 3.0, the object-oriented superset of C developed by Bjarne Stroustrup of AT&T Bell Laboratories. This manual refers to AT&T's previous version as C++ 2.1. In addition to offering many new features and capabilities, C++ often veers from C in varying degrees. These differences are noted. All Borland C++ language features derived from C++ are discussed in Chapter 3.

Borland C++ also fully implements the ANSI C standard, with several extensions as indicated in the text. You can set options in the compiler to warn you if any such extensions are encountered. You can also set the compiler to treat the Borland C++ extension keywords as normal identifiers (see Chapter 3 of the *C++ User's Guide*).

There are also "conforming" extensions provided via the **#pragma** directives offered by ANSI C for handling nonstandard, implementation-dependent features.

1

Lexical elements

These topics provide a formal definition of the Borland C++ lexical elements. They describe the different categories of word-like units (*tokens*) recognized by a language.

The tokens in Borland C++ are derived from a series of operations performed on your programs by the compiler and its built-in preprocessor.

A Borland C++ program starts as a sequence of ASCII characters representing the source code, created by keystrokes using a suitable text editor (such as the Borland C++ editor). The basic program unit in Borland C++ is the file. This usually corresponds to a named file located in RAM or on disk and having the extension .C or .CPP.

The preprocessor first scans the program text for special preprocessor *directives*. For example, the directive **#include** *<inc_file>* adds (or *includes*) the contents of the file *inc_file* to the program before the compilation phase. The preprocessor also expands any macros found in the program and include files.

In the tokenizing phase of compilation, the source code file is *parsed* (that is, broken down) into tokens and whitespace.

Whitespace

the collective name given to spaces (blanks), horizontal and vertical tabs, newline characters, and comments. Whitespace can serve to indicate where tokens start and end, but beyond this function, any surplus whitespace is discarded. For example, the two sequences

```
int i; float f;
```

and

```
int i;
    float f;
```

are lexically equivalent and parse identically to give the six tokens:

- **int**
- *i*
- ;
- **float**
- **f**
- ;

The ASCII characters representing whitespace can occur within *literal strings*, in which case they are protected from the normal parsing process (they remain as part of the string). For example,

```
char name[] = "Borland International";
```

parses to seven tokens, including the single literal-string token "Borland International."

Line splicing with \

A special case occurs if the final newline character encountered is preceded by a backslash (\). The backslash and new line are both discarded, allowing two physical lines of text to be treated as one unit.

```
"Borland\
International"
```

is parsed as "Borland International" (see "String constants" later in this chapter for more information).

Comments

Comments are pieces of text used to annotate a program. Comments are for the programmer's use only; they are stripped from the source text before parsing.

There are two ways to delineate comments: the C method and the C++ method. Both are supported by Borland C++, with an additional, optional extension permitting nested comments. If you are not compiling for ANSI compatibility, you can use any of these kinds of comments in both C and C++ programs.

You should also follow the guidelines on the use of whitespace and delimiters in comments discussed later in this topic to avoid other portability problems.

C comments

A C comment is any sequence of characters placed after the symbol pair /*. The comment terminates at the first occurrence of the pair */ following the initial /*. The entire sequence, including the four comment-delimiter symbols, is replaced by one space *after* macro expansion. Note that some C implementations remove comments without space replacements.

Borland C++ does not support the nonportable *token pasting* strategy using /**/. Token pasting in Borland C++ is performed with the ANSI-specified pair ##, as follows:

```
#define VAR(i,j)   (i/**/j)    /* won't work */
#define VAR(i,j)   (i##j)      /* OK in Borland C++ */
#define VAR(i,j)   (i ## j)    /* Also OK */
```

In Borland C++,

```
int /* declaration */ i /* counter */;
```

parses as these three tokens:

```
int   i;
```

See "Token Pasting with ##" in the online Help for a description of *token pasting*.

C++ comments

C++ allows a single-line comment using two adjacent slashes (//). The comment can start in any position, and extends until the next new line:

```
class X {  // this is a comment
... };
```

You can also use // to create comments in C code. This is specific to Borland C++.

Nested comments

ANSI C doesn't allow nested comments. The attempt to comment out a line

```
/*  int /* declaration */ i /* counter */; */
```

fails, because the scope of the first /* ends at the first */. This gives

```
i ; */
```

which would generate a syntax error.

By default, Borland C++ won't allow nested comments, but you can override this with compiler options. See the C++ *User's Guide*, Chapter 3 for information on enabling nested comments.

Delimiters and whitespace

In rare cases, some whitespace before /* and //, and after */, although not syntactically mandatory, can avoid portability problems. For example, this C++ code:

```
int i = j//* divide by k*/k;
+m;
```

parses as int i = j +m, not as

```
int i = j/k;
+m;
```

as expected under the C convention. The more legible

```
int i = j/ /* divide by k*/ k;
+m;
```

avoids this problem.

Tokens

Tokens are word-like units recognized by a language. Borland C++ recognizes six classes of tokens.

Here is the formal definition of a token:

keyword

identifier

constant

string-literal

operator

punctuator (also known as separators)

As the source code is scanned, tokens are extracted in such a way that the longest possible token from the character sequence is selected. For example, *external* would be parsed as a single identifier, rather than as the keyword **extern** followed by the identifier *al*.

See "Token Pasting with ##" in the online Help for a description of *token pasting*.

Keywords

Keywords are words reserved for special purposes and must not be used as normal identifier names.

You can use options to select ANSI keywords only, UNIX keywords, and so on; see the *C++ User's Guide*, Chapter 3, for information on these options.

If you use non-ANSI keywords in a program and you want the program to be ANSI-compliant, always use the non-ANSI keyword versions that are prefixed with double underscores. Some keywords have a version prefixed with only one underscore; these keywords are provided to facilitate porting code developed with other compilers. For ANSI-specified keywords there is only one version.

Note Note that the keywords _ _**try** and **try** are an exception to the discussion above. The keyword **try** is required to match the **catch** keyword in the C++ exception-handling mechanism. **try** cannot be substituted by _ _**try.** The keyword _ _**try** can only be used to match the _ _**except** or _ _**finally** keywords. See the discussions on C++ exception handling and C-based structured exceptions for more information.

Table of C++-specific keywords

There are several keywords specific to C++. They are not available if you are writing a C-only program.

Table 1.1 All Borland C++ keywords

asm	mutable	this
bool	namespace	throw
catch	new	true
class	operator	try
const_cast	private	typeid
delete	protected	typename
dynamic_cast	public	using
explicit	reinterpret_cast	virtual
false	__rtti	wchar_t
friend	static_cast	
inline	template	

Table 1.2 Table of Borland C++ register pseudovariables

_AH	_CL	_EAX	_ESP
_AL	_CS	_EBP	_FLAGS
_AX	_CX	_EBX	_FS
_BH	_DH	_ECX	_GS
_BL	_DI	_EDI	_SI
_BP	_DL	_EDX	_SP
_BX	_DS	_ES	_SS
_CH	_DX	_ESI	

These pesudovariables are always available to the 32-bit compiler. The 16-bit compiler can use these only whe you use the option to generate 80386 instructions.

Borland C++ keyword extensions

Borland C++ provides additional keywords that are not part of the ANSI or UNIX conventions. You cannot use these keywords in your programs if you set the IDE or command-line options to recognize only ANSI or UNIX keywords.

Table 1.3 Borland C++ keyword extensions

_asm	__except	_interrupt	__rtti
__asm	_export	interrupt	__saveregs
_cdecl	far	_loadds	_saveregs
cdecl	_far	__loadds	__seg
_cs	__huge	near	_seg
__declspec	_huge	__near	_ss
__ds	huge	_near	__thread
_ds	_import	_pascal	__try
__es	__import	__pascal	
_es	__interrupt	pascal	

Identifiers

Here is the formal definition of an identifier:

identifier:

   nondigit

   identifier nondigit

   identifier digit

nondigit: one of

   a b c d e f g h i j k l m n o p q r s t u v w x y z _

   A B C D E F G H I J K L M N O P Q R S T U V W X Y Z

digit: one of

   0 1 2 3 4 5 6 7 8 9

Naming and length restrictions

Identifiers are arbitrary names of any length given to classes, objects, functions, variables, user-defined data types, and so on. (Identifiers can contain the letters *a* to *z* and *A* to *Z*, the underscore character (_), and the digits 0 to 9.) There are only two restrictions:

- The first character must be a letter or an underscore.

- By default, Borland C++ recognizes only the first 32 characters as significant. The number of significant characters can be *reduced* by menu and command-line options, but not increased. See Chapter 3 of the *C++ User's Guide* for information on these options.

Case sensitivity

Borland C++ identifiers are case sensitive, so that *Sum*, *sum*, and *suM* are distinct identifiers.

Global identifiers imported from other modules follow the same naming and significance rules as normal identifiers. However, Borland C++ offers the option of suspending case sensitivity to allow compatibility when linking with case-insensitive languages. With the case-insensitive option, the globals *Sum* and *sum* are considered identical, resulting in a possible `"Duplicate symbol"` warning during linking.

An exception to these rules is that identifiers of type **_ _pascal** are always converted to all uppercase for linking purposes.

Uniqueness and scope

Although identifier names are arbitrary (within the rules stated), errors result if the same name is used for more than one identifier within the same *scope* and sharing the same *name space*. Duplicate names are legal for *different* name spaces regardless of scope rules.

Constants

Constants are tokens representing fixed numeric or character values.

Borland C++ supports four classes of constants: integer, floating point, character (including strings), and enumeration.

Internal representation of numerical types shows how these types are represented internally.

The data type of a constant is deduced by the compiler using such clues as numeric value and the format used in the source code. The formal definition of a constant is shown in the following table.

Table 1.4   Constants: formal definitions

constant
  floating-constant:
  integer-constant
  numeration-constant
  character-constant

floating-constant:
  fractional-constant <exponent-part> <floating-suffix>
  digit-sequence exponent-part <floating-suffix>

fractional-constant:
  <digit-sequence> . digit-sequence
  digit-sequence .

exponent-part:
  e *<sign> digit-sequence*
  E *<sign> digit-sequence*

sign: one of
  + -

digit-sequence:
  digit
  digit-sequence digit

floating-suffix: one of
  f l F L

integer-constant:
  decimal-constant <integer-suffix>
  octal-constant <integer-suffix>
  hexadecimal-constant <integer-suffix>

decimal-constant:
  nonzero-digit
  decimal-constant digit

octal-constant:
  0 |
  octal-constant octal-digit

hexadecimal-constant:
  0 x *hexadecimal-digit*
  0 X *hexadecimal-digit*
  hexadecimal-constant hexadecimal-digit

nonzero-digit: one of
  1 2 3 4 5 6 7 8 9

octal-digit:
one of 0 1 2 3 4 5 6 7

hexadecimal-digit: one of
0 1 2 3 4 5 6 7 8 9
a b c d e f
A B C D E F

integer-suffix:
unsigned-suffix <long-suffix>
long-suffix <unsigned-suffix>

unsigned-suffix: one of
u U

long-suffix: one of
l L

enumeration-constant:
identifier

character-constant:
  c-char-sequence

c-char-sequence:
  c-char
  c-char-sequence c-char

c-char:
Any character in the source character set except the single-quote ('), backslash (\), or newline character *escape-sequence.*

escape-sequence: one of the following
\"   \'   \?   \\
\a   \b   \f   \n
\o   \oo   \ooo \r
\t   \v   \Xh... \xh..

Integer constants

Integer constants can be decimal (base 10), octal (base 8), or hexadecimal (base 16). In the absence of any overriding suffixes, the data type of an integer constant is derived from its value, as shown in Borland C++ integer constants without L or U. Note that the rules vary between decimal and nondecimal constants.

Decimal

Decimal constants from 0 to 4,294,967,295 are allowed. Constants exceeding this limit are truncated. Decimal constants must not use an initial zero. An integer constant that has an initial zero is interpreted as an octal constant. Thus,

```
int i = 10;   /*decimal 10 */
int i = 010;  /*decimal 8 */
int i = 0;    /*decimal 0 = octal 0 */
```

Octal

All constants with an initial zero are taken to be octal. If an octal constant contains the illegal digits 8 or 9, an error is reported. Octal constants exceeding 037777777777 are truncated.

Hexadecimal

All constants starting with 0x (or 0X) are taken to be hexadecimal. Hexadecimal constants exceeding 0xFFFFFFFF are truncated.

long and unsigned suffixes

The suffix *L* (or *l*) attached to any constant forces the constant to be represented as a **long**. Similarly, the suffix *U* (or *u*) forces the constant to be **unsigned**. It is **unsigned long** if the value of the number itself is greater than decimal 65,535, regardless of which base is used. You can use both *L* and *U* suffixes on the same constant in any order or case: *ul, lu, UL*, and so on. See the table of Borland constants.

The data type of a constant in the absence of any suffix (*U, u, L,* or *l*) is the first of the following types that can accommodate its value:

Decimal	**int, long int, unsigned long int**
Octal	**int, unsigned int, long int, unsigned long int**
Hexadecimal	**int, unsigned int, long int, unsigned long int**

If the constant has a *U* or *u* suffix, its data type will be the first of **unsigned int, unsigned long int** that can accommodate its value.

If the constant has an *L* or *l* suffix, its data type will be the first of **long int, unsigned long int** that can accommodate its value.

If the constant has both u and l suffixes (*ul, lu, Ul, lU, uL, Lu, LU, or UL*), its data type will be **unsigned long int**.

Borland C++ integer constants without *L* or *U* summarizes the representations of integer constants in all three bases. The data types indicated assume no overriding *L* or *U* suffix has been used.

Table 1.5   Borland C++ integer constants without L or U

Decimal constants			
0	to	32,767	int
32,768	to	2,147,483,647	long
2,147,483,648	to	4,294,967,295	unsigned long
		> 4294967295	truncated
Octal constants			
00	to	077777	int
010000	to	0177777	unsigned int
02000000	to	017777777777	long
020000000000	to	037777777777	unsigned long
		> 037777777777	truncated
Hexadecimal constants			
0x0000	to	0x7FFF	int
0x8000	to	0xFFFF	unsigned int
0x10000	to	0x7FFFFFFF	long
0x80000000	to	0xFFFFFFFF	unsigned long
		>0xFFFFFFFF	truncated

Floating-point constants

A floating-point constant consists of:

- Decimal integer

- Decimal point

- Decimal fraction

- *e* or *E* and a signed integer exponent (optional)

- Type suffix: *f* or *F* or *l* or *L* (optional)

You can omit either the decimal integer or the decimal fraction (but not both). You can omit either the decimal point or the letter *e* (or *E*) and the signed integer exponent (but not both). These rules allow for conventional and scientific (exponent) notations.

Negative floating constants are taken as positive constants with the unary operator minus (-) prefixed.

Here are some examples:

Constant	Value
23.45e6	23.45×106
.0	0
0.	0
1.	$1.0 \times 100 = 1.0$
-1.23	-1.23
2e-5	$2.0 \times 10\text{-}5$
3E+10	3.0×1010
.09E34	0.09×1034

In the absence of any suffixes, floating-point constants are of type **double**. However, you can coerce a floating constant to be of type **float** by adding an *f* or *F* suffix to the constant. Similarly, the suffix *l* or *L* forces the constant to be data type **long double**. The table below shows the ranges available for **float**, **double**, and **long double**.

Table 1.6 Borland C++ floating constant sizes and ranges

Type	Size (bits)	Range
float	32	3.4×10^{-38} to 3.4×10^{38}
double	64	1.7×10^{-308} to 1.7×10^{308}
long double	80	3.4×10^{-4932} to 1.1×10^{4932}

Character constants

A *character constant* is one or more characters enclosed in single quotes, such as `'A'`, `'+'`, or `'\n'`. In C, single-charactrer constants have data type **int**. The number of bits used to internally represent a character constant is **sizeof(int)**. In a 16-bit program, the upper byte is zero or sign-extended. In C++, a character constant has type **char**. Multicharacter constants in both C and C++ have data type **int**.

To learn more about character constants, see

- "Three char types" later in this chapter

- "Escape sequences" later in this chapter

- "Wide-character and multi-character constants" later in this chapter

Note To compare sizes of character types, compile this as a C program and then as a C++ program.

```
#include <stdio.h>
#define CH 'x'          /* A CHARACTER CONSTANT */
void main(void) {
    char ch = 'x';      /* A char VARIABLE       */
    printf("\nSizeof int    = %d", sizeof(int) );
    printf("\nSizeof char   = %d", sizeof(char) );
    printf("\nSizeof ch     = %d", sizeof(ch) );
    printf("\nSizeof CH     = %d", sizeof(CH) );
```

```
    printf("\nSizeof wchar_t = %d", sizeof(wchar_t) );
}
```

Note   Sizes are in bytes.

Table 1.7   Sizes of character types

Output when compiled as C program			Output when compiled as C++ program		
	16-bit	**32-bit**		**16-bit**	**32-bit**
Sizeof int =	2	4	Sizeof int =	2	4
Sizeof char =	1	1	Sizeof char =	1	1
Sizeof ch =	1	1	Sizeof ch =	1	1
Sizeof CH =	2	4	Sizeof CH =	1	1
Sizeof wchar_t =	2	2	Sizeof wchar_t =	2	2

The three char types

One-character constants, such as 'A', '\t', and '007', are represented as **int** values. In this case, the low-order byte is *sign extended* into the high bit; that is, if the value is greater than 127 (base 10), the upper bit is set to -1 (=0xFF). This can be disabled by declaring that the default **char** type is **unsigned**, which forces the high bit to be zero regardless of the value of the low bit. See Chapter 3 of the *C++ User's Guide* for information on these options.

The three character types, **char**, **signed char**, and **unsigned char,** require an 8-bit (one byte) storage. In C and Borland C++ programs prior to version Borland C++ 4.0 , **char** is treated the same as **signed char**. The behavior of C programs is unaffected by the distinction between the three character types.

Note   To retain the old behavior, use the **-K2** command-line option and Borland C++ 3.1 header files and libraries.

In a C++ program, a function can be overloaded with arguments of type **char**, **signed char**, or **unsigned char**. For example, the following function prototypes are valid and distinct:

```
void func(char ch);
void func(signed char ch);
void func(unsigned char ch);
```

If only one of the above prototypes exists, it will accept any of the three character types. For example, the following is acceptable:

```
void func(unsigned char ch);
void main(void) {
  signed char ch = 'x';
  func(ch);
  }
```

See Chapter 3 of the *C++ User's Guide* for a description of code-generation options.

Escape sequences

The backslash character (\) is used to introduce an *escape sequence*, which allows the visual representation of certain nongraphic characters. For example, the constant **\n** is used to the single newline character.

A backslash is used with octal or hexadecimal numbers to represent the ASCII symbol or control code corresponding to that value; for example, '\03' for *Ctrl-C* or '\x3F' for the question mark. You can use any string of up to three octal or any number of hexadecimal numbers in an escape sequence, provided that the value is within legal range for data type **char** (0 to 0xff for Borland C++). Larger numbers generate the compiler error Numeric constant too large. For example, the octal number \777 is larger than the maximum value allowed (\377) and will generate an error. The first nonoctal or nonhexadecimal character encountered in an octal or hexadecimal escape sequence marks the end of the sequence.

Originally, Turbo C allowed only three digits in a hexadecimal escape sequence. The ANSI C rules adopted in Borland C++ might cause problems with old code that assumes only the first three characters are converted. For example, using Turbo C 1.

```
printf("\x0072.1A Simple Operating System");
```

This is intended to be interpreted as \x007 and "2.1A Simple Operating System". However, Borland C++ compiles it as the hexadecimal number \x0072 and the literal string "1A Simple Operating System".

To avoid such problems, rewrite your code like this:

```
printf("\x007" "2.1A Simple Operating System");
```

Ambiguities might also arise if an octal escape sequence is followed by a nonoctal digit. For example, because 8 and 9 are not legal octal digits, the constant \258 would be interpreted as a two-character constant made up of the characters \25 and 8.

The following table shows the available escape sequences.

Note   You must use \\ to represent an ASCII backslash, as used in operating system paths.

Table 1.8   Borland C++ escape sequences

Sequence	Value	Char	What it does
\a	0x07	BEL	Audible bell
\b	0x08	BS	Backspace
\f	0x0C	FF	Formfeed
\n	0x0A	LF	Newline (linefeed)
\r	0x0D	CR	Carriage return
\t	0x09	HT	Tab (horizontal)
\v	0x0B	VT	Vertical tab
\\	0x5c	\	Backslash
\'	0x27	'	Single quote (apostrophe)
\"	0x22	"	Double quote
\?	0x3F	?	Question mark
\O		any	O=a string of up to three octal digits

Table 1.8   Borland C++ escape sequences

Sequence	Value	Char	What it does
\xH		any	H=a string of hex digits
\XH		any	H=a string of hex digits

Wide-character and multi-character constants

Wide-character types can be used to represent a character that does not fit into the storage space allocated for a **char** type. A wide character is stored in a two-byte space. A character constant preceded immediately by an *L* is a wide-character constant of data type *wchar_t* (defined in stddef.h). For example:

```
wchar_t ch = L'AB';
```

When *wchar_t* is used in a C program it is a type defined in the stddef.h header file. In a C++ program, **wchar_t** is a keyword that can represent distinct codes for any element of the largest extended character set in any of the supported locales. In C++, **wchar_t** is the same size, signedness, and alignment requirement as an **int** type.

A string preceded immediately by an *L* is a wide-character string. The memory allocation for a string is two bytes per character. For example:

```
wchar_t str = L"ABCD";
```

Multi-character constants

Borland C++ also supports multi-character constants. When using the 32-bit compiler, multi-character constants can consist of as many as four characters. The 16-bit compiler is restricted to two-character constants. For example, 'An', '\n\t', and '\007\007' are acceptable in a 16-bit program. The constant, '\006\007\008\009' is valid only in a 32-bit program. When using the 16-bit compiler, these constants are represented as 16-bit **int** values with the first character in the low-order byte and the second character in the high-order byte. For 32-bit compilers, multi-character constants are always 32-bit **int** values. The constants are not portable to other C compilers.

String constants

String constants, also known as string literals, form a special category of constants used to handle fixed sequences of characters. A string literal is of data type array-of-**char** and storage class **static**, written as a sequence of any number of characters surrounded by double quotes:

```
"This is literally a string!"
```

The null (empty) string is written " ".

The characters inside the double quotes can include escape sequences. This code, for example:

```
"\t\t\"Name\"\\\tAddress\n\n"
```

prints like this:

```
        "Name"\        Address
```

"Name" is preceded by two tabs; Address is preceded by one tab. The line is followed by two new lines. The \" provides interior double quotes.

If you compile with the **-A** option for ANSI compatibility, the escape character sequence "\\" is translated to "\" by the compiler.

A literal string is stored internally as the given sequence of characters plus a final null character ('\0'). A null string is stored as a single '\0' character.

Adjacent string literals separated only by whitespace are concatenated during the parsing phase, as in the following example:

```
#include <stdio.h>
int main() {
   char    *p;
   _InitEasyWin();
   p = "This is an example of how Borland C++"
   " will\nconcatenate very long strings for you"
  " automatically, \nresulting in nicer"
   " looking programs.";
   printf(p);
   return(0);
}
```

The output of the program is

```
This is an example of how Borland C++ will
concatenate very long strings for you automatically,
resulting in nicer looking programs.
```

You can also use the backslash (\) as a continuation character to extend a string constant across line boundaries:

```
puts("This is really \
a one-line string");
```

Enumeration constants

Enumeration constants are identifiers defined in **enum** type declarations. The identifiers are usually chosen as mnemonics to assist legibility. Enumeration constants are integer data types. They can be used in any expression where integer constants are valid. The identifiers used must be unique within the scope of the **enum** declaration. Negative initializers are allowed. See the *C++ Language Reference* for a detailed look at **enum** declarations.

The values acquired by enumeration constants depend on the format of the enumeration declaration and the presence of optional *initializers*. In this example,

```
enum team { giants, cubs, dodgers };
```

giants, *cubs*, and *dodgers* are enumeration constants of type *team* that can be assigned to any variables of type *team* or to any other variable of integer type. The values acquired by the enumeration constants are

```
giants = 0, cubs = 1, dodgers = 2
```

in the absence of explicit initializers. In the following example,

```
enum team { giants, cubs=3, dodgers = giants + 1 };
```

the constants are set as follows:

```
giants = 0, cubs = 3, dodgers = 1
```

The constant values need not be unique:

```
enum team { giants, cubs = 1, dodgers = cubs - 1 };
```

Constants and internal representation

ANSI C acknowledges that the size and numeric range of the basic data types (and their various permutations) are implementation-specific and usually derive from the architecture of the host computer. For Borland C++, the target platform is the IBM PC family (and compatibles), so the architecture of the Intel 8088 and 80x86 microprocessors governs the choices of internal representations for the various data types.

The following tables list the sizes and resulting ranges of the data types for Borland C++. Internal representation of numerical types shows how these types are represented internally.

Table 1.9   16-bit data types, sizes, and ranges

Type	Size (bits)	Range	Sample applications
unsigned char	8	0 to 255	Small numbers and full PC character set
char	8	−128 to 127	Very small numbers and ASCII characters
enum	16	−32,768 to 32,767	Ordered sets of values
unsigned int	16	0 to 65,535	Larger numbers and loops
short int	16	−32,768 to 32,767	Counting, small numbers, loop control
int	16	−32,768 to 32,767	Counting, small numbers, loop control
unsigned long	32	0 to 4,294,967,295	Astronomical distances
long	32	−2,147,483,648 to 2,147,483,647	Large numbers, populations
float	32	3.4×10^{-38} to 3.4×10^{38}	Scientific (7-digit precision)
double	64	1.7×10^{-308} to 1.7×10^{308}	Scientific (15-digit precision)
long double	80	3.4×10^{-4932} to 1.1×10^{4932}	Financial (18-digit precision)
near pointer	16	Not applicable	Manipulating memory addresses
far pointer	32	Not applicable	Manipulating addresses outside current segment

Table 1.10   32-bit data types, sizes, and ranges

Type	Size (bits)	Range	Sample applications
unsigned char	8	0 to 255	Small numbers and full PC character set
char	8	−128 to 127	Very small numbers and ASCII characters
short int	16	−32,768 to 32,767	Counting, small numbers, loop control
unsigned int	32	0 to 4,294,967,295	Large numbers and loops
int	32	−2,147,483,648 to 2,147,483,647	Counting, small numbers, loop control
unsigned long	32	0 to 4,294,967,295	Astronomical distances

Table 1.10   32-bit data types, sizes, and ranges (continued)

Type	Size (bits)	Range	Sample applications
enum	32	−2,147,483,648 to 2,147,483,647	Ordered sets of values
long	32	−2,147,483,648 to 2,147,483,647	Large numbers, populations
float	32	3.4×10^{-38} to 1.7×10^{38}	Scientific (7-digit precision)
double	64	1.7×10^{-308} to 3.4×10^{308}	Scientific (15-digit precision)
long double	80	3.4×10^{-4932} to 1.1×10^{4932}	Financial (18-digit precision)

Figure 1.1   Internal representations of numerical types

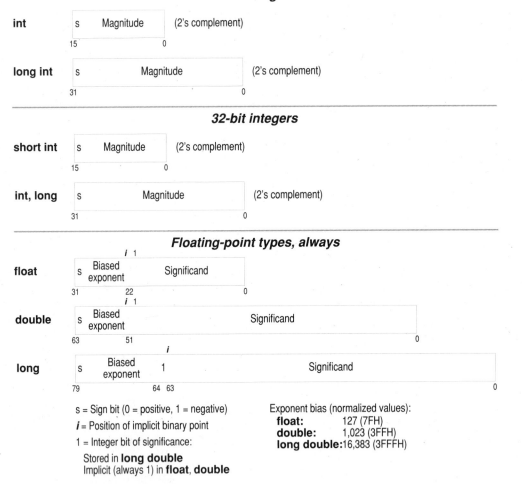

Constant expressions

A constant expression is an expression that always evaluates to a constant (and it must evaluate to a constant that is in the range of representable values for its type). Constant expressions are evaluated just as regular expressions are. You can use a constant expression anywhere that a constant is legal. The syntax for constant expressions is:

constant-expression:

    Conditional-expression

Constant expressions cannot contain any of the following operators, unless the operators are contained within the operand of a **sizeof** operator:

- Assignment
- Comma
- Decrement
- Function call
- Increment

Punctuators

The punctuators (also known as separators) in Borland C++ are defined as follows:

punctuator: one of

```
[ ]  ( )  { }  ,  ;  :  ...  *  =  #
```

Brackets

Open and close brackets [ ] indicate single and multidimensional array subscripts:

```
char ch, str[] = "Stan";
int mat[3][4];              /* 3 x 4 matrix */
ch = str[3];                /* 4th element */
    ⋮
```

Parentheses

Open and close parentheses ( ) are used to group expressions, isolate conditional expressions, and indicate function calls and function parameters:

```
d = c * (a + b);      /* override normal precedence */

if (d == z) ++x;      /* essential with conditional statement */

func();               /* function call, no args */
int (*fptr)();        /* function pointer declaration */
fptr = func;          /* no () means func pointer */

void func2(int n);    /* function declaration with parameters */
```

Parentheses are recommended in macro definitions to avoid potential precedence problems during expansion:

```
#define CUBE(x) ((x) * (x) * (x))
```

The use of parentheses to alter the normal operator precedence and associativity rules is covered in "Expressions" in the online Help.

Braces

Open and close braces { } indicate the start and end of a compound statement:

```
if (d == z)
{
   ++x;
   func();
}
```

The closing brace serves as a terminator for the compound statement, so a ; (semicolon) is not required after the }, except in structure or class declarations. Often, the semicolon is illegal, as in

```
if (statement)
   {};                      /*illegal semicolon*/
else
```

Comma

The comma (,) separates the elements of a function argument list:

```
void func(int n, float f, char ch);
```

The comma is also used as an operator in *comma expressions*. Mixing the two uses of comma is legal, but you must use parentheses to distinguish them:

```
func(i, j);                               /* call func with two args */
func((exp1, exp2), (exp3, exp4, exp5));  /* also calls func with two args! */
```

Semicolon

The semicolon (;) is a statement terminator. Any legal C or C++ expression (including the empty expression) followed by a semicolon is interpreted as a statement, known as an *expression statement*. The expression is evaluated and its value is discarded. If the expression statement has no side effects, Borland C++ might ignore it.

```
a + b;     /* maybe evaluate a + b, but discard value */
++a;       /* side effect on a, but discard value of ++a */
;          /* empty expression = null statement */
```

Semicolons are often used to create an *empty statement:*

```
for (i = 0; i < n; i++)
{
   ;
}
```

Colon

Use the colon (:) to indicate a labeled statement:

```
start:    x=0;
   ⋮
goto start;
```

Labels are discussed in "Labeled statements" in the online Help.

Ellipsis

The ellipsis (...) is three successive periods with no intervening whitespace. Ellipses are used in the formal argument lists of function prototypes to indicate a variable number of arguments, or arguments with varying types:

```
void func(int n, char ch,...);
```

This declaration indicates that *func* will be defined in such a way that calls must have at least two arguments, an **int** and a **char**, but can also have any number of additional arguments.

In C++, you can omit the comma before the ellipsis.

Asterisk (pointer declaration)

The asterisk (*) in a variable declaration denotes the creation of a pointer to a type:

```
char *char_ptr;  /* a pointer to char is declared */
```

Pointers with multiple levels of indirection can be declared by indicating a pertinent number of asterisks:

```
int **int_ptr;           /* a pointer to an integer array */
double ***double_ptr;  /* a pointer to a matrix of doubles */
```

You can also use the asterisk as an operator to either dereference a pointer or as the multiplication operator:

```
i = *int_ptr;
a = b * 3.14;
```

Equal sign (initializer)

The equal sign (=) separates variable declarations from initialization lists:

```
char array[5] = { 1, 2, 3, 4, 5 };
int  x = 5;
```

In C++, declarations of any type can appear (with some restrictions) at any point within the code. In a C function, no code can precede any variable declarations.

In a C++ function argument list, the equal sign indicates the default value for a parameter:

```
int f(int i = 0) { ... }  /* Parameter i has default value of zero */
```

The equal sign is also used as the assignment operator in expressions:

```
int a, b, c;
a = b + c;
float *ptr = (float *) malloc(sizeof(float) * 100);
```

Pound sign (preprocessor directive)

The pound sign (#) indicates a preprocessor directive when it occurs as the first nonwhitespace character on a line. It signifies a compiler action, not necessarily associated with code generation. See "Preprocessor directives" in the online Help for more on the preprocessor directives.

and ## (double pound signs) are also used as operators to perform token replacement and merging during the preprocessor scanning phase.

2

Language structure

These topics provide a formal definition of Borland C++ language structure. They describe the legal ways in which tokens can be grouped together to form expressions, statements, and other significant units.

Declarations

This section briefly reviews concepts related to declarations: objects, storage classes, types, scope, visibility, duration, and linkage. A general knowledge of these is essential before tackling the full declaration syntax. Scope, visibility, duration, and linkage determine those portions of a program that can make legal references to an identifier in order to access its object.

Objects

An *object* is an identifiable region of memory that can hold a fixed or variable value (or set of values). (This use of the word *object* is different from the more general term used in object-oriented languages.) Each value has an associated name and type (also known as a *data type*). The name is used to access the object. This name can be a simple identifier, or it can be a complex expression that uniquely "points" to the object. The type is used

- To determine the correct memory allocation required initially.

- To interpret the bit patterns found in the object during subsequent accesses.

- In many type-checking situations, to ensure that illegal assignments are trapped.

Borland C++ supports many standard (predefined) and user-defined data types, including signed and unsigned integers in various sizes, floating-point numbers in various precisions, structures, unions, arrays, and classes. In addition, pointers to most of these objects can be established and manipulated in various memory models.

The Borland C++ standard libraries and your own program and header files must provide unambiguous identifiers (or expressions derived from them) and types so that Borland C++ can consistently access, interpret, and (possibly) change the bit patterns in memory corresponding to each active object in your program.

Objects and declarations

Declarations establish the necessary mapping between identifiers and objects. Each declaration associates an identifier with a data type. Most declarations, known as *defining declarations*, also establish the creation (where and when) of the object; that is, the allocation of physical memory and its possible initialization. Other declarations, known as *referencing declarations*, simply make their identifiers and types known to the compiler. There can be many referencing declarations for the same identifier, especially in a multifile program, but only one defining declaration for that identifier is allowed.

Generally speaking, an identifier cannot be legally used in a program before its *declaration point* in the source code. Legal exceptions to this rule (known as *forward references*) are labels, calls to undeclared functions, and class, struct, or union tags.

lvalues

An *lvalue* is an object locator: an expression that designates an object. An example of an lvalue expression is *P, where P is any expression evaluating to a non-null pointer. A *modifiable lvalue* is an identifier or expression that relates to an object that can be accessed and legally changed in memory. A **const** pointer to a constant, for example, is *not* a modifiable lvalue. A pointer to a constant can be changed (but its dereferenced value cannot).

Historically, the *l* stood for "left," meaning that an lvalue could legally stand on the left (the receiving end) of an assignment statement. Now only modifiable lvalues can legally stand to the left of an assignment statement. For example, if *a* and *b* are nonconstant integer identifiers with properly allocated memory storage, they are both modifiable lvalues, and assignments such as *a* = 1; and *b* = *a* + *b* are legal.

rvalues

The expression *a* + *b* is not an lvalue: *a* + *b* = *a* is illegal because the expression on the left is not related to an object. Such expressions are often called *rvalues* (short for right values).

Storage classes and types

Associating identifiers with objects requires each identifier to have at least two attributes: *storage class* and *type* (sometimes referred to as data type). The Borland C++ compiler deduces these attributes from implicit or explicit declarations in the source code.

Storage class dictates the location (data segment, register, heap, or stack) of the object and its duration or lifetime (the entire running time of the program, or during execution of some blocks of code). Storage class can be established by the syntax of the declaration, by its placement in the source code, or by both of these factors.

The type determines how much memory is allocated to an object and how the program will interpret the bit patterns found in the object's storage allocation. A given data type can be viewed as the set of values (often implementation-dependent) that identifiers of that type can assume, together with the set of operations allowed on those values. The compile-time operator, **sizeof**, lets you determine the size in bytes of any standard or user-defined type. See "The sizeof operator" later in this chapter for more on this operator.

Scope

The scope of an identifier is that part of the program in which the identifier can be used to access its object. There are five categories of scope: *block* (or *local*), *function*, *function prototype*, *file*, and *class* (C++ only). These depend on how and where identifiers are declared.

- **Block**. The scope of an identifier with block (or local) scope starts at the declaration point and ends at the end of the block containing the declaration (such a block is known as the *enclosing* block). Parameter declarations with a function definition also have block scope, limited to the scope of the block that defines the function.

- **Function**. The only identifiers having function scope are statement labels. Label names can be used with **goto** statements anywhere in the function in which the label is declared. Labels are declared implicitly by writing *label_name:* followed by a statement. Label names must be unique within a function.

- **Function prototype**. Identifiers declared within the list of parameter declarations in a function prototype (not part of a function definition) have function prototype scope. This scope ends at the end of the function prototype.

- **File**. File scope identifiers, also known as *globals*, are declared outside of all blocks and classes; their scope is from the point of declaration to the end of the source file.

- **Class** (C++). A class is a named collection of members, including data structures and functions that act on them. Class scope applies to the names of the members of a particular class. Classes and their objects have many special access and scoping rules.

- **Condition** (C++). Declarations in conditions are supported. Variables can be declared within the expression of **if**, **while**, and **switch** statements. The scope of the variable is that of the statement. In the case of an **if** statement, the variable is also in scope for the **else** block.

Name spaces

Name space is the scope within which an identifier must be unique. C uses four distinct classes of identifiers:

- **goto** label names. These must be unique within the function in which they are declared.

- Structure, union, and enumeration tags. These must be unique within the block in which they are defined. Tags declared outside of any function must be unique within all.

- Structure and union member names. These must be unique within the structure or union in which they are defined. There is no restriction on the type or offset of members with the same member name in different structures.

- Variables, **typedef**s, functions, and enumeration members. These must be unique within the scope in which they are defined. Externally declared identifiers must be unique among externally declared variables.

Note   Structures, classes, and enumerations are in the same name space in C++.

Visibility

The *visibility* of an identifier is that region of the program source code from which legal access can be made to the identifier's associated object.

Scope and visibility usually coincide, although there are circumstances under which an object becomes temporarily *hidden* by the appearance of a duplicate identifier: the object still exists but the original identifier cannot be used to access it until the scope of the duplicate identifier is ended.

Note   Visibility cannot exceed scope, but scope can exceed visibility.

```
  ⋮
  {
     int i; char ch;  // auto by default
     i = 3;           // int i and char ch in scope and visible
  ⋮
  {

        double i;
        i = 3.0e3;    // double i in scope and visible
                      // int i=3 in scope but hidden
        ch = 'A';     // char ch in scope and visible
     }
                      // double i out of scope
     i += 1;          // int i visible and = 4
  ⋮
  // char ch still in scope & visible = 'A'
  }
  ⋮
  // int i and char ch out of scope
```

Again, special rules apply to hidden class names and class member names: C++ operators allow hidden identifiers to be accessed under certain conditions.

Duration

Duration, closely related to storage class, defines the period during which the declared identifiers have real, physical objects allocated in memory. We also distinguish between compile-time and run-time objects. Variables, for instance, unlike **typedef**s and types, have real memory allocated during run time. There are three kinds of duration: *static*, *local*, and *dynamic*.

Static

Memory is allocated to objects with *static* duration as soon as execution is underway; this storage allocation lasts until the program terminates. Static duration objects usually reside in fixed data segments allocated according to the memory model in force. All functions, wherever defined, are objects with static duration. All variables with file scope have static duration. Other variables can be given static duration by using the explicit **static** or **extern** storage class specifiers.

Static duration objects are initialized to zero (or null) in the absence of any explicit initializer or, in C++, constructor.

Don't confuse static duration with file or global scope. An object can have static duration and local scope.

Local

Local duration objects, also known as *automatic* objects, lead a more precarious existence. They are created on the stack (or in a register) when the enclosing block or function is entered. They are deallocated when the program exits that block or function. Local duration objects must be explicitly initialized; otherwise, their contents are unpredictable. Local duration objects must always have local or function scope. The storage class specifier **auto** can be used when declaring local duration variables, but is usually redundant, because **auto** is the default for variables declared within a block. An object with local duration also has local scope, because it does not *exist* outside of its enclosing block. The converse is not true: a local scope object can have static duration.

When declaring variables (for example, **int**, **char**, **float**), the storage class specifier **register** also implies **auto**; but a request (or hint) is passed to the compiler that the object be allocated a register if possible. Borland C++ can be set to allocate a register to a local integral or pointer variable, if one is free. If no register is free, the variable is allocated as an **auto**, local object with no warning or error.

Note   The Borland C++ compiler can ignore requests for register allocation. Register allocation is based on the compiler's analysis of how a variable is used.

Dynamic

Dynamic duration objects are created and destroyed by specific function calls during a program. They are allocated storage from a special memory reserve known as the heap, using either standard library functions such as *malloc*, or by using the C++ operator **new**. The corresponding deallocations are made using *free* or **delete**.

Translation units

The term *translation unit* refers to a source code file together with any included files, but less any source lines omitted by conditional preprocessor directives. Syntactically, a translation unit is defined as a sequence of external declarations:

translation-unit:

> *external-declaration*

> *translation-unit external-declaration*

external-declaration

    function-definition

    declaration

The word *external* has several connotations in C; here it refers to declarations made outside of any function, and which therefore have file scope. (External linkage is a distinct property; see the section "Linkage.") Any declaration that also reserves storage for an object or function is called a definition (or defining declaration). For more details, see "External declarations and definitions."

Linkage

An executable program is usually created by compiling several independent translation units, then linking the resulting object files with preexisting libraries. A problem arises when the same identifier is declared in different scopes (for example, in different files), or declared more than once in the same scope. Linkage is the process that allows each instance of an identifier to be associated correctly with one particular object or function. All identifiers have one of three linkage attributes, closely related to their scope: external linkage, internal linkage, or no linkage. These attributes are determined by the placement and format of your declarations, together with the explicit (or implicit by default) use of the storage class specifier **static** or **extern**.

Each instance of a particular identifier with *external linkage* represents the same object or function throughout the entire set of files and libraries making up the program. Each instance of a particular identifier with *internal linkage* represents the same object or function within one file only. Identifiers with *no linkage* represent unique entities.

External and internal linkage rules

- Any object or file identifier having file scope will have internal linkage if its declaration contains the storage class specifier **static**.

- For C++, if the same identifier appears with both internal and external linkage within the same file, the identifier will have external linkage. In C, it will have internal linkage.

- If the declaration of an object or function identifier contains the storage class specifier **extern**, the identifier has the same linkage as any visible declaration of the identifier with file scope. If there is no such visible declaration, the identifier has external linkage.

- If a function is declared without a storage class specifier, its linkage is determined as if the storage class specifier **extern** had been used.

- If an object identifier with file scope is declared without a storage class specifier, the identifier has external linkage.

Identifiers with no linkage attribute:

- Any identifier declared to be other than an object or a function (for example, a **typedef** identifier)

- Function parameters

- Block scope identifiers for objects declared without the storage class specifier **extern**

Name mangling

When a C++ module is compiled, the compiler generates function names that include an encoding of the function's argument types. This is known as *name mangling*. It makes overloaded functions possible, and helps the linker catch errors in calls to functions in other modules. However, there are times when you won't want name mangling. When compiling a C++ module to be linked with a module that does not have mangled names, the C++ compiler has to be told not to mangle the names of the functions from the other module. This situation typically arises when linking with libraries or .OBJ files compiled with a C compiler.

To tell the C++ compiler not to mangle the name of a function, declare the function as `extern "C"`, like this:

```
extern "C" void Cfunc( int );
```

This declaration tells the compiler that references to the function *Cfunc* should not be mangled.

You can also apply the `extern "C"` declaration to a block of names:

```
extern "C" {
    void Cfunc1( int );
    void Cfunc2( int );
    void Cfunc3( int );
};
```

As with the declaration for a single function, this declaration tells the compiler that references to the functions *Cfunc1*, *Cfunc2*, and *Cfunc3* should not be mangled. You can also use this form of block declaration when the block of function names is contained in a header file:

```
extern "C" {
    #include "locallib.h"
};
```

Introduction to declaration syntax

All six interrelated attributes (storage classes, types, scope, visibility, duration, and linkage) are determined in diverse ways by *declarations*.

Declarations can be *defining declarations* (also known as *definitions*) or *referencing declarations* (sometimes known as *nondefining declarations*). A defining declaration, as the name implies, performs both the duties of declaring and defining; the nondefining declarations require a definition to be added somewhere in the program. A referencing declaration introduces one or more identifier names into a program. A definition actually allocates memory to an object and associates an identifier with that object.

Tentative definitions

The ANSI C standard supports the concept of the *tentative definition*. Any external data declaration that has no storage class specifier and no initializer is considered a tentative definition. If the identifier declared appears in a later definition, then the tentative definition is treated as if the **extern** storage class specifier were present. In other words, the tentative definition becomes a simple referencing declaration.

If the end of the translation unit is reached and no definition has appeared with an initializer for the identifier, then the tentative definition becomes a full definition, and the object defined has uninitialized (zero-filled) space reserved for it. For example,

```
int x;

int x;          /*legal, one copy of x is reserved */
int y;
int y = 4;      /* legal, y is initialized to 4 */
int z = 5;
int z = 6;      /* not legal, both are initialized definitions */
```

Unlike ANSI C, C++ doesn't have the concept of a tentative declaration; an external data declaration without a storage class specifier is always a definition.

Possible declarations

The range of objects that can be declared includes

- Variables

- Functions

- Classes and class members (C++)

- Types

- Structure, union, and enumeration tags

- Structure members

- Union members

- Arrays of other types

- Enumeration constants

- Statement labels

- Preprocessor macros

The full syntax for declarations is shown in Tables 2.1 through 2.3. The recursive nature of the declarator syntax allows complex declarators. You'll probably want to use **typedefs** to improve legibility.

In Borland C++ declaration syntax, note the restrictions on the number and order of modifiers and qualifiers. Also, the modifiers listed are the only addition to the declarator syntax that are not ANSI C or C++. These modifiers are each discussed in greater detail in "Variable modifiers," "Pointer modifiers," and "Function modifiers."

Table 2.1   Borland C++ declaration syntax

declaration:	*elaborated-type-specifier:*
<decl-specifiers> <declarator-list>;	*class-key identifier*
asm-declaration	*class-key class-name*
function-declaration	**enum** *enum-name*
linkage-specification	*class-key:* (C++ specific)
decl-specifier:	**class**
storage-class-specifier	**struct**
type-specifier	**union**
function-specifier	*enum-specifier:*
friend (C++ specific)	**enum** *<identifier>* { *<enum-list>* }
typedef	*enum-list:*
decl-specifiers:	*enumerator*
<decl-specifiers> decl-specifier	*enumerator-list , enumerator*
storage-class-specifier:	*enumerator:*
auto	*identifier*
register	*identifier = constant-expression*
static	*constant-expression:*
extern	*conditional-expression*
function-specifier: (C++ specific)	*linkage-specification:* (C++ specific)
inline	**extern** *string* { *<declaration-list>* }
virtual	**extern** *string declaration*
simple-type-name:	*type-specifier:*
class-name	*simple-type-name*
typedef-*name*	*class-specifier*
char	*enum-specifier*
short	*elaborated-type-specifier*
int	**const**
long	**volatile**
signed	*declaration-list:*
unsigned	*declaration*
float	*declaration-list ; declaration*
double	
void	
declarator-list:	*type-name:*
init-declarator	*type-specifier <abstract-declarator>*
declarator-list , init-declarator	*abstract-declarator:*
init-declarator:	*pointer-operator <abstract-declarator>*
declarator <initializer>	*<abstract-declarator> (argument-declaration-list)*
declarator:	*<cv-qualifier-list>*
dname	*<abstract-declarator> [<constant-expression>]*

Table 2.1   Borland C++ declaration syntax

modifier-list	(*abstract-declarator*)
pointer-operator declarator	*argument-declaration-list:*
declarator (*parameter-declaration-list*)	<arg-declaration-list>
<*cv-qualifier-list* >	*arg-declaration-list* , ...
(The <cv-qualifier-list > is for C++ only.)	<arg-declaration-list> ... (C++ specific)
declarator [<*constant-expression*>]	*arg-declaration-list:*
(*declarator*)	*argument-declaration*
modifier-list:	*arg-declaration-list* , *argument-declaration*
modifier	*argument-declaration:*
modifier-list modifier	*decl-specifiers declarator*
modifier:	*decl-specifiers declarator* = *expression*
_ _cdecl	(C++ specific)
_ _pascal	*decl-specifiers* <*abstract-declarator*>
_ _interrupt	*decl-specifiers* <*abstract-declarator*> = *expression*
_ _near	(C++ specific)
_ _far	*function-definition:*
_ _huge	*function-body:*
pointer-operator:	*compound-statement*
* <*cv-qualifier-list*>	*initializer:*
& <*cv-qualifier-list*> (C++ specific)	= *expression*
class-name :: * <*cv-qualifier-list*>	= { *initializer-list* }
(C++ specific)	(*expression-list*) (C++ specific)
cv-qualifier-list:	*initializer-list:*
cv-qualifier <*cv-qualifier-list*>	*expression*
cv-qualifier	*initializer-list* , *expression*
const	{ *initializer-list* <,> }
volatile	
dname:	
name	
class-name (C++ specific)	
~ *class-name* (C++ specific)	
type-defined-name	

External declarations and definitions

The storage class specifiers auto and register cannot appear in an external declaration. For each identifier in a translation unit declared with internal linkage, no more than one external definition can be given.

An external definition is an external declaration that also defines an object or function; that is, it also allocates storage. If an identifier declared with external linkage is used in an expression (other than as part of the operand of sizeof), then exactly one external definition of that identifier must be somewhere in the entire program.

Borland C++ allows later re-declarations of external names, such as arrays, structures, and unions, to add information to earlier declarations. Here's an example:

```
int a[];               // no size

struct mystruct;       // tag only, no member declarators
    ⋮
int a[3] = {1, 2, 3}; // supply size and initialize
struct mystruct {
   int i, j;
};                     // add member declarators
```

Table 2.2 covers class declaration syntax. In the section on classes (beginning with "Classes"), you can find examples of how to declare a class. Referencing covers C++ reference types (closely related to pointer types) in detail.

Table 2.2　　Borland C++ class declaration syntax (C++ only)

class-specifier	base-specifier
class-head { <member-list> }	: base-list
class-head:	base-list:
class-key <identifier> <base-specifier>	base-specifier
class-key class-name <base-specifier>	base-list , base-specifier
member-list:	base-specifier:
member-declaration <member-list>	class-name
access-specifier : <member-list>	**virtual** <access-specifier> class-name
member-declaration:	access-specifier <**virtual**> class-name
<decl-specifiers> <member-declarator-list> ;	access-specifier:
function-definition <;>	**private**
qualified-name ;	**protected**
member-declarator-list:	**public**
member-declarator	conversion-function-name:
member-declarator-list, member-declarator	**operator** conversion-type-name
member-declarator:	conversion-type-name:
declarator <pure-specifier>	type-specifiers <pointer-operator>
<identifier> : constant-expression	constructor-initializer:
pure-specifier:	: member-initializer-list
= 0	
member-initializer-list:	operator-name: one of
member-initializer	**new delete 1 typeid**
member-initializer , member-initializer-list	+ - * / % ^
member-initializer:	& │ ~ ! = <>
class name (<argument-list>)	+= -= =* /= %= ^=
identifier (<argument-list>)	&= │= << >> >>= <<=
operator-function-name:	== != <= >= && ││
operator operator-name	++ __ , ->* -> ()
	[] .*

Type specifiers

The *type specifier* with one or more optional *modifiers* is used to specify the type of the declared identifier:

```
int i;                   // declare i as a signed integer
unsigned char ch1, ch2;  // declare two unsigned chars
```

By long-standing tradition, if the type specifier is omitted, type **signed int** (or equivalently, **int**) is the assumed default. However, in C++, a missing type specifier can lead to syntactic ambiguity, so C++ practice requires you to explicitly declare all **int** type specifiers.

Type categories

The four basic type categories (and their subcategories) are as follows:

- Aggregate
  - Array
  - **struct**
  - **union**
  - **class** (C++ only)
- Function
- Scalar
  - Arithmetic
  - Enumeration
  - Pointer
  - Reference (C++ only)
- **void**

Types can also be viewed in another way: they can be *fundamental* or *derived* types. The fundamental types are **void**, **char**, **int**, **float**, and **double**, together with **short**, **long**, **signed**, and **unsigned** variants of some of these. The derived types include pointers and references to other types, arrays of other types, function types, class types, structures, and unions.

A class object, for example, can hold a number of objects of different types together with functions for manipulating these objects, plus a mechanism to control access and inheritance from other classes.

Given any nonvoid type **type** (with some provisos), you can declare derived types as follows:

Table 2.3   Declaring types

Declaration	Description
type t;	An object of type *type*
type array[10];	Ten *type*s: *array*[0] - *array*[9]
type *ptr;	*ptr* is a pointer to *type*
type &ref = t;	*ref* is a reference to *type* (C++)
type func(**void**);	*func* returns value of type *type*
void *func1*(*type t*);	*func1* takes a type *type* parameter
struct st {*type t1*; *type t2*};	structure **st** holds two *type*s

Note   *type& var*, *type &var*, and *type & var* are all equivalent.

Type void

Syntax

```
void identifier
```

Description

void is a special type indicating the absence of any value. Use the **void** keyword as a function return type if the function does not return a value.

```
void hello(char *name)
{
  printf("Hello, %s.",name);
}
```

Use **void** as a function heading if the function does not take any parameters.

```
int init(void)
{
  return 1;
}
```

Void pointers

Generic pointers can also be declared as **void**, meaning that they can point to any type.

void pointers cannot be dereferenced without explicit casting because the compiler cannot determine the size of the pointer object.

Example

```
int x;
float r;
void *p = &x;          /* p points to x */
int main (void)

  *(int *) p = 2;
```

```
    p = &r;              /* p points to r */
    *(float *)p = 1.1;
}
```

The fundamental types

The fundamental type specifiers are built from the following keywords:

char	**int**	**signed**
double	**long**	**unsigned**
float	**short**	

From these keywords you can build the integral and floating-point types, which are together known as the *arithmetic* types. The modifiers **long**, **short**, **signed**, and **unsigned** can be applied to the integral types. The include file limits.h contains definitions of the value ranges for all the fundamental types.

Integral types

char, **short**, **int**, and **long**, together with their unsigned variants, are all considered *integral* data types. Integral types shows the integral type specifiers, with synonyms listed on the same line.

Table 2.4   Integral types

char, signed char	Synonyms if default **char** set to **signed**.
unsigned char	
char, unsigned char	Synonyms if default **char** set to **unsigned**.
signed char	
int, signed int	
unsigned, unsigned int	
short, short int, signed short int	
unsigned short, unsigned short int	
long, long int, signed long int	
unsigned long, unsigned long int	

Note   These synonyms are not valid in C++. See "The three char types" in Chapter 1.

Only **signed** or **unsigned** can be used with **char**, **short**, **int**, or **long**. The keywords **signed** and **unsigned**, when used on their own, mean **signed int** and **unsigned int**, respectively.

In the absence of **unsigned**, **signed** is usually assumed. An exception arises with **char**. Borland C++ lets you set the default for **char** to be **signed** or **unsigned**. (The default, if you don't set it yourself, is **signed**.) If the default is set to **unsigned**, then the declaration char ch declares *ch* as **unsigned**. You would need to use signed char ch to override the default. Similarly, with a **signed** default for **char**, you would need an explicit unsigned char ch to declare an **unsigned char**.

Only **long** or **short** can be used with **int**. The keywords **long** and **short** used on their own mean **long int** and **short int**.

ANSI C does not dictate the sizes or internal representations of these types, except to indicate that **short**, **int**, and **long** form a nondecreasing sequence with **"short <= int <= long."** All three types can legally be the same. This is important if you want to write portable code aimed at other platforms.

In a Borland C++ 16-bit program, the types **int** and **short** are equivalent, both being 16 bits. In a Borland C++ 32-bit program, the types **int** and **long** are equivalent, both being 32 bits. The signed varieties are all stored in two's complement format using the most significant bit (MSB) as a sign bit: 0 for positive, 1 for negative (which explains the ranges shown in 16-bit data types, sizes, and ranges and 32-bit data types, sizes, and ranges). In the unsigned versions, all bits are used to give a range of 0 - (2 - 1), where n is 8, 16, or 32.

Floating-point types

The representations and sets of values for the floating-point types are implementation dependent; that is, each implementation of C is free to define them. Borland C++ uses the IEEE floating-point formats. See Chapter 12, "ANSI Implementation-specific standards," for more information.

float and **double** are 32- and 64-bit floating-point data types, respectively. **long** can be used with **double** to declare an 80-bit precision floating-point identifier: **long double** *test_case*, for example.

16-bit data types, sizes, and ranges and 32-bit data types, sizes, and ranges indicate the storage allocations for the floating-point types.

Standard arithmetic conversions

When you use an arithmetic expression, such as $a + b$, where a and b are different arithmetic types, Borland C++ performs certain internal conversions before the expression is evaluated. These standard conversions include promotions of "lower" types to "higher" types in the interests of accuracy and consistency.

Here are the steps Borland C++ uses to convert the operands in an arithmetic expression:

1 Any small integral types are converted as shown in Table 2.5. After this, any two values associated with an operator are either **int** (including the **long** and **unsigned** modifiers), or they are of type **double**, **float**, or **long double**.

2 If either operand is of type **long double**, the other operand is converted to **long double**.

3 Otherwise, if either operand is of type **double**, the other operand is converted to **double**.

4 Otherwise, if either operand is of type **float**, the other operand is converted to **float**.

5 Otherwise, if either operand is of type **unsigned long**, the other operand is converted to **unsigned long**.

6 Otherwise, if either operand is of type **long**, then the other operand is converted to **long**.

7 Otherwise, if either operand is of type **unsigned**, then the other operand is converted to **unsigned**.

8 Otherwise, both operands are of type **int**.

The result of the expression is the same type as that of the two operands.

Table 2.5   Methods used in standard arithmetic conversions

Type	Converts to	Method
char	int	Zero or sign-extended (depends on default char type)
unsigned char	int	Zero-filled high byte (always)
signed char	int	Sign-extended (always)
short	int	Same value; sign extended
unsigned short	unsigned int	Same value; zero filled
enum	int	Same value

Special char, int, and enum conversions

Note The conversions discussed in this section are specific to Borland C++.

Assigning a signed character object (such as a variable) to an integral object results in automatic sign extension. Objects of type **signed char** always use sign extension; objects of type **unsigned char** always set the high byte to zero when converted to **int**.

Converting a longer integral type to a shorter type truncates the higher order bits and leaves low-order bits unchanged. Converting a shorter integral type to a longer type either sign-extends or zero-fills the extra bits of the new value, depending on whether the shorter type is **signed** or **unsigned**, respectively.

Initialization

Initializers set the initial value that is stored in an object (variables, arrays, structures, and so on). If you don't initialize an object, and it has static duration, it will be initialized by default in the following manner:

- To zero if it is an arithmetic type
- To null if it is a pointer type

Note If the object has automatic storage duration, its value is indeterminate.

Syntax for initializers

initializer

> *= expression*

> *= {initializer-list} <,>}*

> *(expression list)*

initializer-list

expression

initializer-list, expression

{initializer-list} <,>}

Rules governing initializers

- The number of initializers in the initializer list cannot be larger than the number of objects to be initialized.

- The item to be initialized must be an object (for example, an array) of unknown size.

- For C (not required for C++), all expressions must be constants if they appear in one of these places:

  - In an initializer for an object that has static duration.

  - In an initializer list for an array, structure, or union (expressions using **sizeof** are also allowed).

- If a declaration for an identifier has block scope, and the identifier has external or internal linkage, the declaration cannot have an initializer for the identifier.

- If a brace-enclosed list has fewer initializers than members of a structure, the remainder of the structure is initialized implicitly in the same way as objects with static storage duration.

Scalar types are initialized with a single expression, which can optionally be enclosed in braces. The initial value of the object is that of the expression; the same constraints for type and conversions apply as for simple assignments.

For unions, a brace-enclosed initializer initializes the member that first appears in the union's declaration list. For structures or unions with automatic storage duration, the initializer must be one of the following:

- An initializer list (as described in "Arrays, structures, and unions").

- A single expression with compatible union or structure type. In this case, the initial value of the object is that of the expression.

Arrays, structures, and unions

You initialize arrays and structures (at declaration time, if you like) with a brace-enclosed list of initializers for the members or elements of the object in question. The initializers are given in increasing array subscript or member order. You initialize unions with a brace-enclosed initializer for the first member of the union. For example, you could declare an array *days*, which counts how many times each day of the week appears in a month (assuming that each day will appear at least once), as follows:

```
int days[7] = { 1, 1, 1, 1, 1, 1, 1 }
```

The following rules initialize character arrays and wide character arrays:

- You can initialize arrays of character type with a literal string, optionally enclosed in braces. Each character in the string, including the null terminator, initializes successive elements in the array. For example, you could declare

```
char name[] = { "Unknown" };
```

which sets up an eight-element array, whose elements are 'U' (for *name*[0]), 'n' (for *name*[1]), and so on (and including a null terminator).

- You can initialize a wide character array (one that is compatible with *wchar_t*) by using a wide string literal, optionally enclosed in braces. As with character arrays, the codes of the wide string literal initialize successive elements of the array.

Here is an example of a structure initialization:

```
struct mystruct {
    int i;
    char str[21];
    double d;
    } s = { 20, "Borland", 3.141 };
```

Complex members of a structure, such as arrays or structures, can be initialized with suitable expressions inside nested braces.

Declarations and declarators

A *declaration* is a list of names. The names are sometimes referred to as *declarators* or *identifiers*. The declaration begins with optional storage class specifiers, type specifiers, and other modifiers. The identifiers are separated by commas and the list is terminated by a semicolon.

Simple declarations of variable identifiers have the following pattern:

   data-type var1 <=init1>, var2 <=init2>, ...;

where *var1, var2, ...* are any sequence of distinct identifiers with optional initializers. Each of the variables is declared to be of type *data-type*. For example,

```
int x = 1, y = 2;
```

creates two integer variables called *x* and *y* (and initializes them to the values 1 and 2, respectively).

These are all defining declarations; storage is allocated and any optional initializers are applied.

The initializer for an automatic object can be any legal expression that evaluates to an assignment-compatible value for the type of the variable involved. Initializers for static objects must be constants or constant expressions.

In C++, an initializer for a static object can be any expression involving constants and previously declared variables and functions.

The format of the declarator indicates how the declared *name* is to be interpreted when used in an expression. If **type** is any type, and *storage class specifier* is any storage class specifier, and if *D1* and *D2* are any two declarators, then the declaration

   storage-class-specifier **type** *D1, D2;*

indicates that each occurrence of D1 or D2 in an expression will be treated as an object of type **type** and storage class *storage class specifier*. The type of the *name* embedded in the declarator will be some phrase containing *type*, such as "*type*," "pointer to *type*," "array of *type*," "function returning *type*," or "pointer to function returning *type*," and so on.

For example, in Table 2.6, each of the declarators could be used as rvalues (or possibly lvalues in some cases) in expressions where a single **int** object would be appropriate. The types of the embedded identifiers are derived from their declarators as follows:

Table 2.6   Declaration syntax examples

Declaration syntax	Implied type of name	Example
type name;	type	int count;
type name[];	(open) array of **type**	int count[];
type name[3];	Fixed array of three elements, all of **type** (*name*[0], *name*[1], and *name*[2])	int count[3];
type *name;	Pointer to **type**	int *count;
type *name[];	(open) array of pointers to **type**	int *count[];
type *(name[]);	Same as above	int *(count[]);
type (*name)[];	Pointer to an (open) array of **type**	int (*count) [];
type &name;	Reference to **type** (C++ only)	int &count;
type name();	Function returning **type**	int count();
type *name();	Function returning pointer to **type**	int *count();
type *(name());	Same as above	int *(count());
type (*name)();	Pointer to function returning **type**	int (*count) ();

Note the need for parentheses in (*name)[ ] and (*name)( ); this is because the precedence of both the array declarator [ ] and the function declarator ( ) is higher than the pointer declarator *. The parentheses in *(name*[ ]) are optional.

Note   See Table 2.1 for the declarator syntax. The definition covers both identifier and function declarators.

Storage class specifiers

Storage classes specifiers are also called *type specifiers*. They dictate the location (data segment, register, heap, or stack) of an object and its duration or lifetime (the entire running time of the program, or during execution of some blocks of code). Storage class can be established by the declaration syntax, by its placement in the source code, or by both of these factors.

The keyword **mutable** does not affect the lifetime of the class member to which it is applied.

The storage class specifiers in Borland C++ are:

auto	mutable	typedef
__declspec	register	
extern	static	

Variable modifiers

In addition to the storage class specifier keywords, a declaration can use certain *modifiers* to alter some aspect of the identifier. The modifiers available with Borland C++ are summarized in Table 2.8.

const

Syntax

```
const <variable name> [ = <value> ] ;
<function name> ( const <type>*<variable name> ;)
<function name> const;
```

Description

Use the **const** modifier to make a variable value unmodifiable.

Use the **const** modifier to assign an initial value to a variable that cannot be changed by the program. Any future assignments to a **const** result in a compiler error.

A **const** pointer cannot be modified, though the object to which it points can be changed. Consider the following examples.

```
const float pi   = 3.14;
const  maxint = 12345;   // When used by itself, const is equivalent to int.
char *const str1 = "Hello, world";          // A constant pointer
char const *str2 = "Borland International";  // A pointer to a constant
                                            // character string.
```

Given these declarations, the following statements are legal.

```
pi   = 3.0;        // Assigns a value to a const.
i    = maxint++;   // Increments a const.
str1 = "Hi, there!" // Points str1 to something else.
```

Using the const keyword in C++ programs

C++ extends **const** to include classes and member functions. In a C++ class definition, use the **const** modifier following a member function declaration. The member function is prevented from modifying any data in the class.

A class object defined with the **const** keyword attempts to use only member functions that are also defined with **const**. If you call a member function that is not defined as **const**, the compiler issues a warning that the a non-**const** function is being called for a **const** object. Using the **const** keyword in this manner is a safety feature of C.

Warning   A pointer can indirectly modify a **const** variable, as in the following:

```
*(int *)&my_age = 35;
```

If you use the **const** modifier with a pointer parameter in a function's parameter list, the function cannot modify the variable that the pointer points to. For example,

```
int printf (const char *format, ...);
```

printf is prevented from modifying the format string.

Example 1

```
class X  {
    int j;
public:
  X::X() { j = 0; };
    int lowerBound() const;          // DOES NOT MODIFY ANY DATA MEMBERS
    int dimension(X x1, const X &x2) { // x2 DATA MEMBERS WON'T BE MODIFIED
        x1.j = 3;        // OKAY; x1 OBJECT IS MODIFIABLE
        x2.j = 5;        // ERROR; x2 IS NOT MODIFIABLE
        return x2.j;
        }
};
```

Example 2

```
#include <iostream.h>

class Alpha {
    int num;
public:
    Alpha(int j = 0) { num = j; }
    int func(int i) const {
        cout << "Non-modifying function." << endl;
        return i++;
        }
    int func(int i) {
        cout << "Modify private data" << endl;
        return num = i;
        }
    int f(int i) { cout << "Non-const function called with i = " << i << endl; return i;}
};

void main() {
    Alpha alpha_mod;         // Calls the non-const functions.
    const Alpha alpha_inst;  // Attempts to call the const functions.

    alpha_mod.func(1);
    alpha_mod.f(1);          // Causes a compiler warning.

    alpha_inst.func(1);
    alpha_inst.f(1);
    }
```

Output

```
Modify private data
Non-const function called with i = 1
Non-modifying function.
Non-const function called with i = 1
```

volatile

Syntax

```
volatile <data definition> ;
```

Description

Use the **volatile** modifier to indicate that a variable can be changed by a background routine, an interrupt routine, or an I/O port. Declaring an object to be **volatile** warns the compiler not to make assumptions concerning the value of the object while evaluating expressions in which it occurs because the value could change at any moment. It also prevents the compiler from making the variable a register variable.

The routines in this example (assuming *timer* has been properly associated with a hardware clock interrupt) implement a timed wait of ticks specified by the argument *interval*. A highly optimizing compiler might not load the value of *ticks* inside the test of the **while** loop since the loop doesn't change the value of *ticks*.

Note   C++ extends **volatile** to include classes and member functions. If you've declared a **volatile** object, you can use only its **volatile** member functions.

Mixed-language calling conventions

Borland C++ allows your programs to easily call routines written in other languages, and vice versa. When you mix languages, you have to deal with two important issues: identifiers and parameter passing.

By default, Borland C++ saves all global identifiers in their original case (lower, upper, or mixed) with an underscore "_" prepended to the front of the identifier. To remove the default, you can select the **-u** command-line option, or uncheck the compiler option setting in the IDE.

Note   The section "Linkage" tells how to use **extern**, which allows C names to be referenced from a C++ program.

Table 2.7 summarizes the effects of a modifier applied to a called function. For every modifier, the table shows the order in which the function parameters are pushed on the stack. Next, the table shows whether the calling program (the *caller*) or the called function (the *callee*) is responsible for popping the parameters off the stack. Finally, the table shows the effect on the name of a global function.

Table 2.7   Calling conventions

Modifier	Push parameters	Pop parameters	Name change
__cdecl[1]	Right first	Caller	'_' prepended
__fastcall	Left first	Callee	'@' prepended
__pascal	Left first	Callee	Uppercase
__stdcall	Right first	Callee	No change

1. This is the default.

Note _ _**fastcall** and _ _**stdcall** are subject to name mangling. See the description of the **-VC** option .

cdecl, _cdecl, _ _cdecl

Syntax

```
cdecl <data/function definition> ;
_cdecl <data/function definition> ;
_ _cdecl <data/function definition> ;
```

Description

Use a **cdecl**, **_cdecl**, or _ _**cdecl** modifier to declare a variable or a function using the C-style naming conventions (case-sensitive, with a leading underscore appended). When you use **cdecl**, **_cdecl**, or _ _**cdecl** in front of a function, it effects how the parameters are passed (last parameter is pushed first, and the caller cleans up the stack). The _ _**cdecl** modifier overrides the compiler directives and IDE options and allows the function to be called as a regular C function.

The **cdecl**, **_cdecl**, and _ _**cdecl** keywords are specific to Borland C++.

Example

```
int cdecl FileCount;
long far cdecl HisFunc(int x);
```

pascal, _pascal, _ _pascal

Syntax

```
pascal <data-definition/function-definition> ;
_pascal <data-definition/function-definition> ;
_ _pascal <data-definition/function-definition> ;
```

Description

Use the **pascal**, **_pascal**, and _ _**pascal** keywords to declare a variable or a function using a Pascal-style naming convention (the name is in uppercase).

In addition, **pascal** declares Pascal-style parameter-passing conventions when applied to a function header (first parameter pushed first; the called function cleans up the stack).

In C++ programs, functions declared with the **pascal** modifer will still be mangled.

Examples

```
int pascal FileCount;
far pascal long ThisFunc(int x, char *s);
```

_stdcall, _ _stdcall

Syntax

```
_ _stdcall <function-name>
_stdcall <function-name>
```

Description

The **_stdcall** and **_ _stdcall** keywords force the compiler to generate function calls using the Standard calling convention.The resulting function calls are smaller and faster. Functions must pass the correct number and type of arguments; this is unlike normal C use, which permits a variable number of function arguments. Such functions comply with the standard WIN32 argument-passing convention.

Note   The **_ _stdcall** modifier is subject to name mangling. See the description of the **-VC** option.

_fastcall, _ _fastcall

Syntax

```
_fastcall function-name
_ _fastcall function-name
```

Description

Use the **_fastcall** modifiers to declare functions that expect parameters to be passed in registers.

The compiler treats this calling convention as a new language specifier, along the lines of **_cdecl** and **_pascal**.

Functions declared using **_cdecl** or **_pascal** cannot also have the **_fastcall** modifiers because they use the stack to pass parameters. Likewise, the **_fastcall** modifiers cannot be used together with **_export** or **_loadds**.

The compiler generates a warning if you mix functions of these types or if you use the **_fastcall** modifiers in a dangerous situation. You can, however, use functions that use the **_fastcall** or **_ _fastcall** conventions in overlaid modules (for example, with modules that will use VROOMM).

The compiler prefixes the **_fastcall** function name with an at-sign (@). This prefix applies to both unmangled C function names and to mangled C++ function names.

Note   The **_ _fastcall** modifier is subject to name mangling. See the description of the **-VC** option.

Multithread variables

The keyword **_ _thread** is used in multithread programs to preserve a unique copy of global and static class variables. Each program thread maintains a private copy of a **_ _thread** variable for each threaded process.

The syntax is *Type _ _***thread** *variable_ _name*. For example

```
int _ _thread x;
```

declares an integer type variable that will be global but private to each thread in the program in which the statement occurs.

The _ _**thread** modifier can be used with global (file-scope) and static variables. The modifier cannot be used with pointers or functions. (However, you can have pointers to _ _**thread** objects.) A program element that requires run-time initialization or run-time finalization cannot be declared to be a _ _**thread** type. The following declarations require run-time initialization and are therefore illegal.

```
int f( );
int _ _thread x = f( );   // illegal
```

Instantiation of a class with a user-defined constructor or destructor requires run-time initialization and is therefore illegal.

```
class X  {
   X( );
   ~X( );
};
X _ _thread myclass;    // illegal
```

Pointer modifiers

Borland C++ has modifiers that affect the pointer declarator (*); that is, they modify pointers to data. These are _ _**near**, _ _**far**, _ _**huge**, _ _**cs**, _ _**ds**, _ _**es**, _ _**seg**, and _ _**ss**.

You can compile a program using one of several memory models. The model you use determines (among other things) the internal format of pointers. For example, if you use a small data model (small or medium), all data pointers contain a 16-bit offset from the data segment (DS) register. If you use a large data model (compact or large), all pointers to data are 32 bits long and give both a segment address and an offset.

Sometimes when you're using one size of data model, you want to declare a pointer to be of a different size or format than the current default. You do so using the pointer modifiers.

See _ _**near**, _ _**far**, and _ _**huge** for an in-depth explanation of these types of pointers, and a description of normalized pointers. Also see the additional discussions of _ _**cs**, _ _**ds**, _ _**es**, _ _**seg**, and _ _**ss**.

Function modifiers

This section presents descriptions of the Borland C++ function modifiers

In addition to their use as pointer modifiers, the _ _**near**, _ _**far**, and _ _**huge** modifiers can also be used as function type modifiers; that is, they can modify functions and function pointers as well as data pointers. In addition, you can use the _ _**loadds**, _ _**export**, _ _**import**, and _ _**saveregs** modifiers to modify functions.

Note   Tiny and huge memory models are not supported in Windows programs.

Also see "Class memory model specifications" in Chapter 3.

In a 16-bit program, the _ _import can be used only as a modifier for class declarations. In 32-bit programs the keyword can be applied to class, function, and variable declarations.

The _ _near, _ _far, and _ _huge function modifiers can be combined with _ _cdecl or _ _pascal, but not with _ _interrupt.

Functions of type _ _huge are useful when interfacing with code in assembly language that doesn't use the same memory allocation as Borland C++.

A function that is not an _ _interrupt type can be declared to be _ _near, _ _far, or _ _huge in order to override the default settings for the current memory model.

A _ _near function uses _ _near calls; a _ _far or _ _huge function uses _ _far call instructions.

In the small and compact memory models, an unqualified function defaults to type _ _near. In the medium and large models, an unqualified function defaults to type _ _far.

A _ _huge function is the same as a _ _far function, except that the DS register is set to the data segment address of the source module when a _ _huge function is entered, but left unset for a _ _far function.

The _ _export modifier makes the function exportable from Windows. The _ _import modifier makes a function available to a Windows program. The keywords are used in an executable (if you don't use smart callbacks) or in a DLL.

The _ _loadds modifier indicates that a function should set the **DS_register**, just as a _ _huge function does, but does not imply _ _near or _ _far calls. Thus, _ _loadds _ _far is equivalent to _ _huge.

The _ _saveregs modifier causes the function to preserve all **register** values and restore them before returning (except for explicit return values passed in registers such as AX or DX).

The _ _loadds and _ _saveregs modifiers are useful for writing low-level interface routines, such as mouse support routines.

Functions declared with the _ _fastcall modifier have different names than their non-_ _fastcall counterparts. The compiler prefixes the _ _fastcall function name with an @. This prefix applies to both unmangled C function names and to mangled C++ function names.

Table 2.8   Borland C++ modifiers

Modifier	Use with	Description
const[1]	Variables	Prevents changes to object.
volatile[1]	Variables	Prevents register allocation and some optimization. Warns compiler that object might be subject to outside change during evaluation.
_ _cdecl[2]	Functions	Forces C argument-passing convention. Affects Linker and link-time names.

Table 2.8   Borland C++ modifiers

Modifier	Use with	Description
__cdecl[2]	Variables	Forces global identifier case-sensitivity and leading underscores.
__interrupt	Functions	Function compiles with the additional register-housekeeping code needed when writing interrupt handlers.
__pascal	Functions	Forces Pascal argument-passing convention. Affects Linker and link-time names.
__pascal	Variables	Forces global identifier case-insensitivity with no leading underscores.
__near, __far, __huge	Pointer types	Overrides the default pointer type specified by the current memory model.
__cs, __ds, __es, __seg, __ss	Pointer types	Segment pointers.
__near, __far, __huge	Functions	Overrides the default function type specified by the current memory model.
__near, __far	Variables	Directs the placement of the object in memory.
__export	Functions/classes	Tells the compiler which functions or classes to export.
__import	Functions/classes	Tells the compiler which functions or classes to import. (In 16-bit programs, this keyword can be used only for class declarations.)
__loadds	Functions	Sets DS to point to the current data segment.
__saveregs	Functions	Preserves all register values (except for return values) during execution of the function.
__fastcall	Functions	Forces register parameter passing convention. Affects the linker and link-time names.
__stdcall	Functions	Forces the standard WIN32 argument-passing convention.

[1] C++ extends **const** and **volatile** to include classes and member functions.

[2] This is the default.

__interrupt functions

Syntax

```
interrupt <function-definition> ;
_interrupt <function-definition> ;
_ _interrupt <function-definition> ;
```

Description

Use the **__interrupt** function modifier to define a function as an interrupt handler.

The _ _**interrupt** modifier is specific to Borlalnd C++. _ _**interrupt** functions are designed to be used with interrupt vectors.

Interrupt functions compile with extra function entry and exit code so that all CPU registers are saved. The BP, SP, SS, CS, and IP registers are preserved as part of the C-calling sequence or as part of the interrupt handling itself. The function uses an IRET instruction to return, so that the function can be used as harware and software interrupts.

Declare interrupt functions to be of type **void** and can be declared in any memory model. For all memory models except huge, DS is set to the program data segment. For the huge memory model, DS is set to the module's data segment.

Example

```
void interrupt myhandler()
{
  ...
}
```

Pointers

Pointers fall into two main categories: pointers to objects and pointers to functions. Both types of pointers are special objects for holding memory addresses.

The two pointer classes have distinct properties, purposes, and rules for manipulation, although they do share certain Borland C++ operations. Generally speaking, pointers to functions are used to access functions and to pass functions as arguments to other functions; performing arithmetic on pointers to functions is not allowed. Pointers to objects, on the other hand, are regularly incremented and decremented as you scan arrays or more complex data structures in memory.

Although pointers contain numbers with most of the characteristics of unsigned integers, they have their own rules and restrictions for assignments, conversions, and arithmetic. The examples in the next few sections illustrate these rules and restrictions.

Note   See "Referencing" in Chapter 3 for a discussion of referencing and dereferencing.

Pointers to objects

A pointer of type "pointer to object of *type*" holds the address of (that is, points to) an object of *type*. Since pointers are objects, you can have a pointer pointing to a pointer (and so on). Other objects commonly pointed at include arrays, structures, unions, and classes.

The size of pointers to objects is dependent on the memory model and the size and disposition of your data segments, possibly influenced by the optional pointer modifiers (discussed starting with "Pointer modifiers").

Pointers to functions

A pointer to a function is best thought of as an address, usually in a code segment, where that function's executable code is stored; that is, the address to which control is transferred when that function is called. The size and disposition of your code segments is determined by the memory model in force, which in turn dictates the size of the function pointers needed to call your functions.

A pointer to a function has a type called "pointer to function returning *type*," where *type* is the function's return type. For example,

```
void (*func)();
```

In C++, this is a pointer to a function taking no arguments, and returning **void**. In C, it's a pointer to a function taking an unspecified number of arguments and returning **void**. In this example,

```
void (*func)(int);
```

func is a pointer to a function taking an **int** argument and returning **void**.

For C++, such a pointer can be used to access static member functions. Pointers to class members must use pointer-to-member operators. See "static_cast typecast operator" in Chapter 3 for details.

Pointer declarations

A pointer must be declared as pointing to some particular type, even if that type is **void** (which really means a pointer to anything). Once declared, though, a pointer can usually be reassigned so that it points to an object of another type. Borland C++ lets you reassign pointers like this without typecasting, but the compiler will warn you unless the pointer was originally declared to be of type pointer to void. And in C, but not C++, you can assign a **void*** pointer to a non-**void*** pointer. See "Type void" earlier in this chapter for details.

Warning! You need to initialize pointers before using them.

If *type* is any predefined or user-defined type, including **void**, the declaration

```
type *ptr;    /* Uninitialized pointer */
```

declares *ptr* to be of type "pointer to *type*." All the scoping, duration, and visibility rules apply to the *ptr* object just declared.

A null pointer value is an address that is guaranteed to be different from any valid pointer in use in a program. Assigning the integer constant 0 to a pointer assigns a null pointer value to it.

The mnemonic NULL (defined in the standard library header files, such as stdio.h) can be used for legibility. All pointers can be successfully tested for equality or inequality to NULL.

The pointer type "pointer to **void**" must not be confused with the null pointer. The declaration

```
void *vptr;
```

declares that *vptr* is a generic pointer capable of being assigned to by any "pointer to *type*" value, including null, without complaint. Assignments without proper casting between a "pointer to *type1*" and a "pointer to *type2*," where *type1* and *type2* are different types, can invoke a compiler warning or error. If *type1* is a function and *type2* isn't (or vice versa), pointer assignments are illegal. If *type1* is a pointer to **void**, no cast is needed. Under C, if *type2* is a pointer to **void**, no cast is needed.

Assignment restrictions also apply to pointers of different sizes (_ _**near**, _ _**far**, and _ _**huge**). You can assign a smaller pointer to a larger one without error, but you can't assign a larger pointer to a smaller one unless you are using an explicit cast. For example,

```
char _ _near *ncp;
char _ _far  *fcp;
char _ _huge *hcp;
fcp = ncp;                // legal
hcp = fcp;                // legal
fcp = hcp;                // not legal
ncp = fcp;                // not legal
ncp = (char _ _near*)fcp; // now legal
```

Pointer constants

A pointer or the pointed-at object can be declared with the **const** modifier. Anything declared as a **const** cannot be have its value changed. It is also illegal to create a pointer that might violate the nonassignability of a constant object. Consider the following examples:

```
int i;                        // i is an int
int * pi;                     // pi is a pointer to int (uninitialized)
int * const cp = &i;          // cp is a constant pointer to int
const int ci = 7;             // ci is a constant int
const int * pci;              // pci is a pointer to constant int
const int * const cpc = &ci;  // cpc is a constant pointer to a
                              // constant int
```

The following assignments are legal:

```
i = ci;          // Assign const-int to int
*cp = ci;        // Assign const-int to
                 // object-pointed-at-by-a-const-pointer
++pci;           // Increment a pointer-to-const
pci = cpc;       // Assign a const-pointer-to-a-const to a
                 // pointer-to-const
```

The following assignments are illegal:

```
ci = 0;          // NO--cannot assign to a const-int
ci--;            // NO--cannot change a const-int
*pci = 3;        // NO--cannot assign to an object
                 // pointed at by pointer-to-const
cp = &ci;        // NO--cannot assign to a const-pointer,
                 // even if value would be unchanged
cpc++;           // NO--cannot change const-pointer
pi = pci;        // NO--if this assignment were allowed,
```

```
// you would be able to assign to *pci
// (a const value) by assigning to *pi.
```

Similar rules apply to the **volatile** modifier. Note that **const** and **volatile** can both appear as modifiers to the same identifier.

Pointer arithmetic

Pointer arithmetic is limited to addition, subtraction, and comparison. Arithmetical operations on object pointers of type "pointer to *type*" automatically take into account the size of *type*; that is, the number of bytes needed to store a *type* object.

The internal arithmetic performed on pointers depends on the memory model in force and the presence of any overriding pointer modifiers.

When performing arithmetic with pointers, it is assumed that the pointer points to an array of objects. Thus, if a pointer is declared to point to *type*, adding an integral value to the pointer advances the pointer by that number of objects of *type*. If *type* has size 10 bytes, then adding an integer 5 to a pointer to *type* advances the pointer 50 bytes in memory. The difference has as its value the number of array elements separating the two pointer values. For example, if *ptr1* points to the third element of an array, and *ptr2* points to the tenth element, then the result of `ptr2 - ptr1` would be 7.

The difference between two pointers has meaning only if both pointers point into the same array.

When an integral value is added to or subtracted from a "pointer to *type*," the result is also of type "pointer to *type*."

There is no such element as "one past the last element," of course, but a pointer is allowed to assume such a value. If P points to the last array element, P + 1 is legal, but P + 2 is undefined. If P points to one past the last array element, P - 1 is legal, giving a pointer to the last element. However, applying the indirection operator * to a "pointer to one past the last element" leads to undefined behavior.

Informally, you can think of P + *n* as advancing the pointer by (*n* * **sizeof**(*type*)) bytes, as long as the pointer remains within the legal range (first element to one beyond the last element).

Subtracting two pointers to elements of the same array object gives an integral value of type *ptrdiff_t* defined in stddef.h (**signed long** for _ _**huge** and _ _**far** pointers; **signed int** for all others). This value represents the difference between the subscripts of the two referenced elements, provided it is in the range of *ptrdiff_t*. In the expression *P1 - P2*, where *P1* and *P2* are of type pointer to type (or pointer to qualified type), *P1* and *P2* must point to existing elements or to one past the last element. If *P1* points to the *i*-th element, and *P2* points to the *j*-th element, *P1 - P2* has the value (*i - j*).

Pointer conversions

Pointer types can be converted to other pointer types using the typecasting mechanism:

```
char *str;
int *ip;
str = (char *)ip;
```

More generally, the cast (*type**) will convert a pointer to type "pointer to *type*."
See Chapter 3 for a discussion of C++ typecast mechanisms.

C++ reference declarations

C++ reference types are closely related to pointer types. *Reference types* create aliases for objects and let you pass arguments to functions by reference. C passes arguments only by *value*. In C++ you can pass arguments by value or by reference. See "Referencing" for complete details.

Arrays

The declaration

type declarator [*<constant-expression>*]

declares an array composed of elements of *type*. An array consists of a contiguous region of storage exactly large enough to hold all of its elements.

If an expression is given in an array declarator, it must evaluate to a positive constant integer. The value is the number of elements in the array. Each of the elements of an array is numbered from 0 through the number of elements minus one.

Multidimensional arrays are constructed by declaring arrays of array type. The following example shows one way to declare a two-dimensional array. The implementation is for three rows and five columns but it can be very easily modified to accept run-time user input.

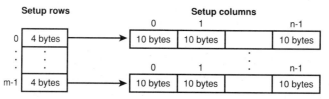

```
/* DYNAMIC MEMORY ALLOCATION FOR A MULTIDIMENSIONAL OBJECT. */
#include <stdio.h>
#include <stdlib.h>

typedef long double TYPE;
typedef TYPE *OBJECT;
unsigned int rows = 3, columns = 5;

void de_allocate(OBJECT);

int main(VOID) {
  OBJECT matrix;
  unsigned int i, j;

  /* STEP 1: SET UP THE ROWS. */
```

```
        matrix = (OBJECT) calloc( rows, sizeof(TYPE *));

        /* STEP 2: SET UP THE COLUMNS. */
        for (i = 0; i < rows; ++i)
          matrix[i] = (TYPE *) calloc( columns, sizeof(TYPE));

          for (i = 0; i < rows; i++)
            for (j = 0; j < columns; j++)
              matrix[i][j] = i + j;     /* INITIALIZE */

        for (i = 0; i < rows; ++i) {
          printf("\n\n");
          for (j = 0; j < columns; ++j)
            printf("%5.2Lf", matrix[i][j]);
        de_allocate(matrix);
        return 0;
        }

    void de_allocate(OBJECT x) {
      int i;

      for (i = 0; i < rows; i++)      /* STEP 1: DELETE THE COLUMNS */
        free(x[i]);

      free(x);      /* STEP 2: DELETE THE ROWS. */
      }
```

This code produces the following output:

```
0.00 1.00 2.00 3.00 4.00
1.00 2.00 3.00 4.00 5.00
2.00 3.00 4.00 5.00 6.00
```

Note   See Chapter 2 in the *C++ Language Reference* for a description of *calloc*, *free*, and *printf*.

In certain contexts, the first array declarator of a series might have no expression inside the brackets. Such an array is of indeterminate size. This is legitimate in contexts where the size of the array is not needed to reserve space.

For example, an **extern** declaration of an array object does not need the exact dimension of the array; neither does an array function parameter. As a special extension to ANSI C, Borland C++ also allows an array of indeterminate size as the final member of a structure. Such an array does not increase the size of the structure, except that padding can be added to ensure that the array is properly aligned. These structures are normally used in dynamic allocation, and the size of the actual array needed must be explicitly added to the size of the structure in order to properly reserve space.

Except when it is the operand of a **sizeof** or **&** operator, an array type expression is converted to a pointer to the first element of the array.

Functions

Functions are central to C and C++ programming. Languages such as Pascal distinguish between procedure and function. For C and C++, functions play both roles.

Declarations and definitions

Each program must have a single external function named *main* marking the entry point of the program. Functions are usually declared as prototypes in standard or user-supplied header files, or within program files. Functions are **external** by default and are normally accessible from any file in the program. They can be restricted by using the **static** storage class specifier (see "Linkage").

Functions are defined in your source files or made available by linking precompiled libraries.

A given function can be declared several times in a program, provided the declarations are compatible. Nondefining function declarations using the function prototype format provide Borland C++ with detailed parameter information, allowing better control over argument number and type checking, and type conversions.

Note In C++ you must always use function prototypes. We recommend that you also use them in C.

Excluding C++ function overloading, only one definition of any given function is allowed. The declarations, if any, must also match this definition. (The essential difference between a definition and a declaration is that the definition has a function body.)

Declarations and prototypes

In the Kernighan and Ritchie style of declaration, a function could be implicitly declared by its appearance in a function call, or explicitly declared as follows:

<*type*> *func*()

where *type* is the optional return type defaulting to **int**. In C++, this declaration means <*type*> *func*(**void**). A function can be declared to return any type except an array or function type. This approach does not allow the compiler to check that the type or number of arguments used in a function call match the declaration.

This problem was eased by the introduction of function prototypes with the following declaration syntax:

<*type*> *func*(*parameter-declarator-list*);

Note You can enable a warning within the IDE or with the command-line compiler:
`Function called without a prototype.`

Declarators specify the type of each function parameter. The compiler uses this information to check function calls for validity. The compiler is also able to coerce arguments to the proper type. Suppose you have the following code fragment:

```
extern long lmax(long v1, long v2); /* prototype */
foo()
{
    int limit = 32;
    char ch = 'A';
    long mval;
    mval = lmax(limit,ch);    /* function call */
}
```

Since it has the function prototype for *lmax*, this program converts *limit* and *ch* to **long**, using the standard rules of assignment, before it places them on the stack for the call to *lmax*. Without the function prototype, *limit* and *ch* would have been placed on the stack as an integer and a character, respectively; in that case, the stack passed to *lmax* would not match in size or content what *lmax* was expecting, leading to problems. The classic declaration style does not allow any checking of parameter type or number, so using function prototypes aids greatly in tracking down programming errors.

Function prototypes also aid in documenting code. For example, the function *strcpy* takes two parameters: a source string and a destination string. The question is, which is which? The function prototype

```
char *strcpy(char *dest, const char *source);
```

makes it clear. If a header file contains function prototypes, then you can print that file to get most of the information you need for writing programs that call those functions. If you include an identifier in a prototype parameter, it is used only for any later error messages involving that parameter; it has no other effect.

A function declarator with parentheses containing the single word **void** indicates a function that takes no arguments at all:

```
func(void);
```

In C++, *func*() also declares a function taking no arguments.

A function prototype normally declares a function as accepting a fixed number of parameters. For functions that accept a variable number of parameters (such as *printf*), a function prototype can end with an ellipsis (...), like this:

```
f(int *count, long total, ...)
```

With this form of prototype, the fixed parameters are checked at compile time, and the variable parameters are passed with no type checking.

Note   stdarg.h and varargs.h contain macros that you can use in user-defined functions with variable numbers of parameters.

Here are some more examples of function declarators and prototypes:

```
int  f();   * In C, a function returning an int with
               no information about parameters.
            This is the K&R "classic style." */

int f();   * In C++, a function taking no arguments */

int  f(void);   * A function returning an int that takes    no parameters. */
```

```
int  p(int,long);/  * A function returning an int that
         accepts two parameters: the first,
         an int; the second, a long. */

int  _ _pascal q(void); /* A pascal function returning
         an int that takes no parameters at all. */

char _ _far *s(char *source, int kind);  /*A function returning
            a farpointer to a char
            and accepting two parameters:
            the first,a pointer to
            a char;the second, an int. */      .

int  printf(char *format,...;  /*  function returning an int and
            accepting a pointer to a char fixed
            parameter and any number of additional
            parameters of unknown type. */

int  (*fp)(int)     /* A pointer to a function returning an int
            and accepting a single int parameter. */
```

Definitions

Table 2.9 gives the general syntax for external function definitions.

Table 2.9　　External function definitions

file
externaldefinition
file externaldefinition
externaldefinition:
functiondefinition
declaration
asmstatement
functiondefinition:
<declarationspecifiers> declarator <declaraionlist>
compoundstatement

In general, a function definition consists of the following sections (the grammar allows for more complicated cases):

1 Optional storage class specifiers: **extern** or **static**. The default is **extern**.

2 A return type, possibly **void**. The default is **int**.

3 Optional modifiers: _ _**pascal**, _ _**cdecl**, _ _**export**, _ _**interrupt**, _ _**near**, _ _**far**, _ _**huge**, _ _**loadds**, _ _**saveregs**. The defaults depend on the memory model and compiler option settings.

4 The name of the function.

5 A parameter declaration list, possibly empty, enclosed in parentheses. In C, the preferred way of showing an empty list is `func(void)`. The old style of *func* is legal in C but antiquated and possibly unsafe.

6 A function body representing the code to be executed when the function is called.

Note   You can mix elements from 1 and 2.

Formal parameter declarations

The formal parameter declaration list follows a syntax similar to that of the declarators found in normal identifier declarations. Here are a few examples:

```
int func(void) {                    // no args
int func(T1 t1, T2 t2, T3 t3=1) {   // three simple parameters, one
                                    // with default argument
int func(T1* ptr1, T2& tref) {      // A pointer and a reference arg
int func(register int i) {          // Request register for arg
int func(char *str,...) {           / * One string arg with a variable number of other
                        args, or with a fixed number of args with varying types */
```

In C++, you can give default arguments as shown. Parameters with default values must be the last arguments in the parameter list. The arguments' types can be scalars, structures, unions, or enumerations; pointers or references to structures and unions; or pointers to functions or classes.

The ellipsis (...) indicates that the function will be called with different sets of arguments on different occasions. The ellipsis can follow a sublist of known argument declarations. This form of prototype reduces the amount of checking the compiler can make.

The parameters declared all have automatic scope and duration for the duration of the function. The only legal storage class specifier is **register**.

The **const** and **volatile** modifiers can be used with formal parameter declarators.

Function calls and argument conversions

A function is called with actual arguments placed in the same sequence as their matching formal parameters. The actual arguments are converted as if by initialization to the declared types of the formal parameters.

Here is a summary of the rules governing how Borland C++ deals with language modifiers and formal parameters in function calls, both with and without prototypes:

- The language modifiers for a function definition must match the modifiers used in the declaration of the function at all calls to the function.

- A function can modify the values of its formal parameters, but this has no effect on the actual arguments in the calling routine, except for reference arguments in C++.

When a function prototype has not been previously declared, Borland C++ converts integral arguments to a function call according to the integral widening (expansion) rules described in Standard arithmetic conversions. When a function prototype is in scope, Borland C++ converts the given argument to the type of the declared parameter as if by assignment.

When a function prototype includes an ellipsis (...), Borland C++ converts all given function arguments as in any other prototype (up to the ellipsis). The compiler widens any arguments given beyond the fixed parameters, according to the normal rules for function arguments without prototypes.

If a prototype is present, the number of arguments must match (unless an ellipsis is present in the prototype). The types need to be compatible only to the extent that an assignment can legally convert them. You can always use an explicit cast to convert an argument to a type that is acceptable to a function prototype.

Note   If your function prototype does not match the actual function definition, Borland C++ will detect this if and only if that definition is in the same compilation unit as the prototype. If you create a library of routines with a corresponding header file of prototypes, consider including that header file when you compile the library, so that any discrepancies between the prototypes and the actual definitions will be caught. C++ provides type-safe linkage, so differences between expected and actual parameters will be caught by the linker.

Structures

A *structure* is a derived type usually representing a user-defined collection of named members (or components). The members can be of any type, either fundamental or derived (with some restrictions to be noted later), in any sequence. In addition, a structure member can be a bit field type not allowed elsewhere. The Borland C++ structure type lets you handle complex data structures almost as easily as single variables. Structure initialization is discussed in "Arrays, structures, and unions" earlier in this chapter.

In C++, a structure type is treated as a class type with certain differences: default access is public, and the default for the base class is also public. This allows more sophisticated control over access to structure members by using the C++ access specifiers: **public** (the default), **private**, and **protected**. Apart from these optional access mechanisms, and from exceptions as noted, the following discussion on structure syntax and usage applies equally to C and C++ structures.

Structures are declared using the keyword **struct**. For example

```
struct mystruct { ... }; // mystruct is the structure tag
    ⋮
    struct mystruct s, *ps, arrs[10];
/* s is type struct mystruct; ps is type pointer to struct mystruct;
    arrs is array of struct mystruct. */
```

Untagged structures and typedefs

If you omit the structure tag, you can get an untagged structure. You can use untagged structures to declare the identifiers in the comma-delimited *struct-id-list* to be of the given structure type (or derived from it), but you cannot declare additional objects of this type elsewhere:

```
struct { ... } s, *ps, arrs[10]; // untagged structure
```

It is possible to create a **typedef** while declaring a structure, with or without a tag:

```
typedef struct mystruct { ... } MYSTRUCT;
MYSTRUCT s, *ps, arrs[10];        // same as struct mystruct s, etc.
typedef struct { ... } YRSTRUCT; // no tag
YRSTRUCT y, *yp, arry[20];
```

Usually, you don't need both a tag and a **typedef**: either can be used in structure declarations.

Untagged structure and union members are ignored during initialization.

Structure member declarations

The *member-decl-list* within the braces declares the types and names of the structure members using the declarator syntax shown in Borland C++ declaration syntax.

A structure member can be of any type, with two exceptions:

- The member type cannot be the same as the **struct** type being currently declared:

```
struct mystruct { mystruct s } s1, s2; // illegal
```

  However, a member can be a pointer to the structure being declared, as in the following example:

```
struct mystruct { mystruct *ps } s1, s2; // OK
```

  Also, a structure can contain previously defined structure types when declaring an instance of a declared structure.

- Except in C++, a member cannot have the type "function returning...," but the type "pointer to function returning..." is allowed. In C++, a **struct** can have member functions.

Note   You can omit the **struct** keyword in C++.

Structures and functions

A function can return a structure type or a pointer to a structure type:

```
mystruct func1(void);  // func1() returns a structure
mystruct *func2(void); // func2() returns pointer to structure
```

A structure can be passed as an argument to a function in the following ways:

```
void func1(mystruct s);       // directly
void func2(mystruct *sptr);   // via a pointer
void func3(mystruct &sref);   // as a reference (C++ only)
```

Structure member access

Structure and union members are accessed using the following two selection operators:

. (period)

-> (right arrow)

Suppose that the object *s* is of struct type *S*, and *sptr* is a pointer to *S*. Then if *m* is a member identifier of type *M* declared in *S*, the expressions *s.m* and *sptr->m* are of type *M*, and both represent the member object *m* in *S*. The expression *sptr->m* is a convenient synonym for `(*sptr).m`.

The operator . is called the direct member selector and the operator -> is called the indirect (or pointer) member selector. For example:

```
struct mystruct
{
    int i;
    char str[21];
    double d;
} s, *sptr = &s;
        ⋮
s.i = 3;              // assign to the i member of mystruct s
sptr -> d = 1.23;     // assign to the d member of mystruct s
```

The expression *s.m* is an lvalue, provided that s is an lvalue and *m* is not an array type. The expression *sptr->m* is an lvalue unless *m* is an array type.

If structure *B* contains a field whose type is structure *A*, the members of *A* can be accessed by two applications of the member selectors:

```
struct A {
    int j;
    double x;
};
struct B {
    int i;
    struct A a;
    double d;
} s, *sptr;
        ⋮
s.i = 3;              // assign to the i member of B
s.a.j = 2;           // assign to the j member of A
sptr->d = 1.23;      // assign to the d member of B
(sptr->a).x = 3.14   // assign to x member of A
```

Each structure declaration introduces a unique structure type, so that in

```
struct A {
    int i,j;
    double d;
} a, a1;
struct B {
    int i,j;
```

```
      double d;
   } b;
```

the objects *a* and *a1* are both of type struct *A*, but the objects *a* and *b* are of different structure types. Structures can be assigned only if the source and destination have the same type:

```
a = a1;   // OK: same type, so member by member assignment
a = b;    // ILLEGAL: different types
a.i = b.i; a.j = b.j; a.d = b.d /* but you can assign member-by-member */
```

Structure word alignment

Memory is allocated to a structure member-by-member from left to right, from low to high memory address. In this example,

```
struct mystruct {
   int i;
   char str[21];
   double d;
} s;
```

the object *s* occupies sufficient memory to hold a 2-byte integer for a 16-bit program, or a 4-byte integer for a 32-bit program, a 21-byte string, and an 8-byte **double**. The format of this object in memory is determined by selecting the word alignment option. Without word alignment, *s* will be allocated 31 contiguous bytes (by the 16-bit compiler) or 33 contiguous bytes (by the 32-bit compiler).

Word alignment is off by default. If you turn on word alignment, Borland C++ pads the structure with bytes to ensure the structure is aligned as follows:

1 The structure will start on a word boundary (even address).

2 Any non-**char** member will have an even byte offset from the start of the structure.

3 A final byte is added (if necessary) at the end to ensure that the whole structure contains an even number of bytes.

For the 16-bit compiler, with word alignment on, the structure would therefore have a byte added before the **double**, making a 32-byte object.

1 The structure boundaries are defined by 4-byte multiples.

2 For any non-**char** member, the offset will be a multiple of the member size. A **short** will be at an offset that is some multiple of 2 **ints** from the start of the structure.

3 One to three bytes can be added (if necessary) at the end to ensure that the whole structure contains a 4-byte multiple.

For the 32-bit compiler, with word alignment on, three bytes would be added before the **double**, making a 36-byte object.

Structure name spaces

Structure tag names share the same name space with union tags and enumeration tags (but **enums** within a structure are in a different name space in C++). This means that such tags must be uniquely named within the same scope. However, tag names need not differ from identifiers in the other three name spaces: the label name space, the member name space(s), and the single name space (which consists of variables, functions, **typedef** names, and enumerators).

Member names within a given structure or union must be unique, but they can share the names of members in other structures or unions. For example,

```
goto s;
    ⋮
s:              // Label
struct s {      // OK: tag and label name spaces different
   int s;       // OK: label, tag and member name spaces different
   float s;     // ILLEGAL: member name duplicated
} s;            // OK: var name space different. In C++, this can only
                // be done if s does not have a constructor.
union s {       // ILLEGAL: tag space duplicate
   int s;       // OK: new member space
   float f;
} f;            // OK: var name space
struct t {
   int s;       // OK: different member space
     ⋮
} s;            // ILLEGAL: var name duplicate
```

Incomplete declarations

A pointer to a structure type *A* can legally appear in the declaration of another structure *B* before *A* has been declared:

```
struct A;                  // incomplete
struct B { struct A *pa };
struct A { struct B *pb };
```

The first appearance of *A* is called *incomplete* because there is no definition for it at that point. An incomplete declaration is allowed here, because the definition of *B* doesn't need the size of *A*.

Bit fields

When you write an application for a 16-bit platform, you can declare **signed** or **unsigned** integer members as bit fields from 1 to 16 bits wide. For 32-bit platforms, a bit field can be as much as 32 bits wide. You specify the bit-field width and optional identifier as follows:

type-specifier<bitfield-id> : width;

where *type-specifier<bitfield-id>* is **char, unsigned char, int,** or **unsigned int**. Bit fields are allocated from low-order to high-order bits within a word. The expression *width* must be present and must evaluate to a constant integer in the range 1 to 32, depending on the target platform.

If the bit field identifier is omitted, the number of bits specified in *width* is allocated, but the field is not accessible. This lets you match bit patterns in, say, hardware registers where some bits are unused. For example:

```
struct mystruct
    int       i  :  2;
    unsigned      j  :  5;
    int        :  4;
    int       k  :  1;
    unsigned      m  :  4;
) a, b, c;
```

produces the following layout:

15	14	13	12	11	10	9	8	7	6	5	4	3	2	1	0
X	X	X	X	X	X	X	X	X	X	X	X	X	X	X	X
<------------------------->	<->	<------------------------->	<-------------------------------------->	<--------->
m		k	(unused)		j		i

Integer fields are stored in two's-complement form, with the leftmost bit being the MSB (most significant bit). With **int** (for example, **signed**) bit fields, the MSB is interpreted as a sign bit. A bit field of width 2 holding binary 11, therefore, would be interpreted as 3 if **unsigned**, but as -1 if **int**. In the previous example, the legal assignment a.i = 6 would leave binary 10 = -2 in a.i with no warning. The signed int field k of width 1 can hold only the values -1 and 0, because the bit pattern 1 is interpreted as -1.

Bit fields can be declared only in structures, unions, and classes. They are accessed with the same member selectors (. and ->) used for non-bit-field members. Also, bit fields pose several problems when writing portable code, since the organization of bits-within-bytes and bytes-within-words is machine dependent.

The expression *&mystruct.x* is illegal if *x* is a bit field identifier, because there is no guarantee that *mystruct.x* lies at a byte address.

Unions

Union types are derived types sharing many of the syntactical and functional features of structure types. The key difference is that a union allows only one of its members to be "active" at any one time. The size of a union is the size of its largest member. The value of only one of its members can be stored at any time. In the following simple case,

```
union myunion {      /* union tag = myunion */
    int i;
    double d;
    char ch;
} mu, *muptr=&mu;
```

the identifier *mu*, of type **union** *myunion*, can be used to hold a 2-byte **int**, an 8-byte **double**, or a single-byte **char**, but only one of these at the same time.

Note   Unions correspond to the variant record types of Pascal and Modula-2.

sizeof(union *myunion*) and **sizeof**(*mu*) both return 8, but 6 bytes are unused (padded) when *mu* holds an **int** object, and 7 bytes are unused when *mu* holds a **char**. You access union members with the structure member selectors (. and >), but care is needed:

```
mu.d = 4.016;
printf("mu.d = %f\n",mu.d); //OK: displays mu.d = 4.016
printf("mu.i = %d\n",mu.i); //peculiar result
mu.ch = 'A';
printf("mu.ch = %c\n",mu.ch); //OK: displays mu.ch = A
printf("mu.d = %f\n",mu.d); //peculiar result
muptr->i = 3;
printf("mu.i = %d\n",mu.i); //OK: displays mu.i = 3
```

The second *printf* is legal, since *mu.i* is an integer type. However, the bit pattern in *mu.i* corresponds to parts of the **double** previously assigned, and will not usually provide a useful integer interpretation.

When properly converted, a pointer to a union points to each of its members, and vice versa.

Anonymous unions (C++ only)

A union that doesn't have a tag and is not used to declare a named object (or other type) is called an *anonymous union*. It has the following form:

```
union { member-list };
```

Its members can be accessed directly in the scope where this union is declared, without using the x.y or p->y syntax.

Anonymous unions can't have member functions and at file level must be declared static. In other words, an anonymous union cannot have external linkage.

Union declarations

The general declaration syntax for unions is similar to that for structures. The differences are

- Unions can contain bit fields, but only one can be active. They all start at the beginning of the union. (*Note that, because bit fields are machine dependent, they can pose problems when writing portable code.*)

- Unlike C++ structures, C++ union types cannot use the class access specifiers: **public**, **private**, and **protected**. All fields of a union are public.

- Unions can be initialized only through their first declared member:

```
union local87 {
        int i;
        double d;
        } a = { 20 };
```

- A union can't participate in a class hierarchy. It can't be derived from any class, nor can it be a base class. A union *can* have a constructor.

Enumerations

An enumeration data type is used to provide mnemonic identifiers for a set of integer values. For example, the following declaration,

```
enum days { sun, mon, tues, wed, thur, fri, sat } anyday;
```

establishes a unique integral type, **enum days**, a variable *anyday* of this type, and a set of enumerators (*sun*, *mon*, ...) with constant integer values

Borland C++ is free to store enumerators in a single byte when `Treat enums as ints is unchecked` (O | C | Code Generation) or the **-b** flag is used. The default is on (meaning **enums** are always **ints**) if the range of values permits, but the value is always promoted to an **int** when used in expressions. The identifiers used in an enumerator list are implicitly of type **signed char**, **unsigned char**, or **int**, depending on the values of the enumerators. If all values can be represented in a **signed** or **unsigned char**, that is the type of each enumerator.

In C, a variable of an enumerated type can be assigned any value of type **int**—no type checking beyond that is enforced. In C++, a variable of an enumerated type can be assigned only one of its enumerators. That is,

```
anyday = mon;        // OK
anyday = 1;          // illegal, even though mon == 1
```

The identifier *days* is the optional enumeration tag that can be used in subsequent declarations of enumeration variables of type **enum days**:

```
enum days payday, holiday; // declare two variables
```

In C++, you can omit the **enum** keyword if **days** is not the name of anything else in the same scope.

As with **struct** and **union** declarations, you can omit the tag if no further variables of this **enum** type are required:

```
enum { sun, mon, tues, wed, thur, fri, sat } anyday;
/* anonymous enum type */
```

The enumerators listed inside the braces are also known as *enumeration constants*. Each is assigned a fixed integral value. In the absence of explicit initializers, the first enumerator (*sun*) is set to zero, and each succeeding enumerator is set to one more than its predecessor (*mon* = 1, *tues* = 2, and so on). See "Enumeration constants" in Chapter 1 for more on enumeration constants.

With explicit integral initializers, you can set one or more enumerators to specific values. Any subsequent names without initializers will then increase by one. For example, in the following declaration,

```
/* Initializer expression can include previously declared enumerators */
enum coins { penny = 1, tuppence, nickel = penny + 4, dime = 10,
             quarter = nickel * nickel } smallchange;
```

tuppence would acquire the value 2, *nickel* the value 5, and *quarter* the value 25.

The initializer can be any expression yielding a positive or negative integer value (after possible integer promotions). These values are usually unique, but duplicates are legal.

enum types can appear wherever **int** types are permitted:

```
enum days { sun, mon, tues, wed, thur, fri, sat } anyday;

enum days payday;
typedef enum days DAYS;
DAYS *daysptr;
int i = tues;
anyday = mon;        // OK
*daysptr = anyday;   // OK
mon = tues;          // ILLEGAL: mon is a constant
```

Enumeration tags share the same name space as structure and union tags. Enumerators share the same name space as ordinary variable identifiers:

```
int mon = 11;
{
    enum days { sun, mon, tues, wed, thur, fri, sat } anyday;
    /* enumerator mon hides outer declaration of int mon */
    struct days { int i, j;};    // ILLEGAL: days duplicate tag
    double sat;                  // ILLEGAL: redefinition of sat
}
mon = 12;                        // back in int mon scope
```

In C++, enumerators declared within a class are in the scope of that class.

In C++ it is possible to overload most operators for an enumeration. However, because the =, [ ], ( ), and -> operators must be overloaded as member functions, it is not possible to overload them for an **enum**. See the following example on how to overload the postfix and prefix increment operators.

How to overload enum operators

```
// OVERLOAD THE POSTFIX AND PREFIX INCREMENT OPERATORS FOR enum

#include <iostream.h>
enum _SEASON { spring, summer, fall, winter };
_SEASON operator++(_SEASON &s) {       // PREFIX INCREMENT
    _SEASON tmp = s; // SAVE THE ORIGINAL VALUE
    // DO MODULAR ARITHMETIC AND CAST THE RESULT TO _SEASON TYPE
    s = _SEASON( (s + 1) % 4 );         // INCREMENT THE ORIGINAL
    return s;                           // RETURN THE OLD VALUE
    }
// UNNAMED int ARGUMENT IS NOT USED
_SEASON operator++(_SEASON &s, int) { // POSTFIX INCREMENT
    _SEASON tmp = s;
    switch (s) {
        case spring: s = summer; break;
        case summer: s = fall; break;
        case fall:   s = winter; break;
        case winter: s = spring; break;
        }
    return (tmp);
    }
```

```
int main(void) {
    _SEASON season = fall;
    cout << "\nThe season is " << season;
    cout << "\nIncrement the season: "<< ++season;
    cout << "\nNo change yet when using postfix: " << season++;
    cout << "\nFinally:" << season;
    return 0;
    }
```

This code produces the following output:

```
The season is 2
Increment the season: 3
No change yet when using postfix: 3
Finally:0
```

Assignment to enum types

The rules for expressions involving **enum** types have been made stricter. The compiler enforces these rules with error messages if the compiler switch **-A** is turned on (which means strict ANSI C++).

Assigning an integer to a variable of **enum** type results in an error:

```
enum color

{
   red, green, blue
};

int f()
{
   color c;
   c = 0;
   return c;
}
```

The same applies when passing an integer as a parameter to a function. Notice that the result type of the expression flag1 | flag2 is **int**:

```
enum e

{
   flag1 = 0x01,
   flag2 = 0x02
};

void p(e);

void f()
{
   p(flag1|flag2);
}
```

To make the example compile, the expression flag1 I flag2 must be cast to the **enum** type: `e (flag1|flag2)`.

Expressions

An *expression* is a sequence of operators, operands, and punctuators that specifies a computation. The formal syntax, listed in Table 2.10, indicates that expressions are defined recursively: subexpressions can be nested without formal limit. (However, the compiler will report an out-of-memory error if it can't compile an expression that is too complex.)

Note   Borland C++ expressions, shows how identifiers and operators are combined to form grammatically legal "phrases."

Expressions are evaluated according to certain conversion, grouping, associativity, and precedence rules that depend on the operators used, the presence of parentheses, and the data types of the operands. The standard conversions are detailed in Table 2.5. The way operands and subexpressions are grouped does not necessarily specify the actual order in which they are evaluated by Borland C++ (see "Evaluation order").

Expressions can produce an lvalue, an rvalue, or no value. Expressions might cause side effects whether they produce a value or not.

The precedence and associativity of the operators are summarized in associativity and precidence in Borland C++ operators. The grammar in Table 2.10, completely defines the precedence and associativity of the operators.

Table 2.10   Borland C++ expressions

primary-expression:
  literal
  this (C++ specific)
  :: *identifier* (C++ specific)
  :: *operator-function-name* (C++ specific)
  :: *qualified-name* (C++ specific)
  (expression)
  name
literal:
  integer-constant
  character-constant
  floating-constant
  string-literal
name:
  identifier
  operator-function-name (C++ specific)
  conversion-function-name (C++ specific)
  ~ class-name (C++ specific)
  qualified-name (C++ specific)

Table 2.10   Borland C++ expressions (continued)

qualified-name: (C++ specific)

  qualified-class-name **::** *name*

postfix-expression:

  primary-expression

  postfix-expression [expression]

  postfix-expression (<expression-list>)

  simple-type-name   (<expression-list>) (C++ specific)

  postfix-expression . name

  postfix-expression -> name

  postfix-expression ++

  postfix-expression --

  const_cast *< type-id > (expression)* (C++ specific)

  dynamic_cast *< type-id > (expression)* (C++ specific)

  reinterpret_cast *< type-id > (expression)* (C++ specific)

  static_cast *< type-id > (expression)* (C++ specific)

  typeid *(expression)* (C++ specific)

  typeid *(type-name)* (C++ specific)

expression-list:

  assignment-expression

  expression-list , assignment-expression

unary-expression:

  postfix-expression

  ++ *unary-expression*

  - - *unary-expression*

  unary-operator cast-expression

  sizeof *unary-expression*

  sizeof *(type-name)*

  allocation-expression (C++ specific)

  deallocation-expression (C++ specific)

unary-operator: one of **&** ***** **+** **-** **!**

allocation-expression: (C++ specific)

  <::> **new** *<placement> new-type-name <initializer>*

  <::> **new** *<placement> (type-name) <initializer>*

placement: (C++ specific)

  (expression-list)

new-type-name: (C++ specific)

  type-specifiers <new-declarator>

new-declarator: (C++ specific)

  ptr-operator <new-declarator>

  new-declarator [<expression>]

deallocation-expression: (C++ specific)

  <::> **delete** *cast-expression*

  <::> **delete** *[ ] cast-expression*

Table 2.10   Borland C++ expressions (continued)

cast-expression:
　unary-expression
　(type-name) cast-expression
pm-expression:
　cast-expression
　pm-expression .* cast-expression (C++ specific)
　pm-expression ->* cast-expression (C++ specific)
multiplicative-expression:
　pm-expression
　multiplicative-expression * pm-expression
　multiplicative-expression / pm-expression
　multiplicative-expression % pm-expression
additive-expression:
　multiplicative-expression
　additive-expression + multiplicative-expression
　additive-expression - multiplicative-expression
shift-expression:
　additive-expression
　shift-expression << additive-expression
　shift-expression >> additive-expression
relational-expression:
　shift-expression
　relational-expression < shift-expression
　relational-expression > shift-expression
　relational-expression <= shift-expression
　relational-expression >= shift-expression
equality-expression:
　relational-expression
　equality expression == relational-expression
　equality expression != relational-expression
AND-expression:
　equality-expression
　AND-expression & equality-expression
exclusive-OR-expression:
　AND-expression
　exclusive-OR-expression ^ AND-expression
inclusive-OR-expression:
　exclusive-OR-expression
　inclusive-OR-expression | exclusive-OR-expression

Table 2.10   Borland C++ expressions (continued)

logical-AND-expression:
  inclusive-OR-expression
  logical-AND-expression && inclusive-OR-expression
logical-OR-expression:
  logical-AND-expression
  logical-OR-expression || logical-AND-expression
conditional-expression:
  logical-OR-expression
  logical-OR-expression ? expression : conditional-expression
assignment-expression:
  conditional-expression
  unary-expression assignment-operator assignment-expression
assignment-operator: one of
  = *= /= %= += -=
  << => >= &= ^= |=
expression:
  assignment-expression
  expression , assignment-expression
constant-expression:
  conditional-expression

Precedence of operators

There are 17 precedence categories, some of which contain only one operator. Operators in the same category have equal precedence with each other.

Where duplicates of operators appear in the table, the first occurrence is unary, the second binary. Each category has an associativity rule: left to right, or right to left. In the absence of parentheses, these rules resolve the grouping of expressions with operators of equal precedence.

The precedence of each operator category in the following table is indicated by its order in the table. The first category (the first line) has the highest precedence.

Table 2.11   Associativity and precedence of Borland C++ operators

Operators	Associativity
( ) [ ] -> :: .	Left to right
! ~ + - ++ -- & * (*typecast*)	Right to left
sizeof new delete typeid	Right to left
.* ->*	Left to right
* / %	Left to right
+ -	Left to right
<< >>	Left to right
< <= > >=	Left to right
== !=	Left to right

Table 2.11   Associativity and precedence of Borland C++ operators (continued)

Operators	Associativity
&	Left to right
^	Left to right
|	Left to right
&&	Left to right
||	Left to right
?: (conditional expression)	Right to left
= *= /= %= += −= &= ^= |= <<= >>=	Right to left
,	Left to right

Expressions and C++

C++ allows the overloading of certain standard C operators. An overloaded operator is defined to behave in a special way when applied to expressions of class type. For instance, the equality operator == might be defined in class *complex* to test the equality of two complex numbers without changing its normal usage with non-class data types.

An overloaded operator is implemented as a function; this function determines the operand type, lvalue, and evaluation order to be applied when the overloaded operator is used. However, overloading cannot change the precedence of an operator. Similarly, C++ allows user-defined conversions between class objects and fundamental types. Keep in mind, then, that some of the C language rules for operators and conversions might not apply to expressions in C++.

Evaluation order

The order in which Borland C++ evaluates the operands of an expression is not specified, except where an operator specifically states otherwise. The compiler will try to rearrange the expression in order to improve the quality of the generated code. Care is therefore needed with expressions in which a value is modified more than once. In general, avoid writing expressions that both modify and use the value of the same object. For example, consider the expression

```
i = v[i++];  // i is undefined
```

The value of *i* depends on whether *i* is incremented before or after the assignment. Similarly,

```
int total = 0;
sum = (total = 3) + (++total); // sum = 4 or sum = 7 ??
```

is ambiguous for *sum* and *total*. The solution is to revamp the expression, using a temporary variable:

```
int temp, total = 0;
temp = ++total;
sum = (total = 3) + temp;
```

Where the syntax does enforce an evaluation sequence, it is safe to have multiple evaluations:

```
sum = (i = 3, i++, i++); // OK: sum = 4, i = 5
```

Each subexpression of the comma expression is evaluated from left to right, and the whole expression evaluates to the rightmost value.

Borland C++ regroups expressions, rearranging associative and commutative operators regardless of parentheses, in order to create an efficiently compiled expression; in no case will the rearrangement affect the value of the expression.

You can use parentheses to force the order of evaluation in expressions. For example, if you have the variables a, b, c, and f, then the expression $f = a + (b + c)$ forces $(b + c)$ to be evaluated before adding the result to a.

Errors and overflows

Associativity and precedence of Borland C++ operators summarizes the precedence and associativity of the operators. During the evaluation of an expression, Borland C++ can encounter many problematic situations, such as division by zero or out-of-range floating-point values. Integer overflow is ignored (C uses modulo 2^n arithmetic on n-bit registers), but errors detected by math library functions can be handled by standard or user-defined routines. See _matherr_ and _signal_.

Operators summary

Operators are tokens that trigger some computation when applied to variables and other objects in an expression.

- Arithmetic
- Assignment
- Bitwise
- C++ specific
- Comma
- Conditional
- Equality
- Logical
- Postfix Expression
- Primary Expression
- Preprocessor
- Reference/Indirect
- Relational

- sizeof

- typeid

All operators can be overloaded except the following:

.	C++ direct component selector
. *	C++ dereference
: :	C++ scope access/resolution
? :	Conditional

Depending on context, the same operator can have more than one meaning. For example, the ampersand (&) can be interpreted as:

- a bitwise AND (A & B)

- an address operator (&A)

- in C++, a reference modifier

Note No spaces are allowed in compound operators. Spaces change the meaning of the operator and will generate an error.

Primary expression operators

For ANSI C, the primary expressions are *literal* (also sometimes referred to as *constant*), identifier, and (*expression*). The C++ language extends this list of primary expressions to include the keyword **this**, scope resolution operator ::, *name*, and the class destructor ~ (tilde).

The primary expressions are summarized in the following list.

primary-expression:
  literal
  this (C++ specific)
    :: *identifier* (C++ specific)
    :: *operator-function-name* (C++ specific)
    :: *qualified-name* (C++ specific)
    (*expression)*
    name
literal:
  integer-constant
  character-constant
    floating-constant
    string-literal
name:
  identifier
  operator-function-name (C++ specific)
    conversion-function-name (C++ specific)

> *~ class-name* (C++ specific)
>   *qualified-name* (C++ specific)   ˙
> *qualified-name:* (C++ specific)
>   *qualified-class-name* :: *name*

For a discussion of the primary expression **this**, see Chapter 3. The keyword **this** cannot be used outside a class member function body.

The scope resolution operator allows reference to a type, object, function, or enumerator even though its identifier is hidden.

The parentheses surrounding an *expression* do not change the unadorned expression itself.

The primary expression *name* is restricted to the category of primary expressions that sometimes appear after the member access operators **.** (dot) and **–>** . Therefore, *name* must be either an lvalue or a function. See also the discussion of member access operators.

An *identifier* is a primary expression, provided it has been suitably declared. The description and formal definition of identifiers is shown in Chapter 1.

See "Constructors and destructors," in Chapter 3 on how to use the destructor operator ~ (tilde).

Postfix expression operators

Syntax

```
postfix-expression(<arg-expression-list>)
array declaration [constant-expression]
compound statement { statement list }
postfix-expression . identifier
postfix-expression -> identifier
```

Remarks

( )   use to group expressions, isolate conditional expressions, indicate function calls and function parameters

{ }   use as the start and end of compound statements

[ ]   use to indicate single and multidimensional array subscripts

.   use to access structure and union members

->   use to access structure and union members

The following postfix expressions let you make safe, explicit typecasts in a C++ program:

const_cast< T > (expression)

dynamic_cast< T > (expression)

reinterpret_cast< T > (expression)

static_cast< T > (expression)

To obtain run-time type identification (RTTI), use the **typeid()** operator. The syntax is as follows:

typeid(expression)

typeid(type-name)

Array subscript operator

Brackets ([ ]) indicate single and multidimensional array subscripts. The expression

```
<exp1>[exp2]
```

is defined as

```
*((exp1) + (exp2))
```

where either:

- *exp1* is a pointer and *exp2* is an integer or
- *exp1* is an integer and *exp2* is a pointer

Function call operator

Syntax

```
postfix-expression(<arg-expression-list>)
```

Remarks
Parentheses ()

- group expressions
- isolate conditional expressions
- indicate function calls and function parameters

The value of the function call expression, if it has a value, is determined by the return statement in the function definition.

This is a call to the function given by the postfix expression.

arg-expression-list is a comma-delimited list of expressions of any type representing the actual (or real) function arguments.

Direct member selector

Syntax

```
postfix-expression . identifier
```

postfix-expression must be of type union or structure.

identifier must be the name of a member of that structure or union type.

Remarks

Use the selection operator (.) to access structure and union members.

Suppose that the object *s* is of struct type *S* and *sptr* is a pointer to *S*. Then, if *m* is a member identifier of type *M* declared in *S*, this expression:

```
s.m
```

are of type *M*, and represent the member object *m* in *s*.

Example

```
struct mystruct {
    int i
    char str[21]
    double d
} s, *sptr=&s
  ...
s.i = 3          // assign to the i member of mystruct s
```

The expression *s.m* is an lvalue, provided that *s* is not an lvalue and *m* is not an array type.

If structure B contains a field whose type is structure A, the members of A can be accessed by two applications of the member selectors.

Indirect member selector

Syntax

```
postfix-expression -> identifier
```

postfix-expression must be of type pointer to structure or pointer to union.

identifier must be the name of a member of that structure or union type.

The expression designates a member of a structure or union object. The value of the expression is the value of the selected member it will be an lvalue if and only if the postfix expression is an lvalue.

Remarks

You use the selection operator -> to access structure and union members.

Suppose that the object *s* is of struct type *S* and *sptr* is a pointer to *S*. Then, if *m* is a member identifier of type *M* declared in *S*, this expression:

```
sptr->m
```

is of type *M*, and represents the member object *m* in *s*.

The expression

```
s->sptr
```

is a convenient synonym for *(*sptr).m*.

Example

```
struct mystruct {
    int i
    char str[21]
    double d
} s, *sptr=&s
    ⋮
sptr->d = 1.23    // assign to the d member of mystruct s
```

The expression *sptr->m* is an lvalue unless *m* is an array type.

If structure B contains a field whose type is structure A, the members of A can be accessed by two applications of the member selectors.

Increment/decrement operators

Increment operator (++)

Syntax

```
postfix-expression ++        (postincrement)
++ unary-expression          (preincrement)
```

The expression is called the operand it must be of scalar type (arithmetic or pointer types) and must be a modifiable lvalue.

Postincrement operator

The value of the whole expression is the value of the postfix expression before the increment is applied.

After the postfix expression is evaluated, the operand is incremented by 1.

Preincrement operator

The operand is incremented by 1 before the expression is evaluated the value of the whole expression is the incremented value of the operand.

The increment value is appropriate to the type of the operand.

Pointer types follow the rules for pointer arithmetic.

Decrement operator (--)

Syntax

```
postfix-expression --          (postdecrement)
-- unary-expression            (predecrement)
```

The decrement operator follows the same rules as the increment operator, except that the operand is decremented by 1 after or before the whole expression is evaluated.

Unary operators

Syntax

```
<unary-operator> <unary expression>
```

or

```
<unary-operator> <type><unary expression>
```

Remarks
Unary operators group right-to-left.

Borland C++ provides the following unary operators:

- ! Logical negation

- * Indirection

- ++ Increment

- ~ Bitwise complement

- -- Decrement

- - Unary minus

- + Unary plus

Reference/indirect operators

Syntax

```
& cast-expression
* cast-expression
```

Remarks

The & and * operators work together to reference and dereference pointers that are passed to functions.

Referencing operator (&)
Use the reference operator to pass the address of a pointer to a function outside of *main()*.

The cast-expression operand must be one of the following:

- a function designator
- an lvalue designating an object that is not a bit field and is not declared with a register storage class specifier

If the operand is of type <*type*>, the result is of <*type*> pointer to type.

Some non-lvalue identifiers, such as function names and array names, are automatically converted into "pointer-to-X" types when they appear in certain contexts. The **&** operator can be used with such objects, but its use is redundant and therefore discouraged.

Consider the following example:

```
T t1 = 1, t2 = 2;

T *ptr = &t1;        // Initialized pointer
*ptr = t2;              // Same effect as t1 = t2
```

`T *ptr = &t1` is treated as

```
T *ptr;
ptr = &t1;
```

So it is *ptr*, or **ptr*, that gets assigned. Once *ptr* has been initialized with the address *&t1*, it can be safely dereferenced to give the lvalue **ptr*.

Indirection operator (*)

Use the asterisk (*) in a variable expression to create pointers. And use the indirect operator in external functions to get a pointer's value that was passed by reference.

If the operand is of type *pointer to function*, the result is a function designator.

If the operand is a pointer to an object, the result is an lvalue designating that object.

The result of indirection is undefined if either of the following occur:

- The *cast-expression* is a null pointer.
- The *cast-expression* is the address of an automatic variable and execution of its block has terminated.

Note   & can also be the bitwise AND operator.

* can also be the multiplication operator.

Plus operator +

In the expression

> + *cast-expression*

the *cast-expression* operand must be of arithmetic type. The result is the value of the operand after any required integral promotions.

Minus operator –

In the expression

– cast-expression

the *cast-expression* operand must be of arithmetic type. The result is the negative of the value of the operand after any required integral promotions.

Bitwise complement operator ~

In the expression

~ cast-expression

the *cast-expression* operand must be of integral type. The result is the bitwise complement of the operand after any required integral promotions. Each 0 bit in the operand is set to 1, and each 1 bit in the operand is set to 0.

Logical negation operator !

In the expression

! cast-expression

the *cast-expression* operand must be of scalar type. The result is of type **int** and is the logical negation of the operand: 0 if the operand is nonzero; 1 if the operand is zero. The expression *!E* is equivalent to (0 == E).

Increment operator ++

In the expressions

++ unary-expression
unary-expression ++

the unary expression is the operand; it must be of scalar type and must be a modifiable lvalue. The first expression shows the syntax for the prefix increment operator, also known as the *preincrement* operator. The operand is incremented by 1 *before* the expression is evaluated; the value of the whole expression is the incremented value of the operand. The 1 used to increment is the appropriate value for the type of the operand. Pointer types follow the rules of pointer arithmetic.

The second expression shows the syntax for the postfix increment operator (also known as the *postincrement* operator). The operand is incremented by 1 *after* the expression is evaluated.

Decrement operator – –

The following expressions show the syntax for prefix and postfix decrementation. The prefix decrement is also known as the *predecrement*; the postfix decrement is also known as the *postdecrement*.

– – unary-expression
unary-expression – –

The operator follows the same rules as the increment operator, except that the operand is decremented by 1.

The sizeof operator

The **sizeof** operator has two distinct uses:

sizeof *unary-expression*
sizeof (*type-name*)

The result in both cases is an integer constant that gives the size in bytes of how much memory space is used by the operand (determined by its type, with some exceptions). The amount of space that is reserved for each type depends on the machine. In the first use, the type of the operand expression is determined without evaluating the expression (and therefore without side effects). When the operand is of type **char** (**signed** or **unsigned**), **sizeof** gives the result 1. When the operand is a non-parameter of array type, the result is the total number of bytes in the array (in other words, an array name is *not* converted to a pointer type). The number of elements in an array equals **sizeof** *array* / **sizeof** *array*[0].

If the operand is a parameter declared as array type or function type, **sizeof** gives the size of the pointer. When applied to structures and unions, **sizeof** gives the total number of bytes, including any padding.

sizeof cannot be used with expressions of function type, incomplete types, parenthesized names of such types, or with an lvalue that designates a bit field object.

The integer type of the result of **sizeof** is *size_t*, defined as **unsigned int** in stddef.h.

You can use **sizeof** in preprocessor directives; this is specific to Borland C++.

In C++, **sizeof**(*classtype*), where *classtype* is derived from some base class, returns the size of the object (remember, this includes the size of the base class).

Source

```
/*  USE THE sizeof OPERATOR TO GET SIZES OF DIFFERENT DATA TYPES. */
#include <stdio.h>

struct st {
    char *name;      /* 2 BYTES IN SMALL-DATA MODELS; 4 BYTES IN LARGE-DATA MODEL */
    int age;         /* 2 BYTES IN SMALL-DATA MODELS; 4 BYTES IN LARGE-DATA MODEL */
    double height;   /* EIGHT BYTES */
        };

struct st St_Array[]= {  /* AN ARRAY OF structs */
    { "Jr.",     4,  34.20 },  /* ST_Array[0] */
    { "Suzie",  23,  69.75 },  /* ST_Array[1] */
    };

int main() {
    long double LD_Array[] = { 1.3, 501.09, 0.0007, 90.1, 17.08 };
```

```
printf("("\nNumber of elements in LD_Array = %d",
        sizeof(LD_Array) / sizeof(LD_Array[0]));

/****  THE NUMBER OF ELEMENTS IN THE ST_Array. ****/
printf("\nSt_Array has %d elements",
        sizeof(St_Array)/sizeof(St_Array[0]));

/****  THE NUMBER OF BYTES IN EACH ST_Array ELEMENT.  ****/
printf("\nSt_Array[0] = %d", sizeof(St_Array[0]));

/****  THE TOTAL NUMBER OF BYTES IN ST_Array.  ****/
   printf("\nSt_Array=%d", sizeof(St_Array));
return 0;
}
```

Output

```
Number of elements in LD_Array = 5
St_Array has 2 elements
St_Array[0] = 12
St_Array= 24
```

Binary operators

This section presents the binary operators, which are operators that require two operands.

Table 2.12 Binary operators

Type of operator	Binary operator	Description
Additive	+	Binary plus (addition)
	—	Binary minus (subtraction)
Multiplicative	*	Multiply
	/	Divide
	%	Remainder
Shift	<<	Shift left
	>>	Shift right
Bitwise	&	Bitwise AND
	^	Bitwise XOR (exclusive OR)
	|	Bitwise inclusive OR
Logical	&&	Logical AND
	||	Logical OR
Assignment	=	Assignment
	*=	Assign product
	/=	Assign quotient
	%=	Assign remainder (modulus)
	+=	Assign sum
	—=	Assign difference
	<<=	Assign left shift
	>>=	Assign right shift

Table 2.12   Binary operators (continued)

Type of operator	Binary operator	Description
	&=	Assign bitwise AND
	^=	Assign bitwise XOR
	|=	Assign bitwise OR
Relational	<	Less than
	>	Greater than
	<=	Less than or equal to
	>=	Greater than or equal to
Equality	==	Equal to
	!=	Not equal to
		Direct component selector
Component selection	.	
	->	Indirect component selector
C++ operators	::	Scope access/resolution
	.*	Dereference pointer to class member
	->*	Dereference pointer to class member
	:	Class initializer
Conditional	$a\,?\,x:y$	"if a then x; else y"
Comma	,	Evaluate; for example, a, b, c; from left to right

Additive operators

There are two additive operators: + and –. The syntax is

additive-expression:
  multiplicative-expression
  additive-expression + *multiplicative-expression*
  additive-expression – *multiplicative-expression*

Addition +

The legal operand types for *op1* + *op2* are

- Both *op1* and *op2* are of arithmetic type.
- *op1* is of integral type, and *op2* is of pointer to object type.
- *op2* is of integral type, and *op1* is of pointer to object type.

In the first case, the operands are subjected to the standard arithmetical conversions, and the result is the arithmetical sum of the operands. In the second and third cases, the rules of pointer arithmetic apply.

Subtraction –

The legal operand types for *op1* – *op2* are

- Both *op1* and *op2* are of arithmetic type.

- Both *op1* and *op2* are pointers to compatible object types. The unqualified type **type** is considered to be compatible with the qualified types **const** **type**, **volatile** **type**, and **const volatile** **type**.

- *op1* is of pointer to object type, and *op2* is integral type.

In the first case, the operands are subjected to the standard arithmetic conversions, and the result is the arithmetic difference of the operands. In the second and third cases, the rules of pointer arithmetic apply.

Multiplicative operators

There are three multiplicative operators: *, /, and %. The syntax is

> *multiplicative-expression:*
>   *cast-expression*
>   *multiplicative-expression cast-expression*
>   *multiplicative-expression* / *cast-expression*
>   *multiplicative-expression* % *cast-expression*

The operands for *(multiplication) and / (division) must be of arithmetical type. The operands for % (modulus, or remainder) must be of integral type. The usual arithmetic conversions are made on the operands.

The result of (*op1* * *op2*) is the product of the two operands. The results of (*op1* / *op2*) and (*op1* % *op2*) are the quotient and remainder, respectively, when *op1* is divided by *op2*, provided that *op2* is nonzero. Use of / or % with a zero second operand results in an error.

When *op1* and *op2* are integers and the quotient is not an integer, the results are as follows:

- If *op1* and *op2* have the same sign, *op1* / *op2* is the largest integer less than the true quotient, and *op1* % *op2* has the sign of *op1*.

- If *op1* and *op2* have opposite signs, *op1* / *op2* is the smallest integer greater than the true quotient, and *op1* % *op2* has the sign of *op1*.

Note   Rounding is always toward zero.

Bitwise logic operators

There are three bitwise logical operators: &, ^, and |.

AND &
The syntax is

> *AND-expression:*
>   *equality-expression*
>   *AND-expression* **&** *equality-expression*

In the expression $E1$ & $E2$, both operands must be of integral type. The usual arithmetical conversions are performed on $E1$ and $E2$, and the result is the bitwise AND of $E1$ and $E2$. Each bit in the result is determined as shown in Table 2.13.

Table 2.13   Bitwise operators truth table

Bit value in $E1$	Bit value in $E2$	$E1$ & $E2$	$E1$ ^ $E2$	$E1$ | $E2$
0	0	0	0	0
1	0	0	1	1
0	1	0	1	1
1	1	1	0	1

Exclusive OR ^

The syntax is

exclusive-OR-expression:
   AND-expression
   exclusive-OR-expression ^ *AND-expression*

In the expression $E1$ ^ $E2$, both operands must be of integral type. The usual arithmetic conversions are performed on $E1$ and $E2$, and the result is the bitwise exclusive OR of $E1$ and $E2$. Each bit in the result is determined as shown in Table 2.13.

Inclusive OR |

The syntax is

inclusive-OR-expression:
   exclusive-OR-expression
   inclusive-OR-expression | *exclusive-OR-expression*

In the expression $E1$ | $E2$, both operands must be of integral type. The usual arithmetic conversions are performed on $E1$ and $E2$, and the result is the bitwise inclusive OR of $E1$ and $E2$. Each bit in the result is determined as shown in Table 2.13.

Bitwise shift operators

There are two bitwise shift operators: << and >>. The syntax is

shift-expression:
   additive-expression
   shift-expression << *additive-expression*
   shift-expression >> *additive-expression*

Shift (<< and >>)

In the expressions $E1$ << $E2$ and $E1$ >> $E2$, the operands $E1$ and $E2$ must be of integral type. The normal integral promotions are performed on $E1$ and $E2$, and the type of the result is the type of the promoted $E1$. If $E2$ is negative or is greater than or equal to the width in bits of $E1$, the operation is undefined.

The result of $E1$ << $E2$ is the value of $E1$ left-shifted by $E2$ bit positions, zero-filled from the right if necessary. Left shifts of an **unsigned long** $E1$ are equivalent to multiplying

E1 by 2^{E2}, reduced modulo ULONG_MAX + 1; left shifts of **unsigned int**s are equivalent to multiplying by 2^{E2} reduced modulo UINT_MAX + 1. If *E1* is a signed integer, the result must be interpreted with care, because the sign bit might change.

Note The constants ULONG_MAX and UINT_MAX are defined in limits.h.

The result of *E1* >> *E2* is the value of *E1* right-shifted by *E2* bit positions. If *E1* is of **unsigned** type, zero-fill occurs from the left if necessary. If *E1* is of **signed** type, the fill from the left uses the sign bit (0 for positive, 1 for negative *E1*). This sign-bit extension ensures that the sign of *E1* >> *E2* is the same as the sign of *E1*. Except for signed types, the value of *E1* >> *E2* is the integral part of the quotient $E1/2^{E2}$.

Relational operators

There are four relational operators: <, >, <=, and >=. The syntax for these operators is

relational-expression:
   shift-expression
   relational-expression < *shift-expression*
   relational-expression > *shift-expression*
   relational-expression <= *shift-expression*
   relational-expression >= *shift-expression*

Less-than <

In the expression *E1* < *E2*, the operands must conform to one of the following sets of conditions:

- Both *E1* and *E2* are of arithmetic type.

- Both *E1* and *E2* are pointers to qualified or unqualified versions of compatible object types.

- Both *E1* and *E2* are pointers to qualified or unqualified versions of compatible incomplete types.

In the first case, the usual arithmetic conversions are performed. The result of *E1* < *E2* is of type **int**. If the value of *E1* is less than the value of *E2*, the result is 1 (true); otherwise, the result is zero (false).

In the second and third cases, in which *E1* and *E2* are pointers to compatible types, the result of *E1* < *E2* depends on the relative locations (addresses) of the two objects being pointed at. When comparing structure members within the same structure, the "higher" pointer indicates a later declaration. Within arrays, the "higher" pointer indicates a larger subscript value. All pointers to members of the same union object compare as equal.

Normally, the comparison of pointers to different structure, array, or union objects, or the comparison of pointers outside the range of an array object give undefined results; however, an exception is made for the "pointer beyond the last element" situation. If *P* points to an element of an array object, and *Q* points to the last element, the expression *P* < *Q* + 1 is allowed, evaluating to 1 (true), even though *Q* + 1 does not point to an element of the array object.

Greater-than >

The expression *E1* > *E2* gives 1 (true) if the value of *E1* is greater than the value of *E2*; otherwise, the result is 0 (false), using the same interpretations for arithmetic and pointer comparisons as are defined for the less-than operator. The same operand rules and restrictions also apply.

Less-than or equal-to <=

Similarly, the expression *E1* <= *E2* gives 1 (true) if the value of *E1* is less than or equal to the value of *E2*. Otherwise, the result is 0 (false), using the same interpretations for arithmetic and pointer comparisons as are defined for the less-than operator. The same operand rules and restrictions also apply.

Greater-than or equal-to >=

Finally, the expression *E1* >= *E2* gives 1 (true) if the value of *E1* is greater than or equal to the value of *E2*. Otherwise, the result is 0 (false), using the same interpretations for arithmetic and pointer comparisons as are defined for the less-than operator. The same operand rules and restrictions also apply.

Equality operators

There are two equality operators: == and !=. They test for equality and inequality between arithmetic or pointer values, following rules very similar to those for the relational operators.

Note   Notice that == and != have a lower precedence than the relational operators < and >, <=, and >=. Also, == and != can compare certain pointer types for equality and inequality where the relational operators would not be allowed.

The syntax is

> *equality-expression*:
>   *relational-expression*
>   *equality-expression* == *relational-expression*
>   *equality-expression* != *relational-expression*

Equal-to ==

In the expression *E1* == *E2*, the operands must conform to one of the following sets of conditions:

- Both *E1* and *E2* are of arithmetic type.

- Both *E1* and *E2* are pointers to qualified or unqualified versions of compatible types.

- One of *E1* and *E2* is a pointer to an object or incomplete type, and the other is a pointer to a qualified or unqualified version of **void**.

- One of *E1* or *E2* is a pointer and the other is a null pointer constant.

If *E1* and *E2* have types that are valid operand types for a relational operator, the same comparison rules just detailed for *E1* < *E2*, *E1* <= *E2*, and so on, apply.

In the first case, for example, the usual arithmetic conversions are performed, and the result of *E1* == *E2* is of type **int**. If the value of *E1* is equal to the value of *E2*, the result is 1 (true); otherwise, the result is zero (false).

In the second case, *E1* == *E2* gives 1 (true) if *E1* and *E2* point to the same object, or both point "one past the last element" of the same array object, or both are null pointers.

If *E1* and *E2* are pointers to function types, *E1* == *E2* gives 1 (true) if they are both null or if they both point to the same function. Conversely, if *E1* == *E2* gives 1 (true), then either *E1* and *E2* point to the same function, or they are both null.

In the fourth case, the pointer to an object or incomplete type is converted to the type of the other operand (pointer to a qualified or unqualified version of **void**).

Inequality !=

The expression *E1* != *E2* follows the same rules as those for *E1* == *E2*, except that the result is 1 (true) if the operands are unequal, and 0 (false) if the operands are equal.

Logical operators

There are two logical operators: **&&** and **| |**.

AND &&

The syntax is

> *logical-AND-expression:*
>   *inclusive-OR-expression*
>   *logical-AND-expression* **&&** *inclusive-OR-expression*

In the expression *E1* **&&** *E2*, both operands must be of scalar type. The result is of type **int**, and the result is 1 (true) if the values of *E1* and *E2* are both nonzero; otherwise, the result is 0 (false).

Unlike the bitwise **&** operator, **&&** guarantees left-to-right evaluation. *E1* is evaluated first; if *E1* is zero, *E1* **&&** *E2* gives 0 (false), and *E2* is not evaluated.

OR ||

The syntax is

> *logical-OR-expression:*
>   *logical-AND-expression*
>   *logical-OR-expression* **| |** *logical-AND-expression*

In the expression *E1* **| |** *E2*, both operands must be of scalar type. The result is of type **int**, and the result is 1 (true) if either of the values of *E1* and *E2* are nonzero. Otherwise, the result is 0 (false).

Unlike the bitwise **|** operator, **| |** guarantees left-to-right evaluation. *E1* is evaluated first; if *E1* is nonzero, *E1* **| |** *E2* gives 1 (true), and *E2* is not evaluated.

Conditional ? :

The syntax is

conditional-expression
  logical-OR-expression
  logical-OR-expression **?** *expression* **:** *conditional-expression*

In the expression *E1* **?** *E2* **:** *E3*, the operand *E1* must be of scalar type. The operands *E2* and *E3* must obey one of the following rules:

- Rule 1: Both are of arithmetic type.

- Rule 2: Both are of compatible structure or union types.

- Rule 3: Both are of **void** type.

- Rule 4: Both are of type pointer to qualified or unqualified versions of compatible types.

- Rule 5: One operand is of pointer type, the other is a null pointer constant.

- Rule 6: One operand is of type pointer to an object or incomplete type, the other is of type pointer to a qualified or unqualified version of **void**.

Note   In C++, the result is an lvalue.

First, *E1* is evaluated; if its value is nonzero (true), then *E2* is evaluated and *E3* is ignored. If *E1* evaluates to zero (false), then *E3* is evaluated and *E2* is ignored. The result of *E1* **?** *E2* **:** *E3* will be the value of whichever of *E2* and *E3* is evaluated.

In rule 1, both *E2* and *E3* are subject to the usual arithmetic conversions, and the type of the result is the common type resulting from these conversions. In rule 2, the type of the result is the structure or union type of *E2* and *E3*. In rule 3, the result is of type **void**.

In rules 4 and 5, the type of the result is a pointer to a type qualified with all the type qualifiers of the types pointed to by both operands. In rule 6, the type of the result is that of the nonpointer-to-void operand.

Assignment operators

There are 11 assignment operators. The = operator is the simple assignment operator; the other 10 are known as compound assignment operators.

The syntax is

assignment-expression:
  conditional-expression
  unary-expression assignment-operator assignment-expression

assignment-operator: one of

=	*=	/=	%=	+=	-=
<<=	>>=	&=	^=	| =	

Simple assignment =

In the expression $E1 = E2$, $E1$ must be a modifiable lvalue. The value of $E2$, after conversion to the type of $E1$, is stored in the object designated by $E1$ (replacing $E1$'s previous value). The value of the assignment expression is the value of $E1$ after the assignment. The assignment expression is not itself an lvalue.

The operands $E1$ and $E2$ must obey one of the following rules:

- Rule 1: $E1$ is of qualified or unqualified arithmetic type and $E2$ is of arithmetic type.

- Rule 2: $E1$ has a qualified or unqualified version of a structure or union type compatible with the type of $E2$.

- Rule 3: $E1$ and $E2$ are pointers to qualified or unqualified versions of compatible types, and the type pointed to by the left has all the qualifiers of the type pointed to by the right.

- Rule 4: One of $E1$ or $E2$ is a pointer to an object or incomplete type and the other is a pointer to a qualified or unqualified version of **void**. The type pointed to by the left has all the qualifiers of the type pointed to by the right.

- Rule 5: $E1$ is a pointer and $E2$ is a null pointer constant.

Note   In C++, the result is an lvalue.

Compound assignment

The compound assignments *op=*, where *op* can be any one of the 10 operator symbols * / % + - << >> & ^ |, are interpreted as follows:

$E1$ *op= E2*

has the same effect as

$E1 = E1$ *op E2*

except that the lvalue $E1$ is evaluated only once. (For example, $E1 += E2$ is the same as $E1 = E1 + E2$.)

The rules for compound assignment are therefore covered in the previous section (on the simple assignment operator =).

Comma operator

The syntax is

expression:
 assignment-expression
 expression , assignment-expression

In the comma expression

$E1, E2$

the left operand *E1* is evaluated as a **void** expression, then *E2* is evaluated to give the result and type of the comma expression. By recursion, the expression

E1, E2, ..., En

results in the left-to-right evaluation of each *Ei*, with the value and type of *En* giving the result of the whole expression. To avoid potential ambiguity (which might arise from the commas being used in both function arguments and in initializer lists), parentheses must be used. For example,

```
func(i, (j = 1, j + 4), k);
```

calls *func* with three arguments, not four. The arguments are *i*, 5, and *k*.

Note In C++, the result is an lvalue.

C++ specific operators

The operators specific to C++ are:

::	scope access (or resolution) operator
.*	dereference pointers to class members
->*	dereference pointers to pointers to class members
const_cast	adds or removes the **const** or **volatile** modifier from a type
delete	dynamically deallocates memory
dynamic_cast	converts a pointer to a desired type
new	dynamically allocates memory
reinterpret_cast	replaces casts for conversions that are unsafe or implementation dependent
static_cast	converts a pointer to a desired type
typeid	gets run-time identification of types and expressions

Use the scope access (or resolution) operator ::(two semicolons) to access a global (or file duration) name even if it is hidden by a local redeclaration of that name.

Use the .* and ->* operators to dereference pointers to class members and pointers to pointers to class members.

Statements

Statements specify the flow of control as a program executes. In the absence of specific jump and selection statements, statements are executed sequentially in the order of appearance in the source code. Borland C++ statements shows the syntax for statements.

Table 2.14   Borland C++ Statements

---

statement:
  labeled-statement
  compound-statement
  expression-statement
  selection-statement
  iteration-statement
  jump-statement
  asm-statement
  declaration (C++ specific)
labeled-statement:
  identifier : statement
  case *constant-expression : statement*
  default *: statement*
compound-statement:
  { <declaration-list> <statement-list> }
declaration-list:
  declaration
  declaration-list declaration
statement-list:
  statement
  statement-list statement
expression-statement:
  <expression> ;
asm-statement:
  asm *tokens newline*
  asm *tokens;*
  asm *{ tokens; <tokens;>= <tokens;>}*
selection-statement:
  if *(expression) statement*
  if *(expression) statement else statement*
  switch *(expression) statement*
iteration-statement:
  while *(expression) statement*
  do *statement while (expression) ;*
  for *(for-init-statement <expression> ; <expression>) statement*
for-init-statement:
  expression-statement
  declaration (C++ specific)
jump-statement:
  goto *identifier ;*
  continue *;*

Table 2.14   Borland C++ Statements

break ;
return *<expression>* ;

Blocks

A compound statement, or *block*, is a list (possibly empty) of statements enclosed in matching braces ({ }). Syntactically, a block can be considered to be a single statement, but it also plays a role in the scoping of identifiers. An identifier declared within a block has a scope starting at the point of declaration and ending at the closing brace. Blocks can be nested to any depth.

Labeled statements

A statement can be labeled in two ways:

- *label-identifier* **:** *statement*

  The label identifier serves as a target for the unconditional **goto** statement. Label identifiers have their own name space and have function scope. In C++ you can label both declaration and non-declaration statements.

- **case** *constant-expression* **:** *statement*

  default : *statement*

  Case and default labeled statements are used only in conjunction with switch statements.

Expression statements

Any expression followed by a semicolon forms an *expression statement*:

> *<expression>*;

Borland C++ executes an expression statement by evaluating the expression. All side effects from this evaluation are completed before the next statement is executed. Most expression statements are assignment statements or function calls.

The *null statement* is a special case, consisting of a single semicolon (;). The null statement does nothing, and is therefore useful in situations where the Borland C++ syntax expects a statement but your program does not need one.

Selection statements

Selection or flow-control statements select from alternative courses of action by testing certain values. There are two types of selection statements: the **if...else** and the **switch**.

Iteration statements

Iteration statements let you loop a set of statements. There are three forms of iteration in Borland C++: **while**, **do while**, and **for** loops.

Jump statements

A jump statement, when executed, transfers control unconditionally. There are four such statements: **break**, **continue**, **goto**, and **return.**

The main() function

Every C and C++ program must have a program-startup function.

- Console-based programs call the *main* function at startup.
- Windows GUI programs call the WinMain function at startup.

Where you place the startup function is a matter of preference. Some programmers place *main* at the beginning of the file, others at the end. Regardless of its location, the following points about *main* always apply:

- Arguments to main
- Wildcard arguments
- Using -p (Pascal calling conventions)
- Value main( ) returns

Arguments to main()

Three parameters (arguments) are passed to *main* by the Borland C++ startup routine: *argc, argv*, and *env*.

- *argc*, an integer, is the number of command-line arguments passed to *main*, including the name of the executable itself.
- *argv* is an array of pointers to strings (**char** *[]).
  - *argv*[0] is the full path name of the program being run.
  - *argv*[1] points to the first string typed on the operating system command line after the program name.
  - *argv*[2] points to the second string typed after the program name.
  - *argv*[*argc*-1] points to the last argument passed to *main*.
  - *argv*[*argc*] contains NULL.
- *env* is also an array of pointers to strings. Each element of *env*[] holds a string of the form ENVVAR=value.
  - ENVVAR is the name of an environment variable, such as PATH or COMSPEC.

- *value* is the value to which ENVVAR is set, such as C:\APPS;C:\TOOLS; (for PATH) or C:\DOS\COMMAND.COM (for COMSPEC).

If you declare any of these parameters, you *must* declare them exactly in the order given: *argc, argv, env*. For example, the following are all valid declarations of arguments to *main*:

```
int main()
int main(int argc)                        /* legal but very unlikely */
int main(int argc, char * argv[])
int main(int argc, char * argv[], char * env[])]
```

The declaration *int main(int argc)* is legal, but it is very unlikely that you would use *argc* in your program without also using the elements of *argv*.

The argument *env* is also available through the global variable **_environ**.

For all platforms, *argc* and *argv* are also available via the global variables **_argc** and **_argv**.

Example of how arguments are passed to main( )

Here is an example that demonstrates a simple way of using these arguments passed to *main()*:

```
/* Program ARGS.C */
#include <stdio.h>
#include <stdlib.h>

int main(int argc, char *argv[], char *env[]) {
   int i;

   printf("The value of argc is %d \n\n", argc);
   printf("These are the %d command-line arguments passed to"
          " main:\n\n", argc);

   for (i = 0; i < argc; i++)
      printf("   argv[%d]: %s\n", i, argv[i]);

   printf("\nThe environment string(s) on this system are:\n\n");

   for (i = 0; env[i] != NULL; i++)
      printf("   env[%d]: %s\n", i, env[i]);
   return 0;
   }
```

Suppose you run ARGS.EXE at the command prompt with the following command line:

```
C:> args first_arg "arg with blanks" 3  4 "last but one" stop!
```

Notice that you can pass arguments with embedded blanks by surrounding them with quotes, as shown by "argument with blanks" and "last but one" in this example command line.

The output of ARGS.EXE (assuming that the environment variables are set as shown here) would then be like this:

```
The value of argc is 7

These are the 7 command-line arguments passed to main:

    argv[0]: C:\BC4\ARGS.EXE
    argv[1]: first_arg
    argv[2]: arg with blanks
    argv[3]: 3
    argv[4]: 4
    argv[5]: last but one
    argv[6]: stop!

The environment string(s) on this system are

    env[0]: COMSPEC=C:\COMMAND.COM
    env[1]: PROMPT=$p $g
    env[2]: PATH=C:\SPRINT;C:\DOS;C:\BC4
```

The maximum combined length of the command-line arguments passed to *main* (including the space between adjacent arguments and the program name itself) is

- 128 for DOS

- 260 for Win16

- 255 for Win32

Wildcard arguments

Command-line arguments containing wildcard characters can be expanded to all the matching file names, much the same way DOS expands wildcards when used with commands like COPY. All you have to do to get wildcard expansion is to link your program with the WILDARGS.OBJ object file, which is included with Borland C++.

Note   Wildcard arguments are used only in console-mode applications.

Once WILDARGS.OBJ is linked into your program code, you can send wildcard arguments (such as *.*) to your *main* function. The argument will be expanded (in the *argv* array) to all files matching the wildcard mask. The maximum size of the *argv* array varies, depending on the amount of memory available in your heap.

If no matching files are found, the argument is passed unchanged. (That is, a string consisting of the wildcard mask is passed to *main*.)

Arguments enclosed in quotes ("...") are not expanded.

Example of using wildcard arguments with main( )

The following commands compile the file ARGS.C and link it with the wildcard expansion module WILDARGS.OBJ, then run the resulting executable file ARGS.EXE:

```
BCC   ARGS.C   WILDARGS.OBJ
ARGS   C:\BC4\INCLUDE\*.H   "*.C"
```

When you run ARGS.EXE, the first argument is expanded to the names of all the *.H
files in your Borland C++ INCLUDE directory. Note that the expanded argument
strings include the entire path. The argument *.C is not expanded because it is enclosed
in quotes.

In the IDE, simply specify a project file from the Project menu that contains the
following lines:

```
ARGS
WILDARGS.OBJ
```

If you prefer the wildcard expansion to be the default, modify your standard
CW32?.LIB library files to have WILDARGS.OBJ linked automatically. To do so, remove
SETARGV and INITARGS from the libraries and add WILDARGS. The following
commands invoke the Turbo librarian (TLIB) to modify all the standard library files
(assuming the current directory contains the standard C and C++ libraries and
WILDARGS.OBJ):

Windows users

```
tlib   CW32          -setargv  +wildargs
tlib   CW32MT        -setargv  +wildargs
tlib   -setargv      +wildargs
```

DOS users

```
tlib   cs   -setargv  +wildargs
tlib   cc   -setargv  +wildargs
tlib   cm   -setargv  +wildargs
tlib   cl   -setargv  +wildargs
tlib   ch   -setargv  +wildargs
```

Using _ _p (Pascal calling conventions)

If you compile your program using Pascal calling conventions, you must remember to
explicitly declare *main* as a C type. Do this with the _ _cdecl keyword, like this:

```
int  _ _cdecl main(int argc, char* argv[], char* envp[])
```

The value main() returns

The value returned by *main* is the status code of the program: an **int**. If, however, your
program uses the routine *exit* (or *_exit*) to terminate, the value returned by *main* is the
argument passed to the call to *exit* (or to *_exit*).

For example, if your program contains the call

```
exit(1)
```

the status is 1.

Passing file information to child processes

If your program uses the *exec* or *spawn* functions to create a new process, the new process will normally inherit all of the open file handles created by the original process. Some information, however, about these handles will be lost, including the access mode used to open the file. For example, if your program opens a file for read-only access in binary mode, and then spawns a child process, the child process might corrupt the file by writing to it, or by reading from it in text mode.

To allow child processes to inherit such information about open files, you must link your program with the object file FILEINFO.OBJ.

For example:

```
BCC32 TEST.C \BC4\LIB\FILEINFO.OBJ
```

The file information is passed in the environment variable _C_FILE_INFO. This variable contains encoded binary information. Your program should not attempt to read or modify its value. The child program must have been built with the C++ run-time library to inherit this information correctly.

Other programs can ignore _C_FILE_INFO, and will not inherit file information.

Multithread programs

32-bit programs can create more than one thread of execution. If your program creates multiple threads, and these threads also use the C++ run-time library, you must use the CW32MT.LIB or CW32MTI library instead.

The multithread libraries provide the following functions that you use to create threads:

- *_beginthread*
- *_beginthreadNT*

The multithread libraries also provide

| *_endthread* | a function that terminates threads |
| *_threadid* | a global variable that contains the current identification number of the thread (also known as the *thread ID*). |

The header file stddef.h contains the declaration of *_threadid*.

When you compile or link a program that uses multiple threads, you must use the **-WM** compiler switch. For example:

```
BCC32 -WM THREAD.C
```

Note   Take special care when using the signal function in a multithread program. The SIGINT, SIGTERM, and SIGBREAK signals can be used only by the main thread (thread one) in a non-Win32 application. When one of these signals occurs, the currently executing thread is suspended, and control transfers to the signal handler (if any) set up by thread one. Other signals can be handled by any thread.

A signal handler should not use C++ run-time library functions because a semaphore deadlock might occur. Instead, the handler should simply set a flag or post a semaphore and return immediately.

3

C++ specifics

C++ is an object-oriented programming language based on C. Generally speaking, you can compile C programs under C++, but you can't compile a C++ program under C if the program uses any constructs specific to C++. Some situations require special care. For example, the same function *func* declared twice in C with different argument types invokes a duplicated name error. Under C++, however, *func* will be interpreted as an overloaded function; whether or not this is legal depends on other circumstances.

Although C++ introduces new keywords and operators to handle classes, some of the capabilities of C++ have applications outside of any class context. This topic discusses the aspects of C++ that can be used independently of classes, then describes the specifics of classes and class mechanisms.

See "C++ exception handling" and "C-based structured exceptions" in Chapter 4 for details on compiling C and C++ programs with exception handling.

Namespaces

Most nontrivial applications consist of more than one source file. The files can be authored and maintained by more than one developer. Eventually, the separate files are organized and linked to produce the final application.

Traditionally, the file organization requires all names that aren't encapsulated within a defined name space (such as function or class body, or translation unit) to share the same global name space. Therefore, multiple definitions of names discovered while linking separate modules require some way to distinguish each name. *C++ namespaces* provide the solution to the problem of name clashes in the global scope.

Namespaces allow an application to be partitioned into a number of subsystems. Each subsystem can define and operate within its own scope. Each developer can introduce whatever identifiers are convenient within a subsystem without worrying about whether such identifiers are being used by someone else. The subsystem scope is known throughout the application by a unique identifier.

It takes only two steps to use C++ namespaces:

1 You must uniquely identify a name space using the keyword **namespace**.

2 You can then access the elements of an identified namespace by applying the **using** keyword.

Defining a namespace

The grammar for defining a namespace is

original-namespace-name:
  identifier
namespace-definition:
  original-namespace-definition
  extension-namespace-definition
  unnamed-namespace-definition

Grammatically, there are three ways to define a namespace with the namespace keyword:

original-namespace-definition:
    namespace *identifier* { *namespace-body* }
extension-namespace-definition:
    namespace *original-namespace-name* { *namespace-body* }
unnamed-namespace-definition:
    namespace { *namespace-body* }

The body is an optional sequence of declarations. The grammar is

namespace-body:
  declaration-seq opt

Example

```
// An example of the using directive
#include <iostream.h>
  namespace F {
    float x = 9;
    }
  namespace G {
    using namespace F;
    float y = 2.0;
      namespace INNER_G {
        float z = 10.01;
        }
    }

  int main() {
    using namespace G;  // THIS DIRECTIVE GIVES YOU EVERYTHING DECLARED IN "G"
    using namespace G::INNER_G;  // THIS DIRECTIVE GIVES YOU ONLY "INNER_G"
```

```
          float x = 19.1;      // LOCAL DECLARATION TAKES PRECEDENCE
          cout << "x = " << x << endl;
          cout << "y = " << y << endl;
          cout << "z = " << z << endl;
          return 0;
          }
```

Output:

```
x = 19.1
y = 2
z = 10.01
```

Declaring a namespace

An original namespace declaration should use an identifier that has not been previously used as a global identifier.

```
namespace ALPHA {  /* ALPHA is the identifier of this namespace. */
    /* your program declarations */
    long double LD;
    float f(float y) { return y; }
    }
```

A namespace identifier must be known in all translation units where you intend to access its elements.

Namespace alias

You can use an alternate name to refer to a namespace identifier. An alias is useful when you need to refer to a long, unwieldy namespace identifier.

```
namespace BORLAND_INTERNATIONAL {
    /* namespace-body */
    namespace NESTED_BORLAND_INTERNATIONAL {
       /* namespace-body */
       }
    }

// Alias namespace
namespace BI = BORLAND_INTERNATIONAL;

// Use access qualifier to alias a nested namespace
namespace NBI = BORLAND_INTERNATIONAL::NESTED_BORLAND_INTERNATIONAL;
```

Extending a namespace

Namespaces are discontinuous and open for additional development. If you redeclare a namespace, you extend the original namespace by adding new declarations. Any extensions that are made to a namespace after a using declaration will not be known at the point at which the using declaration occurs. Therefore, all overloaded versions of some function should be included in the namespace before you declare the function to be in use.

Example for extending namespaces

```
// An example for extending namespaces
#include <iostream.h>
  struct S { };
  class C  { };

  namespace ALPHA {  // ALPHA is an original identifier.
    void g(struct S) {
      cout << "Processing a structure argument" << endl;
      }
    }

  using ALPHA::g;  // using declaration

  /*** After the using declaration above, subsequent attempts
       to overload the g() function are ignored. ***/
  namespace ALPHA { // Extending the ALPHA namespace
    void g( C& ) { // Overloaded version of function
      cout << "Processing a class argument." << endl;
      }
    }

  int main() {
    S mystruct;
    C myclass;

    g(mystruct);

    // The following function call fails at compile-time
    // because there is no overloaded version for this case.
//      g(myclass);
    return 0;
  }
```

Output:

```
Processing a structure argument
```

Anonymous namespaces

The C++ grammar allows you to define anonymous namespaces. To do this, you use the keyword **namespace** with no identifier before the enclosing brace.

```
namespace {         // Anonymous namespace
  // Declarations
  }
```

All anonymous, unnamed namespaces in global scope (that is, unnamed namespaces that are not nested) of the same translation unit share the same namespace. This way you can make static declarations without using the **static** keyword.

Each identifier that is enclosed within an unnamed namespace is unique within the translation unit in which the unnamed namespace is defined.

Example

In file ANON1.CPP:

```
#include <iostream.h>
extern void func(void);

namespace {             // Anonymous
    float pi = 3.14;  // Unique identifier known only in this file
    }

void main() {
    float pi = 0.1;
    cout << "pi = " << pi << endl;
    func();
    }
```

In file ANON2.CPP:

```
#include <iostream.h>

namespace {               // Anonymous namespace
    float pi = 10.0001;  // Unique identifier known only in this file
    void func(void) {
        cout << "First func() called; pi = " << pi;
        }
    }
    void func(void) {
        cout << "Second func() called; pi = " << pi;
        }
```

Program output:

```
pi = 0.1
Second func() called; pi = 10.0001
```

Accessing elements of a namespace

You can access the elements of a namespace in three ways:

- By explicit access qualification
- By the using declaration
- By the using directive

Remember that no matter which namespace you add to your local scope, identifiers in global scope (global scope is just another namespace) are still accessible by using the scope resolution operator ::.

Accessing namespaces in classes

You cannot use a **using** directive inside a class. However, the **using** declarative is allowed and can be quite useful.

Using directive

If you want to use several (or all of) the members of a namespace, C++ provides an easy way to get access to the complete namespace. The using directive specifies that all identifiers in a namespace are in scope at the point that the using directive statement is made. The grammar for the using directive is as follows:

using-directive:

using namespace :: opt *nested-name-specifier* opt *namespace-name*;

The using directive is transitive. That means that when you apply the using directive to a namespace that contains using directives within itself, you get access to those namespaces as well. For example, if you apply the using directive in your program, you also get namespaces *A*, *ONE*, and *TWO*.

```
namespace A {
using namespace ONE;  // This has been defined previously
using namespace TWO;  // This also has been defined previously
}
```

The using directive does not add any identifiers to your local scope. Therefore, an identifier defined in more than one namespace won't be a problem until you actually attempt to use it. Local scope declarations take precedence by hiding all other similar declarations.

Using declaration

You can access namespace members individually with the using declaration syntax. When you make a using declaration, you add the declared identifier to the local namespace. The grammar is

using-declaration:

using :: *unqualified-identifier*;

Example

```
// An example of the using declaration.
// The function g() is defined in two different namespaces.
#include <iostream.h>

namespace ALPHA {  /* ALPHA is the name of this namespace. */
    float f(float y) { return y; }
    void g() { cout << "ALPHA version" << endl; }
    }
namespace BETA {  /* BETA is the name of this namespace. */
    void g() { cout << "BETA version" << endl; }
    }

void main(void) {
// The using declaration identifies the desired version of g().
        using ALPHA::f;  // Qualified declaration
        using BETA::g;   // Qualified declaration
```

```
    float x = 0;

    // Access qualifiers are no longer needed.
    x = f(2.1);
    g();
    }
```

Explicit access qualification

You can explicitly qualify each member of a namespace. To do so, you use the namespace identifier together with the :: scope resolution operator followed by the member name. For example, to access a specific member of namespace *ALPHA*, you write:

```
ALPHA::LD;   // Access a variable
ALPHA::f;    // Access a function
```

Explicit access qualification can always be used to resolve ambiguity. No matter which namespace (except anonymous namespace) is being used in your subsystem, you can apply the scope resolution operator :: to access identifiers in any namespace (including a namespace already being used in the local scope) or the global namespace. Therefore, any identfier in the application can be accessed with sufficient qualification.

Example

```
// An example for accessing a namespace within a class.
// This allows us to overload a function which is a base class member.

#include <iostream.h>
    class A {
    public:
        void func(char ch) { cout << "char = " << ch << endl; }
    };

    class B : public A {
    public:
//      using namespace A;    // ERROR. The using directive isn't allowed
        void func(char *str) { cout << "string = " << str << endl; }

        // The using declarative
        using A::func;         // Overload B::func()
    };

    int main() {
        B b;

        b.func('c');  // Calls A::func()
        b.func("c");  // Calls B::func()
        return 0;
    }
```

New-style typecasting

This section presents a discussion of alternate methods for making a typecast. The methods presented here augment the earlier cast expressions available in the C language.

Types cannot be defined in a cast.

const_cast

Syntax

```
const_cast< T > (arg)
```

Description
Use the const_cast operator to add or remove the const or volatile modifier from a type. In the statement,

```
const_cast< T > (arg)
```

T and arg must be of the same type except for const and volatile modifiers. The cast is resolved at compile time. The result is of type T. Any number of const or volatile modifiers can be added or removed with a single const_cast expression.

A pointer to const can be converted to a pointer to non-const that is in all other respects an identical type. If successful, the resulting pointer refers to the original object.

A const object or a reference to const_cast results in a non-const object or reference that is otherwise an identical type.

The const_cast operator performs similar typecasts on the volatile modifier. A pointer to volatile object can be cast to a pointer to non-volatile object without otherwise changing the type of the object. The result is a pointer to the original object. A volatile-type object or a reference to volatile-type can be converted into an identical non-volatile type.

dynamic_cast

In the expression,

```
dynamic_cast< T > (ptr)
```

T must be a pointer or a reference to a defined class type or void*. The argument ptr must be an expression that resolves to a pointer or reference.

If T is void* then ptr must also be a pointer. In this case, the resulting pointer can access any element of the class that is the most derived element in the hierarchy. Such a class cannot be a base for any other class.

Conversions from a derived class to a base class, or from one derived class to another, are as follows: if T is a pointer and ptr is a pointer to a non-base class that is an element of a class hierarchy, the result is a pointer to the unique subclass. References are treated similarly. If T is a reference and ptr is a reference to a non-base class, the result is a reference to the unique subclass.

A conversion from a base class to a derived class can be performed only if the base is a polymorphic type. The conversion to a base class is resolved at compile time. A conversion from a base class to a derived class, or a conversion across a hierarchy is resolved at run time.

If successful, dynamic_cast< T > (ptr) converts ptr to the desired type. If a pointer cast fails, the returned pointer is valued 0. If a cast to a reference type fails, the Bad_cast exception is thrown.

Note   Run-time type identification (RTTI) is required for dynamic_cast.

Example

```
// HOW TO MAKE DYNAMIC CASTS
// This program must be compiled with the -RT (Generate RTTI) option.
#include <iostream.h>
#include <typeinfo.h>
class Base1
{
    // In order for the RTTI mechanism to function correctly,
    // a base class must be polymorphic.
    virtual void f(void) { /* A virtual function makes the class polymorphic */ }
};
class Base2 { };
class Derived : public Base1, public Base2 { };
int main(void) {
    try {
        Derived d, *pd;
        Base1 *b1 = &d;
        // Perform a downcast from a Base1 to a Derived.
        if ((pd = dynamic_cast<Derived *>(b1)) != 0) {
            cout << "The resulting pointer is of type "
                << typeid(pd).name() << endl;
        }
        else throw Bad_cast();
        // Attempt cast across the hierarchy.  That is, cast from
        // the first base to the most derived class and then back
        // to another accessible base.
        Base2 *b2;
        if ((b2 = dynamic_cast<Base2 *>(b1)) != 0) {
            cout << "The resulting pointer is of type "
                << typeid(b2).name() << endl;
        }
        else throw Bad_cast();
    }
    catch (Bad_cast) {
        cout << "dynamic_cast failed" << endl;
        return 1;
    }
    catch (...) {
        cout << "Exception handling error." << endl;
        return 1;
    }
```

```
        return 0;
}
```

reinterpret_cast

Syntax

```
reinterpret_cast< T > (arg)
```

Description
In the statement,

```
reinterpret_cast< T > (arg)
```

T must be a pointer, reference, arithmetic type, pointer to function, or pointer to member.

A pointer can be explicitly converted to an integral type. An integral arg can be converted to a pointer. Converting a pointer to an integral type and back to the same pointer type results in the original value. A yet undefined class can be used in a pointer or reference conversion.

A pointer to a function can be explicitly converted to a pointer to an object type provided the object pointer type has enough bits to hold the function pointer. A pointer to an object type can be explicitly converted to a pointer to a function only if the function pointer type is large enough to hold the object pointer.

Example
```
// Use reinterpret_cast<Type>(expr) to replace (Type)expr casts
// for conversions that are unsafe or implementation dependent.
void func(void *v) {
        // Cast from pointer type to integral type.
        int i = reinterpret_cast<int>(v);
?
}
void main() {
    // Cast from an integral type to pointer type.
    func(reinterpret_cast<void *>(5));
    // Cast from a pointer to function of one type to
    // pointer to function of another type.
    typedef void (* PFV)();
    PFV pfunc = reinterpret_cast<PFV>(func);
    pfunc();
    }
```

static_cast

Syntax

```
static_cast< T > (arg)
```

Description

In the statement,

```
static_cast< T > (arg)
```

T must be a pointer, reference, arithmetic type, or enum type. The arg-type must match the T-type. Both T and arg must be fully known at compile time.

If a complete type can be converted to another type by some conversion method already provided by the language, then making such a conversion by using static_cast achieves exactly the same thing.

Integral types can be converted to enum types. A request to convert arg to a value that is not an element of enum is undefined. The null pointer is converted to itself. A pointer to one object type can be converted to a pointer to another object type. Note that merely pointing to similar types can cause access problems if the similar types are not similarly aligned.

You can explicitly convert a pointer to a class X to a pointer to some class Y if X is a base class for Y. A static conversion can be made only under the following conditions:

- If an unambiguous conversion exists from Y to X

- If X is not a virtual base class

An object can be explicitly converted to a reference type X& if a pointer to that object can be explicitly converted to an X*. The result of the conversion is an lvalue. No constructors or conversion functions are called as the result of a cast to a reference.

An object or a value can be converted to a class object only if an appropriate constructor or conversion operator has been declared.

A pointer to a member can be explicitly converted into a different pointer-to-member type only if both types are pointers to members of the same class or pointers to members of two classes, one of which is unambiguously derived from the other.

When T is a reference, the result of static_cast< T > (arg) is an lvalue. The result of a pointer or reference cast refers to the original expression.

Run-time type identification (RTTI)

Run-time type identification (RTTI) lets you write portable code that can determine the actual type of a data object at run time even when the code has access only to a pointer or reference to that object. This makes it possible, for example, to convert a pointer to a virtual base class into a pointer to the derived type of the actual object. Use the dynamic_cast operator to make run-time casts.

The RTTI mechanism also lets you check whether an object is of some particular type and whether two objects are of the same type. You can do this with typeid operator, which determines the actual type of its argument and returns a reference to an object of type const typeinfo, which describes that type.

You can also use a type name as the argument to typeid, and typeid will return a reference to a const typeinfo object for that type. The class *typeinfo* provides an operator

== and an **operator !=** that you can use to determine whether two objects are of the same type. Class *typeinfo* also provides a member function name that returns a pointer to a character string that holds the name of the type.

For more information, refer to the *Bad_typeid* class, the **-RT** option and destructors, and the *typeinfo* class.

Example

```
/* How to get RTTI for polymorphic classes.*/
#include <iostream.h>
#include <typeinfo.h>
class __rtti Alpha {          /* Provide RTTI for this class and */
                              /* all classes derived from it */
    virtual void func() {};   /* A virtual function makes */
                              /* Alpha a polymorphic class. */
};
class B : public Alpha {};
int main(void) {
    B Binst;            // Instantiate class B
    B *Bptr;            // Declare a B-type pointer
    Bptr = &Binst;      // Initialize the pointer
    // THESE TESTS ARE DONE AT RUN TIME
    try {
        if (typeid( *Bptr ) == typeid( B ) )
            // Ask "WHAT IS THE TYPE FOR *Bptr?"
            cout << "Name is " << typeid( *Bptr).name();
        if (typeid( *Bptr ) != typeid( Alpha ) )
            cout << "\nPointer is not an Alpha-type.";
        return 0;
        }
    catch (Bad_typeid) {
        cout << "typeid() has failed.";
        return 1;
        }
    }
```

Program output

```
Name is B
Pointer is not an Alpha-type.
```

The typeid operator

Syntax

```
typeid( expression )

typeid( type-name )
```

Description

You can use typeid to get run-time identification of types and expressions. A call to typeid returns a reference to an object of type const typeinfo. The returned object represents the type of the typeid operand.

If the typeid operand is a dereferenced pointer or a reference to a polymorphic type, typeid returns the dynamic type of the actual object pointed or referred to. If the operand is non-polymorphic, typeid returns an object that represents the static type.

You can use the typeid operator with fundamental data types as well as user-defined types. If the typeid operand is a dereferenced NULL pointer, the Bad_typeid exception is thrown.

For more information, see the *Bad_typeid* class and **_ _rtti**.

Example

```
// HOW TO USE operator typeid, Type_info::before(), AND
Type_info::name()
#include <iostream.h>
#include <typeinfo.h>
class A { };
class B : A { };
void main() {
   char C;
   float X;
   // USE THE typeinfo::operator==()TO MAKE COMPARISON
   if (typeid( C ) == typeid( X ))
      cout << "C and X are the same type." << endl;
   else cout << "C and X are NOT the same type." << endl;
   // USE true AND false LITERALS TO MAKE COMPARISON
   cout << typeid(int).name();
   cout << " before " << typeid(double).name() << ": " <<
        (typeid(int).before(typeid(double)) ? true : false) << endl;
   cout << typeid(double).name();
   cout << " before " << typeid(int).name() << ": " <<
        (typeid(double).before(typeid(int)) ? true : false) << endl;
   cout << typeid(A).name();
   cout << " before " << typeid(B).name() << ": " <<
        (typeid(A).before(typeid(B)) ? true : false) << endl;
   }
```

Program output

```
C and X are NOT the same type.
int before double: 0
double before int: 1
A before B: 1
```

_ _rtti and the -RT option

RTTI is enabled by default in Borland C++. You can use the **-RT** command-line option to disable it (**-RT-**) or to enable it (**-RT**). If RTTI is disabled or if the argument to typeid is a pointer or a reference to a non-polymorphic class, typeid returns a reference to a const typeinfo object that describes the declared type of the pointer or reference, and not the actual object that the pointer or reference is bound to.

In addition, even when RTTI is disabled, you can force all instances of a particular class and all classes derived from that class to provide polymorphic run-time type identification (where appropriate) by using the Borland C++ keyword _ _rtti in the class definition.

When you use the **-RT-** compiler option, if any base class is declared _ _rtti, then all polymorphic base classes must also be declared _ _rtti.

```
struct _ _rtti S1 { virtual s1func(); };   /* Polymorphic */
struct _ _rtti S2 { virtual s2func(); };   /* Polymorphic */
struct X : S1, S2 { };
```

If you turn off the RTTI mechanism (by using the **-RT-** compiler option), RTTI might not be available for derived classes. When a class is derived from multiple classes, the order and type of base classes determines whether or not the class inherits the RTTI capability.

When you have polymorphic and non-polymorphic classes, the order of inheritance is important. If you compile the following declarations with **-RT-**, you should declare X with the _ _rtti modifier. Otherwise, switching the order of the base classes for the class X results in the compile-time error: Can't inherit non-RTTI class from RTTI base 'S1'.

```
struct _ _rtti S1 { virtual func(); };   /* Polymorphic class */
struct S2 { };                           /*  Non-polymorphic class */
struct _ _rtti X : S1, S2 { };
```

Note The class X is explicitly declared with _ _rtti. This makes it safe to mix the order and type of classes.

In the following example, class X inherits only non-polymorphic classes. Class X does not need to be declared _ _rtti.

```
struct _ _rtti S1 {  };   // Non-polymorphic class
struct S2 { };
struct X : S2, S1 { };    // The order is not essential
```

Applying either _ _rtti or using the **-RT** compiler option will not make a static class into a polymorphic class.

-RT option and destructors

When **-xd** is enabled, a pointer to a class with a virtual destructor can't be deleted if that class is not compiled with **-RT**. The **-RT** and **-xd** options are on by default.

Example

```
class Alpha {
public:
    virtual ~Alpha( ) { }
};
void func( Alpha *Aptr ) {
    delete Aptr;          // Error.  Alpha is not a polymorphic class
```

```
type
    }
```

Referencing

While in C, you pass arguments only by value; in C++, you can pass arguments by value or by reference. C++ reference types, closely related to pointer types, create aliases for objects and let you pass arguments to functions by reference.

Note   C++ specific pointer referencing and dereferencing is discussed in C++ specific operators.

Simple references

The reference declarator can be used to declare references outside functions:

```
int  i  = 0;

int &ir = i;    // ir is an alias for i
ir = 2;         // same effect as i = 2
```

Note that type& var, type &var, and type & var are all equivalent.

This creates the lvalue *ir* as an alias for *i*, provided the initializer is the same type as the reference. Any operations on *ir* have precisely the same effect as operations on *i*. For example, `ir = 2` assigns 2 to *i*, and `&ir` returns the address of *i*.

Reference arguments

The reference declarator can also be used to declare reference type parameters within a function:

```
void func1 (int i);

void func2 (int &ir);      // ir is type "reference to int"
    ⋮
int sum=3;
func1(sum);                // sum passed by value
func2(&sum);               // sum passed by reference
```

The *sum* argument passed by reference can be changed directly by *func2*. On the other hand, *func1* gets a copy of the *sum* argument (passed by value), so *sum* itself cannot be altered by *func1*.

When an actual argument *x* is passed by value, the matching formal argument in the function receives a copy of *x*. Any changes to this copy within the function body are not reflected in the value of *x* itself. Of course, the function can return a value that could be used later to change *x*, but the function cannot directly alter a parameter passed by value.

The C method for changing *x* uses the actual argument &*x*, the address of *x*, rather than *x* itself. Although &*x* is passed by value, the function can access x through the copy of &x it receives. Even if the function does not need to change *x*, it is still useful (though subject to potentially dangerous side effects) to pass &x, especially if *x* is a large data structure. Passing *x* directly by value involves wasteful copying of the data structure.

Compare the three implementations of the function *treble*:

Implementation 1

```
int treble_1(int n)
{
    return 3 * n;
}
    ⋮
int x, i = 4;
x = treble_1(i);        // x now = 12, i = 4
    ⋮
```

Implementation 2

```
void treble_2(int* np)
{
    *np = (*np) * 3;
}
    ⋮
treble_2(int& i);       // i now = 12
```

Implementation 3

```
void treble_3(int& n)      // n is a reference type
{
    n = 3 * n;
}
    ⋮
treble_3(i);               // i now = 36
```

The formal argument declaration *type*& t (or equivalently, *type*& t) establishes *t* as type "reference to *type*." So, when *treble_3* is called with the real argument *i*, *i* is used to initialize the formal reference argument *n*. *n* therefore acts as an alias for *i*, so n = 3*n also assigns 3 * *i* to *i*.

If the initializer is a constant or an object of a different type than the reference type, create a temporary object for which the reference acts as an alias:

```
int& ir = 6;    /* temporary int object created, aliased by ir, gets value 6 */

float f;
int& ir2 = f;   /* creates temporary int object aliased by ir2; f converted
                   before assignment */
ir2 = 2.0       // ir2 now = 2, but f is unchanged
```

The automatic creation of temporary objects permits the conversion of reference types when formal and actual arguments have different (but assignment-compatible) types. When passing by value, of course, there are fewer conversion problems, since the copy of the actual argument can be physically changed before assignment to the formal argument.

Scope resolution operator ::

The scope access (or resolution) operator :: (two colons) lets you access a global (or file duration) member name even if it is hidden by a local redeclaration of that name. For example:

```
int i;                      // global i
    ⋮
void func(void) {
        int i=0;            // local i hides global i
        i = 3;              // this i is the local i
        ::i = 4;            // this i is the global i
        printf ("%d",i);    // prints out 3
        }
```

Note   This code also works if the global i is a file-level static.

The :: operator has other uses with class types, as discussed throughout this chapter.

You also can use a global identifier by prefixing it with the resolution operator.

You access a nested member name by specifying the class name and using the resolution operator. Therefore, *Alpha::func( )* and *Beta::func( )* are two different functions.

The new and delete operators

The **new** and **delete** operators offer dynamic storage allocation and deallocation, similar but superior to the standard library functions *malloc* and *free*. See the *C++ Language Reference*, Chapter 3, for information on *malloc* and *free*.

Operator new

Syntax

```
<::> new <placement> type-name <(initializer)>

<::> new <placement> (type-name) <(initializer)>
```

Description

The **new** operator offers dynamic storage allocation, similar but superior to the standard library function *malloc*.

The **new** operator must always be supplied with a data type in place of *type-name*. Items surrounded by angle brackets are optional. The optional arguments can be as follows:

• The :: operator invokes the global version of **new**.

• *placement* can be used to supply additional arguments to **new**. You can use this syntax only if you have an overloaded version of **new** that matches the optional arguments. See the discussion of the placement syntax.

- *initializer*, if present, is used to initialize the allocation. Arrays cannot be initialized by the allocation operator.

A request for non-array allocation uses the appropriate operator **new()** function. Any request for array allocation will call the appropriate operator **new[]()** function. The selection of the allocation operator is done as shown below.

Allocation of arrays of *Type*:

1 Attempts to use a class-specific array allocator:

Type::**operator new[]()**

2 If the class-specific array allocator is not defined, the global version is used:

::**operator new[]()**

Allocation of non-arrays of *Type*:

1 Attempts to use the class-specific allocator:

Type::**operator new()**

2 If the class-specific array allocator is not defined, the global version is used:

::**operator new()**

Allocation of single objects (that are not class-type) which are not held in arrays:

1 Memory allocation for a non-array object is by using the ::**operator new()**. Note that this allocation function is always used for the predefined types. It is possible to overload this global operator function. However, this is generally not advised.

Allocation of arrays:

1 Use the global allocation operator:

::**operator new[] ()**

Note Arrays of classes require the default constructor.

new tries to create an object of type *Type* by allocating (if possible) **sizeof(*Type*)** bytes in free store (also called the heap). **new** calculates the size of *Type* without the need for an explicit **sizeof** operator. Further, the pointer returned is of the correct type, "pointer to *Type*," without the need for explicit casting. The storage duration of the new object is from the point of creation until the operator **delete** destroys it by deallocating its memory, or until the end of the program.

If successful, **new** returns a pointer to the allocated memory. By default, an allocation failure (such as insufficient or fragmented heap memory) results in the predefined exception xalloc being thrown. Your program should always be prepared to catch the xalloc exception before trying to access the new object (unless you use a new-handler).

A request for allocation of 0 bytes returns a non-null pointer. Repeated requests for zero-size allocations return distinct, non-null pointers.

Operator delete

Syntax

```
<::> delete <cast-expression>
<::> delete [ ] <cast-expression>
delete <array-name> [ ];
```

Description

The **delete** operator offers dynamic storage deallocation, deallocating a memory block allocated by a previous call to new. It is similar but superior to the standard library function *free*.

You should use the **delete** operator to remove arrays that you no longer need. Failure to free memory can result in memory leaks.

Example of the new and delete operators

The following example shows you one way to allocate and delete memory for a two-dimensional array. The order of operations taken to allocate the space must be reversed when you delete the space. The illustration shows the amount of space allocated for 32-bit programs.

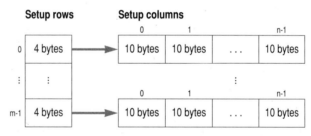

```
// ALLOCATE A TWO-DIMENSIONAL SPACE, INITIALIZE, AND DELETE IT.
#include <except.h>
#include <iostream.h>
void display(long double **);
void de_allocate(long double **);
int m = 3;                              // THE NUMBER OF ROWS.
int n = 5;                              // THE NUMBER OF COLUMNS.
int main(void) {
   long double **data;
   try {                                // TEST FOR EXCEPTIONS.
      data = new long double*[m];       // STEP 1: SET UP THE ROWS.
      for (int j = 0; j < m; j++)
         data[j] = new long double[n];  // STEP 2: SET UP THE COLUMNS
      }
   catch (xalloc) {  // ENTER THIS BLOCK ONLY IF xalloc IS THROWN.
      // YOU COULD REQUEST OTHER ACTIONS BEFORE TERMINATING
      cout << "Could not allocate. Bye ...";
      exit(-1);
      }
```

```
        for (int i = 0; i < m; i++)
            for (int j = 0; j < n; j++)
                data[i][j] = i + j;               // ARBITRARY INITIALIZATION
        display(data);
        de_allocate(data);
        return 0;
        }
    void display(long double **data) {
        for (int i = 0; i < m; i++) {
            for (int j = 0; j < n; j++)
                    cout << data[i][j] << " ";
            cout << "\n" << endl;
            }
        }
    void de_allocate(long double **data) {
        for (int i = 0; i < m;   i++)
            delete[] data[i];                     // STEP 1: DELETE THE COLUMNS
        delete[] data;                            // STEP 2: DELETE THE ROWS
        }
```

Output

```
0 1 2 3 4
1 2 3 4 5
2 3 4 5 6
```

Operator new placement syntax

The placement syntax for operator **new( )** can be used only if you have overloaded the allocation operator with the appropriate arguments. You can use the placement syntax when you want to use and reuse a memory space which you set up once at the beginning of your program.

When you use the overloaded operator **new( )** to specify where you want an allocation to be placed, you are responsible for deleting the allocation. Because you call your version of the allocation operator, you cannot depend on the global ::operator **delete( )** to do the cleanup.

To release memory, you make an explicit call on the destructor. This method for cleaning up memory should be used only in special situations and with great care. If you make an explicit call of a destructor before an object that has been constructed on the stack goes out of scope, the destructor will be called again when the stackframe is cleaned up.

Operator new placement syntax example

```
    // An example of the placement syntax for operator new()
    #include <iostream.h>
    class Alpha {
      union {
        char  ch;
        char  buf[10];
        };
```

```
public:
    Alpha(char c = '\0') : ch(c) {
        cout << "character constructor" << endl;
        }
    Alpha(char *s) {
        cout << "string constructor" << endl;
        strcpy(buf,s);
        }
    ~Alpha( ) { cout << "Alpha::~Alpha() " << endl; }
    void * operator new(size_t, void * buf) {
        return buf;
        }
};
void main() {
    char *str = new char[sizeof(Alpha)];
    // Place 'X' at start of str.
    Alpha* ptr = new(str) Alpha('X');
    cout << "str[0] = " << str[0] << endl;
    // Explicit call of the destructor
    ptr -> Alpha::~Alpha();
    // Place a string in str buffer.
    ptr = new(str) Alpha("my string");
    cout << "\n str = " << str << endl;
    // Explicit call of the destructor
    ptr -> Alpha::~Alpha();
    delete[] str;
    }
```

Output

```
character constructor
str[0] = X
Alpha::~Alpha()
string constructor
 str = my string
Alpha::~Alpha()
```

Operator new with arrays

If *Type* is an array, the pointer returned by operator **new[]()** points to the first element of the array. When creating multidimensional arrays with **new**, all array sizes must be supplied (although the leftmost dimension doesn't have to be a compile-time constant):

```
mat_ptr = new int[3][10][12];     // OK
mat_ptr = new int[n][10][12];     // OK
mat_ptr = new int[3][][12];       // illegal
mat_ptr = new int[][10][12];      // illegal
```

Although the first array dimension can be a variable, all following dimensions must be constants.

Operator delete with arrays

Arrays are deleted by operator **delete[]()**. You must use the syntax `delete [] expr` when deleting an array. After C++ 2.1, the array dimension should not be specified within the brackets:

```
char * p;
void func()
{
    p = new char[10];    //  allocate 10 chars
    delete[] p;          // delete 10 chars
}
```

C++ 2.0 code required the array size. In order to allow 2.0 code to compile, Borland C++ issues a warning and simply ignores any size that is specified. For example, if the preceding example reads `delete[10] p` and is compiled, the warning is as follows:

```
Warning: Array size for 'delete' ignored in function func()
```

::operator new

By default, if there is no overloaded version of **new**, a request for dynamic memory allocation always uses the global version of **new**, **::operator new()**. A request for array allocation calls **::operator new[]()**. With class objects of type *name*, a specific operator called *name*::**operator new()** or *name*::**operator new[]()** can be defined. When **new** is applied to class name objects it invokes the appropriate *name*::**operator new** if it is present; otherwise, the global **::operator new** is used.

Only the operator **new()** function will accept an optional initializer. The array allocator version, **operator new[]()**, will not accept initializers. In the absence of explicit initializers, the object created by **new** contains unpredictable data (garbage). The objects allocated by **new**, other than arrays, can be initialized with a suitable expression in parentheses:

```
int_ptr = new int(3);
```

Arrays of classes with constructors are initialized with the default constructor. The user-defined **new** operator with customized initialization plays a key role in C++ constructors for class-type objects.

Overloading the operator new

The global **::operator new()** and **::operator new[]()** can be overloaded. Each overloaded instance must have a unique signature. Therefore, multiple instances of a global allocation operator can coexist in a single program.

Class-specific memory allocation operators can also be overloaded. The operator **new** can be implemented to provide alternative free storage (heap) memory-management routines, or implemented to accept additional arguments. A user-defined operator **new** must return a **void*** and must have a *size_t* as its first argument. To overload the **new** operators, use the following prototypes declared in the new.h header file.

```
void * operator new(size_t Type_size);    // For Non-array
void * operator new[](size_t Type_size);  // For arrays
```

The Borland C++ compiler provides *Type_size* to the **new** operator. You can substitute any data type for *Type_size* except function names (although a pointer to function is permitted), class declarations, enumeration declarations, const, and volatile.

Overloading the operator delete

The global operators, **::operator delete()** and **::operator delete[]()**, cannot be overloaded. However, you can override the default version of each of these operators with your own implementation. Only one instance of the each global delete function can exist in the program.

The user-defined operator **delete** must have a **void** return type and **void*** as its first argument; a second argument of *type size_t* is optional. A class *T* can define at most one version of each of *T*::**operator delete[]()** and *T*::**operator delete()**. To overload the delete operators, use the following prototypes.

```
void operator delete(void *Type_ptr, [size_t Type_size]);    // For non-array
void operator delete[](size_t Type_ptr, [size_t Type_size]); // For arrays
```

Example of overloading the new and delete operators

```
#include <stdlib.h>
class X {
    ?
public:
    void* operator new(size_t size) { return newalloc(size);}
    void operator delete(void* p) { newfree(p); }
    X() { /* initialize here */ }
    X(char ch) { /* and here */ }
    ~X() { /* clean up here */ }
    ?
};
```

Note   Destructors are called only if you use the **–xd** compiler option and an exception is thrown.

The *size* argument gives the size of the object being created, and *newalloc* and *newfree* are user-supplied memory allocation and deallocation functions. Constructor and destructor calls for objects of **class** *X* (or objects of classes derived from *X* that do not have their own overloaded operators **new** and **delete**) invoke the matching user-defined *X*::**operator new()** and *X*::**operator delete()**, respectively.

The *X*::**operator new()**, *X*::**operator new[]()**, *X*::**operator delete()** and *X*::**operator delete[]()** operator functions are static members of *X* whether explicitly declared as **static** or not, so they cannot be virtual functions.

The standard, predefined (global) **new()**, **new[]()**, **delete()**, and **delete[]()** operators can still be used within the scope of *X*, either explicitly with the global scope operator

(**::operator new()**, **::operator new[]()**, **::operator delete()**, and **::operator delete[]()**), or implicitly when creating and destroying non-*X* or non-*X*-derived class objects.

For example, you could use the standard **new** and **delete** when defining the overloaded versions:

```
void* X::operator new(size_t s)
{
    void* ptr = new char[s]; // standard new called
        ⋮
    return ptr;
}

void X::operator delete(void* ptr)
{
        ⋮
    delete (void*) ptr;      // standard delete called
}
```

The reason for the *size* argument is that classes derived from *X* inherit the *X*::**operator new()** and *X*::**operator new[]()**. The size of a derived class object might differ from that of the base class.

Classes

C++ classes offer extensions to the predefined type system. Each class type represents a unique set of objects and the operations (methods) and conversions available to create, manipulate, and destroy such objects. Derived classes can be declared that *inherit* the members of one or more *base* (or parent) classes.

In C++, structures and unions are considered as classes with certain access defaults.

A simplified, "first-look" syntax for class declarations is

class-key {<*distance-attrib*> <*distance-attrib*>} <*type-info*> *class-name*

<: *base-list*> { <*member-list*> };

class-key is one of **class**, **struct**, or **union**.

The optional *type-info* indicates a request for run-time type information about the class. You can compile with the **–RT** compiler option, or you can use the **_ _rtti** keyword. See the discussion of class *typeinfo* for more information.

The optional *base-list* lists the base class or classes from which the class *class-name* will derive (or *inherit*) objects and methods. If any base classes are specified, the class *class-name* is called a derived class. The *base-list* has default and optional overriding *access specifiers* that can modify the access rights of the derived class to members of the base classes.

The optional *member-list* declares the class members (data and functions) of *class-name* with default and optional overriding access specifiers that can affect which functions can access which members.

Class memory model specifications

For 16-bit applications only, distance modifiers can be applied to a class declaration. The modifier(s) applied to a class declaration determine the addressing of the class's **this** pointer and the class's table of virtual functions (*vtable*). The distance modifiers allowed for class declarations, and their effect on the addressing of **this** and the vtable are as follows:

Table 3.1   Class memory model specifications

Modifier	*this	vtable
_ _near	near	near
_ _far	far	near
_ _huge	far	far
_ _huge _ _near	near	far
_ _export	far	far
_ _import	far	far

If you're importing classes that are declared with the modifier _ _**huge**, you must change the modifier to the keyword _ _**import**. The _ _**huge** modifier merely causes far addressing of the virtual tables (the same effect as the **–Vf** compiler option). The _ _**import** modifier makes all function and static addresses default to far.

See "Exporting and importing classes" in Chapter 6 for a discussion of declaration of classes used in DLLs.

Class names

class-name is any identifier unique within its scope. With structures, classes, and unions, *class-name* can be omitted. See "Untagged structures and typedefs" in Chapter 6 for discussion of untagged structures.

Class types

The declaration creates a unique type, class type *class-name*. This lets you declare further *class objects* (or *instances*) of this type, and objects derived from this type (such as pointers to, references to, arrays of *class-name*, and so on):

```
class X { ... };

X x, &xr, *xptr, xarray[10];
/* four objects: type X, reference to X, pointer to X and array of X */
struct Y { ... };
Y y, &yr, *yptr, yarray[10];
// C would have
// struct Y y, *yptr, yarray[10];
union Z { ... };
Z z, &zr, *zptr, zarray[10];
// C would have
// union Z z, *zptr, zarray[10];
```

Note the difference between C and C++ structure and union declarations: The keywords **struct** and **union** are essential in C, but in C++, they are needed only when the class names, *Y* and *Z*, are hidden.

Class name scope

The scope of a class name is local. There are some special requirements if the class name appears more than once in the same scope. Class name scope starts at the point of declaration and ends with the enclosing block. A class name hides any class, object, enumerator, or function with the same name in the enclosing scope. If a class name is declared in a scope containing the declaration of an object, function, or enumerator of the same name, the class can be referred to only by using the *elaborated type specifier*. This means that the class key, **class**, **struct**, or **union**, must be used with the class name. For example,

```
struct S { ... };

int S(struct S *Sptr);
void func(void) {
   S t;          // ILLEGAL declaration: no class key and function S in scope
   struct S s;   // OK: elaborated with class key
   S(&s);        // OK: this is a function call
}
```

C++ also allows an incomplete class declaration:

```
class X;   // no members, yet!
```

Incomplete declarations permit certain references to class name *X* (usually references to pointers to class objects) before the class has been fully defined. See "Structure member declarations" for more information. Of course, you must make a complete class declaration with members before you can define and use class objects.

Class objects

Class objects can be assigned (unless copying has been restricted), passed as arguments to functions, returned by functions (with some exceptions), and so on. Other operations on class objects and members can be user-defined in many ways, including definition of member and friend functions and the redefinition of standard functions and operators when used with objects of a certain class.

Redefined functions and operators are said to be *overloaded*. Operators and functions that are restricted to objects of a certain class (or related group of classes) are called *member functions* for that class. C++ offers the overloading mechanism that allows the same function or operator name can be called to perform different tasks, depending on the type or number of arguments or operands.

Class member list

The optional *member-list* is a sequence of data declarations (of any type, including enumerations, bit fields, and other classes), function declarations, and definitions, all with optional storage class specifiers and access modifiers. The objects thus defined are called *class members*. The storage class specifiers **auto**, **extern**, and **register** are not allowed. Members can be declared with the **static** storage class specifiers.

Member functions

A function declared without the **friend** specifier is known as a *member function* of the class. Functions declared with the **friend** modifier are called *friend functions*.

The same name can be used to denote more than one function, provided they differ in argument type or number of arguments.

The keyword this

Nonstatic member functions operate on the class type object they are called with. For example, if x is an object of class X and *f()* is a member function of X, the function call x.f() operates on x. Similarly, if *xptr* is a pointer to an X object, the function call xptr->f() operates on *xptr*. But how does *f* know which instance of X it is operating on? C++ provides *f* with a pointer to x called **this**. **this** is passed as a hidden argument in all calls to nonstatic member functions.

this is a local variable available in the body of any nonstatic member function. **this** does not need to be declared and is rarely referred to explicitly in a function definition. However, it is used implicitly within the function for member references. If *x.f(y)* is called, for example, where y is a member of X, **this** is set to *&x* and y is set to **this->y**, which is equivalent to *x.y*.

Static members

The storage class specifier **static** can be used in class declarations of data and function members. Such members are called *static members* and have distinct properties from nonstatic members. With nonstatic members, a distinct copy "exists" for each instance of the class; with static members, only one copy exists, and it can be accessed without reference to any particular object in its class. If x is a static member of class X, it can be referenced as *X::x* (even if objects of class X haven't been created yet). It is still possible to access x using the normal member access operators. For example, *y.x* and *yptr->x*, where y is an object of class X and *yptr* is a pointer to an object of class X, although the expressions y and *yptr* are not evaluated. In particular, a static member function can be called with or without the special member function syntax:

```
class X {
    int member_int;
public:
    static void func(int i, X* ptr);
};
void g(void); {
    X obj;
    func(1, &obj);       // error unless there is a global func()
                         // defined elsewhere
    X::func(1, &obj);    // calls the static func() in X
                         // OK for static functions only
```

```
obj.func(1, &obj);   // so does this (OK for static and
                     // nonstatic functions)
}
```

Because static member functions can be called with no particular object in mind, they don't have a **this** pointer, and therefore cannot access nonstatic members without explicitly specifying an object with **.** or **->**. For example, with the declarations of the previous example, *func* might be defined as follows:

```
void X::func(int i, X* ptr)
{
    member_int = i;        // which object does member_int
                           // refer to? Error
    ptr->member_int = i;   // OK: now we know!
}
```

Apart from inline functions, static member functions of global classes have external linkage. Static member functions cannot be virtual functions. It is illegal to have a static and nonstatic member function with the same name and argument types.

The declaration of a static data member in its class declaration is not a definition, so a definition must be provided elsewhere to allocate storage and provide initialization.

Static members of a class declared local to some function have no linkage and cannot be initialized. Static members of a global class can be initialized like ordinary global objects, but only in file scope. Static members, nested to any level, obey the usual class member access rules, except they can be initialized.

```
class X {
    static int x;
    class inner {
        static float f;
        void func(void);      // nested declaration
        };
    };
int X::x = 1;
float X::inner::f = 3.14;  // initialization of nested static
X::inner::func(void) {     /*  define the nested function */  }
```

The principal use for static members is to keep track of data common to all objects of a class, such as the number of objects created, or the last-used resource from a pool shared by all such objects. Static members are also used to

- Reduce the number of visible global names

- Make obvious which static objects logically belong to which class

- Permit access control to their names

Inline functions

You can declare a member function within its class and define it elsewhere. Alternatively, you can both declare and define a member function within its class in which case it is called an *inline function*.

Borland C++ can sometimes reduce the normal function call overhead by substituting the function call directly with the compiled code of the function body. This process, called an *inline expansion* of the function body, does not affect the scope of the function name or its arguments. Inline expansion is not always possible or feasible. The **inline** specifier indicates to the compiler you would like an inline expansion.

Note The Borland C++ compiler can ignore requests for inline expansion.

Explicit and implicit **inline** requests are best reserved for small, frequently used functions, such as the operator functions that implement overloaded operators. For example, the following class declaration of *func*:

```
int i;                           // global int

class X {
public:
    char* func(void) { return i; }  // inline by default
    char* i;
};
```

is equivalent to:

```
inline char* X::func(void) { return i; }
```

func is defined outside the class with an explicit **inline** specifier. The *i* returned by *func* is the **char*** *i* of class *X* (see "Member scope" later in this chapter).

Inline functions and exceptions

An inline function with an exception-specification will never be expanded inline by Borland C++. For example,

```
inline void f1() throw(int)
    {
    // Warning: Functions with exception specifications are not expanded inline
    }
```

The remaining restrictions apply only when destructor cleanup is enabled.

Note Destructors are called by default.

An inline function that takes at least one parameter that is of type 'class with a destructor' will not be expanded inline. Note that this restriction does not apply to classes that are passed by reference. Example:

```
struct foo {
    foo();
    ~foo();
    };
inline void f2(foo& x) {
    // no warning, f2() can be expanded inline
    }
inline void f3(foo x) {
    // Warning: Functions taking class-by-value argument(s) are
    //          not expanded inline in function f3(foo)
    }
```

An inline function that returns a class with a destructor by value will not be expanded inline whenever there are variables or temporaries that need to be destructed within the return expression:

```
struct foo {
    foo();
    ~foo();
    };
inline foo f4() {
    return foo();
    // no warning, f4() can be expanded inline
    }
inline foo f5() {
    foo X;
    return foo(); // Object X needs to be destructed
    // Warning: Functions containing some return statements are
    //          not expanded inline in function f5()
    }
inline foo f6() {
    return ( foo(), foo() );  // temporary in return value
    // Warning:Functions containing some return statements are
    //          not expanded inline in function f6()
    }
```

Member scope

The expression X::func() in the example in the "Inline functions and exceptions" section earlier in this chapter uses the class name *X* with the scope access modifier to signify that *func*, although defined "outside" the class, is indeed a member function of *X* and exists within the scope of *X*. The influence of *X*:: extends into the body of the definition. This explains why the *i* returned by *func* refers to *X::i*, the **char*** *i* of *X*, rather than the global **int** *i*. Without the *X*:: modifier, the function *func* would represent an ordinary non-class function, returning the global **int** *i*.

All member functions, then, are in the scope of their class, even if defined outside the class.

Data members of class *X* can be referenced using the selection operators **.** and **->** (as with C structures). Member functions can also be called using the selection operators (see "The keyword this" earlier in this chapter). For example:

```
class X {
public:
    int i;
    char name[20];
    X *ptr1;
    X *ptr2;
    void Xfunc(char*data, X* left, X* right);    // define elsewhere
};
void f(void);
{
    X x1, x2, *xptr=&x1;
    x1.i = 0;
```

```
        x2.i = x1.i;
        xptr->i = 1;
        x1.Xfunc("stan", &x2, xptr);
    }
```

If *m* is a member or base member of class *X*, the expression *X::m* is called a *qualified name*; it has the same type as *m*, and it is an lvalue only if *m* is an lvalue. It is important to note that, even if the class name *X* is hidden by a non-type name, the qualified name *X::m* will access the correct class member, *m*.

Class members cannot be added to a class by another section of your program. The class *X* cannot contain objects of class *X*, but can contain pointers or references to objects of class *X* (note the similarity with C's structure and union types).

Nested types

Tag or **typedef** names declared inside a class lexically belong to the scope of that class. Such names can, in general, be accessed only by using the *xxx::yyy* notation, except when in the scope of the appropriate class.

A class declared within another class is called a *nested class*. Its name is local to the enclosing class; the nested class is in the scope of the enclosing class. This is a purely lexical nesting. The nested class has no additional privileges in accessing members of the enclosing class (and vice versa).

Classes can be nested in this way to an arbitrary level. Nested classes can be declared inside some class and defined later. For example,

```
struct outer
{
    typedef int t;   // 'outer::t' is a typedef name
    struct inner     // 'outer::inner' is a class
    {
        static int x;
    };
    static int x;
        int f();
    class deep;      // nested declaration
};
int outer::x;        // define static data member
int outer::f() {
    t x;             // 't' visible directly here
    return x;
    }
int outer::inner::x;      // define static data member
outer::t x;              //  have to use 'outer::t' here
class outer::deep { };  // define the nested class here
```

With Borland C++ 2.0, any tags or **typedef** names declared inside a class actually belong to the global (file) scope. For example:

```
struct foo
{
    enum bar { x };   // 2.0 rules: 'bar' belongs to file scope
                      // 2.1 rules: 'bar' belongs to 'foo' scope
```

```
};
bar x;
```

The preceding fragment compiles without errors. But because the code is illegal under the 2.1 rules, a warning is issued as follows:

```
Warning: Use qualified name to access nested type 'foo::bar'
```

Member access control

Members of a class acquire access attributes either by default (depending on class key and declaration placement) or by the use of one of the three access specifiers: **public**, **private**, and **protected**. The significance of these attributes is as follows:

public   The member can be used by any function.

private   The member can be used only by member functions and friends of the class it's declared in.

protected   Same as for **private**. Additionally, the member can be used by member functions and friends of classes *derived* from the declared class, but only in objects of the derived type. (Derived classes are explained in "Base and derived class access.")

Note   Friend function declarations are not affected by access specifiers (see "Friends of classes" later in this chapter for more information).

Members of a class are **private** by default, so you need explicit **public** or **protected** access specifiers to override the default.

Members of a **struct** are **public** by default, but you can override this with the **private** or **protected** access specifier.

Members of a **union** are **public** by default; this cannot be changed. All three access specifiers are illegal with union members.

A default or overriding access modifier remains effective for all subsequent member declarations until a different access modifier is encountered. For example,

```
class X {
    int i;    // X::i is private by default
    char ch;  // so is X::ch
public:
    int j;    // next two are public
    int k;
protected:
    int l;    // X::l is protected
};
struct Y {
    int i;    // Y::i is public by default
private:
    int j;    // Y::j is private
public:
    int k;    // Y::k is public
};
```

```
union Z {
    int i;    // public by default; no other choice
    double d;
};
```

Note   The access specifiers can be listed and grouped in any convenient sequence. You can save typing effort by declaring all the private members together, and so on.

Base and derived class access

When you declare a derived class *D*, you list the base classes *B1, B2, ...* in a comma-delimited *base-list*:

> *class-key D : base-list { <member-list> }*

D inherits all the members of these base classes. (Redefined base class members are inherited and can be accessed using scope overrides, if needed.) *D* can use only the **public** and **protected** members of its base classes. But, what will be the access attributes of the inherited members as viewed by *D*? *D* might want to use a **public** member from a base class, but make it **private** as far as outside functions are concerned. The solution is to use access specifiers in the *base-list*.

Note   Since a base class can itself be a derived class, the access attribute question is recursive: you backtrack until you reach the basest of the base classes, those that do not inherit.

When declaring *D*, you can use the access specifier **public, protected**, or **private** in front of the classes in the *base-list*:

```
class D : public B1, private B2, ... {
    ⋮
}
```

These modifiers do not alter the access attributes of base members as viewed by the base class, though they can alter the access attributes of base members as viewed by the derived class.

The default is private if D is a class declaration, and public if D is a struct declaration.

Note   Unions cannot have base classes, and unions cannot be used as base classes.

The derived class inherits access attributes from a base class as follows:

- **public** base class: **public** members of the base class are **public** members of the derived class. **protected** members of the base class are **protected** members of the derived class. **private** members of the base class remain **private** to the base class.

- **protected** base class: Both **public** and **protected** members of the base class are **protected** members of the derived class. **private** members of the base class remain **private** to the base class.

- **private** base class: Both **public** and **protected** members of the base class are **private** members of the derived class. **private** members of the base class remain **private** to the base class.

Note that **private** members of a base class are always inaccessible to member functions of the derived class *unless* **friend** declarations are explicitly declared in the base class granting access. For example,

```
/* class X is derived from class A */
```

```
class X : A {                // default for class is private A
  ⋮
}
/* class Y is derived (multiple inheritance) from B and C
   B defaults to private B */
class Y : B, public C {      // override default for C
  ⋮
}
/* struct S is derived from D */
struct S : D {               // default for struct is public D
  ⋮
}
/* struct T is derived (multiple inheritance) from D and E
   E defaults to public E */
struct T : private D, E {    // override default for D
                             // E is public by default
  ⋮
}
```

The effect of access specifiers in the base list can be adjusted by using a *qualified-name* in the public or protected declarations of the derived class. For example:

```
class B {
    int a;                  // private by default
public:
    int b, c;
    int Bfunc(void);
};
class X : private B {       // a, b, c, Bfunc are now private in X
    int d;                  // private by default, NOTE: a is not
                            // accessible in X
public:
    B::c;                   // c was private, now is public
    int e;
    int Xfunc(void);
};
int Efunc(X& x);            // external to B and X
```

The function *Efunc()* can use only the public names *c, e*, and *Xfunc()*.

The function *Xfunc()* is in *X*, which is derived from **private** *B*, so it has access to

- The "adjusted-to-public" *c*
- The "private-to-*X*" members from *B*: *b* and *Bfunc()*
- *X*'s own private and public members: *d, e*, and *Xfunc()*

However, *Xfunc()* cannot access the "private-to-*B*" member, *a*.

Virtual base classes

A **virtual** class is a base class that is passed to more than one derived class, as might happen with multiple inheritance.

You cannot specify a base class more than once in a derived class:

```
class B { ...};
class D : B, B { ... };  // ILLEGAL
```

However, you can indirectly pass a base class to the derived class more than once:

```
class X : public B { ... }
class Y : public B { ... }
class Z : public X, public Y { ... }  // OK
```

In this case, each object of class *Z* has two sub-objects of class *B*.

If this causes problems, add the keyword **virtual** to the base class specifier. For example,

```
class X : virtual public B { ... }
class Y : virtual public B { ... }
class Z : public X, public Y { ... }
```

B is now a virtual base class, and class *Z* has only one sub-object of class *B*.

Constructors for virtual base classes

Constructors for virtual base classes are invoked before any non-virtual base classes.

If the hierarchy contains multiple virtual base classes, the virtual base class constructors invoke in the order they were declared.

Any non-virtual bases are then constructed before the derived class constructor is called.

If a virtual class is derived from a non-virtual base, that non-virtual base will be first, so that the virtual base class can be properly constructed. For example, this code

```
class X : public Y, virtual public Z
   X one;
```

produces this order:

```
Z();   // virtual base class initialization
Y();   // non-virtual base class
X();   // derived class
```

Friends of classes

A **friend** *F* of a class *X* is a function or class, although not a member function of *X*, with full access rights to the private and protected members of *X*. In all other respects, *F* is a normal function with respect to scope, declarations, and definitions.

Since *F* is not a member of *X*, it is not in the scope of *X*, and it cannot be called with the *x.F* and *xptr->F* selector operators (where *x* is an *X* object and *xptr* is a pointer to an *X* object).

If the specifier **friend** is used with a function declaration or definition within the class *X*, it becomes a friend of *X*.

friend functions defined within a class obey the same inline rules as member functions (see Inline functions). **friend** functions are not affected by their position within the class or by any access specifiers. For example:

```
class X {
    int i;                              // private to X
    friend void friend_func(X*, int);
/* friend_func is not private, even though it's declared in the private section */
public:
    void member_func(int);
};
/* definitions; note both functions access private int i */
void friend_func(X* xptr, int a) { xptr->i = a; }
void X::member_func(int a) { i = a; }

X xobj;
/* note difference in function calls */
friend_func(&xobj, 6);
xobj.member_func(6);
```

You can make all the functions of class *Y* into friends of class *X* with a single declaration:

```
class Y;                            // incomplete declaration

class X {
    friend Y;
    int i;
    void member_funcX();
};
class Y; {                          // complete the declaration
    void friend_X1(X&);
    void friend_X2(X*);
        :
};
```

The functions declared in *Y* are friends of *X*, although they have no **friend** specifiers. They can access the private members of *X*, such as *i* and *member_funcX*.

It is also possible for an individual member function of class *X* to be a friend of class *Y*:

```
class X {
        :
    void member_funcX();
}
class Y {
    int i;
    friend void X::member_funcX();
        :
};
```

Class friendship is not transitive: *X* friend of *Y* and *Y* friend of *Z* does not imply *X* friend of *Z*. Friendship is not inherited.

Constructors and destructors

There are several special member functions that determine how the objects of a class are created, initalized, copied, and destroyed. Constructors and destructors are the most important of these. They have many of the characteristics of normal member functions—you declare and define them within the class, or declare them within the class and define them outside—but they have some unique features:

- They do not have return value declarations (not even **void**).

- They cannot be inherited, though a derived class can call the base class's constructors and destructors.

- Constructors, like most C++ functions, can have default arguments or use member initialization lists.

- Destructors can be **virtual**, but constructors cannot. (See "Virtual destructors" later in this chapter.)

- You can't take their addresses.

```
int main (void)
{
  ⋮
  void *ptr = base::base;     // illegal
  ⋮
}
```

- Constructors and destructors can be generated by Borland C++ if they haven't been explicitly defined; they are also invoked on many occasions without explicit calls in your program. Any constructor or destructor generated by the compiler will be public.

- You cannot call constructors the way you call a normal function. Destructors can be called if you use their fully qualified name.

```
{
  ⋮
  X *p;
  ⋮
  p->X::~X();                // legal call of destructor
  X::X();                    // illegal call of constructor
  ⋮
}
```

- The compiler automatically calls constructors and destructors when defining and destroying objects.

- Constructors and destructors can make implicit calls to operator **new** and operator **delete** if allocation is required for an object.

- An object with a constructor or destructor cannot be used as a member of a union.

- If no constructor has been defined for some class X to accept a given type, no attempt is made to find other constructors or conversion functions to convert the assigned value into a type acceptable to a constructor for class X. Note that this rule applies only to any constructor with *one* parameter and no initializers that use the "=" syntax.

```
class X { /* ... */ X(int); };
class Y { /* ... */ Y(X); };
Y a = 1;                     // illegal: Y(X(1)) not tried
```

If **class** *X* has one or more constructors, one of them is invoked each time you define an object *x* of **class** *X*. The constructor creates *x* and initializes it. Destructors reverse the process by destroying the class objects created by constructors.

Constructors are also invoked when local or temporary objects of a class are created; destructors are invoked when these objects go out of scope.

Constructors

Constructors are distinguished from all other member functions by having the same name as the class they belong to. When an object of that class is created or is being copied, the appropriate constructor is called implicitly.

Constructors for global variables are called before the *main* function is called. When the **#pragma startup** directive is used to install a function prior to the *main* function, global variable constructors are called prior to the startup functions.

Local objects are created as the scope of the variable becomes active. A constructor is also invoked when a temporary object of the class is created.

```
class X {
public:
    X();   // class X constructor
};
```

A **class** *X* constructor cannot take *X* as an argument:

```
class X {
public:
    X(X);                    // illegal
};
```

The parameters to the constructor can be of any type except that of the class it's a member of. The constructor can accept a reference to its own class as a parameter; when it does so, it is called the copy constructor . A constructor that accepts no parameters is called the default constructor .

Constructor defaults

The default constructor for **class** *X* is one that takes no arguments; it usually has the form X::X(). If no user-defined constructors exist for a class, Borland C++ generates a default constructor. On a declaration such as *X x*, the default constructor creates the object *x*.

Like all functions, constructors can have default arguments. For example, the constructor

```
X::X(int, int = 0)
```

can take one or two arguments. When presented with one argument, the missing second argument is assumed to be a zero **int**. Similarly, the constructor

```
X::X(int = 5, int = 6)
```

could take two, one, or no arguments, with appropriate defaults. However, the default constructor X::X() takes no arguments and must not be confused with, say,

`X::X(int = 0)`, which can be called with *no* arguments as a default constructor, or can take an argument.

You should avoid ambiguity in calling constructors. In the following case, the two default constructors are ambiguous:

```
class X
{
public:
    X();
    X(int i = 0);
};
int main() {
    X one(10);   // OK; uses X::X(int)
    X two;       // illegal; ambiguous whether to call X::X() or
                 // X::X(int = 0)
    return 0;
}
```

The copy constructor

A copy constructor for **class** *X* is one that can be called with a single argument of type *X* as follows:

```
X::X(X&)
```

or

```
X::X(const X&)
```

or

```
X::X(const X&, int = 0)
```

Default arguments are also allowed in a copy constructor. Copy constructors are invoked when initializing a class object, typically when you declare with initialization by another class object:

```
X x1;
X x2 = x1;
X x3(x1);
```

Borland C++ generates a copy constructor for **class** *X* if one is needed and no other constructor has been defined in **class** *X*. The copy constructor that is generated by the Borland C++ compiler lets you safely start programming with simple data types. You need to make your own definition of the copy constructor if your program creates aggregate, complex types such as **class**, **struct**, and arrays. The copy constructor is also called when you pass a class argument by value to a function.

See also the discussion of member-by-member class assignment later in this chapter. You should define the copy constructor if you overload the assignment operator.

Overloading constructors

Constructors can be overloaded, allowing objects to be created, depending on the values being used for initialization.

```
class X {
    int     integer_part;
    double double_part;
public:
    X(int i)    { integer_part = i; }
    X(double d) { double_part = d; }
};
int main() {
    X one(10);    // invokes X::X(int) and sets integer_part to 10
    X one(3.14); // invokes X::X(double) setting double_part to 3.14
    return 0;
}
```

Order of calling constructors

In the case where a class has one or more base classes, the base class constructors are invoked before the derived class constructor. The base class constructors are called in the order they are declared.

For example, in this setup,

```
class Y {...}
class X : public Y {...}
X one;
```

the constructors are called in this order:

```
Y();    // base class constructor
X();    // derived class constructor
```

For the case of multiple base classes,

```
class X : public Y, public Z
X one;
```

the constructors are called in the order of declaration:

```
Y();  // base class constructors come first
Z();
X();
```

Constructors for virtual base classes are invoked before any nonvirtual base classes. If the hierarchy contains multiple virtual base classes, the virtual base class constructors are invoked in the order in which they were declared. Any nonvirtual bases are then constructed before the derived class constructor is called.

If a virtual class is derived from a nonvirtual base, that nonvirtual base will be first so that the virtual base class can be properly constructed. The code:

```
class X : public Y, virtual public Z
X one;
```

produces this order:

```
Z();    // virtual base class initialization
Y();    // nonvirtual base class
X();    // derived class
```

Or, for a more complicated example:

```
class base;
class base2;
class level1 : public base2, virtual public base;
class level2 : public base2, virtual public base;
class toplevel : public level1, virtual public level2;
toplevel view;
```

The construction order of view would be as follows:

```
base();      // virtual base class highest in hierarchy
             // base is constructed only once
base2();     // nonvirtual base of virtual base level2
             // must be called to construct level2
level2();    // virtual base class
base2();     // nonvirtual base of level1
level1();    // other nonvirtual base
toplevel();
```

If a class hierarchy contains multiple instances of a virtual base class, that base class is constructed only once. If, however, there exist both virtual and nonvirtual instances of the base class, the class constructor is invoked a single time for all virtual instances and then once for each nonvirtual occurrence of the base class.

Constructors for elements of an array are called in increasing order of the subscript.

Class initialization

An object of a class with only public members and no constructors or base classes (typically a structure) can be initialized with an initializer list. If a class has a constructor, its objects must be either initialized or have a default constructor. The latter is used for objects not explicitly initialized.

Objects of classes with constructors can be initialized with an expression list in parentheses. This list is used as an argument list to the constructor. An alternative is to use an equal sign followed by a single value. The single value can be the same type as the first argument accepted by a constructor of that class, in which case either there are no additional arguments, or the remaining arguments have default values. It could also be an object of that class type. In the former case, the matching constructor is called to create the object. In the latter case, the copy constructor is called to initialize the object.

```
class X
{
   int i;
public:
   X();          // function bodies omitted for clarity
   X(int x);
   X(const X&);
};
void main()
{
   X one;        // default constructor invoked
   X two(1);     // constructor X::X(int) is used
   X three = 1;  // calls X::X(int)
```

```
    X four = one; // invokes X::X(const X&) for copy
    X five(two);   // calls X::X(const X&)
}
```

The constructor can assign values to its members in two ways:

- It can accept the values as parameters and make assignments to the member variables within the function body of the constructor:

```
class X
{
    int a, b;
public:
    X(int i, int j) { a = i; b = j }
};
```

- An initializer list can be used prior to the function body:

```
class X
{
    int a, b, &c;   // Note the reference variable.
public:
    X(int i, int j) : a(i), b(j), c(a) {}
};
```

The initializer list is the only place to initialize a reference variable.

In both cases, an initialization of X x(1, 2) assigns a value of 1 to *x::a* and 2 to *x::b*. The second method, the initializer list, provides a mechanism for passing values along to base class constructors.

Note   Base class constructors must be declared as either **public** or **protected** to be called from a derived class.

```
class base1
{
    int x;
public:
    base1(int i) { x = i; }
};

class base2
{
    int x;
public:
    base2(int i) : x(i) {}
};
class top : public base1, public base2
{
    int a, b;
public:
    top(int i, int j) : base1(i*5), base2(j+i), a(i) { b = j;}
};
```

With this class hierarchy, a declaration of `top one(1, 2)` would result in the initialization of *base1* with the value 5 and *base2* with the value 3. The methods of initialization can be intermixed.

As described previously, the base classes are initialized in declaration order. Then the members are initialized, also in declaration order, independent of the initialization list.

```
class X
{
   int a, b;
public:
   X(int i, j) :  a(i), b(a+j) {}
};
```

With this class, a declaration of `X x(1,1)` results in an assignment of 1 to *x::a* and 2 to *x::b*.

Base class constructors are called prior to the construction of any of the derived classes members. If the values of the derived class are changed, they will have no effect on the creation of the base class.

```
class base
{
   int x;
public:
   base(int i) : x(i) {}
};
class derived : base
{
   int a;
public:
   derived(int i) : a(i*10), base(a) { } // Watch out! Base will be
                                         // passed an uninitialized 'a'
};
```

With this class setup, a call of `derived d(1)` will *not* result in a value of 10 for the base class member *x*. The value passed to the base class constructor will be undefined.

When you want an initializer list in a non-inline constructor, don't place the list in the class definition. Instead, put it at the point at which the function is defined.

```
derived::derived(int i) : a(i)
   {
      ⋮
   }
```

Destructors

The destructor for a class is called to free members of an object before the object is itself destroyed. The destructor is a member function whose name is that of the class preceded by a tilde (~). A destructor cannot accept any parameters, nor will it have a return type or value declared.

```
#include <stdlib.h>
class X
```

```
{
public:
    ~X(){};  // destructor for class X
};
```

If a destructor isn't explicitly defined for a class, the compiler generates one.

Invoking destructors

A destructor is called implicitly when a variable goes out of its declared scope.
Destructors for local variables are called when the block they are declared in is no longer
active. In the case of global variables, destructors are called as part of the exit procedure
after the main function.

When pointers to objects go out of scope, a destructor is not implicitly called. This
means that the **delete** operator must be called to destroy such an object.

Destructors are called in the exact opposite order from which their corresponding
constructors were called (see "Order of calling constructors" earlier in this chapter).

atexit, #pragma exit, and destructors

All global objects are active until the code in all exit procedures has executed. Local
variables, including those declared in the *main* function, are destroyed as they go out of
scope. The order of execution at the end of a Borland C++ program is as follows:

- *atexit()* functions are executed in the order they were inserted.

- **#pragma exit** functions are executed in the order of their priority codes.

- Destructors for global variables are called.

exit and destructors

When you call *exit* from within a program, destructors are not called for any local
variables in the current scope. Global variables are destroyed in their normal order.

abort and destructors

If you call *abort* anywhere in a program, no destructors are called, not even for variables
with a global scope.

A destructor can also be invoked explicitly in one of two ways: indirectly through a call
to **delete**, or directly by using the destructor's fully qualified name. You can use **delete**
to destroy objects that have been allocated using **new**. Explicit calls to the destructor are
necessary only for objects allocated a specific address through calls to **new**:

```
#include <stdlib.h>
class X {
public:
    :
    ~X(){};
    :
};
```

```
void* operator new(size_t size, void *ptr)
{
    return ptr;
}
char buffer[sizeof(X)];
void main() {
    X* pointer = new X;
    X* exact_pointer;
    exact_pointer = new(&buffer) X;  // pointer initialized at
                                     // address of buffer
   ⋮
    delete pointer;                  // delete used to destroy pointer
    exact_pointer->X::~X();          // direct call used to deallocate
}
```

Virtual destructors

A destructor can be declared as **virtual**. This allows a pointer to a base class object to call the correct destructor in the event that the pointer actually refers to a derived class object. The destructor of a class derived from a class with a **virtual** destructor is itself **virtual**.

```
/* How virtual affects the order of destructor calls.
   Without a virtual destructor in the base class, the derived
   class destructor won't be called. */
#include <iostream.h>
class color {
public:
    virtual ~color() {  // Virtual destructor
        cout << "color dtor\n";
        }
};
class red : public color {
public:
    ~red() {  // This destructor is also virtual
        cout << "red dtor\n";
        }
};
class brightred : public red {
public:
    ~brightred() {  // This destructor is also virtual
        cout << "brightred dtor\n";
        }
};
int main() {
    color *palette[3];
    palette[0] = new red;
    palette[1] = new brightred;
    palette[2] = new color;

    // The destructors for red and color are called.
    delete palette[0];
    cout << endl;
```

```
// The destructors for bright red, red, and color are called.
delete palette[1];
cout << endl;

// The destructor for color is called.
delete palette[2];
return 0;
}
```

Program output

```
red dtor
color dtor

brightred dtor
red dtor
color dtor

color dtor
```

However, if no destructors are declared as virtual, **delete** *palette*[0], **delete** *palette*[1], and **delete** *palette*[2] would all call only the destructor for class *color*. This would incorrectly destruct the first two elements, which were actually of type *red* and *brightred*.

Overloading operators

C++ lets you redefine the actions of most operators, so that they perform specified functions when used with objects of a particular class. As with overloaded C++ functions in general, the compiler distinguishes the different functions by noting the context of the call: the number and types of the arguments or operands.

All operators can be overloaded except for:

.   .*   ::   ?:

The following preprocessing symbols cannot be overloaded.

##

The =, [ ], ( ), and -> operators can be overloaded only as nonstatic member functions. These operators cannot be overloaded for enum types. Any attempt to overload a global version of these operators results in a compile-time error.

The keyword operator followed by the operator symbol is called the operator function name; it is used like a normal function name when defining the new (overloaded) action for the operator.

A function operator called with arguments behaves like an operator working on its operands in an expression. The operator function cannot alter the number of arguments or the precedence and associativity rules applying to normal operator use.

Example for overloading operators

The following example extends the class *complex* to create complex-type vectors. Several of the most useful operators are overloaded to provide some customary mathematical operations in the usual mathematical syntax.

Some of the issues illustrated by the example are:

- The default constructor is defined. This is provided by the compiler only if you have not defined it or any other constructor.

- The copy constructor is defined explicitly. Normally, if you have not defined any constructors, the compiler will provide one. You should define the copy constructor if you are overloading the assignment operator.

- The assignment operator is overloaded. If you do not overload the assignment operator, the compiler calls a default assignment operator when required. By overloading assignment of cvector types, you specify exactly the actions to be taken. Note that the assignment operator function cannot be inherited by derived classes.

- The subscript operator is defined as a member function (a requirement when overloading) with a single argument. The const version assures the caller that it will not modify its argument—this is useful when copying or assigning. This operator should check that the index value is within range—a good place to implement exception handling.

- The addition operator is defined as a member function. It allows addition only for cvector types. Addition should always check that the operands' sizes are compatible.

- The multiplication operator is declared a friend. This lets you define the order of the operands. An attempt to reverse the order of the operands is a compile-time error.

- The stream insertion operator is overloaded to naturally display a cvector. Large objects that don't display well on a limited size screen might require a different display strategy.

Source

```
/* HOW TO EXTEND THE complex CLASS AND OVERLOAD THE REQUIRED OPERATORS. */
#pragma warn -inl     // IGNORE not expanded inline WARNINGS.
#include <complex.h>  // THIS ALREADY INCLUDES iostream.h
// COMPLEX VECTORS
class cvector {
   int size;
   complex *data;
public:
   cvector() { size = 0; data = NULL; };
   cvector(int i = 5) : size(i) {     // DEFAULT VECTOR SIZE.
      data = new complex[size];
      for (int j = 0; j < size; j++)
          data[j] = j + (0.1 * j);  // ARBITRARY INITIALIZATION.
      };
   /* THIS VERSION IS CALLED IN main() */
   complex& operator [](int i) { return data[i]; };
   /* THIS VERSION IS CALLED IN ASSIGNMENT OPERATOR AND COPY THE CONSTRUCTOR */
```

```cpp
        const complex& operator [](int i) const { return data[i]; };
        cvector operator +(cvector& A) {   // ADDITION OPERATOR
            cvector result(A.size);   // DO NOT MODIFY THE ORIGINAL
            for (int i = 0; i < size; i++)
                result[i] = data[i] + A.data[i];
            return result;
            };
        /* BECAUSE scalar * vector MULTIPLICATION IS NOT COMMUTATIVE, THE ORDER OF
            THE ELEMENTS MUST BE SPECIFIED. THIS FRIEND OPERATOR FUNCTION WILL ENSURE
            PROPER MULTIPLICATION. */
        friend cvector operator *(int scalar, cvector& A) {
            cvector result(A.size);   // DO NOT MODIFY THE ORIGINAL
            for (int i = 0; i < A.size; i++)
                result.data[i] = scalar * A.data[i];
            return result;
            }
        /* THE STREAM INSERTION OPERATOR. */
        friend ostream& operator <<(ostream& out_data, cvector& C) {
            for (int i = 0; i < C.size; i++)
                out_data << "[" << i << "]=" << C.data[i] << "    ";
            cout << endl;
            return out_data;
            };
        cvector( const cvector &C ) {   // COPY CONSTRUCTOR
            size = C.size;
            data = new complex[size];
            for (int i = 0; i < size; i++)
                data[i] = C[i];
            }
        cvector& operator =(const cvector &C) {  // ASSIGNMENT OPERATOR.
            if (this == &C) return *this;
            delete[] data;
            size = C.size;
            data = new complex[size];
            for (int i = 0; i < size; i++)
                data[i] = C[i];
            return *this;
            };
        virtual ~cvector() { delete[] data; }; // DESTRUCTOR
        };
int main(void) { /* A FEW OPERATIONS WITH complex VECTORS. */
    cvector cvector1(4), cvector2(4), result(4);
    // CREATE complex NUMBERS AND ASSIGN THEM TO complex VECTORS
    cvector1[3] = complex(3.3, 102.8);
    cout << "Here is cvector1:" << endl;
    cout << cvector1;
    cvector2[3] = complex(33.3, 81);
    cout << "Here is cvector2:" << endl;
    cout << cvector2;
    result = cvector1 + cvector2;
    cout << "The result of vector addition:" << endl;
    cout << result;
```

```
result = 10 * cvector2;
cout << "The result of 10 * cvector2:" << endl;
cout << result;
return 0;
}
```

Output

```
Here is cvector1:
[0]=(0, 0)    [1]=(1.1, 0)    [2]=(2.2, 0)    [3]=(3.3, 102.8)
Here is cvector2:
[0]=(0, 0)    [1]=(1.1, 0)    [2]=(2.2, 0)    [3]=(33.3, 81)
The result of vector addition:
[0]=(0, 0)    [1]=(2.2, 0)    [2]=(4.4, 0)    [3]=(36.6, 183.8)
The result of 10 * cvector2:
[0]=(0, 0)    [1]=(11, 0)    [2]=(22, 0)    [3]=(333, 810)
```

Overloading operator functions

Operator functions can be called directly, although they are usually invoked indirectly by the use of the overload operator:

```
c3 = c1.operator + (c2);    // same as c3 = c1 + c2
```

Apart from **new** and **delete**, which have their own rules, an operator function must either be a nonstatic member function or have at least one argument of class type. The operator functions =, ( ), [ ], and -> must be nonstatic member functions.

Enumerations can have overloaded operators. However, the operator functions =, ( ), [ ], and -> cannot be overloaded for enumerations.

Overloaded operators and inheritance

With the exception of the assignment function **operator =( )**, all overloaded operator functions for class X are inherited by classes derived from X, with the standard resolution rules for overloaded functions. If X is a base class for Y, an overloaded operator function for X could possibly be further overloaded for Y.

Overloading unary operators

You can overload a prefix or postfix unary operator by declaring a nonstatic member function taking no arguments, or by declaring a nonmember function taking one argument. If @ represents a unary operator, @x and x@ can both be interpreted as either x.**operator@**() or **operator@**(x), depending on the declarations made. If both forms have been declared, standard argument matching is applied to resolve any ambiguity.

- Under C++ 2.0, an overloaded **operator ++** or -- is used for both prefix and postfix uses of the operator.

- With C++ 2.1, when an **operator++** or **operator- -** is declared as a member function with no parameters, or as a nonmember function with one parameter, it only overloads the prefix **operator++** or **operator- -**. You can only overload a postfix

operator++ or **operator--** by defining it as a member function taking an int parameter or as a nonmember function taking one class and one int parameter.

When only the prefix version of an **operator++** or **operator--** is overloaded and the operator is applied to a class object as a postfix operator, the compiler issues a warning. Then it calls the prefix operator, allowing 2.0 code to compile. The preceding example results in the following warnings:

```
Warning: Overloaded prefix 'operator ++' used as a postfix operator in function
func()

Warning: Overloaded prefix 'operator --' used as a postfix operator in function
func()
```

Overloading binary operators

You can overload a binary operator by declaring a nonstatic member function taking one argument, or by declaring a non-member function (usually friend) taking two arguments. If @ represents a binary operator, x@y can be interpreted as either x.**operator**@(y) or **operator**@(x,y) depending on the declarations made. If both forms have been declared, standard argument matching is applied to resolve any ambiguity.

Overloading the assignment operator =

The assignment **operator=( )** can be overloaded by declaring a nonstatic member function. For example,

```
class String {
    ⋮
    String& operator = (String& str);
    ⋮
    String (String&);
    ~String();
}
```

This code, with suitable definitions of String::**operator =()**, allows string assignments str1 = str2 in the usual sense. Unlike the other operator functions, the assignment operator function cannot be inherited by derived classes. If, for any class X, there is no user-defined **operator =**, the **operator =** is defined by default as a member-by-member assignment of the members of class X:

```
X& X::operator = (const X& source)
{
    // memberwise assignment
}
```

Overloading the function call operator ( )

Syntax

```
postfix-expression ( <expression-list> )
```

Description

In its ordinary use as a function call, the postfix-expression must be a function name, or a pointer or reference to a function. When the postfix-expression is used to make a member function call, postfix-expression must be a class member function name or a pointer-to-member expression used to select a class member function. In either case, the postfix-expression is followed by the optional expression-list (possibly empty).

A call X(arg1, arg2), where X is an object class X, is interpreted as X.**operator**()(arg1, arg2).

The function call operator, **operator()()**, can only be overloaded as a nonstatic member function.

Overloading the subscript operator [ ]

Syntax

```
postfix-expression [ expression ]
```

Description

The corresponding operator function is **operator[]()** this can be user-defined for a class X (and any derived classes). The expression X[y], where X is an object of class X, is interpreted as x.operator[](y).

The **operator[]()** can only be overloaded as a nonstatic member function.

Overloading the class member access operator ->

Syntax

```
postfix-expression -> primary-expression
```

Description

The expression x->m, where x is a class X object, is interpreted as (x.**operator->**())->m, so that the function **operator->()** must either return a pointer to a class object or return an object of a class for which **operator->** is defined.

The **operator->()** can only be overloaded as a nonstatic member function.

Polymorphic classes

Classes that provide an identical interface, but can be implemented to serve different specific requirements, are referred to as polymorphic classes. A class is polymorphic if it declares or inherits at least one virtual (or pure virtual) function. The only types that can support polymorphism are **class** and **struct**.

Virtual functions

virtual functions allow derived classes to provide different versions of a base class function. You can use the **virtual** keyword to declare a **virtual** function in a base class. By declaring the function prototype in the usual way and then prefixing the declaration with the **virtual** keyword. To declare a *pure* function (which automatically declares an abstract class), prefix the prototype with the **virtual** keyword, and set the function equal to zero.

```
virtual int funct1(void);        // A virtual function declaration.
virtual int funct2(void) = 0;    // A pure function declaration.
virtual void funct3(void) = 0 {  // This is a valid declaration.
   // Some code here.
   };
```

Note See "Abstract classes" later in this chapter for a discussion of pure virtual functions.

When you declare **virtual** functions, keep these guidelines in mind:

• They can be member functions only.

• They can be declared a **friend** of another class.

• They cannot be a static member.

A **virtual** function does not need to be redefined in a derived class. You can supply one definition in the base class so that all calls will access the base function.

To redefine a **virtual** function in any derived class, the number and type of arguments must be the same in the base class declaration and in the derived class declaration. (The case for redefined **virtual** functions differing only in return type is discussed below.) A redefined function is said to *override* the base class function.

You can also declare the functions int Base::Fun(int) and int Derived::Fun(int) even when they are not **virtual**. In such a case, int Derived::Fun(int) is said to *hide* any other versions of Fun(int) that exist in any base classes. In addition, if class *Derived* defines other versions of *Fun()*, (that is, versions of *Fun()* with different signatures) such versions are said to be *overloaded* versions of *Fun()*.

Virtual function return types

Generally, when redefining a **virtual** function, you cannot change just the function return type. To redefine a **virtual** function, the new definition (in some derived class) must exactly match the return type and formal parameters of the initial declaration. If two functions with the same name have different formal parameters, C++ considers them different, and the **virtual** function mechanism is ignored.

However, for certain virtual functions in a base class, their overriding version in a derived class can have a return type that is different from the overridden function. This is possible only when *both* of the following conditions are met:

• The overridden **virtual** function returns a pointer or reference to the base class.

• The overriding function returns a pointer or reference to the derived class.

If a base class *B* and class *D* (derived publicly from *B*) each contain a **virtual** function *vf*, then if *vf* is called for an object *d* of *D*, the call made is D::vf(), even when the access is via a pointer or reference to *B*. For example,

```
struct X {};// Base class.
struct Y : X {};// Derived class.
struct B {
```

```
    virtual void vf1();
    virtual void vf2();
    virtual void vf3();
    void f();
    virtual X* pf();// Return type is a pointer to base. This can
    //  be overridden.
    };
class D : public B {
public:
    virtual void vf1();// Virtual specifier is legal but redundant.
    void vf2(int);// Not virtual, since it's using a different
        //  arg list. This hides B::vf2().
// char vf3();// Illegal: return-type-only change!
    void f();
    Y*  pf();// Overriding function differs only
    //  in return type. Returns a pointer to
        //  the derived class.
    };
void extf() {
    D d;// Instantiate D
    B* bp = &d;// Standard conversion from D* to B*
    // Initialize bp with the table of functions
        // provided for object d. If there is no entry for a
    // function in the d-table, use the function
        //  in the B-table.
    bp->vf1();   // Calls D::vf1
    bp->vf2();   // Calls B::vf2 since D's vf2 has different args
    bp->f();     // Calls B::f (not virtual)
    X* xptr = bp->pf();// Calls D::pf() and converts the result
    //  to a pointer to X.
    D* dptr = &d;
    Y* yptr = dptr->pf();// Calls D::pf() and initializes yptr.
    //  No further conversion is done.
    }
```

The overriding function *vf1* in *D* is automatically **virtual**. The **virtual** specifier *can* be used with an overriding function declaration in the derived class. If other classes will be derived from *D*, the **virtual** keyword is required. If no further classes will be derived from *D*, the use of **virtual** is redundant.

The interpretation of a **virtual** function call depends on the type of the object it is called for; with nonvirtual function calls, the interpretation depends only on the type of the pointer or reference denoting the object it is called for.

virtual functions exact a price for their versatility: each object in the derived class needs to carry a pointer to a table of functions in order to select the correct one at run time (late binding).

Abstract classes

An *abstract class* is a class with at least one pure **virtual** function. A **virtual** function is specified as pure by setting it equal to zero.

An abstract class can be used only as a base class for other classes. No objects of an abstract class can be created. An abstract class cannot be used as an argument type or as a function return type. However, you can declare pointers to an abstract class. References to an abstract class are allowed, provided that a temporary object is not needed in the initialization. For example,

```
class shape {          // abstract class

    point center;
        ⋮
public:
    where() { return center; }
    move(point p) { center = p; draw(); }
    virtual void rotate(int) = 0; // pure virtual function
    virtual void draw() = 0;      // pure virtual function
    virtual void hilite() = 0;    // pure virtual function
        ⋮
}
    shape x;// ERROR: attempt to create an object of an abstract class
        shape* sptr;// pointer to abstract class is OK
        shape f();// ERROR: abstract class cannot be a return type
    int g(shape s);// ERROR: abstract class cannot be a function argument type
    shape& h(shape&);// reference to abstract class as return
            // value or function argument is OK
```

Suppose that *D* is a derived class with the abstract class *B* as its immediate base class. Then for each pure virtual function pvf in *B*, if *D* doesn't provide a definition for *pvf*, *pvf* becomes a pure member function of *D*, and *D* will also be an abstract class.

For example, using the class *shape* previously outlined,

```
class circle : public shape {// circle derived from abstract class

    int radius;// private
public:
    void rotate(int) { }// virtual function defined: no action
            //  to rotate a circle
    void draw();       // circle::draw must be defined somewhere
}
```

Member functions can be called from a constructor of an abstract class, but calling a pure virtual function directly or indirectly from such a constructor provokes a run-time error.

C++ scope

The lexical scoping rules for C++, apart from class scope, follow the general rules for C, with the proviso that C++, unlike C, permits both data and function declarations to appear wherever a statement might appear. The latter flexibility means that care is needed when interpreting such phrases as "enclosing scope" and "point of declaration."

Class scope

The name M of a member of a class X has class scope "local to X"; it can be used only in the following situations:

- In member functions of X

- In expressions such as `x.M`, where x is an object of X

- In expressions such as *xptr->M*, where *xptr* is a pointer to an object of X

- In expressions such as `X::M` or `D::M`, where D is a derived class of X

- In forward references within the class of which it is a member

Names of functions declared as friends of X are not members of X; their names simply have enclosing scope.

Hiding

A name can be hidden by an explicit declaration of the same name in an enclosed block or in a class. A hidden class member is still accessible using the scope modifier with a class name: `X::M`. A hidden file scope (global) name can be referenced with the unary operator :: (for example, *::g*). A class name X can be hidden by the name of an object, function, or enumerator declared within the scope of X, regardless of the order in which the names are declared. However, the hidden class name X can still be accessed by prefixing X with the appropriate keyword: **class**, **struct**, or **union**.

The point of declaration for a name x is immediately after its complete declaration but before its initializer, if one exists.

C++ scoping rules summary

The following rules apply to all names, including **typedef** names and class names, provided that C++ allows such names in the particular context discussed:

- The name itself is tested for ambiguity. If no ambiguities are detected within its scope, the access sequence is initiated.

- If no access control errors occur, the type of the object, function, class, **typedef**, and so on, is tested.

- If the name is used outside any function and class, or is prefixed by the unary scope access operator ::, *and* if the name is not qualified by the binary :: operator or the member selection operators **.** and ->, then the name must be a global object, function, or enumerator.

- If the name n appears in any of the forms $X::n$, $x.n$ (where x is an object of X or a reference to X), or *ptr->n* (where *ptr* is a pointer to X), then n is the name of a member of X or the member of a class from which X is derived.

- Any name that hasn't been discussed yet and that is used in a static member function must either be declared in the block it occurs in or in an enclosing block, or be a global name. The declaration of a local name *n* hides declarations of *n* in enclosing blocks and global declarations of *n*. Names in different scopes are not overloaded.

- Any name that hasn't been discussed yet and that is used in a nonstatic member function of class *X* must either be declared in the block it occurs in or in an enclosing block, be a member of class *X* or a base class of *X*, or be a global name. The declaration of a local name *n* hides declarations of *n* in enclosing blocks, members of the function's class, and global declarations of *n*. The declaration of a member name hides declarations of the same name in base classes.

- The name of a function argument in a function definition is in the scope of the outermost block of the function. The name of a function argument in a nondefining function declaration has no scope at all. The scope of a default argument is determined by the point of declaration of its argument, but it can't access local variables or nonstatic class members. Default arguments are evaluated at each point of call.

- A constructor initializer is evaluated in the scope of the outermost block of its constructor, so it can refer to the constructor's argument names.

Using templates

Templates, also called *generics* or *parameterized* types, let you construct a family of related functions or classes.

Note   For complete examples of templates and template-driven classes, see the source files for the ObjectWindows classes in the SOURCE\OWL directories.

This section introduces the basic concept of templates, then provides some specific points.

Template syntax

Use templates to construct a family of related functions or classes. The template syntax is shown below.

Syntax

```
template-declaration:
    template < template-argument-list > declaration
template-argument-list:
    template-argument
    template-argument-list, template argument
template-argument:
    type-argument
    argument-declaration
type-argument:
    class identifier
template-class-name:
    template-name < template-arg-list >
template-arg-list:
```

```
      template-arg
      template-arg-list , template-arg
  template-arg:
      expression
      type-name
  < template-argument-list > declaration
```

Template body parsing

Earlier versions of the compiler didn't check the syntax of a template body unless the template was instantiated. A template body is now parsed immediately when seen like every other declaration.

```
template <class T> class X : T

{

  Int  j;  // Error: Type name expected in template X<T>

};
```

Let's assume that *Int* hasn't been defined so far. This means that *Int* must be a member of the template argument *T*. But it also might just be a typing error and should be **int** instead of *Int*. Because the compiler can't guess the right meaning it issues an error message.

If you want to access types defined by a template argument you should use a **typedef** to make your intention clear to the compiler:

```
template <class T> class X : T

{

  typedef  T::Int  Int;

  Int  j;

};
```

You cannot just write

```
    typedef   T::Int;
```

as in earlier versions of the compiler. Not giving the **typedef** name was acceptable, but this now causes an error message.

All other templates mentioned inside the template body are declared or defined at that point. Therefore, the following example is ill-formed and will not compile:

```
template <class T> class  X

{

  void f(NotYetDefinedTemplate<T> x);

};
```

All template definitions must end with a semicolon. Earlier versions of the compiler did not complain if the semicolon was missing.

Function templates

Consider a function *max(x, y)* that returns the larger of its two arguments. *x* and *y* can be of any type that has the ability to be ordered. But, since C++ is a strongly typed language, it expects the types of the parameters *x* and *y* to be declared at compile time. Without using templates, many overloaded versions of *max* are required, one for each data type to be supported even though the code for each version is essentially identical. Each version compares the arguments and returns the larger.

One way around this problem is to use a macro:

```
#define max(x,y) ((x > y) ? x : y)
```

However, using the **#define** circumvents the type-checking mechanism that makes C++ such an improvement over C. In fact, this use of macros is almost obsolete in C++. Clearly, the intent of *max(x, y)* is to compare compatible types. Unfortunately, using the macro allows a comparison between an **int** and a **struct**, which are incompatible.

Another problem with the macro approach is that substitution will be performed where you don't want it to be. By using a template instead, you can define a pattern for a family of related overloaded functions by letting the data type itself be a parameter:

```
template <class T> T max(T x, T y){
    return (x > y) ? x : y;
    };
```

The data type is represented by the template argument **<class T>**. When used in an application, the compiler generates the appropriate code for the *max* function according to the data type actually used in the call:

```
int i;
Myclass a, b;

int j = max(i,0);       // arguments are integers
Myclass m = max(a,b);   // arguments are type Myclass
```

Any data type (not just a class) can be used for **<class T>**. The compiler takes care of calling the appropriate **operator>()**, so you can use *max* with arguments of any type for which **operator>()** is defined.

Overriding a template function

The previous example is called a *function template* (or *generic function*, if you like). A specific instantiation of a function template is called a *template function*. Template function instantiation occurs when you take the function address, or when you call the function with defined (non-generic) data types. You can override the generation of a template function for a specific type with a non-template function:

```
#include <string.h>

char *max(char *x, char *y){
    return(strcmp(x,y) > 0) ? x : y;
}
```

If you call the function with string arguments, it's executed in place of the automatic template function. In this case, calling the function avoided a meaningless comparison between two pointers.

Only trivial argument conversions are performed with compiler-generated template functions.

The argument type(s) of a template function must use all of the template formal arguments. If it doesn't, there is no way of deducing the actual values for the unused template arguments when the function is called.

Implicit and explicit template functions

When doing overload resolution (following the steps of looking for an exact match), the compiler ignores template functions that have been generated implicitly by the compiler.

```
template<class T> T max(T a, T b){
        return   (a > b) ? a : b;
};

void     f(int i, char c){
        max(i, i);              // calls max(int ,int )
        max(c, c);              // calls max(char,char)
        max(i, c);              // no match for max(int,char)
        max(c, i);              // no match for max(char,int)
}
```

This code results in the following error messages:

```
Could not find a match for 'max(int,char)' in function f(int,char)
Could not find a match for 'max(char,int)' in function f(int,char)
```

If the user explicitly declares a template function, this function, on the other hand, will participate fully in overload resolution. See the following example of explicit template function.

```
template<class T> T max(T a, T b) {
        return   (a > b) ? a : b;
};

// Declare explicit template function
int     max(int,int);

void     f(int i, char c)
{
        max(i, i);              // calls max(int ,int )
        max(c, c);              // calls max(char,char)
        max(i, c);              // calls max(int,int)
        max(c, i);              // calls max(int,int)
}
```

When searching for an exact match for template function parameters, trivial conversions are considered to be exact matches. See the following example on trivial conversions.

```
template <class T> void func(const T)
{
    ⋮
};
func(0);   // This is illegal under ANSI C++: unresolved func(int).
// However, Borland C++  allows func(const int) to be called.
```

Template functions with derived class pointer or reference arguments are permitted to match their public base classes. See the following example of base class referencing.

```
template <class T> class B
{
   // class declarations
};
template <class T> class D : public B<T>
{
   // class declarations
};

template <class T> void func(B <T> *b)
{
   // function body
}
// This is illegal under ANSI C++: unresolved func( int )
// However, Borland C++ calls func( B<int> * ).
func( new D<int> );
```

Class templates

A class template (also called a *generic class* or *class generator*) lets you define a pattern for class definitions. Consider the following example of a vector class (a one-dimensional array). Whether you have a vector of integers or any other type, the basic operations performed on the type are the same (insert, delete, index, and so on). With the element type treated as a type parameter to the class, the system will generate type-safe class definitions on the fly.

```
// An example for defining a template class.
template <class T> class Vector
{
   T *data;
   int size;
public:
   Vector(int);
   ~Vector( ) { delete[ ] data; }
   T& operator[ ] (int i) { return data[i]; }
};
// Note the syntax for out-of-line definitions.
template <class T> Vector<T>::Vector(int n)
{
   data = new T[n];
   size = n;
};

int main()
{
   Vector<int> x(5);    // Generate a vector to store five integers
   for (int i = 0; i < 5; ++i)
      x[i] = i;              //  Initialize the vector.
   return 0;
}
```

As with function templates, an explicit *template class* definition can be provided to override the automatic definition for a given type:

```
class Vector<char *> { ... };
```

The symbol *Vector* must always be accompanied by a data type in angle brackets. It cannot appear alone, except in some cases in the original template definition.

Template arguments

Multiple arguments are allowed as part of the class template declaration. Template arguments can also represent values in addition to data types:

```
template<class T, int size = 64> class Buffer { ... };
```

Non-type template arguments such as *size* can have default values. The value supplied for a non-type template argument must be a constant expression:

```
const int N = 128;
int i = 256;


Buffer<int, 2*N> b1;// OK
Buffer<float, i> b2;// Error: i is not constant
```

Since each instantiation of a template class is indeed a class, it receives its own copy of static members. Similarly, template functions get their own copy of static local variables.

Using angle brackets in templates

Be careful when using the right angle bracket character upon instantiation:

```
Buffer<char, (x > 100 ? 1024 : 64)> buf;
```

In the preceding example, without the parentheses around the second argument, the > between x and 100 would prematurely close the template argument list.

Using type-safe generic lists in templates

In general, when you need to write lots of nearly identical things, consider using templates. The problems with the following class definition, a generic list class,

```
class GList
{
 public:
   void insert( void * );
   void *peek();
     ⋮
};
```

are that it isn't type-safe and common solutions need repeated class definitions. Since there's no type checking on what gets inserted, you have no way of knowing what results you'll get. You can solve the type-safe problem by writing a wrapper class:

```
class FooList : public Glist {
 public:
   void insert( Foo *f ) { GList::insert( f ); }
   Foo *peek() { return (Foo *)GList::peek(); }
     ⋮
};
```

This is type-safe. *insert* will only take arguments of type pointer-to-*Foo* or object-derived-from-*Foo*, so the underlying container will only hold pointers that in fact point to something of type *Foo*. This means that the cast in *FooList::peek()* is always safe, and you've created a true *FooList*. Now, to do the same thing for a *BarList*, a *BazList*, and so on, you need repeated separate class definitions. To solve the problem of repeated class definitions and be type-safe, you can once again use templates. See the following example for type-safe generic list class.

```
template <class T> class List : public GList
{
public:
    void insert( T *t ) { GList::insert( t ); }
    T *peek() { return (T *)GList::peek(); }
        ⋮
};

    // Create a List object of Foo types and name it fList.
    List<Foo> fList;

// Create a List object of Bar types and name it bList.
    List<Bar> bList;

// Create a List object of Baz types and name it zList.
    List<Baz> zList;
```

By using templates, you can create whatever type-safe lists you want, as needed, with a simple declaration. And there's no code generated by the type conversions from each wrapper class so there's no run-time overhead imposed by this type safety.

Eliminating pointers in templates

Another design technique is to include actual objects, making pointers unnecessary. This can also reduce the number of **virtual** function calls required, since the compiler knows the actual types of the objects. This is beneficial if the **virtual** functions are small enough to be effectively inlined. It's difficult to inline **virtual** functions when called through pointers, because the compiler doesn't know the actual types of the objects being pointed to.

```
template <class T> aBase {
    ⋮
private:
    T buffer;
};

class anObject : public aSubject, public aBase<aFilebuf> {
    ⋮
};
```

All the functions in *aBase* can call functions defined in *aFilebuf* directly, without having to go through a pointer. And if any of the functions in *aFilebuf* can be inlined, you'll get a speed improvement, because templates allow them to be inlined.

Compiler template switches

The **-Jg** family of switches controls how instances of templates are generated by the compiler. Every template instance that the compiler encounters is affected by the value of the switch when the compiler sees the first occurrence of that instance.

For template functions the switch applies to the function instances; for template classes, it applies to all member functions and static data members of the template class. In all cases, this switch applies only to compiler-generated template instances and never to user-defined instances. It can be used, however, to tell the compiler which instances will be user-defined so that they aren't generated from the template.

-Jg Default value of the switch. All template instances first encountered when this switch value is in effect are generated, such that if several compilation units generate the same template instance, the linker merges them to produce a single copy of the instance. This is the most convenient approach to generating template instances because it's almost entirely automatic. Note, though, that to be able to generate the template instances, the compiler must have the function body (in case of a template function) or bodies of member functions and definitions for static data members (in case of a template class).

-Jgd Instructs the compiler to generate public definitions for template instances. This is similar to **-Jg**, but if more than one compilation unit generates a definition for the same template instance, the linker will report public symbol redefinition errors.

-Jgx Instructs the compiler to generate external references to template instances. Some other compilation unit must generate a public definition for that template instance (using the **-Jgd** switch) so that the external references can be satisfied.

Using template switches

When using the **-Jg** family of switches, there are two basic approaches for generating template instances:

Approach 1

Include the function body (for a function template) or member function and static data member definitions (for a template class) in the header file that defines the particular template, and use the default setting of the template switch (**-Jg**). If some instances of the template are user-defined, the declarations (prototypes, for example) for them should be included in the same header but preceded by **#pragma option -Jgx**.

```
// Declare a template function and define it's body.
/* When this header file is included in a C++ source file, the sort template can
be used without worrying about how the various instances are generated (with the
exception of sort for integer arrays which is a user-defined instance. Its
definition must be provided by the user. */
template<class T> void sort (T* array, int size)
{
    // Body of template goes here.
}
// Sorting of integer elements done by user-define instance.
#pragma option -Jgx
extern void sort(int *array, int size);
// Restore the template switch to its original state.
#pragma option -Jg
```

Approach 2

Compile all of the source files comprising the program with the **-Jgx** switch (causing external references to templates to be generated). In order to provide the definitions for all of the template instances, add a file (or files) to the program that includes the template bodies (including any user-defined instance definitions), and list all the template instances needed in the rest of the program to provide the necessary public symbol definitions. Compile the file (or files) with the **-Jgd** switch. See the example for separate file template compilation in the next section.

Separate file template compilation

```
// In vector.h
template <class elem, int size> class vector
{
    elem * value;
public:
    vector();
    elem & operator [ ] (int index) {
        return value[index];
        }
};


// In main.cpp source file.
#include "vector.h"
/** Let the compiler know that the following template instances will be defined
elsewhere. **/
#pragma option -Jgx
// Use two instances of the vector template class.
vector<int, 100> int_100;
vector<char, 10> char_10;
int main( )
{
    return int_100[ 0 ] + char_10[ 0 ];
}


// In template.cpp source file.
#include <string.h>
#include "vector.h"
// Define any template bodies.
template <class elem, int size> vector <elem, size> :: vector()
{
    value = new elem[size];
    memset(value, 0, size * sizeof(elem) );
}
// Generate the necessary instances.
#pragma option -Jgd
typedef vector<int, 100> fake_int_100;
typedef vector<char, 10> fake_char_10;
```

Exporting and importing templates

The declaration of a template function or template class needs to be sufficiently flexible so it can be used in either a DLL or an EXE file. The same template declaration should be available as an import and/or export, or without a modifier. To be completely flexible, the header file template declarations should not use _ _**export** or _ _**import** modifiers. This allows you to apply the appropriate modifier at the point of instantiation depending on how the instantiation is to be used.

The following steps demonstrate exporting and importing of templates. The source code is organized in three files. Using the header file, code is generated in the DLL. A DLL library is created and linked to an EXE file.

Exportable/importable template declarations

The header file contains all template class and template function declarations. An export/import version of the templates can be instantiated by defining the appropriate macro at compile time.

For example:

```
// In file EXPORTER.H
#include<iostream.h>
# if defined (BUILD_DLL_EXPORTS)
#       define DECLSPEC __export
# elif defined (USING_DLL_IMPORTS)
#       define DECLSPEC __import
# endif
/////////////////////////////////////////////////
// Receive CLASS DEFINITIONS
template <class T> class Receive
{
  T value;
public:
  Receive(const T val) : value(val){}
    T display();
};
template<class T> T Receive<T>::display()
{
  return value;
}
// TEMPLATE FUNCTION DEFINITION
template <class T>
T another_min(T a, T b) { return a < b ? a : b;}
#if (defined (BUILD_DLL_EXPORTS) || defined(USING_DLL_IMPORTS) )
////// INSTANTIATED TEMPLATE CLASSES /////
template class DECLSPEC Receive<double>;
template class DECLSPEC Receive<int>;
template class DECLSPEC Receive<char>;
////// INSTANTIATED TEMPLATE FUNCTIONS /////
template int DECLSPEC another_min<int>(int, int);
template double DECLSPEC another_min<double>(double, double);
#endif
```

Compiling exportable templates

Write the source code for a DLL. When compiled, this DLL has reusable export code.

For example:

```
// In file DLL_SRC.CPP.
// GENERATE CODE FOR EXPORTABLE CLASSES AND FUNCTIONS.
// TO COMPILE THIS FILE, USE BCC32 -tWD -DBUILD_DLL_EXPORTS
DLL_SRC.CPP
#define STRICT
#include <windows.h>
#include "exporter.h"
BOOL WINAPI DllEntryPoint(HINSTANCE hinstdll,
                          DWORD fdwReason, LPVOID lpvReserved)
{
  return 1;
}
```

Using import templates

Now you can write a calling function that uses templates. This file is linked to the DLL. Only objects that are not declared in the header file and which are instantiated in the main function cause the compiler to generate new code. Code for a newly instantiated object is written into the MAIN.OBJ file.

For example:

```
// Before you compile this file you need to create the dynamic link library.
// You can use the command IMPLIB DLL_SRC.LIB DLL_SRC.DLL
// TO COMPILE THIS FILE, USE BCC32 -DUSING_DLL_IMPORTS MAIN
DLL_SRC.LIB
#include <iostream.h>
#include "exporter.h"
int main () {
    int small = 5;
    int big = 10;
    double smalld = 1.2;
    double bigd = 12.3;
    // No new code is generated for these objects.
    Receive <double> Test_d(0.01);
    Receive <int> Test_i(5);
   // Generate code in MAIN.OBJ for this object.
  Receive <float> Test_f(3.14);
    cout << "Test_d.display() = " <<  Test_d.display() << endl;
    cout << "Test_i.display() = " <<  Test_i.display() << endl;
    cout << "min(5, 10): " << another_min(small, big) << endl;
    cout << "min(12.3, 1.2): " << another_min(bigd, smalld)<<endl;
    cout << "Test_f.display() = " <<  Test_f.display() << endl;
    return 0;
}
```

Program output

```
Test_d.display() = 0.01
Test_i.display() = 5
min(5, 10): 5
min(12.3, 1.2): 1.2
Test_f.display() = 3.14
```

4

Exception handling

This chapter describes the Borland C++ error-handling mechanisms generally referred to as *exception handling*. The Borland C++ implementation of C++ exception handling is consistent with the proposed ANSI specification. The exception-handling mechanisms that are available in C programs are referred to as *structured exceptions*. Borland C++ provides full compiling, linking, and debugging support for C programs with structured exceptions. See the section "C-based structured exceptions" later in this chapter, and the *C++ User's Guide* for a discussion of compiler options for programming with exceptions.

C++ exception handling

The C++ language defines a standard for exception handling. The standard ensures that the power of object-oriented design is supported throughout your program.

In accordance with the specifications of the ANSI/ISO C++ working paper, Borland C++ supports the termination exception-handling model. When an abnormal situation arises at run time, the program could terminate. However, throwing an exception lets you gather information at the throw point that could be useful in diagnosing the causes that led to failure. You can also specify in the exception handler the actions to be taken before the program terminates. Only synchronous exceptions are handled, meaning that the cause of failure is generated from within the program. An event such as *Ctrl-C* (which is generated from outside the program) is not considered to be a synchronous exception.

C++ exceptions can be handled only in a **try**/**catch** construct.

Syntax:

> *try-block:*
>   **try** *compound-statement handler-list*
>
> *handler-list:*
>   *handler handler-list* _{opt}

handler:
> **catch** *(exception-declaration) compound-statement*

exception-declaration:
> *type-specifier-list declarator*
> *type-specifier-list abstract-declarator*
> *type-specifier-list*
>
> *...*

throw-expression:
> **throw** *assignment-expression* $_{opt}$

Note The **catch** and **throw** keywords are not allowed in a C program.

The *try-block* is a statement that specifies the flow of control as the program executes. The try-block is designated by the **try** keyword. Braces after the keyword surround a program block that can generate exceptions. The language structure specifies that any exceptions that occur should be raised within the *try-block*. See Chapter 2 for a discussion about statements.

The handler is a block of code designed to handle an exception. The C++ language requires that at least one handler be available immediately after the try-block. There should be a handler for each exception that the program can generate.

When the program encounters an abnormal situation for which it is not designed, you can transfer control to some other part of the program that is designed to deal with the problem. This is done by throwing an exception.

The exception-handling mechanism requires the use of three keywords: **try**, **catch**, and **throw**. The *try-block* specified by **try** must be followed immediately by the *handler* specified by **catch**. If an exception is thrown in the *try-block*, program control is transferred to the appropriate exception handler. The program should attempt to catch any exception that is thrown by any function. Failure to do so could result in abnormal termination of the program.

Exception declarations

Although C++ allows an exception to be of almost any type, it is useful to make exception classes. The exception object is treated exactly the way any object would be treated. An exception carries information from the point where the exception is thrown to the point where the exception is caught. This is information that the program user will want to know when the program encounters some anomaly at run time.

Predefined exceptions, specified by the C++ language, are documented in the *C++ Language Reference*, Chapter 16. Borland C++ provides additional support for exceptions. These extensions are also documented in the *C++ Language Reference*, Chapter 11. See also Chapter 3 of this book for a discussion of the **new** operator and the predefined *xalloc* exception.

Throwing an exception

A block of code in which an exception can occur must be prefixed by the keyword **try**. Following the **try** keyword is a block of code enclosed by braces. This indicates that the program is prepared to test for the existence of exceptions. If an exception occurs, the program flow is interrupted. The sequence of steps taken is as follows:

1 The program searches for a matching handler
2 If a handler is found, the stack is unwound to that point
3 Program control is transferred to the handler

If no handler is found, the program will call the *terminate* function. If no exceptions are thrown, the program executes in the normal fashion.

A *throw expression* is also referred to as a throw-point. You can specify whether an exception can be thrown by using one of the following syntax specifications:

```
1. throw throw_expression;
2. throw;
3. void my_func1() throw (A, B)
   {
   // Body of function.
   }
4. void my_func2() throw ()
   {
   // Body of this function.
   }
```

The first case specifies that *throw_expression* is to be passed to a handler.

The second case specifies that the exception currently being handler is to be thrown again. An exception must currently exist. Otherwise, *terminate* is called.

The third case specifies a list of exceptions that *my_func1* can throw. No other exceptions should propagate out of *my_func1*. If an exception other than *A* or *B* is generated within *my_func1*, it is considered to be an unexpected exception and program control will be transferred to the *unexpected* function. By default, the *unexpected* function ends with a call to *abort* but it can throw an exception. See the *C++ Language Reference*, Chapter 16, for a description of *unexpected*.

The final case specifies that *my_func2* should throw no exceptions. If some other function (for example, **operator new**) in the body of *my_func2* throws an exception, such an exception should be caught and handled within the body of *my_func2*. Otherwise, such an exception is a violation of *my_func2* exception specification. The *unexpected* function is then called.

When an exception occurs, the throw expression initializes a temporary object of the type *T* (to match the type of argument *arg*) used in *throw(T arg)*. Other copies can be generated as required by the compiler. Consequently, it can be useful to define a copy constructor for the exception object.

Handling an exception

The exception handler is indicated by the **catch** keyword. The handler must be placed immediately after the try-block. The keyword **catch** can also occur immediately after another **catch**. Each handler will only handle an exception that matches, or can be converted to, the type specified in its argument list. The possible conversions are listed after the try-block syntaxes.

The following syntaxes, following the try-block, are valid:

```
try {
    // Include any code that might throw an exception
}
```

1. ```
   catch (T X)
   {
   // Take some actions
   }
   ```
2. ```
   catch ( ... )
   {
   // Take some actions
   }
   ```

The first statement is specifically defined to handle an object of type *T*. If the argument is *T*, *T&*, **const** *T*, or **const** *T&*, the handler will accept an object of type *X* if any of the following are true:

- *T* and *X* are of the same type
- *T* is an accessible base class for *X* in the throw expression
- *T* is a pointer type and *X* is a pointer type that can be converted to *T* by a standard pointer conversion at the throw point

The statement **catch** (…) will handle any exception, regardless of type. This statement, if used, must be the last handler for its try-block.

Every exception thrown by the program must be caught and processed by the exception handler. If the program fails to provide an exception handler for a thrown exception, the program will call *terminate*.

Exception handlers are evaluated in the order that they are encountered. An exception is caught when its type matches the type in the **catch** statement. Once a type match is made, program control is transferred to the handler. The stack will have been unwound upon entering the handler. The handler specifies what actions should be taken to deal with the program anomaly.

A **goto** statement can be used to transfer program control out of a handler or try-block but such a statement can never be used to enter a handler or try-block.

After the handler has executed, the program can continue at the point after the last handler for the current try-block. No other handlers are evaluated for the current exception.

Exception specifications

The C++ language makes it possible for you to specify any exceptions that a function can throw. This *exception specification* can be used as a suffix to the function declaration. The syntax for exception specification is as follows:

exception-specification:
    throw *(type-id-list $_{opt}$)*

type-id-list:

type-id
type-id-list, type-id

The function suffix is not considered to be part of the function's type. Consequently, a pointer to a function is not affected by the function's exception specification. Such a pointer checks only the function's return and argument types. Therefore, the following is legal:

```
void f2(void) throw();        // Should not throw exceptions
void f3(void) throw (BETA);  // Should only throw BETA objects
void (* fptr)();              // Pointer to a function returning void
fptr = f2;
fptr = f3;
```

Extreme care should be taken when overriding virtual functions. Again, because the exception specification is not considered part of the function type, it is possible to violate the program design. In the following example, the derived class *BETA::vfunc* is defined so that it throws an exception—a departure from the original function declaration.

```
class ALPHA {
public:
    virtual void vfunc(void) throw () {};  // Exception specification
};

class BETA : public ALPHA {
    struct BETA_ERR {};
    void vfunc(void) throw( BETA_ERR ) {}; // Exception specification is changed
};
```

The following are examples of functions with exception specifications.

```
void f1();                // The function can throw any exception

void f2() throw();        // Should not throw any exceptions

void f3() throw( A, B* ); // Can throw exceptions publicly derived from A,
                          // or a pointer to publicly derived B
```

The definition and all declarations of such a function must have an exception specification containing the same set of type-id's. If a function throws an exception not listed in its specification, the program will call *unexpected*. This is a run-time issue—it will not be flagged at compile time. Therefore, care must be taken to handle any exceptions that can be thrown by elements called within a function.

Example 2

```
// HOW TO MAKE EXCEPTION-SPECIFICATIONS AND HANDLE ALL EXCEPTIONS
#include <iostream.h>


// EXCEPTION DECLARATIONS
class Alpha {
    // Include something that shows why you chose to throw this exception.
};
Alpha alpha_inst;

class Beta {
    // Include something that shows why you chose to throw this exception.
```

```
};
Beta beta_inst;

// THROW ONLY Alpha OR Beta TYPE OBJECTS
void f3(char c) throw (Alpha, Beta) {
    cout << "f3() was called" << endl;
    if (c == 'a')
        throw( alpha_inst );
    if (c == 'b')
        throw( beta_inst );
    else ; // DO NOTHING WITH OTHER CHARACTERS
    }

// SHOULD NOT THROW EXCEPTIONS
void f2(char ch) throw() {
    try {                           // WRAP ALL CODE IN A TRY-BLOCK
        cout << "f2() was called" << endl;
        f3(ch);
        }
    // HERE ARE HANDLERS FOR THE EXCEPTIONS WE KNOW COULD BE THROWN
    catch (Alpha& alpha_inst) { cout << "Caught Alpha exception.";}
    catch (Beta& beta_inst) { cout << "Caught Beta exception.";}

    // IF THE CODE IS MODIFIED LATER SO THAT SOME
    // OTHER EXCEPTION IS THROWN, IT IS HANDLED HERE
    // AND WE AVOID VIOLATING THE f2() THROW SPECIFICATION
    catch ( ... ) {
        // BUT, WE POST OURSELVES A WARNING MESSAGE.
        cout << "Warning: f2() has elements with exceptions!" << endl;
        }
    }

int main(void) {
    char trigger;

    try {
        cout << "Input a character:";
        cin >> trigger;
        f2(trigger);
        cout << "\nSuccess.";
        return 0;  // WE GET HERE ONLY IF EVERYTHING EXECUTES WELL.
        }
    catch ( ... ) {
        cout << "Need more handlers!";
        return 1;
        }
    }
```

Sample output when 'a' is the input

```
Input a character: a
f2() was called
```

```
f3() was called
Caught Alpha exception.
Success.
```

If an exception is thrown that is not listed in the exception specification, the *unexpected* function will be called. The following diagrams illustrate the sequence of events that can occur when *unexpected* is called. See the C++ *Language Reference*, Chapter 15, for a description of the *set_terminate*, *set_unexpected*, and unexpected functions. The chapter also describes the *terminate_function* and *unexpected_function* types.

Program behavior when a function is registered with *set_unexpected*():

```
unexpected()   // CALLED AUTOMATICALLY
   |
   |
   |                 // DEFINE YOUR UNEXPECTED HANDLER
   |                 unexpected_function my_unexpected( void )
   |                 {
   |                     // DEFINE ACTIONS TO TAKE
   |                     // POSSIBLY MAKE ADJUSTMENTS
   |                 }
   |
   |                 // REGISTER YOUR HANDLER
   |                 set_unexpected( my_unexpected );
   |
my_unexpected();
```

Program behavior when no function is registered with *set_unexpected*() but there is a function registered with *set_terminate*():

```
unexpected()   // CALLED AUTOMATICALLY
   |
terminate()
   |
   |             // DEFINE YOUR TERMINATION SCHEME
   |             terminate_function my_terminate( void )
   |                {
   |                // TAKE ACTIONS BEFORE TERMINATING
   |                // SHOULD NOT THROW EXCEPTIONS
   |                exit(1); // MUST END SOMEHOW.
   |                }
   |
   |             // REGISTER YOUR TERMINATION FUNCTION
   |             set_terminate( my_terminate )
   |
   |
my_terminate()
// PROGRAM ENDS.
```

Constructors and destructors

When an exception is thrown, the copy constructor is called for the thrown value. The copy constructor is used to initialize a temporary object at the throw point. Other copies can be generated by the program. See Chapter 3 for a discussion of the copy constructor.

When program flow is interrupted by an exception, destructors are called for all automatic objects that were constructed since the beginning of the try-block was entered. If the exception was thrown during construction of some object, destructors will be called only for those objects that were fully constructed. For example, if an array of objects was under construction when an exception was thrown, destructors will be called only for the array elements that were already fully constructed.

Note Destructors are called by default. See the C++ *User's Guide* for information about exception-handling switches.

When a C++ exception is thrown, the stack is unwound. By default, during stack unwinding, destructors are called for automatic objects. You can use the **–xd** compiler option to switch the default off.

Unhandled exceptions

If an exception is thrown and no handler has found it, the program will call the *terminate* function. The following diagram illustrates the series of events that can occur when the program encounters an exception for which no handler can be found. See the C++ *Language Reference*, Chapter 16, for a description of the *terminate* function.

Default program behavior for unhandled exceptions:

```
terminate();
   |
   |
abort();
// PROGRAM ENDS.
```

C-based structured exceptions

Borland C++ provides support for program development that makes use of structured exceptions. You can compile and link a C source file that contains an implementation of structured exceptions. In a C program, the ANSI-compatible keywords used to implement structured exceptions are _ _**except**, _ _**finally**, and _ _**try**. Note that the _ _**finally** and _ _**try** keywords can appear only in C programs.

Note For portability, you can use the *try* and *except* macros defined in excpt.h.

For try-except exception-handling implementations the syntax is as follows:

try-block:
    _ _**try** *compound-statement* (in a C module)
    try *compound-statement* (in a C++ module)

handler:
    _ _**except** *(expression) compound-statement*

For try-finally termination implementations the syntax is as follows:

try-block:
    _ _**try** *compound-statement*

termination:
    _ _**finally** *compound-statement*

Using C-based exceptions in C++

Borland C++ supports substantial interaction between C and C++ error handling mechanisms. The implementation of exception handling mechanisms lets you port code across platforms. The following interactions are supported:

- C structured exceptions can be used in C++ programs.

- C++ exceptions cannot be caught in a C module because C++ exceptions require that their handler be specified by the **catch** keyword, and **catch** is not allowed in a C program.

- An exception generated by a call to the *RaiseException* function is handled by a **try**/ **_ _except** or **_ _try**/**_ _except** block. All handlers of **try**/**catch** blocks are ignored when *RaiseException* is called.

The following C exception support functions can be used in C and C++ programs:

- *GetExceptionCode*
- *GetExceptionInformation*
- *SetUnhandledExceptionFilter*
- *UnhandledExceptionFilter*

Note   Borland C++ does not require that the *UnhandledExceptionFilter* function be used only in the except filter of **_ _try**/**_ _except** or **try**/**_ _except** blocks.However, program behavior is undefined when this function is called outside of the **_ _try**/**_ _except** or **try**/ **_ _except** block.

Handling C-based exceptions

The full functionality of an **_ _except** block is allowed in C++. If an exception is generated in a C module, it is possible to provide a handler-block in a separate calling C++ module.

If a handler can be found for the generated structured exception, the following actions can be taken:

- Execute the actions specified by the handler
- Ignore the generated exception and resume program execution
- Continue the search for some other handler (regenerate the exception)

These actions are consistent with the design of structured exceptions. The following example shows how to mix C and C++ exceptions. Note that the C mechanism uses the **try** and **_ _except** keywords. The C++ mechanism uses the required **try** and **catch** keywords.

```
/* In PROG.C */
void func(void) {
    ⋮
    /* generate an exception */
RaiseException( /* specify your arguments */ );
    ⋮
}

// In CALLER.CPP
```

```
// How to test for C++ or C-based exceptions.
#include <excpt.h>
#include <iostream.h>

int main(void) {
  try
  {                // test for C++ exceptions
    try
    {              // test for C-based structured exceptions
      func();
    }
    _ _except( /* filter-expression */ )
    {
    cout << "A structured exception was generated.";
    :
    /* specify actions to take for this structured exception */
    return -1;
    }
    return 0;
  }
  catch ( ... )
  {
  // handler for any C++ exception
  cout << "A C++ exception was thrown.";
  return 1;
  }
}
```

Structured exceptions also allow you to program a termination handler. The termination handler can be used only in a C module and is specified by the _ _**finally** keyword. The termination handler ensures that the code in the _ _**finally** block is executed no matter how the flow within the _ _**try** exits. The _ _**finally** keyword is not allowed in a C++ program. Consequently the _ _**try**/_ _**finally** block is not supported in a C++ program.

Even though the _ _**try**/_ _**finally** block is not supported in a C++ program, a C-based exception generated by the operating system or the program will still result in proper stack unwinding of objects with destructors. You can use this to emulate a _ _**finally** block by creating a local object whose destructor does the necessary cleanup. Any module compiled with the **–xd** compiler option (this option is on by default) will have destructors invoked for all objects with **auto** storage. Stack unwinding occurs from the point where the exception is thrown to the point where the exception is caught.

Note   Destructors are called by default. See the C++ *User's Guide* for information about exception-handling switches.

5

Programming for portability

If you are new to programming, or need to know about moving 16-bit applications to Windows NT or Windows 95, this topic is for you. This topic describes a variety of 16-bit and 32-bit programming topics, including

- Resource script files

- Module definition files

- Import libraries

- The Borland heap manager

- 32-bit Windows programming

In addition to compiling source code and linking .OBJ files, a Windows programmer must compile resource script files, and bind resources to an executable. A Windows programmer must also know about dynamic linking, dynamic link libraries (DLLs), and import libraries. Also, if you are using the Borland C++ IDE, it is helpful to know how to use the Borland project manager which uses project files to automate and manage application building. See the discussion of compiling and linking a Windows program for an illustration of the process of building a Windows application.

Note The intricacies of designing and developing Windows applications go beyond the scope of this document.

Compiling and linking a Windows program

These are the steps for compiling and linking a Windows program:

1 Source code is compiled or assembled producing .OBJ files.

2 Module definition files (.DEF) tell the linker what kind of executable you want to produce.

3 Resource Workshop (or some other resource editor) creates resources, like icons or bitmaps. A resource file (.RC) is produced. See *Part II* of the *C++ User's Guide.*

4 The .RC file is compiled by a resource compiler or Resource Workshop, and a binary .RES file is output.

5 Linking produces an .EXE file with bound resources.

Resource script files

Windows applications typically use *resources*. Resources are icons, menus, dialog boxes, fonts, cursors, bitmaps, or other user-defined resources. Resources are defined in a file called a resource script file, also known as a resource file. These files have the file name extension .RC.

To make use of resources, you must use the Borland Resource Compiler (BRC32) to compile your .RC file into a binary format. Resource compilation creates a .RES file. TLINK32 then binds the .RES file to the .EXE file output by the linker. This process also marks the .EXE file as a Windows executable.

Note   See the discussion of BRCC32.EXE in Chapter 10 of the *C++ User's Guide.*

Module definition files

A module definition (.DEF) file provides information to the linker about the contents and system requirements of a Windows application. This information includes heap and stack size, and code and data characteristics. .DEF files also list functions that are to be made available for other modules (export functions), and functions that are needed from other modules (import functions). Because Borland linkers have other ways of finding out the information contained in a module definition file, module definition files are not always required for Borland's linker to create a Windows application.

Here's the module definition file for the WHELLO example:

```
NAME            WHELLO

DESCRIPTION     'C++ Windows Hello World'

EXETYPE         WINDOWS
CODE            PRELOAD MOVEABLE
DATA            PRELOAD MOVEABLE MULTIPLE
HEAPSIZE        1024
STACKSIZE       5120
```

Let's take this file apart, statement by statement:

• NAME specifies a name for a program. If you want to build a DLL instead of a program, you would use the LIBRARY statement. Every module definition file should have either a NAME statement or a LIBRARY statement, but never both. The name specified must be the same name as the executable file. WINDOWAPI identifies this program as a Windows executable.

• DESCRIPTION lets you specify a string that describes your application or library.

- EXETYPE marks the executable as a Windows executable. This is necessary for all Windows executables.

- CODE describes attributes of the executable's code segment. The PRELOAD option instructs the loader to load this portion of the image when the application is loaded into memory. The MOVEABLE option means Windows can move the code around in memory.

- DATA defines the default attributes of data segments. The MULTIPLE option ensures that each instance of the application has its own data segment.

- HEAPSIZE specifies the size of the application's local heap.

- STACKSIZE specifies the size of the application's local stack. You can't use the STACKSIZE statement to create a stack for a DLL.

Two important statements not used in this .DEF file are the EXPORTS and IMPORTS statements.

The EXPORTS statement lists functions in a program or DLL that will be called by other applications or by Windows. These functions are known as export functions, callbacks, or callback functions. Exported functions are identified by the linker and entered into an export table.

To help you avoid the necessity of creating and maintaining long EXPORTS sections in your module definition files, Borland C++ provides the _ _**export** keyword. Functions flagged with _ _**export** will be identified by the linker and entered into the export table for the module. This is why the WHELLO example has no EXPORT statement in its module definition file.

Note   Prior to Borland C++ 5.0, the _ _**export** keyword was required to immediately precede the function name. To help port applications that use a different syntax for funtion modifiers, Borland C++ now provides the _ _**declspec** keyword.

The WHELLO application doesn't have an IMPORTS statement either because the only functions it calls from other modules are those from the Windows Application Program Interface (API); those functions are imported via the automatic inclusion of the IMPORT.LIB or IMPORT32.LIB import libraries. When an application needs to call other external functions, these functions must be listed in the IMPORTS statement, or included via an import library.

Import libraries

When you use DLLs, you must give the linker definitions of the functions you want to import from DLLs. This information temporarily satisfies the external references to the functions called by the compiled code, and tells the Windows loader where to find the functions at run time.

There are two ways to tell the linker about import functions:

- You can add an IMPORTS section to the module definition file and list every DLL function that the module will use.

- You can include an import library for the DLLs when you link the module.

An import library contains import definitions for some or all of the exported functions for one or more DLLs. A utility called IMPLIB creates import libraries for DLLs. IMPLIB creates import libraries directly from DLLs or from a DLL's module definition files, or from a combination of the two.

Import libraries can be substituted for all or part of the IMPORTS section of a module definition file.

WinMain

Syntax

```
int PASCAL WinMain(HINSTANCE hCurInstance, HINSTANCE hPrevInstance,
                   LPSTR lpCmdLine, int nCmdShow)
```

Description
This function is the main entry point for a Windows application. It must be supplied by the user.

Type	Parameter	Description
HINSTANCE	*hCurInstance*	The instance handle of the application. Each instance of an application has a unique instance handle. It is used as an argument to several Windows functions and can be used to distinguish between multiple instances of a given application.
HINSTANCE	*hPrevInstance*	The handle of the previous instance of this application. This value is NULL if this is the first instance.
LPSTR	*lpCmdLine*	A far pointer to a null-terminated command-line. Specify this value when invoking the application from the program manager or from a call to **WinExec**.
int	*nCmdShow*	An integer that specifies the application's window display. Pass this value to **ShowWindow**.

Under Win32, there are two differences in the values passed through these parameters:

- *hPrevInstance* always returns NULL.

- *lpCmdLine* points to a string containing the entire command line, not just the parameters.

Return Value
The return value from *WinMain* is not currently used by Windows. It is useful during debugging because you can display this value upon termination of your program.

Prologs and epilogs

When you compile a module for Windows, the compiler needs to know what kind of prolog and epilog needs to be created for each of a module's functions. IDE settings and command-line compiler options control the creation of the prolog and epilog. The prolog and epilog perform several duties, including ensuring that the correct data segment is active during callback functions, and marking stack frames for the Windows stack-crawling mechanism.

The prolog/epilog code is automatically generated by the compiler, though various compiler options or IDE settings dictate which sets of instructions are contained in the generated code.

See the following topics for further discussion:

- The **_export** keyword
- The **_import** keyword
- Prologs, epilogs, and exports: a summary
- Entry/exit code options

Figure 5.1   Compiling and linking a Windows program

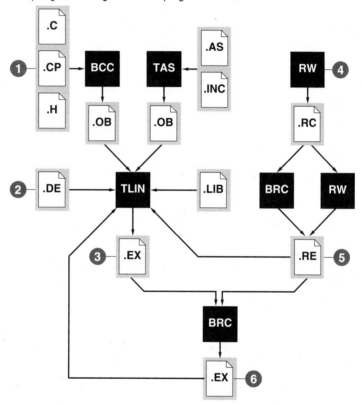

_export, _ _export

Form 1

```
class _export <class name>
```

Form 2

```
return_type _export <function name>
```

Form 3

```
data_type _export <data name>
```

Description

These modifiers are used to export classes, functions, and data.

The linker enters functions flagged with **_export** or **_ _export** into an export table for the module.

Using **_export** or **_ _export** eliminates the need for an EXPORTS section in your module definition file.

Note   Exported functions must be declared as **_ _far**. You can use the **FAR** type, defined in windows.h.

Functions that are not modified with **_export** or **_ _export** receive abbreviated prolog and epilog code, resulting in a smaller object file and slightly faster execution.

Note   If you use **_export** or **_ _export** to export a function, that function will be exported by name rather than by ordinal (ordinal is usually more efficient).

If you want to change various attributes from the default, you'll need a module definition file.

_import, _ _import

Form 1

```
class _import <class name>
class __import <class name>
```

Form 2

```
return_type _import <function name> //32-bit only
return_type __import <function name> //32-bit only
```

Form 3

```
data_type _import <data name> //32-bit only
data_type __import <data name> //32-bit only
```

Description

This keyword can be used as a class modifier for 16-bit programs; and as a class, function, or data modifier in 32-bit programs. If you're importing classes that are declared with the modifier **_ _huge**, you must change the modifier to the keyword **_ _import**. The **_ _huge** modifier merely causes far addressing of the virtual tables (the same effect as the -Vf compiler option). The **_ _import** modifier makes all function and static addresses default to **_far**.

Prologs, epilogs, and exports: a summary

Prologs and epilogs are required when exporting functions in a 16-bit Windows application. They ensure that the correct data segment is active during callback functions and mark near and far stack frames for Windows stack crawling.

Two steps are required to export a function.

1 The compiler must create the correct prolog and epilog for the function.

2 The linker must create an entry for every export function in the header section of the executable.

In 32-bit Windows the binding of data segments does not apply. However, DLLs must have entries in the header so the loader can find the function to link to when an .EXE loads the DLL.

If a function is flagged with the _ _**export** keyword and any of the Windows compiler options are used, it will be compiled as exportable and linked as an export.

If a function is *not* flagged with the _ _**export** keyword, then one of the following situations will determine whether the function is exportable:

- If you compile with the -tW/-tWC or -tWD/-tWCD option (or with the All Functions Exportable IDE equivalent), the function will be compiled as exportable.

- If the function is listed in the EXPORTS section of the module definition file, the function will be linked as an export. If it is not listed in the module definition file, or if no module definition file is linked, it won't be linked as an export.

- If you compile with the -tWE or -tWDE/-tWCDE option (or with the Explicit Functions Exported IDE equivalent), the function will *not* be compiled as exportable. Including this function in the EXPORTS section of the module definition will cause it be exported, but, because the prolog is incorrect, the program will run incorrectly. You may get a Windows error message in the 16-bit environment.

See the table, Compiler options and the _export keyword, for a summary of the effect of the combination of the Windows compiler options and the _ _**export** keyword.

Compiler options and the _ _export keyword

This table summarizes the effect of the combination of various Windows options and the _ _**export** keyword:

The compiler option is: *	-tW or -tWD	-tWE or -tWDE	-tW or -tWD	-tWE or -tWDE	-tW or -tWD	-tWE or -tWDE	-tW or -tWD
Function flagged with __export?	Yes	Yes	Yes	Yes	No	No	No
Function listed in EXPORTS?	Yes	Yes	No	No	Yes	Yes	No
Is function exportable?	Yes	Yes	Yes	Yes	Yes	No	Yes
Will function be exported?	**Yes**	**Yes**	**Yes**	**Yes**	**Yes**	**Yes ****	**No *****

* Or the 32-bit console-mode application equivalents.

** The function will be exported in some sense, but because the prolog and epilog will not be correct, the function will not work as expected.

*** This combination also makes little sense. It is inefficient to compile all functions as exportable if you do not actually export some of them.

The Borland heap manager

Windows supports dynamic memory allocations on two different heaps: the *global heap* and the *local heap*.

The global heap is a pool of memory available to all applications. Although global memory blocks of any size can be allocated, the global heap is intended only for large memory blocks (256 bytes or more). Each global memory block carries an overhead of at least 20 bytes, and under the Windows standard and 386 enhanced modes, there is a system-wide limit of 8192 global memory blocks, only some of which are available to any given application.

The local heap is a pool of memory available only to your application. It exists in the upper part of an application's data segment. The total size of local memory blocks that can be allocated on the local heap is 64K minus the size of the application's stack and static data. For this reason, the local heap is best suited for small memory blocks (256 bytes or less). The default size of the local heap is 4K, but you can change this in your applications .DEF file.

Borland C++ includes a *heap manager* which implements the **new**, *delete*, *malloc*, and **free** functions. The heap manager uses the global heap for all allocations. Because the global heap has a system-wide limit of 8192 memory blocks (which certainly is less than what some applications might require), the Borland C++ heap manager includes a *sub-allocator* algorithm to enhance performance and allow a substantially larger number of blocks to be allocated.

This is how the segment sub-allocator works: When allocating a large block, the heap manager simply allocates a global memory block using the Windows *GlobalAlloc* routine. When allocating a small block, the heap manager allocates a larger global memory block and then divides (sub-allocates) that block into smaller blocks as required. Allocations of small blocks reuse all available sub-allocation space before the heap manager allocates a new global memory block, which, in turn, is further sub-allocated.

The *HeapLimit* variable defines the threshold between small and large heap blocks. *HeapLimit* is set at 64K bytes. The *HeapBlock* variable defines the size the heap manager uses when allocating blocks to be assigned to the sub-allocator. *HeapBlock* is set at 4096 bytes.

32-bit Windows programming

The following topics briefly describe the Win32 and Windows programming environment, and explain how to port your code to this environment. This port makes your code compilable to run on both 16- and 32-bit versions of Windows, and compilable for future processors hosting Windows.

Borland C++ 32-bit tools support the production of 32-bit .OBJ and .EXE files in the portable executable (PE) file format, which is the executable file format for Win32 and Windows NT programs. Win32-conforming executables will run unchanged on Windows NT.

Note See the topic on building Win32 executables for a discussion of 32-bit tool names, options, and libraries.

Win32

Win32 is an operating system extension to Windows 3.1 that provides support for developing and running Windows 32-bit executables. Win32 is a set of DLLs that handle mapping 32-bit application program interface (API) calls to their 16-bit counterparts, a virtual device driver (VxD) to handle memory management, and a revised API called the Win32 API. The DLL and VxD are transparent.

To make sure your code will compile and run under Win32 you should

1 Make sure your code adheres to the Win32 API.

2 Write portable code using types and macros provided in the windows.h, and windowsx.h files.

See the topic on writing portable Windows code for some help in writing portable Windows code.

The Win32 API

The Win32 API widens most of the existing 16-bit Windows API to 32 bits and adds new API calls compatible with Windows NT. The Win32 API is a subset of the Win32 API for Windows NT. Those 16-bit API calls that have been converted to and are callable in the 32-bit environment, and those 32-bit API calls implementable in the 16-bit Windows environment make up the Win32 API.

If a Win32 executable calls any of the Win32 API functions not supported under Win32, appropriate error codes are returned at runtime. Writing applications that conform to the Win32 API, and using the porting tips described under Writing portable Windows code means your application will be portable across 16- and 32-bit Windows environments.

For complete descriptions of Win32 API functions, see the Microsoft Windows documentation.

Writing portable Windows code

This topic provides information about portability constructs introduced in Windows 3.1 that will assist you in producing portable Windows code. Explanations of several compiler error and warning messages you might likely see when developing portable code are also included.

Existing Windows 16-bit code can be ported to Win32 and Windows NT with minimal changes. Most changes revolve around substituting new macros and types for old, and replacing any 16-bit–specific API calls with analogous Win32 API calls. Once these changes have been made, your code can compile and run under 16- or 32-bit Windows.

A compile-time environment variable, STRICT, has been provided to assist you in making your code portable.

STRICT

Windows 3.1 introduced support in windows.h for defining STRICT. Defining STRICT enables strict compiler error checking. For example, if STRICT is not defined, passing an *HWND* to a function that requires an *HDC* will not cause a compiler warning. Define STRICT, and you will get a compiler error.

Using STRICT enables

- Strict handle type checking

- Correct and consistent parameter and return value type declarations

- Fully prototyped type definitions for callback function types (window, dialog, and hook procedures)

- ANSI-compliant declaration of COMM, DCB, and COMSTAT structures

STRICT is Windows 3.0 backward compatible. It can be used with the 3.1 windows.h for creating applications that will run under Windows 3.0.

Defining STRICT will assist you in locating and correcting type incompatibilities that arise when migrating your code to 32 bits, and will aid portability between 16- and 32-bit Windows.

New types, constants, and macros have been provided so you can change your source code to be STRICT-compliant. The table of STRICT-compliant types provides a list of the types, macros, and handle types that you can use to make your application STRICT-compliant.

Table 5.1   STRICT-compliant types, constants, helper macros, and handles

Types and constants	Description
CALLBACK	Use instead of FAR PASCAL in your callback routines (for example, window and dialog procedures).
LPARAM	Declares all 32-bit polymorphic parameters.
LPCSTR	Same as LPSTR, except that is used for read-only string pointers.
LRESULT	Declares all 32-bit polymorphic return values.
UINT	Portable unsigned integer type whose size is determined by the targeted environment. Represents a 16-bit value on Windows 3.1, and a 32-bit value on Win32.
WINAPI	Use instead of FAR PASCAL for API declarations. If you are writing a DLL with exported API entry points, you can use this for the API declarations.
WPARAM	Declares all 16-bit polymorphic parameters.
Macros	**Description**
FIELDOFFSET(type, field)	Calculates the field offsets in a structure. type is the structure type, and field is the field name.
MAKELP(sel,off)	Takes a selector and offset and produces a FAR VOID*.
MAKELPARAM(low,high)	Makes an LPARAM out of two 16-bit values.
MAKERESULT(low,high)	Makes an LRESULT out of two 16-bit values.
OFFSETOF(lp)	Extracts the offset of a far pointer and returns a UINT.
SELECTOROF(lp)	Extracts the selector for a far pointer and returns a UINT.
Handles	**Description**
HACCEL	Accelerator table handle
HDRVR	Driver handle (Windows 3.1 only)
HDWP	DeferWindowPost() handle
HFILE	File handle
HGDIOBJ	Generic GDI object handle
HGLOBAL	Global handle
HINSTANCE	Instance handle
HLOCAL	Local handle
HMETAFILE	Metafile handle
HMODULE	Module handle
HRSRC	Resource handle
HTASK	Task handle

Making your code STRICT-compliant

This steps will help to make your application STRICT-compliant.

1 Decide what code you want to be STRICT-compliant. Converting your code to STRICT can be done in stages.

2 Turn on the compiler's highest error/warning level. In the IDE, use the Make | Break Make On options. On the command line, use the –w switch to display warnings. You might want to compile at this stage, before taking the next step.

3 #define STRICT before including windows.h and compile, or use –DSTRICT on the command line.

Note Because of C++ type-safe linking, linking STRICT and non-STRICT modules may cause linker errors in C++ applications.

STRICT conversion hints

This topic describes some common coding practices you should use when converting your code to STRICT compliance.

- Change *HANDLE* to the appropriate specific handle type, for example, *HMODULE*, *HINSTANCE*, and so on.

- Change *WORD* to *UINT* except where you specifically want a 16-bit value on a 32-bit platform.

- Change *WORD* to *WPARAM*.

- Change *LONG* to *LPARAM* or *LRESULT* as appropriate.

- Change *FARPROC* to *WNDPROC*, *DLGPROC*, or *HOOKPROC* as appropriate.

- For 16-bit Windows always declare function pointers with the proper function type, rather than *FARPROC*. You'll need to cast function pointers to and from the proper function type when using *MakeProcInstance*, *FreeProcInstance*, and other functions that take or return a *FARPROC*, for example:

```
BOOL CALLBACK DlgProc(HWND hwnd, UINT msg,
                      WPARAM wParam,
                      LPARAM lParam);
                      DLGPROC lpfnDlg;
lpfnDlg=(DLGPROC)MakeProcInstance(DlgProc, hinst);
...
FreeProcInstance((FARPROC)lpfnDlg);
```

- Take special care with *HMODULE*s and *HINSTANCE*s. For the most part, the Kernel module management functions use *HINSTANCE*s, but there are a few APIs that return or accept only *HMODULE*s.

- If you've copied any API function declarations from windows.h, they may have changed, and your local declaration may be out of date. Remove your local declarations.

- Cast the results of *LocalLock* and *GlobalLock* to the proper kind of data pointer. Parameters to these and other memory management functions should be cast to *LOCALHANDLE* or *GLOBALHANDLE*, as appropriate.

- Cast the result of *GetWindowWord* and *GetWindowLong* and the parameters to *SetWindowWord* and *SetWindowLong*.

- When casting *SendMessage*, *DefWindowProc*, and *SendDlgItemMsg*, or any other function that returns an *LRESULT* or *LONG* to a handle of some kind, you must first cast the result to a *UINT*:

```
HBRUSH hbr;
hbr = (HBRUSH)(UINT)SendMessage(hwnd, WM_CTLCOLOR, ..., ...);
```

- The *CreateWindow* and *CreateWindowEx* hmenu parameter is sometimes used to pass an integer control ID. In this case you must cast this to an *HMENU*:

```
HWND hwnd;
int id;
hwnd = CreateWindow("Button", "Ok", BS_PUSHBUTTON,
                    x, y, cx, cy, hwndParent,
                    (HMENU)id,    //Cast required here
                    hinst, NULL);
```

- Polymorphic data types (*WPARAM, LPARAM, LRESULT,* **void** *FAR**) should be assigned to variables as soon as possible. You should avoid using them in your own code when the type of the value is known. This will minimize the number of potentially unsafe and non-32-bit-portable casting you will have to do in your code. The macro APIs and message cracker mechanisms provided in windowsx.h will take care of almost all packing and unpacking of these data types in a 32-bit portable way.

- Become familiar with the common compiler warnings and errors that you're likely to encounter as you convert to STRICT.

Some of the most common compiler errors and warnings you might encounter are described under "The UINT and WORD types."

See also the description of message crackers later in this chapter.

The UINT and WORD types

The type *UINT* has been created and used extensively in the API to create a data type portable from Windows 3.*x*. *UINT* is defined as

```
typedef unsigned int UINT;
```

UINT is needed because of the difference in int sizes between 16-bit Windows and Win32. For 16-bit Windows, **int** is a 16-bit unsigned integer; for Win32 **int** is a 32-bit unsigned integer. Use *UINT* to declare integer objects expected to widen from 16 to 32 bits when compiling 32-bit applications.

The type *WORD* is defined as

```
typedef unsigned short WORD;
```

WORD declares a 16-bit value on both 16-bit Windows and Win32. Use *WORD* to create objects that will remain 16 bits wide across both platforms. Note that because Win32 handles are widened to 32 bits, *WORD* can no longer be used for handles.

The WINAPI and CALLBACK calling conventions

The windows.h macro WINAPI defines the calling convention. WINAPI resolves to the appropriate calling convention for the targeted platform. WINAPI should be used in place of FAR PASCAL.

For example, here is an important change necessary for window procedure definitions. The following is code as it would appear in 16-bit Windows:

```
LONG FAR PASCAL WindowProc(HANDLE hWnd, unsigned message
                    WORD wParam, LONG lParam)
```

Here is the Win32 version:

```
LONG WINAPI WindowProc(HWND hWnd, UINT message
                       UINT wParam, LONG lParam)
```

Using WINAPI allows specifying alternative calling conventions. Currently, Win32 uses **_stdcall**. The fundamental type **unsigned** is changed to the more portable *UINT*. *WORD* is also changed to *UINT*, in this case illustrating the expansion of *wParam* to 32 bits. Not making this change to *wParam* will result in application failure during initial window creation.

Use the CALLBACK calling convention in your callback function declarations. This replaces FAR PASCAL.

Extracting message data

In 32-bit Windows code you need to change the way you unpack message data from *lParam* and *wParam*. In Win32 *wParam* grows from 16 to 32 bits in size, while *lParam* remains 32 bits wide. But since *lParam* frequently contains a handle and another value in 16-bit Windows, and a handle grows to 32 bits under Win32, another packing scheme was necessary for *wParam* and *lParam*.

For example, WM_COMMAND is one of the messages affected by the changes to extra parameter size. Under Windows 3.*x wParam* contains a 16-bit identifier, and *lParam* contains both a 16-bit window handle and a 16-bit command.

Under Win32 *lParam* contains the window handle, but nothing else since window handles are now 32 bits. So the 16-bit command is moved from *lParam* to the low-order 16 bits of *wParam* (now 32 bits), with the high order 16 bits of *wParam* containing the identifier. This repacking means changing the way you extract information from these parameters. An easy, portable way of extracting message data is by using message crackers.

Message crackers

Message crackers are a portable way of extracting messages from *wParam* and *lParam*. Depending on your environment (16-bit Windows or Win32), message crackers use an appropriate technique for extracting the message data. Each Windows message has a set of message crackers.

For example, here is the 32-bit version of the WM_COMMAND message crackers:

```
#define GET_WM_COMMAND_ID(wp, lp)                 LOWORD(wp)

#define GET_WM_COMMAND_HWND(wp, lp)               (HWND)(lp)

#define GET_WM_COMMAND_CMD(wp, lp)                HIWORD(wp)
#define GET_WM_COMMAND_MPS(id, hwnd, cmd)    \
                    (WPARAM) MAKELONG(id, cmd),
                    (LONG) (hwnd)
```

And here is the 16-bit version of the WM_COMMAND message crackers:

```
#define GET_WM_COMMAND_ID(wp, lp)                 (wp)

#define GET_WM_COMMAND_HWND(wp, lp)               (HWND)LOWORD(lp)
```

```
#define GET_WM_COMMAND_CMD(wp, lp)          HIWORD(lp)
#define GET_WM_COMMAND_MPS(id, hwnd, cmd)   \
                       (WPARAM)(id), MAKELONG(hwnd, cmd)
```

Using these message-cracker macros will ensure that your message extraction code is portable to either platform.

Porting DOS system calls

Windows 3.0 provided the *DOS3Call* API function for calling DOS file I/O functions. This function, and other INT 21H DOS functions, are replaced in Win32 by named 32-bit calls. See the list of DOS INT 21H calls and their equivalent Win32 API functions.

Table 5.2   INT 21H and Win32 equivalent functions

INT 21H function	DOS operation	Win32 API equivalent
0EH	Select disk	*SetCurrentDirectory*
19H	Get current disk	*GetCurrentDirectory*
2AH	Get date	*GetDateAndTime*
2BH	Set date	*SetDateAndTime*
2CH	Get time	*GetDateAndTime*
2DH	Set time	*SetDateAndTime*
36H	Get disk free space	*GetDiskFreeSpace*
39H	Create directory	*CreateDirectory*
3AH	Remove directory	*RemoveDirectory*
3BH	Set current directory	*SetCurrentDirectory*
3CH	Create handle	*CreateFile*
3DH	Open handle	*CreateFile*
3EH	Close handle	*CloseHandle*
3FH	Read handle	*ReadFile*
40H	Write handle	*WriteFile*
41H	Delete file	*DeleteFile*
42H	Move file pointer	*SetFilePointer*
43H	Get file attributes	*GetAttributesFile*
43H	Set file attributes	*SetAttributesFile*
47H	Get current directory	*GetCurrentDirectory*
4EH	Find first file	*FindFirstFile*
4FH	Find next file	*FindNextFile*
56H	Change directory entry	*MoveFile*
57H	Get file date/time	*GetDateAndTimeFile*
57H	Set file date/time	*SetDateAndTimeFile*
59H	Get extended error	*GetLastError*
5AH	Create unique file	*GetTempFileName*
5BH	Create new file	*CreateFile*
5CH	Lock file	*LockFile*
5CH	Unlock file	*UnlockFile*
67H	Set handle count	*SetHandleCount*

Common compiler errors and warnings

This topic describes some of the common compiler errors and warnings you might get when trying to make your application compile cleanly with all messages enabled, and with or without STRICT defined.

Warning: Call to function *funcname* with no prototype

This means that a function was used before it was prototyped, or declared. It can also arise when a function that takes no arguments is not prototyped with **void**:

```
void bar(); /* Should be: bar(void) */

void main(void)

{
   bar();
}
```

Warning: Conversion may lose significant digits

This warning results when a value is converted by the compiler, such as from LONG to **int**. You're being warned because you might lose information from this cast. If you're sure there are no information-loss problems, you can suppress this warning with the appropriate explicit cast to the smaller type.

Warning: Function should return a value

This warning means that a function declared to return a value does not return a value. In older, non-ANSI C code, it was common to declare functions that did not return a value with no return type:

```
foo(i)
int i;
{
...
}
```

Functions declared in this manner are treated by the compiler as being declared to return an **int**. If the function does not return anything, it should be declared **void**:

```
void foo(int i)
{
...
}
```

Error: Lvalue required
Error: Type mismatch in parameter

These errors indicate that you are trying to assign or pass a non-pointer type when a pointer type is required. With STRICT defined, all handle types as well as *LRESULT*, *WPARAM*, and *LPARAM* are internally declared as pointer types, so trying to pass an int, *WORD*, or *LONG* as a handle will result in these errors.

These errors should be fixed by properly declaring the non-pointer values you're assigning or passing. In the case of special constants such as (HWND)1 to indicate "insert at bottom" to the window positioning functions, you should use the new macro (such as HWND_BOTTOM). Only in rare cases should you suppress a type mismatch error with a cast. This can often generate incorrect code.

Error: **Type mismatch in redeclaration of** *paramname*

This error will result if you have inconsistent declarations of a variable, parameter, or function in your source code.

Warning: **Conversion may lose significant digits**

This warning results when a value is converted by the compiler, such as from LONG to **int**. You're being warned because you may lose information from this cast. If you're sure there are no information-loss problems, you can suppress this warning with the appropriate explicit cast to the smaller type.

Warning: **Non-portable pointer conversion**

This error results when you cast a near pointer or a handle to a 32-bit value such as *LRESULT, LPARAM, LONG,* or *DWORD*. This warning almost always represents a bug, because the high order 16 bits of the value will contain a non-zero value. The compiler first converts the 16-bit near pointer to a 32-bit far pointer by placing the current data segment value in the high 16 bits, then converts this far pointer to the 32-bit value.

To avoid this warning and ensure that a 0 is placed in the high 16 bits, you must first cast the handle to a *UINT*:

```
HWND hwnd;
LRESULT result = (LRESULT)(UINT)hwnd;
```

In cases where you do want the 32-bit value to contain a far pointer, you can **avoid** the warning with an explicit cast to a far pointer:

```
char near* pch;
LPARAM lParam = (LPARAM)(LPSTR)pch;
```

Error: **Size of the type is unknown or zero**

This error results from trying to change the value of a **void** pointer with + or +=. These typically result from the fact that certain Windows functions that return pointers to arbitrary types (such as *GlobalLock* and *LocalLock*) are defined to return void FAR* rather than LPSTR.

To solve these problems, you should assign the **void*** value to a properly declared variable (with the appropriate cast):

```
BYTE FAR* lpb = (BYTE FAR*)GlobalLock(h);
lpb += sizeof(DWORD);
```

Error: **Not an allowed type**

This error typically results from trying to dereference a **void** pointer. This usually results from directly using the return value of *GlobalLock* or *LocalLock* as a pointer. To solve this problem, assign the return value to a variable of the appropriate type (with the appropriate cast) before using the pointer:

```
BYTE FAR* lpb = (BYTE FAR*)GlobalLock(h);
*lpb = 0;
```

Warning: **Parameter** *paramname* **is never used**

This message can result in callback functions when your code does not use certain parameters. You can either turn off this warning, use **#pragma argsused** to suppress it, or you can omit the name of the parameter in the function definition.

By adhering to the Win32 API, and using STRICT to make code changes, you will make your Windows code portable.

Building Win32 executables

You must use the proper tools, switches, libraries, and startup code to build a Win32 application. The following table lists the compiler (BCC32) and linker (TLINK32) switches, libraries, and startup code commonly needed when linking, and the resulting executable type (.DLL or .EXE).

Table 5.3 Win32 options, startup code, and libraries

BCC32 options	TLINK32 option	Libraries	Startup code	Creates this executable type
–tW, –tWE	/Tpe	cw32.lib import32.lib	c0w32.obj	.EXE
–tWD, –tWDE	/Tpd	cw32.lib import32.lib	c0d32.obj	.DLL
–tWC	/Tpe /ap	cw32.lib import32.lib	c0x32.obj	Console .EXE
–tWCD, –tWCDE	/Tpd /ap	cw32.lib import32.lib	c0d32.obj	.DLL

6

Using dynamic-link libraries

Using DLLs in your applications reduces .EXE file size, conserves system memory, and provides more flexibility in changing, extending, or upgrading your applications. Windows supports both dynamic linking and static linking.

Creating a DLL

You create a DLL in much the same way you create an EXE:

- Source files containing your code are compiled into .OBJ files

- .OBJ files are linked together

The DLL, however, has no *main* function, and is therefore linked differently.

The following topics describe how to write a DLL:

- Borland DLLs

- DLLs and 16-bit Memory Models

- Exporting and Importing Classes

- Exporting and Importing Functions

- LibMain and DllEntryPoint

- WEP (Windows Exit Procedure)

Static linking

When an application uses a function from a static-link library (for example, the C runtime library), a copy of that function is bound to your application by TLINK at link time. Two applications running simultaneously that use the same function would each have their own copy of that function. It is more efficient, however, if both applications shared a single copy of the function. Dynamic linking provides this capability by resolving your application's references to external functions at run time.

Dynamic linking

When a program uses a function from a DLL, the function code is not linked into the .EXE. Instead, dynamic linking uses a two-step method:

1 At link time, TLINK binds import records (which contain DLL and procedure-location information) to your .EXE. This temporarily satisfies any external references to DLL functions in your code. These import records are supplied by module-definition files or import libraries.

2 At run time, the import-record information is used to locate and bind the DLL functions to your program.

With dynamic linking, your applications are smaller because:

• Only one copy of the function code is linked into your application.

• System memory is conserved because DLL code and resources are shared among applications.

DLL

A DLL is an executable library module containing functions or resources for use by applications or other DLLs. A DLL has no *main* function, which is the usual entry point for an application. Instead, a DLL has multiple entry points, one for each exported function.

When a DLL is loaded by the operating system, the DLL can be shared among multiple applications; one loaded copy of the DLL is all that's necessary.

LibMain and DllEntryPoint

Syntax

```
int FAR PASCAL LibMain  (HINSTANCE hInstance, WORD wDataSeg, WORD cbHeapSize,
                LPSTR lpCmdLine)
```

Description

You must supply the *LibMain* function for 16-bit programs, or the *DllEntryPoint* (32-bit Windows API) function for 32-bit programs as the main entry point for a DLL.

• For 16-bit programs, Windows calls *LibMain* once, when the library is first loaded. *LibMain* performs initialization for the DLL.

• For 32-bit programs, Windows calls *DllEntryPoint* each time the DLL is loaded and unloaded (it replaces WEP for 32-bit applications), each time a process attaches to or detaches from the DLL, or each time a thread within the process is created or destroyed.

DLL initialization depends almost entirely on the function of the particular DLL, but might include the following typical tasks:

- Unlocking the data segment with *UnlockData*, if it has been declared as MOVEABLE.
- Setting up global variables for the DLL, if it uses any.

The initialization code is executed only for the first application using the DLL.

The DLL startup code initializes the local heap automatically; you don't need to include code in *LibMain* to do this.

The following parameters (defined in windows.h) are passed to *LibMain*:

Parameter	Type	Description
HANDLE	*hInstance*	Instance handle of the DLL.
WORD	*wDataSeg*	Value of the data segment (DS) register.
WORD	*cbHeapSize*	Size of the local heap specified in the module definition file for the DLL.
LPSTR	*lpCmdLine*	A far pointer to the command line specified when the DLL was loaded.
		This value is almost always null because DLLs are typically loaded automatically with no parameters. It is possible, however, to supply a command line to a DLL when it is loaded explicitly.

Return value

On success, *LibMain* returns 1 (successful initialization).

On error, it returns 0 (failure in initialization).

Note If *LibMain* returns 0, Windows unloads the DLL from memory.

WEP (Windows Exit Procedure)

Syntax

```
int FAR PASCAL WEP (int nParameter)
```

where *nParameter* is either

- WEP_SYSTEM_EXIT (indicates that all of Windows is shutting down)
- WEP_FREE_DLL (indicates that only this DLL is being unloaded)

Description

The exit point for a 16-bit DLL is the function *WEP* (Windows Exit Procedure). This function is not required in a DLL (because the Borland C++ run-time libraries provide a default), but you can supply your own *WEP* to perform any DLL cleanup before the DLL is unloaded from memory. Windows calls *WEP* just prior to unloading the DLL.

Under Borland C++, *WEP* does not need to be exported. Borland C++ defines its own *WEP* that calls your *WEP* (if you have defined one), and then performs system cleanup.

Return value

WEP returns 1 to indicate success. Windows currently does not do anything with this return value.

Exporting and importing functions

To make your DLL functions accessible to other applications (.EXEs or other DLLs), the function names must be *exported*. To use exported functions, the function names must be *imported*.

Exporting functions

There are two ways to export functions:

- Create a module-definition file with an EXPORTS section listing all functions that will be used by other applications. The IMPDEF tool can help you do this.

- Precede every function name to be exported in the DLL with the keyword **_export** in the function definition.

A function must be exported from a DLL before it can be imported to another DLL or application.

Importing functions

If a Windows application module or another DLL uses functions from a DLL, you must tell the linker that you want to import the functions. There are three ways to do this:

- Add an IMPORTS section to the module-definition file and list every DLL function that the module will use.

- Include the import library for the DLLs when you link the module. The IMPLIB tool creates an import library for one or more DLLs.

- Define your function using the **_import** keyword (32-bit applications only).

DLLs and 16-bit memory models

Functions in a DLL are not linked directly into a Windows application. They are called at run time instead. Calls to DLL functions, therefore, will be far calls because the DLL will have a different code segment than the application. The data used by called DLL functions also need to be far.

Suppose you have a Windows application called APP1, a DLL defined by LSOURCE1.C, and a header file for that DLL called lsource1.h. Function *f1*, which operates on a string, is called by the application.

If you want the function to work correctly regardless of the memory model used to compile the DLL, you need to explicitly make the function and its data far. In the header file lsource1.h, the function prototype would take this form:

```
extern int _export FAR f(char FAR *dstring);
```

In the DLL source LSOURCE1.C, the implementation of the function would take this form:

```
int FAR f1(char far *dstring)

{
    ⋮
}
```

For the application to use the function, the function must be compiled as exportable and then exported. To accomplish this, you can either compile the DLL with all functions exportable (**-WD**) and list *f1* in the EXPORTS section of the module-definition file, or you can flag the function with the **_export** keyword, as follows:

```
int FAR _export f1(char far *dstring)

{
    ⋮
}
```

If you compile the DLL under the large model (far data, far code), then you don't need to explicitly define the function or its data as far in the DLL. In the header file, the prototype would still take the form shown here because the prototype would need to be correct for a module compiled with a smaller memory model:

```
extern int FAR f1(char FAR *dstring);
```

In the DLL, however, the function could be defined like this:

```
int _export f1(char *dstring)

{
    ⋮
}
```

Remember that before an application can use *f1*, it has to be imported into the application, either by listing *f1* in the IMPORTS section of a module-definition file or by linking with an import library for the DLL.

Exporting and importing classes

To use classes in a DLL, the class must be exported from the .DLL file and imported by the .EXE file. Conditionalized macro expansion can be used to support both of these circumstances. For example, include something similar to the following code in a header file:

```
#if defined (BUILDING_YOUR_DLL)

    #define _YOURCLASS _export
#elif defined(USING_YOUR_DLL)
    #define _YOURCLASS _import
#else
    #define _YOURCLASS
#endif
```

In your definitions, define your classes like this:

```
class _YOURCLASS class1 {

    // ...

};
```

Define BUILD_YOUR_DLL (with the **-D** option, for example) when you are building your DLL. The _YOURCLASS macro will expand to **_import**. Define USE_YOUR_DLL when you are building the .EXE which will use the DLL. The _YOURCLASS macro will expand to **_import**.

See also the discussion on using **_export** with C++ classes.

Static data in 16-bit DLLs

Through the functions in a DLL, all applications using the DLL have access to the global data in the DLL. In 16-bit DLLs, a particular function will use the same data, regardless of the application that called it (unlike 32-bit DLLs where all data is private to the process). If you want a 16-bit DLL's global data to be protected for use by a single application, you need to write that protection yourself. The DLL itself does not have a mechanism for making global data available to a single application. If you need data to be private for a given caller of a DLL, you need to dynamically allocate the data and manage the access to that data manually. Static data in a 16-bit DLL is global to all callers of a DLL.

Borland DLLs

General forms of compiler and linker command lines that use the DLL versions of the Borland run-time libraries and class libraries are described below.

Here is a 16-bit compile and link using the DLL version of the run-time library:

```
bcc -c -D_RTLDLL -ml source.cpp

tlink -C -Twe c0wl source, , , import crtldll
```

Note that the macro _RTLDLL and the **-ml** switch are use.

Here is the 32-bit version:

```
bcc32 -c -D_RTLDLL source.cpp

tlink32 -Tpe -ap c0x32 source, , , import32 cw32i
```

Here is a 16-bit compile and link using the DLL version of the class library:

```
bcc -c -D_BIDSDLL -ml source.cpp

tlink -C -Twe c0wl source, , , import bidsi crtldll
```

Here is a 32-bit compile and link using the DLL version of the class library:

```
bcc32 -c -D_BIDSDLL source.cpp
tlink32 -Tpe -ap c0x32 source, , , import32 bidsfi cw32i
```

7

Using inline assembly

Inline assembly is assembly-language instructions embedded within your C or C++ code. Inline assembly instructions are compiled or assembled along with your code rather than being assembled in separate assembly modules.

This chapter describes how to use inline assembly with Borland C++. The following topics are discussed:

- Inline assembly syntax and usage
  - Using the **asm** keyword to place an assembly instruction within your C/C++ code
  - Using C symbols in your **asm** statements to reference data and functions
  - Using register variables, offsets, and size overrides
  - Using C structure members
  - Using jump instructions and labels

- Using the **–B** compiler option and **#pragma inline** statement to compile inline assembly

- Using the built-in assembler (BASM)

See the C++ *User's Guide* for the IDE equivalents of command-line options.

Inline assembly syntax and usage

This section describes inline assembly syntax, and how to use inline assembly instructions with C++ structures, pointers, and identifiers.

To place an assembly instruction in your C/C++ code, use the **asm** keyword. The format is

> **asm** *opcode operands* ; or *newline*

where

- *opcode* is a valid 80x86 instruction.

- *operands* contains the operand(s) acceptable to the *opcode*, and can reference C constants, variables, and labels.

- The end of the **asm** statement is signaled by either ; (semicolon) or by *newline* (a new line).

A new **asm** statement can be placed on the same line, following a semicolon, but no **asm** statement can continue to the next line. To include multiple **asm** statements, surround them with braces. The initial brace must appear on the same line as the **asm** keyword.

Three **asm** statements are shown here; two on one line, and one below them.

```
asm {
    pop ax; pop ds
    iret
}
```

Semicolons are not used to start comments (as they are in TASM). When commenting **asm** statements, use C-style comments, like this:

```
asm mov ax,ds;                  /* This comment is OK */
asm {pop ax; pop ds; iret;}     /* This comment is also legal */
asm push ds                     ;THIS COMMENT IS INVALID!!
```

The assembly-language portion of the statement is copied straight to the output, embedded in the assembly language that Borland C++ is generating from your C or C++ instructions. Any C symbols are replaced with appropriate assembly language equivalents.

Each **asm** statement is considered to be a C statement. For example, the following construct is a valid C **if** statement:

```
myfunc()
{
    int  i;
    int x;

    if  (i > 0)
        asm  mov  x,4
    else
        i = 7;
}
```

Note that a semicolon isn't needed after the *mov x,4* instruction. **asm** statements are the only statements in C that depend on the occurrence of a new line to indicate that they have ended. Although this isn't in keeping with the rest of the C language, it is the convention adopted by several UNIX-based compilers.

An **asm** statement can be used as an executable statement inside a function, or as an external declaration outside of a function. **asm** statements located inside functions are placed in the code segment, and **asm** statements located outside functions are placed in the data segment.

Inline assembly references to data and functions

You can use any C symbol in your **asm** statements, including automatic (local) variables, register variables, and function parameters. Borland C++ automatically converts these symbols to the appropriate assembly-language operands and appends underscores onto identifier names.

In general, you can use a C symbol in any position where an address operand would be legal. Of course, you can use a register variable wherever a register would be a legal operand.

If the assembler encounters an identifier while parsing the operands of an inline-assembly instruction, it searches for the identifier in the C symbol table. The names of the 80x86 registers are excluded from this search. Either uppercase or lowercase forms of the register names can be used.

Inline assembly and register variables

Inline assembly code can freely use SI or DI as scratch registers. If you use SI or DI in inline assembly code, the compiler won't use these registers for register variables.

In 16-bit code BX is available for use as a scratch register. In 32-bit code, the corresponding EBX is not available for use as a scratch register.

When you use BCC32 or BCC32A to compile a C or C++ source file, including files with inline assembly, the compiler preserves the EBX register. However, when you compile an assembly .ASM source file, you are responsible for preserving the EBX register. This is true whether you compile the .ASM source file with a 32-bit compiler or use TASM32.

Inline assembly, offsets, and size overrides

When programming, you don't need to be concerned with the exact offsets of local variables: using the variable name will include the correct offsets.

It might be necessary, however, to include appropriate WORD PTR, BYTE PTR, or other size overrides on assembly instruction. A DWORD PTR override is needed on LES or indirect far call instructions.

Using C structure members

You can reference structure members in an inline-assembly statement in the usual way (that is, with *variable.member*). When you do this, you are working with variables, and you can store or retrieve values in these structure members. However, you can also directly reference the member name (without the variable name) as a form of numeric constant. In this situation, the constant equals the offset (in bytes) from the start of the structure containing that member. Consider the following program fragment:

```
struct myStruct {
    int a_a;
    int a_b;
    int a_c;
} myA ;

myfunc()
```

```
{
    ...
    asm {mov  ax, WORD PTR myA.a_b
         mov  bx, WORD PTR myA.a_c
        }
    ...
}
```

This fragment declares a structure type named *myStruct* with three members: *a_a*, *a_b*, and *a_c*. It also declares a variable *myA* of type *myStruct*. The first inline-assembly statement moves the value contained in *myA.a_b* into the register AX. The second moves the value at the address *[di] + offset(a_c)* into the register BX (it takes the address stored in DI and adds to it the offset of *a_c* from the start of *myStruct*). In this sequence, these assembler statements produce the following code:

```
mov  ax, DGROUP : myA+2
mov  bx, [di+4]
```

This way, if you load a register (such as DI) with the address of a structure of type *myStruct*, you can use the member names to directly reference the members. The member name can be used in any position where a numeric constant is allowed in an assembly-statement operand.

The structure member must be preceded by a dot (.) to signal that a member name, rather than a normal C symbol, is being used. Member names are replaced in the assembly output by the numeric offset of the structure member (the numeric offset of *a_c* is 4), but no type information is retained. Thus members can be used as compile-time constants in assembly statements.

There is one restriction, however: if two structures that you're using in inline assembly have the same member name, you must distinguish between them. Insert the structure type (in parentheses) between the dot and the member name, as if it were a cast. For example,

```
asm   mov   bx,[di].(struct tm)tm_hour
```

Using jump instructions and labels

You can use any of the conditional and unconditional jump instructions, plus the loop instructions, in inline assembly. These instructions are valid only inside a function. Since no labels can be defined in the **asm** statements, jump instructions must use C **goto** labels as the object of the jump. If the label is too far away, the jump will not be automatically converted to a long-distance jump. For this reason, you should be careful when inserting conditional jumps. You can use the **-B** switch to check your jumps. Direct far jumps cannot be generated.

In the following code, the jump goes to the C **goto** label *a*.

```
int   x()
{
a:                          /* This is the goto label "a" */
    ...
    asm jmp  a              /* Goes to label "a" */
    ...
}
```

Indirect jumps are also allowed. To use an indirect jump, use a register name as the operand of the jump instruction.

Compiling with inline assembly

There are two ways Borland C++ can handle inline assembly code in your C or C++ code.

- Borland C++ can convert your C or C++ code into assembly language, then transfer to TASM to produce an .OBJ file. (This method is described in this section.)

- Borland C++ can use its built-in assembler (BASM) to insert your assembly statements directly into the compiler's instruction stream (16-bit compiler only). (This method is described in the following section.)

You can use the **–B** compiler option for inline assembly in your C or C++ program. If you use this option, the compiler first generates an assembly file, then invokes TASM on that file to produce the .OBJ file.

Note By default **–B** invokes TASM or TASM32. You can override it with –E*xxx*, where *xxx* is another assembler. See the *C++ User's Guide* for details.

You can invoke TASM while omitting the **–B** option if you include the **#pragma inline** statement in your source code. This statement enables the **–B** option for you when the compiler encounters it. You will save compile time if you put **#pragma inline** at the top of your source file.

The **–B** option and **#pragma inline** tell the compiler to produce an .ASM file, which might contain your inline assembly instructions, and then transfer to TASM to assemble the .OBJ file. The 16-bit Borland C++ compiler has another method, BASM, that allows the compiler, not TASM, to assemble you inline assembly code.

Using the built-in assembler (BASM)

The 16-bit compiler can assemble your inline assembly instructions using the built-in assembler (BASM). This assembler is part of the compiler, and can do most of the things TASM can do, with the following restrictions:

- It can't use assembler macros.
- It can't handle 80386 or 80486 instructions.
- It doesn't permit Ideal mode syntax.
- It allows only a limited set of assembler directives (see page 216).

Because BASM isn't a complete assembler, it might not accept some assembly-language constructs. If this happens, Borland C++ will issue an error message. You then have two choices: you can simplify your inline assembly-language code so the assembler will accept it, or you can use the **–B** option to invoke TASM to catch whatever errors there might be. TASM might not identify the location of errors, however, because the original C source line number is lost.

Opcodes

You can include any of the 80x86 instruction opcodes as inline-assembly statements. There are four classes of instructions allowed by the Borland C++ compiler:

- Normal instructions—the regular 80x86 opcode set
- String instructions—special string-handling codes
- Jump instructions—various jump opcodes
- Assembly directives—data allocation and definition

All operands are allowed by the compiler, even if they are erroneous or disallowed by the assembler. The exact format of the operands is not enforced by the compiler.

Table 7.1 lists all allowable BASM opcodes. For 80286 instructions, use the **–2** command-line compiler option.

Note If you're using inline assembly in routines that use floating-point emulation (the command-line compiler option **–f**), the opcodes marked with * aren't supported.

Table 7.1 BASM opcode mnemonics

aaa	fdivrp	fpatan	lsl
aad	feni	fprem	mov
aam	ffree*	fptan	mul
aas	fiadd	frndint	neg
adc	ficom	frstor	nop
add	ficomp	fsave	not
and	fidiv	fscale	or
bound	fidivr	fsqrt	out
call	fild	fst	pop
cbw	fimul	fstcw	popa
clc	fincstp*	fstenv	popf
cld	finit	fstp	push
cli	fist	fstsw	pusha
cmc	fistp	fsub	pushf
cmp	fisub	fsubp	rcl
cwd	fisubr	fsubr	rcr
daa	fld	fsubrp	ret
das	fld1	ftst	rol
dec	fldcw	fwait	ror
div	fldenv	fxam	sahf
enter	fldl2e	fxch	sal
f2xm1	fldl2t	fxtract	sar
fabs	fldlg2	fyl2x	sbb
fadd	fldln2	fyl2xp1	shl
faddp	fldpi	hlt	shr
fbld	fldz	idiv	smsw
fbstp	fmul	imul	stc
fchs	fmulp	in	std

Table 7.1   BASM opcode mnemonics (continued)

fclex	fnclex	inc	sti
fcom	fndisi	int	sub
fcomp	fneni	into	test
fcompp	fninit	iret	verr
fdecstp	fnop	lahf	verw
fdisi	fnsave	lds	wait
fdiv	fnstcw	lea	xchg
fdivp	fnstenv	leave	xlat
fdivr	fnstsw	les	xor

* Not supported if you're using inline assembly in routines that use floating-point emulation (the command-line compiler option –f).

When using 80186 instruction mnemonics in your inline-assembly statements, you must include the –1 command-line option. This forces appropriate statements into the assembly-language compiler output so that the assembler will expect the mnemonics. If you're using an older assembler, these mnemonics might not be supported.

String instructions

In addition to the opcodes listed in Table 7.1, the string instructions given in Table 7.2 can be used alone or with repeat prefixes.

Table 7.2   BASM string instructions

cmps	insw	movsb	outsw	stos
cmpsb	lods	movsw	scas	stosb
cmpsw	lodsb	scasb	stosw	
lodsw	outsb	scasw		
insb	movs			

The following prefixes can be used with the string instructions:

```
lock   rep   repe   repne   repnz   repz
```

Jump instructions

Jump instructions are treated specially. Because a label can't be included on the instruction itself, jumps must go to C labels (see the "Using jump instructions and labels" section on page 212). The allowed jump instructions are given in the next table.

Table 7.3   Jump instructions

ja	jge	jnc	jns	loop
jae	jl	jne	jnz	loope
jb	jle	jng	jo	loopne
jbe	jmp	jnge	jp	loopnz
jc	jna	jnl	jpe	loopz
jcxz	jnae	jnle	jpo	

Table 7.3   Jump instructions (continued)

je	jnb	jno	js
jg	jnbe	jnp	jz

Assembly directives

The following assembly directives are allowed in Borland C++ inline-assembly statements:

```
db      dd      dw      extrn
```

8

Header files summary

Header files, also called include files, provide function prototype declarations for library functions. Data types and symbolic constants used with the library functions are also defined in them, along with global variables defined by Borland C++ and by the library functions. The Borland C++ library follows the ANSI C standard on names of header files and their contents.

Note   The middle column indicates C++ header files and header files defined by ANSI C.

alloc.h		Declares memory-management functions (allocation, deallocation, and so on).
assert.h	ANSI C	Defines the assert debugging macro.
bcd.h	C++	Declares the C++ class *bcd* and the overloaded operators for *bcd* and *bcd* math functions.
bios.h		Declares various functions used in calling IBM-PC ROM BIOS routines.
bwcc.h		Defines the Borland Windows Custom Control interface.
checks.h	C++	Defines the class diagnostic macros.
complex.h	C++	Declares the C++ complex math functions.
conio.h		Declares various functions used in calling the operating system console I/O routines.
constrea.h	C++	Defines the *conbuf* and *constream* classes.
cstring.h	C++	Defines the *string* classes.
ctype.h	ANSI C	Contains information used by the character classification and character conversion macros (such as *isalpha* and *toascii*).
date.h	C++	Defines the *date* class.

_defs.h		Defines the calling conventions for different application types and memory models.
dir.h		Contains structures, macros, and functions for working with directories and path names.
direct.h		Defines structures, macros, and functions for dealing with directories and path names.
dirent.h		Declares functions and structures for POSIX directory operations.
dos.h		Defines various constants and gives declarations needed for DOS and 8086-specific calls.
errno.h	ANSI C	Defines constant mnemonics for the error codes.
except.h	C++	Declares the exception-handling classes and functions.
excpt.h		Declares C structured exception support.
fcntl.h		Defines symbolic constants used in connection with the library routine open.
file.h	C++	Defines the *file* class.
float.h	ANSI C	Contains parameters for floating-point routines.
fstream.h	C++	Declares the C++ stream classes that support file input and output.
generic.h	C++	Contains macros for generic class declarations.
io.h		Contains structures and declarations for low-level input/output routines.
iomanip.h	C++	Declares the C++ streams I/O manipulators and contains templates for creating parameterized manipulators.
iostream.h	C++	Declares the basic C++ streams (I/O) routines.
limits.h	ANSI C	Contains environmental parameters, information about compile-time limitations, and ranges of integral quantities.
locale.h	ANSI C	Declares functions that provide country- and language-specific information.
malloc.h		Declares memory-management functions and variables.
math.h	ANSI C	Declares prototypes for the math functions and math error handlers.
mem.h		Declares the memory-manipulation functions. (Many of these are also defined in string.h.)
memory.h		Contains memory-manipulation functions.
new.h	C++	Access to *_new_handler* and *set_new_handler*.

_nfile.h		Defines the maximum number of open files.
_null.h		Defines the value of NULL.
process.h		Contains structures and declarations for the *spawn...* and *exec...* functions.
search.h		Declares functions for searching and sorting.
setjmp.h	ANSI C	Declares the functions *longjmp* and *setjmp* and defines a type *jmp_buf* that these functions use.
share.h		Defines parameters used in functions that make use of file-sharing.
signal.h	ANSI C	Defines constants and declarations for use by the *signal* and *raise* functions.
stdarg.h	ANSI C	Defines macros used for reading the argument list in functions declared to accept a variable number of arguments (such as *vprintf*, *vscanf*, and so on).
stddef.h	ANSI C	Defines several common data types and macros.
stdio.h	ANSI C	Defines types and macros needed for the standard I/O package defined in Kernighan and Ritchie and extended under UNIX System V. Defines the standard I/O predefined streams *stdin*, *stdout*, *stdprn*, and *stderr* and declares stream-level I/O routines.
stdiostr.h	C++	Declares the C++ (version 2.0) stream classes for use with *stdio FILE* structures. You should use iostream.h for new code.
stdlib.h	ANSI C	Declares several commonly used routines such as conversion routines and search/sort routines.
string.h	ANSI C	Declares several string-manipulation and memory-manipulation routines.
strstrea.h	C++	Declares the C++ stream classes for use with byte arrays in memory.
sys\locking.h		Contains definitions for mode parameter of *locking* function.
sys\stat.h		Defines symbolic constants used for opening and creating files.
sys\timeb.h		Declares the function *ftime* and the structure *timeb* that ftime returns.
sys\types.h		Declares the type *time_t* used with time functions.
thread.h	C++	Defines the thread classes.
time.h	ANSI C	Defines a structure filled in by the time-conversion routines *asctime*, *localtime*, and *gmtime*, and a type used by the routines *ctime*, *difftime*, *gmtime*, *localtime*, and *stime*. It also provides prototypes for these routines.

typeinfo.h	C++	Declares the run-time type information classes.
utime.h		Declares the *utime* function and the *utimbuf* struct that it returns.
values.h		Defines important constants, including machine dependencies; provided for UNIX System V compatibility.
varargs.h		Definitions for accessing parameters in functions that accept a variable number of arguments. Provided for UNIX compatibility; you should use stdarg.h for new code.

Using precompiled headers

Borland C++ can generate (and subsequently use) precompiled headers to speed up your project compile times.

Precompiled headers are header files that are compiled once, then used over and over again in their compiled state.

You can use a precompiled header if a compilation uses one or more of the same header files, the same compiler options, the same macro defines, and so on, as is contained in the precompiled header file.

To control the use of precompiled headers, do one of the following:

- From within the IDE, turn on the Precompiled Headers option in the Compiler settings page of the Project Options dialog box. The IDE bases the name of the precompiled header file on the project name, creating*<PROJECT_NAME>*.CSM. From the command line, use the following command-line options: **-H=<filename>**, **-Hc**, **-H<filename>**, and **-Hu**. See Chapter 3 for more information.

- From within your code, use the **hdrfile** and **hdrstop** pragmas.

Setting file names

The compilers store all precompiled headers in one file, using the following naming conventions:

- The 16-bit command-line compiler names the precompiled header file BCDEF.CSM.

- The 32-bit command-line compiler names the precompiled header file BC32DEF.CSM.

- The IDE names the precompiled header file *<PROJECT_NAME>*.CSM.

Note   To explicitly set the precompiled file name from the command line, use the **-H=<filename>** option or the #pragma **hdrfile** directive.

Precompiled header file overview

When compiling C and C++ programs, the compiler can spend up to half its time parsing header files. When the compiler parses a header file, it enters declarations and definitions into its symbol table.

Precompiled headers cut this process short by creating and storing a binary image of the symbol table on disk. By directly loading a binary image of the symbol table, the compiler can increase the speed of this step by over ten times. The disadvantage is that precompiled header files can become quite large because they can contain the symbol table images for all the **#include** files encountered in your sources.

If, while compiling a source file, Borland C++ discovers that the first **#include** files are identical to those of a previous compilation (of either the same or different source), it loads the binary image for those **#include** files and parses the remaining **#include** files.

For a given module, either all or none of the precompiled headers are used—if compilation of any included header file fails, the precompiled header file isn't updated for that module.

Precompiled header limits

When using precompiled headers, BCDEF.CSM can become very large because it contains symbol table images for all sets of includes encountered in your sources. If you don't have sufficient disk space, you'll get a warning saying the write failed because of the precompiled headers. To fix this, you must provide more disk space and retry the compile. For information on reducing the size of the BCDEF.CSM file, see "Optimizing precompiled headers."

If you're using large macros in a makefile in addition to using precompiled headers, there is a limit on the macro size: 4K for 16-bit applications and 16K for 32-bit applications.

If a header file contains any code, it can't be precompiled. For example, although C++ class definitions can appear in header files, you should ensure that only inline member functions are defined in the header and heed warnings such as `Functions containing reserved word are not expanded inline`.

Precompiled header rules

The following rules apply when you create and use precompiled headers:

- A header that contains code can't be precompiled. For example, although C++ class definitions can appear in header files, make sure that only inline member functions are defined in the header. Heed warnings such as `Functions containing 'for' are not expanded inline`.

- In order to use a previously generated precompiled header, the source file must:
  - Have the same set of include files, in the same order, as the precompiled header.

- Have the same macros defined with identical values as the precompiled header.
- Use the same language (C or C++) as the precompiled header.
- Use header files with identical time stamps as the precompiled header.

- In addition, the following option settings must be identical to those used when you generated the precompiled header:
  - Memory model, including SS != DS (**-m**x)
  - Underscores on externs (**-u**)
  - Maximum identifier length (**-iL**)
  - Target DOS or Windows (**-W** or **-W**x)
  - Generate word alignment (**-a**)
  - Pascal calls (**-p**)
  - Treat enums as integers (**-b**)
  - Default char is unsigned (**-K**)
  - Virtual table control (**-V**x and **-Vm**x)
  - Expand intrinsic functions inline (**-Oi**)
  - Templates (**-J**x)
  - String literals in code segment (**-dc**, 16-bit only)
  - Debugging information (**-v**, **-vi**, and **-R**)
  - Far variables (**-F**x)
  - Language compilance (**-A**)
  - C++ compile (**-P**)
  - DOS overlay-compatible code (**-Y**)

- If you're using large macros in addition to using precompiled headers, the compiler limits the size of the macros as following:
  - 4K macros for 16-bit applications
  - 16K macros for 32-bit applications

Optimizing precompiled headers

For the most efficiently compiled precompiled headers, follow these rules:

- Arrange your header files in the same sequence in all source files.

- Put the largest header files first.

- Prime the precompiled header file with often-used initial sequences of header files.

- Use #pragma **hdrstop** to terminate the list of header files at well-chosen places. This lets you make the list of header files in different sources look similar to the compiler.

For example, suppose you have the following two source files (A_SOURCE.CPP and B_SOURCE.CPP), which both include windows.h and myhdr.h:

```
/* A_SOURCE.CPP */

#include <windows.h>
#include "myhdr.h"
#include "xxx.h"
// ...


/* B_SOURCE.CPP */
#include "yyy.h"
#include <string.h>
#include "myhdr.h"
#include <windows.h>
// ...
```

To optimize the precompiled headers for these source files, you would rearrange the beginning of B_SOURCE.CPP as follows:

```
/* Revised B_SOURCE.CPP */
#include <windows.h>
#include "myhdr.h"
#include "yyy.h"
#include <string.h>
// ...
```

Now, windows.h and myhdr.h are in the same order in both A_SOURCE.CPP and B_SOURCE.CPP, and they are both located at the beginning of the **#include** list.

In addition, you could also create a new source file called PREFIX.CPP which contains only the matching header files, like this:

```
/* PREFIX.CPP */
#include <windows.h>
#include "myhdr.h"
```

If you compile PREFIX.CPP first (or insert a #pragma hdrstop in both A_SOURCE.CPP and B_SOURCE.CPP), the net effect is that after the initial compilation of PREFIX.CPP, both A_SOURCE.CPP and B_SOURCE.CPP will be able to load the symbol table produced by PREFIX.CPP. The compiler will then need to parse only xxx.h for A_SOURCE.CPP, and yyy.h and strings.h for B_SOURCE.CPP.

alloc.h

Declares memory-management functions (allocation, deallocation, and so on).

Functions

- calloc
- farcalloc
- farfree
- farmalloc
- farrealloc
- free
- heapcheck

- heapcheckfree
- heapchecknode
- heapfillfree
- heapwalk
- malloc
- realloc

Constants, data types, and global variables

- NULL
- ptrdiff_t
- size_t

assert.h

Defines the assert debugging macro.

Functions

- assert

bios.h

Declares various functions used in calling IBM-PC ROM BIOS routines.

Functions

- _bios_equip
- _bios_disk (in Borland C++ DOS Support Help)
- _bios_equiplist
- _bios_keybrd (in Borland C++ DOS Support Help)
- _bios_memsize
- _bios_serialcom (in Borland C++ DOS Support Help)
- _bios_timeofday
- bioscom (in Borland C++ DOS Support Help)
- biosequip
- bioskey (in Borland C++ DOS Support Help)
- biosmemory
- biosprint (in Borland C++ DOS Support Help)
- biostime

conio.h

Declares various functions used in calling the operating system console I/O routines.

Functions

- cgets
- clreol
- clrscr
- cprintf
- cputs
- cscanf
- delline
- getch
- getche
- getpass
- gettext
- gettextinfo
- gotoxy
- highvideo
- inp
- inport
- inportb
- inpw
- insline
- kbhit
- lowvideo
- movetext
- normvideo
- outp
- outport
- outportb
- outpw
- putch
- puttext
- _setcursortype
- textattr
- textbackground
- textcolor
- textmode
- ungetch
- wherex
- wherey
- window

ctype.h

Contains information used by the character classification and character conversion macros.

Functions and macros

- isalnum
- isalpha
- isascii
- iscntrl
- isdigit
- isgraph
- islower
- isprint
- ispunct
- isspace
- isupper
- isxdigit
- toascii
- _tolower
- tolower
- _toupper
- toupper

Constants, data types, and global variables

- _IS_CTL
- _IS_DIG
- _IS_HEX
- _IS_LOW
- _IS_PUN
- _IS_SP
- _IS_UPP

dir.h

Contains structures, macros, and functions for working with directories and path names.

Functions

- chdir
- findfirst
- findnext
- fnmerge
- fnsplit
- getcurdir
- getcwd
- getdisk
- mkdir
- mktemp

- rmdir
- searchpath
- setdisk

Constants, data types, and global variables

- DIRECTORY
- DRIVE
- EXTENSION
- ffblk
- FILENAME
- MAXDIR
- MAXDRIVE
- MAXEXT
- MAXFILE
- MAXPATH

direct.h

Defines structures, macros, and functions for dealing with directories and path names.

Includes

- DIR.H

Functions

- _chdrive
- _getdcwd

dirent.h

Declares functions and structures for POSIX directory operations.

Functions

- closedir
- opendir
- readdir
- rewinddir

dos.h

Defines various constants and gives declarations needed for DOS and 8086-specific calls.

Functions

- allocmem (in Borland C++ DOS Support Help)
- bdos
- bdosptr
- _chain_intr
- _chmod
- country
- ctrlbrk
- delay (in Borland C++ DOS Support Help)
- disable
- _dos_allocmem (in Borland C++ DOS Support Help)
- _dos_close
- _dos_commit
- _dos_creat
- _dos_creatnew
- dosexterr
- _dos_findfirst
- _dos_findnext
- _dos_freemem (in Borland C++ DOS Support Help)
- _dos_getdate
- _dos_getdiskfree
- _dos_getdrive
- _dos_getfileattr
- _dos_getftime
- _dos_gettime
- _dos_getvect
- _dos_keep (in Borland C++ DOS Support Help)
- _dos_open
- _dos_read
- _dos_setblock (in Borland C++ DOS Support Help)
- _dos_setdate
- _dos_setdrive
- _dos_setfileattr
- _dos_settime
- _dos_setvect
- dostounix
- _dos_write
- _emit_
- enable
- FP_OFF
- FP_SEG
- geninterrupt
- getcbrk
- getdate
- getdfree
- getdta

- getfat
- getfatd
- getftime
- getpsp
- gettime
- getvect
- getverify
- _harderr (in Borland C++ DOS Support Help)
- _hardresume (in Borland C++ DOS Support Help)
- _hardretn (in Borland C++ DOS Support Help)
- inport
- inportb
- int86
- int86x
- intdos
- intdosx
- intr
- keep (in Borland C++ DOS Support Help)
- MK_FP
- nosound (in Borland C++ DOS Support Help)
- outport
- outportb
- parsfnm
- peek
- peekb
- poke
- pokeb
- randbrd (in Borland C++ DOS Support Help)
- randbwr (in Borland C++ DOS Support Help)
- segread
- setcbrk
- setdate
- setdta
- settime
- setvect
- setverify
- sleep
- sound (in Borland C++ DOS Support Help)
- unixtodos
- unlink

Constants, data types, and global variables

- _8087
- _argc
- _argv
- COUNTRY

- date
- devhdr
- dfree
- diskfree_t
- dosdate_t
- DOSERROR
- dostime_t
- _doserrno
- dosSearchInfo
- errno
- _environ
- fatinfo
- fcb
- FA_*
- ffblk
- _heaplen (in Borland C++ DOS Support Help)
- NFDS
- _osmajor
- _osminor
- _osversion
- _ovrbuffer (in Borland C++ DOS Support Help)
- _psp
- REGPACK
- REGS
- SEEK_CUR
- SEEK_END
- SEEK_SET
- SREGS
- _stklen (in Borland C++ DOS Support Help)
- time
- _version
- xfcb

errno.h

Defines constant mnemonics for the error codes.

Constants, data types, and global variables

- _doserrno
- errno
- _sys_errlist
- _sys_nerr
- error number definitions

fcntl.h

Defines open flags for open and similar library functions.

Functions

- _fmode
- _pipe

Constants

- O_APPEND
- O_BINARY
- O_CHANGED
- O_CREAT
- O_DENYALL
- O_DENYNONE
- O_DENYREAD
- O_DENYWRITE
- O_DEVICE
- O_EXCL
- O_NOINHERIT
- O_RDONLY
- O_RDWR
- O_TEXT
- O_TRUNC
- O_WRONLY

float.h

Contains parameters for floating-point routines.

Functions

- _clear87
- _fpreset
- _status87

Constants, data types, and global variables

- CW_DEFAULT
- FPE_EXPLICITGEN
- FPE_INEXACT
- FPE_INTDIV0
- FPE_INTOVFLOW
- FPE_INVALID
- FPE_OVERFLOW

- FPE_UNDERFLOW
- FPE_ZERODIVIDE
- ILL_EXECUTION
- ILL_EXPLICITGEN
- SEGV_BOUND
- SEGV_EXPLICITGEN

generic.h

Contains macros for generic class declarations.

io.h

Contains structures and declarations for low-level input/output routines.

Functions

- access
- chmod
- chsize
- close
- creat
- creatnew
- creattemp
- dup
- dup2
- eof
- filelength
- _get_osfhandle
- getftime
- _InitEasyWin
- ioctl
- isatty
- lock
- locking
- lseek
- mktemp
- open
- _open_osfhandle
- _pipe
- read
- remove
- rename
- _rtl_chmod
- _rtl_close

- _rtl_creat
- _rtl_open
- _rtl_read
- _rtl_write
- setftime
- setmode
- sopen
- tell
- umask
- unlink
- unlock
- write

Constants, data types, and global variables

- ftime structure
- HANDLE_MAX
- fseek/lseek modes

iomanip.h

Declares the C++ streams I/O manipulators and contains macros for creating parameterized manipulators.

Includes

- iostream.h

Classes

- iapply
- imanip
- ioapp
- iomanip
- oapp
- omanip
- sapp
- smanip

Overloaded operators

<<   >>

limits.h

Contains environmental parameters, information about compile-time limitations, and ranges of integral quantities.

Constants, data types, and global variables

- CHAR_BIT
- CHAR_MAX
- CHAR_MIN
- INT_MAX
- INT_MIN
- LONG_MAX
- LONG_MIN
- SCHAR_MAX
- SCHAR_MIN
- SHRT_MAX
- SHRT_MIN
- UCHAR_MAX
- UINT_MAX
- ULONG_MAX
- USHRT_MAX

locale.h

Declares functions that provide information specific to languages and countries.

Functions

- localeconv
- setlocale

Constants, data types, and global variables

- LC_ALL
- LC_COLLATE
- LC_CTYPE
- LC_MONETARY
- LC_NUMERIC
- LC_TIME
- lconv (struct)
- NULL

malloc.h

Declares memory-management functions and variables.

Includes

ALLOC.H

Functions

- _heapchk
- _heapmin
- _heapset
- _msize
- _rtl_heapwalk
- stackavail

math.h

Declares prototypes for the math functions and math error handlers.

Functions

- abs
- acos, acosl
- asin, asinl
- atan, atanl
- atan2, atan2l
- atof, _atold
- cabs, cabsl
- ceil, ceill
- cos, cosl
- cosh, coshl
- exp, expl
- fabs, fabsl
- floor, floorl
- fmod, fmodl
- frexp, frexpl
- hypot, hypotl
- labs
- ldexp, ldexpl
- log, logl
- log10, log10l
- _matherr, _matherrl
- modf, modfl
- poly, polyl
- pow, powl
- pow10, pow10l
- sin, sinl
- sinh, sinhl
- sqrt, sqrtl
- tan, tanl
- tanh, tanhl

Constants, data types, and global variables

- complex (struct)
- _complexl (struct)
- EDOM
- ERANGE
- exception (struct)
- _exceptionl (struct)
- HUGE_VAL
- M_E
- M_LOG2E
- M_LOG10E
- M_LN2
- M_LN10
- M_PI
- M_PI_2
- M_PI_4
- M_1_PI
- M_2_PI
- M_1_SQRTPI
- M_2_SQRTPI
- M_SQRT2
- M_SQRT_2
- _mexcep

mem.h

Declares the memory-manipulation functions. (Many of these are also defined in string.h.)

Functions

- _fmemccpy
- _fmemchr
- _fmemcmp
- _fmemcpy
- _fmemicmp
- _fmemmove
- _fmemset
- _fmovmem
- memccpy
- memchr
- memcmp
- memcpy
- memicmp
- memmove

- memset
- movedata
- movmem
- setmem

Constants, data types, and global variables

- NULL
- ptrdiff_t
- size_t

memory.h

Contains memory-manipulation functions.

Includes

- MEM.H

new.h

Provides access to the the following functions:

- set_new_handler
- _new_handler (global variable)

process.h

Contains structures and declarations for the spawn... and exec... functions.

Functions

- abort
- _beginthread
- _beginthreadNT
- _c_exit
- _cexit
- cwait
- _endthread
- execl
- execle
- execlp
- execlpe
- execv
- execve
- execvp

- execvpe
- exit
- _exit
- getpid
- spawnl
- spawnle
- spawnlp
- spawnlpe
- spawnv
- spawnve
- spawnvp
- spawnvpe
- wait

Constants, data types, and global variables

- P_DETACH
- P_NOWAIT
- P_NOWAITO
- P_OVERLAY
- P_WAIT

search.h

Declares functions for searching and sorting.

Functions

- bsearch
- lfind
- lsearch
- qsort

setjmp.h

Declares the functions longjmp and setjmp and defines a type jmp_bufj that these functions use.

Functions

- longjmp
- setjmp

Constants, data types, and global variables

- jmp_buf

share.h

Defines parameters used in functions that make use of file-sharing.

Constants, data types, and global variables

- SH_COMPAT
- SH_DENYNO
- SH_DENYNONE
- SH_DENYRD
- SH_DENYRW
- SH_DENYWR

signal.h

Defines constants and declarations for use by the signal and raise functions.

Functions

- raise
- signal

Constants, data types, and global variables

- predefined signal handlers
- sig_atomic_t type
- SIG_DFL
- SIG_ERR
- SIG_IGN
- SIGABRT
- SIGFPE
- SIGILL
- SIGINT
- SIGSEGV
- SIGTERM

stdarg.h

Defines macros used for reading the argument list in functions declared to accept a variable number of arguments (such as vprintf, vscanf, and so on).

Macros

- va_arg
- va_end
- va_start

Constants, data types, and global variables

- va_list

stddef.h

Defines several common data types and macros.

Functions

- offsetof

Constants, data types, and global variables

- NULL
- ptrdiff_t
- size_t
- _threadid
- wchar_t

stdio.h

Defines types and macros needed for the standard I/O package defined in Kernighan and Ritchie and extended under UNIX System V. It defines the standard I/O predefined streams stdin, stdout, stdprn, and stderr, and declares stream-level I/O routines.

Functions

clearerr	_fstrncpy	spawnlp
fclose	ftell	spawnlpe
fcloseall	fwrite	spawnv
fdopen	getc	spawnve
feof	getchar	spawnvp
ferror	gets	spawnvpe
fflush	getw	sprintf
fgetc	_pclose	sscanf
fgetchar	perror	strerror
fgetpos	_popen	_strerror
fgets	printf	strncpy
fileno	putc	tempnam
flushall	putchar	tmpfile
fopen	puts	tmpnam
fprintf	putw	ungetc
fputc	remove	unlink
fputchar	rename	vfprintf
fputs	rewind	vfscanf
fread	rmtmp	vprintf
freopen	scanf	vscanf
fscanf	setbuf	vsprintf
fseek	setvbuf	vsscanf
fsetpos	spawnl	
_fsopen	spawnle	

Constants, data types, and global variables

buffering modes	_F_TERM	SEEK_CUR
BUFSIZ	_F_WRIT	SEEK_END
EOF	FILE	SEEK_SET
_F_BIN	fpos_t	size_t
_F_BUF	fseek/lseek modes	stdaux
_F_EOF	_IOFBF	stderr
_F_ERR	_IOLBF	stdin
_F_IN	_IONBF	stdout
_F_LBUF	L_ctermid	stdprn
_F_OUT	L_tmpnam	SYS_OPEN
_F_RDWR	NULL	TMP_MAX
_F_READ	FOPEN_MAX	

stdiostr.h

Declares the C++ (version 2.0) stream classes for use with stdio FILE structures. You should use iostream.h for new code.

Includes

IOSTREAM.H

STDIO.H

stdlib.h

Declares several commonly used routines such as conversion routines and search/sort routines.

Functions

abort	labs	realloc
abs	ldiv	_rotl
atexit	lfind	_rotr
atof	_lrotl	_searchenv
atoi	_lrotr	_searchstr
atol	lsearch	_splitpath
bsearch	ltoa	srand
calloc	_makepath	strtod
_crotr	malloc	strtol
div	max	_strtold
ecvt	mblen	strtoul
exit	mbstowcs	swab
_exit	mbtowc	system
fcvt	min	time
free	putenv	ultoa
_fullpath	qsort	wcstombs
gcvt	rand	wctomb
getenv	random	
itoa	randomize	

Constants, data types, and global variables

- div_t
- _doserrno
- environ
- errno
- EXIT_FAILURE

- EXIT_SUCCESS
- _fmode
- ldiv_t
- NULL
- _osmajor
- _osminor
- RAND_MAX
- size_t
- sys_errlist
- sys_nerr
- _version
- wchar_t

string.h

Declares several string-manipulation and memory-manipulation routines.

Includes

LOCALE.H

Functions

_fmemccpy	_fstrrev	strcspn
_fmemchr	_fstrset	strdup
_fmemcmp	_fstrspn	strerror
_fmemcpy	_fstrstr	_strerror
_fmemicmp	_fstrtok	stricmp
_fmemset	_fstrupr	strlen
_fstr*	memccpy	strlwr
_fstrcat	memchr	strncat
_fstrchr	memcmp	strncmp
_fstrcmp	memcpy	strncmpi
_fstrcpy	memicmp	strncpy
_fstrcspn	memmove	strnicmp
_fstrdup	memset	strnset
_fstricmp	movedata	strpbrk
_fstrlen	movmem	strrchr
_fstrlwr	setmem	strrev
_fstrncat	stpcpy	strset
_fstrncmp	strcat	strspn
_fstrncpy	strchr	strstr
_fstrnicmp	strcmp	strtok
_fstrnset	strcmpi	strupr
_fstrpbrk	strcoll	strxfrm
_fstrrchr	strcpy	

Constants, data types, and global variables

- size_t

sys\locking.h

Contains definitions for mode parameter of locking function.

Constants

- LK_LOCK
- LK_NBLCK
- LK_NBRLCK
- LK_RLCK
- LK_UNLCK

sys\stat.h

Defines symbolic constants used for opening and creating files.

Includes

SYS\TYPES.H

Functions

- chmod
- fstat
- stat

Constants, data types, and global variables

- file status bits
- stat structure

sys\timeb.h

Functions

- ftime

Constants, data types, and global variables

- timeb structure
- _timezone

sys\types.h

Constants, data types, and global variables

- time_t

time.h

Defines a structure filled in by time-conversion routines asctime, localtime, and gmtime, and a type used by the routines ctime, difftime, gmtime, localtime, and stime. It also provides prototypes for these routines.

Functions

- asctime

- clock
- ctime
- difftime
- gmtime
- localtime
- mktime
- randomize
- stime
- _strdate
- strftime
- _strtime
- time
- tzset

Constants, data types, and global variables

- CLK_TCK
- clock_t
- daylight
- size_t
- time_t
- timezone
- tm
- tzname

Classes

- Time classes

utime.h

Declares the utime function and the utimbuf struct that it returns.

Function

- utime

Constants, data types, and global variables

- time_t
- utimbuf

values.h

Defines UNIX-compatible constants for limits to float and double values.

- BITSPERBYTE

- DMAXEXP
- DMAXPOWTWO
- DMINEXP
- DSIGNIF
- FMAXEXP
- FMAXPOWTWO
- FMINEXP
- FSIGNIF
- _FEXPLEN
- HIBITI
- HIBITL
- HIBITS
- _LENBASE
- MAXDOUBLE
- MAXFLOAT
- MAXINT
- MAXLONG
- MAXSHORT
- MINDOUBLE
- MINFLOAT

varargs.h

Definitions for accessing parameters in functions that accept a variable number of arguments.

These macros are compatible with UNIX System V.

Use STDARG.H for ANSI C compatibility.

Note   You can't include both STDARG.H and VARARGS.H.

Macros

- va_start
- va_arg
- va_end

Type

- va_list

excpt.h

The excpt.h header file contains the declarations and prototypes for structured exception-handling values, types, and routines. Consult the Windows API documentation for more details.

bwcc.h

The bwcc.h header file defines the interface for Borland Windows Custom Control library (BWCC).

For details on using the Borland Windows Custom Control library, see the *C++ Language Reference*, Part VI.

_defs.h

The _defs.h header file contains common definitions for pointer size and calling conventions.

Calling Conventions

_RTLENTRY   Specifies the calling convention used by the Standard Run-time Library.

_USERENTRY   Specifies the calling convention the Standard Run-time Library expects user-compiled functions to use for callbacks.

Export (and size for DOS) information

_EXPCLASS   Exports the class if you are building a DLL version of a library.

_EXPDATA   Exports the data if you are building a DLL version of a library.

_EXPFUNC   Exports the function if you are building a DLL version of a library.

Note   These export macros are provided as examples only and should not be used to create user-defined functions.

_nfile.h

The _nfile.h header file defines _NFILE_, which specifies the maximum number of open files you can have.

NFILE is defined as 50 for all applications.

_null.h

The _null.h defines the value of NULL for different memory models and applications types:

Model	Value	
Flat	((void *)0)	if not C++ or Windows application
Flat	0	

Using EasyWin

Borland C++ provides EasyWin, a feature that lets you compile standard DOS applications which use traditional TTY style input and output so they can run as true Windows programs. With EasyWin, you do not need to change a DOS program to run it under Windows.

Note You cannot use EasyWin with the DLL version of the run-time library.

EasyWin includes:

clreol	*gotoxy*	*wherey*
clrscr	*wherex*	

These functions have the same names (and uses) as functions in conio.h header file. Classes in constrea.h provide console I/O functionality for use with C++ streams.

The following routines can be ported to EasyWin programs but are not available in 16-bit Windows programs:

fgetchar	*kbhit*	*puts*
getch	*perror*	*scanf*
getchar	*printf*	*vprintf*
getche	*putch*	*vscanf*
gets	*putchar*	

These functions are provided to simplify porting of existing DOS code into 16-bit Windows applications.

Converting DOS applications to Windows

To convert console-based applications that use standard files or *iostream* functions, check the EasyWin Target Type using TargetExpert in the IDE. Borland C++ will detect that your program does not contain a *WinMain* function (normally required for Windows applications) and link the EasyWin library. When you run your program in the Windows environment, a standard window is created, and your program takes input and produces output for that window as if it were the standard screen.

You can use the EasyWin window any time to request input to or specify output from a TTY device. This means that in addition to *stdin* and *stdout*, all *stderr*, *stdaux*, and *cerr* devices are all connected to this window.

EasyWin C example

```
#include <stdio.h>


int main()
{
  printf("Hello Windows\n");
  return 0;
}
```

EasyWin C++ example

```
#include <iostream.h>


int main()
{
  cout << "Hello Windows\n";
  return 0;
}
```

Using EasyWin from within a Windows program

Borland C++ provides EasyWin so you can quickly and easily convert your DOS applications to 16-bit Windows programs.

You can also use EasyWin from within 16-bit Windows programs. For example, you can add *printf* functions to your program code to help debug a Windows program.

To use EasyWin from within a Windows program, call *_InitEasyWin()* before performing any standard input or output.

_InitEasyWin example

```
#include <stdio.h>
#include <windows.h>

#pragma argsused
```

```
int PASCAL WinMain( HANDLE hInstance, HANDLE hPrevInstance,
                    LPSTR lpszCmdParam, int nCmdShow )
{
    char *p;

    _InitEasyWin();

    p = "This is an example of how Borland C++"
        " will automatically\nconcatenate"
        " very long strings,\nresulting in nicer"
        " looking programs.";

    printf(p);

    return(0);
}
```

EasyWin features

EasyWin now has support for several new features:

- Printing support lets you print the contents of the EasyWin window.

- Viewable scrolling buffer stores either 100 or 400 lines of text (depending on the memory model). This buffer automatically scrolls as you move the vertical or horizontal scroll bar thumb tabs.

- Redirects output to a file of your choice when the buffer runs out of space.

- Full Windows Clipboard support, lets you paste to standard input and copy from the buffer onto the Clipboard, using either the keyboard or the mouse.

Printing

Use the Print command on the system menu to print the contents of an EasyWin window. It activates the standard Print dialog from which you can specify printing options.

By default, EasyWin prints 80 columns and approximately 54 lines on U.S. Letter size (8.5" x 11") paper.

Note The Print command is grayed if you do not have a default printer installed under Windows. If you have a printer installed but it is not the default, make it the default printer before attempting to print from an EasyWin application.

If you have trouble printing on a dot-matrix printer, add the following global variable to your main source file:

```
BOOL _UseDefaultPrinterFont;
```

Set this variable to TRUE and EasyWin will print using the default font for your printer instead of the standard EasyWin printer font.

You should declare this variable as external and set it to TRUE within your *main()* function:

```
extern BOOL _UseDefaultPrinterFont;
  ⋮
int main()
{
  _UseDefaultPrinterFont = TRUE;
  ⋮
}
```

Note   This variable is not recommended for use with laser or inkjet printers.

Scrolling buffer

EasyWin caches your screen output into a buffer of either:

- 400 lines (for compact and large memory models)
- 100 lines (for small and medium memory models)

You can view the buffer any time by using the scroll bar or any of the standard window movement keys.

You can change the buffer size of your EasyWin application by declaring the following global variable in your main source file with the appropriate initializer:

```
POINT _BufferSize = { X, Y };
```

where:

X   is the number of columns you want. Setting X to a value other than 80 is not recommended as the results are unpredictable.

Y   is the number of lines you want. If you need to specify a value for Y greater than 100, use the compact or large memory model. The small and medium memory models have limited local heap space for the buffer.

Autoscrolling

If you click and drag either the vertical or horizontal scroll bar thumb tab, the text in the buffer automatically scrolls up and down or left and right. This is a useful feature when you want to quickly scan large amounts of data in the EasyWin window.

Saving text in an output file

If you want to redirect the output of your program to a file, add the following global variable to your main source file:

```
char *_OutputFileName = "C:\\myoutput.txt";
```

Make _OutputFileName the name of the file in which to store the redirected output.

Note If the output file you specified already exists, it is deleted without warning.

Clipboard support

EasyWin lets you cut, copy, and paste text from an EasyWin application window.

To select text, use the Edit command from the system menu and choose Mark. This puts you in Mark mode. You can use the mouse or the keyboard to select text. You can move the cursor and select text using the standard rules and keystrokes for this feature.

Table 9.1   Actions that implement the Clipboard.

Action	Explanation
Enter	Exits Mark mode. Any marked text is copied to the Clipboard.
Escape	Exits Mark mode. No text is selected.
Right mouse button	Same as Enter.
Edit l Copy	Same as Enter.
Edit l Paste	Pastes text into *stdin*, receiving the contents of the Clipboard as input to your program, merging it with any keyboard input.

Example

If you are writing a program that requests its data from the keyboard via *scanf*, *cin*, or other similar *stdio/conio* functions:

- Write a data file that contains your entire input.

- Load that file into NotePad, select it, and copy it to the Clipboard.

- Run your program, go to the system Edit menu, and choose Paste.

Your program accepts the contents of Clipboard as input.

Note The Paste command is grayed if the Clipboard contains no objects of type CF_TEXT or if your program has terminated.

- The Copy command is grayed if you have not selected a block of text.

10

Math

This chapter describes the floating-point options and explains how to use *complex* and *bcd* numerical types.

Floating-point I/O

Floating-point output requires linking of conversion routines used by *printf, scanf,* and any variants of these functions. To reduce executable size, the floating-point formats are not automatically linked. However, this linkage is done automatically whenever your program uses a mathematical routine or the address is taken of some floating-point number. If neither of these actions occur, the missing floating-point formats can result in a run-time error.

The following program illustrates how to set up your program to properly execute.

```
/* PREPARE TO OUTPUT FLOATING-POINT NUMBERS. */
    #include <stdio.h>

    #pragma extref _floatconvert

    void main() {
        printf("d = %f\n", 1.3);
        }
```

Floating-point options

There are two types of numbers you work with in C: integer (**int, short, long,** and so on) and floating point (**float, double,** and **long double**). Your computer's processor can easily handle integer values, but more time and effort are required to handle floating-point values.

However, the iAPx86 family of processors has a corresponding family of math coprocessors, the 8087, the 80287, and the 80387. We refer to this entire family of math coprocessors as the 80x87, or "the coprocessor."

The 80x87 is a special hardware numeric processor that can be installed in your PC. It executes floating-point instructions very quickly. If you use floating point a lot, you'll probably want a coprocessor. The CPU in your computer interfaces to the 80x87 via special hardware lines.

Note If you have an 80486 or Pentium processor, the numeric coprocessor is probably already built in.

Emulating the 80x87 chip

The default Borland C++ code-generation option is *emulation* (the **–f** command-line compiler option). This option is for programs that might or might not have floating point, and for machines that might or might not have an 80x87 math coprocessor.

With the emulation option, the compiler will generate code as if the 80x87 were present, but will also link in the emulation library (EMU.LIB). When the program runs, it uses the 80x87 if it is present; if no coprocessor is present at run time, it uses special software that emulates the 80x87. This software uses 512 bytes of your stack, so make allowance for it when using the emulation option and set your stack size accordingly.

Using the 80x87 code

If your program is going to run only on machines that have an 80x87 math coprocessor, you can save a small amount in your .EXE file size by omitting the 80x87 autodetection and emulation logic. Choose the 80x87 floating-point code-generation option (the **–f87** command-line compiler option). Borland C++ will then link your programs with FP87.LIB instead of with EMU.LIB.

No floating-point code

If there is no floating-point code in your program, you can save a small amount of link time by choosing None for the floating-point code-generation option (the **–f–** command-line compiler option). Then Borland C++ will not link with EMU.LIB, FP87.LIB, or MATH*x*.LIB.

Fast floating-point option

Borland C++Borland C++ has a fast floating-point option (the **–ff** command-line compiler option). It can be turned off with **–ff–** on the command line. Its purpose is to allow certain optimizations that are technically contrary to correct C semantics. For example,

```
double x;
x = (float)(3.5*x);
```

To execute this correctly, *x* is multiplied by 3.5 to give a **double** that is truncated to **float** precision, then stored as a **double** in *x*. Under the fast floating-point option, the **long**

double product is converted directly to a **double**. Since very few programs depend on the loss of precision in passing to a narrower floating-point type, fast floating point is the default.

The 87 environment variable

If you build your program with 80x87 emulation, which is the default, your program will automatically check to see if an 80x87 is available, and will use it if it is.

There are some situations in which you might want to override this default autodetection behavior. For example, your own run-time system might have an 80x87, but you might need to verify that your program will work as intended on systems without a coprocessor. Or your program might need to run on a PC-compatible system, but that particular system returns incorrect information to the autodetection logic (saying that a nonexistent 80x87 is available, or vice versa).

Borland C++ provides an option for overriding the start-up code's default autodetection logic; this option is the 87 environment variable.

You set the 87 environment variable at the DOS prompt with the SET command, like this:

```
C>, SET 87=N
```

or like this:

```
C> SET 87=Y
```

Don't include spaces on either side of the =. Setting the 87 environment variable to N (for No) tells the start-up code that you do not want to use the 80x87, even though it might be present in the system.

Note Setting the 87 environment variable to *Y* (for Yes) means that the coprocessor is there, and you want the program to use it. *Let the programmer beware:* If you set 87 = *Y* when, in fact, there is no 80x87 available on that system, your system will hang.

If the 87 environment variable has been defined (to any value) but you want to undefine it, enter the following at the DOS prompt:

```
C> SET 87=
```

Press *Enter* immediately after typing the equal sign.

Registers and the 80x87

When you use floating point, make note of these points about registers:

- In 80x87 emulation mode, register wraparound and certain other 80x87 peculiarities are not supported.

- If you are mixing floating point with inline assembly, you might need to take special care when using 80x87 registers. Unless you are sure that enough free registers exist, you might need to save and pop the 80x87 registers before calling functions that use the coprocessor.

Disabling floating-point exceptions

By default, Borland C++ programs abort if a floating-point overflow or divide-by-zero error occurs. You can mask these floating-point exceptions by a call to _control87 in *main*, before any floating-point operations are performed. For example,

```
#include <float.h>
main() {
    _control87(MCW_EM,MCW_EM);
      ⋮
}
```

You can determine whether a floating-point exception occurred after the fact by calling _status87 or _clear87. See the C++ *Library Reference* entries for these functions for details.

Certain math errors can also occur in library functions; for instance, if you try to take the square root of a negative number. The default behavior is to print an error message to the screen, and to return a NAN (an IEEE not-a-number). Use of the NAN is likely to cause a floating-point exception later, which will abort the program if unmasked. If you don't want the message to be printed, insert the following version of _matherr into your program:

```
#include <math.h>
int _matherr(struct _exception *e)
{
    return 1;              /* error has been handled */
}
```

Any other use of _matherr to intercept math errors is not encouraged; it is considered obsolete and might not be supported in future versions of Borland C++.

Using complex types

Complex numbers are numbers of the form $x + yi$, where x and y are real numbers, and i is the square root of -1. Borland C++ has always had a type

```
struct complex
{
    double x, y;
};
```

defined in math.h. This type is convenient for holding complex numbers, because they can be considered a pair of real numbers. However, the limitations of C make arithmetic with complex numbers rather cumbersome. With the addition of C++, complex math is much simpler.

A significant advantage to using the Borland C++ *complex* numerical type is that all of the ANSI C Standard mathematical routines are defined to operate with it. These mathematical routines are not defined for use with the C **struct complex**.

Note See Part III of the C++ *Language Reference* for more information.

To use complex numbers in C++, all you have to do is to include complex.h. In complex.h, all the following have been overloaded to handle complex numbers:

- All of the binary arithmetic operators.
- The input and output operators, >> and <<.
- The ANSI C math functions.

The complex library is invoked only if the argument is of type *complex*. Thus, to get the complex square root of -1, use

```
sqrt(complex(-1))
```

and not

```
sqrt(-1)
```

The following functions are defined by class *complex*:

```
double  arg(complex&);       // angle in the plane
complex conj(complex&);      // complex conjugate
double  imag(complex&);      // imaginary part
double  norm(complex&);      // square of the magnitude
double  real(complex&);      // real part
// Use polar coordinates to create a complex.
complex polar(double mag, double angle = 0);
```

Using bcd types

Borland C++, along with almost every other computer and compiler, does arithmetic on binary numbers (that is, base 2). This can sometimes be confusing to people who are used to decimal (base 10) representations. Many numbers that are exactly representable in base 10, such as 0.01, can only be approximated in base 2.

Note   See Part III of the *C++ Language Reference* for more information.

Binary numbers are preferable for most applications, but in some situations the round-off error involved in converting between base 2 and 10 is undesirable. The most common example of this is a financial or accounting application, where the pennies are supposed to add up. Consider the following program to add up 100 pennies and subtract a dollar:

```
#include <stdio.h>
int i;
float x = 0.0;
for (i = 0; i < 100; ++i)
    x += 0.01;
x -= 1.0;
printf("100*.01 - 1 = %g\n",x);
```

The correct answer is 0.0, but the computed answer is a small number close to 0.0. The computation magnifies the tiny round-off error that occurs when converting 0.01 to base 2. Changing the type of *x* to **double** or **long double** reduces the error, but does not eliminate it.

To solve this problem, Borland C++ offers the C++ type *bcd*, which is declared in bcd.h. With *bcd*, the number 0.01 is represented exactly, and the *bcd* variable *x* provides an exact penny count.

```
#include <bcd.h>
int i;
bcd x = 0.0;
for (i = 0; i < 100; ++i)
    x += 0.01;
x -= 1.0;
cout << "100*.01 - 1 = " << x << "\n";
```

Here are some facts to keep in mind about *bcd*:

- *bcd* does not eliminate all round-off error: A computation like 1.0/3.0 will still have round-off error.

- *bcd* types can be used with ANSI C math functions.

- *bcd* numbers have about 17 decimal digits precision, and a range of about 1×10^{-125} to 1×10^{125}.

Converting bcd numbers

bcd is a defined type distinct from **float**, **double**, or **long double**; decimal arithmetic is performed only when at least one operand is of the type *bcd*.

Note   The *bcd* member function *real* is available for converting a *bcd* number back to one of the usual formats (**float**, **double**, or **long double**), though the conversion is not done automatically. *real* does the necessary conversion to **long double**, which can then be converted to other types using the usual C conversions. For example, a *bcd* can be printed using any of the following four output statements with *cout* and *printf*.

```
/* PRINTING bcd NUMBERS */
/* This must be compiled as a C++ program. */
#include <bcd.h>
#include <iostream.h>
#include <stdio.h>

void main(void) {
    bcd a = 12.1;
    double x = real(a); // This conversion required for printf().

    printf("\na = %g", x);
    printf("\na = %Lg", real(a));
    printf("\na = %g", (double)real(a));
    cout << "\na = " << a; // The preferred method.
    }
```

Note that since *printf* doesn't do argument checking, the format specifier must have the *L* if the **long double** value *real(a)* is passed.

Number of decimal digits

You can specify how many decimal digits after the decimal point are to be carried in a conversion from a binary type to a *bcd*. The number of places is an optional second argument to the constructor *bcd*. For example, to convert $1000.00/7 to a *bcd* variable rounded to the nearest penny, use

```
bcd a = bcd(1000.00/7, 2)
```

where 2 indicates two digits following the decimal point. Thus,

```
1000.00/7               =       142.85714...

bcd(1000.00/7, 2)       =       142.860

bcd(1000.00/7, 1)       =       142.900

bcd(1000.00/7, 0)       =       143.000

bcd(1000.00/7, -1)      =       140.000

bcd(1000.00/7, -2)      =       100.000
```

The number is rounded using banker's rounding (as specified by IEEE), which rounds to the nearest whole number, with ties being rounded to an even digit. For example,

```
bcd(12.335, 2)          =       12.34

bcd(12.345, 2)          =       12.34

bcd(12.355, 2)          =       12.36
```

11

16-bit memory management

This chapter discusses

- What to do when you receive "Out of memory" errors.

- What memory models are: how to choose one, and why you would (or wouldn't)
  want to use a particular memory model.

Running out of memory

Borland C++ does not generate any intermediate data structures to disk when it is
compiling (Borland C++ writes only .OBJ files to disk); instead it uses RAM for
intermediate data structures between passes. Because of this, you might encounter the
message "Out of memory" if there isn't enough memory available for the compiler.

The solution to this problem is to make your functions smaller, or to split up the file that
has large functions.

Memory models

Borland C++ gives you six memory models, each suited for different program and code
sizes. Each memory model uses memory differently. What do you need to know to use
memory models? To answer that question, you need to take a look at the computer
system you're working on. Its central processing unit (CPU) is a microprocessor
belonging to the Intel iAPx86 family; an 80286, 80386, 80486, or Pentium. For now, we'll
just refer to it as an 8086.

Note   See page 269 for a summary of each memory model.

The 8086 registers

The following figure shows some of the registers found in the 8086 processor. There are other registers—because they can't be accessed directly, they aren't shown here.

Figure 11.1   8086 registers

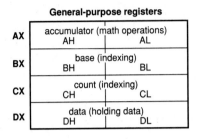

General-purpose registers

AX	accumulator (math operations) AH · AL
BX	base (indexing) BH · BL
CX	count (indexing) CH · CL
DX	data (holding data) DH · DL

Segment address registers

CS	code segment pointer
DS	data segment pointer
SS	stack segment pointer
ES	extra segment pointer

Special-purpose registers

SP	stack pointer
BP	base pointer
SI	source index
DI	destination index

General-purpose registers

The general-purpose registers are the registers used most often to hold and manipulate data. Each has some special functions that only it can do. For example,

- Some math operations can only be done using AX.
- BX can be used as an index register.
- CX is used by LOOP and some string instructions.
- DX is implicitly used for some math operations.

But there are many operations that all these registers can do; in many cases, you can freely exchange one for another.

Segment registers

The segment registers hold the starting address of each of the four segments. As described in the next section, the 16-bit value in a segment register is shifted left 4 bits (multiplied by 16) to get the true 20-bit address of that segment.

Special-purpose registers

The 8086 also has some special-purpose registers:

- The SI and DI registers can do many of the things the general-purpose registers can, plus they are used as index registers. They're also used by Borland C++ for register variables.

- The SP register points to the current top-of-stack and is an offset into the stack segment.

- The BP register is a secondary stack pointer, usually used to index into the stack in order to retrieve arguments or automatic variables.

Borland C++ functions use the base pointer (BP) register as a base address for arguments and automatic variables. Parameters have positive offsets from BP, which vary depending on the memory model. BP points to the saved previous BP value if there is a stack frame. Functions that have no arguments will not use or save BP if the Standard Stack Frame option is *Off*.

Automatic variables are given negative offsets from BP. The offsets depend on how much space has already been assigned to local variables.

The flags register

The 16-bit flags register contains all pertinent information about the state of the 8086 and the results of recent instructions.

Figure 11.2   Flags register of the 80x86 processors

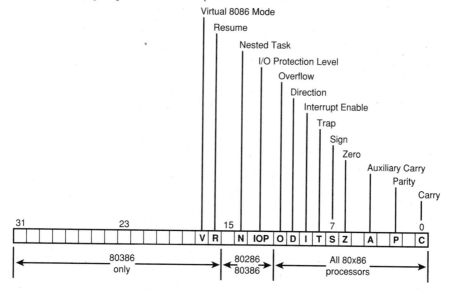

For example, if you wanted to know whether a subtraction produced a zero result, you would check the *zero flag* (the Z bit in the flags register) immediately after the instruction; if it were set, you would know the result was zero. Other flags, such as the *carry* and *overflow flags*, similarly report the results of arithmetic and logical operations.

Other flags control the 8086 operation modes. The *direction flag* controls the direction in which the string instructions move, and the *interrupt flag* controls whether external hardware, such as a keyboard or modem, is allowed to halt the current code temporarily so that urgent needs can be serviced. The *trap flag* is used only by software that debugs other software.

The flags register isn't usually modified or read directly. Instead, the flags register is generally controlled through special assembler instructions (such as **CLD**, **STI**, and **CMC**) and through arithmetic and logical instructions that modify certain flags. Likewise, the contents of certain bits of the flags register affect the operation of instructions such as **JZ**, **RCR**, and **MOVSB**. The flags register is not really used as a storage location, but rather holds the status and control data for the 8086.

Memory segmentation

The Intel 8086 microprocessor has a *segmented memory architecture*. It has a total address space of 1 MB, but is designed to directly address only 64K of memory at a time. A 64K chunk of memory is known as a segment; hence the phrase "segmented memory architecture."

- The 8086 keeps track of four different segments: *code*, *data*, *stack*, and *extra*. The code segment is where the machine instructions are; the data segment is where information is; the stack is, of course, the stack; and the extra segment is also used for extra data.

- The 8086 has four 16-bit segment registers (one for each segment) named CS, DS, SS, and ES; these point to the code, data, stack, and extra segments, respectively.

- A segment can be located anywhere in memory. In DOS real mode it can be located almost anywhere. For reasons that will become clear as you read on, a segment must start on an address that's evenly divisible by 16 (in decimal).

Address calculation

Note   This whole section is applicable only to real mode under DOS. You can safely ignore it for Windows development.

A complete address on the 8086 is composed of two 16-bit values: the segment address and the offset. Suppose the data segment address—the value in the DS register—is 2F84 (base 16), and you want to calculate the actual address of some data that has an offset of 0532 (base 16) from the start of the data segment: how is that done?

Address calculation is done as follows: Shift the value of the segment register 4 bits to the left (equivalent to one hex digit), then add in the offset.

The resulting 20-bit value is the actual address of the data, as illustrated here:

```
DS register (shifted):  0010 1111 1000 0100 0000  =  2F840
Offset:                      0000 0101 0011 0010  =  00532
```

```
      _ _ _ _ _ _ _ _ _ _ _        _ _ _ _ _ _ _ _ _ _ _ _ _ _
      address:                     0010 1111 1101 0111 0010  =  2FD72
```

Note   A chunk of 16 bytes is known as a *paragraph*, so you could say that a segment always starts on a paragraph boundary.

The starting address of a segment is always a 20-bit number, but a segment register only holds 16 bits—so the bottom 4 bits are always assumed to be all zeros. This means segments can only start every 16 bytes through memory, at an address where the last 4 bits (or last hex digit) are zero. So, if the DS register is holding a value of 2F84, then the data segment actually starts at address 2F840.

The standard notation for an address takes the form *segment:offset*; for example, the previous address would be written as 2F84:0532. Note that since offsets can overlap, a given segment:offset pair is not unique; the following addresses all refer to the same memory location:

```
0000:0123
0002:0103
0008:00A3
0010:0023
0012:0003
```

Segments can overlap (but don't have to). For example, all four segments could start at the same address, which means that your entire program would take up no more than 64K—but that's all the space you'd have for your code, your data, and your stack.

Pointers

Although you can declare a pointer or function to be a specific type regardless of the model used, by default the type of memory model you choose determines the default type of pointers used for code and data. There are four types of pointers: *near* (16 bits), *far* (32 bits), *huge* (also 32 bits), and *segment* (16 bits).

Near pointers

A near pointer (16-bits) relies on one of the segment registers to finish calculating its address; for example, a pointer to a function would add its 16-bit value to the left-shifted contents of the code segment (CS) register. In a similar fashion, a near data pointer contains an offset to the data segment (DS) register. Near pointers are easy to manipulate, since any arithmetic (such as addition) can be done without worrying about the segment.

Far pointers

A far pointer (32-bits) contains not only the offset within the segment, but also the segment address (as another 16-bit value), which is then left-shifted and added to the offset. By using far pointers, you can have multiple code segments; this, in turn, allows you to have programs larger than 64K. You can also address more than 64K of data.

When you use far pointers for data, you need to be aware of some potential problems in pointer manipulation. As explained in the section on address calculation, you can have many different segment:offset pairs refer to the same address. For example, the far pointers 0000:0120, 0010:0020, and 0012:0000 all resolve to the same 20-bit address. However, if you had three different far pointer variables—*a*, *b*, and *c*—containing those three values respectively, then all the following expressions would be *false*:

```
if (a == b) · · ·
if (b == c) · · ·
if (a == c) · · ·
```

A related problem occurs when you want to compare far pointers using the >, >=, <, and <= operators. In those cases, only the offset (as an **unsigned**) is used for comparison purposes; given that *a*, *b*, and *c* still have the values previously listed, the following expressions would all be *true*:

```
if (a > b) · · ·
if (b > c) · · ·
if (a > c) · · ·
```

The equals (==) and not-equal (!=) operators use the 32-bit value as an **unsigned long** (not as the full memory address). The comparison operators (<=, >=, <, and >) use just the offset.

The == and != operators need all 32 bits, so the computer can compare to the NULL pointer (0000:0000). If you used only the offset value for equality checking, any pointer with 0000 offset would be equal to the NULL pointer, which is not what you want.

Note   If you add values to a far pointer, only the offset is changed. If you add enough to cause the offset to exceed FFFF (its maximum possible value), the pointer just wraps around back to the beginning of the segment. For example, if you add 1 to 5031:FFFF, the result would be 5031:0000 (not 6031:0000). Likewise, if you subtract 1 from 5031:0000, you would get 5031:FFFF (not 5030:000F).

If you want to do pointer comparisons, it's safest to use either near pointers—which all use the same segment address—or huge pointers, described next.

Huge pointers

Huge pointers are also 32 bits long. Like far pointers, they contain both a segment address and an offset. Unlike far pointers, they are *normalized* to avoid the problems associated with far pointers.

A normalized pointer is a 32-bit pointer that has as much of its value in the segment address as possible. Since a segment can start every 16 bytes (10 in base 16), this means that the offset will only have a value from 0 to 15 (0 to F in base 16).

To normalize a pointer, convert it to its 20-bit address, then use the right 4 bits for your offset and the left 16 bits for your segment address. For example, given the pointer 2F84:0532, you would convert that to the absolute address 2FD72, which you would then normalize to 2FD7:0002. Here are a few more pointers with their normalized equivalents:

```
0000:0123    0012:0003
0040:0056    0045:0006
500D:9407    594D:0007
7418:D03F    811B:000F
```

There are three reasons why it is important to always keep huge pointers normalized:

1 For any given memory address there is only one possible huge address (segment:offset) pair. That means that the == and != operators return correct answers for any huge pointers.

2 In addition, the >, >=, <, and <= operators are all used on the full 32-bit value for huge pointers. Normalization guarantees that the results of these comparisons will also be correct.

3 Finally, because of normalization, the offset in a huge pointer automatically wraps around every 16 values, but—unlike far pointers—the segment is adjusted as well. For example, if you were to increment 811B:000F, the result would be 811C:0000; likewise, if you decrement 811C:0000, you get 811B:000F. It is this aspect of huge pointers that allows you to manipulate data structures greater than 64K in size. This ensures that, for example, if you have a huge array of **struct**s that's larger than 64K, indexing into the array and selecting a **struct** field will always work with structs of any size.

There is a price for using huge pointers: additional overhead. Huge pointer arithmetic is done with calls to special subroutines. Because of this, huge pointer arithmetic is significantly slower than that of far or near pointers.

The six memory models

Borland C++ gives you six memory models for 16-bit DOS programs: tiny, small, medium, compact, large, and huge. Your program requirements determine which one you pick. Here's a brief summary of each:

- **Tiny.** As you might guess, this is the smallest of the memory models. All four segment registers (CS, DS, SS, ES) are set to the same address, so you have a total of 64K for all of your code, data, and stack. Near pointers are always used. Tiny model programs can be converted to .COM format by linking with the /t option. Use this model when memory is at an absolute premium.

- **Small.** The code and data segments are different and don't overlap, so you have 64K of code and 64K of data and stack. Near pointers are always used. This is a good size for average applications.

- **Medium.** Far pointers are used for code, but not for data. As a result, data plus stack are limited to 64K, but code can occupy up to 1 MB. This model is best for large programs without much data in memory.

- **Compact.** The inverse of medium: Far pointers are used for data, but not for code. Code is then limited to 64K, while data has a 1 MB range. This model is best if code is small but needs to address a lot of data.

- **Large.** Far pointers are used for both code and data, giving both a 1 MB range. Large and huge are needed only for very large applications.

- **Huge.** Far pointers are used for both code and data. Borland C++ normally limits the size of all static data to 64K; the huge memory model sets aside that limit, allowing data to occupy more than 64K.

Figures 111.3 through 111.8 show how memory in the 8086 is apportioned for the Borland C++ memory models. To select these memory models, you can either use menu selections from the IDE or you can type options invoking the command-line compiler version of Borland C++Borland C++.

Figure 11.3 Tiny model memory segmentation

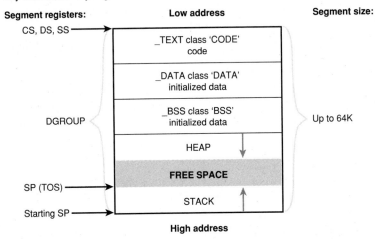

Figure 11.4 Small model memory segmentation

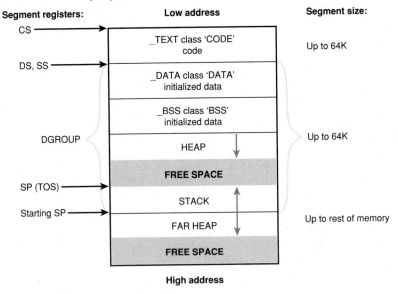

Figure 11.5   Medium model memory segmentation

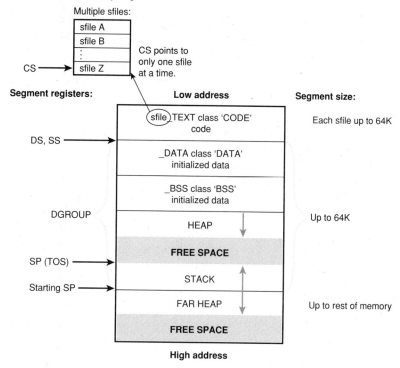

Figure 11.6   Compact model memory segmentation

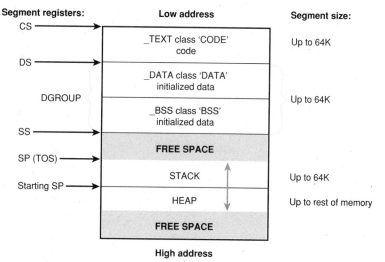

Figure 11.7 Large model memory segmentation

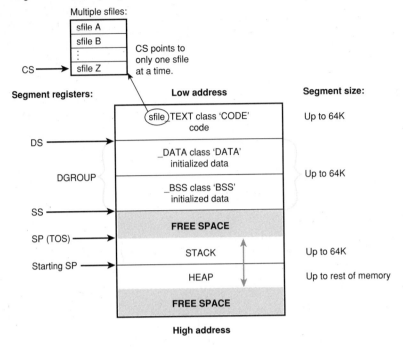

Figure 11.8 Huge model memory segmentation

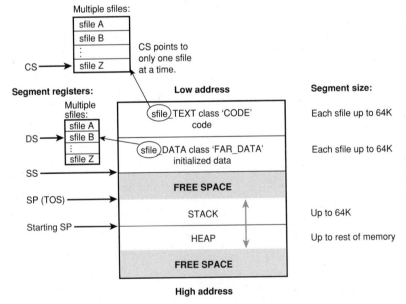

Table 1.1 summarizes the different models and how they compare to one another. The models are often grouped according to whether their code or data models are *small* (64K) or *large* (16 MB); these groups correspond to the rows and columns in Table 1.1.

Table 11.1   Comparison of models

	Code size	
Data size	**64K**	**16MB**
64K	Tiny (data, code overlap; total size = 64K)	
	Small (no overlap; total size = 128K)	Medium (small data, large code)
16 MB	Compact (large data, small code)	Large (large data, code)
		Huge (same as large but static data > 64K)

The models tiny, small, and compact are small code models because, by default, code pointers are near; likewise, compact, large, and huge are large data models because, by default, data pointers are far.

When you compile a module (a given source file with some number of routines in it), the resulting code for that module cannot be greater than 64K, since it must all fit inside of one code segment. This is true even if you're using one of the larger code models (medium, large, or huge). If your module is too big to fit into one (64K) code segment, you must break it up into different source code files, compile each file separately, then link them together. Similarly, even though the huge model permits static data to total more than 64K, it still must be less than 64K in *each* module.

Mixed-model programming: Addressing modifiers

Borland C++ introduces eight new keywords not found in standard ANSI C. These keywords are _ _**near**, _ _**far**, _ _**huge**, _ _**cs**, _ _**ds**, _ _**es**, _ _**ss**, and _ _**seg**. These keywords can be used as modifiers to pointers (and in some cases, to functions), with certain limitations and warnings.

In Borland C++, you can modify the declarations of pointers, objects, and functions with the keywords _ _**near**, _ _**far**, or _ _**huge**. The _ _**near**, _ _**far**, and _ _**huge** data pointers are described earlier in this chapter. You can declare far objects using the _ _**far** keyword. _ _**near** functions are invoked with near calls and exit with near returns. Similarly, _ _**far** functions are called _ _**far** and return far values. _ _**huge** functions are like _ _**far** functions, except that _ _**huge** functions set DS to a new value, and _ _**far** functions do not.

There are also four special _ _**near** data pointers: _ _**cs**, _ _**ds**, _ _**es**, and _ _**ss**. These are 16-bit pointers that are specifically associated with the corresponding segment register. For example, if you were to declare a pointer to be

```
char _ss *p;
```

then *p* would contain a 16-bit offset into the stack segment.

Functions and pointers within a given program default to near or far, depending on the memory model you select. If the function or pointer is near, it is automatically associated with either the CS or DS register.

The next table shows how this works. Note that the size of the pointer corresponds to whether it is working within a 64K memory limit (near, within a segment) or inside the general 1 MB memory space (far, has its own segment address).

Table 11.2   Defaults for functions and pointers

Memory model	Function pointers	Data pointers
Tiny	near, _cs	near, _ds
Small	near, _cs	near, _ds
Medium	far	near, _ds
Compact	near, _cs	far
Large	far	far
Huge	far	far

Segment pointers

Use _ _**seg** in segment pointer type declarators. The resulting pointers are 16-bit segment pointers. The syntax for _ _**seg** is:

datatype _seg **identifier*;

For example,

```
int _seg *name;
```

Any indirection through *identifier* has an assumed offset of 0. In arithmetic involving segment pointers the following rules hold true:

1 You can't use the ++, – –, +=, or –= operators with segment pointers.

2 You cannot subtract one segment pointer from another.

3 When adding a near pointer to a segment pointer, the result is a far pointer that is formed by using the segment from the segment pointer and the offset from the near pointer. Therefore, the two pointers must either point to the same type, or one must be a pointer to void. There is no multiplication of the offset regardless of the type pointed to.

4 When a segment pointer is used in an indirection expression, it is also implicitly converted to a far pointer.

5 When adding or subtracting an integer operand to or from a segment pointer, the result is a far pointer, with the segment taken from the segment pointer and the offset found by multiplying the size of the object pointed to by the integer operand. The arithmetic is performed as if the integer were added to or subtracted from the far pointer.

6 Segment pointers can be assigned, initialized, passed into and out of functions, compared and so forth. (Segment pointers are compared as if their values were

unsigned integers.) In other words, other than the above restrictions, they are treated exactly like any other pointer.

Declaring far objects

You can declare far objects in Borland C++. For example,

```
int far x = 5;
int far z;
extern int far y = 4;
static long j;
```

The command-line compiler options **–zE**, **–zF**, and **–zH** (which can also be set using **#pragma option**) affect the far segment name, class, and group, respectively. When you use **#pragma option**, you can make them apply to any ensuing far object declarations. Thus you could use the following sequence to create a far object in a specific segment:

```
#pragma option -zEmysegment -zHmygroup -zFmyclass
int far x;
#pragma option -zE* -zH* -zF*
```

This will put *x* in segment MYSEGMENT 'MYCLASS' in the group 'MYGROUP', then reset all of the far object items to the default values. Note that by using these options, several far objects can be forced into a single segment:

```
#pragma option -zEcombined -zFmyclass
int far x;
double far y;
#pragma option -zE* -zF*
```

Both *x* and *y* will appear in the segment COMBINED 'MYCLASS' with no group.

Declaring functions to be near or far

On occasion, you'll want (or need) to override the default function type of your memory model.

For example, suppose you're using the large memory model, but you have a recursive (self-calling) function in your program, like this:

```
double power(double x,int exp) {
   if (exp <= 0)
      return(1);
   else
      return(x * power(x, exp-1));
   }
```

Every time *power* calls itself, it has to do a far call, which uses more stack space and clock cycles. By declaring power as _ _**near**, you eliminate some of the overhead by forcing all calls to that function to be near:

```
double _ _near power(double x,int exp)
```

This guarantees that *power* is callable only within the code segment in which it was compiled, and that all calls to it are near calls.

This means that if you're using a large code model (medium, large, or huge), you can only call *power* from within the module where it is defined. Other modules have their own code segment and thus cannot call _ _**near** functions in different modules. Furthermore, a near function must be either defined or declared before the first time it is used, or the compiler won't know it needs to generate a near call.

Conversely, declaring a function to be far means that a far return is generated. In the small code models, the far function must be declared or defined before its first use to ensure it is invoked with a far call.

Look back at the *power* example at the beginning of this section. It is wise to also declare *power* as static, since it should be called only from within the current module. That way, being a static, its name will not be available to any functions outside the module.

Declaring pointers to be near, far, or huge

You've seen why you might want to declare functions to be of a different model than the rest of the program. For the same reasons given in the preceding section, you might want to modify pointer declarations: either to avoid unnecessary overhead (declaring _ _**near** when the default would be _ _**far**) or to reference something outside of the default segment (declaring _ _**far** or _ _**huge** when the default would be _ _**near**).

There are, of course, potential pitfalls in declaring functions and pointers to be of nondefault types. For example, say you have the following small model program:

```
void myputs(s) {
    char *s;
    int  i;
    for (i = 0; s[i] != 0; i++) putc(s[i]);
    }
main() {
    char  near *mystr;
mystr = "Hello, world\n"
    myputs(mystr);
    }
```

This program works fine. In fact, the _ _**near** declaration on *mystr* is redundant, since all pointers, both code and data, will be near.

But what if you recompile this program using the compact (or large or huge) memory model? The pointer *mystr* in *main* is still near (it's still a 16-bit pointer). However, the pointer *s* in *myputs* is now far, because that's the default. This means that *myputs* will pull two words out of the stack in an effort to create a far pointer, and the address it ends up with will certainly not be that of *mystr*.

How do you avoid this problem? If you're going to explicitly declare pointers to be of type _ _**far** or _ _**near**, be sure to use function prototypes for any functions that might use them. The solution is to define *myputs* in ANSI C style, like this:

```
void myputs(char *s) {
    /* body of myputs */
    }
```

Now when Borland C++ compiles your program, it knows that *myputs* expects a pointer to **char**; and since you're compiling under the large model, it knows that the pointer must be _ _**far**. Because of that, Borland C++ will push the data segment (DS) register onto the stack along with the 16-bit value of *mystr*, forming a far pointer.

How about the reverse case: arguments to *myputs* declared as _ _**far** and compiled with a small data model? Again, without the function prototype, you will have problems, because *main* will push both the offset and the segment address onto the stack, but *myputs* will expect only the offset. With the prototype-style function definitions, though, *main* will only push the offset onto the stack.

Pointing to a given segment:offset address

You can make a far pointer point to a given memory location (a specific segment:offset address). You can do this with the macro *MK_FP*, which takes a segment and an offset and returns a far pointer. For example,

```
MK_FP(segment_value, offset_value)
```

Given a _ _**far** pointer, *fp*, you can get the segment component with *FP_SEG(fp)* and the offset component with *FP_OFF(fp)*. For more information about these three Borland C++ library routines, refer to the C++ *Library Reference*.

Using library files

Borland C++ offers a version of the standard library routines for each of the six memory models. Borland C++ is smart enough to link in the appropriate libraries in the proper order, depending on which model you've selected. However, if you're using the Borland C++ linker, TLINK, directly (as a standalone linker), you need to specify which libraries to use. See the online Help for how to do this.

Linking mixed modules

Suppose you compiled one module using the small memory model and another module using the large model, then wanted to link them together. This would present some problems, but they can be solved.

The files would link together fine, but the problems you would encounter would be similar to those described in the earlier section, "Declaring functions to be near or far." If a function in the small module called a function in the large module, it would do so with a near call, which would probably be disastrous. Furthermore, you could face the same problems with pointers as described in the earlier section, "Declaring pointers to be near, far, or huge," since a function in the small module would expect to pass and receive _ _**near** pointers, and a function in the large module would expect _ _**far** pointers.

The solution, again, is to use function prototypes. Suppose that you put *myputs* into its own module and compile it with the large memory model. Then create a header file called myputs.h (or some other name with a .h extension), which would have the following function prototype in it:

```
void far myputs(char far *s);
```

Now, put *main* into its own module (called MYMAIN.C), and set things up like this:

```
#include <stdio.h>
#include "myputs.h"

main() {
    char  near *mystr;

    mystr = "Hello, world\n";
    myputs(mystr);
    }
```

When you compile this program, Borland C++ reads in the function prototype from myputs.h and sees that it is a _ _**far** function that expects a _ _**far** pointer. Therefore, it generates the proper calling code, even if it's compiled using the small memory model.

What if, on top of all this, you need to link in library routines? Your best bet is to use one of the large model libraries and declare everything to be _ _**far**. To do this, make a copy of each header file you would normally include (such as stdio.h), and rename the copy to something appropriate (such as fstdio.h).

Then edit each function prototype in the copy so that it is explicitly _ _**far**, like this:

```
int far cdecl printf(char far * format, ...);
```

That way, not only will _ _**far** calls be made to the routines, but the pointers passed will also be _ _**far** pointers. Modify your program so that it includes the new header file:

```
#include <fstdio.h>

void main() {
    char  near *mystr;
    mystr = "Hello, world\n";
    printf(mystr);
}
```

Compile your program with the command-line compiler BCC and then link it with TLINK, specifying a large model library, such as CL.LIB. Mixing models is tricky, but it can be done; just be prepared for some difficult bugs if you do things wrong.

12

ANSI implementation-specific standards

Certain aspects of the ANSI C standard are not defined exactly by ANSI. Instead, each implementor of a C compiler is free to define these aspects individually. This topic describes how Borland has chosen to define these implementation-specific standards. The section numbers refer to the February 1990 ANSI Standard. Remember that there are differences between C and C++; this topic provides you with information on the C language implementation.

2.1.1.3 How to identify a diagnostic.

When the compiler runs with the correct combination of options, any messages it issues beginning with the words *Fatal, Error,* or *Warning* are diagnostics in the sense that ANSI specifies. The options needed to ensure this interpretation are as follows:

Table 12.1   Identifying diagnostics in Borland C++

Option	Action
–A	Enable only ANSI keywords.
–C–	No nested comments allowed.
–i32	At least 32 significant characters in identifiers.
–p–	Use C calling conventions.
–w–	Turn off all warnings except the following.
–wbei	Turn on warning about inappropriate initializers.
–wbig	Turn on warning about constants being too large.
–wcpt	Turn on warning about nonportable pointer comparisons.
–wdcl	Turn on warning about declarations without type or storage class.
–wdup	Turn on warning about duplicate nonidentical macro definitions.
–wext	Turn on warning about variables declared both as external and as static.
–wfdt	Turn on warning about function definitions using a typedef.
–wrpt	Turn on warning about nonportable pointer conversion.

Table 12.1   Identifying diagnostics in Borland C++ (continued)

Option	Action
–wstu	Turn on warning about undefined structures.
–wsus	Turn on warning about suspicious pointer conversion.
–wucp	Turn on warning about mixing pointers to signed and unsigned char.
–wvrt	Turn on warning about void functions returning a value.

You cannot use the following options:

–ms!	SS must be the same as DS for small data models.
–mm!	SS must be the same as DS for small data models.
–mt!	SS must be the same as DS for small data models.
–zG*xx*	The BSS group name cannot be changed.
–zS*xx*	The data group name cannot be changed.

Other options not specifically mentioned here can be set to whatever you want.

2.1.2.2.1   The semantics of the arguments to *main*.

The value of *argv*[0] is a pointer to a null byte when the program is run on DOS versions prior to version 3.0. For DOS version 3.0 or later, *argv*[0] points to the program name.

The remaining *argv* strings point to each component of the DOS command-line arguments. Whitespace separating arguments is removed, and each sequence of contiguous non-whitespace characters is treated as a single argument. Quoted strings are handled correctly (that is, as one string containing spaces).

2.1.2.3   What constitutes an interactive device.

An interactive device is any device that looks like the console.

2.2.1   The collation sequence of the execution character set.

The collation sequence for the execution character set uses the signed value of the character in ASCII.

2.2.1   Members of the source and execution character sets.

The source and execution character sets are the extended ASCII set supported by the IBM PC. Any character other than Ctrl+Z can appear in string literals, character constants, or comments.

2.2.1.2   Multibyte characters.

Multibyte characters are supported in Borland C++.

2.2.2   The direction of printing.

Printing is from left-to-right, the normal direction for the PC.

2.2.4.2   The number of bits in a character in the execution character set.

There are 8 bits per character in the execution character set.

3.1.2 The number of significant initial characters in identifiers.

The first 32 characters are significant, although you can use a command-line option (–i) to change that number. Both internal and external identifiers use the same number of significant characters. (The number of significant characters in C++ identifiers is unlimited.)

3.1.2 Whether case distinctions are significant in external identifiers.

The compiler normally forces the linker to distinguish between uppercase and lowercase. You can use a command-line option (–l–c) to suppress the distinction.

3.1.2.5 The representations and sets of values of the various types of integers.

Table 12.2   Identifying diagnostics in C++

Type	16-bit minimum value	16-bit maximum value	32-bit minimum value	32-bit maximum value
signed char	–128	127	–128	127
unsigned char	0	255	0	255
signed short	–32,768	32,767	–32,768	32,767
unsigned short	0	65,535	0	65,535
signed int	–32,768	32,767	–2,147,483,648	–2,147,483,647
unsigned int	0	65,535	0	4,294,967,295
signed long	–2,147,483,648	2,147,483,647	–2,147,483,648	2,147,483,647
unsigned long	0	4,294,967,295	0	4,294,967,295

All **char** types use one 8-bit byte for storage.

All **short** and **int** types use 2 bytes (in 16-bit programs).

All **short** and **int** types use 4 bytes (in 32-bit programs).

All **long** types use 4 bytes.

If alignment is requested (–a), all non**char** integer type objects will be aligned to even byte boundaries. If the requested alignment is –a4, the result is 4-byte alignment. Character types are never aligned.

3.1.2.5 The representations and sets of values of the various types of floating-point numbers.

The IEEE floating-point formats as used by the Intel 8087 are used for all Borland C++ floating-point types. The **float** type uses 32-bit IEEE real format. The **double** type uses 64-bit IEEE real format. The **long double** type uses 80-bit IEEE extended real format.

3.1.3.4 The mapping between source and execution character sets.

Any characters in string literals or character constants remain unchanged in the executing program. The source and execution character sets are the same.

3.1.3.4 The value of an integer character constant that contains a character or escape sequence not represented in the basic execution character set or the extended character set for a wide character constant.

Wide characters are supported.

3.1.3.4 **The current locale used to convert multibyte characters into corresponding wide characters for a wide character constant.**

Wide character constants are recognized.

3.1.3.4 **The value of an integer constant that contains more than one character, or a wide character constant that contains more than one multibyte character.**

Character constants can contain one or two characters. If two characters are included, the first character occupies the low-order byte of the constant, and the second character occupies the high-order byte.

3.2.1.2 **The result of converting an integer to a shorter signed integer, or the result of converting an unsigned integer to a signed integer of equal length, if the value cannot be represented.**

These conversions are performed by simply truncating the high-order bits. Signed integers are stored as two's complement values, so the resulting number is interpreted as such a value. If the high-order bit of the smaller integer is nonzero, the value is interpreted as a negative value; otherwise, it is positive.

3.2.1.3 **The direction of truncation when an integral number is converted to a floating-point number that cannot exactly represent the original value.**

The integer value is rounded to the nearest representable value. Thus, for example, the **long** value $(2^{31} -1)$ is converted to the **float** value 2^{31}. Ties are broken according to the rules of IEEE standard arithmetic.

3.2.1.4 **The direction of truncation or rounding when a floating-point number is converted to a narrower floating-point number.**

The value is rounded to the nearest representable value. Ties are broken according to the rules of IEEE standard arithmetic.

3.3 **The results of bitwise operations on signed integers.**

The bitwise operators apply to signed integers as if they were their corresponding unsigned types. The sign bit is treated as a normal data bit. The result is then interpreted as a normal two's complement signed integer.

3.3.2.3 **What happens when a member of a union object is accessed using a member of a different type.**

The access is allowed and the different type member will access the bits stored there. You'll need a detailed understanding of the bit encodings of floating-point values to understand how to access a floating-type member using a different member. If the member stored is shorter than the member used to access the value, the excess bits have the value they had before the short member was stored.

3.3.3.4 **The type of integer required to hold the maximum size of an array.**

For a normal array, the type is **unsigned int**, and for huge arrays the type is **signed long**.

3.3.4 **The result of casting a pointer to an integer or vice versa.**

When converting between integers and pointers of the same size, no bits are changed. When converting from a longer type to a shorter type, the high-order bits are truncated. When converting from a shorter integer type to a longer pointer type, the integer is first widened to an integer type the same size as the pointer type.

Thus signed integers will sign-extend to fill the new bytes. Similarly, smaller pointer types being converted to larger integer types will first be widened to a pointer type as wide as the integer type.

3.3.5   The sign of the remainder on integer division.

The sign of the remainder is negative when only one of the operands is negative. If neither or both operands are negative, the remainder is positive.

3.3.6   The type of integer required to hold the difference between two pointers to elements of the same array, ptrdiff_t.

The type is signed **int** when the pointers are **near** (or the program is a 32-bit application), or **signed long** when the pointers are **far** or **huge**. The type of ptrdiff_t depends on the memory model in use. In small data models, the type is **int**. In large data models, the type is **long**.

3.3.7   The result of a right shift of a negative signed integral type.

A negative signed value is sign extended when right shifted.

3.5.1   The extent to which objects can actually be placed in registers by using the *register* storage-class specifier.

Objects declared with any two-byte integer or pointer types can be placed in registers. The compiler places any small auto objects into registers, but objects explicitly declared as register take precedence. At least two and as many as six registers are available. The number of registers actually used depends on what registers are needed for temporary values in the function.

3.5.2.1   Whether a plain int bit field is treated as a signed int or as an unsigned int bit field.

Plain **int** bit fields are treated as **signed int** bit fields.

3.5.2.1   The order of allocation of bit fields within an int.

Bit fields are allocated from the low-order bit position to the high-order.

3.5.2.1   The padding and alignment of members of structures.

By default, no padding is used in structures. If you use the word alignment option (–**a**), structures are padded to even size, and any members that do not have character or character array type are aligned to an even multiple offset.

3.5.2.1   Whether a bit field can straddle a storage-unit boundary.

When alignment (–**a**) is not requested, bit fields can straddle word boundaries, but are never stored in more than two adjacent bytes.

3.5.2.2   The integer type chosen to represent the values of an enumeration type.

Store all enumerators as full **int**s. Store the enumerations in a **long** or **unsigned long** if the values don't fit into an **int**. This is the default behavior as specified by –**b** compiler option.

The **–b–** behavior specifies that enumerations should be stored in the smallest integer type that can represent the values. This includes all integral types, for example, **signed char, unsigned char, signed short, unsigned short, signed int, unsigned int, signed long,** and **unsigned long**.

For C++ compliance, **–b–** must be specified because it is not correct to store all enumerations as **int**s for C++.

3.5.3 What constitutes an access to an object that has volatile-qualified type.

Any reference to a volatile object will access the object. Whether accessing adjacent memory locations will also access an object depends on how the memory is constructed in the hardware. For special device memory, such as video display memory, it depends on how the device is constructed. For normal PC memory, volatile objects are used only for memory that might be accessed by asynchronous interrupts, so accessing adjacent objects has no effect.

3.5.4 The maximum number of declarators that can modify an arithmetic, structure, or union type.

There is no specific limit on the number of declarators. The number of declarators allowed is fairly large, but when nested deeply within a set of blocks in a function, the number of declarators will be reduced. The number allowed at file level is at least 50.

3.6.4.2 The maximum number of case values in a switch statement.

There is no specific limit on the number of cases in a switch. As long as there is enough memory to hold the case information, the compiler will accept them.

3.8.1 Whether the value of a single-character character constant in a constant expression that controls conditional inclusion matches the value of the same character constant in the execution character set. Whether such a character constant can have a negative value.

All character constants, even constants in conditional directives, use the same character set (execution). Single-character character constants will be negative if the character type is signed (default and **–K** not requested).

3.8.2 The method for locating includable source files.

For include file names given with angle brackets, if include directories are given in the command line, then the file is searched for in each of the include directories. Include directories are searched in this order: first, using directories specified on the command line, then using directories specified in TURBOC.CFG or BCC32.CFG. If no include directories are specified, then only the current directory is searched.

3.8.2 The support for quoted names for includable source files.

For quoted file names, the file is first searched for in the current directory. If not found, searches for the file as if it were in angle brackets.

3.8.2 The mapping of source file name character sequences.

Backslashes in include file names are treated as distinct characters, not as escape characters. Case differences are ignored for letters.

3.8.8 The definitions for _ _DATE_ _ and _ _TIME_ _ when they are unavailable.

The date and time are always available and will use the operating system date and time.

4.1.1 The decimal point character.

The decimal point character is a period (.).

4.1.5 The type of the sizeof operator, *size_t*.

The type *size_t* is **unsigned**.

4.1.5 The null pointer constant to which the macro NULL expands.

For a 16-bit application, an integer or a long zero, depending on the memory model.

For 32-bit applications, NULL expands to an **int** zero or a **long** zero. Both are 32-bit **signed** numbers.

4.2 The diagnostic printed by and the termination behavior of the assert function.

The diagnostic message printed is "Assertion failed: *expression*, file *filename*, line *nn*," where *expression* is the asserted expression that failed, *filename* is the source file name, and *nn* is the line number where the assertion took place.

Abort is called immediately after the assertion message is displayed.

4.3 The implementation-defined aspects of character testing and case-mapping functions.

None, other than what is mentioned in 4.3.1.

4.3.1 The sets of characters tested for by the *isalnum, isalpha, iscntrl, islower, isprint,* and *isupper* functions.

First 128 ASCII characters for the default C locale. Otherwise, all 256 characters.

4.5.1 The values returned by the mathematics functions on domain errors.

An IEEE NAN (not a number).

4.5.1 Whether the mathematics functions set the integer expression *errno* to the value of the macro ERANGE on underflow range errors.

No, only for the other errors—domain, singularity, overflow, and total loss of precision.

4.5.6.4 Whether a domain error occurs or zero is returned when the *fmod* function has a second argument of zero.

No; fmod(x,0) returns 0.

4.7.1.1 The set of signals for the *signal* function.

SIGABRT, SIGFPE, SIGILL, SIGINT, SIGSEGV, and SIGTERM.

4.7.1.1 The semantics for each signal recognized by the *signal* function.

See the description of *signal*.

4.7.1.1 The default handling and the handling at program startup for each signal recognized by the *signal* function.

See the description of *signal*.

4.7.1.1   If the equivalent of *signal(sig, SIG_DFL)* is not executed prior to the call of a signal handler, the blocking of the signal that is performed.

The equivalent of *signal(sig, SIG_DFL)* is always executed.

4.7.1.1   Whether the default handling is reset if the SIGILL signal is received by a handler specified to the *signal* function.

No, it is not.

4.9.2   Whether the last line of a text stream requires a terminating newline character.

No, none is required.

4.9.2   Whether space characters that are written out to a text stream immediately before a newline character appear when read in.

Yes, they do.

4.9.2   The number of null characters that may be appended to data written to a binary stream.

None.

4.9.3   Whether the file position indicator of an append mode stream is initially positioned at the beginning or end of the file.

The file position indicator of an append-mode stream is initially placed at the beginning of the file. It is reset to the end of the file before each write.

4.9.3   Whether a write on a text stream causes the associated file to be truncated beyond that point.

A write of 0 bytes might or might not truncate the file, depending on how the file is buffered. It is safest to classify a zero-length write as having indeterminate behavior.

4.9.3   The characteristics of file buffering.

Files can be fully buffered, line buffered, or unbuffered. If a file is buffered, a default buffer of 512 bytes is created upon opening the file.

4.9.3   Whether a zero-length file actually exists.

Yes, it does.

4.9.3   Whether the same file can be open multiple times.

Yes, it can.

4.9.4.1   The effect of the *remove* function on an open file.

No special checking for an already open file is performed; the responsibility is left up to the programmer.

4.9.4.2   The effect if a file with the new name exists prior to a call to *rename*.

Rename returns a –1 and *errno* is set to EEXIST.

4.9.6.1 The output for %p conversion in *fprintf*.

In near data models, four hex digits (XXXX). In far data models, four hex digits, colon, four hex digits (XXXX:XXXX). (For 16-bit programs.)

Eight hex digits (XXXXXXXX). (For 32-bit programs.)

4.9.6.2 The input for %p conversion in *fscanf*.

See 4.9.6.1.

4.9.6.2 The interpretation of a –(hyphen) character that is neither the first nor the last character in the scanlist for a %[conversion in *fscanf*.

See the description of *scanf*.

4.9.9.1 The value the macro ERRNO is set to by the *fgetpos* or *ftell* function on failure.

EBADF   Bad file number.

4.9.10.4 The messages generated by perror.

Table 12.3   Messages generated in both Win16 and Win32

Arg list too big	Math argument
Attempted to remove current directory	Memory arena trashed
Bad address	Name too long
Bad file number	No child processes
Block device required	No more files
Broken pipe	No space left on device
Cross-device link	No such device
Error 0	No such device or address
Exec format error	No such file or directory
Executable file in use	No such process
File already exists	Not a directory
File too large	Not enough memory
Illegal seek	Not same device
Inappropriate I/O control operation	Operation not permitted
Input/output error	Path not found
Interrupted function call	Permission denied
Invalid access code	Possible deadlock
Invalid argument	Read-only file system
Invalid data	Resource busy
Invalid environment	Resource temporarily unavailable
Invalid format	Result too large
Invalid function number	Too many links
Invalid memory block address	Too many open files
Is a directory	

Table 12.4   Messages generated only in Win32

Bad address	No child processes
Block device required	No space left on device
Broken pipe	No such device or address
Executable file in use	No such process
File too large	Not a directory
Illegal seek	Operation not permitted
Inappropriate I/O control operation	Possible deadlock
Input/output error	Read-only file system
Interrupted function call	Resource busy
Is a directory	Resource temporarily unavailable
Name too long	Too many links

4.10.3   The behavior of *calloc, malloc,* or *realloc* if the size requested is zero.

calloc and *malloc* will ignore the request and return 0. *realloc* will free the block.

4.10.4.1   The behavior of the *abort* function with regard to open and temporary files.

The file buffers are not flushed and the files are not closed.

4.10.4.3   The status returned by *exit* if the value of the argument is other than zero, EXIT_SUCCESS, or EXIT_FAILURE.

Nothing special. The status is returned exactly as it is passed. The status is a represented as a **signed char.**

4.10.4.4   The set of environment names and the method for altering the environment list used by *getenv*.

The environment strings are those defined in the operating system with the SET command. *putenv* can be used to change the strings for the duration of the current program, but the SET command must be used to change an environment string permanently.

4.10.4.5   The contents and mode of execution of the string by the *system* function.

The string is interpreted as an operating system command. COMSPEC is used or COMMAND.COM is executed (for 16-bit programs) or CMD.EXE (for 32-bit programs) and the argument string is passed as a command to execute. Any operating system built-in command, as well as batch files and executable programs, can be executed.

4.11.6.2   The contents of the error message strings returned by *strerror*.

See 4.9.10.4.

4.12.1   The local time zone and Daylight Saving Time.

Defined as local PC time and date.

4.12.2.1   The era for clock.

Represented as clock ticks, with the origin being the beginning of the program execution.

4.12.3.5 The formats for date and time.

Borland C++ implements ANSI formats.

Borland C++ DOS programmer's guide

Part II provides information you might need to develop 16-bit applications that are targeted to run DOS.

This part is organized into the following chapters:

Chapter 13, "DOS memory management," describes overlays. Overlays are supported only in DOS applications. See also Chapter 11, "16-bit memory management."

Chapter 14, "Video functions," discusses graphics in Borland C++. The topics discussed in this chapter are available only for 16-bit DOS applications.

13

DOS memory management

This chapter discusses

- How overlays work, and how to use them.
- How to overlay modules with exception-handling constructs.

Overlays (VROOMM) for DOS

Overlays are used only in 16-bit DOS programs; you can mark the code segments of a Windows application as discardable to decrease memory consumption. *Overlays* are parts of a program's code that share a common memory area. Only the parts of the program that are required for a given function reside in memory at the same time.

Overlays can significantly reduce a program's total run-time memory requirements. With overlays, you can execute programs that are much larger than the total available memory, since only parts of the program reside in memory at any given time.

How overlays work

Borland C++'s overlay manager (called VROOMM for Virtual Run-time Object-Oriented Memory Manager) is highly sophisticated; it does much of the work for you. In a conventional overlay system, modules are grouped together into a base and a set of overlay units. Routines in a given overlay unit can call other routines in the same unit and routines in the base, but not routines in other units. The overlay units are overlaid against each other; that is, only one overlay unit can be in memory at a time, and each unit occupies the same physical memory. The total amount of memory needed to run the program is the size of the base plus the size of the largest overlay.

This conventional scheme is quite inflexible. It requires complete understanding of the possible calling dependencies in the program, and requires you to have the overlays grouped accordingly. It might be impossible to break your program into overlays if you can't split it into separable calling dependencies.

VROOMM's scheme is quite different. It provides *dynamic segment swapping*. The basic swapping unit is the segment. A segment can be one or more modules. More importantly, any segment can call *any other* segment.

Memory is divided into an area for the base plus a swap area. Whenever a function is called in a segment that is neither in the base nor in the swap area, the segment containing the called function is brought into the swap area, possibly displacing other segments. This is a powerful approach—it is like software virtual memory. You no longer have to break your code into static, distinct, overlay units. You just let it run!

Suppose a segment needs to be brought into the swap area. If there is room for the segment, execution continues. If there is not, then one or more segments in the swap area must be thrown out to make room.

The algorithm for deciding which segment to throw out is quite sophisticated. Here's a simplified version: if there is an inactive segment, choose it for removal. Inactive segments are those without executing functions. Otherwise, pick an active segment and swap it out. Keep swapping out segments until there is enough room available. This technique is called *dynamic swapping*.

The more memory you provide for the swap area, the better the program performs. The swap area acts like a cache; the bigger the cache, the faster the program runs. The best setting for the size of the swap area is the size of the program's *working set*.

Once an overlay is loaded into memory, it is placed in the overlay buffer, which resides in memory between the stack segment and the far heap. By default, the size of the overlay buffer is estimated and set at startup, but you can change it using the global variable *_ovrbuffer* (see the C++ *Language Reference*, Chapter 9, "DOS global variables"). If there isn't enough available memory, an error message is displayed by DOS ("Program too big to fit in memory") or by the C startup code ("Not enough memory to run program").

One important option of the overlay manager is the ability to swap the modules to expanded or extended memory when they are discarded from the overlay buffer. Next time the module is needed, the overlay manager can copy it from where the module was swapped to instead of reading from the file. This makes the overlay manager much faster.

When using overlays, memory is used as shown in Figure 13.1.

Figure 13.1   Memory maps for overlays

	Medium model		Large model		Huge model
	Class CODE	Resident code	**Class CODE**	Resident code	**Class CODE**
	Class OVRINFO	Overlay control data	Class OVRINFO	Overlay control data	Class OVRINFO
These segments are generated automatically by the linker	Class STUBSEG	One stub segment for each overlay segment	Class STUBSEG	One stub segment for each overlay segment	Class STUBSEG
	_DATA Class DATA		_DATA Class Data	Multiple data segments	
Near heap and stack share data segment	NEAR HEAP	Seperate stack segment	STACK	Seperate stack segment	STACK
	STACK				
	Overlay buffer (allocated at startup)		Overlay buffer (allocated at startup)		Overlay buffer (allocated at startup)
	FAR HEAP		FAR HEAP		FAR HEAP

Guidelines for using Borland C++ overlays effectively

To get the best out of Borland C++ overlays,

- Minimize resident code (resident run-time library, interrupt handlers, and device drivers are a good starting point).

- Set overlay buffer size to be a comfortable working set (start with 128K and adjust up and down to see the speed/size tradeoff). See page 297 for more information on setting the size of the overlay buffer.

- Think versatility and variety: take advantage of the overlay system to provide support for special cases, interactive help, and other end-user benefits you couldn't consider before.

Requirements

To create overlays, you'll need to remember a few rules:

- The smallest part of a program that can be made into an overlay is a segment.

- Overlaid applications must use the medium, large, or huge programming models; the tiny, small, and compact models are not supported.

- Normal segment merging rules govern overlaid segments. That is, several .OBJ modules can contribute to the same overlaid segment.

The link-time generation of overlays is completely separated from the run-time overlay management; the linker does *not* automatically include code to manage the overlays. In fact, from the linker's point of view, the overlay manager is just another piece of code that gets linked in. The only assumption the linker makes is that the overlay manager takes over an interrupt vector (typically INT 3FH) through which all dynamic loading is controlled. This level of transparency makes it very easy to implement custom-built overlay managers that suit the particular needs of each application.

Exception handling and overlays

If you overlay a C++ program that contains exception-handling constructs, there are a number of situations that you must avoid. The following program elements cannot contain an exception-handling construct:

- Inline functions that are not expanded inline
- Template functions
- Member functions of template classes

Exception-handling constructs include user-written **try/catch** and **_ _try/_ _except** blocks. In addition, the compiler can insert exception handlers for blocks with automatic class variables, exception specifications, and some **new/delete** expressions.

If you attempt to overlay any of the above exception-handling constructs, the linker identifies the function and module with the following message:

```
Error: Illegal local public in function_name in module module_name
```

When this error is caused by an inline function, you can rewrite the function so that it is not inline. If the error is caused by a template function, you can do the following:

- Remove all exception-handling constructs from the function
- Remove the function from the overlay module

You need to pay special attention when overlaying a program that uses multiple inheritance. An attempt to overlay a module that defines or uses class constructors or destructors that are required for a multiple inheritance class can cause the linker to generate the following message:

```
Error: Illegal local public in class_name:: in module module_name
```

When such a message is generated, the module identified by the linker message should not be overlaid.

The container classes (in the BIDS?.LIB) have the exception-handling mechanism turned off by default. However, the diagnostic version of BIDS throws exceptions and should not be used with overlays. By default, the *string* class can throw exceptions and should not be used in programs that use overlays. See the C++ *Language Reference*, Part III, "Borland C++ class libraries reference," for a discussion of BIDS and the *string* class.

Using overlays

Overlays can be used only in 16-bit DOS programs. To overlay a program, all of its modules must be compiled with the **–Y** compiler option enabled. To make a particular module into an overlay, it needs to be compiled with the **–Yo** option. (**–Yo** automatically enables **–Y**.)

The **–Yo** option applies to all modules and libraries that follow it on the command line; you can disable it with **–Yo–**. These are the only command line options that are allowed to follow file names. For example, to overlay the module OVL.C but not the library GRAPHICS.LIB, either of the following command lines could be used:

```
BCC -ml -Yo ovl.c -Yo- graphics.lib
```

or

```
BCC -ml graphics.lib -Yo ovl.c
```

If TLINK is invoked explicitly to link the .EXE file, the **/o** linker option must be specified on the linker command line or response file. See Chapter 3 of the *C++ User's Guide* for details on how to use the **/o** option.

Overlay example

Suppose that you want to overlay a program consisting of three modules: MAIN.C, O1.C, and O2.C. Only the modules O1.C and O2.C should be made into overlays. (MAIN.C contains time-critical routines and interrupt handlers, so it should stay resident.) Let's assume that the program uses the large memory model.

The following command accomplishes the task:

```
BCC -ml -Y main.c -Yo o1.c o2.c
```

The result will be an executable file MAIN.EXE, containing two overlays.

Note   See the discussion of TargetExpert in the *C++ User's Guide*, Chapter 2, for information on programming with overlays.

Overlaid programs

This section discusses issues vital to well-behaved overlaid applications.

The far call requirement

Use a large code model (medium, large, or huge) when you want to compile an overlay module. At any call to an overlaid function in another module, you *must* guarantee that all currently active functions are far.

You *must* compile all overlaid modules with the **–Y** option, which makes the compiler generate code that can be overlaid.

Note   Failing to observe the far call requirement in an overlaid program will cause unpredictable and possibly catastrophic results when the program is executed.

Buffer size

The default overlay buffer size is twice the size of the largest overlay. This is adequate for some applications. But imagine that a particular function of a program is implemented through many modules, each of which is overlaid. If the total size of those modules is larger than the overlay buffer, a substantial amount of swapping will occur if the modules make frequent calls to each other.

The solution is to increase the size of the overlay buffer so that enough memory is available at any given time to contain all overlays that make frequent calls to each other. You can do this by setting the _ovrbuffer_ global variable (see the C++ _Language Reference,_ Chapter 9) to the required size in paragraphs. For example, to set the overlay buffer to 128K, include the following statement in your code:

```
unsigned _ovrbuffer = 0x2000;
```

There is no general formula for determining the ideal overlay buffer size.

What not to overlay

Exception-handling constructs in overlays require special attention. See page 296 for a discussion of exception handling.

Don't overlay modules that contain interrupt handlers, or small and time-critical routines. Due to the non-reentrant nature of the DOS operating system, modules that might be called by interrupt functions should not be overlaid.

Borland C++'s overlay manager fully supports passing overlaid functions as arguments, assigning and initializing function pointer variables with addresses of overlaid functions, and calling overlaid routines via function pointers.

Debugging overlays

Most debuggers have very limited overlay debugging capabilities, if any at all. Not so with Borland C++'s Turbo Debugger, the standalone debugger. The debugger fully supports single-stepping and breakpoints in overlays in a manner completely transparent to you. By using overlays, you can easily engineer and debug huge applications—all by using Turbo Debugger.

Note   Overlays should not be used with any diagnostic version of the BIDS libraries.

External routines in overlays

Like normal C functions, **external** assembly language routines must observe certain programming rules to work correctly with the overlay manager.

If an assembly language routine makes calls to _any_ overlaid functions, the assembly language routine _must_ be declared FAR, and it _must_ set up a stack frame using the BP register. For example, assuming that _OtherFunc_ is an overlaid function in another module, and that the assembly language routine _ExternFunc_ calls it, then _ExternFunc_ must be FAR and set up a stack frame, as shown:

```
ExternFunc      PROC    FAR
    push    bp                  ;Save BP
    mov     bp,sp               ;Set up stack frame
    sub     sp,LocalSize        ;Allocate local variables
    :
    call    OtherFunc           ;Call another overlaid module
    :
    mov     sp,bp               ;Dispose local variables
    pop     bp                  ;Restore BP
    RET                         ;Return
ExternFunc      ENDP
```

where *LocalSize* is the size of the local variables. If *LocalSize* is zero, you can omit the two lines to allocate and dispose local variables, but you must not omit setting up the BP stack frame even if you have no arguments or variables on the stack.

These requirements are the same if *ExternFunc* makes *indirect* references to overlaid functions. For example, if *OtherFunc* makes calls to overlaid functions, but is not itself overlaid, *ExternFunc* must be FAR and still has to set up a stack frame.

In the case where an assembly language routine doesn't make any direct or indirect references to overlaid functions, there are no special requirements; the assembly language routine can be declared NEAR. It does not have to set up a stack frame.

Overlaid assembly language routines should *not* create variables in the code segment, since any modifications made to an overlaid code segment are lost when the overlay is disposed. Likewise, pointers to objects based in an overlaid code segment cannot be expected to remain valid across calls to other overlays, since the overlay manager freely moves around and disposes overlaid code segments.

Swapping

If you have expanded or extended memory available, you can tell the overlay manager to use it for swapping. If you do so, when the overlay manager has to discard a module from the overlay buffer (because it should load a new module and the buffer is full), it can store the discarded module in this memory. Any later loading of this module is reduced to in-memory transfer, which is significantly faster than reading from a disk file.

In both cases there are two possibilities: the overlay manager can either detect the presence of expanded or extended memory and can take it over by itself, or it can use an already detected and allocated portion of memory. For extended memory, the detection of the memory use is not always successful because of the many different cache and RAM disk programs that can take over extended memory without any mark. To avoid this problem, you can tell the overlay manager the starting address of the extended memory and how much of it is safe to use.

Borland C++ provides two functions that allow you to initialize expanded and extended memory. See the *C++ Language Reference*, Chapter 7, for a description of the *_OvrInitEms* and *_OvrInitExt* functions.

14

Video functions

Borland C++ comes with a complete library of graphics functions, so you can produce onscreen charts and diagrams. The graphics functions are available for 16-bit DOS-only applications. This chapter briefly discusses video modes and windows, then explains how to program in graphics mode.

Video modes

Your PC has some type of video adapter. This can be a Monochrome Display Adapter (MDA) for text-only display, or it can be a graphics adapter, such as a Color/Graphics Adapter (CGA), an Enhanced Graphics Adapter (EGA), a Video Graphics Array adapter (VGA), or a Hercules Monochrome Graphics Adapter. Each adapter can operate in a variety of modes; the mode specifies whether the screen displays 80 or 40 columns (text mode only), the display resolution (graphics mode only), and the display type (color or black and white).

The screen's operating mode is defined when your program calls one of the mode-defining functions *textmode*, *initgraph*, or *setgraphmode*.

- In *text mode*, your PC's screen is divided into cells (80 or 40 columns wide by 25, 43, or 50 lines high). Each cell consists of a character and an attribute. The character is the displayed ASCII character; the attribute specifies *how* the character is displayed (its color, intensity, and so on). Borland C++ provides a full range of routines for manipulating the text screen, for writing text directly to the screen, and for controlling cell attributes.

- In *graphics mode*, your PC's screen is divided into pixels; each pixel displays a single dot onscreen. The number of pixels (the resolution) depends on the type of video adapter connected to your system and the mode that adapter is in. You can use functions from Borland C++'s graphics library to create graphic displays onscreen: You can draw lines and shapes, fill enclosed areas with patterns, and control the color of each pixel.

In text modes, the upper left corner of the screen is position (1,1), with x-coordinates increasing from left to right, and y-coordinates increasing from screen-top to screen-bottom. In graphics modes, the upper left corner is position (0,0), with the x- and y-coordinate values increasing in the same manner.

Windows and viewports

Borland C++ provides functions for creating and managing windows on your screen in text mode (and viewports in graphics mode). If you aren't familiar with windows and viewports, you should read this brief overview. Borland C++'s window- and viewport-management functions are explained in the "Programming in graphics mode" section.

A *window* is a rectangular area defined on your PC's video screen when it's in a text mode. When your program writes to the screen, its output is restricted to the active window. The rest of the screen (outside the window) remains untouched.

The default window is a full-screen text window. Your program can change this default window to a text window smaller than the full screen (with a call to the *window* function, which specifies the window's position in terms of screen coordinates).

In graphics mode, you can also define a rectangular area on your PC's video screen; this is a *viewport*. When your graphics program outputs drawings and so on, the viewport acts as the virtual screen. The rest of the screen (outside the viewport) remains untouched. You define a viewport in terms of screen coordinates with a call to the *setviewport* function.

Except for these window- and viewport-defining functions, all *coordinates* for text-mode and graphics-mode functions are given in window- or viewport-relative terms, not in absolute screen coordinates. The upper left corner of the text-mode window is the coordinate origin, referred to as (1,1); in graphics modes, the viewport coordinate origin is position (0,0).

Programming in graphics mode

This section provides a brief summary of the functions used in graphics mode. For more detailed information about these functions, refer to the *C++ Language Reference*, Chapter 6, "Borland graphics interface."

Borland C++ provides a separate library of over 70 graphics functions, ranging from high-level calls (like *setviewport*, *bar3d*, and *drawpoly)* to bit-oriented functions (like *getimage* and *putimage*). The graphics library supports numerous fill and line styles, and provides several text fonts that you can size, justify, and orient horizontally or vertically.

These functions are in the library file GRAPHICS.LIB, and they are prototyped in the header file graphics.h. In addition to these two files, the graphics package includes graphics device drivers (*.BGI files) and stroked character fonts (*.CHR files); these files are discussed in following sections.

To use the graphics functions with the BCC.EXE command-line compiler, you have to list GRAPHICS.LIB on the command line. For example, if your program MYPROG.C uses graphics, the BCC command line would be

```
BCC MYPROG GRAPHICS.LIB
```

See the C++ *User's Guide* discussion of TargetExpert in Chapter 2 for a description of DOS programming with graphics. When you make your program, the linker automatically links in the Borland C++ graphics library.

Note   Because graphics functions use **far** pointers, graphics aren't supported in the tiny memory model.

There is only one graphics library, not separate versions for each memory model (in contrast to the standard libraries CS.LIB, CC.LIB, CM.LIB, and so on, which are memory-model specific). Each function in GRAPHICS.LIB is a **far** function, and those graphics functions that take pointers take **far** pointers. For these functions to work correctly, it is important that you **#include** graphics.h in every module that uses graphics.

The graphics library functions

There are seven categories of Borland C++ graphics functions:

- Graphics system control
- Drawing and filling
- Manipulating screens and viewports
- Text output
- Color control
- Error handling
- State query

Graphics system control

Here's a summary of the graphics system control:

Function	Description
closegraph	Shuts down the graphics system.
detectgraph	Checks the hardware and determines which graphics driver to use; recommends a mode.
graphdefaults	Resets all graphics system variables to their default settings.
_graphfreemem	Deallocates graphics memory; hook for defining your own routine.
_graphgetmem	Allocates graphics memory; hook for defining your own routine.
getgraphmode	Returns the current graphics mode.
getmoderange	Returns lowest and highest valid modes for specified driver.
initgraph	Initializes the graphics system and puts the hardware into graphics mode.
installuserdriver	Installs a vendor-added device driver to the BGI device driver table.
installuserfont	Loads a vendor-added stroked font file to the BGI character file table.
registerbgidriver	Registers a linked-in or user-loaded driver file for inclusion at link time.
restorecrtmode	Restores the original (pre-*initgraph*) screen mode.

Function	Description
setgraphbufsize	Specifies size of the internal graphics buffer.
setgraphmode	Selects the specified graphics mode, clears the screen, and restores all defaults.

Borland C++'s graphics package provides graphics drivers for the following graphics adapters (and true compatibles):

- Color/Graphics Adapter (CGA)
- Multi-Color Graphics Array (MCGA)
- Enhanced Graphics Adapter (EGA)
- Video Graphics Array (VGA)
- Hercules Graphics Adapter
- AT&T 400-line Graphics Adapter
- 3270 PC Graphics Adapter
- IBM 8514 Graphics Adapter

To start the graphics system, you first call the *initgraph* function. *initgraph* loads the graphics driver and puts the system into graphics mode.

You can tell *initgraph* to use a particular graphics driver and mode, or to autodetect the attached video adapter at run time and pick the corresponding driver. If you tell *initgraph* to autodetect, it calls *detectgraph* to select a graphics driver and mode. If you tell *initgraph* to use a particular graphics driver and mode, you must be sure that the hardware is present. If you force *initgraph* to use hardware that is not present, the results will be unpredictable.

Once a graphics driver has been loaded, you can use the *gerdrivername* function to find out the name of the driver and the *getmaxmode* function to find out how many modes a driver supports. *getgraphmode* will tell you which graphics mode you are currently in. Once you have a mode number, you can find out the name of the mode with *getmodename*. You can change graphics modes with *setgraphmode* and return the video mode to its original state (before graphics was initialized) with *restorecrtmode*. *restorecrtmode* returns the screen to text mode, but it does not close the graphics system (the fonts and drivers are still in memory).

graphdefaults resets the graphics state's settings (viewport size, draw color, fill color and pattern, and so on) to their default values.

installuserdriver and *installuserfont* let you add new device drivers and fonts to your BGI.

Finally, when you're through using graphics, call *closegraph* to shut down the graphics system. *closegraph* unloads the driver from memory and restores the original video mode (via *restorecrtmode*).

A more detailed discussion

The previous discussion provided an overview of how *initgraph* operates. In the following paragraphs, we describe the behavior of *initgraph*, *_graphgetmem*, and *_graphfreemem* in some detail.

Normally, the *initgraph* routine loads a graphics driver by allocating memory for the driver, then loading the appropriate .BGI file from disk. As an alternative to this dynamic loading scheme, you can link a graphics driver file (or several of them) directly into your executable program file. You do this by first converting the .BGI file to an .OBJ file (using the BGIOBJ utility), then placing calls to *registerbgidriver* in your source code (before the call to *initgraph*) to *register* the graphics driver(s). When you build your program, you need to link the .OBJ files for the registered drivers.

After determining which graphics driver to use (via *detectgraph*), *initgraph* checks to see if the desired driver has been registered. If so, *initgraph* uses the registered driver directly from memory. Otherwise, *initgraph* allocates memory for the driver and loads the .BGI file from disk.

Note Using *registerbgidriver* is an advanced programming technique, not recommended for novice programmers. This function is described in more detail in the C++ *Language Reference*, Chapter 6.

During run time, the graphics system might need to allocate memory for drivers, fonts, and internal buffers. If this is necessary, it calls *_graphgetmem* to allocate memory and *_graphfreemem* to free memory. By default, these routines call *malloc* and *free*, respectively.

You can override this default behavior by defining your own *_graphgetmem* and *_graphfreemem* functions. By doing this, you can control graphics memory allocation yourself. You must, however, use the same names for your own versions of these memory-allocation routines: they will override the default functions with the same names that are in the standard C libraries.

Note If you provide your own *_graphgetmem* or *_graphfreemem*, you might get a "duplicate symbols" warning message. Just ignore the warning.

Drawing and filling

Here's a quick summary of the drawing and filling functions:

Drawing functions	Description
arc	Draws a circular arc.
circle	Draws a circle.
drawpoly	Draws the outline of a polygon.
ellipse	Draws an elliptical arc.
getarccoords	Returns the coordinates of the last call to *arc* or *ellipse*.
getaspectratio	Returns the aspect ratio of the current graphics mode.
getlinesettings	Returns the current line style, line pattern, and line thickness.
line	Draws a line from (*x0,y0*) to (*x1,y1*).
linerel	Draws a line to a point some relative distance from the current position (CP).
lineto	Draws a line from the current position (CP) to (*x,y*).
moveto	Moves the current position (CP) to (*x,y*).
moverel	Moves the current position (CP) a relative distance.
rectangle	Draws a rectangle.
setaspectratio	Changes the default aspect ratio-correction factor.
setlinestyle	Sets the current line width and style.

Filling functions	Description
bar	Draws and fills a bar.
bar3d	Draws and fills a 3-D bar.
fillellipse	Draws and fills an ellipse.
fillpoly	Draws and fills a polygon.
floodfill	Flood-fills a bounded region.
getfillpattern	Returns the user-defined fill pattern.
getfillsettings	Returns information about the current fill pattern and color.
pieslice	Draws and fills a pie slice.
sector	Draws and fills an elliptical pie slice.
setfillpattern	Selects a user-defined fill pattern.
setfillstyle	Sets the fill pattern and fill color.

With Borland C++'s drawing and painting functions, you can draw colored lines, arcs, circles, ellipses, rectangles, pie slices, two- and three-dimensional bars, polygons, and regular or irregular shapes based on combinations of these. You can fill any bounded shape (or any region surrounding such a shape) with one of eleven predefined patterns, or your own user-defined pattern. You can also control the thickness and style of the drawing line, and the location of the current position (CP).

You draw lines and unfilled shapes with the functions *arc*, *circle*, *drawpoly*, *ellipse*, *line*, *linerel*, *lineto*, and *rectangle*. You can fill these shapes with *floodfill*, or combine drawing and filling into one step with *bar*, *bar3d*, *fillellipse*, *fillpoly*, *pieslice*, and *sector*. You use *setlinestyle* to specify whether the drawing line (and border line for filled shapes) is thick or thin, and whether its style is solid, dotted, and so forth, or some other line pattern you've defined. You can select a predefined fill pattern with *setfillstyle*, and define your own fill pattern with *setfillpattern*. You move the CP to a specified location with *moveto*, and move it a specified displacement with *moverel*.

To find out the current line style and thickness, call *getlinesettings*. For information about the current fill pattern and fill color, call *getfillsettings*; you can get the user-defined fill pattern with *getfillpattern*.

You can get the aspect ratio (the scaling factor used by the graphics system to make sure circles come out round) with *getaspectratio*, and the coordinates of the last drawn arc or ellipse with *getarccoords*. If your circles aren't perfectly round, use *setaspectratio* to correct them.

Manipulating the screen and viewport

Here's a quick summary of the screen-, viewport-, image-, and pixel-manipulation functions.

Function	Description
Screen manipulation	
cleardevice	Clears the screen (active page).
setactivepage	Sets the active page for graphics output.
setvisualpage	Sets the visual graphics page number.

Function	Description
Viewport manipulation	
clearviewport	Clears the current viewport.
getviewsettings	Returns information about the current viewport.
setviewport	Sets the current output viewport for graphics output.
Image manipulation	
getimage	Saves a bit image of the specified region to memory.
imagesize	Returns the number of bytes required to store a rectangular region of the screen.
putimage	Puts a previously saved bit image onto the screen.
Pixel manipulation	
getpixel	Gets the pixel color at (x,y).
putpixel	Plots a pixel at (x,y).

Besides drawing and painting, the graphics library offers several functions for manipulating the screen, viewports, images, and pixels. You can clear the whole screen in one step with a call to *cleardevice*; this routine erases the entire screen and homes the CP in the viewport, but leaves all other graphics system settings intact (the line, fill, and text styles; the palette; the viewport settings; and so on).

Depending on your graphics adapter, your system has between one and four screen-page buffer; these are areas in memory where individual whole-screen images are stored dot-by-dot. You can specify the active screen page (where graphics functions place their output) with *setactivepage* and the visual page (the one displayed onscreen) with *setvisualpage*.

Once your screen is in graphics mode, you can define a viewport (a rectangular "virtual screen") on your screen with a call to *setviewport*. You define the viewport's position in terms of absolute screen coordinates and specify whether clipping is on (active) or off. You clear the viewport with *clearviewport*. To find out the current viewport's absolute screen coordinates and clipping status, call *getviewsettings*.

You can capture a portion of the onscreen image with *getimage*, call *imagesize* to calculate the number of bytes required to store that captured image in memory, then put the stored image back on the screen (anywhere you want) with *putimage*.

The coordinates for all output functions (drawing, filling, text, and so on) are viewport-relative.

You can also manipulate the color of individual pixels with the functions *getpixel* (which returns the color of a given pixel) and *putpixel* (which plots a specified pixel in a given color).

Text output in graphics mode

Here's a quick summary of the graphics-mode text output functions:

Function	Description
gettextsettings	Returns the current text font, direction, size, and justification.
outtext	Sends a string to the screen at the current position (CP).

Function	Description
outtextxy	Sends a string to the screen at the specified position.
registerbgifont	Registers a linked-in or user-loaded font.
settextjustify	Sets text justification values used by *outtext* and *outtextxy*.
settextstyle	Sets the current text font, style, and character magnification factor.
setusercharsize	Sets width and height ratios for stroked fonts.
textheight	Returns the height of a string in pixels.
textwidth	Returns the width of a string in pixels.

The graphics library includes an 8×8 bit-mapped font and several stroked fonts for text output while in graphics mode.

- In a *bit-mapped* font, each character is defined by a matrix of pixels.

- In a *stroked* font, each character is defined by a series of vectors that tell the graphics system how to draw that character.

The advantage of using a stroked font is apparent when you start to draw large characters. Since a stroked font is defined by vectors, it retains good resolution and quality when the font is enlarged. On the other hand, when you enlarge a bit-mapped font, the matrix is multiplied by a scaling factor; as the scaling factor becomes larger, the characters' resolution becomes coarser. For small characters, the bit-mapped font should be sufficient, but for larger text you should select a stroked font.

You output graphics text by calling either *outtext* or *outtextxy*, and you control the justification of the output text (with respect to the CP) with *settextjustify*. You choose the character font, direction (horizontal or vertical), and size (scale) with *settextstyle*. You can find out the current text settings by calling *gettextsettings*, which returns the current text font, justification, magnification, and direction in a *textsettings* structure. *setusercharsize* lets you modify the character width and height of stroked fonts.

If clipping is *on*, all text strings output by *outtext* and *outtextxy* are clipped at the viewport borders. If clipping is *off*, these functions throw away bit-mapped font output if any part of the text string would go off the screen edge; stroked font output is truncated at the screen edges.

To determine the onscreen size of a given text string, call *textheight* (which measures the string's height in pixels) and *textwidth* (which measures its width in pixels).

The default 8×8 bit-mapped font is built into the graphics package, so it's always available at run time. The stroked fonts are each kept in a separate .CHR file; they can be loaded at run time or converted to .OBJ files (with the BGIOBJ utility) and linked into your .EXE file.

Normally, the *settextstyle* routine loads a font file by allocating memory for the font, then loading the appropriate .CHR file from disk. As an alternative to this dynamic loading scheme, you can link a character font file (or several of them) directly into your executable program file. You do this by first converting the .CHR file to an .OBJ file (using the BGIOBJ utility), then placing calls to *registerbgifont* in your source code (before the call to *settextstyle*) to *register* the character font(s). When you build your program, you need to link in the .OBJ files for the stroked fonts you register.

Note Using *registerbgifont* is an advanced programming technique, not recommended for novice programmers.

Color control

Here's a quick summary of the color control functions:

Function	Description
Get color information	
getbkcolor	Returns the current background color.
getcolor	Returns the current drawing color.
getdefaultpalette	Returns the palette definition structure.
getmaxcolor	Returns the maximum color value available in the current graphics mode.
getpalette	Returns the current palette and its size.
getpalettesize	Returns the size of the palette look-up table.
Set one or more colors	
setallpalette	Changes all palette colors as specified.
setbkcolor	Sets the current background color.
setcolor	Sets the current drawing color.
setpalette	Changes one palette color as specified by its arguments.

Before summarizing how these color control functions work, we first present a basic description of how colors are actually produced on your graphics screen.

Pixels and palettes

The graphics screen consists of an array of pixels; each pixel produces a single (colored) dot onscreen. The pixel's value does not specify the precise color directly; it is an index into a color table called a *palette*. The palette entry corresponding to a given pixel value contains the exact color information for that pixel.

This indirection scheme has a number of implications. Though the hardware might be capable of displaying many colors, only a subset of those colors can be displayed at any given time. The number of colors in this subset is equal to the number of entries in the palette (the palette's *size*). For example, on an EGA, the hardware can display 64 different colors, but only 16 of them at a time; the EGA palette's *size* is 16.

The *size* of the palette determines the range of values a pixel can assume, from 0 to (*size* –1). *getmaxcolor* returns the highest valid pixel value (*size* –1) for the current graphics driver and mode.

When we discuss the Borland C++'s graphics functions, we often use the term *color*, such as the current drawing color, fill color and pixel color. In fact, this color is a pixel's value: it's an index into the palette. Only the palette determines the true color on the screen. By manipulating the palette, you can change the actual color displayed on the screen even though the pixel values (drawing color, fill color, and so on) haven't changed.

Background and drawing color

The *background color* always corresponds to pixel value 0. When an area is cleared to the background color, that area's pixels are set to 0.

The *drawing color* is the value to which pixels are set when lines are drawn. You choose a drawing color with `setcolor(n)`, where *n* is a valid pixel value for the current palette.

Color control on a CGA

Due to graphics hardware differences, how you actually control color differs quite a bit between CGA and EGA, so they're presented separately. Color control on the AT&T driver, and the lower resolutions of the MCGA driver is similar to CGA.

On the CGA, you can choose to display your graphics in low resolution (320×200), which allows you to use four colors, or in high resolution (640×200), in which you can use two colors.

CGA low resolution

In the low-resolution modes, you can choose from four predefined four-color palettes. In any of these palettes, you can set only the first palette entry; entries 1, 2, and 3 are fixed. The first palette entry (color 0) is the background color; it can be any one of the 16 available colors (see the following table of CGA background colors).

You choose which palette you want by selecting the appropriate mode (CGAC0, CGAC1, CGAC2, CGAC3); these modes use color palette 0 through color palette 3, as detailed in the following table. The CGA drawing colors and the equivalent constants are defined in graphics.h.

Palette number	Constant assigned to color number (pixel value):		
	1	**2**	**3**
0	CGA_LIGHTGREEN	CGA_LIGHTRED	CGA_YELLOW
1	CGA_LIGHTCYAN	CGA_LIGHTMAGENTA	CGA_WHITE
2	CGA_GREEN	CGA_RED	CGA_BROWN
3	CGA_CYAN	CGA_MAGENTA	CGA_LIGHTGRAY

To assign one of these colors as the CGA drawing color, call **setcolor** with either the color number or the corresponding constant name as an argument; for example, if you're using palette 3 and you want to use cyan as the drawing color:

```
setcolor(1);
```

or

```
setcolor(CGA_CYAN);
```

The available CGA background and foreground colors, defined in graphics.h, are listed in the following table:

Numeric value	Symbolic name	Numeric value	Symbolic name
0	BLACK	8	DARKGRAY
1	BLUE	9	LIGHTBLUE
2	GREEN	10	LIGHTGREEN
3	CYAN	11	LIGHTCYAN
4	RED	12	LIGHTRED
5	MAGENTA	13	LIGHTMAGENTA
6	BROWN	14	YELLOW
7	LIGHTGRAY	15	WHITE

To assign one of these colors to the CGA background color, use *setbkcolor(color)*, where *color* is one of the entries in the preceding table. For CGA, this color is not a pixel value (palette index); it directly specifies the actual color to be put in the first palette entry.

CGA high resolution

In high-resolution mode (640×200), the CGA displays two colors: a black background and a colored foreground. Pixels can take on values of either 0 or 1. Because of a quirk in the CGA itself, the foreground color is actually what the hardware thinks of as its background color; you set it with the *setbkcolor* routine. (Strange, but true.)

The colors available for the colored foreground are those listed in the preceding table. The CGA uses this color to display all pixels whose value equals 1.

The modes that behave in this way are CGAHI, MCGAMED, MCGAHI, ATT400MED, and ATT400HI.

CGA palette routines

Because the CGA palette is predetermined, you shouldn't use the *setallpalette* routine on a CGA. Also, you shouldn't use *setpalette(index, actual_color)*, except for *index* = 0. (This is an alternate way to set the CGA background color to *actual_color*.)

Color control on the EGA and VGA

On the EGA, the palette contains 16 entries from a total of 64 possible colors; each entry is user-settable. You can retrieve the current palette with *getpalette*, which fills in a structure with the palette's size (16) and an array of the actual palette entries (the "hardware color numbers" stored in the palette). You can change the palette entries individually with *setpalette*, or all at once with *setallpalette*.

The default EGA palette corresponds to the 16 CGA colors, as given in the previous color table: black is in entry 0, blue in entry 1, ..., white in entry 15. There are constants defined in graphics.h that contain the corresponding hardware color values: these are EGA_BLACK, EGA_WHITE, and so on. You can also get these values with *getpalette*.

The *setbkcolor(color)* routine behaves differently on an EGA than on a CGA. On an EGA, *setbkcolor* copies the actual color value that's stored in entry #*color* into entry #0.

As far as colors are concerned, the VGA driver behaves like the EGA driver; it just has higher resolution (and smaller pixels).

Error handling in graphics mode

Here's a quick summary of the graphics-mode error-handling functions:

Function	Description
grapherrormsg	Returns an error message string for the specified error code.
graphresult	Returns an error code for the last graphics operation that encountered a problem.

If an error occurs when a graphics library function is called (such as a font requested with *settextstyle* not being found), an internal error code is set. You retrieve the error code for the last graphics operation that reported an error by calling *graphresult*. A call to *grapherrormsg(graphresult())* returns the error strings listed in the following table.

The error return-code accumulates, changing only when a graphics function reports an error. The error return code is reset to 0 only when *initgraph* executes successfully or when you call *graphresult*. Therefore, if you want to know which graphics function returned which error, you should store the value of *graphresult* into a temporary variable and then test it.

Error code	*graphics_errors* constant	Corresponding error message string
0	grOk	No error
-1	grNoInitGraph	(BGI) graphics not installed (use *initgraph*)
-2	grNotDetected	Graphics hardwaren't detected
-3	grFileNotFound	Device driver file not found
-4	grInvalidDriver	Invalid device driver file
-5	grNoLoadMem	Not enough memory to load driver
-6	grNoScanMem	Out of memory in scan fill
-7	grNoFloodMem	Out of memory in flood fill
-8	grFontNotFound	Font file not found
-9	grNoFontMem	Not enough memory to load font
-10	grInvalidMode	Invalid graphics mode for selected driver
-11	grError	Graphics error
-12	grIOerror	Graphics I/O error
-13	grInvalidFont	Invalid font file
-14	grInvalidFontNum	Invalid font number
-15	grInvalidDeviceNum	Invalid device number
-18	grInvalidVersion	Invalid version of file

State query

The following table summarizes the graphics mode state query functions:

Table 14.1 Graphics mode state query functions

Function	Returns
getarccoords	Information about the coordinates of the last call to *arc* or *ellipse*.
getaspectratio	Aspect ratio of the graphics screen.
getbkcolor	Current background color.
getcolor	Current drawing color.
getdrivername	Name of current graphics driver.
getfillpattern	User-defined fill pattern.
getfillsettings	Information about the current fill pattern and color.
getgraphmode	Current graphics mode.
getlinesettings	Current line style, line pattern, and line thickness.
getmaxcolor	Current highest valid pixel value.
getmaxmode	Maximum mode number for current driver.
getmaxx	Current *x* resolution.
getmaxy	Current *y* resolution.
getmodename	Name of a given driver mode.
getmoderange	Mode range for a given driver.
getpalette	Current palette and its size.
getpixel	Color of the pixel at *x,y*.
gettextsettings	Current text font, direction, size, and justification.
getviewsettings	Information about the current viewport.
getx	*x* coordinate of the current position (CP).
gety	*y* coordinate of the current position (CP).

Each of Borland C++'s graphics function categories has at least one state query function. These functions are mentioned under their respective categories and also covered here. Each of the Borland C++ graphics state query functions is named get something (except in the error-handling category). Some of them take no argument and return a single value representing the requested information; others take a pointer to a structure defined in graphics.h, fill that structure with the appropriate information, and return no value.

The state query functions for the graphics system control category are *getgraphmode*, *getmaxmode*, and *getmoderange*: the first returns an integer representing the current graphics driver and mode, the second returns the maximum mode number for a given driver, and the third returns the range of modes supported by a given graphics driver. *getmaxx* and *getmaxy* return the maximum *x* and *y* screen coordinates for the current graphics mode.

The drawing and filling state query functions are *getarccoords, getaspectratio, getfillpattern, getfillsettings,* and *getlinesettings. getarccoords* fills a structure with coordinates from the last call to *arc* or *ellipse; getaspectratio* tells the current mode's aspect ratio, which the graphics system uses to make circles come out round. *getfillpattern* returns the current user-defined fill pattern. *getfillsettings* fills a structure with the current fill pattern and fill color. *getlinesettings* fills a structure with the current line style (solid, dashed, and so on), line width (normal or thick), and line pattern.

In the screen- and viewport manipulation category, the state query functions are *getviewsettings*, *getx*, *gety*, and *getpixel*. When you have defined a viewport, you can find out its absolute screen coordinates and whether clipping is active by calling *getviewsettings*, which fills a structure with the information. *getx* and *gety* return the (viewport-relative) x- and y-coordinates of the CP. *getpixel* returns the color of a specified pixel.

The graphics mode text-output function category contains one all-inclusive state query function: *gettextsettings*. This function fills a structure with information about the current character font, the direction in which text will be displayed (horizontal or bottom-to-top vertical), the character magnification factor, and the text-string justification (both horizontal and vertical).

Borland C++'s color-control function category includes four state query functions. *getbkcolor* returns the current background color, and *getcolor* returns the current drawing color. *getpalette* fills a structure with the size of the current drawing palette and the palette's contents. *getmaxcolor* returns the highest valid pixel value for the current graphics driver and mode (palette *size* −1).

Finally, *getmodename* and *getdrivername* return the name of a given driver mode and the name of the current graphics driver, respectively.

Borland C++ class libraries guide

Part III is a programmer's guide to using the container classes, iostreams classes, persistent streams classes, and mathematical classes. It is divided into the following chapters:

- **Chapter 15, "Using Borland C++ container classes,"** explains how to use the container class library, also known as Borland International Data Structures (BIDS), which is a large collection of classes that encapsulate commonly used data structures. Each container class encapsulates a specific type of data structure (for example, a stack), and the operations that characterize that type of data structure (for example, push and pop operations).

- **Chapter 16, "Using iostreams classes,"** explains how to use the C++ input and output classes, commonly known as iostreams. With the arrival of C++ and object-oriented design, input and output operations became encapsulated in a series of classes. Each iostreams class encapsulates some form of input, output, or input and output from low-level character transfer to higher-level, file-oriented input/output operations.

- **Chapter 17, "Using persistent streams classes,"** explains how to use classes that support persistence. In computer programs, an example of persistence is retaining information between application invocations—your application comes up in the same state you left it in the day before.

- **Chapter 18, "Using the mathematical classes,"** explains how to use the mathematical classes, which encapsulate binary-coded decimal numbers (*bcd* class) and complex numbers (*complex* class).

15

Using Borland container classes

This chapter describes the Borland C++ container class library. It contains sections describing container library organization, class naming conventions, and the programming interface. See Chapter 10 of the *C++ Language Reference* for information describing specific classes in this library.

A container is an object that can hold any number of other objects of a single specified type. The specified type can be a built-in type like an **int** or a **float**, or it can be a user-defined type, like a record containing fields of different types, or an object instantiated from a C++ class you have defined.

Borland C++ containers place stored objects into one of thirteen predefined data structures. Container classes support standard operations on data structures through a coding interface that is easy to use and strongly standardized. You will not need to create code defining a data structure or its operations. To use a data structure to store data, instantiate a container object and then use existing container members to add, search, find, change or remove data.

Borland C++ containers also manage some operations without your intervention. Borland C++ containers manage pointers to data stored in a list, tree or other data structure, can resize the container, can sort stored data, can support your custom memory manager class, and can throw exceptions for you.

Note   A data structure is a collection of data items, where items are placed in a predefined relationship to each other. This predefined relationship implies that a collection of operations exists to manage that data. For example, a stack is a data structure designed to store data in the order received, and to provide the last data item stored. Data placed in a stack structure is accessed by using *push* and *pop* operations.

Container library implementation

The Borland C++ container class library includes 187 templates. They are organized into a flat hierarchy. This minimizes your design and coding effort and makes these classes easier to use.

The container class library is templatized, to make it easy for you to store objects of any type. Because the library is templatized, you do not need to subclass a container class to store data of your selected type. Simply pass your data type to the container class template when you instantiate the container object.

The container class library also minimizes the use of virtual functions, which would require you to write specialized code defining those members before they are used, and could require you to subclass a class. In most cases, virtual functions are present in class declarations to implement private mechanisms which have already been coded for you.

To make it easier to select a class, Borland C++ has divided the library into thirteen families of class templates. Each family includes a set of similar class templates which support the same data structure. To create a Borland container, you will select the best family to use for your purposes; identify the specialized class template within that family to use; and then use that class template to instantiate a container object that stores objects of your selected data type.

All container objects are specialized to perform a variety of data management tasks. Specialized containers can manage pointers instead of objects; sort objects as they are inserted into the container; maintain a running count of objects inserted into the container; or accept your own memory manager class as an input parameter.

ADT and FDS classes

The container class library is composed of two interdependent collections of families: The Abstract Data Types (ADT) class families, and the Fundamental Data Structures (FDS) class families.

ADT classes

ADT families focus on conceptual operations performed on data structures. ADT families exist for stacks, queues, deques, bags, sets, arrays, and dictionaries. All ADT classes rely on an FDS (Fundamental Data Structures) class to implement the data structure they manage. For most coding purposes, you should select a class belonging to an ADT family. The following table lists and describes ADT class families.

See "Class naming conventions" later in this chapter for ADS class naming conventions.

Table 15.1 ADT class families

Family	Header file	Description
Array	arrays.h	Stores data into a resizable, contiguous block of memory. Data at any array position can be added, removed, or inspected at any time. Supports index operators.
Association	assoc.h	Designed to support the dictionary family. This class contains two data members: a key and a value. Given a key, an association class returns a value. Key and value data may be of different user types.

Table 15.1 ADT class families (continued)

Family	Header file	Description
Bag	bags.h	Stores objects as an unordered, undefined group. A bag is the simplest structure that the container families support. A bag can accept duplicate values.
Deque	deques.h	Stores data in a chain. Objects are placed into this structure in the order received, into either head or tail positions (FIFO). Data can be pushed and popped from either end of the queue.
Dictionary	dict.h	Stores Association objects. When given a key, dictionary containers return the value associated with that key.
Queue	queues.h	Stores data in a chain. Objects are placed into this structure in the order received. Objects are pushed onto the head of the queue and popped from the tail (FIFO).
Set	sets.h	Stores data in an unsequenced group. A set is a bag structure that does not accept objects with duplicated values.
Stack	stacks.h	Stores data in a chain. Objects are placed into this structure in the order received, into the top position. Objects are pushed and popped from the top of the stack (LIFO).

FDS classes

FDS families emphasize the way classes are stored in memory. These classes do not have specialized members contained in ADT classes. FDS families support vectors, lists, hash tables, and binary trees. The following table lists and describes FDS class families.

Table 15.2 FDS class families

Family	Header file	Description
Double List	dlistimp.h	Stores data in a linked chain of nodes, where each node contains pointers to the previous and to the next node in the list.
Hash Table	hashimp.h	Stores objects in a hash table data structure. The hash table family implements the ADT Dictionary family.
List	listimp.h	Stores objects in a linked chain of nodes, where each node contains a pointer to the next node in the list.
Vector	vectimp.h	Stores objects in a collection of blocks of contiguous memory. The vector family implements most ADT class families.

Class naming conventions

A Borland C++ ADT class name is formatted to express the functions it performs for you automatically, together with the FDS class family it uses to perform those functions. An FDS class name is similarly formatted.

The following figures use typical class names to define and illustrate this naming format:

Figure 15.1 Format of a typical ADT name

The letter **"T"** precedes all container class names. **"T"** stands for Template.

The ADT class family name corresponds to a data structure name, like **array, stack, set, queue** or **bag**. This class stores data in a one-dimensional array.

The word **"As"** separates the ADT name from the FDS name.

The word **"Iterator"** is appended to the ADT name to identify the Iterator class designed to act on the container class.

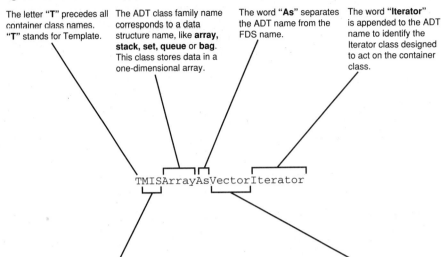

TMISArrayAsVectorIterator

Use your memory manager object or use default memory manager. Class function codes specify whether this class is designed to contain objects or pointers, or can automatically sort or count objects as they are inserted. Some classes have no function codes.

The codes in this example indicate that this class takes your **M**emory Manager as an input parameter, stores pointers (manages objects **I**ndirectly), and places pointers in **S**orted order by object.

The name of the FDS class used to implement this ADT class. This class uses the FDS Vector family to implement its array.

Most ADT classes use the FDS vector family, but some families also use FDS list or double list families. The ADT Dictionary family uses the FDS hash table family.

Figure 15.2 Format of a typical FDS class name

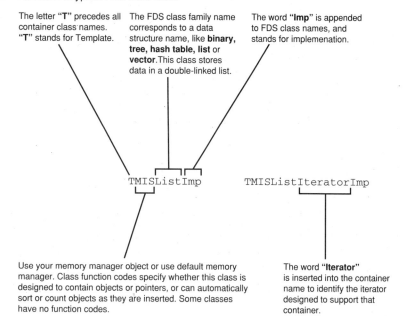

The letter "**T**" precedes all container class names. "**T**" stands for Template.

The FDS class family name corresponds to a data structure name, like **binary, tree, hash table, list** or **vector**. This class stores data in a double-linked list.

The word "**Imp**" is appended to FDS class names, and stands for implemenation.

TMISListImp   TMISListIteratorImp

Use your memory manager object or use default memory manager. Class function codes specify whether this class is designed to contain objects or pointers, or can automatically sort or count objects as they are inserted. Some classes have no function codes.

The codes in this example indicate that this class takes your **M**emory Manager as an input parameter, stores pointers (manages objects indirectly), and places pointers in **S**orted order by object.

The word "**Iterator**" is inserted into the container name to identify the iterator designed to support that container.

Class function codes

Every class template name is encoded with the mechanisms it uses to manage stored objects. The following table lists and defines these mechanisms.

Table 15.3 Class function codes

Abbreviation	Description
T	Borland class library prefix. All container classes start with 'T'.
M	Supports a user-supplied memory manager.
I	Stores pointers to objects rather than the objects themselves (Indirect container).
S	Places objects in sorted order as they are placed into the container. Indirect containers hold pointers in sorted order by object.
C	Keeps a count of objects stored in the container.
D	Stores objects themselves (Direct container). Used in Association classes.

Simplified class template names

To simplify coding, the container class library includes a brief set of simplified class names, that stand for the most commonly used container classes. The following table lists these names together with the classes they stand for.

Table 15.4   Simplified class template names

Simplified name	Class name
TArray	TArrayAsVector
TArrayIterator	TArrayAsVectorIterator
TBag	TBagAsVector
TBagIterator	TBagAsVectorIterator
TBinaryTree	TBinaryTreeImp
TBinaryTreeIterator	TBinaryTreeIteratorImp
TDictionary	TDictionaryAsHashTable
TDictionaryIterator	TDictionaryAsHashTableIterator
TDeque	TDequeAsVector
TDequeIterator	TDequeAsVectorIterator
TDoubleList	TDoubleListImp
TDoubleListListIterator	TDoubleListIteratorImp
TList	TListImp
TListIterator	TListIteratorImp
TQueue	TQueueAsVector
TQueueIterator	TQueueAsVectorIterator
TSet	TSetAsVector
TSetIterator	TSetAsVectorIterator
TStack	TStackAsVector
TStackIterator	TStackAsVectorIterator

Using containers

This section reviews major tasks involving containers, describes operations on data stored in containers, and lists a general procedure you can follow to use container classes in your program.

Using class templates

Borland C++ container classes are implemented using C++ templates. A template is a class declaration that accepts a number of data types as input parameters, and produces an instance of that class that supports those data types. You may specify a predefined data type like a **float**, or you can specify the name of a class you have designed, declared and named yourself. All Borland C++ templates take the data type of the object to be stored in the container object, as a template parameter. Some Borland C++ containers also take the data type of your memory-manager class as well.

A class template instantiates a class that stores objects of the type you have specified as the template parameter. It instantiates a class, not an object. You may create an object at the same time you instantiate the class using the syntax in the following example:

```
TArrayAsVector<float> FloatArray(10);
```

This example instantiates an instance of the *TArrayAsVector* class that stores **float**s. It then instantiates an object of that class called *FloatArray*, that stores 10 **float**s. The *FloatArray* object contains all the members you need to call, to add, search, change and remove **float**s from the array—you don't need to write them.

Using direct and indirect classes

Containers can store copies of objects (direct containers) or pointers to objects (indirect containers). Indirect containers contain the letter *I* in their template names. Class template names without the letter *I* in their name instantiate direct containers. See the following examples:

- This example instantiates a *TArrayAsVector* object that stores ten **float**s. This is a direct container.

  ```
  TArrayAsVector<float> FloatArray(10);
  ```

- This example instantiates a *TIArrayAsVector* object that stores ten pointers to **float**s. The container manages pointers for you. This is an indirect container that works almost exactly like the direct containe in the previous example.

  ```
  TIArrayAsVector<float> FloatArray(10)
  ```

The type of object you need to store helps determine whether you need to use a direct or indirect container. You would probably select a direct container to store an array of **float**s because a **float** does not use much memory. You would probably use an indirect container to store a group of **struct**s, to reduce copying time.

The choice between direct and indirect containers is often not easy. Performance tuning requires you to compare performance of different container implementations, and this can involve lots of recoding. You can reduce this recoding effort by using Borland C++ containers, because direct and indirect containers in the same family use the same members to perform the same data operations.

If your program includes a stored object that is accessed by more than one container, then you will need use indirect containers to store pointers to that object. You must take care not to delete that stored object from memory until all containers have finished using that object. Refer to "Deleting container objects" later in this chapter for details.

If you plan to store objects of your own defined type in either a direct or indirect container, then you must supply a valid == operator, a default constructor, a less-than (<) operator, and an assignment (=) operator within the class definition for your object. Refer to the reference selection defining the container class you have selected to use, for details concerning operators and methods you must provide before using.

Handling pointers in direct and indirect containers

In most cases, you should use an indirect container to store pointers—but it is still possible to use a direct container to store pointers. Direct and indirect containers handle pointers differently.

When using the == and < operators to determine whether two objects are equal:

- Direct containers containing pointers to objects compare pointer values. The == operator returns **true** only if two pointer objects contain the same address.

- Indirect containers compare dereferenced object values. The == operator returns **true** only if the target objects contain the same value.

A direct container does not automatically dereference objects. It sorts pointers by memory location, rather than by object value. When a direct object goes out of scope, it automatically destroys the pointers to objects it held—you must provide code to maintain access to those objects.

Using memory-managed classes

All containers can use the default memory manager class *TStandardAllocator* to manage memory. You do not need to pass this default class to an unmanaged container—the compiler handles this for you.

Some containers can support your own memory manager. If you use your own memory manager class, you must use a managed container class template, and then pass the class name of this memory manager to your managed class template when you instantiate an object of that class.

Your custom memory manager must include static operator members. Because they are static, you never instantiate your memory manager class. You must call memory manager methods directly.

Because it will support stored objects of your own data type, your custom memory manager class must define a class-specific **new** operator, a placement *new* operator that takes a **void*** argument as its second parameter, and a **delete** operator. Use the *TStandardAllocator* prototypes in alloctr.h as an example for building your own overloaded operators.

The following example uses a class template in the queue family that accepts your memory manager of type *MyMemManager* as a template parameter. It instantiates a queue object that can hold 100 objects of type *MyClass*.

```
TMQueueAsVector <MyClass, MyMemManager> MyQueue(100);
```

Using sorted classes

Some containers can automatically store objects in sorted order. Indirect sorted containers store pointers sorted by object.

If you plan to store objects of your own defined type in either a direct or indirect container, then you must supply a valid < operator within the class definition for your object. The *Add* member needs this < operator to resolve element ordering when it adds an object to its container.

Using iterator classes

Many operations require you to iterate through all objects stored in a container object. To simplify iteration, every class family includes a set of iterator class templates that correspond to individual container class templates in the family. To iterate, pass a reference to your container object to its iterator object.

Container iterators implement the following members:

- *Current* is a member function which returns the current object.

- *Restart* is a member function which resets the iterator to the first object in the container.

- ++ pre- and postincrement operators move the object pointed to by *Current*, to the next object in the container.

- The deque family iterator classes also contain pre- and postdecrement operators.

Note   You may also iterate without using iterators, by calling the *ForEach, FirstThat,* or *LastThat* members built into your instantiated container object.

This example illustrates the iteration process using an iterator object:

1 Define your container and iterator objects. To minimize typing errors and make your code more readable, you should **typedef** your container and iterator class templates: Also note that the iterator contains a nested template parameter list, ending in two greater-than symbols. The compiler will misinterpret this symbol set as a streams operator unless you place a space between these two symbols.

```
typedef TArrayAsVector<float> arrayType;
typedef TArrayAsVectorIterator <TArrayAsVector<float> > iteratorType;
                                               ... place a space here.
```

2 Instantiate your container and iterator objects. Instantiate the container before you instantiate an iterator.

To begin iteration, instantiate an iterator object, and then pass your container to your iterator. This code slice instantiates a container object named *FloatArray* and in iterator object called *iter*. It then passes *FloatArray* to *iter* to begin iterating through the objects that *FloatArray* contains.

```
arrayType FloatArray(10);
   ⋮
iteratorType Iter(FloatArray);
```

3 Iterate through the container using *Current* and ++ iterator members.

For clarity, the example below places iteration activity in a self-contained function, *UseIterator*.

UseIterator instantiates an iterator object named *iter* and passes a reference to the *FloatArray* container to it. First, it uses the *iter.Current* member to return data stored at the object the iterator is currently pointing to. Then it prints that **float** value to your screen and increments the *Current* pointer to the next object, until all **float**s stored in

FloatArray have been printed to your screen. If you have stored objects of a type you have defined, then you must overload the << operator to support that data type.

Note An iterator does not interate through a container automatically. You must increment the iterator object in your code. This is not true for the *ForEach* container member function, which iterate automatically. Refer to the *ForEach* member description for the container class template you have selected to use, for details.

```
void UseIterator ( const arrayType & FloatArray )
{
    iteratorType Iter(FloatArray);

    // loop through all objects in the
    // FloatArray container

    while (Iter != 0);
        {

        // print data stored in the current object
        // to the screen.

        cout << Iter.Current ( ) << endl;

        // increment the Current pointer to the next object.
        // Current returns zero when it reaches the end.
        // operator int returns zero in an empty container
        // before Current is called.

        Iter++;
        }
}
```

Using iterator members

Most container classes contain the members *FirstThat*, *ForEach*, and *LastThat*.

- *ForEach* provides a general mechanism you can use to access all data stored in your container.

  ForEach iterates through all objects your container currently holds. For each object, it calls a callback function, which acts on data stored in that object. Then it procedes to the next object and calls your function again, until it has visited all objects stored in your container.

- *FirstThat* and *LastThat* call a callback function which tests data stored within the current object. These members return either the first object or the last object passing your test condition.

You must write the callback functions called by these methods. They should accept a reference to the type of object stored in your container, and a void pointer. *FirstThat* and *LastThat* require that this function should receive a **const** reference to your type; should be a *const* function; and should return zero if data does not pass your test, and return a nonzero value if data does pass your test.

Note   You must take care never to call *Detach* or *Flush* from within your callback function. *Detach* and *Flush* act on objects, not data, and will resize your container under some conditions. Resizing a container while iterating through the objects it contains will produce undefined results.

Callback functions

Your callback functions must conform precisely to the signature expected by *ForEach*, *FirstThat*, and *LastThat*. For coding convenience, all container classes **typedef** these signatures as follows:

- The *IterFunc* **typedef** defines a function taking a reference to your object type, and a **void** pointer. It defines this function as an **IterFunc*, and uses this **typedef** as the first argument passed to a call to *ForEach* member.

  Your custom *iter* function accesses data via the object reference, and returns nothing.

- The *CondFunc* **typedef** defines a function taking a **const** reference to your object type, and a **void** pointer. It defines this function as a **CondFunc*, and uses this **typedef** as the first argument passed to a call to *FirstThat* and *LastThat* members.

  Your custom *cond* function must access data via the **const** object reference and test data. It must return zero if data fails your conditional test; nonzero if data passes your conditional test.

You must use *IterFunc* and *CondFunc* **typedef**s when calling *ForEach*, *FirstThat*, and *LastThat*.

Deleting container objects

All containers store copies of objects, whether those objects are data, or are pointers to data. Direct containers destroy objects automatically when they are removed, or when the container goes out of scope. Indirect containers destroy the pointers they store, but do not automatically destroy objects referenced by their pointers. You must decide whether these objects should also be destroyed.

This is not a simple design decision. You may design a program that creates several containers, each holding its own pointer to the same object. You may mistakenly delete an object still in use by another indirect container.

In general, you can remove a pointer from an indirect container at any time, but you should delete the object referenced by that pointer from memory only only after the last container is through with that object. You are responsible for writing code that manages the deletion of objects accessed by more than one container.

The container class library provides a mechanism to simplify this object management process, called object ownership. It is described in the following section.

To delete objects from memory, follow these general guidelines:

- For an ADT container, call the *Destroy* member. For containers which do not provide a *Destroy* member, call *Detach* or *Flush* and pass *TShouldDelete::Delete* as an input parameter.

- For an FDS container, call *Detach* or *Flush*, which takes a *del* value as an input parameter. Set *del* equal to some nonzero value.

To remove objects from a container but leave it in memory, follow these guidelines:

- For an ADT container, call *Detach* or *Flush* and pass *TShouldDelete::NoDelete* as a parameter. You should have determined that you can still access this object though a pointer or other container before calling *Detach* or *Flush*.

- For an FDS container, call *Detach* or *Flush* and set the *del* input parameter to zero. You should have determined that you can still access this object though a pointer or other container before calling *Detach* or *Flush*.

Object ownership

Indirect containers in ADT class families use the concept of object ownership to determine if an object should be deleted when it is removed. A container object owns its objects when it has the right to delete them from memory.

Ownership for a container object is determined by an object of the *TShouldDelete* class, which is a base class. Every indirect ADT container object derives from an object of the *TShouldDelete* class. *TShouldDelete* performs two similar tasks, accessed through the members listed below.

TShouldDelete::OwnsElements determines the default behavior for your container's *Detach* and *Flush* functions. If *OwnsElements* specifies ownership, then *Detach* and *Flush* will perform the actions set in the *DeleteType* **enum** defined in *TShouldDelete*. The *DeleteType* value is passed as an input parameter by *Detach* and *Flush*. If *OwnsElements* specifies no ownership, then *Detach* and *Flush* will not delete removed objects from memory.

Set *TShouldDelete::OwnsElements* parameters as follows:

- Pass a zero to the *TShouldDelete::OwnsElements* input parameter for *Detach* and *Flush*, if you do not want its container to own the objects it holds. Stored objects removed from a container will be retained in memory.

- Pass any nonzero value to the *TShouldDelete::OwnsElements* input parameter for *Detach* and *Flush*, if you do want its container to own the objects it holds. When set to a nonzero value, *Detach* and *Flush* perform the task specified by the *DeleteType* **enum**.

The *DeleteType* **enum** overrides behavior set by *OwnsElements* for your container.

- *NoDelete* never deletes objects from memory when they are removed from the container.

- *DefDelete* performs the default behavior for your container. This behavior is listed in the *Flush* and *Delete* member definitions for the class family which defines your container object.

- *Delete* always deletes objects from memory upon being removed from the container.

The user programming interface

This section defines major container class library operations and lists important members used to perform those operations. It does not list all members and does not review all possible operations.

Creating a container object

Create a container object by instantiating it. To create a container, select a container template that supports functions that meet your program requirements and pass the type of the object your container will store, to your class template when you instantiate your container object.

The following example instantiates an empty array container that can store 10 **float**s, and places this object on the stack. This object calls its destructor when it goes out of scope.

```
TArrayAsVector <float> arrayObject(10);
```

The following example instantiates a *TArrayAsVector<float>* pointer and an empty array container that can store ten **float**s. It places the container on the heap and sets the pointer to point to the container. This object persists in your program until you explicitly call the *delete* operator to delete the container from memory.

```
TArrayAsVector <float> *aPointer = new TArrayAsVector<float>(10);
```

Adding objects to a container

All containers are empty when they are created. Use the container *Add* member to add objects to the container. Stack containers use their *Push* member to add objects to the stack. Deques use *PutLeft* and *PutRight*. Queues use *Put*.

Searching for an existing object in a container

Most containers provide a *Find* member, which returns a pointer or a reference to the first occurance of the value you pass to it. Array containers can also return an array index value. The Dictionary *Find* member takes a value of type *Key*, and returns a pointer or a reference to data of type *Value*.

Removing an object from a container

All containers provide a *Detach* member, which searches through stored objects and removes the first object matching the value given as an input parameter. For indirect containers, the stored pointer is always removed from the container, and an object ownership input parameter determines whether its referenced object is also removed from memory. See "Deleting container objects" and "Object ownership" earlier in this chapter for details.

Most containers provide a *Flush* member, which removes all objects from a container. For indirect containers, stored pointers are always removed from the container, and an object ownership input parameter determines whether their referenced objects are also removed from memory. See "Deleting container objects" and "Object ownership" for details.

Retrieving objects from a container

Most containers can use an iterator technique to retrieve a stored value. See the following section.

Some containers provide a *Find* member, which can return a value stored at an array or vector index, or can search for the value passed to it.

Stack objects use *Pop*.

Queue objects use *Get*.

Deque objects use *GetLeft* and *GetRight*.

Iterating through objects stored in a container

The container class library provides two iteration techniques:

- Most container classes provide the member functions *ForEach, FirstThat,* and *LastThat*. For each object, the member function calls a user-written function which accesses the value it stores. To use *ForEach, FirstThat,* and *LastThat*, you must write a function which acts on data stored in the current object. *ForEach* always visits each object stored in a container.

- Each container class has a corresponding iterator class. To iterate, pass the container object to the iterator object. To act upon data stored at a current location within a container, call the iterator *Current* function to return a stored value, write code which acts upon that value, and then use the ++ operator to index the iterator to the next object in the container. An iterator does not automatically visit every object stored in a container.

Displaying data stored in containers

In general, you can use *iostreams* operators for built-in data types, but must supply overridden insertion and extraction operators for your own data types. See the example at the end of this chapter for a container storing user-typed objects that prints values to your terminal screen.

To print data of your own type to your terminal screen, follow these general steps:

1 In a class of your own type, provide an << operator. This function takes a reference to an *ostream* object and a **const** reference to your class type, and returns the ostream. The body of the function formats your data.

2 You can now use *cout* and << to insert objects of your class type into the stream that displays data on your screen.

Container coding guidelines

This section lists some general guidelines you can follow to use containers in your code.

Selecting and defining your container class

1 Determine the type of elements you will store in your container. Decide whether to store objects themselves, or to store pointers to those objects. Decide whether to use the default memory manager or to manage memory yourself.

2 Select the container family that fits your program design. Containers can store data in arrays, vectors, lists, double lists, stacks, queues, double queues, bags, sets, dictionaries, hash tables, and binary trees. You can implement some choices as vectors or as linked lists. You can use an FDS class to implement a data structure of your own design.

3 From within a container template family, select the template that fits your program design. Container classes can store data or pointers to data, can accept either default or user-supplied memory managers, and can automatically sort elements as they are added to the container. Selecting the appropriate family saves you time because you won't have to write the code to accomplish what the container does for you automatically.

For example, if you have chosen to store pointers to **longs** and want to build an array that holds your pointers in sorted order, instantiate an object of the *TISArrayAsVector<long>* class. An object of this class stores pointers to **longs**, and automatically places the pointer for your current object in sorted order in the array. Objects in this class are always sorted.

Modifying your container class

1 Objects that you store in a container must provide functions listed in the reference section of this guide. In general, containers storing predefined types already have access to the functions they need. Containers supporting your user-defined objects usually require you to supply specializations of the logical and streams operators your program uses.

If you intend to use *FirstThat, ForEach,* and *LastThat* members to iterate through objects stored in your container, you must write callback functions to act on that data. Callback function signatures must conform to *cond* and *iter* **typedef**s listed in the reference section.

Dictionary and hash table containers require access to a *HashValue* function. You must supply this function to hash table containers. You may use the default *HashTable* function supplied in a Dictionary container.

For user-defined classes, you must provide a copy constructor, overloaded equivalence and assignment operators, and overridden streams operators for that class. Classes that will be put into sorted containers require an overloaded less-than operator.

2 If you have decided to use your own memory manager, then you must overload the new and delete operator member declarations in your memory manager class.

In all cases, you can declare these members by copying prototypes declared in *TStandardAllocator* into your own class definition and implement them appropriately. Refer to the *TStandardAllocator* class declaration in the alloctr.h file. Also refer to the example at the end of this chapter, which overloads these members to support a class which manages **int**s in an array container.

Coding your program

1 To promote code maintainability, you should **typedef** the container and iterator class templates you have selected to use. This makes it easy to change a class template while minimizing changes you may need to make to your working code. If you change from a direct to an indirect container, you will also need to review your code to change reference calls to pointer calls in appropriate places.

2 Instantiate a container class from the class template you have decided to use. Pass the data type of the data you will store as a parameter to the class template upon instantiation. Also pass the data type of your memory manager class to your class template, if you have decided to use a managed container class template.

3 Instantiate a container object. Pass appropriate constructor parameters to your object upon instantiation.

4 Instantiate an iterator object, if you have decided to use an iterator to access data stored in your container. Pass your container to your iterator object upon instantiation.

Code example

This example uses an array to store objects of your own user-type, *Contained*. *Contained* objects store **int**s.

Note   Passing an **int** directly to a template will create two *Detach* functions with the same **int** parameter. This will generate a compiler error. The solution is to pass a class of your own user-type to a template upon instantiation, and to store **int**s within objects of that new class. This example illustrates proper **int** storage, and also illustrates how to declare, instantiate and store a class of your own user-type in a container of any family.

This example is similar to the array example found in the Array family reference section. That example stored a built-in type (**long**), and did not require overloaded operators, a custom class declaration, or other special handling.

```
#include <iostream.h>
#include <classlib/arrays.h>
/* Declare a custom class that your array container stores.
   This example is named Contained. It contains
   examples of all the members which you are usually
   required to provide any user-written class, including
   three constructors, two logical operators, and an ostream
   operator. Contained also contains the intValue data member which
   makes it possible for you to store ints in an array container.
*/
class Contained
{
public:
    Contained( int i = 0 ) : intValue(i) {}
```

```cpp
        Contained ( const Contained & c )        // copy constructor
            {intValue = c.intValue;}
        int operator == ( const Contained& c ) //comparison operator
            { return intValue == c.intValue; }
        int operator <  ( const Contained& c ) //less-than operator
            { return intValue <  c.intValue; }
    private:
        int intValue;
        friend ostream& operator <<   ( ostream&, const Contained& );
    };
    ostream& operator << ( ostream& os, const Contained& c )
        { return os << c.intValue; }
    /* This is the code for the iteration function required by ForEach member.
       This function, called Show, takes a reference to the current contained
       object c, and prints it to the screen.
    */
    void Show( Contained& c, void * )
        {
        cout << c << endl;
        }
    /* This code illustrates the use of ForEach. It takes a
       Contained-type object and calls the ForEach iteration
       function named Show. Show executes, passes control
       back to ForEach; ForEach iterates to the next object
       in the array automatically, and calls Show again.
       This process repeats until ForEach has visited
       every element in the array.
    */
    void UseForEach ( TArrayAsVector<Contained>& vect )
        {
        vect.ForEach( Show, 0 );
        }
    /* This code illustrates the use of an iterator object. It
       instantiates an array iterator object named iter and
       prints the array contents to your terminal screen.
       The steam operator works because you have
       overloaded it in your Contained class definition.
       Note that you must increment iter in your code to
       advance to the next object.
    */
    void UseIterator( const TArrayAsVector<Contained>& vect )
        {
        TArrayAsVectorIterator<Contained> iter(vect);
        while( iter != 0 )
            {
            cout << iter.Current() << endl;
            iter++;
            }
        }
    /* The main function instantiates an array container
       named vect, which holds ten objects of type Contained.
       It creates several Contained objects and places
```

```
            those objects into the array container. Then, it detaches the
            contained object which holds the number seven.
            It uses the ForEach vect member to print array
            contents to your screen. Then it uses an Iterator
            object to print out the same array contents to your
            screen.
    */
    int main()
    {
        TArrayAsVector<Contained> vect(10);
        /* A Contained-type object is created and int i is added to it.
           The Contained object is in turn added to the array
           container named vect, using the vect Add member.
        */
        for( int i = 0; i < 10; i++ )
            vect.Add( Contained(i) );
        // remove one Contained object from the vect container.
        vect.Detach( Contained(7) );
        // vect calls its own ForEach member to iterate through the array.
        cout << "Using ForEach:\n";
        UseForEach(vect);
        /* vect uses an iterator object to iterate through the array.
           This is a repeat of the UseForEach process.
        */
        cout << "\nUsing Iterator:\n";
        UseIterator(vect);
        return 0;
    }
```

Output

```
Using ForEach member function to iterate:
0
1
2
3
4
5
6
8
9
Using an iterator object to iterate:
0
1
2
3
4
5
6
8
9
```

16

Using iostreams classes

This chapter provides a brief, practical overview of how to use C++ stream I/O. For specific details on the C++ stream classes and their member functions, see the *C++ Language Reference* , Part III.

Stream input/output in C++ (commonly referred to as *iostreams*, or just *streams*) provides all the functionality of the *stdio* library in ANSI C and much more. Iostreams are used to convert typed objects into readable text, and vice versa. Streams can also read and write binary data. The C++ language lets you define or overload I/O functions and operators that are then called automatically for corresponding user-defined types.

What is a stream?

A stream is an abstraction referring to any flow of data from a source (or *producer*) to a *sink* (or *consumer*). We also use the synonyms *extracting*, *getting*, and *fetching* when speaking of inputting characters from a source; and *inserting*, *putting*, or *storing* when speaking of outputting characters to a sink. Classes are provided that support console output (constrea.h), memory buffers (iostream.h), files (fstream.h), and strings (strstrea.h) as sources or sinks (or both).

The iostream library

The *iostream* library has two parallel families of classes: those derived from *streambuf*, and those derived from *ios*. Both are low-level classes, each doing a different set of jobs. All stream classes have at least one of these two classes as a base class. Access from *ios*-based classes to *streambuf*-based classes is through a pointer.

The streambuf class

The *streambuf* class provides an interface to memory and physical devices. *streambuf* provides underlying methods for buffering and handling streams when little or no formatting is required. The member functions of the *streambuf* family of classes are used by the *ios*-based classes. You can also derive classes from *streambuf* for your own functions and libraries. The buffering classes *conbuf*, *filebuf*, and *strstreambuf* are derived from *streambuf*.

Figure 16.1   Class streambuf and its derived classes

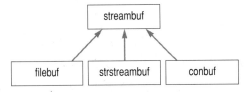

The ios class

The class *ios* (and hence any of its derived classes) contains a pointer to a *streambuf*. It performs formatted I/O with error-checking using a *streambuf*.

An inheritance diagram for all the *ios* family of classes is found in Figure 16.2. For example, the *ifstream* class is derived from the *istream* and *fstreambase* classes, and *istrstream* is derived from *istream* and *strstreambase*. This diagram is not a simple hierarchy because of the generous use of *multiple inheritance*. With multiple inheritance, a single class can inherit from more than one base class. (The C++ language provides for *virtual inheritance* to avoid multiple declarations.) This means, for example, that all the members (data and functions) of *iostream*, *istream*, *ostream*, *fstreambase*, and *ios* are part of objects of the *fstream* class. All classes in the *ios*-based tree use a *streambuf* (or a *filebuf* or *strstreambuf*, which are special cases of a *streambuf*) as its source and/or sink.

C++ programs start with four predefined open streams, declared as objects of *withassign* classes as follows:

```
extern istream_withassign cin;    // Corresponds to stdin; file descriptor 0.
extern ostream_withassign cout;   // Corresponds to stdout; file descriptor 1.
extern ostream_withassign cerr;   // Corresponds to stderr; file descriptor 2.
extern ostream_withassign clog;   // A buffered cerr; file descriptor 2.
```

Figure 16.2   Class ios and its derived classes

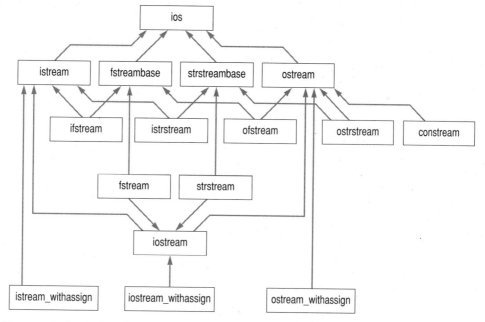

By accepted practice, the arrows point **from** the derived class **to** the base class.

Stream output

Stream output is accomplished with the *insertion* (or *put to)* operator, <<. The standard
left shift operator, <<, is overloaded for output operations. Its left operand is an object of
type *ostream*. Its right operand is any type for which stream output has been defined
(that is, fundamental types or any types you have overloaded it for). For example,

```
cout << "Hello!\n";
```

writes the string "Hello!" to *cout* (the standard output stream, normally your screen)
followed by a new line.

The << operator associates from left to right and returns a reference to the *ostream* object
it is invoked for. This allows several insertions to be cascaded as follows:

```
int i = 8;
double d = 2.34;
    cout << "i = " << i << ", d = " << d << "\n";
```

This will write the following to standard output:

```
i = 8, d = 2.34
```

Fundamental types

The fundamental data types directly supported are **char, short, int, long, char*** (treated
as a string), **float, double, long double**, and **void***. Integral types are formatted

according to the default rules for *printf* (unless you've changed these rules by setting various *ios* flags). For example, the following two output statements give the same result:

```
int i;
long l;
cout << i << " " << l;
printf("%d %ld", i, l);
```

The pointer (**void** *) inserter is used to display pointer addresses:

```
int i;
cout << &i;          // display pointer address in hex
```

Read the description of *ostream* in the C++ *Language Reference*, Chapter 11, for other output functions.

I/O formatting

Formatting for both input and output is determined by various *format state* flags contained in the **class** *ios*. The flags are read and set with the *flags*, *setf*, and *unsetf* member functions.

Output formatting can also be affected by the use of the *fill*, *width*, and *precision* member functions of **class** *ios*.

The format flags are detailed in the description of **class** *ios* in the C++ *Language Reference*, Chapter 11.

Manipulators

A simple way to change some of the format variables is to use a special function-like operator called a *manipulator*. Manipulators take a stream reference as an argument and return a reference to the same stream. You can embed manipulators in a chain of insertions (or extractions) to alter stream states as a side effect without actually performing any insertions (or extractions). Parameterized manipulators must be called for each stream operation. For example,

```
#include <iostream.h>
#include <iomanip.h>   // Required for parameterized manipulators.

int main(void) {
int i = 6789, j = 1234, k = 10;

    cout << setw(6) << i << j << i << k << j;
    cout << "\n";
    cout << setw(6) << i << setw(6) << j << setw(6) << k;
    return(0);
    }
```

produces this output:

```
678912346789101234
6789  1234    10
```

setw is a parameterized manipulator declared in iomanip.h. Other parameterized manipulators, *setbase, setfill, setprecision, setiosflags,* and *resetiosflags,* work in the same way. To make use of these, your program must include iomanip.h. You can write your own manipulators without parameters:

```
#include <iostream.h>

// Tab and prefix the output with a dollar sign.
ostream& money( ostream& output) {
    return output << "\t$";
    }

int main(void) {
    float owed = 1.35, earned = 23.1;
    cout << money << owed << money << earned;
    return(0);
    }
```

produces the following output:

```
$1.35    $23.1
```

The non-parameterized manipulators *dec, hex,* and *oct* (declared in iostream.h) take no arguments and simply change the conversion base (and leave it changed):

```
int i = 36;
cout << dec << i << " " << hex << i << " " << oct << i << endl;
cout << dec;  // Must reset to use decimal base.
// displays 36 24 44
```

Table 16.1   Stream manipulators

Manipulator	Action
dec	Set decimal conversion base format flag.
hex	Set hexadecimal conversion base format flag.
oct	Set octal conversion base format flag.
ws	Extract whitespace characters.
endl	Insert newline and flush stream.
ends	Insert terminal null in string.
flush	Flush an ostream.
setbase(**int** *n*)	Set conversion base format to base *n* (0, 8, 10, or 16). 0 means the default: decimal on output, ANSI C rules for literal integers on input.
resetiosflags(**long** *f*)	Clear the format bits specified by *f*.
setiosflags(**long** *f*)	Set the format bits specified by *f*.
setfill(**int** *c*)	Set the fill character to *c*.
setprecision(**int** *n*)	Set the floating-point precision to *n*.
setw(**int** *n*)	Set field width to *n*.

The manipulator *endl* inserts a newline character and flushes the stream. You can also flush an *ostream* at any time with

```
ostream << flush;
```

Filling and padding

The fill character and the direction of the padding depend on the setting of the fill character and the left, right, and internal flags.

The default fill character is a space. You can vary this by using the function *fill*:

```
int i = 123;
cout.fill('*');
cout.width(6);
cout << i;          // display ***123
```

The default direction of padding gives right-alignment (pad on the left). You can vary these defaults (and other format flags) with the functions *setf* and *unsetf*:

```
int i = 56;
   :
cout.width(6);
cout.fill('#');
cout.setf(ios::left,ios::adjustfield);
cout << i;          // display 56####
```

The second argument, *ios::adjustfield*, tells *setf* which bits to set. The first argument, *ios::left*, tells *setf* what to set those bits to. Alternatively, you can use the manipulators *setfill*, *setiosflags*, and *resetiosflags* to modify the fill character and padding mode. See *ios* data members in the *C++ Language Reference*, Chapter 11, for a list of masks used by *setf*.

Stream input

Stream input is similar to output but uses the overloaded right shift operator, >>, known as the *extraction* (get from) operator or *extractor*. The left operand of >> is an object of type **class** *istream*. As with output, the right operand can be of any type for which stream input has been defined.

By default, >> skips whitespace (as defined by the *isspace* function in ctype.h), then reads in characters appropriate to the type of the input object. Whitespace skipping is controlled by the **ios::skipws** flag in the format state's enumeration. The *skipws* flag is normally set to give whitespace skipping. Clearing this flag (with *setf*, for example) turns off whitespace skipping. There is also a special "sink" manipulator, *ws*, that lets you discard whitespace.

Consider the following example:

```
int i;
double d;
cin >> i >> d;
```

When the last line is executed, the program skips any leading whitespace. The integer value (*i*) is then read. Any whitespace following the integer is ignored. Finally, the floating-point value (*d*) is read.

For type **char** (**signed** or **unsigned**), the effect of the >> operator is to skip whitespace and store the next (non-whitespace) character. If you need to read the next character, whether it is whitespace or not, you can use one of the *get* member functions. See the discussion of *istream* in the *C++ Language Reference*, Chapter 11.

For type **char*** (treated as a string), the effect of the **>>** operator is to skip whitespace and store the next (non-whitespace) characters until another whitespace character is found. A final null character is then appended. Care is needed to avoid "overflowing" a string. You can alter the default width of zero (meaning no limit) using *width* as follows:

```
char array[SIZE];
cin.width(sizeof(array));
cin >> array;              // Avoids overflow.
```

For all input of fundamental types, if only whitespace is encountered, nothing is stored in the target, and the istream state is set to *fail*. The target will retain its previous value; if it was uninitialized, it remains uninitialized.

I/O of user-defined types

To input or output your own defined types, you must overload the extraction and insertion operators. Here is an example:

```
#include <iostream.h>

struct info {
    char *name;
    double val;
    char *units;
    };

// You can overload << for output as follows:
ostream& operator << (ostream& s, info& m) {
    s << m.name << " " << m.val << " " << m.units;
    return s;
    };

// You can overload >> for input as follows:
istream& operator >> (istream& s, info& m) {
    s >> m.name >> m.val >> m.units;
    return s;
    };

int main(void) {
    info x;
    x.name = new char[15];
    x.units = new char[10];

    cout << "\nInput name, value and units:";
    cin >> x;
    cout << "\nMy input:" << x;
    return(0);
    }
```

Simple file I/O

The class *ofstream* inherits the insertion operations from *ostream*, while *ifstream* inherits the extraction operations from *istream*. The file-stream classes also provide constructors and member functions for creating files and handling file I/O. You must include fstream.h in all programs using these classes.

Consider the following example that copies the file FILE.IN to the file FILE.OUT:

```
#include <fstream.h>

int main(void) {
    char ch;
    ifstream f1("FILE.IN");
    ofstream f2("FILE.OUT");

    if (!f1) cerr << "Cannot open FILE.IN for input";
    if (!f2) cerr << "Cannot open FILE.OUT for output";
    while (f2 && f1.get(ch))
        f2.put(ch);
    return(0);
    }
```

Note that if the *ifstream* or *ofstream* constructors are unable to open the specified files, the appropriate stream error state is set.

The constructors let you declare a file stream without specifying a named file. Later, you can associate the file stream with a particular file:

```
ofstream ofile;           // creates output file stream
    :
ofile.open("payroll");  // ofile connects to file "payroll"
// do some payrolling...

ofile.close();            // close the ofile stream
ofile.open("employee"); // ofile can be reused...
```

By default, files are opened in text mode. This means that on input, carriage-return/linefeed sequences are converted to the '\n' character. On output, the '\n' character is converted to a carriage-return/linefeed sequence. These translations are not done in binary mode. The file-opening mode is set with an optional second parameter to the *open* function or in some file-stream constructors. The file opening-mode constants can be used alone or they can be logically ORed together. See the description of **class** *ios* data members in the C++ *Language Reference*, Chapter 11.

String stream processing

The functions defined in strstrea.h support in-memory formatting, similar to *sscanf* and *sprintf*, but much more flexible. All of the *istream* member functions are available for **class** *istrstream* (input *string stream*). This is the same for output: *ostrstream* inherits from *ostream*.

Given a text file with the following format:

```
101 191 Cedar Chest
102 1999.99 Livingroom Set
```

Each line can be parsed into three components: an integer ID, a floating-point price, and a description. The output produced is

```
1: 101   191.00   Cedar Chest
2: 102   1999.99  Livingroom Set
```

Here is the program:

```cpp
#include <fstream.h>
#include <strstrea.h>
#include <iomanip.h>
#include <string.h>

int main(int argc, char **argv) {
    int id;
    float amount;
    char description[41];

    if (argc == 1) {
        cout << "\nInput file name required.";
        return (-1);
    }

    ifstream inf(argv[1]);

    if (inf) {
        char inbuf[81];
        int lineno = 0;

        // Want floats to print as fixed point
        cout.setf(ios::fixed, ios::floatfield);

        // Want floats to always have decimal point
        cout.setf(ios::showpoint);

        while (inf.getline(inbuf,81)) {
            // 'ins' is the string stream:
            istrstream ins(inbuf,strlen(inbuf));
            ins >> id >> amount >> ws;
            ins.getline(description,41);  // Linefeed not copied.
            cout << ++lineno << ": "
                << id << '\t'
                << setprecision(2) << amount << '\t'
                << description << "\n";
        }
    }
    return(0);
}
```

Note the use of format flags and manipulators in this example. The calls to *setf* coupled with *setprecision* allow floating-point numbers to be printed in a money format. The manipulator *ws* skips whitespace before the description string is read.

Screen output streams

The class *constream*, derived from *ostream* and defined in constrea.h, provides the functionality of conio.h for use with C++ streams. This lets you create output streams that write to specified areas of the screen, in specified colors, and at specific locations.

As with conio.h functions, constreams are not available for GUI applications. The screen area created by *constream* is not bordered or otherwise distinguished from the surrounding screen.

Console stream manipulators are provided to facilitate formatting of console streams. These manipulators work in the same way as the corresponding function provided by conio.h. For a detailed description of the manipulators' behavior and valid arguments, see the C++ *Language Reference*, Chapter 11.

Table 16.2   Console stream manipulators

Manipulator	conio function	Action
clreol	*clreol*	Clears to end of line in text window.
delline	*delline*	Deletes line in the text window.
highvideo	*highvideo*	Selects high-intensity characters.
insline	*insline*	Inserts a blank line in the text window.
lowvideo	*lowvideo*	Selects low-intensity characters.
normvideo	*normvideo*	Selects normal-intensity characters.
setattr(**int**)	*textattr*	Sets screen attributes.
setbk(**int**)	*textcolor*	Sets new character color.
setclr(**int**)	*textcolor*	Sets the color.
setcrsrtype(**int**)	*_setcursortype*	Selects cursor appearance.
setxy(**int**, **int**)	*gotoxy*	Positions the cursor at the specified position.

Typical use of parameterized manipulators. See the C++ *Language Reference*, Chapter 11 for a description of **class** *constream*.

```
#include <constrea.h>

int main(void) {
   constream win1;

   win1.window(1, 1, 40, 20); // Initialize the desired space.
   win1.clrscr();             // Clear this rectangle.

   // Use the parameterized manipulator to set screen attributes.
   win1 << setattr((BLUE<<4) | WHITE)
        << "This text is white on blue.";

   // Use this parameterized manipulator to specify output area.
   win1 << setxy(10, 10)
        << "This text is in the middle of the window.";
   return(0);
   }
```

You can create multiple constreams, each writing to its own portion of the screen. Then, you can output to any of them without having to reset the window each time.

```
#include <constrea.h>

int main(void) {
  constream demo1, demo2;

  demo1.window( 1, 2, 40, 10 );
  demo2.window( 1, 12, 40, 20 );

  demo1.clrscr();
  demo2.clrscr();

  demo1 << "Text in first window" << endl;
  demo2 << "Text in second window" << endl;
  demo1 << "Back to the first window" << endl;
  demo2 << "And back to the second window" << endl;
  return(0);
  }
```

17

Using persistent streams classes

This section describes Borland's object streaming support, then explains how to make your objects streamable.

Objects that you create when an application runs—windows, dialog boxes, collections, and so on—are temporary. They are constructed, used, and destroyed as the application proceeds. Objects can appear and disappear as they enter and leave their scope, or when the program terminates. By making your objects streamable you save these objects, either in memory or file streams, so that they *persist* beyond their normal lifespan.

See Chapter 12 of the *C++ Library Reference* for reference details of persistent streams.

There are many applications for persistent objects. When saved in shared memory they can provide interprocess communication. They can be transmitted via modems to other systems. And, most significantly, objects can be saved permanently on disk using file streams. They can then be read back and restored by the same application, by other instances of the same application, or by other applications. Efficient, consistent, and safe streamability is available to all objects.

Building your own streamable classes is straightforward and incurs little overhead. To make your class streamable you need to add specific data members, member functions, and operators. You also must derive your class, either directly or indirectly, from the *TStreamableBase* class. Any derived class is also streamable.

To simplify creating streamable objects, the persistent streams library contains macros that add all the routines necessary to make your classes streamable. The two most important are:

- DECLARE_STREAMABLE
- IMPLEMENT_STREAMABLE

These macros add the boilerplate code necessary to make your objects streamable. In most cases you can make your objects streamable by adding these two macros at appropriate places in your code, as explained later.

What's new with streaming

Object streaming has been significantly changed from Borland's earlier implementation to make it easier to use and more powerful. These changes are compatible with existing code developed with Borland's ObjectWindows and Turbo Vision products.

The new streaming code is easier to use because it provides macros that relieve the programmer of the burden of remembering most of the details needed to create a streamable class. Its other new features include support for multiple inheritance, class versioning, and better system isolation. In addition, the streaming code has been reorganized to make it easier to write libraries that won't force streaming code to be linked in if it isn't used.

There have been several additions to the streaming capabilities. These changes are intended to be backward compatible, so if you compile a working application with the new streaming code, your application should be able to read streams that were written with the old code. There is no provision for writing the old stream format, however. We assume that you'll like the new features so much that you won't want to be without them.

The following sections describe the changes and new capabilities of streaming. Each of these changes is made for you when you use the DECLARE_STREAMABLE and IMPLEMENT_STREAMABLE macros.

Object versioning

Objects in streams now have a version number associated with them. An object version number is a 32-bit value that should not be 0. Whenever an object is written to a stream, its version number will also be written. With versioning you can recognize if there's an older version of the object you're reading in, so you can interpret the stream appropriately.

Reading and writing base classes

In your current code, you might be reading and writing base classes directly, as shown here:

```
void Derived::write( opstream& out )
{
    Base::write( out );
// ...
}
void *Derived::read( ipstream& in )
{
    Base::read( in );
// ...
}
```

This method will continue to work, but it won't write out any version numbers for the base class. To take full advantage of versioning, you should change these calls to use the new template functions that understand about versions:

```
void Derived::Write( opstream& out )
{
    WriteBaseObject( (Base *)this, out );
// ...
}

void *Derived::Read( ipstream& in, uint32 ver )
{
    ReadBaseObject( (Base *)this, in );
// ...
}
```

Note   The cast to a pointer to the base class is essential. If you leave it out, your program may crash.

Reading and writing integers

Old streams wrote **int** and **unsigned** data types as 2-byte values. To move easily to 32-bit platforms, the new streams write **int** and **unsigned** values as 4-byte values. The new streams can read old streams, and will handle the 2-byte values correctly.

The old streams provide two member functions for reading and writing integer values:

```
void writeWord(unsigned);

unsigned readWord();
```

These have been changed in the new streams:

```
void writeWord(uint32);

uint32 readWord();
```

Existing code that uses these functions will continue to work correctly if it is recompiled and relinked, although calls to *readWord* will generate warnings about a loss of precision when the return value is assigned to an **int** or **unsigned** in a 16-bit application. But in new code, all of these functions should be avoided. In general, you probably know the true size of the data being written, so the streaming library now provides separate functions for each data size:

```
void writeWord16(uint16);

void writeWord32(uint32);

uint16 readWord16(unit16);

uint32 readWord32(unit32);
```

Use of these four functions is preferred.

Multiple inheritance and virtual base support

The streaming code now provides four function templates that support virtual base classes and multiple inheritance. The following sections describe these functions.

The ReadVirtualBase and WriteVirtualBase function templates

Any class that has a direct virtual base should use the new *ReadVirtualBase* and *WriteVirtualBase* function templates:

```
void Derived::Write( opstream& out )
{
    WriteVirtualBase( (VirtualBase *)this, out );
// ...
}

void *Derived::Read( ipstream& in, uint32 ver )
{
    ReadVirtualBase( (VirtualBase *)this, in );
// ...
}
```

A class derived from a class with virtual bases does not need to do anything special to deal with those virtual bases. Each class is responsible only for its direct bases.

The ReadBaseObject and WriteBaseObject function templates

Object streams now support multiple inheritance. To read and write multiple bases, use the new *WriteBaseObject* and *ReadBaseObject* function templates for each base:

```
void Derived::Write( opstream& out )
{
    WriteBaseObject( (Base1 *)this, out );
    WriteBaseObject( (Base2 *)this, out ):
// ...
}

void *Derived::Read( ipstream& in, uint32 ver )
{
    ReadBaseObject( (Base1 *)this, in );
    ReadBaseObject( (Base2 *)this, in );
// ...
}
```

Creating streamable objects

The easiest way to make a class streamable is by using the macros supplied in the persistent streams library. The following steps will work for most classes:

1 Make *TStreamableBase* a virtual base of your class, either directly or indirectly.

2 Add the DECLARE_STREAMABLE macro to your class definition.

3 Add the IMPLEMENT_STREAMABLE macro to one of your source files. Adding the IMPLEMENT_CASTABLE macro is also recommended.

4 Write the *Read* and *Write* member function definitions in one of your source files.

The following sections provide details about defining and implementing streamable classes.

Defining streamable classes

To define a streamable class you need to:

- Include objstrm.h
- Base your class on the *TStreamableBase* class
- Include macro DECLARE_STREAMABLE into your class definition. For example,

```
#include <objstrm.h>
class Sample : public TStreamableBase
{
public:
    // member functions, etc.
private:
    int i;
DECLARE_STREAMABLE(IMPEXPMACRO, Sample, 1 );
};
```

Header file objstrm.h provides the classes, templates, and macros that are needed to define a streamable class.

Every streamable class must inherit, directly or indirectly, from the class *TStreamableBase*. In this example, the class *Sample* inherits directly from *TStreamableBase*. A class derived from *Sample* would not need to explicitly inherit from *TStreamableBase* because *Sample* already does. If you are using multiple inheritance, you should make *TStreamableBase* a virtual base instead of a nonvirtual base as shown here. This will make your classes slightly larger, but won't have any other adverse effect on them.

In most cases the DECLARE_STREAMABLE macro is all you need to use when you're defining a streamable class. This macro takes three parameters. The first parameter is used when compiling DLLs. This parameter takes a macro that is meant to expand to either _ _**export**, _ _**import**, or nothing, depending on how the class is to be used in the DLL. See Chapter 12 and Chapter 15 of the C++ *Language Reference* for further explanation. The second parameter is the name of the class that you're defining, and the third is the version number of that class. The streaming code doesn't pay any attention to the version number, so it can be anything that has some significance to you. See the discussion of the nested class *Streamer* for details.

DECLARE_STREAMABLE adds a constructor to your class that takes a parameter of type *StreamableInit*. This is for use by the streaming code; you won't need to use it directly. DECLARE_STREAMABLE also creates two inserters and two extractors for your class so that you can write objects to and read them from persistent streams. For the class *Sample* (shown earlier in this section), these functions have the following prototypes:

```
opstream& operator << ( opstream&, const Sample& );
opstream& operator << ( opstream&, const Sample* );
ipstream& operator >> ( ipstream&, Sample& );
ipstream& operator >> ( ipstream&, Sample*& );
```

The first inserter writes out objects of type *Sample*. The second inserter writes out objects pointed to by a pointer to *Sample*. This inserter gives you the full power of object streaming, because it understands about polymorphism. That is, it will correctly write objects of types derived from *Sample*, and when those objects are read back in using the pointer extractor (the last extractor) they will be read in as their actual types. The extractors are the inverse of the inserters.

Finally, DECLARE_STREAMABLE creates a nested class named *Streamer*, based on the *TStreamer* class, which defines the core of the streaming code.

Implementing streamable classes

Most of the members added to your class by the DECLARE_STREAMABLE macro are inline functions. There are a few, however, that aren't inline; these must be implemented outside of the class. Once again, there are macros to handle these definitions.

The IMPLEMENT_CASTABLE macro provides a rudimentary typesafe downcast mechanism. If you are building with Borland C++ 5.0, you don't need to use this because Borland C++ supports RTTI. However, if you need to build your code with a compiler that does not support RTTI, you will need to use the IMPLEMENT_CASTABLE macro to provide the support that object streaming requires. Although it isn't necessary to use IMPLEMENT_CASTABLE when using Borland C++, you ought to do so anyway if you're concerned about being able to compile your code with another compiler. See Chapter 3 of the C++ *Language Reference* for a discussion of RTTI.

IMPLEMENT_CASTABLE has several variants:

```
IMPLEMENT_CASTABLE( cls )
IMPLEMENT_CASTABLE1( cls, base1 )
IMPLEMENT_CASTABLE2( cls, base1, base2 )
IMPLEMENT_CASTABLE3( cls, base1, base2, base3 )
IMPLEMENT_CASTABLE4( cls, base1, base2, base3, base4 )
IMPLEMENT_CASTABLE5( cls, base1, base2, base3, base4, base5)
```

At some point in your source code you should invoke this macro with the name of your streamable class as its first parameter and the name of all its streamable base classes other than *TStreamableBase* as the succeeding parameters. For example:

```
class Base1 : public virtual TStreamableBase
{
// ...
DECLARE_STREAMABLE( IMPEXPMACRO, Base1, 1 );
};
IMPLEMENT_CASTABLE( Base1 );          // no streamable bases

class Base2 : public virtual TStreamableBase
{
// ...
DECLARE_STREAMABLE( IMPEXPMACRO, Base2, 1 );
};
IMPLEMENT_CASTABLE( Base1 );          // no streamable bases

class Derived : public Base1, public virtual Base2
{
// ...
DECLARE_STREAMABLE( IMPEXPMACRO, Derived, 1 );
};
IMPLEMENT_CASTABLE2( Derived, Base1, Base2 ); //two streamable bases
```

```
class MostDerived : public Derived
{
DECLARE_STREAMABLE( IMPEXPMACRO, MostDerived, 1 );
};
IMPLEMENT_CASTABLE1( MostDerived, Derived ); //one streamable base
```

The class *Derived* uses IMPLEMENT_CASTABLE2 because it has two streamable base classes.

In addition to the IMPLEMENT_CASTABLE macros, you should invoke the appropriate IMPLEMENT_STREAMABLE macro somewhere in your code. The IMPLEMENT_STREAMABLE macro looks like the IMPLEMENT_CASTABLE macros:

```
IMPLEMENT_STREAMABLE( cls )
IMPLEMENT_STREAMABLE1( cls, base1 )
IMPLEMENT_STREAMABLE2( cls, base1, base2 )
IMPLEMENT_STREAMABLE3( cls, base1, base2, base3 )
IMPLEMENT_STREAMABLE4( cls, base1, base2, base3, base4 )
IMPLEMENT_STREAMABLE5( cls, base1, base2, base3, base4, base5 )
```

The IMPLEMENT_STREAMABLE macros have one important difference from the IMPLEMENT_CASTABLE macros: when using the IMPLEMENT_STREAMABLE macros you must list all the streamable base classes of your class in the parameter list, and you must list all virtual base classes that are streamable. This is because the IMPLEMENT_STREAMABLE macros define the special constructor that the object streaming code uses; that constructor must call the corresponding constructor for all of its direct base classes and all of its virtual bases. For example:

```
class Base1 : public virtual TStreamableBase
{
// ...
DECLARE_STREAMABLE( IMPEXPMACRO, Base1, 1 );
};
IMPLEMENT_CASTABLE( Base1 );          // no streamable bases
IMPLEMENT_STREAMABLE( Base1 ); // no streamable bases

class Base2 : public virtual TStreamableBase
{
// ...
DECLARE_STREAMABLE( IMPEXPMACRO, Base2, 1 );
};
IMPLEMENT_CASTABLE( Base1 );          // no streamable bases
IMPLEMENT_STREAMABLE( Base1 ); // no streamable bases

class Derived : public Base1, public virtual Base2
{
// ..
DECLARE_STREAMABLE( IMPEXPMACRO, Derived, 1 );
};
IMPLEMENT_CASTABLE2( Derived, Base1, Base2 );
IMPLEMENT_STREAMABLE2( Derived, Base1, Base2 );

class MostDerived : public Derived
{
// ...
DECLARE_STREAMABLE( IMPEXPMACRO, MostDerived, 1 );
};
```

```
IMPLEMENT_CASTABLE1( MostDerived, Derived );
IMPLEMENT_STREAMABLE2( MostDerived, Derived, Base2 );
```

The nested class Streamer

The nested class *Streamer* is the core of the streaming code for your objects. The
DECLARE_STREAMABLE macro creates *Streamer* inside your class. It is a protected
member, so classes derived from your class can access it. *Streamer* inherits from
TNewStreamer, which is internal to the object streaming system. It inherits the following
two pure **virtual** functions:

```
virtual void Write( opstream& ) const = 0;
virtual void *Read( ipstream&, uint32 ) const = 0;
```

Streamer overrides these two functions, but does not provide definitions for them. You
must write these two functions: *Write* should write any data that needs to be read back
in to reconstruct the object, and *Read* should read that data. *Streamer::GetObject* returns a
pointer to the object being streamed. For example:

```
class Demo : public TStreamableBase
{
    int i;
    int j;
public:
    Demo( int ii, int jj ) : i(ii), j(jj) {}
DECLARE_STREAMABLE( IMPEXPMACRO, Demo, 1 );
};
IMPLEMENT_CASTABLE( Demo );
IMPLEMENT_STREAMABLE( Demo );

void *Demo::Streamer::Read( ipstream& in, uint32 ) const
{
    in >> GetObject()->i >> GetObject()->j;
    return GetObject();
}

void Demo::Streamer::Write( opstream& out ) const
{
    out << GetObject()->i << GetObject()->j;
}
```

Writing the Read and Write functions

It is usually easiest to implement the *Read* function before implementing the *Write*
function. To implement *Read* you need to:

* Know what data you need in order to reconstruct the new streamable object.
* Devise a sensible way of reading that data into the new streamable object.

Then implement *Write* to work in parallel with *Read* so that it sets up the data that *Read*
will later read. The streaming classes provide several operators to make this easier. For
example, *opstream* provides inserters for all the built-in types, just as *ostream* does. So all
you need to do to write out any of the built-in types is to insert them into the stream.

You also need to write out base classes. In the old ObjectWindows and Turbo Vision streaming, this was done by calling the base's *Read* and *Write* functions directly. This doesn't work with code that uses the new streams, because of the way class versioning is handled.

The streaming library provides template functions to use when reading and writing base classes. *ReadVirtualBase* and *WriteVirtualBase* are used for virtual base classes, and *ReadBaseObject* and *WriteBaseObject* are used for nonvirtual bases. Just like IMPLEMENT_CASTABLE, you only need to deal with direct bases. Virtual bases of your base classes will be handled by the base class, as shown in this example:

```
class Base1 : public virtual TStreamableBase
{
int i;
DECLARE_STREAMABLE( IMPEXPMACRO, Base1, 1 );
};
IMPLEMENT_CASTABLE( Base1 );            // no streamable bases
IMPLEMENT_STREAMABLE( Base1 ); // no streamable bases
void Base1::Streamer::Write( opstream& out ) const
{
   out << GetObject()->i;
}

class Base2 : public virtual TStreamableBase
{
int j;
DECLARE_STREAMABLE( IMPEXPMACRO, Base2, 1 );
};
IMPLEMENT_CASTABLE( Base1 );            // no streamable bases
IMPLEMENT_STREAMABLE( Base1 ); // no streamable bases
void Base2::Streamer::Write( opstream& out ) const
{
   out << GetObject()->j;
}

class Derived : public Base1, public virtual Base2
{
int k;
DECLARE_STREAMABLE( IMPEXPMACRO, Derived, 1 );
};
IMPLEMENT_CASTABLE2( Derived, Base1, Base2 );
IMPLEMENT_STREAMABLE2( Derived, Base1, Base2 );
void Derived::Streamer::Write( opstream& out ) const
{
   WriteBaseObject( (Base1 *)this, out );
   WriteVirtualBase( (Base2 *)this, out );
   out << GetObject()->k;
}

class MostDerived : public Derived
{
int m;
DECLARE_STREAMABLE( IMPEXPMACRO, MostDerived, 1 );
};
```

```
IMPLEMENT_CASTABLE1( MostDerived, Derived );
IMPLEMENT_STREAMABLE2( MostDerived, Derived, Base2 );
void MostDerived::Streamer::Write( opstream& out ) const
{
   WriteBaseObject( (Derived *)this, out );
   out << GetObject()->m;
}
```

When you're writing out a base class, don't forget to cast the **this** pointer. Without the cast, the template function will think it's writing out your class and not the base class. The result will be that it calls your *Write* or *Read* function rather than the base's. This results in a lengthy series of recursive calls, which will eventually crash.

Object versioning

You can assign version numbers to different implementations of the same class as you change them in the course of maintenance. This doesn't mean that you can use different versions of the same class in the same program, but it lets you write your streaming code in such a way that a program using the newer version of a class can read a stream that contains the data for an older version of a class. For example:

```
class Sample : public TStreamableBase
{
int i;
DECLARE_STREAMABLE( IMPEXPMACRO, Sample, 1 );
};
IMPLEMENT_CASTABLE( Sample );
IMPLEMENT_STREAMABLE( Sample );
void Sample::Streamer::Write( opstream& out ) const
{
   out << GetObject()->i;
}
void *Sample::Streamer::Read( ipstream& in, uint32 ) const
{
   in >> GetObject()->i;
   return GetObject();
}
```

Suppose you've written out several objects of this type into a file and you discover that you need to change the class definition. You'd do it something like this:

```
class Sample : public TStreamableBase
{
int i;
int j;          // new data member
DECLARE_STREAMABLE( IMPEXPMACRO, Sample, 2 );// new version number
};
IMPLEMENT_CASTABLE( Sample );
IMPLEMENT_STREAMABLE( Sample );
void Sample::Streamer::Write( opstream& out ) const
{
   out << GetObject()->i;
   out << GetObject()->j;
```

```
      }
void *Sample::Streamer::Read( ipstream& in, uint32 ver ) const
{
    in >> GetObject()->i;
    if( ver > 1 )
                in >> GetObject()->j;
    else
                GetObject()->j = 0;
    return GetObject();
}
```

Streams written with the old version of *Sample* will have a version number of 1 for all objects of type *Sample*. Streams written with the new version will have a version number of 2 for all objects of type *Sample*. The code in *Read* checks that version number to determine what data is present in the stream.

The streaming library used in the previous versions of ObjectWindows and Turbo Vision doesn't support object versioning. If you use the new library to read files created with that library, your *Read* function will be passed a version number of 0. Other than that, the version number has no significance to the streaming library, and you can use it however you want.

Using the mathematical classes

This chapter explains how to use *complex* and *bcd* numerical types.

Using complex types

Complex numbers are numbers of the form $x + yi$, where x and y are real numbers, and i is the square root of -1. Borland C++ has always had a type

```
struct complex
{
    double  x, y;
};
```

defined in math.h. This type is convenient for holding complex numbers, because they can be considered a pair of real numbers. However, the limitations of C make arithmetic with complex numbers rather cumbersome. With the addition of C++, complex math is much simpler.

A significant advantage to using the Borland C++ *complex* numerical type is that all of the ANSI C Standard mathematical routines are defined to operate with it. These mathematical routines are not defined for use with the C **struct complex**.

Note   See Part III, "Borland C++ class libraries guide," for more information.

To use complex numbers in C++, all you have to do is to include complex.h. In complex.h, all the following have been overloaded to handle complex numbers:

- All of the binary arithmetic operators.
- The input and output operators, >> and <<.
- The ANSI C math functions.

The complex library is invoked only if the argument is of type *complex*. Thus, to get the complex square root of -1, use

```
sqrt(complex(-1))
```

and not

```
sqrt(-1)
```

The following functions are defined by class *complex*:

```
double  arg(complex&);     // angle in the plane
complex conj(complex&);    // complex conjugate
double  imag(complex&);    // imaginary part
double  norm(complex&);    // square of the magnitude
double  real(complex&);    // real part
// Use polar coordinates to create a complex.
complex polar(double mag, double angle = 0);
```

Using bcd types

Borland C++, along with almost every other computer and compiler, does arithmetic on binary numbers (that is, base 2). This can sometimes be confusing to people who are used to decimal (base 10) representations. Many numbers that are exactly representable in base 10, such as 0.01, can only be approximated in base 2.

Note   See Part III, "Borland C++ class libraries guide," for more information.

Binary numbers are preferable for most applications, but in some situations the round-off error involved in converting between base 2 and 10 is undesirable. The most common example of this is a financial or accounting application, where the pennies are supposed to add up. Consider the following program to add up 100 pennies and subtract a dollar:

```
#include <stdio.h>
int i;
float x = 0.0;
for (i = 0; i < 100; ++i)
    x += 0.01;
x -= 1.0;
printf("100*.01 - 1 = %g\n",x);
```

The correct answer is 0.0, but the computed answer is a small number close to 0.0. The computation magnifies the tiny round-off error that occurs when converting 0.01 to base 2. Changing the type of *x* to **double** or **long double** reduces the error, but does not eliminate it.

To solve this problem, Borland C++ offers the C++ type *bcd*, which is declared in bcd.h. With *bcd*, the number 0.01 is represented exactly, and the *bcd* variable *x* provides an exact penny count.

```
#include <bcd.h>
int i;
bcd x = 0.0;
for (i = 0; i < 100; ++i)
    x += 0.01;
x -= 1.0;
cout << "100*.01 - 1 = " << x << "\n";
```

Here are some facts to keep in mind about *bcd*:

- *bcd* does not eliminate all round-off error: A computation like 1.0/3.0 will still have round-off error.

- *bcd* types can be used with ANSI C math functions.

- *bcd* numbers have about 17 decimal digits precision, and a range of about 1×10^{-125} to 1×10^{125}.

Converting bcd numbers

bcd is a defined type distinct from **float**, **double**, or **long double**; decimal arithmetic is performed only when at least one operand is of the type *bcd*.

Note   The *bcd* member function *real* is available for converting a *bcd* number back to one of the usual formats (**float**, **double**, or **long double**), though the conversion is not done automatically. *real* does the necessary conversion to **long double**, which can then be converted to other types using the usual C conversions. For example, a *bcd* can be printed using any of the following four output statements with *cout* and *printf*.

```
/* PRINTING bcd NUMBERS */
/* This must be compiled as a C++ program. */
#include <bcd.h>
#include <iostream.h>
#include <stdio.h>

void main(void) {
   bcd a = 12.1;
   double x = real(a); // This conversion required for printf().

   printf("\na = %g", x);
   printf("\na = %Lg", real(a));
   printf("\na = %g", (double)real(a));
   cout << "\na = " << a; // The preferred method.
   }
```

Note that since *printf* doesn't do argument checking, the format specifier must have the *L* if the **long double** value *real(a)* is passed.

Number of decimal digits

You can specify how many decimal digits after the decimal point are to be carried in a conversion from a binary type to a *bcd*. The number of places is an optional second argument to the constructor *bcd*. For example, to convert $1000.00/7 to a *bcd* variable rounded to the nearest penny, use

```
bcd a = bcd(1000.00/7, 2)
```

where 2 indicates two digits following the decimal point. Thus,

```
1000.00/7              =      142.85714...
bcd(1000.00/7, 2)      =      142.860
bcd(1000.00/7, 1)      =      142.900
bcd(1000.00/7, 0)      =      143.000
bcd(1000.00/7, -1)     =      140.000
bcd(1000.00/7, -2)     =      100.000
```

The number is rounded using banker's rounding (as specified by IEEE), which rounds to the nearest whole number, with ties being rounded to an even digit. For example,

```
bcd(12.335, 2)         =      12.34
bcd(12.345, 2)         =      12.34
bcd(12.355, 2)         =      12.36
```

Standard class libraries guide

Part IV documents the Rogue Wave Software, Inc., implementation of the *Standard C++ Library*. It assumes that you are already familiar with the basics features of the C++ programming language. If you are new to C++ you may wish to examine an introductory text, such as the book *The C++ Programming Language*, by Bjarne Stroustrup (Addison-Wesley, 1991).

Part IV, "Standard Class Libraries Guide" documents Rogue Wave's implementation of the Standard C++ Library.

Based on ANSI's Working Paper for Draft Proposed International Standard for Information Systems—Programming Language C++. April 28, 1995.

Reading this part

There is a classic "chicken-and-egg" problem associated with the container class portion of the standard library. The heart of the container class library is the definition of the containers themselves, but you can't really appreciate the utility of these structures without an understanding of the algorithms that so greatly extend their functionality. On the other hand, you can't really understand the algorithms without some appreciation of the containers.

Therefore, after reading Chapters 19, 20, and 21 carefully, Chapters 22 through 28 should be read concurrently with Chapters 29 and 30. Alternatively, simply skim over Chapters 22 through 28 and Chapters 29 and 30 to gain a superficial understanding of the overall structure, then go back and read these sections again in more detail.

Typeface conventions used in this part

We have presented both *class_names* and `function_names()` in a distinctive font the first time they are introduced. In addition, when we wish to refer to a function name or algorithm name but not draw attention to the arguments, we will follow the function name with an empty pair of parenthesis. We do this even when the actual function invocation requires additional arguments. We have used the term *algorithm* to refer to the functions in the generic algorithms portion of the standard library, so as to avoid confusion with member functions, argument functions, and functions defined by the programmer. Note that both class names and function names in the standard library follow the convention of using an underline character as a separator. Throughout the text, examples and file names are printed in the same `Courier font` used for function names.

In the text, it is common to omit printing the class name in the distinctive font after it has been introduced. This is intended to make the appearance of the text less visually disruptive. However, we return to the distinctive font to make a distinction between several different possibilities, as for example between the classes *vector* and *list* used as containers in constructing a *stack*.

What is the Standard C++ Library?

The International Standards Organization (ISO) and the American National Standards Institute (ANSI) are completing the process of standardizing the C++ programming language. A major result of this standardization process is the Standard C++ Library, a large and comprehensive collection of classes and functions. This product is *Rogue Wave*'s implementation of the ANSI/ISO Standard Library.

The ANSI/ISO Standard C++ Library includes the following parts:

- A large *set* of data structures and algorithms formerly known as the Standard Template Library (STL).

- An IOStream facility.

- A locale facility.

- A templatized *string* class.

- A templatized class for representing complex numbers.

- A uniform framework for describing the execution environment, through the use of a template class named *numeric_limits* and specializations for each fundamental data type.

- Memory management features.

- Language support features.

- Exception handling features.

This version of the *Rogue Wave Standard C++ Library* includes the data structures and algorithms libraries (STL), and the *string*, *complex*, and *numeric_limits* classes.

Does the Standard C++ Library differ from other libraries?

A major portion of the Standard C++ Library is comprised of a collection of class definitions for standard data structures and a collection of algorithms commonly used to manipulate such structures. This part of the library was formerly known as the Standard Template Library or STL. The organization and design of the STL differs in almost all respects from the design of most other C++ libraries, *because it avoids encapsulation and uses almost no inheritance.*

An emphasis on encapsulation is a key hallmark of object-oriented programming. The emphasis on combining data and functionality into an object is a powerful organization principle in software development; indeed it is *the* primary organizational technique. Through the proper use of encapsulation, even exceedingly complex software systems can be divided into manageable units and assigned to various members of a team of programmers for development.

Inheritance is a powerful technique for permitting code sharing and software reuse, but it is most applicable when two or more classes share a common set of basic features. For example, in a graphical user interface, two types of windows may inherit from a common base window class, and the individual subclasses will provide any required unique features. In another use of inheritance, object-oriented container classes may ensure common behavior and support code reuse by inheriting from a more general class, and factoring out common member functions.

The designers of the STL decided against using an entirely object-oriented approach, and separated the tasks to be performed using common data structures from the representation of the structures themselves. This is why the STL is properly viewed as a collection of algorithms and, separate from these, a collection of data structures that can be manipulated using the algorithms.

What are the effects of non-object-oriented design?

The STL portion of the Standard C++ Library was purposely designed with an architecture that is not object-oriented. This design has some side effects, some advantageous, and some not, that developers must be aware of as they investigate how to most effectively use the library. We'll discuss a few of them here.

Smaller source code

There are approximately fifty different algorithms in the STL, and about a dozen major data structures. This separation of has the effect of reducing the size of source code, and decreasing some of the risk that similar activities will have dissimilar interfaces. Were it not for this separation, for example, each of the algorithms would have to be re-implemented in each of the different data structures, requiring several hundred more member functions than are found in the present scheme.

Flexibility

One advantage of the separation of algorithms from data structures is that such algorithms can be used with conventional C++ pointers and arrays. Because C++ arrays are not objects, algorithms encapsulated within a class hierarchy seldom have this ability.

Efficiency

The STL in particular, and the Standard C++ Library in general, provide a low-level, "nuts and bolts" approach to developing C++ applications. This low-level approach can be useful when specific programs require an emphasis on efficient coding and speed of execution.

Iterators: mismatches and invalidations

The Standard C++ Library data structures use pointer-like objects called iterators to describe the contents of a container. (These are described in detail in Chapter 19, "Iterators".) Given the library's architecture, it is not possible to verify that these iterator elements are matched; i.e., that they are derived from the same container. Using (either intentionally or by accident) a beginning iterator from one container with an ending iterator from another is a recipe for certain disaster.

It is very important to know that iterators can become invalidated as a result of a subsequent insertion or deletion from the underlying container class. This invalidation is not checked, and use of an invalid iterator can produce unexpected results.

Familiarity with the Standard C++ Library will help reduce the number of errors related to iterators.

Templates: errors and "code bloat"

The flexibility and power of templatized algorithms is, with most compilers, purchased at a loss of precision in diagnostics. Errors in the parameter lists to generic algorithms will sometimes be manifest only as obscure compiler errors for internal functions that are defined many levels deep in template expansions. Again, familiarity with the algorithms and their requirements is a key to successful use of the standard library.

Because of its heavy reliance on templates, the STL can cause programs to grow larger than expected. You can minimize this problem by learning to recognize the cost of instantiating a particular template class, and by making appropriate design decisions. Be aware that as compilers become more and more fluent in templates, this will become less of a problem.

Multithreading problems

The Standard C++ Library must be used carefully in a multithreaded environment. Iterators, because they exist independently of the containers they operate on, cannot be safely passed between threads. Since iterators can be used to modify a non `const` container, there is no way to protect such a container if it spawns iterators in multiple threads. Use "thread-safe" wrappers, such as those provided by *Tools.h++*, if you need to access a container from multiple threads.

How should I use the Standard C++ Library?

Within a few years the Standard C++ Library will be the standard set of classes and libraries delivered with all ANSI-conforming C++ compilers. We have noted that the design of a large portion of the Standard C++ Library is in many ways not object-oriented. On the other hand, C++, excels as a language for manipulating objects. How do we integrate the Standard Library's non-object-oriented architecture with C++'s strengths as a language for manipulating objects?

The key is to use the right tool for each task. Object-oriented design methods and programming techniques are almost without peer as guideposts in the development of large complex software. For the large majority of programming tasks, object-oriented techniques will remain the preferred approach. And, products such as Rogue Wave's *Tools.h++ 7.0*, which will encapsulate the Standard C++ Library with a familiar object-oriented interface, will provide you with the power of the Library and the advantages of object-orientation.

Use Standard C++ Library components directly when you need flexibility and/or highly efficient code. Use the more traditional approaches to object-oriented design, such as encapsulation and inheritance, when you need to model larger problem domains, and knit all the pieces into a full solution. When you need to devise an architecture for your application, *always* consider the use of encapsulation and inheritance to compartmentalize the problem. But if you discover that you need an efficient data structure or algorithm for a compact problem, such as data stream manipulation in drivers (the kind of problem that often resolves to a single class), look to the Standard C++ Library. The Standard C++ Library excels in the creation of reusable classes, where low-level constructs are needed, while traditional OOP techniques really shine when those classes are combined to solve a larger problem.

In the future, most libraries will use the Standard C++ Library as their foundation. By using the Standard C++ Library, either directly or through an encapsulation such as *Tools.h++ 7.0*, you help insure interoperability. This is especially important in large projects that may rely on communication between several libraries. A good rule of thumb is to use the highest encapsulation level available to you, but make sure that the Standard C++ Library is available as the base for interlibrary communication and operation.

The C++ language supports a wide range of programming approaches because the problems we need to solve require that range. The language, and now the Standard C++ library that supports it, are designed to give you the power to approach each unique problem from the best possible angle. The Standard C++ Library, when combined with more traditional OOP techniques, puts a very flexible tool into the hands of anyone building a collection of C++ classes, whether those classes are intended to stand alone as a library or are tailored to a specific task.

Using the Standard Library

Because the Standard C++ Library consists largely of template declarations, on most platforms it is only necessary to include in your programs the appropriate header files. These header files will be noted in the text that describes how to use each algorithm or class.

Using the Standard Template Library with Borland C++

This document describes an implementation of the Standard Template Library (STL) that is consistent with the ANSI/ISO C++ working paper. In order to provide a completely flexible library, the working paper specifies the use of two template features that are not yet supported in the current version of Borland C++. The template features which are not yet supported are *member function templates* and the *use of template parameters to define default types*.

Although the documentation includes some information about STL features which are not yet supported, you don't need to take any special actions to start using the library. The header file for each container defines alternate forms which Borland C++ automatically inserts in your code. You must include the necessary header files in the manner described by this document.

Member function templates

Member function templates are used in all containers provided by the Standard Template Library. An example of this is the constructor for *deque<T>* that takes two templated iterators:

```
template <class InputIterator>
 deque (InputIterator, InputIterator);
```

deque also has an insert function of this type. Borland C++ does not support the use of functions that would allow you to use any type of input iterator as arguments. The header file for each container provides substitute functions that let you use an iterator obtained from the same type of container as the one you are constructing (or calling a member function on), or you can use a pointer to the type of element that's in the container.

For example, to avoid member function templates, you can construct a *deque* in the following two ways:

```
int intarray[10];
 deque<int> first_deque(intarray,intarray + 10);

deque<int>
 second_deque(first_deque.begin(),first_deque.end());
```

But you cannot construct a *deque* this way:

```
deque<long>
 long_deque(first_dequef.begin(),first_deque.end());
```

because the `long_deque` and `first_deque` are not the same type.

A container can have other member function templates besides the constructor. In general, the header file for each container provides an alternate non-template function prototype.

Template parameters

A template function can use template parameters that are initialized with a default value. The following topics describe the extent of Borland C++ support and how you should use the STL.

Default template arguments

Borland C++ supports the following form of default template arguments:

```
template < class T = int > class Array;
```

This syntax supports the construction of *Array* objects which, by default, are containers for **int** types. It's possible to use any type in place of **int** including other user-defined types.

Using template parameters to define default types

Borland C++ does not support functions with template parameters which are used to specify default types. Therefore, you must always supply all template arguments that would otherwise use one of their parameters to generate a default type.

For example, there is a version of the *stack* container that uses a template parameter to define a default type for another parameter. In the following declaration, the generic type *T* is used to instantiate a *deque* object. But *deque* is a generic type that depends on a generic type *T*.

The declaration is as follows.

```
template <class T, class Container = deque<T> >
 class stack;  // This form is not supported
```

The stack.h header file provides an alternate form which is supported by Borland C++. This class declaration does not extend the scope of template parameters to define other parameters. The declaration is as follows.

```
template <class T, class Container> class stack;
```

To construct a *stack* type, you must always supply all arguments. You must instantiate your *stack* type by writing something like this:

```
stack<double, deque<double> > MyStack;
```

Using the STL header files

For the STL implementation to work correctly, you must always include files as specified in this document. For example, to use the STL *string* implementation, you must have the following in your code:

```
#include <string>
```

Similarly, to use the STL generic algorithms, you must have the following in your code:

```
#include <algorithm >
```

Running the tutorial programs

All the tutorial programs described in this text have been gathered together and are available as part of the distribution package. You can compile and run these programs, and use them as models for your own programming problems. Many of these example programs have been extended with additional output commands that are not reproduced here in the text. The expected output from each program is also included as part of the distribution.

Terminology used in this part

bidirectional iterator   An iterator that can be used for reading and writing, and which can move in either a forward or backward direction.

binary function   A function that requires two arguments.

binder   A function adaptor that is used to convert a two-argument binary function object into a one-argument unary function object, by binding one of the argument values to a specific constant.

constant iterator   An iterator that can be used only for reading values, which cannot be used to modify the values in a sequence.

container class   A class used to hold a collection of similarly typed values. The container classes provided by the standard library include vector, list, deque, set, map, stack, queue, and priority_queue.

deque   An indexable container class. Elements can be accessed by their position in the container. Provides fast random access to elements. Additions to either the front or the back of a deque are efficient. Insertions into the middle are not efficient.

forward iterator   An iterator that can be used either for reading or writing, but which moves only forward through a collection.

function object   An instance of a class that defines the parenthesis operator as one of its member functions. When a function object is used in place of a function, the parenthesis member function will be executed when the function would normally be invoked.

generic algorithm   A templated algorithm that is not specialized to any specific container type. Because of this, generic algorithms can be used with a wide variety of different forms of container.

heap   A way of organizing a collection so as to permit rapid insertion of new values, and rapid access to and removal of the largest value of the collection.

heterogeneous collection   A collection of values that are not all of the same type. In the standard library a heterogeneous collection can only be maintained by storing pointers to objects, rather than objects themselves.

insert iterator   An adaptor used to convert iterator write operations into insertions into a container.

iterator   A generalization of the idea of a pointer. An iterator denotes a specific element in a container, and can be used to cycle through the elements being held by a container.

generator   A function that can potentially return a different value each time it is invoked. A random number generator is one example.

input iterator   An iterator that can be used to read values in sequence, but cannot be used for writing.

list   A linear container class. Elements are maintained in sequence. Provides fast access only to the first and last elements. Insertions into the middle of a list are efficient.

map   An indexed and ordered container class. Unlike a vector or deque, the index values for a map can be any ordered data type (such as a string or character). Values are maintained in sequence, and can be efficiently inserted, accessed or removed in any order.

multimap   A form of map that permits multiple elements to be indexed using the same value.

multiset   A form of set that permits multiple instances of the same value to be maintained in the collection.

negator   An adaptor that converts a predicate function object, producing a new function object that when invoked yields the opposite value.

ordered collection   A collection in which all values are ordered according to some binary comparison operator. The set data type automatically maintains an ordered collection. Other collections (vector, deque, list) can be converted into an ordered collection.

output iterator   An iterator that can be used only to write elements into a container, it cannot be used to read values.

past the end iterator   An iterator that marks the end of a range of values, such as the end of the set of values maintained by a container.

predicate   A function or function object that when invoked returns a Boolean (true/false) value or an integer value.

predicate function   A predicate.

priority_queue   An adaptor container class, usually built on top of a vector or deque. The priority queue is designed for rapidly accessing and removing the largest element in the collection.

queue   An adaptor container class, usually built on top of a list or deque. The queue provides rapid access to the topmost element. Elements are removed from a queue in the same order they are inserted into the queue.

random access iterator   An iterator that can be subscripted, so as to access the values in a container in any order.

range   A subset of the elements held by a container. A range is typically specified by two iterators.

reverse iterator,   An iterator that moves over a sequence of values in reverse order, such as back to front.

sequence   A portion or all of the elements held by a container. A sequence is usually described by a range.

set   An ordered container class. The set container is optimized for insertions, removals, and tests for inclusion.

stack   An adaptor container class, built usually on top of a vector or deque. The stack provides rapid access to the topmost element. Elements are removed from a stack in the reverse of the order they are inserted into the stack.

stream iterator   An adaptor that converts iterator operations into stream operations. Can be use to either read from or write to an iostream.

unary function   A function that requires only one argument. Applying a binder to a binary function results in a unary function.

vector   An indexable container class. Elements are accessed using a key that represents their position in the container. Provides fast random access to elements. Addition to the end of a vector is efficient. Insertion into the middle is not efficient.

wide string   A string with 16-bit characters. Wide strings are necessary for many non-roman alphabets, i.e., Japanese.

19

Iterators

Note   **Iterators:** *Iterators* are pointer-like objects, used to cycle through the elements stored in a container.

Fundamental to the use of the container classes and the associated algorithms provided by the standard library is the concept of an *iterator*. Abstractly, an iterator is simply a pointer-like object used to cycle through all the elements stored in a container. Because different algorithms need to traverse containers in variety of fashions, there are different forms of iterator. Each container class in the standard library can generate an iterator with functionality appropriate to the storage technique used in implementing the container. It is the category of iterators required as arguments that chiefly distinguishes which algorithms in the standard library can be used with which container classes.

Note   **Range:** A *range* is a sequence of values held in a container. The range is described by a pair of iterators, which define the beginning and end of the sequence.

Just as pointers can be used in a variety of ways in traditional programming, iterators are also used for a number of different purposes. An iterator can be used to denote a specific value, just as a pointer can be used to reference a specific memory location. On the other hand, a *pair* of iterators can be used to describe a *range* of values, in a manner analogous to the way in which two pointers can be used to describe a contiguous region of memory. In the case of iterators, however, the values being described are not necessarily physically in sequence, but are rather logically in sequence, because they are derived from the same container, and the second follows the first in the order in which the elements are maintained by the container.

Conventional pointers can sometimes be *null*, that is, they point at nothing. Iterators, as well, can fail to denote any specific value. Just as it is a logical error to dereference a null pointer, it is an error to dereference an iterator that is not denoting a value.

When two pointers that describe a region in memory are used in a C++ program, it is conventional that the ending pointer is *not* considered to be part of the region. For example, an array named x of length ten is sometimes described as extending from x to x+10, even though the element at x+10 is not part of the array. Instead, the pointer value x+10 is the *past-the-end* value—the element that is the next value *after* the end of the range being described. Iterators are used to describe a range in the same manner. The second value is not considered to be part of the range being denoted. Instead, the second value is a *past-the-end* element, describing the next value in sequence after the final value of the range. Sometimes, as with pointers to memory, this will be an actual value in the container. Other times it may be a special value, specifically constructed for the purpose. In either case, it is not proper to dereference an iterator that is being used to specify the end of a range.

Just as with conventional pointers, the fundamental operation used to modify an iterator is the increment operator (operator ++). When the increment operator is applied to an iterator that denotes the final value in a sequence, it will be changed to the "past-the-end" value. An iterator j is said to be *reachable* from an iterator i if, after a finite sequence of applications of the expression ++i, the iterator i becomes equal to j.

Note   **Iterator ranges:** When iterators are used to describe a range of values in a container, it is assumed (but not verified) that the second iterator is reachable from the first. Errors will occur if this is not true.

Ranges can be used to describe the entire contents of a container, by constructing an iterator to the initial element and a special "ending" iterator. Ranges can also be used to describe subsequences within a single container, by employing two iterators to specific values. Whenever two iterators are used to describe a range it is assumed, but not verified, that the second iterator is reachable from the first. Errors can occur if this expectation is not satisfied.

In the remainder of this section we will describe the different forms of iterators used by the standard library, as well as various other iterator-related functions.

Varieties of iterators

There are five basic forms of iterators used in the standard library:

input iterator	read only, forward moving
output iterator	write only, forward moving
forward iterator	both read and write, forward moving
bidirectional iterator	read and write, forward and backward moving
random access iterator	read and write, random access

Iterator categories are hierarchical. Forward iterators can be used wherever input or output iterators are required, bidirectional iterators can be used in place of forward iterators, and random access iterators can be used in situations requiring bidirectionality.

A second characteristic of iterators is whether or not they can be used to modify the values held by their associated container. A *constant iterator* is one that can be used for access only, and cannot be used for modification. Output iterators are never constant, and input iterators always are. Other iterators may or may not be constant, depending upon how they are created. There are both constant and non-constant bidirectional iterators, both constant and non-constant random access iterators, and so on.

The following table summarizes specific ways that various categories of iterators are generated by the containers in the standard library.

Iterator form	Produced by
input iterator	istream_iterator
output iterator	ostream_iterator
	inserter
	front_inserter
	back_inserter
bidirectional iterator	*list*
	set and *multiset*
	map and *multimap*
random access iterator	ordinary pointers
	vector
	deque

In the following sections we will describe the capabilities and construction of each form of iterator.

Input iterators

Input iterators are the simplest form of iterator. To understand their capabilities, consider an example program. The `find()` generic algorithm (to be described in more detail in "Searching operations"), performs a simple linear search, looking for a specific value being held within a container. The contents of the container are described using two iterators, here called first and last. While first is not equal to last the element denoted by first is compared to the test value. If equal, the iterator, which now denotes the located element, is returned. If not equal, the first iterator is incremented, and the loop cycles once more. If the entire region of memory is examined without finding the desired value, then the algorithm returns the end-of-range iterator.

```
template <class InputIterator, class T>
InputIterator
  find (InputIterator first, InputIterator last, const T& value)
{
 while (first != last && *first != value)
  ++first;
 return first;
}
```

This algorithm illustrates three requirements for an input iterator:

* An iterator can be compared for equality to another iterator. They are equal when they point to the same position, and are otherwise not equal.

* An iterator can be dereferenced using the * operator, to obtain the value being denoted by the iterator.

- An iterator can be incremented, so that it refers to the next element in sequence, using the operator ++.

Notice that these characteristics can all be provided with new meanings in a C++ program, since the behavior of the given functions can all be modified by overloading the appropriate operators. It is because of this overloading that iterators are possible. There are three main varieties of input iterators:

Ordinary pointers. Ordinary pointers can be used as input iterators. In fact, since we can subscript and add to ordinary pointers, they are random access values, and thus can be used either as input or output iterators. The end-of-range pointer describes the end of a contiguous region of memory, and the deference and increment operators have their conventional meanings. For example, the following searches for the value 7 in an array of integers:

```
intdata[100];

   . . .
int * where = find(data, data+100, 7);
```

Note **Ordinary pointers as iterators:** Because ordinary pointers have the same functionality as random access iterators, most of the generic algorithms in the standard library can be used with conventional C++ arrays, as well as with the containers provided by the standard library.

Note that constant pointers, pointers which do not permit the underlying array to be modified, can be created by simply placing the keyword const in a declaration.

```
const int * first = data;
const int * last = data + 100;
 // can't modify location returned by the following
const int * where = find(first, last, 7);
```

Container iterators. All of the iterators constructed for the various containers provided by the standard library are at *least* as general as input iterators. The iterator for the first element in a collection is always constructed by the member function begin(), while the iterator that denotes the "past-the-end" location is generated by the member function end(). For example, the following searches for the value 7 in a list of integers:

```
list<int>::iterator where = find(aList.begin(), aList.end(), 7);
```

Each container that supports iterators provides a type within the class declaration with the name iterator. Using this, iterators can uniformly be declared in the fashion shown. If the container being accessed is constant, or if the description const_iterator is used, then the iterator is a constant iterator.

Input stream iterators. The standard library provides a mechanism to operate on an input *stream* using an input iterator. This ability is provided by the class istream_iterator, and will be described in more detail in "Input stream iterators."

Output iterators

An output iterator has the opposite functionality from an input iterator. Output iterators can be used to assign values in a sequence, but cannot be used to access values. For example, we can use an output iterator in a generic algorithm that copies values from one sequence into another:

```
template <class InputIterator, classOutputIterator>
OutputIterator copy
  (InputIterator first, InputIterator last, OutputIterator result)
{
 while (first != last)
  *result++ = *first++;
    return result;
}
```

Note   **Parallel sequences:** A number of the generic algorithms manipulate two parallel sequences. Frequently the second sequence is described using only a beginning iterator, rather than an iterator pair. It is assumed, but not checked, that the second sequence has at least as many elements as the first.

Two ranges are being manipulated here; the range of source values specified by a pair of input iterators, and the destination range. The latter, however, is specified by only a single argument. It is assumed that the destination is large enough to include all values, and errors will ensue if this is not the case.

As illustrated by this algorithm, an output iterator can modify the element to which it points, by being used as the target for an assignment. Indeed, output iterators can use the dereference operator only in this fashion, and cannot be used to return or access the elements they denote.

As we noted earlier, ordinary pointers, as well as all the iterators constructed by containers in the standard library, can be used as examples of output iterators. (Ordinary pointers are random access iterators, which are a superset of output iterators.) So, for example, the following code fragment copies elements from an ordinary C-style array into an standard library *vector*:

```
int data[100];
vector<int> newdata(100);
  ...
copy (data, data+100, newdata.begin());
```

Just as the `istream_iterator` provided a way to operate on an input stream using the input iterator mechanism, the standard library provides a data type `ostream_iterator`, that permits values to be written to an output stream in an iterator-like fashion. These will be described in "Output stream iterators."

Yet another form of output iterator is an *insert iterator*. An insert iterator changes the output iterator operations of dereferencing/assignment and increment into insertions into a container. This permits operations such as `copy()` to be used with variable length containers, such as lists and sets.

Forward iterators

A forward iterator combines the features of an input iterator and an output iterator. It permits values to both be accessed and modified. One function that uses forward iterators is the `replace()` generic algorithm, which replaces occurrences of specific values with other values. This algorithm is written as follows:

```
template <class ForwardIterator, class T>
void
 replace (ForwardIterator first, ForwardIterator last,
     const T& old_value, const T& new_value)
{
 while (first != last) {
  if (*first == old_value)
   *first = new_value;
  ++first;
    }
}
```

Ordinary pointers, as well as any of the iterators produced by containers in the standard library, can be used as forward iterators. The following, for example, replaces instances of the value 7 with the value 11 in a *vector* of integers.

```
replace (aVec.begin(), aVec.end(), 7, 11);
```

Bidirectional iterators

A bidirectional iterator is similar to a forward iterator, except that bidirectional iterators support the decrement operator (operator --), permitting movement in either a forward or a backward direction through the elements of a container. For example, we can use bidirectional iterators in a function that reverses the values of a container, placing the results into a new container.

```
template <class BidirectionalIterator, class OutputIterator>
OutputIterator
 reverse_copy (BidirectionalIterator first,
      BidirectionalIterator last,
      OutputIterator result)
{
 while (first != last)
  *result++ = *--last;
 return result;
}
```

As always, the value initially denoted by the last argument is not considered to be part of the collection.

The `reverse_copy()` function could be used, for example, to reverse the values of a linked *list*, and place the result into a *vector*:

```
list<int> aList;
  ...
vector<int> aVec (aList.size());
reverse_copy (aList.begin(), aList.end(), aVec.begin() );
```

Random-access iterators

Some algorithms require more functionality than the ability to access values in either a forward or backward direction. Random access iterators permit values to be accessed by subscript, subtracted one from another (to yield the number of elements between their respective values) or modified by arithmetic operations, all in a manner similar to conventional pointers.

When using conventional pointers, arithmetic operations can be related to the underlying memory; that is, $x+10$ is the memory ten elements after the beginning of x. With iterators the logical meaning is preserved ($x+10$ is the tenth element after x), however the physical addresses being described may be different.

Algorithms that use random-access iterators include generic operations such as sorting and binary search. For example, the following algorithm randomly shuffles the elements of a container. This is similar to, although simpler than, the function random_shuffle() provided by the standard library.

```
template <class RandomAccessIterator>
void
 mixup (RandomAccessIterator first, RandomAccessIterator last)
{
 while (first < last) {
  iter_swap(first, first + randomInteger(last - first));
  ++first;
 }
}
```

Note **randomInteger():** The function randomInteger described here is used in a number of the example programs presented in later sections.

The program will cycle as long as first is denoting a position that occurs earlier in the sequence than the one denoted by last. Only random-access iterators can be compared using relational operators, all other iterators can be compared only for equality or inequality. On each cycle through the loop, the expression last - first yields the number of elements between the two limits. The function randomInteger() is assumed to generate a random number between 0 and the argument. Using the standard random number generator, this function could be written as follows:

```
unsigned int randomInteger (unsigned int n)
 // return random integer greater than
 // or equal to 0 and less than n
{
 return rand() % n;
}
```

This random value is added to the iterator first, resulting in an iterator to a randomly selected value in the container. This value is then swapped with the element denoted by the iterator first.

Reverse iterators

An iterator naturally imposes an order on an underlying container of values. For a *vector* or a *map* the order is given by increasing index values. For a *set* it is the increasing order of the elements held in the container. For a *list* the order is explicitly derived from the fashion in which values are inserted.

A *reverse iterator* will yield values in exactly the reverse order of those given by the standard iterators. That is, for a *vector* or a *list*, a reverse iterator will generate the last element first, and the first element last. For a *set* it will generate the largest element first, and the smallest element last. Strictly speaking, reverse iterators are not themselves a new category of iterator. Rather, there are reverse bidirectional iterators, reverse random access iterators, and so on.

The *list*, *set*, and *map* data types provide a pair of member functions that produce reverse bidirectional iterators. The functions rbegin() and rend() generate iterators that cycle through the underlying container in reverse order. Increments to such iterators move backward, and decrements move forward through the sequence.

Similarly, the *vector* and *deque* data types provide functions (also named rbegin() and rend()) that produce reverse random access iterators. Subscript and addition operators, as well as increments to such iterators move backward within the sequence.

Stream iterators

Stream iterators are used to access an existing input or output stream using iterator operations.

Input stream iterators

Note **Stream iterators:** An input stream iterator permits an input stream to be read using iterator operations. An output stream iterator similarly writes to an output stream when iterator operations are executed.

As we noted in the discussion of input iterators, the standard library provides a mechanism to turn an input stream into an input iterator. This ability is provided by the class istream_iterator. When declared, the two template arguments are the element type, and a type that measures the distance between elements. Almost always the latter is the standard type ptrdiff_t. The single argument provided to the constructor for an istream_iterator is the stream to be accessed. Each time the ++ operator is invoked on an input stream iterator a new value from the stream is read (using the >> operator) and stored. This value is then available through the use of the dereference operator (operator *). The value constructed by istream_iterator when no arguments are provided to the constructor can be used as an ending iterator value. The following, for example, finds the first value 7 in a file of integer values:

```
istream_iterator<int, ptrdiff_t> intstream(cin), eof;
istream_iterator<int, ptrdiff_t>::iterator where =
    find(intstream, eof, 7);
```

The element denoted by an iterator for an input stream is valid only until the next element in the stream is requested. Also, since an input stream iterator is an input iterator, elements can only be accessed, they cannot be modified by assignment. Finally, elements can be accessed only once, and only in a forward moving direction. If you want to read the contents of a stream more than one time, you must create a separate iterator for each pass.

Output stream iterators

The output stream iterator mechanism is analogous to the input stream iterator. Each time a value is assigned to the iterator, it will be written on the associated output stream, using the >> operator. To create an output stream iterator you must specify, as an argument with the constructor, the associated output stream. Values written to the output stream must recognize the stream >> operation. An optional second argument to the constructor is a string that will be used as a separator between each pair of values. The following, for example, copies all the values from a *vector* into the standard output, and separates each value by a space:

```
copy (newdata.begin(), newdata.end(),
    ostream_iterator<int> (cout, " "));
```

Simple file transformation algorithms can be created by combining input and output stream iterators and the various algorithms provided by the standard library. The following short program reads a file of integers from the standard input, removes all occurrences of the value 7, and copies the remainder to the standard output, separating each value by a new line:

```
void main()
{
  istream_iterator<int, ptrdiff_t> input (cin), eof;
ostream_iterator<int> output (cout, "\n");

remove_copy (input, eof, output, 7);

}
```

Insert iterators

Assignment to the dereferenced value of an output iterator is normally used to *overwrite* the contents of an existing location. For example, the following invocation of the function copy() transfers values from one *vector* to another, although the space for the second *vector* was already set aside (and even initialized) by the declaration statement:

```
vector<int> a(10);
vector<int> b(10);
  ...
copy (a.begin(), a.end(), b.begin());
```

Even structures such as lists can be overwritten in this fashion. The following assumes that the *list* named c has at least ten elements. The initial ten locations in the *list* will be replaced by the contents of the *vector* a.

```
list<int> c;
...
copy (a.begin(), a.end(), c.begin());
```

With structures such as lists and sets, which are dynamically enlarged as new elements are added, it is frequently more appropriate to *insert* new values into the structure, rather than to *overwrite* existing locations. A type of adaptor called an *insert iterator* allows us to use algorithms such as `copy()` to insert into the associated container, rather than overwrite elements in the container. The output operations of the iterator are changed into insertions into the associated container. The following, for example, inserts the values of the *vector* a into an initially empty *list*:

```
list<int> d;

copy (a.begin(), a.end(), front_inserter(d));
```

There are three forms of insert iterators, all of which can be used to change a *copy* operation into an *insert* operation. The iterator generated using `front_inserter`, shown above, inserts values into the front of the container. The iterator generated by `back_inserter` places elements into the back of the container. Both forms can be used with *lists*, *deques*, and even *vectors*, but not with *sets* or *maps*.

The third, and most general, form is `inserter`, which takes two arguments; a container and an iterator within the container. This form copies elements into the specified location in the container. (For a *list*, this means elements are copied immediately before the specified location). This form can be used with all the structures for which the previous two forms work, as well as with sets and maps.

The following simple program illustrates the use of all three forms of insert iterators. First, the values 3, 2, and 1 are inserted into the front of an initially empty *list*. Note that, as they are inserted each value becomes the new front, so that the resultant *list* is ordered 1, 2, 3. Next, the values 7, 8, and 9 are inserted into the end of the *list*. Finally, the `find()` operation is used to locate an iterator that denotes the 7 value, and the numbers 4, 5, and 6 are inserted immediately prior. The result is the *list* of numbers from 1 to 9 in order.

```
void main() {
  int threeToOne [ ] = {3, 2, 1};
  int fourToSix [ ] = {4, 5, 6};
  int sevenToNine [ ] = {7, 8, 9};

  list<int> aList;

      // first insert into the front
      //note that each value becomes new front
  copy (threeToOne, threeToOne+3, front_inserter(aList));

      // then insert into the back
  copy(sevenToNine, sevenToNine+3, back_inserter(aList));

      // find the seven, and insert into middle
  list<int>::iterator seven = find(aList.begin(), aList.end(), 7);
  copy (fourToSix, fourToSix+3, inserter(aList, seven));

      // copy result to output
  copy (aList.begin(), aList.end(),
```

```
        ostream_iterator<int>(cout, " "));
    cout << endl;
    }
```

Observe that there is an important and subtle difference between the iterators created by `inserter(aList, aList.begin())` and `front_inserter(aList)`. The call on `inserter(aList, aList.begin())` copies values in sequence, adding each one to the front of a *list*, whereas `front_inserter(aList)` copies values making each value the new front. The result is that `front_inserter(aList)` reverses the order of the original sequence, while `inserter(aList, aList.begin())` retains the original order.

Iterator operations

The standard library provides two functions that can be used to manipulate iterators. The function `advance()` takes an iterator and a numeric value as argument, and modifies the iterator by moving the given amount.

```
void advance (InputIterator & iter, Distance & n);
```

For random access iterators this is the same as `iter + n`, however the function is useful because it is designed to operate with all forms of iterator. For forward iterators the numeric distance must be positive, whereas for bidirectional or random access iterators the value can be either positive or negative. The operation is efficient (constant time) only for random access iterators. In all other cases it is implemented as a loop that invokes either the operators ++ or -- on the iterator, and therefore takes time proportional to the distance traveled. The `advance()` function does not check to ensure the validity of the operations on the underlying iterator.

The second function, `distance()`, returns the number of iterator operations necessary to move from one element in a sequence to another. The description of this function is as follows:

```
void distance (InputIterator first, InputIterator last,
    Distance &n);
```

The result is returned in the third argument, which is passed by reference. `Distance` will *increment* this value by the number of times the operator ++ must be executed to move from `first` to `last`. Always be sure that the variable passed through this argument is properly initialized before invoking the function.

Chapter

20

Functions and predicates

This chapter describes functions, including a special function called a predicate.

Functions

A number of algorithms provided in the standard library require functions as arguments. A simple example is the algorithm for_each(), which invokes a function, passed as argument, on each value held in a container. The following, for example, applies the printElement() function to produce output describing each element in a *list* of integer values:

```
void printElement (int value)
{
   cout << "The list contains " << value << endl;
}

main () {
   list<int> aList;
      ...
   for_each (aList.begin(), aList.end(), printElement);
}
```

Binary functions take two arguments, and are often applied to values from two different sequences. For example, suppose we have a *list* of strings, and a *list* of integers. For each element in the first *list* we wish to replicate the string the number of times given by the corresponding value in the second *list*. We could perform this easily using the function transform() from the standard library. First, we define a binary function with the desired characteristics:

```
string stringRepeat (const string & base, int number)
   // replicate base the given number of times
{
   string result;  // initially the result is empty
   while (number--)  result += base;
   return result;
}
```

The following call on `transform()` then produces the desired effect:

```
list<string> words;
list<int> counts;

   ...
transform (words.begin(), words.end(),
    counts.begin(), words.begin(), stringRepeat);
```

Transforming the words `one`, `two`, `three` with the values 3, 2, 3 would yield the result `oneoneone`, `twotwo`, `threethreethree`.

Predicates

A *predicate* is simply a function that returns either a Boolean (true/false) value or an integer value. Following the normal C convention, an integer value is assumed to be true if nonzero, and false otherwise. An example function might be the following, which takes as argument an integer and returns true if the number represents a leap year, and false otherwise:

```
bool isLeapYear (int year)
   // return true if year is leap year
{
    // millenniums are leap years
  if (0 == year % 1000) return true;
    // centuries are not
  if (0 == year % 100) return false;
    // every fourth year is
  if (0 == year % 4) return true;
    // otherwise not
  return false;
}
```

A predicate is used as an argument, for example, in the generic algorithm named `find_if()`. This algorithm returns the first value that satisfies the predicate, returning the end-of-range value if no such element is found. Using this algorithm, the following locates the first leap year in a *list* of years:

```
list<int>::iterator firstLeap =
        find_if(aList.begin(), aList.end(), isLeapYear);
```

Function objects

A *function object* is an instance of a class that defines the parenthesis operator as a member function. There are a number of situations where it is convenient to substitute function objects in place of functions. When a function object is used as a function, the parenthesis operator is invoked whenever the function is called.

To illustrate, consider the following class definition:

```
class biggerThanThree {
  public:
    bool operator () (int val)
```

```
      { return val > 3; }
  };
```

If we create an instance of class *biggerThanThree*, every time we reference this object using the function call syntax, the parenthesis operator member function will be invoked. The next step is to generalize this class, by adding a constructor and a constant data field, which is set by the constructor.

```
class biggerThan {
  public:
    biggerThan (int x) : testValue(x) { }
    const int testValue;

    bool operator () (int val)
      { return val > testValue; }
};
```

The result is a general "bigger than X" function, where the value of X is determined when we create an instance of the class. We can do so, for example, as an argument to one of the generic functions that require a predicate. In this manner the following will find the first value in a *list* that is larger than 12:

```
list<int>::iterator firstBig =
  find_if (aList.begin(), aList.end(), biggerThan(12));
```

Three of the most common reasons to use function objects in place of ordinary functions are when an existing function object provided by the standard library can be employed instead of a new function, to improve execution by inlining function calls, or when the function object must either access or set state information being held by an object. We will give examples of each.

The following table illustrates the function objects provided by the standard library.

Name	Implemented operations
arithmetic functions	
plus	addition $x + y$
minus	subtraction $x - y$
times	multiplication $x * y$
divides	division x / y
modulus	remainder $x \% y$
negate	negation $- x$
comparison functions	
equal_to	equality test $x == y$
not_equal_to	inequality test $x != y$
greater	greater comparison $x > y$
less	less-than comparison $x < y$
greater_equal	greater than or equal comparison $x >= y$
less_equal	less than or equal comparison $x <= y$
logical functions	
logical_and	logical conjunction $x \&\& y$

Name	Implemented operations
logical_or	logical disjunction x ‖ y
logical_not	logical negation ! x

Let's look at a couple of examples that show how these might be used. The first example uses plus() to compute the by-element addition of two lists of integer values, placing the result back into the first *list*. This can be performed by the following:

```
transform (listOne.begin(), listOne.end(), listTwo.begin(),
  listOne.begin(), plus<int>() );
```

The second example negates every element in a *vector* of boolean values:

```
transform (aVec.begin(), aVec.end(), aVec.begin(),
  logical_not<bool>() );
```

Note   **Location of the class definitions:** The class definitions for unary_function and binary_function can be incorporated by #including functional.

The base classes used by the standard library in the definition of the functions shown in preceding table are available for the creation of new unary and binary function objects. These base classes are defined as follows:

```
template <class ArgType, class ResultType>
class unary_function {
  typedef ArgType argument_type;
  typedef ResultType result_type;
};
```

```
template <class ArgType1, class ArgType2, class ResultType>
struct binary_function {
  typedef ArgType1 first_argument_type;
  typedef ArgType2 second_argument_type;
  typedef ResultType result_type;
};
```

An example of the use of these functions is found in Example programs. Here we want to take a binary function of type "Widget" and an argument of type integer, and compare the widget identification number against the integer value. A function to do this is written in the following manner:

```
struct WidgetTester : binary_function<Widget, int, bool> {
public:
  bool operator () (const Widget & wid, int testid) const
    { return wid.id == testid; }
};
```

A second reason to consider using function objects instead of functions is faster code. In many cases an invocation of a function object, such as the examples given in the calls on transform() presented earlier, can be expanded in-line, thereby eliminating the overhead of a function call.

Note   **Using function objects to store references:** A more complex illustration of the use of a function object occurs in the radix sorting example program given as an illustration of the use of the *list* data type in Example program: radix sort. In this program references are initialized in the function object, so that during the sequence of invocations the function object can access and modify local values in the calling program.

The third major reason to use a function object in place of a function is when each invocation of the function must remember some state set by earlier invocations. An example of this occurs in the creation of a generator, to be used with the generic algorithm `generate()`. A *generator* is simply a function that returns a different value each time it is invoked. The most commonly used form of generator is a random number generator, but there are other uses for the concept. A sequence generator simply returns the values of an increasing sequence of natural numbers (1, 2, 3, 4, and so on). We can call this object *iotaGen* after the similar operation in the programming language APL, and define it as follows:

```
class iotaGen {
public:
   iotaGen (int start = 0) : current(start) { }
   int operator () () { return current++; }
private:
   int current;
};
```

An iota object maintains a current value, which can be set by the constructor, or defaults to zero. Each time the function-call operator is invoked, the current value is returned, and also incremented. Using this object, the following call on the standard library function `generate()` will initialize a *vector* of 20 elements with the values 1 through 20:

```
vector<int> aVec(20);
generate (aVec.begin(), aVec.end(), iotaGen(1));
```

Negators and binders

Negators and binders are function adaptors that are used to build new function objects out of existing function objects. Almost always, these are applied to functions as part of the process of building an argument *list* prior to invoking yet another function or generic algorithm.

The negators `not1()` and `not2()` take a unary and a binary predicate function object, respectively, and create a new function object that will yield the complement of the original. For example, using the widget tester function object defined in the previous section, the function object:

```
not2(WidgetTester())
```

yields a binary predicate which takes exactly the same arguments as the widget tester, and which is true when the corresponding widget tester would be false, and false otherwise. Negators work only with function objects defined as subclasses of the classes `unary_function` and `binary_function`, given earlier.

Note   **A hot idea:** The idea here described by the term binder is in other contexts often described by the term *curry*. This is not, as some people think, because it is a hot idea. Instead, it is named after the computer scientist Haskell P. Curry, who used the concept extensively in an influential book on the theory of computation in the 1930s. Curry himself attributed the idea to Moses Schönfinkel, leaving one to wonder why we don't instead refer to binders as "Schönfinkels."

A binder takes a two-argument function, and binds either the first or second argument to a specific value, thereby yielding a one argument function. The underlying function must be a subclass of class `binary_function`. The binder `bind1st()` binds the first argument, while the binder `bind2nd()` binds the second.

For example, the binder `bind2nd(greater<int>(), 5)` creates a function object that tests for being larger than 5. This could be used in the following, which yields an iterator representing the first value in a *list* larger than 5:

```
list<int>::iterator where = find_if(aList.begin(), aList.end(),
    bind2nd(greater<int>(), 5));
```

Combining a binder and a negator, we can create a function that is true if the argument is divisible by 3, and false otherwise. This can be used to remove all the multiples of 3 from a *list*.

```
list<int>::iterator where = remove_if (aList.begin(), aList.end(),
    not1(bind2nd(modulus<int>(), 3)));
```

A binder is used tie the widget number of a call on the binary function `WidgetTester()`, yielding a one-argument function that takes only a widget as argument. This is used to find the first widget that matches the given widget type:

```
list<Widget>::iterator wehave =

find_if(on_hand.begin(), on_hand.end(),
    bind2nd(WidgetTester(), wid));
```

Container classes

The standard library provides no fewer than ten alternative forms of container. In this chapter we will briefly describe the varieties, considering the characteristics of each, and discuss how you might go about selecting which container to use in solving a particular problem. Subsequent chapters will then go over each of the different containers in more detail.

The following chart shows the ten container types provided by the standard library, and gives a short description of the most significant characteristic for each.

Name	Characteristic
vector	random access to elements, efficient insertions at end
list	efficient insertion and removal throughout
deque	random access, efficient insertion at front or back
set	elements maintained in order, efficient test for inclusion, insertion and removal
multiset	set with repeated copies
map	access to values via keys, efficient insertion and removal
multimap	*map* permitting duplicate keys
stack	insertions and removals only from top
queue	insertion at back, removal from front
priority queue	efficient access and removal of largest value

Selecting a container

The following series of questions can help you determine which type of container is best suited for solving a particular problem.

How are values going to be accessed?

If random access is important, than a *vector* or a *deque* should be used. If sequential access is sufficient, then one of the other structures may be suitable.

Is the order in which values are maintained in the collection important?

There are a number of different ways in which values can be sequenced. If a strict ordering is important throughout the life of the container, then the *set* data structure is an obvious choice, as insertions into a *set* are automatically placed in order. On the other hand, if this ordering is important only at one point (for example, at the end of a long series of insertions), then it might be easier to place the values into a *list* or *vector*, then sort the resulting structure at the appropriate time. If the order that values are held in the structure is related to the order of insertion, then a *stack*, *queue*, or *list* may be the best choice.

Will the size of the structure vary widely over the course of execution?

If true, then a *list* or *set* might be the best choice. A *vector* or *deque* will continue to maintain a large buffer even after elements have been removed from the collection. Conversely, if the size of the collection remains relatively fixed, than a *vector* or *deque* will use less memory than will a *list* or *set* holding the same number of elements.

Is it possible to estimate the size of the collection?

The *vector* data structure provides a way to preallocate a block of memory of a given size (using the `reserve()` member function). This ability is not provided by the other containers.

Is testing to see whether a value is contained in the collection a frequent operation?

If so, then the *set* or *map* containers would be a good choice. Testing to see whether a value is contained in a *set* or *map* can be performed in a very small number of steps (logarithmic in the size of the container), whereas testing to see if a value is contained in one of the other types of collections might require comparing the value against every element being stored by the container.

Is the collection indexed? That is, can the collection be viewed as a series of key/value pairs?

If the keys are integers between 0 and some upper limit, then a *vector* or *deque* should be employed. If, on the other hand, the key values are some other ordered data type (such as characters, strings, or a user-defined type), then the *map* container can be used.

Can values be related to each other?

All values stored in any container provided by the standard library must be able to test for equality against another similar value, but not all need to recognize the relational less-than operator. However, if values cannot be ordered using the relational less-than operator, then they cannot be stored in a *set* or a *map*.

Is finding and removing the largest value from the collection a frequent operation?

If this is true, then the priority queue is the best data structure to use.

At what positions are values inserted into or removed from the structure?

If values are inserted into or removed from the middle, then a list is the best choice. If values are inserted only at the beginning, then a *deque* or a list is the preferred choice. If values are inserted or removed only at the end, then a stack or queue may be a logical choice.

Is a frequent operation the merging of two or more sequences into one?

If true then a *set* or a *list* would seem to be the best choice, depending upon whether or not the collection is maintained in order. Merging two sets is a very efficient operation. If the collections are not ordered, but the efficient `splice()` member function from class list can be used, then the list data type is to be preferred, since this operation is not provided in the other containers.

In many situations any number of different containers may be applicable to a given problem. In such cases one possibility is to compare actual execution timings to determine which alternative is best.

Memory management issues

Containers in the standard library can maintain a variety of different types of elements. These include the fundamental data types (`integer`, `char`, and so on), pointers, or user defined types. Containers cannot hold references. In general, memory management is handled automatically by the standard container classes, with little interaction by the programmer.

Values are placed into a container using the copy constructor. For most container classes, the element type held by the container must also define a default constructor. Generic algorithms that copy into a container (such as `copy()`) use the assignment operator.

When an entire container is duplicated (for example, through invoking a copy constructor or as the result of an assignment), every value is copied into the new structure using (depending on the structure) either the assignment operator or a copy constructor. Whether such a result is a "deep copy" or a "shallow copy" is controlled by the programmer, who can provide the assignment operator with whatever meaning is desired. Memory for structures used internally by the various container classes is allocated and released automatically and efficiently.

If a destructor is defined for the element type, this destructor will be invoked when values are removed from a container. When an entire collection is destroyed, the destructor will be invoked for each remaining value being held by the container.

A few words should be said about containers that hold pointer values. Such collections are not uncommon. For example, a collection of pointers is the only way to store values that can potentially represent either instances of a class or instances of a subclass. Such a collection is encountered in an example problem discussed in "Application: event-driven simulation."

In these cases the container is responsible only for maintaining the pointer values themselves. It is the responsibility of the programmer to manage the memory for the values being referenced by the pointers. This includes making certain the memory values are properly allocated (usually by invoking the new operator), that they are not released while the container holds references to them, and that they are properly released once they have been removed from the container.

Container types not found in the standard library

There are a number of "classic" container types that are not found in the standard library. In most cases, the reason is that the containers that have been provided can easily be adapted to a wide variety of uses, including those traditionally solved by these alternative collections.

There is no *tree* collection that is described as such. However, the *set* data type is internally implemented using a form of binary search tree. For most problems that would be solved using trees, the *set* data type is an adequate substitute.

The *set* data type is specifically ordered, and there is no provision for performing *set* operations (union, intersection, and so on) on a collection of values that cannot be ordered (for example, a *set* of complex numbers). In such cases a list can be used as a substitute, although it is still necessary to write special *set* operation functions, as the generic algorithms cannot be used in this case.

There are no *multidimensional arrays*. However, *vectors* can hold other *vectors* as elements, so such structures can be easily constructed.

There are no *graphs*. However, one representation for graphs can be easily constructed as a *map* that holds other maps. This type of structure is described in the sample problem discussed in "Example program: graphs."

There are no *sparse arrays*. A novel solution to this problem is to use the graph representation discussed in "Example program: graphs."

There are no *hash tables*. A hash table provides amortized constant time access, insertion and removal of elements, by converting access and removal operations into indexing operations. However, hash tables can be easily constructed as a *vector* (or *deque*) that holds lists (or even sets) as elements. A similar structure is described in the radix sort sample problem discussed in "Example program: radix sort," although this example does not include invoking the hash function to convert a value into an index.

In short, while not providing every conceivable container type, the containers in the standard library represent those used in the solution of most problems, and a solid foundation from which further structures can be constructed.

22

vector and vector<bool>

This chapter describes the *vector* container class, including the special case of Boolean *vectors*.

The vector data abstraction

The *vector* container class generalizes the concept of an ordinary C array. Like an array, a *vector* is an indexed data structure, with index values that range from 0 to one less than the number of elements contained in the structure. Also like an array, values are most commonly assigned to and extracted from the *vector* using the subscript operator. However, the *vector* differs from an array in the following important respects:

- A *vector* has more "self-knowledge" than an ordinary array. In particular, a *vector* can be queried about its size, about the number of elements it can potentially hold (which may be different from its current size), and so on.

- The size of the *vector* can change dynamically. New elements can be inserted on to the end of a *vector*, or into the middle. Storage management is handled efficiently and automatically. It is important to note, however, that while these abilities are provided, insertion into the middle of a *vector* is not as efficient as insertion into the middle of a list (The list data abstraction). If many insertion operations are to be performed, the list container should be used instead of the *vector* data type.

The *vector* container class in the standard library should be compared and contrasted to the *deque* container class we will describe in more detail in *deque* data abstraction. Like a *vector*, a *deque* (pronounced "deck") is an indexed data structure. The major difference between the two is that a *deque* provides efficient insertion at either the beginning or the end of the container, while a *vector* provides efficient insertion only at the end. In many situations, either structure can be used. Use of a *vector* generally results in a smaller executable file, while, depending upon the particular set of operations being performed, use of a *deque* may result in a slightly faster program.

Vector include files

Whenever you use a *vector*, you must include the *vector* header file.

```
# include <vector>
```

Vector operations

The following chart summarizes the member functions provided by the *vector* data type. Each will shortly be described in more detail. Note that while member functions provide basic operations, the utility of the data structure is greatly extended through the use of the generic algorithms described in Chapter 29.

Result	Name	Arguments
	vector	()
	vector	(size)
	vector	(size, value_type)
	vector	template<class Iterator> (Iterator, Iterator)
	vector	(const vector)
	vector	template<class Iterator>assign (Iterator, Iterator)
	vector	template<class Size, class T> assign (Size, T)
reference	at	(size_type)
value_type	back	()
RandomAccessIterator	begin	()
size_type	capacity	()
bool	empty	()
RandomAccessIterator	end	()
void	erase	(iterator)
void	erase	(iterator, iterator)
value_type	front	()
void	insert	(iterator, size_type, value_type)
iterator	insert	(iterator, value_type)
void	insert	template <class Iterator> (iterator,Iterator, Iterator)
size_type	max_size	()
void	pop_back	()
void	push_back	(value_type)
RandomAccessIterator	rbegin	()
RandomAccessIterator	rend	()
void	reserve	(size_type)
void	resize	(size_type, value_type)
size_type	size	()
void	swap	(vector)
reference	operator[]	(size_type)
vector	operator =	(vector)

In subsequent chapters we will illustrate the basic operations that can be performed with *vectors*.

Declaration and initialization of vectors

Note **Requirements of an element type:** Elements that are held by a *vector* must define a default constructor (constructor with no arguments), as well as a copy constructor. Although not used by functions in the *vector* class, some of the generic algorithms also require *vector* elements to recognize either the equivalence operator (operator ==) or the relational less-than operator (operator <).

Because it is a template class, the declaration of a *vector* must include a designation of the component type. This can be a primitive language type (such as integer or double), a pointer type, or a user-defined type. In the latter case, the user-defined type *must* implement a default constructor, as this constructor is used to initialize newly created elements. A copy constructor, either explicitly or implicitly defined, must also exist for the container element type. Like an array, a *vector* is most commonly declared with an integer argument that describes the number of elements the *vector* will hold:

```
vector<int> vec_one(10);
```

The constructor used to create the *vector* in this situation is declared as `explicit`, which prevents it being used as a conversion operator. (This is generally a good idea, since otherwise an integer might unintentionally be converted into a *vector* in certain situations.)

There are a variety of other forms of constructor that can also be used to create *vectors*. In addition to a size, the constructor can provide a constant value that will be used to initialize each new *vector* location. If no size is provided, the *vector* initially contains no elements, and increases in size automatically as elements are added. The copy constructor creates a clone of a *vector* from another *vector*.

```
vector<int> vec_two(5, 3);  // copy constructor
vector<int> vec_three;
vector<int> vec_four(vec_two);  //  initialization by assignment
```

A *vector* can also be initialized using elements from another collection, by means of a beginning and ending iterator pair. The arguments can be any form of iterator, thus collections can be initialized with values drawn from any of the container classes in the standard library that support iterators.

```
vector <int> vec_five (aList.begin(), aList.end());
```

Note **Constructors and iterators:** Because it requires the ability to define a method with a template argument different from the class template, some compilers may not yet support the initialization of containers using iterators. In the mean time, while compiler technology catches up with the standard library definition, the Rogue Wave version of the standard library will support conventional pointers and *vector* iterators in this manner.

A *vector* can be assigned the values of another *vector*, in which case the target receives a copy of the argument *vector*.

```
vec_three = vec_five;
```

The `assign()` member function is similar to an assignment, but is more versatile and, in some cases, requires more arguments. Like an assignment, the existing values in the container are deleted, and replaced with the values specified by the arguments. There are two forms of `assign()`. The first takes two iterator arguments that specify a subsequence of an existing container. The values from this subsequence then become the new elements in the receiver. The second version of `assign()` takes a count and an optional value of the container element type. After the call the container will hold only the number of elements specified by the count, which are equal to either the default value for the container type or the initial value specified.

```
vec_six.assign(list_ten.begin(), list_ten.end());
vec_four.assign(3, 7); // three copies of the value 7
vec_five.assign(12); // twelve copies of value zero
```

If a destructor is defined for the container element type, the destructor will be called for each value removed from the collection.

Finally, two *vectors* can exchange their entire contents by means of the `swap()` operation. The argument container will take on the values of the receiver, while the receiver will assume those of the argument. A swap is very efficient, and should be used, where appropriate, in preference to an explicit element-by-element transfer.

```
vec_three.swap(vec_four);
```

Type definitions

The class *vector* includes a number of type definitions. These are most commonly used in declaration statements. For example, an iterator for a *vector* of integers can be declared in the following fashion:

```
vector<int>::iterator location;
```

In addition to `iterator`, the following types are defined:

`value_type`	The type associated with the elements the *vector* maintains.
`const_iterator`	An iterator that does not allow modification of the underlying sequence.
`reverse_iterator`	An iterator that moves in a backward direction.
`const_reverse_iterator`	A combination constant and reverse iterator.
`reference`	A reference to an underlying element.
`const_reference`	A reference to an underlying element that will not permit the element to be modified.
`size_type`	An unsigned integer type, used to refer to the size of containers.
`difference_type`	A signed integer type, used to describe to distances between iterators.

Subscripting a vector

The value being maintained by a *vector* at a specific index can be accessed or modified using the subscript operator, just like an ordinary array. And, like arrays, there currently are no attempts to verify the validity of the index values (although this may change in future releases). Indexing a constant *vector* yields a constant reference. Attempts to index a *vector* outside the range of legal values will generate unpredictable and spurious results:

```
cout << vec_five[1] << endl;
vec_five[1] = 17;
```

The member function `at()` can be used in place of the subscript operator. It takes exactly the same arguments as the subscript operator, and returns exactly the same values.

The member function `front()` returns the first element in the *vector*, while the member function `back()` yields the last. Both also return constant references when applied to constant *vectors*.

```
cout << vec_five.front() << " ... " << vec_five.back() << endl;
```

Extent and size-changing operations

There are, in general, three different "sizes" associated with any *vector*. The first is the number of elements currently being held by the *vector*. The second is the maximum size to which the *vector* can be expanded without requiring that new storage be allocated. The third is the upper limit on the size of any *vector*. These three values are yielded by the member functions `size()`, `capacity()`, and `max_size()`, respectively.

```
cout << "size: " << vec_five.size() << endl;
cout << "capacity: " << vec_five.capacity() << endl;
cout << "max_size: " << vec_five.max_size() << endl;
```

The maximum size is usually limited only by the amount of available memory, or the largest value that can be described by the data type `size_type`. The current size and capacity are more difficult to characterize. As we will note in the next section, elements can be added to or removed from a *vector* in a variety of ways. When elements are removed from a *vector*, the memory for the *vector* is generally not reallocated, and thus the size is decreased but the capacity remains the same. A subsequent insertion does not force a reallocation of new memory if the original capacity is not exceeded.

Note   **Memory management:** A *vector* stores values in a single large block of memory. A *deque*, on the other hand, employs a number of smaller blocks. This difference may be important on machines that limit the size of any single block of memory, because in such cases a *deque* will be able to hold much larger collections than are possible with a *vector*.

An insertion that causes the size to exceed the capacity generally results in a new block of memory being allocated to hold the *vector* elements. Values are then copied into this new memory using the assignment operator appropriate to the element type, and the old memory is deleted. Because this can be a potentially costly operation, the *vector* data type provides a means for the programmer to specify a value for the capacity of a *vector*. The member function `reserve()` is a directive to the *vector*, indicating that the *vector* is expected to grow to at least the given size. If the argument used with `reserve()` is larger than the current capacity, then a reallocation occurs and the argument value becomes the new capacity. (It may subsequently grow even larger; the value given as argument need not be a bound, just a guess.) If the capacity is already in excess of the argument, then no reallocation takes place. Invoking `reserve()` does not change the size of the *vector*, nor the element values themselves (with the exception that they may potentially be moved should reallocation take place).

```
vec_five.reserve(20);
```

A reallocation invalidates all references, pointers, and iterators referring to elements being held by a *vector*.

The member function `empty()` returns true if the *vector* currently has a size of zero (regardless of the capacity of the *vector*). Using this function is generally more efficient than comparing the result returned by `size()` to zero.

```
cout << "empty is " << vec_five.empty() << endl;
```

The member function `resize()` changes the size of the *vector* to the value specified by the argument. Values are either added to or erased from the end of the collection as necessary. An optional second argument can be used to provide the initial value for any new elements added to the collection. If a destructor is defined for the element type, the destructor will be called for any values that are removed from the collection.

```
         // become size 12, adding values of 17 if necessary
vec_five.resize (12, 17);
```

Inserting and removing elements

As we noted earlier, the class *vector* differs from an ordinary array in that a *vector* can, in certain circumstances, increase or decrease in size. When an insertion causes the number of elements being held in a *vector* to exceed the capacity of the current block of memory being used to hold the values, then a new block is allocated and the elements are copied to the new storage.

Note **Costly insertions:** Even adding a single element to a *vector* can, in the worst case, require time proportional to the number of elements in the *vector*, as each element is moved to a new location. If insertions are a prominent feature of your current problem, then you should explore the possibility of using containers, such as lists or sets, which are optimized for insert operations.

A new element can be added to the back of a *vector* using the function `push_back()`. If there is space in the current allocation, this operation is very efficient (constant time).

```
vec_five.push_back(21);   // add element 21 to end of collection
```

The corresponding removal operation is `pop_back()`, which decreases the size of the *vector*, but does not change its capacity. If the container type defines a destructor, the destructor will be called on the value being eliminated. Again, this operation is very efficient. (The class *deque* permits values to be added and removed from both the back and the front of the collection. These functions are described in *deque* data abstraction, which discusses deques in more detail.)

More general insertion operations can be performed using the `insert()` member function. The location of the insertion is described by an iterator; insertion takes place immediately preceding the location denoted. A fixed number of constant elements can be inserted by a single function call. It is much more efficient to insert a block of elements in a single call, than to perform a sequence of individual insertions, because with a single call at most one allocation will be performed.

```
                    // find the location of the 7
        vector<int>::iterator where =
            find(vec_five.begin(), vec_five.end(), 7);
                    // then insert the 12 before the 7
        vec_five.insert(where, 12);
        vec_five.insert(where, 6, 14);    // insert six copies of 14
```

The most general form of the `insert()` member function takes a position and a pair of iterators that denote a subsequence from another container. The range of values described by the sequence is inserted into the *vector*. Again, because at most a single allocation is performed, using this function is preferable to using a sequence of individual insertions.

```
        vec_five.insert (where, vec_three.begin(), vec_three.end());
```

Note **Iterator invalidation:** Once more, it is important to remember that should reallocation occur as a result of an insertion, all references, pointers, and iterators that denoted a location in the now-deleted memory block that held the values before reallocation become invalid.

In addition to the `pop_back()` member function, which removes elements from the end of a *vector*, a function exists that removes elements from the middle of a *vector*, using an iterator to denote the location. The member function that performs this task is `erase()`. There are two forms; the first takes a single iterator and removes an individual value, while the second takes a pair of iterators and removes all values in the given range. The size of the *vector* is reduced, but the capacity is unchanged. If the container type defines a destructor, the destructor will be invoked on the eliminated values.

```
        vec_five.erase(where);
                    // erase from the 12 to the end
        where = find(vec_five.begin(), vec_five.end(), 12);
        vec_five.erase(where, vec_five.end());
```

Iteration

The member functions `begin()` and `end()` yield random access iterators for the container. Again, we note that the iterators yielded by these operations can become invalidated after insertions or removals of elements. The member functions `rbegin()` and `rend()` return similar iterators, however these access the underlying elements in reverse order. Constant iterators are returned if the original container is declared as constant, or if the target of the assignment or parameter is constant.

Vector test for inclusion

A *vector* does not directly provide any method that can be used to determine if a specific value is contained in the collection. However, the generic algorithms `find()` or `count()` ("Find an element satisfying a condition" and "Count the number of elements that satisfy a condition") can be used for this purpose. The following statement, for example, tests to see whether an integer *vector* contains the element 17.

Note Note that `count()` returns its result through an argument that is passed by reference. It is important that this value be properly initialized before invoking this function.

```
int num = 0;
count (vec_five.begin(), vec_five.end(), 17, num);

if (num)
  cout << "contains a 17" << endl;
else
  cout << "does not contain a 17" << endl;
```

Sorting and sorted vector operations

A *vector* does not automatically maintain its values in sequence. However, a *vector* can be placed in order using the generic algorithm sort() ("Sorting algorithms"). The simplest form of sort uses for its comparisons the less-than operator for the element type. An alternative version of the generic algorithm permits the programmer to specify the comparison operator explicitly. This can be used, for example, to place the elements in descending rather than ascending order:

```
// sort ascending
sort (aVec.begin(), aVec.end());

// sort descending, specifying the ordering function explicitly
sort (aVec.begin(), aVec.end(), greater<int>() );

// alternate way to sort descending
sort (aVec.rbegin(), aVec.rend());
```

A number of the operations described in Chapter 30 can be applied to a *vector* holding an ordered collection. For example, two *vectors* can be merged using the generic algorithm merge() ("Merge ordered sequences").

```
// merge two vectors, printing output
merge (vecOne.begin(), vecOne.end(), vecTwo.begin(), vecTwo.end(),
  ostream_iterator<int> (cout, " "));
```

Sorting a *vector* also lets us use the more efficient binary search algorithms ("Binary search"), instead of a linear traversal algorithm such as find().

Useful generic algorithms

Most of the algorithms described in Chapter 29 can be used with *vectors*. The following table summarizes a few of the more useful of these. For example, the maximum value in a *vector* can be determined as follows:

```
vector<int>::iterator where =
  max_element (vec_five.begin(), vec_five.end());
cout << "maximum is " << *where << endl;
```

Purpose	Name
Fill a *vector* with a given initial value	fill
Copy one sequence into another	copy
Copy values from a generator into a *vector*	generate
Find an element that matches a condition	find
Find consecutive duplicate elements	adjacent_find

Purpose	Name
Find a subsequence within a *vector*	search
Locate maximum or minimum element	max_element, min_element
Reverse order of elements	reverse
Replace elements with new values	replace
Rotate elements around a midpoint	rotate
Partition elements into two groups	partition
Generate permutations	next_permutation
Inplace merge within a *vector*	Inplace_merge
Randomly shuffle elements in *vector*	random_shuffle
Count number of elements that satisfy condition	count
Reduce *vector* to a single value	accumulate
Inner product of two *vectors*	inner_product
Test two *vectors* for pairwise equality	equal
Lexical comparison	lexicographical_compare
Apply transformation to a *vector*	transform
Partial sums of values	partial_sum
Adjacent differences of value	adjacent_difference
Execute function on each element	for_each

Boolean vectors

Vectors of bit values (Boolean 1/0 values) are handled as a special case by the standard library, so that they can be efficiently packed several elements to a word. The operations for a Boolean *vector*, *vector<bool>*, are a superset of those for an ordinary *vector*, only the implementation is more efficient.

One new member function added to the Boolean *vector* data type is flip(). When invoked, this function inverts all the bits of the *vector*. Boolean *vectors* also return as reference an internal value that also supports the flip() member function.

```
vector<bool> bvec(27);
bvec.flip();         // flip all values
bvec[17].flip();     // flip bit 17
```

vector<bool> also supports an additional swap() member function.

Example program: sieve of Eratosthenes

Note   **Obtaining the source:** Source for this program is found in the file sieve.cpp.

An example program that illustrates the use of *vectors* is the classic algorithm, called the *sieve of Eratosthenes*, used to discover prime numbers. A list of all the numbers up to some bound is represented by an integer *vector*. The basic idea is to strike out (set to zero) all those values that cannot be primes; thus all the remaining values will be the prime numbers. To do this, a loop examines each value in turn, and for those that are set to one (and thus have not yet been excluded from the *set* of candidate primes) strikes out all multiples of the number. When the outermost loop is finished, all remaining prime values have been discovered. The program is as follows:

```cpp
void main() {
    // create a sieve of integers, initially set
    const int sievesize = 100;
    vector<int> sieve(sievesize, 1);

    // now search for 1 bit positions
    for (int i = 2; i * i < sievesize; i++)
        if (sieve[i])
            for (int j = i + i; j < sievesize; j += i)
                sieve[j] = 0;

    // finally, output the values that are set
    for (int j = 2; j < sievesize; j++)
        if (sieve[j])
            cout << j << " ";
    cout << endl;
}
```

23

list

The list data abstraction

The *vector* data structure is a container of relatively fixed size. While the standard library provides facilities for dynamically changing the size of a *vector*, such operations are costly and should be used only rarely. Yet in many problems, the size of a collection may be difficult to predict in advance, or may vary widely during the course of execution. In such cases an alternative data structure should be employed. In this section we will examine an alternative data structure that can be used in these circumstances, the list data type.

A list corresponds to the intuitive idea of holding elements in a linear (although not necessarily ordered) sequence. New values can be added or removed either to or from the front of the list, or to or from the back. By using an iterator to denote a position, elements can also be added or removed to or from the middle of a list. In all cases the insertion or removal operations are efficient; they are performed in a constant amount of time that is independent of the number of elements being maintained in the collection. Finally, a list is a linear structure. The contents of the list cannot be accessed by subscript, and, in general, elements can only be accessed by a linear traversal of all values.

List include files

Whenever you use a list, you must include the list header file.

```
# include <list>
```

List operations

The following chart summarizes the member functions provided by the list data type. Each will shortly be described in more detail. Note that while member functions provide basic operations, the utility of the data structure is greatly extended through the use of the generic algorithms described in Chapters 29 and 30, respectively.

Result	Name	Arguments
	`list`	`()`
	`list`	`(size)`
	`list`	`(size, value_type)`
	`list`	`template <class Iterator>` `(Iterator, Iterator)`
	`list`	`(const list)`
	`list`	`template<class Iterator>` `assign (Iterator, Iterator)`
	`list`	`template<class Size,class T>` `assign (Size, T)`
`value_type`	`back`	`()`
`BidirectionalIterator`	`begin`	`()`
`bool`	`empty`	`()`
`BidirectionalIterator`	`end`	`()`
`void`	`erase`	`(iterator)`
`void`	`erase`	`(iterator, iterator)`
`value_type`	`front`	`()`
`iterator`	`insert`	`(iterator, size_type, value_type)`
`iterator`	`insert`	`(iterator, value_type)`
`void`	`insert`	`template <class Iterator>` `(iterator, Iterator, Iterator)`
`size_type`	`max_size`	`()`
`void`	`merge`	`(list)`
`void`	`pop_back`	`()`
`void`	`pop_front`	`()`
`void`	`push_back`	`(value_type)`
`void`	`push_front`	`(value_type)`
`BidirectionalIterator`	`rbegin`	`()`
`void`	`remove`	`(value_type)`
`void`	`remove_if`	`(predicate)`
`BidirectionalIterator`	`rend`	`()`
`void`	`reverse`	`()`
`size_type`	`size`	`()`
`void`	`sort`	`()`
`void`	`splice`	`(iterator, list)`
`void`	`splice`	`(iterator, list, iterator)`
`void`	`splice`	`(iterator, list, iterator iterator)`
`void`	`swap`	`(list)`
`void`	`unique`	`()`
`void`	`unique`	`(predicate)`
`list`	`operator =`	`(list)`

In subsequent sections, we will illustrate the basic operations that can be performed with lists.

Declaration and initialization of lists

Note **Memory management:** Note that if you declare a container as holding pointers, you are responsible for managing the memory for the objects pointed to. The container classes will not, for example, automatically free memory for these objects when an item is erased from the container.

There are a variety of ways to declare a list. In the simplest form, a list is declared by simply stating the type of element the collection will maintain. This can be a primitive language type (such as `integer` or `double`), a pointer type, or a user-defined type. In the latter case, the user-defined type *must* implement a default constructor (a constructor with no arguments), as this constructor is in some cases used to initialize newly created elements. A collection declared in this fashion will initially not contain any elements.

```
list <int> list_one;
list <Widget *> list_two;
list <Widget> list_three;
```

An alternative form of declaration creates a collection that initially contains some number of equal elements. The constructor for this form is declared as `explicit`, meaning it cannot be used as a conversion operator. This prevents integers from inadvertently being converted into lists. The constructor for this form takes two arguments, a size and an initial value. The second argument is optional. If only the number of initial elements to be created is given, these values will be initialized with the default constructor; otherwise the elements will be initialized with the value of the second argument:

```
list <int> list_four (5);   // five elements, initialized to zero
list <double> list_five (4, 3.14);   // 4 values, initially 3.14
list <Widget> wlist_six (4);   // default constructor, 4 elements
list <Widget> list_six (3, Widget(7));   // 3 copies of Widget(7)
```

Lists can also be initialized using elements from another collection, using a beginning and ending iterator pair. The arguments can be any form of iterator, thus collections can be initialized with values drawn from any of the container classes in the standard library that support iterators. Because this requires the ability to specialize a member function using a template, some compilers may not yet support this feature. In these cases an alternative technique using the `copy()` generic algorithm can be employed. When a list is initialized using `copy()`, an *insert iterator* must be constructed to convert the output operations performed by the copy operation into list insertions (see "Insert iterators" in Chapter 19). The inserter requires two arguments; the list into which the value is to be inserted, and an iterator indicating the location at which values will be placed. Insert iterators can also be used to copy elements into an arbitrary location in an existing list.

```
list <double> list_seven (aVector.begin(), aVector.end());
    // the following is equivalent to the above

list <double> list_eight;
copy (aVector.begin(), aVector.end(),
    inserter(list_eight, list_eight.begin()));
```

The `insert()` operation, to be described in "Placing elements into a list" in this chapter, can also be used to place values denoted by an iterator into a list. Insert iterators can be used to initialize a list with a sequence of values produced by a *generator* (see "Initialize a sequence with generated values" in Chapter 29). This is illustrated by the following:

```
list <int> list_nine;  // initialize list 1 2 3 ... 7
generate_n (inserter(list_nine, list_nine.begin()),
    7, iotaGen(1));
```

A *copy constructor* can be used to initialize a list with values drawn from another list. The assignment operator performs the same actions. In both cases the assignment operator for the element type is used to copy each new value.

```
list <int> list_ten (list_nine);  // copy constructor
list <Widget> list_eleven;
list_eleven = list_six;  // values copied by assignment
```

The `assign()` member function is similar to the assignment operator, but is more versatile and, in some cases, requires more arguments. Like an assignment, the existing values in the container are deleted, and replaced with the values specified by the arguments. If a destructor is provided for the container element type, it will be invoked for the elements being removed. There are two forms of `assign()`. The first takes two iterator arguments that specify a subsequence of an existing container. The values from this subsequence then become the new elements in the receiver. The second version of assign takes a count and an optional value of the container element type. After the call the container will hold the number of elements specified by the count, which will be equal to either the default value for the container type or the initial value specified.

```
list_six.assign(list_ten.begin(), list_ten.end());
list_four.assign(3, 7);   // three copies of value seven
list_five.assign(12);    // twelve copies of value zero
```

Finally, two lists can exchange their entire contents by means of the operation `swap()`. The argument container will take on the values of the receiver, while the receiver will assume those of the argument. A swap is very efficient, and should be used, where appropriate, in preference to an explicit element-by-element transfer.

```
list_ten.swap(list_nine);   // exchange lists nine and ten
```

Type definitions

The class list includes a number of type definitions. The most common use for these is in declaration statements. For example, an iterator for a list of integers can be declared in the following fashion:

```
list<int>::iterator location;
```

In addition to `iterator`, the following types are defined:

value_type	The type associated with the elements the list maintains.
const_iterator	An iterator that does not allow modification of the underlying sequence.
reverse_iterator	An iterator that moves in a backward direction.

const_reverse_iterator	A combination constant and reverse iterator.
reference	A reference to an underlying element.
const_reference	A reference to an underlying element that will not permit the element to be modified
size_type	An unsigned integer type, used to refer to the size of containers.
difference_type	A signed integer type, used to describe to distances between iterators.

Placing elements into a list

Values can be inserted into a list in a variety of ways. Elements are most commonly added to the front or back of a list. These tasks are provided by the push_front() and push_back() operations, respectively. These operations are efficient (constant time) for both types of containers.

```
list_seven.push_front(1.2);
list_eleven.push_back (Widget(6));
```

In a previous discussion (Insert iterators) we noted how, with the aid of an insert iterator and the copy() or generate() generic algorithm, values can be placed into a list at a location denoted by an iterator. There is also a member function, named insert(), that avoids the need to construct the inserter. As we will describe shortly, the values returned by the iterator generating functions begin() and end() denote the beginning and end of a list, respectively. An insert using one of these is equivalent to push_front() or push_back(), respectively. If we specify only one iterator, the default element value is inserted.

```
        // insert default widget at beginning of list
list_eleven.insert(list_eleven.begin());
        // insert widget 8 at end of list
list_eleven.insert(list_eleven.end(), Widget(8));
```

Note   **Iterator invalidation:** Unlike a *vector* or *deque*, insertions or removals from the middle of a *list* will not invalidate references or pointers to other elements in the container. This property can be important if two or more iterators are being used to refer to the same container.

An iterator can denote a location in the middle of a list. There are several ways to produce this iterator. For example, we can use the result of any of the searching operations described in "Searching operations" later in this chapter, such as an invocation of the find() generic algorithm. The new value is inserted immediately *prior* to the location denoted by the iterator. The insert() operation itself returns an iterator denoting the location of the inserted value. This result value was ignored in the invocations shown above.

```
        // find the location of the first 5 value in list
list<int>::iterator location =
    find(list_nine.begin(), list_nine.end(), 5);
        // and insert an 11 immediate before it
location = list_nine.insert(location, 11);
```

It is also possible to insert a fixed number of copies of an argument value. This form of `insert()` does not yield the location of the values.

```
line_nine.insert (location, 5, 12);    // insert five twelve's
```

Finally, an entire sequence denoted by an iterator pair can be inserted into a list. Again, no useful value is returned as a result of the `insert()`.

```
     // insert entire contents of list_ten into list_nine
list_nine.insert (location, list_ten.begin(), list_ten.end());
```

There are a variety of ways to *splice* one list into another list. A splice differs from an insertion in that the item is simultaneously added to the receiver list and removed from the argument list. For this reason, a splice can be performed very efficiently, and should be used whenever appropriate. As with an insertion, the member function `splice()` uses an iterator to indicate the location in the receiver list where the splice should be made. The argument is either an entire list, a single element in a list (denoted by an iterator), or a subsequence of a list (denoted by a pair of iterators).

```
     // splice the last element of list ten
list_nine.splice (location, list_ten, list_ten.end());
     // splice all of list ten
list_nine.splice (location,  list_ten);
     // splice list 9 back into list 10
list_ten.splice (list_ten.begin(), list_nine,
    list_nine.begin(), location);
```

Two ordered lists can be combined into one using the `merge()` operation. Values from the argument list are merged into the ordered list, leaving the argument list empty. The merge is stable; that is, elements retain their relative ordering from the original lists. As with the generic algorithm of the same name ("Merge ordered sequences" in Chapter 30), two forms are supported. The second form uses the binary function supplied as argument to order values. Not all compilers support the second form. If the second form is desired and not supported, the more general generic algorithm can be used, although this is slightly less efficient.

```
     // merge with explicit compare function
list_eleven.merge(list_six, widgetCompare);

     //the following is similar to the above

list<Widget> list_twelve;
merge (list_eleven.begin(), list_eleven.end(),
    list_six.begin(), list_six.end(),
    inserter(list_twelve, list_twelve.begin()), widgetCompare);
list_eleven.swap(list_twelve);
```

Removing elements

Just as there are a number of different ways to insert an element into a list, there are a variety of ways to remove values from a list. The most common operations used to remove a value are `pop_front()` or `pop_back()`, which delete the single element from the front or the back of the list, respectively. These member functions simply remove the given element, and do not themselves yield any useful result. If a destructor is defined for the element type it will be invoked as the element is removed. To look at the values before deletion, use the member functions front() or back().

The erase() operation can be used to remove a value denoted by an iterator. For a list, the argument iterator, and any other iterators that denote the same location, become invalid after the removal, but iterators denoting other locations are unaffected. We can also use erase() to remove an entire subsequence, denoted by a pair of iterators. The values beginning at the initial iterator and up to, but not including, the final iterator are removed from the list. Erasing elements from the middle of a list is an efficient operation, unlike erasing elements from the middle of a *vector* or a *deque*.

```
list_nine.erase (location);
    // erase values between the first 5 and the following 7
location = find(list_nine.begin(), list_nine.end(), 5);
list<int>::iterator location2 =
    find(location, list_nine.end(), 7);
list_nine.erase (location, location2);
```

The remove() member function removes all occurrences of a given value from a list. A variation, remove_if(), removes all values that satisfy a given predicate. An alternative to the use of either of these is to use the remove() or remove_if() generic algorithms (Remove unwanted elements). The generic algorithms do not reduce the size of the list, instead they move the elements to be retained to the front of the list, leave the remainder of the list unchanged, and return an iterator denoting the location of the first unmodified element. This value can be used in conjunction with the erase() member function to remove the remaining values.

```
list_nine.remove(4);    // remove all fours
list_nine.remove_if(divisibleByThree);    //remove any div by 3

        // the following is equivalent to the above
list<int>::iterator location3 =
   remove_if(list_nine.begin(), list_nine.end(),
      divisibleByThree);
list_nine.erase(location3, list_nine.end());
```

The operation unique() will erase all but the first element from every consecutive group of equal elements in a list. The list need not be ordered. An alternative version takes a binary function, and compares adjacent elements using the function, removing the second value in those situations were the function yields a true value. As with remove_if(), not all compilers support the second form of unique(). In this case the more general unique() generic algorithm can be used (see "Remove runs of similar values" in Chapter 29). In the following example the binary function is the greater-than operator, which will have the effect of removing all elements smaller than a preceding element.

```
        // remove first from consecutive equal elements
list_nine.unique();

        // explicitly give comparison function
list_nine.unique(greater<int>());

        // the following is equivalent to the above
location3 =
   unique(list_nine.begin(), list_nine.end(), greater<int>());
list_nine.erase(location3, list_nine.end());
```

Extent operations

The member function `size()` will return the number of elements being held by a container. The function `empty()` will return true if the container is empty, and is more efficient than comparing the size against the value zero.

```
cout << "Number of elements: " << list_nine.size () << endl;
if ( list_nine.empty () )
  cout << "list is empty " << endl;
else
  cout << "list is not empty " << endl;
```

The member function `resize()` changes the size of the list to the value specified by the argument. Values are either added or erased from the end of the collection as necessary. An optional second argument can be used to provide the initial value for any new elements added to the collection.

```
        // become size 12, adding values of 17 if necessary
list_nine.resize (12, 17);
```

Access and iteration

The member functions `front()` and `back()` return, but do not remove, the first and last items in the container, respectively. For a list, access to other elements is possible only by removing elements (until the desired element becomes the front or back) or through the use of iterators.

There are two types of iterators that can be constructed for lists. The functions `begin()` and `end()` construct iterators that traverse the list in forward order. For the list data type `begin()` and `end()` create bidirectional iterators. The alternative functions `rbegin()` and `rend()` construct iterators that traverse in reverse order, moving from the end of the list to the front.

List test for inclusion

The list data types do not directly provide any method that can be used to determine if a specific value is contained in the collection. However, either the generic algorithms `find()` or `count()` (see "Find an element satisfying a condition" and "Count the number of elements that satisfy a condition" in Chapter 29) can be used for this purpose. The following statements, for example, test to see whether an integer list contains the element 17.

```
int num = 0;
count(list_five.begin(), list_five.end(), 17, num);
if (num > 0)
  cout << "contains a 17" << endl;
else
  cout << "does not contain a 17" << endl;

if (find(list_five.begin(), list_five.end(), 17) != list_five.end())
  cout << "contains a 17" << endl;
else
  cout << "does not contain a 17" << endl;
```

Sorting and sorted list operations

The member function `sort()` places elements into ascending order. If a comparison operator other than < is desired, it can be supplied as an argument.

```
list_ten.sort ( );   // place elements into sequence
list_twelve.sort (widgetCompare);   // sort with widget compare function
```

Once a list has been sorted, a number of the generic algorithms for ordered collections can be used with lists. These are described in detail in Ordered collection algorithms overview.

Searching operations

The various forms of searching functions, namely `find()`, `find_if()`, `adjacent find()`, `mismatch()`, `max_element()`, `min_element()` or `search()` can be applied to list. In all cases the result is an iterator, which can be dereferenced to discover the denoted element, or used as an argument in a subsequent operation.

Note   **Verify search results:** The searching algorithms in the standard library will always return the end of range iterator if no element matching the search condition is found. Unless the result is guaranteed to be valid, it is a good idea to check for the end of range condition.

In-place transformations

A number of operations can be applied to lists in order to transform them in place. Some of these are provided as member functions. Others make use of some of the generic functions described in Chapter 29.

For a list, the member function reverse() reverses the order of elements in the list.

```
list_ten.reverse();   // elements are now reversed
```

The generic algorithm `transform()` (see "Transform one or two sequences" in Chapter 29) can be used to modify every value in a container, by simply using the same container as both input and as result for the operation. The following, for example, increments each element of a list by one. To construct the necessary unary function, the first argument of the binary integer addition function is bound to the value one. The version of `transform()` that manipulates two parallel sequences can be used in a similar fashion.

```
transform(list_ten.begin(), list_ten.end(),
    list_ten.begin(), bind1st(plus<int>(), 1));
```

In an analogous manner, the functions `replace()` and `replace_if()` (see "Replace certain elements with fixed value" in Chapter 29) can be used to replace elements of a list with specific values. Rotations (see "Rotate elements around a midpoint" in Chapter 29) and partitions (see "Partition a sequence into two groups" in Chapter 29), can also be performed with lists.

```
// find the location of the 5 value, and rotate around it
location = find(list_ten.begin(), list_ten.end(), 5);
```

```
    rotate(list_ten.begin(), location, list_ten.end());
      // now partition using values greater than 7
    partition(list_ten.begin(), list_ten.end(),
        bind2nd(greater<int>(), 7));
```

The functions `next_permutation()` and `prev_permutation()` (see "Generate permutations in sequence" in Chapter 29) can be used to generate the next permutation (or previous permutation) of a collection of values.

```
    next_permutation (list_ten.begin(), list_ten.end());
```

Other operations

The algorithm `for_each()` (see "Apply a function to all elements in a collection" in Chapter 29) will apply a function to every element of a collection. An illustration of this use will be given in the radix sort example program in the section on the *deque* data structure.

The `accumulate()` generic algorithm reduces a collection to a scalar value (see "Reduce sequence to a single value" in Chapter 29). This can be used, for example, to compute the sum of a list of numbers. A more unusual use of `accumulate()` will be illustrated in the radix sort example.

```
    cout << "Sum of list is: " <<
        accumulate(list_ten.begin(), list_ten.end(), 0) << endl;
```

Two lists can be compared against each other. They are equal if they are the same size and all corresponding elements are equal. A list is less than another list if it is lexicographically smaller (see "Lexical comparison" in Chapter 29).

Example program: an inventory system

Note   **Obtaining the sample program:** The executable version of the widget works program is contained in file widwork.cpp on the distribution disk.

We will use a simple inventory management system to illustrate the use of several list operations. Assume a business, named *World Wide Widget Works*, requires a software system to manage their supply of widgets. Widgets are simple devices, distinguished by different identification numbers:

```
    class  Widget {
    public:
      Widget(int a = 0) : id(a) { }
      void operator = (const Widget& rhs) { id = rhs.id; }
      int id;
      friend ostream & operator << (ostream & out,const Widget & w)
        { return out << "Widget " << w.id; }
      friend bool operator == (const Widget&lhs, const Widget& rhs)
        { return lhs.id == rhs.id; }
      friend bool operator< (const Widget&llhs, const Widget& rhs)
        { return lhs.id < rhs.id; }
    };
```

The state of the inventory is represented by two lists. One list represents the stock of widgets on hand, while the second represents the type of widgets that customers have backordered. The first is a list of widgets, while the second is a list of widget identification types. To handle our inventory we have two commands; the first, `order()` processes orders, while the second, `receive()`, processes the shipment of a new widget.

```
class inventory {
public:
  void order (int wid);   // process order for widget type wid
  void receive (int wid);   // receive widget of type wid in shipment
private:
  list<Widget> on_hand;
  list<int> on_order;
};
```

When a new widget arrives in shipment, we compare the widget identification number with the list of widget types on backorder. We use `find()` to search the backorder list, immediately shipping the widget if necessary. Otherwise it is added to the stock on hand.

```
void inventory::receive (int wid)
{
  cout << "Received shipment of widget type " << wid << endl;
  list<int>::iterator weneed =
      find (on_order.begin(), on_order.end(), wid);
  if (weneed != on_order.end()) {
    cout << "Ship " << Widget(wid)
        << " to fill back order" << endl;
    on_order.erase(weneed);
    }
  else
    on_hand.push_front(Widget(wid));
}
```

When a customer orders a new widget, we scan the list of widgets in stock to determine if the order can be processed immediately. We can use the function `find_if()` to search the list. To do so we need a binary function that takes as its argument a widget and determines whether the widget matches the type requested. We can do this by taking a general binary widget testing function, and binding the second argument to the specific widget type. To use the function `bind2nd()`, however, requires that the binary function be an instance of the class binary_function. The general widget testing function is written as follows:

```
class WidgetTester : public binary_function<Widget, int, bool> {
public:
  bool operator () (const Widget & wid, int testid) const
    { return wid.id == testid; }
};
```

The widget order function is then written as follows:

```
void inventory::order (int wid)
{
  cout << "Received order for widget type " << wid << endl;
  list<Widget>::iterator wehave =
```

```
        find_if (on_hand.begin(), on_hand.end(),
            bind2nd(WidgetTester(), wid));
    if (wehave != on_hand.end()) {
      cout << "Ship " << *wehave << endl;
      on_hand.erase(wehave);
      }
    else {
      cout << "Back order widget of type "  << wid  << endl;
      on_order.push_front(wid);
      }
}
```

24

deque

Deque data abstraction

The name *"deque"* is short for "double-ended queue," and is pronounced like "deck." Traditionally, the term is used to describe any data structure that permits both insertions and removals from either the front or the back of a collection. The *deque* container class permits this, as well as much more. In fact, the capabilities of the *deque* data structure are almost a union of those provided by the *vector* and *list* classes.

- Like a *vector*, the *deque* is an indexed collection. Values can be accessed by subscript, using the position within the collection as a key (a capability not provided by the list class).

- Like a *list*, values can be efficiently added either to the front or to the back of a *deque* (a capability provided only in part by the *vector* class).

- As with both the *list* and *vector* classes, insertions can be made into the middle of the sequence held by a *deque*. Such insertion operations are not as efficient as with a *list*, but slightly more efficient that they are in a *vector*.

In short, a *deque* can often be used both in situations that require a *vector* and in those that call for a *list*. Often, the use of a *deque* in place of either a *vector* or a *list* will result in faster programs. To determine which data structure should be used, you can refer to the set of questions described in "Selecting a container" in Chapter 21.

Deque include files

The *deque* header file must appear in all programs that use the *deque* data type.

```
# include <deque>
```

Deque operations

The following table summarizes the member functions provided by the *deque* data type. You will note the close similarity between this chart and the ones provided earlier for the *vector* and *list* data types. No further discussion will be provided for those operations which match either the *vector* or *list* member functions discussed earlier.

Result	Name	Arguments
	deque	()
	deque	(size_type)
	deque	(size_type, value_type)
	deque	template <class Iterator> (Iterator, Iterator)
	deque	template <class Iterator> assign (Iterator, Iterator)
	deque	template <class Size,class T> assign (Size, T)
	deque	(const deque)
reference	at	(size_type)
reference	back	()
RandomAccessIterator	begin	()
bool	empty	()
RandomAccessIterator	end	()
void	erase	(iterator)
void	erase	(iterator,iterator)
reference	front	()
iterator	insert	(iterator, value_type)
void	insert	(iterator, size_type, value_type)
void	insert	template <class Iterator> (iterator, Iterator, Iterator)
size_type	max_size	()
void	pop_back	()
void	pop_front	()
void	push_back	(value_type)
void	push_front	(value_type)
RandomAccessIterator	rbegin	()
RandomAccessIterator	rend	()
void	resize	(size_type, value_type)
size_type	size	()
void	swap	(deque)
reference	operator []	size_type
deque	operator =	deque

A *deque* is declared in the same fashion as a *vector,* and includes within the class the same type definitions as *vector.*

Notice that the `begin()` and `end()` member functions return random access iterator, rather than bidirectional iterators, as they do for lists.

An insertion (either `insert()`, `push_front()`, or `push_back()`) can potentially invalidate all outstanding iterators and references to elements in the *deque*. As with the *vector* data type, this is a much more restrictive condition than insertions into a list.

If the underlying element type provides a destructor, then the destructor will be invoked when a value is erased from a *deque*.

Since the *deque* data type provides random access iterators, all the generic algorithms that operate with *vectors* can also be used with deques.

A *vector* holds elements in a single large block of memory. A *deque*, on the other hand, uses a number of smaller blocks. This may be important on systems that restrict the size of memory blocks, as it will permit a *deque* to hold many more elements than a *vector*.

As values are inserted, the index associated with any particular element in the collection will change. For example, if a value is inserted into position 3, then the value formerly indexed by 3 will now be found at index location 4, the value formerly at 4 will be found at index location 5, and so on.

Example program: radix sort

The radix sort algorithm is a good illustration of how lists and deques can be combined with other containers. In the case of radix sort, a *vector* of deques is manipulated, much like a hash table.

Note   **Obtaining the sample program:** The complete radix sort program is found in the file `RADIX.CPP` in the tutorial distribution disk.

Radix sorting is a technique for ordering a list of positive integer values. The values are successively ordered on digit positions, from right to left. This is accomplished by copying the values into "buckets," where the index for the bucket is given by the position of the digit being sorted. Once all digit positions have been examined, the list must be sorted.

The following table shows the sequences of values found in each bucket during the four steps involved in sorting the list 624 852 426 987 269 146 415 301 730 78 593. During pass 1 the one's place digits are ordered. During pass 2 the ten's place digits are ordered, retaining the relative positions of values set by the earlier pass. On pass 3 the hundred's place digits are ordered, again retaining the previous relative ordering. After three passes the result is an ordered list.

bucket	pass 1	pass 2	pass 3
0	730	301	78
1	301	415	146
2	852	624, 426	269
3	593	730	301
4	624	146	415, 426
5	415	852	593

bucket	pass 1	pass 2	pass 3
6	426, 146	269	624
7	987	78	730
8	78	987	852
9	269	593	987

The radix sorting algorithm is simple. A `while` loop is used to cycle through the various passes. The value of the variable `divisor` indicates which digit is currently being examined. A Boolean flag is used to determine when execution should halt. Each time the `while` loop is executed a *vector* of deques is declared. By placing the declaration of this structure inside the `while` loop, it is reinitialized to empty each step. Each time the loop is executed, the values in the list are copied into the appropriate bucket by executing the function `copyIntoBuckets()` on each value. Once distributed into the buckets, the values are gathered back into the list by means of an accumulation.

```
void radixSort(list<unsigned int> & values)
{
  bool flag = true;
  int divisor = 1;

  while (flag) {
    vector< deque<unsigned int> > buckets(10);
    flag = false;
    for_each(values.begin(), values.end(),
        copyIntoBuckets(...));
    accumulate(buckets.begin(), buckets.end(),
        values.begin(), listCopy);
    divisor *= 10;
    }
}
```

The use of the function `accumulate()` here is slightly unusual. The "scalar" value being constructed is the list itself. The initial value for the accumulation is the iterator denoting the beginning of the list. Each bucket is processed by the following binary function:

```
list<unsigned int>::iterator
    listCopy(list<unsigned int>::iterator c,
      deque<unsigned int> & lst)
{
    // copy list back into original list, returning end
  return copy(lst.begin(), lst.end(), c);
}
```

The only difficulty remaining is defining the function `copyIntoBuckets()`. The problem here is that the function must take as its argument only the element being inserted, but it must also have access to the three values `buckets`, `divisor`, and `flag`. In languages that permit functions to be defined within other functions the solution would be to define `copyIntoBuckets()` as a local function within the `while` loop. But C++ has no such facilities. Instead, we must create a class definition, which can be initialized with references to the appropriate values. The parenthesis operator for this class is then used as the function for the `for_each()` invocation in the radix sort program.

```
class copyIntoBuckets {
public:
  copyIntoBuckets
    (int d, vector< deque<unsigned int> > & b, bool & f)
      : divisor(d), buckets(b), flag(f) {}

  int divisor;
  vector<deque<unsigned int> > & buckets;
  bool & flag;

  void operator () (unsigned int v)
      {  int index = (v / divisor) % 10;
        // flag is set to true if any bucket
        // other than zeroth is used
        if (index) flag = true;
        buckets[index].push_back(v);
      }
};
```

25

set, multiset, and bit_set

The set data abstraction

Note **Sets, ordered and not:** Although the abstract concept of a *set* does not necessarily imply an ordered collection, the *set* data type is always ordered. If necessary, a collection of values that cannot be ordered can be maintained in, for example, a list.

A *set* is a collection of values. Because the container used to implement the *set* data structure maintains values in an ordered representation, sets are optimized for insertion and removal of elements, and for testing to see whether a particular value is contained in the collection. Each of these operations can be performed in a logarithmic number of steps, whereas for a *list*, *vector*, or *deque*, each operation requires in the worst case an examination of every element held by the container. For this reason, sets should be the data structure of choice in any problem that emphasizes insertion, removal, and test for inclusion of values. Like a *list*, a *set* is not limited in size, but rather expands and contracts as elements are added to or removed from the collection.

There are two varieties of sets provided by the standard library. In the *set* container, every element is unique. Insertions of values that are already contained in the *set* are ignored. In the *multiset* container, on the other hand, multiple occurrences of the same value are permitted.

Set include files

Whenever you use a *set* or a *multiset*, you must include the *set* header file.

```
# include <set>
```

Set and multiset operations

Note **Sets and bags:** In other programming languages, a *multiset* is sometimes referred to as a *bag*.

The following chart summarizes the member functions provided by the *set* and *multiset* data types. Each will shortly be described in more detail. Note that while member functions provide basic operations, the utility of these data structures is greatly extended through the use of the generic algorithms described in Chapters 29 and 30.

Result	Name	Arguments
	set	()
	multiset	()
	set	(Compare)
	multiset	(Compare)
	set	template <class Iterator> (Iterator, Iterator)
	multiset	template <class Iterator> (Iterator, Iterator)
	set	(const set)
	multiset	(const multiset)
BidirectionalIterator	begin	()
size_type	count	(value_type)
bool	empty	()
BidirectionalIterator	end	()
pair<iterator, iterator>	equal_range	(value_type)
void	erase	(iterator)
size_type	erase	(value_type)
void	erase	(iterator, iterator)
iterator	find	(value_type)
pair<iterator, bool>	insert	(value_type)
iterator	insert	(iterator, value_type)
void	insert	template <class Iterator> (Iterator, Iterator)
iterator	lower_bound	(value_type)
size_type	max_size	()
BidirectionalIterator	rbegin	()
BidirectionalIterator	rend	()
size_type	size	()
void	swap	(set)
iterator	upper_bound	(key_type)
Function	value_comp	()
set	operator =	(set)

Creation and initialization

A *set* is a template data structure, specialized by the type of the elements it contains, and the operator used to compare keys. The latter argument is optional, and, if it is not provided, the less than operator for the key type will be assumed. The element type can be a primitive language type (such as integer or double), a pointer type, or a user-defined type. The element type must recognize both the equality testing operator (operator ==) and the less than comparison operator (operator <).

Note **Initializing sets with iterators:** As we noted in the earlier discussion on *vectors* and lists, the initialization of containers using a pair of iterators requires a mechanism that is still not widely supported by compilers. If not provided, the equivalent effect can be produced by declaring an empty *set* and then using the `copy()` generic algorithm to copy values into the *set*.

Sets can be declared with no initial elements, or they can be initialized from another container by providing a pair of iterators. An optional argument in both cases is an alternative comparison function; this value overrides the value provided by the template parameter. This mechanism is useful if a program contains two or more sets with the same values but different orderings, as it prevents more than one copy of the *set* member function from being instantiated. The copy constructor can be used to form a new *set* that is a clone, or copy, of an existing *set*.

```
set <int> set_one;
set <int, greater<int> > set_two;
set <int> set_three(greater<int>());

set <gadget, less<gadget>() > gset;
set <gadget> gset(less<gadget>())

set <int> set_four (aList.begin(), aList.end());
set <int> set_five
    (aList.begin(), aList.end(), greater<int>() );
set <int> set_six (set_four);  // copy constructor
```

A *set* can be assigned to another *set*, and two sets can exchange their values using the `swap()` operation (in a manner analogous to other standard library containers).

```
set_one = set_five;
set_six.swap(set_two);
```

Type definitions

The classes *set* and *multiset* include a number of type definitions. The most common use for these is in a declaration statement. For example, an iterator for a *set* of integers can be declared in the following fashion:

```
set<int>::iterator location;
```

In addition to `iterator`, the following types are defined:

`value_type`	The type associated with the elements the *set* maintains.
`const_iterator`	An iterator that does not allow modification of the underlying sequence.
`reverse_iterator`	An iterator that moves in a backward direction.
`const_reverse_iterator`	A combination constant and reverse iterator.
`reference`	A reference to an underlying element.
`const_reference`	A reference to an underlying element that will not permit modification.
`size_type`	An unsigned integer type, used to refer to the size of containers.

| value_compare | A function that can be used to compare two elements. |
| difference_type | A signed integer type, used to describe the distance between iterators. |

Insertion

Note **Pairs:** See the discussion of maps in the section "The *map* data abstraction" in Chapter 26 for a description of the pair data type.

Unlike a list or *vector*, there is only one way to add a new element to a *set*. A value can be inserted into a *set* or a *multiset* using the `insert()` member function. With a *multiset*, the function returns an iterator that denotes the value just inserted. Insert operations into a *set* return a pair of values, in which the first field contains an iterator, and the second field contains a Boolean value that is true if the element was inserted, and false otherwise. Recall that in a *set*, an element will not be inserted if it matches an element already contained in the collection.

```
set_one.insert (18);

if (set_one.insert(18).second)
  cout << "element was inserted" << endl;
else
  cout << "element was not inserted " << endl;
```

Insertions of several elements from another container can also be performed using an iterator pair:

```
set_one.insert (set_three.begin(), set_three.end());
```

Removal of elements from a set

Values are removed from a *set* using the member function `erase()`. The argument can be either a specific value, an iterator that denotes a single value, or a pair of iterators that denote a range of values. When the first form is used on a *multiset*, all arguments matching the argument value are removed, and the return value indicates the number of elements that have been erased.

```
   // erase element equal to 4
set_three.erase(4);

   // erase element five
stesttype::iterator five = set_three.find(5);
set_three.erase(five);

   // erase all values between seven and eleven
stesttype::iterator seven = set_three.find(7);
stesttype::iterator eleven = set_three.find(11);
set_three.erase (seven, eleven);
```

If the underlying element type provides a destructor, then the destructor will be invoked prior to removing the element from the collection.

Searching and counting

The member function `size()` will yield the number of elements held by a container. The member function `empty()` will return a Boolean true value if the container is empty, and is generally faster than testing the size against zero.

The member function `find()` takes an element value, and returns an iterator denoting the location of the value in the *set* if it is present, or a value matching the end-of-*set* (the value yielded by the function `end()`) if it is not. If a *multiset* contains more than one matching element, the value returned can be any appropriate value.

```
list<int>::iterator five = set_three.find(5);
if (five != set_three.end())
    cout << "set contains a five" << endl;
```

The member functions `lower_bound()` and `upper_bound()` are most useful with multisets, as with sets they simply mimic the function `find()`. The member function `lower_bound()` yields the first entry that matches the argument key, while the member function `upper_bound()` returns the first value past the last entry matching the argument. Finally, the member function `equal_range()` returns a pair of iterators, holding the lower and upper bounds.

The member function `count()` returns the number of elements that match the argument. For a *set* this value is either zero or one, whereas for a *multiset* it can be any nonnegative value. Since a non-zero integer value is treated as true, the `count()` function can be used to test for inclusion of an element, if all that is desired is to determine whether or not the element is present in the *set*. The alternative, using `find()`, requires testing the result returned by `find()` against the end-of-collection iterator.

```
if (set_three.count(5))
    cout << "set contains a five" << endl;
```

Iterators

Note   **No iterator invalidation:** Unlike a *vector* or *deque*, the insertion or removal of values from a *set* does not invalidate iterators or references to other elements in the collection.

The member functions `begin()` and `end()` produce iterators for both sets and multisets. The iterators produced by these functions are constant to insure that the ordering relation for the *set* is not inadvertently or intentionally destroyed by assigning a new value to a *set* element. Elements are generated by the iterators in sequence, ordered by the comparison operator provided when the *set* was declared. The member functions `rbegin()` and `rend()` produce iterators that yield the elements in reverse order.

Set operations

The traditional *set* operations of subset test, *set* union, *set* intersection, and *set* difference are not provided as member functions, but are instead implemented as generic algorithms that will work with any ordered structure. These functions are described in more detail in *set* operations. The following summary describes how these functions can be used with the *set* and *multiset* container classes.

Subset test

The function `includes()` can be used to determine if one *set* is a subset of another; that is, if all elements from the first are contained in the second. In the case of multisets the number of matching elements in the second *set* must exceed the number of elements in the first. The four arguments are a pair of iterators representing the (presumably) smaller *set*, and a pair of iterators representing the (potentially) larger *set*.

```
if (includes(set_one.begin(), set_one.end(),
    set_two.begin(), set_two.end()))
        cout << "set is a subset" << endl;
```

The less than operator (operator <) will be used for the comparison of elements, regardless of the operator used in the declaration of the *set*. Where this is inappropriate, an alternative version of the `includes()` function is provided. This form takes a fifth argument, which is the comparison function used to order the elements in the two sets.

Set union or intersection

The function `set_union()` can be used to construct a union of two sets. The two sets are specified by iterator pairs, and the union is copied into an output iterator that is supplied as a fifth argument. To form the result as a *set*, an *insert iterator* must be used to form the output iterator. (See "Insert iterators" in Chapter 19 for a discussion of insert iterators.) If the desired outcome is a union of one *set* with another, then a temporary *set* can be constructed, and the results swapped with the argument *set* prior to deletion of the temporary *set*.

```
    // union two sets, copying result into a vector
vector<int> v_one (set_one.size() + set_two.size());

set_union(set_one.begin(), set_one.end(),
    set_two.begin(), set_two.end(), v_one.begin());

    // form union in place
{
set<int> temp_set;
set_union(set_one.begin(), set_one.end(),
    set_two.begin(), set_two.end(),
    inserter(temp_set, temp_set.begin()));
set_one.swap(temp_set);  // temp_set will be deleted
}
```

The function `set_intersection()` is similar, and forms the intersection of the two sets.

As with the `includes()` function, the less than operator (operator <) is used to compare elements in the two argument sets, regardless of the operator provided in the declaration of the sets. Should this be inappropriate, alternative versions of both the `set_union()` or `set_intersection()` functions permit the comparison operator used to form the *set* to be given as a sixth argument.

The operation of taking the union of two multisets should be distinguished from the operation of merging two sets. Imagine that one argument *set* contains three instances of the element 7, and the second *set* contains two instances of the same value. The union will contain only three such values, while the merge will contain five. To form the merge, the function `merge()` can be used (see "Merge ordered sequences" in Chapter 30). The arguments to this function exactly match those of the `set_union()` function.

Set difference

There are two forms of *set* difference. A simple *set* difference represents the elements in the first *set* that are not contained in the second. A symmetric *set* difference is the union of the elements in the first *set* that are not contained in the second, with the elements in the second that are not contained in the first. These two values are constructed by the functions `set_difference()` and `set_symmetric_difference()`, respectively. The use of these functions is similar to the use of the `set_union()` function described earlier.

Other generic algorithms

Because sets are ordered and have constant iterators, a number of the generic functions described in Chapter 29 either are not applicable to sets or are not particularly useful. However, the following table gives a few of the functions that can be usefully used in conjunction with the *set* data type.

Purpose	Name
Copy one sequence into another	copy
Find an element that matches a condition	find_if
Find a subsequence within a *set*	search
Count number of elements that satisfy condition	count_if
Reduce *set* to a single value	accumulate
Execute function on each element	for_each

Example program: a spelling checker

Note   **Obtaining the sample program:** This program can be found in the file spell.cpp in the tutorial distribution.

A simple example program that uses a *set* is a spelling checker. The checker takes as arguments two input streams; the first representing a stream of correctly spelled words (that is, a dictionary), and the second a text file. First, the dictionary is read into a *set*. This is performed using a `copy()` and an input stream iterator, copying the values into an inserter for the dictionary. Next, words from the text are examined one by one, to see if they are in the dictionary. If they are not, then they are added to a *set* of misspelled words. After the entire text has been examined, the program outputs the list of misspelled words.

```
void spellCheck (istream & dictionary, istream & text)
{
  typedef set <string, less<string> > stringset;
  stringset words, misspellings;
  string word;
```

```
        istream_iterator<string, ptrdiff_t> dstream(dictionary), eof;

          // first read the dictionary
        copy (dstream, eof, inserter(words, words.begin()));

          // next read the text
        while (text >> word)
          if (! words.count(word))
            misspellings.insert(word);

          // finally, output all misspellings
        cout << "Misspelled words:" << endl;
        copy (misspellings.begin(), misspellings.end(),
          ostream_iterator<string>(cout, "\n"));

    }
```

An improvement would be to suggest alternative words for each misspelling. There are various heuristics that can be used to discover alternatives. The technique we will use here is to simply exchange adjacent letters. To find these, a call on the following function is inserted into the loop that displays the misspellings.

```
    void findMisspell(stringset & words, string & word)
    {
      for (int i = 1; i < word.length(); i++) {
        swap(word[i-1], word[i]);
        if (words.count(word))
          cout << "Suggestion: " << word << endl;
          // put word back as before
        swap(word[i-1], word[i]);
        }
    }
```

The class bit_set

A *bit_set* is really a cross between a *set* and a *vector*. Like the *vector* abstraction *vector<bool>*, the abstraction represents a *set* of binary (0/1 bit) values. However, *set* operations can be performed on bitsets using the logical bit-wise operators. The class *bit_set* does not provide any iterators for accessing elements.

Initialization and creation

A *bit_set* is a template class abstraction. The template argument is not, however, a type, but an integer value. The value represents the number of bits the *set* will contains.

```
    bit_set<126> bset_one;  // create a set of 126 bits
```

An alternative technique permits the size of the *set* to be specified as an argument to the constructor. The actual size will be the smaller of the value used as template argument and the constructor argument. This technique is useful when a program contains two or more bit *vectors* of differing sizes. Consistently using the larger size for the template argument means that only one *set* of methods for the class will be generated. The actual size, however, will be determined by the constructor.

```
    bit_set<126> bset_two(100);  // this set has only 100 elements
```

A third form of constructor takes as argument a string of 0 and 1 characters. A bit_set is created that has as many elements as are characters in the string, and is initialized with the values from the string.

```
bit_set<126> small_set("10101010");  // this set has 8 elements
```

Accessing and testing elements

An individual bit in the bit_set can be accessing using the subscript operation. Whether the bit is one or not can be determined using the member function test(). Whether any bit in the bit_set is on is tested using the member function any(), which yields a boolean value. The inverse of any() is returned by the member function none().

```
bset_one[3] = 1;
if (bset_one.test(4))
  cout << "bit position 4 is set" << endl;
if (bset_one.any())
  cout << "some bit position is set" << endl;
```

The function set() can be used to set a specific bit. bset_one.set(i) is equivalent to bset_one[i] = true. Invoking the function without any arguments sets all bit positions to true. The function reset() is similar, and sets the indicated positions to false (sets all positions to false if invoked with no argument). The function flip() flips either the indicated position, or all positions if no argument is provided. The function flip() is also provided as a member function for the individual bit references.

```
bset_one.flip();  // flip the entire set
bset_one.flip(12);  // flip only bit 12
bset_one[12].flip();  // reflip bit 12
```

The member function size() returns the size of the bit_set, while the member function count() yields the number of bits that are set.

Set operations

Set operations on bit_sets are implemented using the bit-wise operators, in a manner analogous to the way in which the same operators act on integer arguments.

The negation operator (operator ~) applied to a bit_set returns a new bit_set containing the inverse of elements in the argument *set*.

The intersection of two bit_sets is formed using the and operator (operator &). The assignment form of the operator can be used. In the assignment form the target becomes the disjunction of the two sets.

```
bset_three = bset_two & bset_four;
bset_five &= bset_three;
```

The union of two sets is formed in a similar manner using the *or* operator (operator |). The exclusive-or is formed using the bit-wise exclusive or operator (operator ^).

The left and right shift operators (operator << and >>) can be used to shift a *bit_set* left or right, in a manner analogous to the use of these operators on integer arguments. If a bit is shifted left by an integer value *n*, then the new bit position *i* is the value of the former *i-n*. Zeros are shifted into the new positions.

Conversions

The member function to_ulong() converts a *bit_set* into an unsigned long. It is an error to perform this operation on a *bit_set* containing more elements than will fit into this representation.

The member function to_string() converts a *bit_set* into an object of type *string*. The string will have as many characters as the *bit_set*. Each zero bit will correspond to the character 0, while each one bit will be represented by the character 1.

26

map and multimap

The map data abstraction

Note   **Other names for maps:** In other programming languages, a map-like data structure is sometimes referred to as a *dictionary*, a *table*, or an *associative array*.

A *map* is an indexed data structure, similar to a *vector* or a *deque*. However, maps differ from *vectors* or deques in two important respects. First, in a *map*, unlike a *vector* or *deque*, the index values (called the *key values*) need not be integer, but can be any ordered data type. For example, maps can be indexed by real numbers, or by strings. Any data type for which a comparison operator can be defined can be used as a key. As with a *vector* or *deque*, elements can be accessed through the use of the subscript operator (although there are other techniques). The second important difference is that a *map* is an ordered data structure. This means that elements are maintained in sequence, the ordering being determined by key values. Because they maintain values in order, maps can very rapidly find the element specified by any given key (searching is performed in logarithmic time). Like a list, maps are not limited in size, but expand or contract as necessary as new elements are added or removed.

There are two varieties of maps provided by the standard library. The *map* data structure demands unique keys. That is, there is a one-to-one association between key elements and their corresponding value. In a *map*, the insertion of a new value that uses an existing key is ignored. A *multimap*, on the other hand, permits multiple different entries to be indexed by the same key. Both data structures provide relatively fast (logarithmic time) insertion, deletion, and access operations.

Note   **The pair data type:** If you want to use the pair data type without using maps, you should include the header file named `utility`.

In large part, a *map* can simply be considered to be a *set* that maintains a collection of pairs. The *pair* data structure is a tuple of values. The first value is accessed through the field name `first`, while the second is, naturally, named `second`. A function named `make_pair()` simplifies the task of producing an instance of class *pair*.

```
template <class T1, class T2>
struct pair {
  T1 first;
  T2 second;
  pair (const T1 & x, const T2 & y) : first(x), second(y) { }
};
template <class T1, class T2>
inline pair<T1, T2> make_pair(const T1& x, const T2& y)
  { return pair<T1, T2>(x, y); }
```

In determining the equivalence of keys; for example, to determine if the key portion of a new element matches any existing key, the comparison function for keys is used, and not the equivalence (==) operator. Two keys are deemed equivalent if the comparison function used to order key values yields false in both directions. That is, if Compare(key1, key2) is false, and if Compare(key2, key1) is false, then key1 and key2 are considered equivalent.

Map include files

Whenever you use a *map* or a *multimap*, you must include the *map* or *multimap* header file.

```
# include <map>
```

Map and multimap operations

The following chart summarizes the member functions provided by the *map* and *multimap* data types. Each will shortly be described in more detail. Note that while member functions provide basic operations, the utility of the data structure is greatly extended through the use of the generic algorithms described in Chapter 30.

Result	Name	Arguments
	map	()
	multimap	()
	map	(Compare)
	multimap	(Compare)
	map	template <class Iterator> (Iterator, Iterator)
	multimap	template <class Iterator> (Iterator, Iterator)
	map	(const map)
	multimap	(const multimap)
BidirectionalIterator	begin	()
size_type	count	(key_type)
bool	empty	()
BidirectionalIterator	end	()
pair<iterator, iterator>	equal_range	(key_type)

Result	Name	Arguments
void	erase	(iterator)
size_type	erase	(key_type)
void	erase	(iterator, iterator)
iterator	find	(key_type)
Function	key_comp	()
pair<iterator, bool>	insert	(value_type)
iterator	insert	(iterator, value_type)
void	insert	template <class Iterator> (Iterator, Iterator)
iterator	lower_bound	(key_type)
size_type	max_size	()
BidirectionalIterator	rbegin	()
BidirectionalIterator	rend	()
size_type	size	()
void	swap	(map)
iterator	upper_bound	(key_type)
Function	value_comp	()
reference	operator []	(key_type) (map only)
map	operator =	(map)

Creation and initialization

The declaration of a *map* follows the pattern we have seen repeatedly in the standard library. A *map* is a template data structure, specialized by the type of the key elements, the type of the associated values, and the operator to be used in comparing keys. If your compiler supports default template types (a relatively new feature in C++ not yet supported by all vendors), then the last of these is optional, and if not provided, the less than operator for key type will be assumed. Maps can be declared with no initial elements, or initialized from another container by providing a pair of iterators. In the latter case the iterators must denote values of type pair; the first field in each pair is taken to be a key, while the second field is a value. A copy constructor also permits maps to be created as copies of other maps.

```
    // map indexed by doubles containing strings
map<double, string, less<double> > map_one;
    // map indexed by integers, containing integers
map<int, int> map_two(aContainer.begin(), aContainer.end());
    // create a new map, initializing it from map two
map<int, int> map_three (map_two);// copy constructor
```

A *map* can be assigned to another *map*, and two maps can exchange their values using the swap() operation (in a manner analogous to other standard library containers).

Type definitions

The classes *map* and *multimap* include a number of type definitions. These are most commonly used in declaration statements. For example, an iterator for a *map* of strings to integers can be declared in the following fashion:

```
map<string, int>::iterator location;
```

In addition to `iterator`, the following types are defined:

`key_type`	The type associated with the keys used to index the *map*.
`value_type`	The type held by the container, a key/value pair.
`const_iterator`	An iterator that does not allow modification of the underlying sequence.
`reverse_iterator`	An iterator that moves in a backward direction.
`const_reverse_iterator`	A combination constant and reverse iterator.
`reference`	A reference to an underlying value.
`const_reference`	A reference to an underlying value that will not permit the element to be modified.
`size_type`	An unsigned integer type, used to refer to the size of containers.
`key_compare`	A function object that can be used to compare two keys.
`value_compare`	A function object that can be used to compare two elements.
`difference_type`	A signed integer type, used to describe to the distances between iterators.

Insertion and access

Values can be inserted into a *map* or a *multimap* using the `insert()` operation. Note that the argument must be a key-value pair. This pair is often constructed using the data type value_type associated with the *map*.

```
map_three.insert (map<int>::value_type(5, 7));
```

Insertions can also be performed using an iterator pair, for example as generated by another *map*.

```
map_two.insert (map_three.begin(), map_three.end());
```

With a *map* (but not a *multimap*), values can be accessed and inserted using the subscript operator. Simply using a key as a subscript creates an entry—the default element is used as the associated value. Assigning to the result of the subscript changes the associated binding.

```
cout << "Index value 7 is " << map_three[7] << endl;
   // now change the associated value
map_three[7] = 5;
cout << "Index value 7 is " << map_three[7] << endl;
```

Removal of values

Values can be removed from a *map* or a *multimap* by naming the key value. In a *multimap,* the erasure removes all elements with the associated key. An element to be removed can also be denoted by an iterator; as, for example, the iterator yielded by a find() operation. A pair of iterators can be used to erase an entire range of elements.

```
    // erase element 4
map_three.erase(4);
    // erase element five
mtesttype::iterator five = map_three.find(5);
map_three.erase(five);

    // erase all values between seven and eleven
mtesttype::iterator seven = map_three.find(7);
mtesttype::iterator eleven = map_three.find(11);
map_three.erase (seven, eleven);
```

If the underlying element type provides a destructor, then the destructor will be invoked prior to removing the key and value pair from the collection.

Iterators

Note **No iterator invalidation:** Unlike a *vector* or *deque*, the insertion or removal of elements from a *map* does not invalidate iterators which may be referencing other portions of the container.

The member functions begin() and end() produce bidirectional iterators for both maps and multimaps. Dereferencing a iterator for either a *map* or a *multimap* will yield a pair of key/value elements. The field names first and second can be applied to these values to access the individual fields. The first field is constant, and cannot be modified. The second field, however, can be used to change the value being held in association with a given key. Elements will be generated in sequence, based on the ordering of the key fields.

The member functions rbegin() and rend() produce iterators that yield the elements in reverse order.

Searching and counting

The member function size() will yield the number of elements held by a container. The member function empty() will return a Boolean true value if the container is empty, and is generally faster than testing the size against zero.

The member function find() takes a key argument, and returns an iterator denoting the associated key/value pair. In the case of multimaps, the first such value is returned. In both cases the past-the-end iterator is returned if no such value is found.

```
if (map_one.find(4) != map_end.end())
    cout << "contains a four" << endl;
```

The member function lower_bound() yields the first entry that matches the argument key, while the member function upper_bound() returns the first value past the last entry matching the argument. Finally, the member function `equal_range()` returns a pair of iterators, holding the lower and upper bounds. An example showing the use of these procedures will be presented later in this chapter.

The member function `count()` returns the number of elements that match the key value supplied as the argument. For a *map*, this value is always either zero or one, whereas for a *multimap* it can be any nonnegative value. If you simply want to determine whether or not a collection contains an element indexed by a given key, using `count()` is often easier than using the `find()` function and testing the result against the end-of-sequence iterator.

```
if (map_one.count(4))
   cout << "contains a four" << endl;
```

Element comparisons

The member functions `key_comp()` and `value_comp()`, which take no arguments, return a function that can be used to compare elements of the key or value types. Values used in these comparisons need not be contained in the collection, and neither function will have any effect on the container.

```
if (map_two.key_comp()(i, j))
   cout << "element i is less than j" << endl;
```

Other map operations

Because maps and multimaps are ordered collections, and because the iterators for maps return pairs, many of the functions described in Chapter 30 are meaningless or difficult to use. However, there are a few notable exceptions. The functions `for_each()` ("Apply a function to all elements in a collection"), `adjacent_find()` ("Find consecutive duplicate elements"), and `accumulate()` ("Reduce sequence to a single value") each have their own uses. In all cases it is important to remember that the functions supplied as arguments should take a key/value pair as arguments.

Example programs

We present three example programs that illustrate the use of maps and multimaps. These are a telephone database, graphs, and a concordance.

Example program: a telephone database

Note   **Obtaining the sample program:** The complete example program is included in file `TELE.CPP` in the distribution disk.

A maintenance program for a simple telephone database is a good application for a *map*. The database is simply an indexed structure, where the name of the person or business (a string) is the key value, and the telephone number (a long) is the associated entry. We might write such a class as follows:

```
typedef map<string, long, less<string> > friendMap;
typedef friendMap::value_type entry_type;

class telephoneDirectory {
public:
  void addEntry (string name, long number)// add new entry to database
    { database[name] = number; }

  void remove (string name)// remove entry from database
    { database.erase(name); }

  void update (string name, long number)// update entry
    { remove(name); addEntry(name, number); }

  void displayDatabase()// display entire database
    { for_each(database.begin(), database.end(), printEntry); }

  void displayPrefix(int);// display entries that match prefix

  void displayByPrefix();// display database sorted by prefix
private:
  friendMap database;
};
```

Simple operations on our database are directly implemented by *map* commands.
Adding an element to the database is simply an `insert`, removing an element is an
`erase`, and updating is a combination of the two. To print all the entries in the database
we can use the `for_each()` algorithm, and apply the following simple utility routine to
each entry:

```
void printEntry(const entry_type & entry)
  { cout << entry.first << ":" << entry.second << endl; }
```

We will use a pair of slightly more complex operations to illustrate how a few of the
algorithms described in Chapter 30 can be used with maps. Suppose one wanted to
display all the phone numbers with a certain three digit initial prefix . We will use the
`find_if()` function (which is different from the `find()` member function in class *map*)
to locate the first entry. Starting from this location, subsequent calls on `find_if()` will
uncover each successive entry.

```
void telephoneDirectory::displayPrefix(int prefix)
{
  cout << "Listing for prefix " << prefix << endl;
  friendMap::iterator where;
  where =
    find_if (database.begin(), database.end(),
       checkPrefix(prefix));
  while (where != database.end()) {
    printEntry(*where);
    where = find_if (++where, database.end(),
      checkPrefix(prefix));
    }
  cout << "end of prefix listing" << endl;
}
```

For the predicate to this operation, we require a Boolean function that takes only a single argument (the pair representing a database entry), and tells us whether or not it is in the given prefix. There is no obvious candidate function, and in any case the test prefix is not being passed as an argument to the comparison function. The solution to this problem is to employ a technique that is commonly used with the standard library, defining the predicate function as an instance of a class, and storing the test predicate as an instance variable in the class, initialized when the class is constructed. The desired function is then defined as the function call operator for the class:

```
int prefix(const pair<string, long> entry)
  { return entry.second / 10000; }

class checkPrefix {
public:
  checkPrefix (int p) : testPrefix(p) { }
  const int testPrefix;
  bool operator () const (const entry_type & entry)
    { return prefix(entry) == testPrefix; }
};
```

Our final example will be to display the directory sorted by prefix. It is not possible to alter the way in which maps are themselves ordered. So instead, we create a new *map* with the element types reversed, then copy the values into the new *map*, which will have the effect of ordering the values by prefix. Once the new *map* is created, it is then printed.

```
typedef map<long, string, less<long> > sortedMap;
typedef sortedMap::value_type sorted_entry_type;

void telephoneDirectory::displayByPrefix()

{
  cout << "Display by prefix" << endl;
  sortedMap sortedData;
  friendMap::iterator itr;
  for (itr = database.begin(); itr != database.end(); itr++)
    sortedData.insert(sortedMap::value_type((*itr).second,
        (*itr).first));
  for_each(sortedData.begin(), sortedData.end(), printSortedEntry);
}
```

The function used to print the sorted entries is the following:

```
void printSortedEntry (const sorted_entry_type & entry)
    { cout << entry.first << ":" << entry.second << endl; }
```

Example program: graphs

Note **Obtaining the sample program:** The executable version of this program is found in the file GRAPH.CPP on the distribution disk.

A *map* whose elements are themselves maps is a natural representation for a directed graph. For example, suppose we use strings to encode the names of cities, and we wish to construct a *map* where the value associated with an edge is the distance between two connected cities. We could create such a graph in the following fashion:

```
typedef map<string, int> stringVector;
typedef map<string, stringVector> graph;

string pendleton("Pendleton");// define strings for city names
string pensacola("Pensacola");
string peoria("Peoria");
string phoenix("Phoenix");
string pierre("Pierre");
string pittsburgh("Pittsburgh");
string princeton("Princeton");
string pueblo("Pueblo");

graph cityMap;// declare the graph that holds the map

cityMap[pendleton][phoenix] = 4;// add edges to the graph
cityMap[pendleton][pueblo] = 8;
cityMap[pensacola][phoenix] = 5;
cityMap[peoria][pittsburgh] = 5;
cityMap[peoria][pueblo] = 3;
cityMap[phoenix][peoria] = 4;
cityMap[phoenix][pittsburgh] = 10;
cityMap[phoenix][pueblo] = 3;
cityMap[pierre][pendleton] = 2;
cityMap[pittsburgh][pensacola] = 4;
cityMap[princeton][pittsburgh] = 2;
cityMap[pueblo][pierre] = 3;
```

The type stringVector is a *map* of integers indexed by strings. The type graph is, in effect, a two-dimensional sparse array, indexed by strings and holding integer values. A sequence of assignment statements initializes the graph.

A number of classic algorithms can be used to manipulate graphs represented in this form. One example is Dijkstra's shortest-path algorithm. Dijkstra's algorithm begins from a specific city given as an initial location. A *priority_queue* of distance/city pairs is then constructed, and initialized with the distance from the starting city to itself (namely, zero). The definition for the distance pair data type is as follows:

```
struct DistancePair {
  unsigned int first;
  string second;
  DistancePair() : first(0) { }
  DistancePair(unsigned int f, const string & s)
    : first(f), second(s) { }
};

bool operator < (const DistancePair & lhs, const DistancePair & rhs)
  { return lhs.first < rhs.first; }
```

In the algorithm that follows, note how the conditional test is reversed on the priority queue, because at each step we wish to pull the smallest, and not the largest, value from the collection. On each iteration around the loop we pull a city from the queue. If we have not yet found a shorter path to the city, the current distance is recorded, and by examining the graph we can compute the distance from this city to each of its adjacent cities. This process continues until the priority queue becomes exhausted.

```
void shortestDistance(graph & cityMap,
```

```
                    const string & start, stringVector & distances)
    {
      // process a priority queue of distances to cities
      priority_queue<DistancePair, vector<DistancePair>,
          greater<DinstancePair> > que;
      que.push(DistancePair(0, start));

      while (! que.empty()) {
          // pull nearest city from queue
        int distance = que.top().first;
        string city = que.top().second;
        que.pop();
          // if we haven't seen it already, process it
        if (0 == distances.count(city)) {
            // then add it to shortest distance map
          distances[city] = distance;
            // and put values into queue
          const stringVector & cities = cityMap[city];
          stringVector::const_iterator start = cities.begin();
          stringVector::const_iterator stop = cities.end();
          for (; start != stop; ++start)
            que.push(DinstancePair(distance + (*start).second, (*start).first));
          }
        }
    }
```

Notice that this relatively simple algorithm makes use of *vectors*, maps, strings, and priority queues.

Example program: a concordance

Note **Obtaining the sample program:** An executable version of the concordance program is found on the distribution disk under the name CONCORD.CPP.

A concordance is an alphabetical listing of words in a text, that shows the line numbers on which each word occurs. We develop a concordance to illustrate the use of the *map* and *multimap* container classes. The data values will be maintained in the concordance by a *multimap*, indexed by strings (the words) and will hold integers (the line numbers). A *multimap* is employed because the same word will often appear on several different lines; indeed, discovering such connections is one of the primary purposes of a concordance. An alternative possibility would have been to use a *map* and use a *set* of integer elements as the associated values.

```
class concordance {
  typedef multimap<string, int> wordDictType;
public:
  void addWord (string, int);
  void readText (istream &);
  void printConcordance (ostream &);

private:
  wordDictType wordMap;
};
```

The creation of the concordance is divided into two steps: first the program generates the concordance (by reading lines from an input stream), and then the program prints the result on the output stream. This is reflected in the two member functions `readText()` and `printConcordance()`. The first of these, `readText()`, is written as follows:

```
void concordance::readText (istream & in)
{
  string line;
  for (int i = 1; getline(in, line, Ô\n'); i++) {
    allLower(line);
    list<string> words;
    split (line, " ,.;:", words);
    list<string>::iterator wptr;
    for (wptr = words.begin(); wptr != words.end(); ++wptr)
      addWord(*wptr, i);
  }
}
```

Lines are read from the input stream one by one. The text of the line is first converted into lower case, then the line is split into words, using the function `split()` described in "Example function: split a line into words" in Chapter 34. Each word is then entered into the concordance. The method used to enter a value into the concordance is as follows:

```
void concordance::addWord (string word, int line)
{
    // see if word occurs in list
    // first get range of entries with same key
  wordDictType::iterator low = wordMap.lower_bound(word);
  wordDictType::iterator high = wordMap.upper_bound(word);
    // loop over entries, see if any match current line
  for ( ; low != high; ++low)
    if ((*low).second == line)
      return;
    // didn't occur, add now
  wordMap.insert(wordDictType::value_type(word, line));
}
```

The major portion of `addWord()` is concerned with ensuring values are not duplicated in the word *map* should the same word occur twice on the same line. To assure this, the range of values matching the key is examined; each value is tested, and if any match the line number then no insertion is performed. It is only if the loop terminates without discovering the line number that the new word/line-number pair is inserted.

The final step is to print the concordance. This is performed in the following fashion:

```
void concordance::printConcordance (ostream & out)
{
  string lastword("");
  wordDictType::iterator pairPtr;
  wordDictType::iterator stop = wordMap.end();
  for (pairPtr = wordMap.begin(); pairPtr != stop; ++pairPtr)
      // if word is same as previous, just print line number
```

```
          if (lastword == (*pairPtr).first)
            out << " " << (*pairPtr).second;
          else {// first entry of word
            lastword = (*pairPtr).first;
            cout << endl << lastword << ": " << (*pairPtr).second;
            }
        cout << endl; // terminate last line
    }
```

An iterator loop is used to cycle over the elements being maintained by the word list. Each new word generates a new line of output—thereafter line numbers appear separated by spaces. If, for example, the input was the text:

It was the best of times,

it was the worst of times.

The output, from best to worst, would be:

```
best:1
it:1 2
of:1 2
the:1 2
times:1 2
was:1 2
worst:1
```

27

stack and queue

Most people have a good intuitive understanding of the *stack* and *queue* data abstractions, based on experience with everyday objects. An excellent example of a stack is a pile of papers on a desk, or a stack of dishes in a cupboard. In both cases the important characteristic is that it is the item on the top that is most easily accessed. The easiest way to add a new item to the collection is to place it above all the current items in the stack. In this manner, an item removed from a stack is the item that has been most recently inserted into the stack; for example, the top piece of paper in the pile, or the top dish in the stack.

Note　**LIFO and FIFO:** A stack is sometimes referred to as a LIFO structure, and a queue is called a FIFO structure. The abbreviation LIFO stands for Last In, First Out. This means the first entry removed from a stack is the last entry that was inserted. The term FIFO, on the other hand, is short for First In, First Out. This means the first element removed from a queue is the first element that was inserted into the queue.

An everyday example of a *queue*, on the other hand, is a bank teller line, or a line of people waiting to enter a theater. Here new additions are made to the back of the queue, as new people enter the line, while items are removed from the front of the structure, as patrons enter the theater. The removal order for a queue is the opposite of that for a stack. In a queue, the item that is removed is the element that has been present in the queue for the longest period of time.

In the standard library, both stacks and queues are *adaptors*, built on top of other containers which are used to actually hold the values. A stack can be built out of either a *vector* or a *deque*, while a queue can be built on top of either a list or a *deque*. Elements held by either a stack or queue must recognize both the operators < and ==.

Because neither stacks nor queues define iterators, it is not possible to examine the elements of the collection except by removing the values one by one. The fact that these structures do not implement iterators also implies that most of the generic algorithms described in Generic algorithms overview and Ordered collection algorithms overview cannot be used with either data structure.

The stack data abstraction

As a data abstraction, a stack is traditionally defined as any object that implements the following operations:

`empty()`	return true if the collection is empty
`size()`	return number of elements in collection
`top()`	return (but do not remove) the topmost element in the stack
`push(newElement)`	push a new element onto the stack
`pop()`	remove (but do not return) the topmost element from the stack

Note that accessing the front element and removing the front element are separate operations. Programs that utilize the stack data abstraction should include the file `stack`, as well as the include file for the container type (e.g., `vector`).

```
# include <stack>
# include <vector>
```

Note   **Right angle brackets:** Note that on most compilers it is important to leave a space between the two right angle brackets in the declaration of a stack; otherwise they are interpreted by the compiler as a right shift operator.

A declaration for a stack must specify two arguments; the underlying element type, and the container that will hold the elements. For a stack, the most common container is a *vector* or a *deque*, however a list can also be used. The *vector* version is generally smaller, while the *deque* version may be slightly faster. The following are sample declarations for a stack.

```
stack< int, vector<int> > stackOne;
stack< double, deque<double> > stackTwo;
stack< Part *, list<Part * > > stackThree;
stack< Customer, list<Customer> > stackFour;
```

The last example creates a stack of a programmer-defined type named `Customer`.

Example program: an RPN calculator

A classic application of a stack is in the implementation of calculator. Input to the calculator consists of a text string that represents an expression written in reverse Polish notation (RPN). Operands, that is, integer constants, are pushed on a stack of values. As operators are encountered, the appropriate number of operands are popped off the stack, the operation is performed, and the result is pushed back on the stack.

Note   **Obtaining the sample program:** This program is found in the file CALC.CPP in the distribution package.

We can divide the development of our stack simulation into two parts. A calculator engine is concerned with the actual work involved in the simulation, but does not perform any input or output operations. The name is intended to suggest an analogy to a car engine, or a computer processor—the mechanism performs the actual work, but the user of the mechanism does not normally directly interact with it. Wrapped around this is the calculator program, which interacts with the user, and passes appropriate instructions to the calculator engine.

We can use the following class definition for our calculator engine. Inside the class declaration we define an enumerated list of values to represent each of the possible operators that the calculator is prepared to accept. We have made two simplifying assumptions: all operands will be integer values, and we will handle only binary operators.

```
class calculatorEngine {
public:
  enum binaryOperator {plus, minus, times, divide};

  int currentMemory ()  // return current top of stack
    { return data.top(); }

  void pushOperand (int value)  // push operand value on to stack
    { data.push (value); }

  void doOperator (binaryOperator);  // pop stack and perform operator

protected:
  stack< int, vector<int> > data;
};
```

Note   **Defensive programming:** A more robust program would check to see if the stack was empty before attempting to perform the pop() operation.

The member function doOperator() performs the actual work. It pops values from the stack, performs the operation, then pushes the result back onto the stack.

```
void calculatorEngine::doOperator (binaryOperator theOp)
{
  int right = data.top();  // read top element
  data.pop();  // pop it from stack
  int left = data.top();  // read next top element
  data.pop();  // pop it from stack
  switch (theOp) {
    case plus: data.push(left + right); break;
    case minus: data.push(left - right); break;
    case times: data.push(left * right); break;
    case divide: data.push(left / right); break;
    }
}
```

The main program reads values in reverse Polish notation, invoking the calculator engine to do the actual work:

```
void main() {
  int intval;
  calculatorEngine calc;
```

```
        char c;

        while (cin >> c)
          switch (c) {
            case '0': case '1': case '2': case '3': case '4':
            case '5': case '6': case '7': case '8': case '9':
              cin.putback(c);
              cin >> intval;
              calc.pushOperand(intval);
              break;

            case '+':  calc.doOperator(calculatorEngine::plus);
              break;

            case '-':  calc.doOperator(calculatorEngine::minus);
              break;

            case '*':  calc.doOperator(calculatorEngine::times);
              break;

            case '/':  calc.doOperator(calculatorEngine::divide);
              break;
            case 'p':  cout << calc.currentMemory() << endl;
              break;

            case 'q':  return; // quit program
          }
        }
```

The queue data abstraction

As a data abstraction, a *queue* is traditionally defined as any object that implements the following operations:

empty()	return true if the collection is empty
size()	return number of elements in collection
front()	return (but do not remove) the element at the front of the queue
back()	return the element at the end of the queue
push(newElement)	push a new element on to the end of the queue
pop()	remove (but do not return) the element at the front of the queue

Note that the operations of accessing and of removing the front elements are performed separately. Programs that utilize the queue data abstraction should include the file queue, as well as the include file for the container type (e.g., list).

```
# include <queue>
```

```
# include <list>
```

A declaration for a queue must specify both the element type as well as the container that will hold the values. For a queue the most common containers are a list or a *deque*. The list version is generally smaller, while the *deque* version may be slightly faster. The following are sample declarations for a queue.

```
queue< int, list<int> > queueOne;
queue< double, deque<double> > queueTwo;
queue< Part *, list<Part * > > queueThree;
queue< Customer, list<Customer> > queueFour;
```

The last example creates a queue of a programmer-defined type named Customer. As with the stack container, all objects stored in a queue must understand the operators < and ==.

Because the queue does not implement an iterator, none of the generic algorithms described in Generic algorithms overview or Ordered collection algorithms overview apply to queues.

Example program: bank teller simulation

Note   **Obtaining the sample program:** The complete version of the bank teller simulation program is found in file TELLER.CPP on the distribution disk.

Queues are often found in businesses, such as supermarkets or banks. Suppose you are the manager of a bank, and you need to determine how many tellers to have working during certain hours. You decide to create a computer simulation, basing your simulation on certain observed behavior. For example, you note that during peak hours there is a ninety percent chance that a customer will arrive every minute.

We create a simulation by first defining objects to represent both customers and tellers. For customers, the information we wish to know is the average amount of time they spend waiting in line. Thus, customer objects simply maintain two integer data fields: the time they arrive in line, and the time they will spend at the counter. The latter is a value randomly selected between 2 and 8. (See Chapter 19, "Interators," for a discussion of the randomInteger() function.)

```
class Customer {
public:
  Customer (int at = 0) : arrival_Time(at),
      processTime(2 + randomInteger(6)) {}
  int arrival_Time;
  int processTime;

  bool done()  // are we done with our transaction?
    { return --processTime < 0; }

  operator < (const Customer & c)  // order by arrival time
    { return arrival_Time < c.arrival_Time; }

  operator == (const Customer & c)  // no two customers are alike
    { return false; }
};
```

Because objects can only be stored in standard library containers if they can be compared for equality and ordering, it is necessary to define the < and == operators for customers. Customers can also tell us when they are done with their transactions.

Tellers are either busy servicing customers, or they are free. Thus, each teller value holds two data fields; a customer, and a Boolean flag. Tellers define a member function to answer whether they are free or not, as well as a member function that is invoked when they start servicing a customer.

```
class Teller {
public:
  Teller() { free = true; }

  bool isFree()  // are we free to service new customer?
    { if (free) return true;
      if (customer.done())
        free = true;
      return free;
    }

  void addCustomer(Customer c)  // start serving new customer
    {  customer = c;
       free = false;
    }
private:
  bool free;
  Customer customer;
};
```

The main program is then a large loop, cycling once each simulated minute. Each minute a new customer is, with probability 0.9, entered into the queue of waiting customers. Each teller is polled, and if any are free they take the next customer from the queue. Counts are maintained of the number of customers serviced and the total time they spent in queue. From these two values we can determine, following the simulation, the average time a customer spent waiting in the line.

```
void main() {
  int numberOfTellers = 5;
  int numberOfMinutes = 60;
  double totalWait = 0;
  int numberOfCustomers = 0;
  vector<Teller> teller(numberOfTellers);
  queue< Customer, deque<Customer> > line;

  for (int time = 0; time < numberOfMinutes; time++) {
    if (randomInteger(10) < 9)
      line.push(Customer(time));
    for (int i = 0; i < numberOfTellers; i++) {
      if (teller[i].isFree() & ! line.empty()) {
        Customer & frontCustomer = line.front();
        numberOfCustomers++;
        totalWait += (time - frontCustomer.arrival_Time);
        teller[i].addCustomer(frontCustomer);
        line.pop();
      }
```

```
        }
      }
    cout << "average wait:" <<
        (totalWait / numberOfCustomers) << endl;
  }
```

By executing the program several times, using various values for the number of tellers, the manager can determine the smallest number of tellers that can service the customers while maintaining the average waiting time at an acceptable amount.

28

priority_queue

The priority queue data abstraction

A *priority queue* is a data structure useful in problems where it is important to be able to rapidly and repeatedly find and remove the largest element from a collection of values. An everyday example of a priority queue is the "to do" list of tasks waiting to be performed that most of us maintain to keep ourselves organized. Some jobs, such as "clean desktop," are not imperative and can be postponed arbitrarily. Other tasks, such as "finish report by Monday" or "buy flowers for anniversary," are time-crucial and must be addressed more rapidly. Thus, we sort the tasks waiting to be accomplished in order of their importance (or perhaps based on a combination of their critical importance, their long-term benefit, and the fun we will have doing them) and choose the most pressing.

Note   **A queue that is not a queue:** The term priority *queue* is a misnomer, in that the data structure is not a queue, in the sense that we used the term in Chapter 27, since it does not return elements in a strict first-in, first-out sequence. Nevertheless, the name is now firmly associated with this particular data type.

A more computer-related example of a priority queue is that used by an operating system to maintain a list of pending processes, where the value associated with each element is the priority of the job. For example, it may be necessary to respond rapidly to a key pressed at a terminal, before the data is lost when the next key is pressed. On the other hand, the process of copying a listing to a queue of output waiting to be handled by a printer is something that can be postponed for a short period, as long as it is handled eventually. By maintaining processes in a priority queue, those jobs with urgent priority will be executed prior to any jobs with less urgent requirements.

Simulation programs use a priority queue of "future events." The simulation maintains a virtual "clock," and each event has an associated time when the event will take place. In such a collection, the element with the smallest time value is the next event that should be simulated. These are only a few instances of the types of problems for which a priority queue is a useful tool. You probably have, or will, encounter others.

The priority queue operations

A priority queue is a data structure that can hold elements of type T and that implements the following five operations:

`push(T)`	Add a new value to the collection being maintained
`top()`	Return a reference to the smallest element in the collection
`pop()`	Delete the smallest element from the collection
`size()`	Return the number of elements in the collection
`empty()`	Return true if the collection is empty

Elements of type `T` must be comparable to each other, either through the use of the default less-than operator (the < operator), or through a comparison function passed either as a template argument or as an optional argument on the constructor. The latter form will be illustrated in the example program provided later in this section. As with all the containers in the Standard Library, there are two constructors. The default constructor requires either no arguments or the optional comparison function. An alternative constructor takes an iterator pair, and initializes the values in the container from the argument sequence. Once more, an optional third argument can be used to define the comparison function.

Note   **Initializing queues from other containers:** As we noted in earlier sections, support for initializing containers using a pair of iterators requires a feature that is not yet widely supported by compilers. While we document this form of constructor, it may not yet be available on your system.

The priority queue data type is built on top of a container class, which is the structure actually used to maintain the values in the collection. There are two containers in the standard library that can be used to construct priority queues: *vectors* or deques. The following illustrates the declaration of several priority queues:

```
priority_queue< int, vector<int> > queue_one;
priority_queue< int, vector<int>, greater<int> > queue_two;
priority_queue< double, deque<double> >
    queue_three(aList.begin(), aList.end());
priority_queue< eventStruct, vector<eventStruct> >
    queue_four(eventComparison);
priority_queue< eventStruct, deque<eventStruct> >
    queue_five(aVector.begin(), aVector.end(), eventComparison);
```

Queues constructed out of *vectors* tend to be somewhat smaller, while queues constructed out of deques can be somewhat faster, particularly if the number of elements in the queue varies widely over the course of execution. However, these differences are slight, and either form will generally work in most circumstances.

Programs that utilize the priority queue data abstraction should include the file `queue`, as well as the include file for the container type (e.g., `vector`).

```
# include <queue>
# include <vector>
```

Because the priority queue data structure does not itself know how to construct iterators, very few of the algorithms noted in Chapter 29 can be used with priority queues. Instead of iterating over values, a typical algorithm that uses a priority queue constructs a loop, which repeatedly pulls values from the structure (using the `top()` and `pop()` operations) until the collection becomes empty (tested using the `empty()` operation). The example program described in the next section will illustrate this use.

Note   **Information on heaps:** Details of the algorithms used in manipulating heaps will not be discussed here, however such information is readily available in almost any textbook on data structures.

Priority queues are implemented by internally building a data structure called a *heap*. Abstractly, a heap is a binary tree in which every node possesses the property that the value associated with the node is smaller than or equal to the value associated with either child node.

Application: event-driven simulation

An extended example will illustrate the use of priority queues. The example illustrates one of the more common uses for priority queues, which is to support the construction of a simulation model.

A *discrete event-driven simulation* is a popular simulation technique. Objects in the simulation model objects in the real world, and are programmed to react as much as possible as the real objects would react. A priority queue is used to store a representation of "events" that are waiting to happen. This queue is stored in order, based on the time the event should occur, so the smallest element will always be the next event to be modeled. As an event occurs, it can spawn other events. These subsequent events are placed into the queue as well. Execution continues until all events have been processed.

Note   **Finding smallest elements:** We describe the priority queue as a structure for quickly discovering the *largest* element in a sequence. If, instead, your problem requires the discovery of the *smallest* element, there are various possibilities. One is to supply the inverse operator as either a template argument or the optional comparison function argument to the constructor. If you are defining the comparison argument as a function, as in the example problem, another solution is to simply invert the comparison test.

Events can be represented as subclasses of a base class, which we will call *event*. The base class simply records the time at which the event will take place. A pure virtual function named `processEvent` will be invoked to execute the event.

```
class event {
public:
  event (unsigned int t) : time(t) { }
  const unsigned int time;
  virtual void processEvent() = 0;
};
```

The simulation queue will need to maintain a collection of different types of events. Each different form of event will be represented by a different subclass of class *event*. Not all events will have the same exact type, although they will all be subclasses of class *event*. (This is sometimes called a *heterogeneous* collection.) For this reason the collection must store *pointers* to events, instead of the events themselves. (In theory one could store references, instead of pointers, however the standard library containers cannot hold references).

Since comparison of pointers cannot be specialized on the basis of the pointer types, we must instead define a new comparison function for pointers to events. In the standard library this is accomplished by defining a new structure, the sole purpose of which is to define the function invocation operator (the `()` operator) in the appropriate fashion. Since in this particular example we wish to use the priority queue to return the *smallest* element each time, rather than the largest, the order of the comparison is reversed, as follows:

```
struct eventComparison {
    bool operator () (event * left, event * right) const
        { return left->time > right->time; }
};
```

We are now ready to define the class *simulation*, which provides the structure for the simulation activities. The class *simulation* provides two functions. The first is used to insert a new event into the queue, while the second runs the simulation. A data field is also provided to hold the current simulation "time."

Note   **Storing pointers versus storing values:** Other example programs in this tutorial have all used containers to store values. In this example the container will maintain pointers to values, not the values themselves. Note that a consequence of this is that the programmer is then responsible for managing the memory for the objects being manipulated.

```
class simulation {
public:
    simulation () : eventQueue(), time(0) { }
    void scheduleEvent (event * newEvent)
        { eventQueue.push (newEvent); }
    void run();
    unsigned int time;
protected:
    priority_queue<event *, vector<event *>, eventComparison> eventQueue;
};
```

Notice the declaration of the priority queue used to hold the pending events. In this case we are using a *vector* as the underlying container. We could just as easily have used a *deque*.

The heart of the simulation is the member function `run()`, which defines the event loop. This procedure makes use of three of the five priority queue operations, namely `top()`, `pop()`, and `empty()`. It is implemented as follows:

```
void simulation::run()
{
    while (! eventQueue.empty()) {
        event * nextEvent = eventQueue.top();
        eventQueue.pop();
```

```
      time = nextEvent->time;
      nextEvent->processEvent();
      delete nextEvent;  // free memory used by event
      }
  }
```

An ice cream store simulation

Note   **Obtaining the sample program:** The complete event simulation is found in the file
`icecream.cpp` on the distribution disk.

To illustrate the use of our simulation framework, this example program gives a simple
simulation of an ice cream store. Such a simulation might be used, for example, to
determine the optimal number of chairs that should be provided, based on assumptions
such as the frequency that customers will arrive, the length of time they will stay, and so
on.

Our store simulation will be based around a subclass of class *simulation*, defined as
follows:

```
class storeSimulation : public simulation {
public:
  storeSimulation()
    : freeChairs(35), profit(0.0), simulation() { }

  bool canSeat (unsigned int numberOfPeople);
  void order(unsigned int numberOfScoops);
  void leave(unsigned int numberOfPeople);

private:
  unsigned int freeChairs;
  double profit;
} theSimulation;
```

There are three basic activities associated with the store. These are arrival, ordering and
eating, and leaving. This is reflected not only in the three member functions defined in
the simulation class, but in three separate subclasses of *event*.

The member functions associated with the store simply record the activities taking
place, producing a log that can later be studied to evaluate the simulation.

```
bool storeSimulation::canSeat (unsigned int numberOfPeople)
  // if sufficient room, then seat customers
{
  cout << "Time: " << time;
  cout << " group of " << numberOfPeople << " customers arrives";
  if (numberOfPeople < freeChairs) {
    cout << " is seated" << endl;
    freeChairs -= numberOfPeople;
    return true;
    }
  else {
    cout << " no room, they leave" << endl;
    return false;
    }
}
```

```
void storeSimulation::order (unsigned int numberOfScoops)
  // serve icecream, compute profits
{
  cout << "Time: " << time;
  cout << " serviced order for " << numberOfScoops << endl;
  profit += 0.35 * numberOfScoops;
}

void storeSimulation::leave (unsigned int numberOfPeople)
  // people leave, free up chairs
{
  cout << "Time: " << time;
  cout << " group of size " << numberOfPeople <<
      " leaves" << endl;
  freeChairs += numberOfPeople;
}
```

As we noted already, each activity is matched by a subclass of event. Each subclass of *event* includes an integer data field, which represents the size of a group of customers. The arrival event occurs when a group enters. When executed, the arrival event creates and installs a new instance of order event. The function `randomInteger()` (see "Random access iterators" in Chapter 19) is used to compute a random integer between 1 and the argument value.

```
class arriveEvent : public event {
public:
  arriveEvent (unsigned int time, unsigned int groupSize)
    : event(time), size(groupSize) { }
  virtual void processEvent ();
private:
  unsigned int size;
};
void arriveEvent::processEvent()
{         // see if everybody can be seated
  if (theSimulation.canSeat(size))
    theSimulation.scheduleEvent
      (new orderEvent(time + 1 + randomInteger(4), size));
}
```

An order event similarly spawns a leave event.

```
class orderEvent : public event {
public:
  orderEvent (unsigned int time, unsigned int groupSize)
    : event(time), size(groupSize) { }
  virtual void processEvent ();
private:
  unsigned int size;
};
void orderEvent::processEvent()
{         // each person orders some number of scoops
  for (int i = 0; i < size; i++)
    theSimulation.order(1 + rand(3));
  theSimulation.scheduleEvent
```

```
        (new leaveEvent(time + 1 + randomInteger(10), size));
    };
```

Finally, leave events free up chairs, but do not spawn any new events.

```
    class leaveEvent : public event {
    public:
        leaveEvent (unsigned int time, unsigned int groupSize)
            : event(time), size(groupSize) { }
        virtual void processEvent ();
    private:
        unsigned int size;
    };

    void leaveEvent::processEvent ()
    {           // leave and free up chairs
        theSimulation.leave(size);
    }
```

To run the simulation we simply create some number of initial events (say, 30 minutes worth), then invoke the `run()` member function.

```
    void main() {
        // load queue with some number of initial events
        unsigned int t = 0;
        while (t < 30) {
            t += rand(6);
            theSimulation.scheduleEvent(
                new arriveEvent(t, 1 + randomInteger(4)));
        }
        // then run simulation and print profits
        theSimulation.run();
        cout << "Total profits " << theSimulation.profit << endl;
    }
```

29

Generic algorithms

In this chapter and in Chapter 30, we will examine and illustrate each of the generic algorithms provided by the standard library. The names and a short description of each of the algorithms in this section are given in the following table. We have divided the algorithms into several categories, based on how they are typically used. This division differs from the categories used in the C++ standard definition, which is based upon which algorithms modify their arguments and which do not.

Table 29.1   Algorithms used to initialize a sequence

Name	Purpose
fill	Fill a sequence with an initial value
fill_n	Fill n positions with an initial value
copy	Copy sequence into another sequence
copy_backward	Copy sequence into another sequence
generate	Initialize a sequence using a generator
generate_n	Initialize n positions using generator
swap_ranges	Swap values from two parallel sequences

Table 29.2   Searching algorithms

Name	Purpose
find	Find an element matching the argument
find_if	Find an element satisfying a condition
adjacent_find	Find consecutive duplicate elements
search	Match a subsequence within a sequence
max_element	Find the maximum value in a sequence
min_element	Find the minimum value in a sequence
mismatch	Find first mismatch in parallel sequences

Table 29.3   In-place transformations

Name	Purpose
reverse	Reverse the elements in a sequence
replace	Replace specific values with new value
replace_if	Replace elements matching predicate
rotate	Rotate elements in a sequence around a point
partition	Partition elements into two groups
stable_partition	Partition preserving original ordering
next_permutation	Generate permutations in sequence
prev_permutation	Generate permutations in reverse sequence
inplace_merge	Merge two adjacent streams into one
random_shuffle	Randomly rearrange elements in a sequence

Table 29.4   Removal algorithms

Name	Purpose
remove	Remove elements that match condition
unique	Remove all but first of duplicate values in sequences

Table 29.5   Scalar generating algorithms

Name	Purpose
count	Count number of elements matching value
count_if	Count elements matching predicate
accumulate	Reduce sequence to a scalar value
inner_product	Inner product of two parallel sequences
equal	Check two sequences for equality
lexicographical_compare	Compare two sequences

Table 29.6   Sequence generating algorithms

Name	Purpose
transform	Transform each element
partial_sum	Generate sequence of partial sums
adjacent_difference	Generate sequence of adjacent differences

Table 29.7   Miscellaneous operations

Name	Purpose
for_each	Apply a function to each element of collection

To use any of the generic algorithms you must first include the appropriate header file. The majority of the functions are defined in the header file `algorithm`. The functions `accumulate()`, `inner_product()`, `partial_sum()`, and `adjacent_difference()` are defined in the header file `numeric`.

```
# include <algorithm>
# include <numeric>
```

In this chapter we will illustrate the use of each algorithm with a series of short examples. Many of the algorithms are also used in the sample programs provided in the chapters on the various container classes. These cross references have been noted where appropriate.

All of the short example programs described in this chapter have been collected in a number of files, named `alg1.cpp` through `alg6.cpp`. In the files, the example programs have been augmented with output statements describing the test programs and illustrating the results of executing the algorithms. In order to not confuse the reader with unnecessary detail, we have generally omitted these output statements from the descriptions here. If you wish to see the text programs complete with output statements, you can compile and execute these test files. The expected output from these programs is also included in the distribution.

Initialization algorithms

Note   **Obtaining the source:** The sample programs described in this section can be found in the file `alg1.cpp`.

The first set of algorithms we will cover are those that are chiefly, although not exclusively, used to initialize a newly created sequence with certain values. The standard library provides several initialization algorithms. In our discussion we'll provide examples of how to apply these algorithms, and suggest how to choose one algorithm over another.

Fill a sequence with an initial value

The `fill()` and `fill_n()` algorithms are used to initialize or reinitialize a sequence with a fixed value. Their definitions are as follows:

```
void fill (ForwardIterator first, ForwardIterator last, const T&);
void fill_n (OutputIterator, Size, const T&);
```

Note   **Different initialization algorithms:** The initialization algorithms all overwrite every element in a container. The difference between the algorithms is the source for the values used in initialization. The `fill()` algorithm repeats a single value, the `copy()` algorithm reads values from a second container, and the `generate()` algorithm invokes a function for each new value.

The example program illustrates several uses of the algorithm:

```
void fill_example ()
  // illustrate the use of the fill algorithm
{
    // example 1, fill an array with initial values
  char buffer[100], * bufferp = buffer;
  fill (bufferp, bufferp + 100, '\0');
  fill_n (bufferp, 10, 'x');

    // example 2, use fill to initialize a list
  list<string> aList(5, "nothing");
```

```
        fill_n (inserter(aList, aList.begin()), 10, "empty");

        // example 3, use fill to overwrite values in list
        fill (aList.begin(), aList.end(), "full");

        // example 4, fill in a portion of a collection
        vector<int> iVec(10);
        generate (iVec.begin(), iVec.end(), iotaGen(1));
        vector<int>::iterator & seven =
            find(iVec.begin(), iVec.end(), 7);
        fill (iVec.begin(), seven, 0);
    }
```

In example 1, an array of character values is declared. The `fill()` algorithm is invoked to initialize each location in this array with a null character value. The first 10 positions are then replaced with the character 'x' by using the algorithm `fill_n()`. Note that the `fill()` algorithm requires both starting and past-end iterators as arguments, whereas the `fill_n()` algorithm uses a starting iterator and a count.

Example 2 illustrates how, by using an *insert iterator* (see "Insert iterators" in Chapter 19), the `fill_n()` algorithm can be used to initialize a variable length container, such as a list. In this case the list initially contains five elements, all holding the text `"nothing"`. The call on `fill_n()` then inserts ten instances of the string `"empty"`. The resulting list contains fifteen elements.

The third and fourth examples illustrate how `fill()` can be used to change the values in an existing container. In the third example each of the fifteen elements in the list created in example 2 is replaced by the string `"full"`.

Example 4 overwrites only a portion of a list. Using the algorithm `generate()` and the function object iotaGen, which we will describe in the next section, a *vector* is initialized to the values 1 2 3 ... 10. The `find()` algorithm ("Find an element satisfying a condition") is then used to locate the position of the element 7, saving the location in an iterator appropriate for the *vector* data type. The `fill()` call then replaces all values up to, but not including, the 7 entry with the value 0. The resulting *vector* has six zero fields, followed by the values 7, 8, 9, and 10.

The `fill()` and `fill_n()` algorithm can be used with all the container classes contained in the standard library, although insert iterators must be used with ordered containers, such as a *set*.

Copy one sequence onto another sequence

The algorithms `copy()` and `copy_backward()` are versatile functions that can be used for a number of different purposes, and are probably the most commonly executed algorithms in the standard library. The definitions for these algorithms are as follows:

```
OutputIterator copy (InputIterator first, InputIterator last,
        OutputIterator result);

BidirectionalIterator copy_backward (BidirectionalIterator first,
        BidirectionalIterator last, BidirectionalIterator result);
```

Note **Appending several copies:** The result returned by the copy() function is a pointer to the end of the copied sequence. To make a *catenation* of values, the result of one copy() operation can be used as a starting iterator in a subsequent copy().

Uses of the copy() algorithm include:

- Duplicating an entire sequence by copying into a new sequence
- Creating subsequences of an existing sequence
- Adding elements into a sequence
- Copying a sequence from input or to output
- Converting a sequence from one form into another

These are illustrated in the following sample program.

```
void copy_example()
    // illustrate the use of the copy algorithm
{
  char * source = "reprise";
  char * surpass = "surpass";
  char buffer[120], * bufferp = buffer;

    // example 1, a simple copy
  copy (source, source + strlen(source) + 1, bufferp);

    // example 2, self copies
  copy (bufferp + 2, bufferp + strlen(buffer) + 1, bufferp);
  int buflen = strlen(buffer) + 1;
  copy_backward (bufferp, bufferp + buflen, bufferp + buflen + 3);
  copy (surpass, surpass + 3, bufferp);

    // example 3, copy to output
  copy (bufferp, bufferp + strlen(buffer),
        ostream_iterator<char>(cout));
  cout << endl;

    // example 4, use copy to convert type
  list<char> char_list;
  copy (bufferp, bufferp + strlen(buffer),
        inserter(char_list, char_list.end()));
  char * big = "big ";
  copy (big, big + 4, inserter(char_list, char_list.begin()));

  char buffer2 [120], * buffer2p = buffer2;
  * copy (char_list.begin(), char_list.end(), buffer2p) = '\0';
  cout << buffer2 << endl;
}
```

The first call on copy(), in example 1, simply copies the string pointed to by the variable source into a buffer, resulting in the buffer containing the text "reprise". Note that the ending position for the copy is one past the terminating null character, thus ensuring the null character is included in the copy operation.

The copy() operation is specifically designed to permit self-copies, i.e., copies of a sequence onto itself, as long as the destination iterator does not fall within the range formed by the source iterators. This is illustrated by example 2. Here the copy begins at position 2 of the buffer and extends to the end, copying characters into the beginning of the buffer. This results in the buffer holding the value "prise".

The second half of example 2 illustrates the use of the copy_backward() algorithm. This function performs the same task as the copy() algorithm, but moves elements from the end of the sequence first, progressing to the front of the sequence. (If you think of the argument as a string, characters are moved starting from the right and progressing to the left.) In this case the result will be that buffer will be assigned the value "priprise". The first three characters are then modified by another copy() operation to the values "sur", resulting in buffer holding the value "surprise".

Note   **copy_backwards:** In the copy_backwards algorithm, note that it is the order of transfer, and not the elements themselves that is "backwards;" the relative placement of moved values in the target is the same as in the source.

Example 3 illustrates copy() being used to move values to an output stream (see "Output stream iterators" in Chapter 19). The target in this case is an ostream_iterator generated for the output stream cout. A similar mechanism can be used for input values. For example, a simple mechanism to copy every word in the input stream into a list is the following call on copy():

```
list<string> words;
istream_iterator<string, ptrdiff_t> in_stream(cin), eof;

copy(in_stream, eof, inserter(words, words.begin()));
```

This technique is used in the spell checking program described in "Example program: a spelling checker."

Copy can also be used to convert from one type of stream to another. For example, the call in example 4 of the sample program copies the characters held in the buffer one by one into a list of characters. The call on inserter() creates an insert iterator, used to insert values into the list. The first call on copy() places the string surprise, created in example 2, into the list. The second call on copy() inserts the values from the string "big" onto the front of the list, resulting in the list containing the characters big surprise. The final call on copy() illustrates the reverse process, copying characters from a list back into a character buffer.

Initialize a sequence with generated values

A *generator* is a function that will return a series of values on successive invocations. Probably the generator you are most familiar with is a random number generator. However, generators can be constructed for a variety of different purposes, including initializing sequences.

Like fill() and fill_n(), the algorithms generate() and generate_n() are used to initialize or reinitialize a sequence. However, instead of a fixed argument, these algorithms draw their values from a generator. The definition of these algorithms is as follows:

```
void generate (ForwardIterator, ForwardIterator, Generator);
void generate_n (OutputIterator, Size, Generator);
```

Our example program shows several uses of the generate algorithm to initialize a sequence.

```
string generateLabel () {
   // generate a unique label string of the form L_ddd
   static int lastLabel = 0;
   char labelBuffer[80];
   ostrstream ost(labelBuffer, 80);
   ost << "L_" << lastLabel++ << '\0';
   return string(labelBuffer);
}


void generate_example ()
  // illustrate the use of the generate and generate_n algorithms
{
    // example 1, generate a list of label values
   list<string> labelList;
   generate_n (inserter(labelList, labelList.begin()),
       4, generateLabel);

    // example 2, generate an arithmetic progression
   vector<int> iVec(10);
   generate (iVec.begin(), iVec.end(), iotaGen(2));
   generate_n (iVec.begin(), 5, iotaGen(7));
}
```

A generator can be constructed as a simple function that "remembers" information about its previous history in one or more static variables. An example is shown in the beginning of the example program, where the function generateLabel() is described. This function creates a sequence of unique string labels, such as might be needed by a compiler. Each invocation on the function generateLabel() results in a new string of the form L_ddd, each with a unique digit value. Because the variable named lastLabel is declared as static, its value is remembered from one invocation to the next. The first example of the sample program illustrates how this function might be used in combination with the generate_n() algorithm to initialize a list of four label values.

As we described in "Functions," in the Standard Library a function is any object that will respond to the function call operator. Using this fact, classes can easily be constructed as functions. The class *iotaGen*, which we described in "Function objects," is an example. The *iotaGen* function object creates a generator for an integer arithmetic sequence. In the second example in the sample program, this sequence is used to initialize a *vector* with the integer values 2 through 11. A call on generate_n() is then used to overwrite the first 5 positions of the *vector* with the values 7 through 11, resulting in the *vector* 7 8 9 10 11 7 8 9 10 11.

Swap values from two parallel ranges

The template function swap() can be used to exchange the values of two objects of the same type. It has the following definition:

```
template <class T> void swap (T& a, T& b)
{
  T temp(a);
  a = b;
  b = temp;
}
```

The function is generalized to iterators in the function named `iter_swap()`. The algorithm `swap_ranges()` then extends this to entire sequences. The values denoted by the first sequence are exchanged with the values denoted by a second, parallel sequence. The description of the `swap_ranges()` algorithm is as follows:

```
ForwardIterator swap_ranges
     (ForwardIterator first, ForwardIterator last, ForwardIterator first2);
```

Note **Parallel sequences:** A number of algorithms operate on two parallel sequences. In most cases the second sequence is identified using only a starting iterator, not a starting and ending iterator pair. It is assumed, but never verified, that the second sequence is at least as large as the first. Errors will occur if this condition is not satisfied.

The second range is described only by a starting iterator. It is assumed (but not verified) that the second range has at least as many elements as the first range. We use both functions alone and in combination in the example program.

```
void swap_example ()
    // illustrate the use of the algorithm swap_ranges
{
    // first make two parallel sequences
  int data[] = {12, 27, 14, 64}, *datap = data;
  vector<int> aVec(4);
  generate(aVec.begin(), aVec.end(), iotaGen(1));

    // illustrate swap and iter_swap
  swap(data[0], data[2]);
  vector<int>::iterator last = aVec.end(); last--;
  iter_swap(aVec.begin(), last);

    // now swap the entire sequence
  swap_ranges (aVec.begin(), aVec.end(), datap);
}
```

Searching operations

The next category of algorithms we will describe are those that are used to locate elements within a sequence that satisfy certain properties. Most commonly the result of a search is then used as an argument to a further operation, such as a `copy` ("Partition a sequence into two groups"), a `partition` ("Copy one sequence onto another sequence"), or an `in-place merge` ("Merge two adjacent sequences into one").

Note **Obtaining the source:** The example functions described in this section can be found in the file `alg2.cpp`.

The searching routines described in this section return an iterator that identifies the first element that satisfies the search condition. It is common to store this value in an iterator variable, as follows:

```
list<int>::iterator where;
where = find(aList.begin(), aList.end(), 7);
```

If you want to locate *all* the elements that satisfy the search conditions you must write a loop. In that loop, the value yielded by a previous search is first advanced (since otherwise the value yielded by the previous search would once again be returned), and the resulting value is used as a starting point for the new search. For example, the following loop from the `adjacent_find()` example program ("Find consecutive duplicate elements") will print the value of all repeated characters in a string argument.

Note **Check search results:** The searching algorithms in the standard library all return the end-of-sequence iterator if no value is found that matches the search condition. As it is generally illegal to dereference the end-of-sequence value, it is important to check for this condition before proceeding to use the result of a search.

```
while ((where = adjacent_find(where, stop)) != stop) {
  cout << "double " << *where << " in position "
    << where - start << endl;
  ++where;
  }
```

Many of the searching algorithms have an optional argument that can specify a function to be used to compare elements, in place of the equality operator for the container element type (operator `==`). In the descriptions of the algorithms we write these optional arguments inside a square bracket, to indicate they need not be specified if the standard equality operator is acceptable.

Find an element satisfying a condition

There are two algorithms, `find()` and `find_if()`, that are used to find the first element that satisfies a condition. The definitions of these two algorithms are as follows:

```
InputIterator find_if (InputIterator first, InputIterator last, Predicate);
InputIterator find (InputIterator first, InputIterator last, const T&);
```

The algorithm `find_if()` takes as argument a predicate function, which can be any function that returns a boolean value (see "Predicates" in Chapter 20). The `find_if()` algorithm returns a new iterator that designates the first element in the sequence that satisfies the predicate. The second argument, the past-the-end iterator, is returned if no element is found that matches the requirement. Because the resulting value is an iterator, the dereference operator (the `*` operator) must be used to obtain the matching value. This is illustrated in the example program.

The second form of the algorithm, `find()`, replaces the predicate function with a specific value, and returns the first element in the sequence that tests equal to this value, using the appropriate equality operator (the `==` operator) for the given datatype.

Note **Searching sets and maps:** These algorithms perform a linear sequential search through the associated structures. The *set* and *map* data structures, which are ordered, provide their own `find()` member functions, which are more efficient. Because of this, the generic `find()` algorithm should not be used with *set* and *map*.

The following example program illustrates the use of these algorithms:

```
void find_test ()
  // illustrate the use of the find algorithm
{
  int vintageYears[] = {1967, 1972, 1974, 1980, 1995};
  int * start = vintageYears;
  int * stop = start + 5;
  int * where = find_if (start, stop, isLeapYear);

  if (where != stop)
    cout << "first vintage leap year is " << *where << endl;
  else
    cout << "no vintage leap years" << endl;

  where = find(start, stop, 1995);

  if (where != stop)
    cout << "1995 is position " << where - start
      << " in sequence" << endl;
  else
    cout "1995 does not occur in sequence" << endl;
}
```

Find consecutive duplicate elements

The `adjacent_find()` algorithm is used to discover the first element in a sequence equal to the next immediately following element. For example, if a sequence contained the values 1 4 2 5 6 6 7 5, the algorithm would return an iterator corresponding to the first 6 values. If no value satisfying the condition is found, then the end-of-sequence iterator is returned. The definition of the algorithm is as follows:

```
ForwardIterator adjacent_find (ForwardIterator first,
  ForwardIterator last [, BinaryPredicate ] );
```

The first two arguments specify the sequence to be examined. The optional third argument must be a binary predicate (a binary function returning a Boolean value). If present, the binary function is used to test adjacent elements, otherwise the equality operator (operator ==) is used.

The example program searches a text string for adjacent letters. In the example text these are found in positions 5, 7, 9, 21, and 37. The increment is necessary inside the loop in order to avoid the same position being discovered repeatedly.

```
void adjacent_find_example ()
  // illustrate the use of the adjacent_find instruction
{
  char * text = "The bookkeeper carefully opened the door.";

  char * start = text;
```

```
    char * stop = text + strlen(text);
    char * where = start;

    cout << "In the text: " << text << endl;
    while ((where = adjacent_find(where, stop)) != stop) {
      cout << "double " << *where
        << " in position " << where - start << endl;
      ++where;
    }
  }
```

Find a subsequence within a sequence

The algorithm `search()` is used to locate the beginning of a particular subsequence within a larger sequence. The easiest example to understand is the problem of looking for a particular substring within a larger string, although the algorithm can be generalized to other uses. The arguments are assumed to have at least the capabilities of forward iterators.

```
ForwardIterator search
  (ForwardIterator first1, ForwardIterator last1,
  ForwardIterator first2, ForwardIterator last2
  [, BinaryPredicate ]);
```

Note **Speed of search:** In the worst case, the number of comparisons performed by the algorithm `search()` is the product of the number of elements in the two sequences. Except in rare cases, however, this worst case behavior is highly unlikely.

Suppose, for example, that we wish to discover the location of the string `"ration"` in the string `"dreams and aspirations"`. The solution to this problem is shown in the example program. If no appropriate match is found, the value returned is the past-the-end iterator for the first sequence.

```
void search_example ()
    // illustrate the use of the search algorithm
{
  char * base = "dreams and aspirations";
  char * text = "ration";

  char * where = search(base, base + strlen(base),
      text, text + strlen(text));

  if (*where != '\0')
    cout << "substring position: " << where = base << endl;
  else
    cout << "substring does not occur in text" << endl;
}
```

Note that this algorithm, unlike many that manipulate two sequences, uses a starting and ending iterator pair for both sequences, not just the first sequence.

Like the algorithms `equal()` and `mismatch()`, an alternative version of `search()` takes an optional binary predicate that is used to compare elements from the two sequences.

Locate maximum or minimum element

The functions `max()` and `min()` can be used to find the maximum and minimum of a pair of values. These can optionally take a third argument that defines the comparison function to use in place of the less-than operator (operator <). The arguments are values, not iterators:

```
template <class T>
  const T& max(const T& a, const T& b [, Compare ] );
template <class T>
  const T& min(const T& a, const T& b [, Compare ] );
```

The maximum and minimum functions are generalized to entire sequences by the generic algorithms `max_element()` and `min_element()`. For these functions the arguments are input iterators.

```
ForwardIterator max_element (ForwardIterator first,
    ForwardIterator last [, Compare ] );
ForwardIterator min_element (ForwardIterator first,
    ForwardIterator last [, Compare ] );
```

Note **Largest and smallest elements of a set:** The maximum and minimum algorithms can be used with all the datatypes provided by the standard library. However, for the ordered data types, *set* and *map*, the maximum or minimum values are more easily accessed as the first or last elements in the structure.

These algorithms return an iterator that denotes the largest or smallest of the values in a sequence, respectively. Should more than one value satisfy the requirement, the result yielded is the first satisfactory value. Both algorithms can optionally take a third argument, which is the function to be used as the comparison operator in place of the default operator.

The example program illustrates several uses of these algorithms. The function named `split()` used to divide a string into words in the string example is described in "Example function: split a line into words." The function `randomInteger()` is described in "Random access iterators."

```
void max_min_example ()
  // illustrate use of max_element and min_element algorithms
{
  // make a vector of random numbers between 0 and 99
  vector<int> numbers(25);
  for (int i = 0; i < 25; i++)
    numbers[i] = randomInteger(100);

  // print the maximum
  vector<int>::iterator max =
    max_element(numbers.begin(), numbers.end());
  cout << "largest value was " << * max << endl;

    // example using strings
  string text =
    "It was the best of times, it was the worst of times.";
  list<string> words;
```

```
split (text, " .,!:;", words);
cout << "The smallest word is "
    << * min_element(words.begin(), words.end())
    << " and the largest word is "
    << * max_element(words.begin(), words.end())
    << endl;
}
```

Locate the first mismatched elements in parallel sequences

The name mismatch() might lead you to think that this algorithm was the inverse of the equal() algorithm, which determines if two sequences are equal (see "Test two sequences for pairwise equality"). Instead, the mismatch() algorithm returns a pair of iterators that together indicate the first positions where two parallel sequences have differing elements. (The structure pair is described in "The *map* data abstraction"). The second sequence is denoted only by a starting position, without an ending position. It is assumed (but not checked) that the second sequence contains at least as many elements as the first. The arguments and return type for mismatch() can be described as follows:

```
pair<InputIterator, InputIterator> mismatch
   (InputIterator first1, InputIterator last1,
   InputIterator first2 [, BinaryPredicate ] );
```

The elements of the two sequences are examined in parallel, element by element. When a mismatch is found, that is, a point where the two sequences differ, then a *pair* containing iterators denoting the locations of the two differing elements is constructed and returned. If the first sequence becomes exhausted before discovering any mismatched elements, then the resulting pair contains the ending value for the first sequence, and the last value examined in the second sequence. (The second sequence need not yet be exhausted).

The example program illustrates the use of this procedure. The function mismatch_test() takes as arguments two string values. These are lexicographically compared and a message printed indicating their relative ordering. (This is similar to the analysis performed by the lexicographic_compare() algorithm, although that function simply returns a Boolean value.) Because the mismatch() algorithm assumes the second sequence is at least as long as the first, a comparison of the two string lengths is performed first, and the arguments are reversed if the second string is shorter than the first. After the call on mismatch() the elements of the resulting pair are separated into their component parts. These parts are then tested to determine the appropriate ordering.

```
void mismatch_test (char * a, char * b)
  // illustrate the use of the mismatch algorithm
{
  pair<char *, char *> differPositions(0, 0);
  char * aDiffPosition;
  char * bDiffPosition;

  if (strlen(a) < strlen(b)) {
    // make sure longer string is second
    differPositions = mismatch(a, a + strlen(a), b);
```

```
        aDiffPosition = differPositions.first;
        bDiffPosition = differPositions.second;
        }
    else {
        differPositions = mismatch(b, b + strlen(b), a);
          // note following reverse ordering
        aDiffPosition = differPositions.second;
        bDiffPosition = differPositions.first;

    }
    // compare resulting values
    cout << "string " << a;
    if (*aDiffPosition == *bDiffPosition)
      cout << " is equal to ";
    else if (*aDiffPosition < *bDiffPosition)
      cout << " is less than ";
    else
      cout << " is greater than ";
    cout << b << endl;
    }
```

A second form of the `mismatch()` algorithm is similar to the one illustrated, except it accepts a binary predicate as a fourth argument. This binary function is used to compare elements, in place of the `==` operator.

In-place transformations

Note **Obtaining the source:** The example functions described in this section can be found in the file `alg3.cpp`.

The next category of algorithms in the standard library that we examine are those used to modify and transform sequences without moving them from their original storage locations. A few of these routines, such as `replace()`, include a *copy* version as well as the original in-place transformation algorithms. For the others, should it be necessary to preserve the original, a copy of the sequence should be created before the transformations are applied. For example, the following illustrates how one can place the reversal of one *vector* into another newly allocated *vector*.

```
vector<int> newVec(aVec.size());
copy (aVec.begin(), aVec.end(), newVec.begin());   // first copy
reverse (newVec.begin(), newVec.end());            // then reverse
```

Many of the algorithms described as sequence generating operations, such as `transform()` ("Transform one or two sequences"), or `partial_sum` ("Partial sums"), can also be used to modify a value in place by simply using the same iterator as both input and output specification.

Reverse elements in a sequence

The algorithm `reverse()` reverses the elements in a sequence, so that the last element becomes the new first, and the first element the new last. The arguments are assumed to be bidirectional iterators, and no value is returned.

```
    void reverse (BidirectionalIterator first, BidirectionalIterator last);
```

The example program illustrates two uses of this algorithm. In the first, an array of character values is reversed. The algorithm `reverse()` can also be used with list values, as shown in the second example. In this example, a list is initialized with the values 2 to 11 in increasing order. (This is accomplished using the *iotaGen* function object introduced in "Function objects"). The list is then reversed, which results in the list holding the values 11 to 2 in decreasing order. Note, however, that the list data structure also provides its own `reverse()` member function.

```
    void reverse_example ()
      // illustrate the use of the reverse algorithm
    {
      // example 1, reversing a string
    char * text = "Rats live on no evil star";
    reverse (text, text + strlen(text));
    cout << text << endl;

      // example 2, reversing a list
    list<int> iList;
    generate_n (inserter(iList, iList.begin()), 10, iotaGen(2));
    reverse (iList.begin(), iList.end());
    }
```

Replace certain elements with fixed value

The algorithms `replace()` and `replace_if()` are used to replace occurrences of certain elements with a new value. In both cases the new value is the same, no matter how many replacements are performed. Using the algorithm `replace()`, all occurrences of a particular test value are replaced with the new value. In the case of `replace_if()`, all elements that satisfy a predicate function are replaced by a new value. The iterator arguments must be forward iterators.

The algorithms `replace_copy()` and `replace_copy_if()` are similar to `replace()` and `replace_if()`, however they leave the original sequence intact and place the revised values into a new sequence, which may be a different type.

```
    void replace (ForwardIterator first, ForwardIterator last,
        const T&, const T&);
    void replace_if (ForwardIterator first, ForwardIterator last,
        Predicate, const T&);
    OutputIterator replace_copy (InputIterator, InputIterator,
        OutputIterator, const T&, const T&);
    OutputIterator replace_copy (InputIterator, InputIterator,
        OutputIterator, Predicate, const T&);
```

In the example program, a *vector* is initially assigned the values 0 1 2 3 4 5 4 3 2 1 0. A call on `replace()` replaces the value 3 with the value 7, resulting in the *vector* 0 1 2 7 4 5 4 7 2 1 0. The invocation of `replace_if()` replaces all even numbers with the value 9, resulting in the *vector* 9 1 9 7 9 5 9 7 9 1 9.

```
    void replace_example ()
      // illustrate the use of the replace algorithm
    {
```

```
    // make vector 0 1 2 3 4 5 4 3 2 1 0
vector<int> numbers(11);
for (int i = 0; i < 11; i++)
   numbers[i] = i < 5 ? i : 10 - i;
   // replace 3 by 7
replace (numbers.begin(), numbers.end(), 3, 7);
   // replace even numbers by 9
replace_if (numbers.begin(), numbers.end(), isEven, 9);
   // illustrate copy versions of replace
int aList[] = {2, 1, 4, 3, 2, 5};
int bList[6], cList[6], j;
replace_copy (aList, aList+6, &bList[0], 2, 7);
replace_copy_if (bList, bList+6, &cList[0],
     bind2nd(greater<int>(), 3), 8);
}
```

The example program also illustrates the use of the `replace_copy` algorithms. First, an array containing the values 2 1 4 3 2 5 is created. This is modified by replacing the 2 values with 7, resulting in the array 7 1 4 3 7 5. Next, all values larger than 3 are replaced with the value 8, resulting in the array values 8 1 8 3 8 8. In the latter case the `bind2nd()` adaptor is used, to modify the binary greater-than function by binding the 2nd argument to the constant value 3, thereby creating the unary function $x > 3$.

Rotate elements around a midpoint

A rotation of a sequence divides the sequence into two sections, then swaps the order of the sections, maintaining the relative ordering of the elements within the two sections. Suppose, for example, that we have the values 1 to 10 in sequence:

1 2 3 4 5 6 7 8 9 10

If we were to rotate around the element 7, the values 7 to 10 would be moved to the beginning, while the elements 1 to 6 would be moved to the end. This would result in the following sequence:

7 8 9 10 1 2 3 4 5 6

When you invoke the algorithm `rotate()`, the starting point, midpoint, and past-the-end location are all denoted by forward iterators:

```
void rotate (ForwardIterator first, ForwardIterator middle,
   ForwardIterator last);
```

The prefix portion, the set of elements following the start and not including the midpoint, is swapped with the suffix, the set of elements between the midpoint and the past-the-end location. Note, as in the illustration presented earlier, that these two segments need not be the same length.

```
void rotate_example()
   // illustrate the use of the rotate algorithm
{
   // create the list 1 2 3 ... 10
   list<int> iList;
   generate_n(inserter(iList, iList.begin()), 10, iotaGen(1));
```

```
    // find the location of the seven
list<int>::iterator & middle =
    find(iList.begin(), iList.end(), 7);

    // now rotate around that location
rotate (iList.begin(), middle, iList.end());

    // rotate again around the same location
list<int> cList;
rotate_copy (iList.begin(), middle, iList.end(),
    inserter(cList, cList.begin()));
}
```

The example program first creates a list of the integers in order from 1 to 10. Next, the find() algorithm ("Find an element satisfying a condition") is used to find the location of the element 7. This is used as the midpoint for the rotation.

A second form of rotate() copies the elements into a new sequence, rather than rotating the values in place. This is also shown in the example program, which once again rotates around the middle position (now containing a 3). The resulting list is 3 4 5 6 7 8 9 10 1 2. The values held in iList remain unchanged.

Partition a sequence into two groups

A *partition* is formed by moving all the elements that satisfy a predicate to one end of a sequence, and all the elements that fail to satisfy the predicate to the other end. Partitioning elements is a fundamental step in certain sorting algorithms, such as "quicksort."

```
BidirectionalIterator partition
    (BidirectionalIterator, BidirectionalIterator, Predicate);
BidirectionalIterator stable_partition
    (BidirectionalIterator, BidirectionalIterator, Predicate);
```

There are two forms of partition supported in the standard library. The first, provided by the algorithm partition(), guarantees only that the elements will be divided into two groups. The result value is an iterator that describes the final midpoint between the two groups; it is one past the end of the first group.

Note   **Partitions:** While there is a unique stable partition for any sequence, the partition() algorithm can return any number of values. The following, for example, are all legal partitions of the example problem:

```
2  4  6  8 10  1  3  5  7  9
10  8  6  4  2  5  7  9  3  1
2  6  4  8 10  3  5  7  9  1
6  4  2 10  8  5  3  7  9  1
```

In the example program the initial *vector* contains the values 1 to 10 in order. The partition moves the even elements to the front, and the odd elements to the end. This results in the *vector* holding the values 10 2 8 4 6 5 7 3 9 1, and the midpoint iterator pointing to the element 5.

```
void partition_example ()
  // illustrate the use of the partition algorithm
{
    // first make the vector 1 2 3 ... 10
  vector<int> numbers(10);
  generate(numbers.begin(), numbers.end(), iotaGen(1));

    // now put the even values low, odd high
  vector<int>::iterator result =
    partition(numbers.begin(), numbers.end(), isEven);
  cout << "middle location " << result - numbers.begin() << endl;

    // now do a stable partition
  generate (numbers.begin(), numbers.end(), iotaGen(1));
  stable_partition (numbers.begin(), numbers.end(), isEven);
}
```

The relative order of the elements within a partition in the resulting *vector* may not be the same as the values in the original *vector*. For example the value 4 preceded the element 8 in the original, yet in the result it may follow the element 8. A second version of partition, named `stable_partition()`, guarantees the ordering of the resulting values. For the sample input shown in the example, the stable partition would result in the sequence 2 4 6 8 10 1 3 5 7 9. The `stable_partition()` algorithm is slightly slower and uses more memory than the `partition()` algorithm, so when the order of elements is not important you should use `partition()`.

Generate permutations in sequence

A permutation is a rearrangement of values. If values can be compared against each other (such as integers, characters, or words) then it is possible to systematically construct all permutations of a sequence. There are 2 permutations of two values, for example, and six permutations of three values, and 24 permutations of four values.

Note   **Ordering permutations:** Permutations can be ordered, with the smallest permutation being the one in which values are listed smallest to largest, and the largest being the sequence that lists values largest to smallest. Consider, for example, the permutations of the integers 1 2 3. The six permutations of these values are, in order:

```
1 2 3
1 3 2
2 1 3
2 3 1
3 1 2
3 2 1
```

Notice that in the first permutation the values are all ascending, while in the last permutation they are all descending.

The permutation generating algorithms have the following definition:

```
bool next_permutation (BidirectionalIterator first,
    BidirectionalIterator last, [ Compare ] );
```

```
bool prev_permutation (BidirectionalIterator first,
    BidirectionalIterator last, [ Compare ] );
```

The second example in the sample program illustrates the same idea, only using pointers to character arrays instead of integers. In this case a different comparison function must be supplied, since the default operator would simply compare pointer addresses.

```
bool nameCompare (char * a, char * b) { return strcmp(a, b) <= 0; }

void permutation_example ()
  // illustrate the use of the next_permutation algorithm
{
    // example 1, permute the values 1 2 3
  int start [] = { 1, 2, 3};
  do
    copy (start, start + 3,
        ostream_iterator<int> (cout, " ")), cout << endl;
  while (next_permutation(start, start + 3));

    // example 2, permute words
  char * words = {"Alpha", "Beta", "Gamma"};
  do
    copy (words, words + 3,
        ostream_iterator<char *> (cout, " ")), cout << endl;
  while (next_permutation(words, words + 3, nameCompare));

    // example 3, permute characters backwards
  char * word = "bela";
  do
    cout << word << ' ';
  while (prev_permutation (word, &word[4]));
  cout << endl;
}
```

Example 3 in the sample program illustrates the use of the reverse permutation algorithm, which generates values in reverse sequence. This example also begins in the middle of a sequence, rather than at the beginning. The remaining permutations of the word "bela", are `beal`, `bale`, `bael`, `aleb`, `albe`, `aelb`, `aebl`, `able`, and finally, `abel`.

Merge two adjacent sequences into one

A *merge* takes two ordered sequences and combines them into a single ordered sequence, interleaving elements from each collection as necessary to generate the new list. The `inplace_merge()` algorithm assumes a sequence is divided into two adjacent sections, each of which is ordered. The merge combines the two sections into one, moving elements as necessary. (The alternative `merge()` algorithm, described elsewhere, can be used to merge two separate sequences into one.) The arguments to `inplace_merge()` must be bidirectional iterators.

```
void inplace_merge (BidirectionalIterator first,
    BidirectionalIterator middle,
    BidirectionalIterator last [, BinaryFunction ] );
```

The example program illustrates the use of the `inplace_merge()` algorithm with a *vector* and with a list. The sequence 0 2 4 6 8 1 3 5 7 9 is placed into a *vector*. A `find()` call ("Find an element satisfying a condition") is used to locate the beginning of the odd number sequence. The two calls on `inplace_merge()` then combine the two sequences into one.

```
void inplace_merge_example ()
    // illustrate the use of the inplace_merge algorithm
{
    // first generate the sequence 0 2 4 6 8 1 3 5 7 9
    vector<int> numbers(10);
    for (int i = 0; i < 10; i++)
        numbers[i] = i < 5 ? 2 * i : 2 * (i - 5) + 1;

    // then find the middle location
    vector<int>::iterator midvec =
        find(numbers.begin(), numbers.end(), 1);

    // copy them into a list
    list<int> numList;
    copy (numbers.begin(), numbers.end(),
        inserter (numList, numList.begin()));
    list<int>::iterator midList =
        find(numList.begin(), numList.end, 1);

    // now merge the lists into one
    inplace_merge (numbers.begin(), midvec, numbers.end());
    inplace_merge (numList.begin(), midList, numList.end());
}
```

Randomly rearrange elements in a sequence

The algorithm `random_shuffle()` randomly rearranges the elements in a sequence. Exactly *n* swaps are performed, where *n* represents the number of elements in the sequence. The results are, of course, unpredictable. Because the arguments must be random access iterators, this algorithm can only be used with *vectors*, deques, or ordinary pointers. It cannot be used with lists, sets, or maps.

```
void random_shuffle (RandomAccessIterator first,
    RandomAccessIterator last [, Generator ] );
```

An alternative version of the algorithm uses the optional third argument. This value must be a random number generator. This generator must take as an argument a positive value `m` and return a value between 0 and `m-1`. As with the `generate()` algorithm, this random number function can be any type of object that will respond to the function invocation operator.

```
void random_shuffle_example ()
    // illustrate the use of the random_shuffle algorithm
```

```
{
    // first make the vector containing 1 2 3 ... 10
    vector<int> numbers;
    generate(numbers.begin(), numbers.end(), iotaGen(1));

      // then randomly shuffle the elements
    random_shuffle (numbers.begin(), numbers.end());

      // do it again, with explicit random number generator
    struct RandomInteger {
    {
      operator() (int m) { return rand() % m; }
    } random;

    random_shuffle (numbers.begin(), numbers.end(), random);
}
```

Removal algorithms

Note   **Removal algorithms:** The algorithms in this section set up a sequence so that the
desired elements are moved to the front. The remaining values are not actually
removed, but the starting location for these values is returned, making it possible to
remove these values by means of a subsequent call on `erase()`. *Remember*, the remove
algorithms do not actually remove the unwanted elements.

The following two algorithms can be somewhat confusing the first time they are
encountered. Both claim to remove certain values from a sequence. But, in fact, neither
one reduces the size of the sequence. Both operate by moving the values that are to be
retained to the front of the sequence, and returning an iterator that describes where this
sequence ends. Elements after this iterator are simply the original sequence values, left
unchanged. This is necessary because the generic algorithm has no knowledge of the
container it is working on. It only has a generic iterator. This is part of the price we pay
for generic algorithms. In most cases the user will want to use this iterator result as an
argument to the `erase()` member function for the container, removing the values from
the iterator to the end of the sequence.

Let us illustrate this with a simple example. Suppose we want to remove the even
numbers from the sequence 1 2 3 4 5 6 7 8 9 10, something we could do with the
`remove_if()` algorithm. The algorithm `remove_if()` would leave us with the
following sequence:

```
1 3 5 7 9 | 6 7 8 9 10
```

The vertical bar here represents the position of the iterator returned by the `remove_if()`
algorithm. Notice that the five elements before the bar represent the result we want,
while the five values after the bar are simply the original contents of those locations.
Using this iterator value along with the end-of-sequence iterator as arguments to
`erase()`, we can eliminate the unwanted values, and obtained the desired result.

Both the algorithms described here have an alternative *copy* version. The copy version of
the algorithms leaves the original unchanged, and places the preserved elements into an
output sequence.

Obtaining the source: The example functions described in this section can be found in the file alg4.cpp.

Remove unwanted elements

The algorithm remove() eliminates unwanted values from a sequence. As with the find() algorithm, these can either be values that match a specific constant, or values that satisfy a given predicate. The definition of the argument types is as follows:

```
ForwardIterator remove
    (ForwardIterator first, ForwardIterator last, const T &);
ForwardIterator remove_if
    (ForwardIterator first, ForwardIterator last, Predicate);
```

The algorithm remove() copies values to the front of the sequence, overwriting the location of the removed elements. All elements not removed remain in their relative order. Once all values have been examined, the remainder of the sequence is left unchanged. The iterator returned as the result of the operation provides the end of the new sequence. For example, eliminating the element 2 from the sequence 1 2 4 3 2 results in the sequence 1 4 3 3 2, with the iterator returned as the result pointing at the second 3. This value can be used as argument to erase() in order to eliminate the remaining elements (the 3 and the 2), as illustrated in the example program.

A copy version of the algorithms copies values to an output sequence, rather than making transformations in place.

```
OutputIterator remove_copy
        (InputIterator first, InputIterator last,
        OutputIterator result, const T &);

OutputIterator remove_copy_if
        (InputIterator first, InputIterator last,
        OutputIterator result, Predicate);
```

The use of remove() is shown in the following program.

```
void remove_example ()
  // illustrate the use of the remove algorithm
{
  // create a list of numbers
  int data[] = {1, 2, 4, 3, 1, 4, 2};
  list<int> aList;
  copy (data, data+7, inserter(aList, aList.begin()));

    // remove 2's, copy into new list
  list<int> newList;
  remove_copy (aList.begin(), aList.end(),
    back_inserter(newList), 2);

    // remove 2's in place
  list<int>::iterator where;
  where = remove (aList.begin(), aList.end(), 2);
  aList.erase(where, aList.end());
```

```
    // remove all even values
  where = remove_if (aList.begin(), aList.end(), isEven);
  aList.erase(where, aList.end());
}
```

Remove runs of similar values

The algorithm `unique()` moves through a linear sequence, eliminating all but the first element from every consecutive group of equal elements. The argument sequence is described by forward iterators.

```
ForwardIterator unique (ForwardIterator first,
    ForwardIterator last [, BinaryPredicate ] );
```

As the algorithm moves through the collection, elements are moved to the front of the sequence, overwriting the existing elements. Once all unique values have been identified, the remainder of the sequence is left unchanged. For example, a sequence such as 1 3 3 2 2 2 4 will be changed into 1 3 2 4 | 2 2 4. I have used a vertical bar to indicate the location returned by the iterator result value. This location marks the end of the unique sequence, and the beginning of the left-over elements. With most containers the value returned by the algorithm can be used as an argument in a subsequent call on `erase()` to remove the undesired elements from the collection. This is illustrated in the example program.

A copy version of the algorithm moves the unique values to an output iterator, rather than making modifications in place. In transforming a list or *multiset*, an insert iterator can be used to change the copy operations of the output iterator into insertions.

```
OutputIterator unique_copy
    (InputIterator first, InputIterator last,
     OutputIterator result [, BinaryPredicate ] );
```

These are illustrated in the sample program:

```
void unique_example ()
  // illustrate use of the unique algorithm
{
    // first make a list of values
  int data[] = {1, 3, 3, 2, 2, 4};
  list<int> aList;
  set<int> aSet;
  copy (data, , inserter(aList, aList.begin()));

    // copy unique elements into a set
  unique_copy (aList.begin(), aList.end(),
    inserter(aSet, aSet.begin()));

    // copy unique elements in place
  list<int>::iterator where;
  where = unique(aList.begin(), aList.end());

    // remove trailing values
  aList.erase(where, aList.end());
}
```

Algorithms that produce a scalar result

Note **Obtaining the source:** The example functions described in this section can be found in the file `alg5.cpp`.

The next category of algorithms are those that reduce an entire sequence to a single scalar value.

Remember that two of these algorithms, `accumulate()` and `inner_product()`, are defined in the `numeric` header file, not the `algorithm` header file as are the other generic algorithms.

Count the number of elements that satisfy a condition

The algorithms `count()` and `count_if()` are used to discover the number of elements that match a given value or that satisfy a given predicate, respectively. Both take as argument a reference to a counting value (typically an integer), and increment this value. Note that the count is passed as a by-reference argument, and is *not* returned as the value of the function. The `count()` function itself yields no value.

```
void count (InputIterator first, InputIterator last,
      const T&, Size &);
void count_if (InputIterator first, InputIterator last,
      Predicate, Size &);
```

Note **The resulting count:** Note that the `count()` algorithms do not return the sum as a function result, but instead simply add to the last argument in their parameter list, which is passed by reference. This means successive calls on these functions can be used to produce a cumulative sum. This also means that you must initialize the variable passed to this last argument location prior to calling one of these algorithms.

The example code fragment illustrates the use of these algorithms. The call on `count()` will count the number of occurrences of the letter e in a sample string, while the invocation of `count_if()` will count the number of vowels.

```
void count_example ()
    // illustrate the use of the count algorithm
{
  int eCount = 0;
  int vowelCount = 0;

  char * text = "Now is the time to begin";

  count (text, text + strlen(text), 'e', eCount);
  count_if (text, text + strlen(text), isVowel, vowelCount);

  cout << "There are " << eCount << " letter e's " << endl
      << "and " << vowelCount << " vowels in the text:"
      << text << endl;
}
```

Reduce sequence to a single value

The result generated by the `accumulate()` algorithm is the value produced by placing a binary operator between each element of a sequence, and evaluating the result. By default the operator is the addition operator, +, however this can be replaced by any binary function. An initial value (an identity) must be provided. This value is returned for empty sequences, and is otherwise used as the left argument for the first calculation.

```
ContainerType accumulate (InputIterator first, InputIterator last,
        ContainerType initial [, BinaryFunction ] );
```

The example program illustrates the use of `accumulate()` to produce the sum and product of a *vector* of integer values. In the first case the identity is zero, and the default operator + is used. In the second invocation the identity is 1, and the multiplication operator (named *times*) is explicitly passed as the fourth argument.

```
void accumulate_example ()
  // illustrate the use of the accumulate algorithm
{
  int numbers[] = {1, 2, 3, 4, 5};

    // first example, simple accumulation
  int sum = accumulate (numbers, numbers + 5, 0);
  int product =
      accumulate (numbers, numbers + 5, 1, times<int>());

  cout << "The sum of the first five integers is " << sum << endl;
  cout << "The product is " << product << endl;

    // second example, with different types for initial value
  list<int> nums;
  nums = accumulate (numbers, numbers+5, nums, intReplicate);
}


list<int>& intReplicate (list<int>& nums, int n)
    // add sequence n to 1 to end of list
{
  while (n) nums.push_back(n--);
  return nums;
}
```

Neither the identity value nor the result of the binary function are required to match the container type. This is illustrated in the example program by the invocation of `accumulate()` shown in the second example. Here the identity is an empty list. The function (shown after the example program) takes as argument a list and an integer value, and repeatedly inserts values into the list. The values inserted represent a decreasing sequence from the argument down to 1. For the example input (the same *vector* as in the first example), the resulting list contains the 15 values 1 2 1 3 2 1 4 3 2 1 5 4 3 2 1.

Generalized inner product

Assume we have two sequences of n elements each; $a1, a2, ... an$ and $b1, b2, ... bn$. The *inner product* of the sequences is the sum of the parallel products, that is the value $a1 * b1 + a2 * b2 + ... + an * bn$. Inner products occur in a number of scientific calculations. For example, the inner product of a row times a column is the heart of the traditional matrix multiplication algorithm. A generalized inner product uses the same structure, but permits the addition and multiplication operators to be replaced by arbitrary binary functions. The standard library includes the following algorithm for computing an inner product:

```
ContainerType inner_product
    (InputIterator first1, InputIterator last1,
    InputIterator first2, ContainerType initialValue
    [ , BinaryFunction add, BinaryFunction times ] );
```

The first three arguments to the `inner_product()` algorithm define the two input sequences. The second sequence is specified only by the beginning iterator, and is assumed to contain at least as many elements as the first sequence. The next argument is an initial value, or identity, used for the summation operator. This is similar to the identity used in the `accumulate()` algorithm. In the generalized inner product function the last two arguments are the binary functions that are used in place of the addition operator, and in place of the multiplication operator, respectively.

In the example program the second invocation illustrates the use of alternative functions as arguments. The multiplication is replaced by an equality test, while the addition is replaced by a logical *or*. The result is true if any of the pairs are equal, and false otherwise. Using an *and* in place of the *or* would have resulted in a test which was true only if *all* pairs were equal; in effect the same as the `equal()` algorithm described in the next section.

```
void inner_product_example ()
    // illustrate the use of the inner_product algorithm
{
  int a[] = {4, 3, -2};
  int b[] = {7, 3, 2};

    // example 1, a simple inner product
  int in1 = inner_product(a, a+3, b, 0);
  cout << "Inner product is " << in1 << endl;

    // example 2, user defined operations
  bool anyequal = inner_product(a, a+3, b, true,
      logical_or<bool>(), equal_to<int>());
  cout << "any equal? " << anyequal << endl;
}
```

Test two sequences for pairwise equality

The `equal()` algorithm tests two sequences for pairwise equality. By using an alternative binary predicate, it can also be used for a wide variety of other pair-wise tests of parallel sequences. The arguments are simple input iterators:

```
bool equal (InputIterator first, InputIterator last,
      InputIterator first2 [, BinaryPredicate] );
```

Note   **Equal and mismatch:** By substituting another function for the binary predicate, the `equal` and `mismatch` algorithms can be put to a variety of different uses. Use the `equal()` algorithm if you want a pairwise test that returns a *Boolean* result. Use the `mismatch()` algorithm if you want to discover the *location* of elements that fail the test.

The `equal()` algorithm assumes, but does not verify, that the second sequence contains at least as many elements as the first. A `true` result is generated if all values test equal to their corresponding element. The alternative version of the algorithm substitutes an arbitrary Boolean function for the equality test, and returns `true` if all pair-wise elements satisfy the predicate. In the sample program this is illustrated by replacing the predicate with the `greater_equal()` function, and in this fashion true will be returned only if all values in the first sequence are greater than or equal to their corresponding value in the second sequence.

```
void equal_example ()
  // illustrate the use of the equal algorithm
{
  int a[] = {4, 5, 3};
  int b[] = {4, 3, 3};
  int c[] = {4, 5, 3};

  cout << "a = b is: " << equal(a, a+3, b) << endl;
  cout << "a = c is: " << equal(a, a+3, c) << endl;
  cout << "a pair-wise greater-equal b is: "
    << equal(a, a+3, b, greater_equal<int>()) << endl;
}
```

Lexical comparison

A lexical comparison of two sequences can be described by noting the features of the most common example, namely the comparison of two words for the purposes of placing them in "dictionary order." When comparing two words, the elements (that is, the characters) of the two sequences are compared in a pair-wise fashion. As long as they match, the algorithm advances to the next character. If two corresponding characters fail to match, the earlier character determines the smaller word. So, for example, everybody is smaller than everything, since the b in the former word alphabetically precedes the t in the latter word. Should one or the other sequence terminate before the other, than the terminated sequence is considered to be smaller than the other. So, for example, every precedes both everybody and everything, but comes after eve. Finally, if both sequences terminate at the same time and, in all cases, pair-wise characters match, then the two words are considered to be equal.

The `lexicographical_compare()` algorithm implements this idea, returning `true` if the first sequence is smaller than the second, and `false` otherwise. The algorithm has been generalized to any sequence. Thus the `lexicographical_compare()` algorithm can be used with arrays, strings, *vectors*, lists, or any of the other data structures used in the standard library.

```
bool lexicographical_compare
```

```
(InputIterator first1, InputIterator last1,
 InputIterator first2, InputIterator last2 [, BinaryFunction ] );
```

Unlike most of the other algorithms that take two sequences as argument, the `lexicographical_compare()` algorithm uses a first and a past-end iterator for *both* sequences. A variation on the algorithm also takes a fifth argument, which is the binary function used to compare corresponding elements from the two sequences.

The example program illustrates the use of this algorithm with character sequences, and with arrays of integer values.

```
void lexicographical_compare_example()
  // illustrate the use of the lexicographical_compare algorithm
{
  char * wordOne = "everything";
  char * wordTwo = "everybody";

  cout << "compare everybody to everything " <<
    lexicographical_compare(wordTwo, wordTwo + strlen(wordTwo),
      wordOne, wordOne + strlen(wordOne)) << endl;

  int a[] = {3, 4, 5, 2};
  int b[] = {3, 4, 5};
  int c[] = {3, 5};

  cout << "compare a to b:" <<
    lexicographical_compare(a, a+4, b, b+3) << endl;
  cout << "compare a to c:" <<
    lexicographical_compare(a, a+4, c, c+2) << endl;
}
```

Sequence generating algorithms

Note   **Obtaining the source:** The example functions described in this section can be found in the file `alg6.cpp`.

The algorithms described in this section are all used to generate a new sequence from an existing sequence by performing some type of transformation. In most cases, the output sequence is described by an output iterator. This means these algorithms can be used to overwrite an existing structure (such as a *vector*). Alternatively, by using an insert iterator (see "Insert iterators"), the algorithms can insert the new elements into a variable length structure, such as a *set* or *list*. Finally, in some cases which we will note, the output iterator can be the same as one of the sequences specified by an input iterator, thereby providing the ability to make an in-place transformation.

The functions `partial_sum()` and `adjacent_difference()` are described in the header file `numeric`, while the other functions are described in the header file `algorithm`.

Transform one or two sequences

The algorithm `transform()` is used either to make a general transformation of a single sequence, or to produce a new sequence by applying a binary function in a pair-wise fashion to corresponding elements from two different sequences. The general definition of the argument and result types are as follows:

```
OutputIterator transform (InputIterator first, InputIterator last,
    OutputIterator result, UnaryFunction);
OutputIterator transform
    (InputIterator first1, InputIterator last1,
    InputIterator first2, OutputIterator result, BinaryFunction);
```

The first form applies a unary function to each element of a sequence. In the example program given below, this is used to produce a *vector* of integer values that hold the arithmetic negation of the values in a linked list. The input and output iterators can be the same, in which case the transformation is applied in-place, as shown in the example program.

The second form takes two sequences and applies the binary function in a pair-wise fashion to corresponding elements. The transaction assumes, but does not verify, that the second sequence has at least as many elements as the first sequence. Once more, the result can either be a third sequence, or either of the two input sequences.

```
int square(int n) { return n * n; }

void transform_example ()
    // illustrate the use of the transform algorithm
{
    // generate a list of value 1 to 6
    list<int> aList;
    generate_n (inserter(aList, aList.begin()), 6, iotaGen(1));

    // transform elements by squaring, copy into vector
    vector<int> aVec(6);
    transform (aList.begin(), aList.end(), aVec.begin(), square);

    // transform vector again, in place, yielding 4th powers
    transform (aVec.begin(), aVec.end(), aVec.begin(), square);

    // transform in parallel, yielding cubes
    vector<int> cubes(6);
    transform (aVec.begin(), aVec.end(), aList.begin(),
        cubes.begin(), divides<int>());
}
```

Partial sums

A partial sum of a sequence is a new sequence in which every element is formed by adding the values of all prior elements. For example, the partial sum of the *vector* 1 3 2 4 5 is the new *vector* 1 4 6 10 15. The element 4 is formed from the sum 1 + 3, the element 6 from the sum 1 + 3 + 2, and so on. Although the term "sum" is used in describing the operation, the binary function can, in fact, be any arbitrary function. The example program illustrates this by computing partial products. The arguments to the partial sum function are described as follows:

```
OutputIterator partial_sum
    (InputIterator first, InputIterator last,
     OutputIterator result [, BinaryFunction] );
```

By using the same value for both the input iterator and the result the partial sum can be changed into an in-place transformation.

```
void partial_sum_example ()
  // illustrate the use of the partial sum algorithm
{
    // generate values 1 to 5
  vector<int> aVec(5);
  generate (aVec.begin(), aVec.end(), iotaGen(1));
    // output partial sums
  partial_sum (aVec.begin(), aVec.end(),
    ostream_iterator<int> (cout, " ")), cout << endl;
    // output partial products
  partial_sum (aVec.begin(), aVec.end(),
    ostream_iterator<int> (cout, " "),
    times<int>() );
}
```

Adjacent differences

An adjacent difference of a sequence is a new sequence formed by replacing every element with the difference between the element and the immediately preceding element. The first value in the new sequence remains unchanged. For example, a sequence such as (1, 3, 2, 4, 5) is transformed into (1, 3-1, 2-3, 4-2, 5-4), and in this manner becomes the sequence (1, 2, -1, 2, 1).

As with the algorithm partial_sum(), the term "difference" is not necessarily accurate, as an arbitrary binary function can be employed. The adjacent sums for this sequence are (1, 4, 5, 6, 9), for example. The arguments to the adjacent difference algorithm have the following definitions:

```
OutputIterator adjacent_difference (InputIterator first,
    InputIterator last, OutputIterator result [, BinaryFunction ]);
```

By using the same iterator as both input and output iterator, the adjacent difference operation can be performed in-place.

```
void adjacent_difference_example ()
  // illustrate the use of the adjacent difference algorithm
{
    // generate values 1 to 5
  vector<int> aVec(5);
  generate (aVec.begin(), aVec.end(), iotaGen(1));

    // output adjacent differences
```

```
      adjacent_difference (aVec.begin(), aVec.end(),
        ostream_iterator<int> (cout, " ")), cout << endl;

        // output adjacent sums
      adjacent_difference (aVec.begin(), aVec.end(),
        ostream_iterator<int> (cout, " "),
        plus<int>() );
  }
```

Miscellaneous algorithms

In the final section we describe the remaining algorithms found in the standard library.

Apply a function to all elements in a collection

The algorithm `for_each()` takes three arguments. The first two provide the iterators that describe the sequence to be evaluated. The third is a one-argument function. The `for_each()` algorithm applies the function to each value of the sequence, passing the value as argument.

```
Function for_each
   (InputIterator first, InputIterator last, Function);
```

For example, the following code fragment, which uses the `print_if_leap()` function, will print a list of the leap years that occur between 1900 and 1997:

```
cout << "leap years between 1990 and 1997 are: ";
for_each (1990, 1997, print_if_leap);
cout << endl;
```

Note   **Results produced by side effect:** The function passed as the third argument is not permitted to make any modifications to the sequence, so it can only achieve any result by means of a side effect, such as printing, assigning a value to a global or static variable, or invoking another function that produces a side effect. If the argument function returns any result, it is ignored.

The argument function is guaranteed to be invoked only once for each element in the sequence. The `for_each()` algorithm itself returns the value of the third argument, although this, too, is usually ignored.

The following example searches an array of integer values representing dates, to determine which vintage wine years were also leap years:

```
int vintageYears[] = {1947, 1955, 1960, 1967, 1994};
...
cout << "vintage years which were also leap years are: ";
for_each (vintageYears, vintageYears + 5, print_if_leap);
cout << endl;
```

Side effects need not be restricted to printing. Assume we have a function `countCaps()` that counts the occurrence of capital letters:

```
int capCount = 0;
void countCaps(char c)   { if (isupper(c)) capCount++; }
```

The following example counts the number of capital letters in a string value:

```
string advice = "Never Trust Anybody Over 30!";
for_each(advice.begin(), advice.end(),countCaps);
cout << "upper-case letter count is " << capCount << endl;
```

30

Ordered collection algorithms

In this chapter we will describe the generic algorithms in the standard library that are specific to ordered collections. These are summarized by the following table:

Name	Purpose
Sorting algorithms:	
sort	rearrange sequence, place in order
stable_sort	sort, retaining original order of equal elements
partial_sort	sort only part of sequence
partial_sort_copy	partial sort into copy
Find nth largest element:	
nth_element	locate nth largest element
Binary search:	
binary_search	search, returning boolean
lower_bound	search, returning first position
upper_bound	search, returning last position
equal_range	search, returning both positions
Merge ordered sequences:	
merge	combine two ordered sequences
Set operations:	
set_union	form union of two sets
set_intersection	form intersection of two sets
set_difference	form difference of two sets
set_symmetric_difference	form symmetric difference of two sets
includes	see if one *set* is a subset of another
Heap operations:	
make_heap	turn a sequence into a heap
push_heap	add a new value to the heap

Name	Purpose
pop_heap	remove largest value from the heap
sort_heap	turn heap into sorted collection

Ordered collections can be created using the standard library in a variety of ways. For example:

- The containers *set, multiset, map,* and *multimap* are ordered collections by definition.

- A *list* can be ordered by invoking the `sort()` member function.

- A *vector, deque,* or ordinary C++ array can be ordered by using one of the sorting algorithms described later in this section.

Like the generic algorithms described in the previous section, the algorithms described here are not specific to any particular container class. This means they can be used with a wide variety of types. Many of them do, however, require the use of random-access iterators. For this reason they are most easily used with *vectors*, deques, or ordinary arrays.

Note   **Obtaining the sample programs:** The example programs described in this section have been combined and are included in the file ALG7.CPP in the tutorial distribution. As we did in Chapter 29, we will generally omit output statements from the descriptions of the programs provided here, although they are included in the executable versions.

Almost all the algorithms described in this section have two versions. The first version uses for comparisons the less-than operator (operator <) appropriate to the container element type. The second, and more general, version uses an explicit comparison function object, which we will write as Compare. This function object must be a binary predicate (see "Predicates" in Chapter 20). Since this argument is optional, we will write it within square brackets in the description of the argument types.

A sequence is considered to be ordered if for every valid (that is, denotable) iterator i with a denotable successor j, it is the case that the comparison Compare(*j, *i) is false. Note that this does not necessarily imply that Compare(*i, *j) is true. It is assumed that the relation imposed by Compare is transitive, and induces a total ordering on the values.

In the descriptions that follow, two values x and y are said to be equivalent if both Compare(x, y) and Compare(y, x) are false. Note that this need not imply that x == y.

Algorithm include files

As with the algorithms described in Chapter 29, before you can use any of the algorithms described in this section in a program you must include the algorithm header file:

```
# include <algorithm>
```

Sorting algorithms

There are two fundamental sorting algorithms provided by the standard library, described as follows:

```
void sort (RandomAccessIterator first,
    RandomAccessIterator last [, Compare ] );

void stable_sort (RandomAccessIterator first,
    RandomAccessIterator last [, Compare ] );
```

The sort() algorithm is slightly faster, but it does not guarantee that equal elements in the original sequence will retain their relative orderings in the final result. If order is important, then use the stable_sort() version.

Because these algorithms require random-access iterators, they can be used only with *vectors*, deques, and ordinary C pointers. Note, however, that the list container provides its own sort() member function.

The comparison operator can be explicitly provided when the default operator < is not appropriate. This is used in the example program to sort a list into descending, rather than ascending order. An alternative technique for sorting an entire collection in the inverse direction is to describe the sequence using reverse iterators.

Note **More sorts:** Yet another sorting algorithm is provided by the heap operations, to be described in "Heap operations" later in this chapter.

The following example program illustrates the sort() algorithm being applied to a *vector*, and the sort() algorithm with an explicit comparison operator being used with a *deque*.

```
void sort_example ()
  // illustrate the use of the sort algorithm
{
    // fill both a vector and a deque
    // with random integers
  vector<int> aVec(15);
  deque<int> aDec(15);
  generate (aVec.begin(), aVec.end(), randomValue);
  generate (aDec.begin(), aDec.end(), randomValue);

    // sort the vector ascending
  sort (aVec.begin(), aVec.end());

    // sort the deque descending
  sort (aDec.begin(), aDec.end(), greater<int>() );

    // alternative way to sort descending
  sort (aVec.rbegin(), aVec.rend());
}
```

Partial sort

The generic algorithm `partial_sort()` sorts only a portion of a sequence. In the first version of the algorithm, three iterators are used to describe the beginning, middle, and end of a sequence. If n represents the number of elements between the start and middle, then the smallest n elements will be moved into this range in order. The remaining elements are moved into the second region. The order of the elements in this second region is undefined.

```
void partial_sort (RandomAccessIterator first,
    RandomAccessIterator middle,
    RandomAccessIterator last [ , Compare ]);
```

A second version of the algorithm leaves the input unchanged. The output area is described by a pair of random-access iterators. If n represents the size of this area, then the smallest n elements in the input are moved into the output in order. If n is larger than the input, then the entire input is sorted and placed in the first n locations in the output. In either case the end of the output sequence is returned as the result of the operation.

```
RandomAccessIterator partial_sort_copy
    (InputIterator first, InputIterator last,
    RandomAccessIterator result_first,
    RandomAccessIterator result_last [, Compare ] );
```

Because the input to this version of the algorithm is specified only as a pair of input iterators, the `partial_sort_copy()` algorithm can be used with any of the containers in the standard library. In the example program it is used with a list.

```
void partial_sort_example ()
    // illustrate the use of the partial sort algorithm
{
    // make a vector of 15 random integers
    vector<int> aVec(15);
    generate (aVec.begin(), aVec.end(), randomValue);

    // partial sort the first seven positions
    partial_sort (aVec.begin(), aVec.begin() + 7, aVec.end());

    // make a list of random integers
    list<int> aList(15, 0);
    generate (aList.begin(), aList.end(), randomValue);

    // sort only the first seven elements
    vector<int> start(7);
    partial_sort_copy (aList.begin(), aList.end(),
        start.begin(), start.end(), greater<int>());
}
```

Nth element

Imagine we have the sequence 2 5 3 4 7, and we want to discover the median, or middle element. We could do this with the function `nth_element()`. One result might be the following sequence:

3 2 | 4 | 7 5

The vertical bars are used to describe the separation of the result into three parts; the elements before the requested value, the requested value, and the values after the requested value. Note that the values in the first and third sequences are unordered; in fact, they can appear in the result in any order. The only requirement is that the values in the first part are no larger than the value we are seeking, and the elements in the third part are no smaller than this value.

The three iterators provided as arguments to the algorithm `nth_element()` divide the argument sequence into the three sections we just described. These are the section prior to the middle iterator, the single value denoted by the middle iterator, and the region between the middle iterator and the end. Either the first or third of these may be empty.

The arguments to the algorithm can be described as follows:

```
void nth_element (RandomAccessIterator first,
    RandomAccessIterator nth,
    RandomAccessIterator last [, Compare ] );
```

Following the call on `nth_element()`, the nth largest value will be copied into the position denoted by the middle iterator. The region between the first iterator and the middle iterator will have values no larger than the nth element, while the region between the middle iterator and the end will hold values no smaller than the nth element.

The example program illustrates finding the fifth largest value in a *vector* of random numbers.

```
void nth_element_example ()
    // illustrate the use of the nth_element algorithm
{
    // make a vector of random integers
    vector<int> aVec(10);
    generate (aVec.begin(), aVec.end(), randomValue);

    // now find the 5th largest
    vector<int>::iterator nth = aVec.begin() + 4;
    nth_element (aVec.begin(), nth, aVec.end());

    cout << "fifth largest is " << *nth << endl;
}
```

Binary search

The standard library provides a number of different variations on binary search algorithms. All will perform only approximately `log n` comparisons, where n is the number of elements in the range described by the arguments. The algorithms work best with random access iterators, such as those generated by *vectors* or deques, when they will also perform approximately `log n` operations in total. However, they will also work with non-random access iterators, such as those generated by lists, in which case they will perform a linear number of steps. Although legal, it is not necessary to perform a binary search on a *set* or *multiset* data structure, since those container classes provide their own search methods, which are more efficient.

The generic algorithm `binary_search()` returns `true` if the sequence contains a value that is equivalent to the argument. Recall that to be equivalent means that both `Compare(value, arg)` and `Compare(arg, value)` are false. The algorithm is defined as follows:

```
bool binary_search (ForwardIterator first, ForwardIterator last,
    const T & value [, Compare ] );
```

In other situations it is important to know the position of the matching value. This information is returned by a collection of algorithms, defined as follows:

```
ForwardIterator lower_bound (ForwardIterator first,
    ForwardIterator last, const T& value [ , Compare ] );
```

```
ForwardIterator upper_bound (ForwardIterator first,
    ForwardIterator last, const T& value [, Compare ] );
```

```
pair<ForwardIterator, ForwardIterator> equal_range
    (ForwardIterator first, ForwardIterator last,
        const T& value [, Compare ] );
```

The algorithm `lower_bound()` returns, as an iterator, the first position into which the argument could be inserted without violating the ordering, whereas the algorithm `upper_bound()` finds the last such position. These will match only when the element is not currently found in the sequence. Both can be executed together in the algorithm `equal_range()`, which returns a pair of iterators.

Our example program shows these functions being used with a *vector* of random integers.

```
void binary_search_example ()
    // illustrate the use of the binary search algorithm
{
    // make an ordered vector of 15 random integers
    vector<int> aVec(15);
    generate (aVec.begin(), aVec.end(), randomValue);
    sort (aVec.begin(), aVec.end());

    // see if it contains an eleven
    if (binary_search (aVec.begin(), aVec.end(), 11))
        cout << "contains an 11" << endl;
    else
        cout << "does not contain an 11" << endl;

    // insert an 11 and a 14
    vector<int>::iterator where;
    where = lower_bound (aVec.begin(), aVec.end(), 11);
    aVec.insert (where, 11);

    where = upper_bound (aVec.begin(), aVec.end(), 14);
    aVec.insert (where, 14);
}
```

Merge ordered sequences

The algorithm merge() combines two ordered sequences to form a new ordered sequence. The size of the result is the sum of the sizes of the two argument sequences. This should be contrasted with the set_union() operation, which eliminates elements that are duplicated in both sets. The set_union() function will be described later in this section.

The merge operation is stable. This means, for equal elements in the two ranges, not only is the relative ordering of values from each range preserved, but the values from the first range always precede the elements from the second. The two ranges are described by a pair of iterators, whereas the result is defined by a single output iterator. The arguments are defined as follows:

```
OutputIterator merge (InputIterator first1, InputIterator last1,
   InputIterator first2, InputIterator last2,
   OutputIterator result [, Compare ]);
```

The example program illustrates a simple merge, the use of a merge with an inserter, and the use of a merge with an output stream iterator.

```
void merge_example ()
  // illustrate the use of the merge algorithm
{
    // make a list and vector of 10 random integers
  vector<int> aVec(10);
  list<int> aList(10, 0);
  generate (aVec.begin(), aVec.end(), randomValue);
  sort (aVec.begin(), aVec.end());
  generate_n (aList.begin(), 10, randomValue);
  aList.sort();

    // merge into a vector
  vector<int> vResult (aVec.size() + aList.size());
  merge (aVec.begin(), aVec.end(), aList.begin(), aList.end(),
    vResult.begin());

    // merge into a list
  list<int> lResult;
  merge (aVec.begin(), aVec.end(), aList.begin(), aList.end(),
    inserter(lResult, lResult.begin()));

    // merge into the output
  merge (aVec.begin(), aVec.end(), aList.begin(), aList.end(),
    ostream_iterator<int> (cout, " "));
  cout << endl;
}
```

The algorithm inplace_merge() (Merge two adjacent sequences into one) can be used to merge two sections of a single sequence into one sequence.

Set operations

The operations of *set* union, *set* intersection, and *set* difference were all described when we discussed the *set* container class. However, the algorithms that implement these operations are generic, and applicable to any ordered data structure. The algorithms assume the input ranges are ordered collections that represent multisets; that is, elements can be repeated. However, if the inputs represent sets, then the result will always be a *set*. That is, unlike the merge() algorithm, none of the *set* algorithms will produce repeated elements in the output that were not present in the input sets.

The *set* operations all have the same format. The two input sets are specified by pairs of input iterators. The output *set* is specified by an input iterator, and the end of this range is returned as the result value. An optional comparison operator is the final argument. In all cases it is required that the output sequence not overlap in any manner with either of the input sequences.

```
OutputIterator set_union (InputIterator first1, InputIterator last1,
    InputIterator first2, InputIterator last2,
    OutputIterator result [, Compare ] );
```

The example program illustrates the use of the four *set* algorithms as well as a call on merge() in order to contrast the merge and the *set* union operations. The algorithm includes() is slightly different. Again the two input sets are specified by pairs of input iterators, and the comparison operator is an optional fifth argument. The return value for the algorithm is true if the first *set* is entirely included in the second, and false otherwise.

```
void set_example ()
    // illustrate the use of the generic set algorithms
{
    ostream_iterator<int> intOut (cout, " ");

        // make a couple of ordered lists
    list<int> listOne, listTwo;
    generate_n (inserter(listOne, listOne.begin()), 5, iotaGen(1));
    generate_n (inserter(listTwo, listTwo.begin()), 5, iotaGen(3));

        // now do the set operations
        // union - 1 2 3 4 5 6 7
    set_union (listOne.begin(), listOne.end(),
        listTwo.begin(), listTwo.end(), intOut), cout << endl;
        // merge - 1 2 3 3 4 4 5 5 6 7
    merge (listOne.begin(), listOne.end(),
        listTwo.begin(), listTwo.end(), intOut), cout << endl;
        // intersection - 3 4 5
    set_intersection (listOne.begin(), listOne.end(),
        listTwo.begin(), listTwo.end(), intOut), cout << endl;
        // difference - 1 2
    set_difference (listOne.begin(), listOne.end(),
        listTwo.begin(), listTwo.end(), intOut), cout << endl;
        // symmetric difference - 1 2 6 7
    set_symmetric_difference (listOne.begin(), listOne.end(),
        listTwo.begin(), listTwo.end(), intOut), cout << endl;
```

```
if (includes (listOne.begin(), listOne.end(),
    listTwo.begin(), listTwo.end()))
        cout << "set is subset" << endl;
    else
        cout << "set is not subset" << endl;
}
```

Heap operations

A *heap* is a binary tree in which every node is larger than the values associated with either child. A heap (and, for that matter, a binary tree) can be very efficiently stored in a *vector*, by placing the children of node i in positions 2 * i + 1 and 2 * i + 2.

Using this encoding, the largest value in the heap will always be located in the initial position, and can therefore be very efficiently retrieved. In addition, efficient (logarithmic) algorithms exist that both permit a new element to be added to a heap and the largest element removed from a heap. For these reasons, a heap is a natural representation for the *priority queue* data type, described in "The priority queue data abstraction" in Chapter 28. The default operator is the less-than operator (operator <) appropriate to the element type. If desired, an alternative operator can be specified. For example, by using the greater-than operator (operator >), one can construct a heap that will locate the smallest element in the first location, instead of the largest.

Note   **Heaps and ordered collections:** Note that an ordered collection is a heap, but a heap need not necessarily be an ordered collection. In fact, a heap can be constructed in a sequence much more quickly than the sequence can be sorted.

The algorithm make_heap() takes a range, specified by random access iterators, and converts it into a heap. The number of steps required is a linear function of the number of elements in the range.

```
void make_heap (RandomAccessIterator first,
    RandomAccessIterator last [, Compare ]);
```

A new element is added to a heap by inserting it at the end of a range (using the push_back() member function of a *vector* or *deque*, for example), followed by an invocation of the algorithm push_heap(). The push_heap() algorithm restores the heap property, performing at most a logarithmic number of operations.

```
void push_heap (RandomAccessIterator first,
    RandomAccessIterator last [, Compare ]);
```

The algorithm pop_heap() swaps the first and final elements in a range, then restores to a heap the collection without the final element. The largest value of the original collection is therefore still available as the last element in the range (accessible, for example, using the back() member function in a *vector*, and removable using the pop_back() member function), while the remainder of the collection continues to have the heap property. The pop_heap() algorithm performs at most a logarithmic number of operations.

```
void pop_heap (RandomAccessIterator first,
    RandomAccessIterator last [, Compare ]);
```

Finally, the algorithm `sort_heap()` converts a heap into a ordered (sorted) collection. Note that a sorted collection is still a heap, although the reverse is not the case. The sort is performed using approximately `n log n` operations, where `n` represents the number of elements in the range. The `sort_heap()` algorithm is not stable.

```
void sort_heap (RandomAccessIterator first,
    RandomAccessIterator last [, Compare ]);
```

Here is an example program that illustrates the use of these functions.

```
void heap_example ()
  // illustrate the use of the heap algorithms
{
    // make a heap of 15 random integers
  vector<int> aVec(15);
  generate (aVec.begin(), aVec.end(), randomValue);
  make_heap (aVec.begin(), aVec.end());
  cout << "Largest value " << aVec.front() << endl;

    // remove largest and reheap
  pop_heap (aVec.begin(), aVec.end());
  aVec.pop_back();

    // add a 97 to the heap
  aVec.push_back (97);
  push_heap (aVec.begin(), aVec.end());

    // finally, make into a sorted collection
  sort_heap (aVec.begin(), aVec.end());
}
```

31

Exception handling

The Standard C++ Library provides a *set* of classes for reporting errors. These classes use the exception handling facility of the language. The library implements a particular error model, which divides errors in two broad categories: logic errors and runtime errors.

Logic errors are errors that are due to problems in the internal logic of the program. They are generally preventable.

Runtime errors, on the other hand, are generally not preventable, or at least not predictable. These are errors that are generated by circumstances outside the control of the program, such as peripheral hardware faults.

The standard exception hierarchy

The library implements the two-category error model described above with a *set* of classes. These classes are defined in the stdexcept header file. They can be used to catch exceptions thrown by the library and to throw exceptions from your own code.

The classes are related through inheritance. The inheritance hierarchy looks like this:

exception

   logic_error

      domain_error

      invalid_argument

      length_error

      out_of_range

   runtime_error

      range_error

      overflow_error

Classes *logic_error* and *runtime_error* inherit from class *exception*. All other exception classes inherit from either *logic_error* or *runtime_error*.

Using exceptions

All exceptions that are thrown explicitly by any element of the library are guaranteed to be part of the standard exception hierarchy. Review the reference for these classes to determine which functions throw which exceptions. You can then choose to catch particular exceptions, or catch any that might be thrown (by specifying the base class exception).

For instance, if you are going to call the `insert` function on *string* with a position value that could at some point be invalid, then you should use code like this:

```
string s;
int n;
...
try
{
s.insert(n,"Howdy");
}
catch (const exception& e)
{
    // deal with the exception
}
```

To throw your own exceptions, simply construct an exception of an appropriate type, assign it an appropriate message, and throw it. For example:

```
...
if (n > max)
    throw out_of_range("Your past the end, bud");
```

Theclass *exception* serves as the base class for all other exception classes. As such it defines a standard interface. This interface includes the `what()` member function, which returns a null-terminated string that represents the message that was thrown with the exception. This function is likely to be most useful in a catch clause, as demonstrated in the example program at the end of this section.

The class *exception* does not contain a constructor that takes a message string, although it can be thrown without a message. Calling `what()` on an exception object will return a default message. All classes derived from *exception* *do* provide a constructor that allows you to specify a particular message.

To throw a base exception you would use the following code:

```
throw exception;
```

This is generally not very useful, since whatever catches this exception will have no idea what kind of error has occurred. Instead of a base exception, you will usually throw a derived class such as *logic_error* or one of its derivations (such as *out_of_range* as shown in the example above). Better still, you can extend the hierarchy by deriving your own classes. This allows you to provide error reporting specific to your particular problem. For instance:

```
class bad_packet_error : public runtime_error
{
  public:
    bad_packet_error(const string& what);
};

if (bad_packet())
  throw bad_packet_error("Packet size incorrect");
```

This demonstrates how the Standard C++ exception classes provide you with a basic error model. From this foundation you can build the right error detection and reporting methods required for your particular application.

Example program: exception handling

Note   **Obtaining the sample program:** This program can be found in the file EXCEPTN.CPP in your code distribution.

This following example program demonstrates the use of exceptions.

```
#include <stdexcept>
#include <string>

static void f() { throw runtime_error("a runtime error"); }

int main ()
{
 string s;

 // First we'll try to incite then catch an exception from
 // the standard library string class.
 // We'll try to replace at a position that is non-existent.
 //
 // By wrapping the body of main in a try-catch block we can be
 // assured that we'll catch all exceptions in the exception
 // hierarchy. You can simply catch exception as is done below,
 // or you can catch each of the exceptions in which you have an
 // interest.
 try
 {
  s.replace(100,1,1,'c');
 }
 catch (const exception& e)
 {
  cout << "Got an exception: " << e.what() << endl;
 }

 // Now we'll throw our own exception using the function
 // defined above.
 try
 {
```

```
  f();
}
catch (const exception& e)
{
  cout << "Got an exception: " << e.what() << endl;
}

return 0;
}
```

32

auto_ptr

The *auto_ptr* class wraps any pointer obtained through new and provides automatic deletion of that pointer. The pointer wrapped by an *auto_ptr* object is deleted when the *auto_ptr* itself is destroyed.

Creating and using auto pointers

Include the utility header file to access the *auto_ptr* class.

You attach an *auto_ptr* object to a pointer either by using one of the constructors for *auto_ptr*, by assigning one *auto_ptr* object to another, or by using the reset member function. Only one *auto_ptr* "owns" a particular pointer at any one time, except for the NULL pointer (which all *auto_ptr*s own by default). Any use of *auto_ptr*'s copy constructor or assignment operator transfers ownership from one *auto_ptr* object to another. For instance, suppose we create *auto_ptr* a like this:

```
auto_ptr<string> a(new string);
```

The *auto_ptr* object a now "owns" the newly created pointer. When a is destroyed (such as when it goes out of scope) the pointer will be deleted. But, if we assign a to b, using the assignment operator:

```
auto_ptr<string> b = a;
```

b now owns the pointer. Use of the assignment operator causes a to release ownership of the pointer. Now if a goes out of scope the pointer will not be affected. However, the pointer *will* be deleted when b goes out of scope.

The use of new within the constructor for a may seem a little odd. Normally we avoid constructs like this since it puts the responsibility for deletion on a different entity than the one responsible for allocation. But in this case, the *auto_ptr*'s sole responsibility is to manage the deletion. This syntax is actually preferable since it prevents us from accidentally deleting the pointer ourselves.

Use operator*, operator->, or the member function get() to access the pointer held by an *auto_ptr*. For instance, we can use any of the three following statements to assign "What's up Doc" to the string now pointed to by the *auto_ptr* b.

```
*b = "What's up Doc";
*(b.get()) = "What's up Doc";
b->assign("What's up Doc");
```

auto_ptr also provides a release member function that releases ownership of a pointer. Any *auto_ptr* that does not own a specific pointer is assumed to point to the NULL pointer, so calling release on an *auto_ptr* will set it to the NULL pointer. In the example above, when a is assigned to b, the pointer held by a is released and a is set to the NULL pointer.

Example program: auto_ptr

This program illustrates the use of *auto_ptr* to ensure that pointers held in a *vector* are deleted when they are removed. Often, we might want to hold pointers to strings, since the strings themselves may be quite large and we'll be copying them when we put them into the *vector*. Particularly in contrast to a string, an *auto_ptr* is quite small: hardly bigger than a pointer.

Note   **Obtaining the sample program:** You can find this program in the file AUTOPTR.CPP in the tutorial distribution.

```
#include <vector>
#include <utility>
#include <string>

int main()
{
 {
  // First the wrong way
  vector<string*> v;
  v.insert(v.begin(), new string("Florence"));
  v.insert(v.begin(), new string("Milan"));
  v.insert(v.begin(), new string("Venice"));

  // Now remove the first element

  v.erase(v.begin());

  // Whoops, memory leak
  // string("Venice") was removed, but not deleted
  // We were supposed to handle that ourselves
 }
 {
  // Now the right way
  vector<auto_ptr<string> > v;
  v.insert(v.begin(),
       auto_ptr<string>(new string("Florence")));
  v.insert(v.begin(), auto_ptr<string>(new string("Milan")));
```

```
        v.insert(v.begin(), auto_ptr<string>(new string("Venice")));

        // Everything is fine since auto_ptrs transfer ownership of
        // their pointers when copied

        // Now remove the first element
        v.erase(v.begin());
        // Success
        // When auto_ptr(string("Venice")) is erased (and destroyed)
        // string("Venice") is deleted
    }

    return 0;
}
```

33

Complex

The class complex is a template class, used to create objects for representing and manipulating complex numbers. The operations defined on complex numbers allow them to be freely intermixed with the other numeric types available in the C++ language, thereby permitting numeric software to be easily and naturally expressed.

Creating and using complex numbers

In the following sections we will describe the operations used to create and manipulate complex numbers.

Header files

Programs that use complex numbers must include the complex header file.

```
# include <complex>
```

Declaring complex numbers

The template argument is used to define the types associated with the real and imaginary fields. This argument must be one of the floating point number data types available in the C++ language, either float, double, or long double.

There are several constructors associated with the class. A constructor with no arguments initializes both the real and imaginary fields to zero. A constructor with a single argument initializes the real field to the given value, and the imaginary value to zero. A constructor with two arguments initializes both real and imaginary fields. Finally, a copy constructor can be used to initialize a complex number with values derived from another complex number.

```
complex<double> com_one;   // value 0 + 0i
complex<double> com_two(3.14);   // value 3.14 + 0i
complex<double> com_three(1.5, 3.14)   // value 1.5 + 3.14i
complex<double> com_four(com_two);   // value is also 3.14 + 0i
```

A complex number can be assigned the value of another complex number. Since the one-argument constructor is also used for a conversion operator, a complex number can also be assigned the value of a real number. The real field is changed to the right hand side, while the imaginary field is set to zero.

```
com_one = com_three;   // becomes 1.5 + 3.14i
com_three = 2.17;   // becomes 2.17 + 0i
```

The function `polar()` can be used to construct a complex number with the given magnitude and phase angle.

```
com_four = polar(5.6, 1.8);
```

The conjugate of a complex number is formed using the function `conj()`. If a complex number represents $x + yi$, then the conjugate is the value $y + xi$.

```
complex<double> com_five = conj(com_four);
```

Accessing complex number values

The member functions `real()` and `imag()` return the real and imaginary fields of a complex number, respectively. These functions can also be invoked as ordinary functions with complex number arguments.

Note   **Functions and member functions:** With the exception of the member functions `real()` and `imag()`, most operations on complex numbers are performed using ordinary functions, not member functions.

```
// the following should be the same
cout << com_one.real() << "+" << com_one.imag() << "i" << endl;
cout << real(com_one) << "+" << imag(com_one) << "i" << endl;
```

Arithmetic operations

The arithmetic operators +, -, *, and / can be used to perform addition, subtraction, multiplication, and division of complex numbers. All four work either with two complex numbers, or with a complex number and a real value. Assignment operators are also defined for all four.

```
cout << com_one + com_two << endl;
cout << com_one - 3.14 << endl;
cout << 2.75 * com_two << endl;
com_one += com_three / 2.0;
```

The unary operators + and – can also be applied to complex numbers.

Comparing complex values

Two complex numbers can be compared for equality or inequality, using the operators == and !=. Two values are equal if their corresponding fields are equal. Complex numbers are not well-ordered, and thus cannot be compared using any other relational operator.

Stream input and output

Complex numbers can be written to an output stream, or read from an input stream, using the normal stream I/O conventions. A value is written in parenthesis, either as (u) or (u,v), depending upon whether or not the imaginary value is zero. A value is read as a parenthesis surrounding two numeric values.

Norm and absolute value

The function norm() returns the norm of the complex number. This is the sum of the squares of the real and imaginary parts. The function abs() returns the absolute value, which is the square root of the norm. Note that both are ordinary functions that take the complex value as an argument, not member functions.

```
cout << norm(com_two) << endl;
cout << abs(com_two) << endl;
```

The directed phase angle of a complex number is yielded by the function arg().

```
cout << com_four << " in polar coordinates is "
  << arg(com_four) << " and " << norm(com_four) << endl;
```

Trigonometric functions

The trigonometric functions defined for floating point values (namely, sin(), cos(), tan(), asin(), acos(), atan(), sinh(), cosh(), and tanh()), have all been extended to complex number arguments. Each takes a single complex number as argument and returns a complex number as result. The function atan2() takes two complex number arguments, or a complex number and a real value (in either order), and returns a complex number result.

Transcendental functions

The transcendental functions exp(), log(), log10(), and sqrt() have been extended to complex arguments. Each takes a single complex number as argument, and returns a complex number as result.

The standard library defines several variations of the exponential function pow(). Versions exist to raise a complex number to an integer power, to raise a complex number to a complex power or to a real power, or to raise a real value to a complex power.

Example program: roots of a polynomial

Note **Obtaining the sample program:** This program is found in the file COMPLX.CPP in the distribution.

The roots of a polynomial a x2 + b x + c = 0 are given by the formula:

```
x = (-b ± sqrt(b2 - 4ac))/2a
```

The following program takes as input three double precision numbers, and returns the complex roots as a pair of values.

```
typedef complex<double> dcomplex;

pair<dcomplex, dcomplex> quadratic
      (dcomplex a, dcomplex b, dcomplex c)
        // return the roots of a quadratic equation
{
  dcomplex root = sqrt(b * b - 4.0 * a * c);
  a *= 2.0;
  return make_pair(
    (-b + root)/a,
    (-b - root)/a);
}
```

34

string

The string abstraction

A *string* is basically an indexable sequence of characters. In fact, although a string is not declared as a subclass of *vector*, almost all of the *vector* operators discussed in *vector* operations can be applied to string values. However, a string is also a much more abstract quantity, and, in addition to simple *vector* operators, the string datatype provides a number of useful and powerful high level operations.

In the standard library, a string is actually a template class, named `basic_string`. The template argument represents the type of character that will be held by the string container. By defining strings in this fashion, the standard library not only provides facilities for manipulating sequences of normal 8-bit ASCII characters, but also for manipulating other types of character-like sequences, such as 16-bit wide characters. The data types string and `wstring` (for wide string) are simply typedefs of `basic_string`, defined as follows:

```
typedef basic_string<char,strint_char_traits<char> > string;
typedef basic_string<wchar_t> wstring;
```

Note **Strings and wide strings:** In the remainder of this section we will refer to the string data type, however all the operations we will introduce are equally applicable to wide strings.

As we have already noted, a string is similar in many ways to a *vector* of characters. Like the *vector* data type, there are two sizes associated with a string. The first represents the number of characters currently being stored in the string. The second is the *capacity*, the maximum number of characters that can potentially be stored into a string without reallocation of a new internal buffer. As it is in the *vector* data type, the capacity of a string is a dynamic quantity. When string operations cause the number of characters being stored in a string value to exceed the capacity of the string, a new internal buffer is allocated and initialized with the string values, and the capacity of the string is increased. All this occurs behind the scenes, requiring no interaction with the programmer.

String include files

Programs that use strings must include the `string` header file:

```
# include <string>
```

String operations

In the following sections, we'll examine the standard library operations used to create and manipulate strings.

Declaring string variables

The simplest form of declaration for a string simply names a new variable, or names a variable along with the initial value for the string. This form was used extensively in the example graph program in Example program: graphs. A copy constructor also permits a string to be declared that takes its value from a previously defined string.

```
string s1;
string s2 ("a string");
string s3 = "initial value";
string s4 (s3);
```

In these simple cases the capacity is initially exactly the same as the number of characters being stored. Alternative constructors let you explicitly set the initial capacity. Yet another form allows you to set the capacity and initialize the string with repeated copies of a single character value.

```
string s6 ("small value", 100);   // holds 11 values, can hold 100
string s7 (10, '\n');   // holds ten newline characters
```

Note **Initializing from iterators:** Remember, the ability to initialize a container using a pair of iterators requires the ability to declare a template member function using template arguments independent of those used to declare the container. At present not all compilers support this feature.

Finally, like all the container classes in the standard library, a string can be initialized using a pair of iterators. The sequence being denoted by the iterators must have the appropriate type of elements.

```
string s8 (aList.begin(), aList.end());
```

Resetting size and capacity

As with the *vector* data type, the current size of a string is yielded by the `size()` member function, while the current capacity is returned by `capacity()`. The latter can be changed by a call on the `reserve()` member function, which (if necessary) adjusts the capacity so that the string can hold at least as many elements as specified by the argument. The member function `max_size()` returns the maximum string size that can be allocated. Usually this value is limited only by the amount of available memory.

```
cout << s6.size() << endl;
```

```
cout << s6.capacity() << endl;
s6.reserve(200);   // change capacity to 200
cout << s6.capacity() << endl;
cout << s6.max_size() << endl;
```

The member function `length()` is simply a synonym for `size()`. The member function `resize()` changes the size of a string, either truncating characters from the end or inserting new characters. The optional second argument for `resize()` can be used to specify the character inserted into the newly created character positions.

```
s7.resize(15, '\t');   // add tab characters at end
cout << s7.length() << endl;   // size should now be 15
```

The member function `empty()` returns `true` if the string contains no characters, and is generally faster than testing the length against a zero constant.

```
if (s7.empty())
   cout << "string is empty" << endl;
```

Assignment, append, and swap

A string variable can be assigned the value of either another string, a literal C-style character array, or an individual character.

```
s1 = s2;
s2 = "a new value";
s3 = 'x';
```

The operator `+=` can also be used with any of these three forms of argument, and specifies that the value on the right hand side should be *appended* to the end of the current string value.

```
s3 += "yz";   // s3 is now xyz
```

The more general `assign()` and `append()` member functions let you specify a subset of the right hand side to be assigned to or appended to the receiver. A single integer argument n indicates that only the first n characters should be assigned/appended, while two arguments, `pos` and `n`, indicate that the n values following position `pos` should be used.

```
s4.assign (s2, 3);   // assign first three characters
s4.append (s5, 2, 3);   // append characters 2, 3 and 4
```

The addition operator `+` is used to form the catenation of two strings. The `+` operator creates a copy of the left argument, then appends the right argument to this value.

```
cout << (s2 + s3) << endl;   // output catenation of s2 and s3
```

As with all the containers in the standard library, the contents of two strings can be exchanged using the `swap()` member function.

```
s5.swap (s4);   // exchange s4 and s5
```

Character access

An individual character from a string can be accessed or assigned using the subscript operator. The member function `at()` is a synonym for this operation.

```
cout << s4[2] << endl;  // output position 2 of s4
s4[2] = 'x';  // change position 2
cout << s4.at(2) << endl;  // output updated value
```

The member function `c_str()` returns a pointer to a null terminated character array, whose elements are the same as those contained in the string. This lets you use strings with functions that require a pointer to a conventional C-style character array. The resulting pointer is declared as constant, which means that you cannot use `c_str()` to modify the string. In addition, the value returned by `c_str()` might not be valid after any operation that may cause reallocation (such as `append()` or `insert()`). The member function `data()` returns a pointer to the underlying character buffer.

```
char d[256];
strcpy(d, s4.c_str());  // copy s4 into array d
```

Iterators

The member functions `begin()` and `end()` return beginning and ending random-access iterators for the string. The values denoted by the iterators will be individual string elements. The functions `rbegin()` and `rend()` return backwards iterators.

Note   **Invalidating iterators:** Note that the contents of an iterator are not guaranteed to be valid after any operation that might force a reallocation of the internal string buffer, such as an append or an insertion.

Insertion, removal, and replacement

The string member functions `insert()` and `remove()` are similar to the *vector* functions `insert()` and `erase()`. Like the *vector* versions, they can take iterators as arguments, and specify the insertion or removal of the ranges specified by the arguments. The function `replace()` is a combination of remove and insert, in effect replacing the specified range with new values.

```
s2.insert(s2.begin()+2, aList.begin(), aList.end());
s2.remove(s2.begin()+3, s2.begin()+5);
s2.replace(s2.begin()+3, s2.begin()+6, s3.begin(), s3.end());
```

In addition, the functions also have non-iterator implementations. The `insert()` member function takes as argument a position and a string, and inserts the string into the given position. The `remove` function takes two integer arguments, a position and a length, and removes the characters specified. And the `replace` function takes two similar integer arguments as well as a string and an optional length, and replaces the indicated range with the string (or an initial portion of a string, if the length has been explicitly specified).

```
s3.insert (3, "abc");  //insert abc after position 3
s3.remove (4, 2);  // remove positions 4 and 5
s3.replace (4, 2, "pqr");  //replace positions 4 and 5 with pqr
```

Copy and substring

The member function `copy()` generates a substring of the receiver, then assigns this substring to the target given as the first argument. The range of values for the substring is specified either by an initial position, or a position and a length.

```
s3.copy (s4, 2);     // assign to s4 positions 2 to end of s3
s5.copy (s4, 2, 3);  // assign to s4 positions 2 to 4 of s5
```

The member function `substr()` returns a string that represents a portion of the current string. The range is specified by either an initial position, or a position and a length.

```
cout << s4.substr(3) << endl;     // output 3 to end
cout << s4.substr(3, 2) << endl;  // output positions 3 and 4
```

String comparisons

Note **Comparing strings:** Although the function is accessible, users will seldom invoke the member function `compare()` directly. Instead, comparisons of strings are usually performed using the conventional comparison operators, which in turn make use of the function `compare()`.

The member function `compare()` is used to perform a lexical comparison between the receiver and an argument string. Optional arguments permit the specification of a different starting position or a starting position and length of the argument string. See Lexical comparison for a description of lexical ordering. The function returns a negative value if the receiver is lexicographically smaller than the argument, a zero value if they are equal and a positive value if the receiver is larger than the argument.

The relational and equality operators (<, <=, ==, !=, >=, and >) are all defined using the comparison member function. Comparisons can be made either between two strings, or between strings and ordinary C-style character literals.

Searching operations

The member function `find()` determines the first occurrence of the argument string in the current string. An optional integer argument lets you specify the starting position for the search. (Remember that string index positions begin at zero.) If the function can locate such a match, it returns the starting index of the match in the current string. Otherwise, it returns a value out of the range of the set of legal subscripts for the string. The function `rfind()` is similar, but scans the string from the end, moving backwards.

```
s1 = "mississippi";
cout << s1.find("ss") << endl;     // returns 2
cout << s1.find("ss", 3) << endl;  // returns 5
cout << s1.rfind("ss") << endl;    // returns 5
cout << s1.rfind("ss", 4) << endl; // returns 2
```

The functions `find_first_of()`, `find_last_of()`, `find_first_not_of()`, and `find_last_not_of()` treat the argument string as a *set* of characters. As with many of the other functions, one or two optional integer arguments can be used to specify a subset of the current string. These functions find the first (or last) character that is either present (or absent) from the argument *set*. The position of the given character, if located, is returned. If no such character exists then a value out of the range of any legal subscript is returned.

```
i = s2.find_first_of ("aeiou");   // find first vowel
j = s2.find_first_not_of ("aeiou", i);  // next non-vowel
```

Example function: split a line into words

Note **Obtaining the sample program:** The split function can be found in the concordance program in file CONCORD.CPP.

In this section we will illustrate the use of some of the string functions by defining a function to split a line of text into individual words. We have already made use of this function in the concordance example program in Example program: a concordance.

There are three arguments to the function. The first two are strings, describing the line of text and the separators to be used to differentiate words, respectively. The third argument is a list of strings, used to return the individual words in the line.

```
void split
    (string & text, string & separators, list<string> & words)
{
    int n = text.length();
    int start, stop;

    start = text.find_first_not_of(separators);
    while ((start >= 0) && (start < n)) {
        stop = text.find_first_of(separators, start);
        if ((stop < 0) || (stop > n)) stop = n;
        words.push_back(text.substr(start, stop - start));
        start = text.find_first_not_of(separators, stop+1);
    }
}
```

The program begins by finding the first character that is not a separator. The loop then looks for the next following character that is a separator, or uses the end of the string if no such value is found. The difference between these two is then a word, and is copied out of the text using a substring operation and inserted into the list of words. A search is then made to discover the start of the next word, and the loop continues. When the index value exceeds the limits of the string, execution stops.

35

Numeric limits

Numeric limits overview

A new feature of the C++ Standard Library is an organized mechanism for describing the characteristics of the fundamental types provided in the execution environment. In older C and C++ libraries, these characteristics were often described by large collections of symbolic constants. For example, the smallest representable value that could be maintained in a character would be found in the constant named CHAR_MIN, while the similar constant for a short would be known as SHRT_MIN, for a float FLT_MIN, and so on.

Note **Two mechanisms, one purpose:** For reasons of compatibility, the numeric_limits mechanism is used as an addition to the symbolic constants used in older C++ libraries, rather than a strict replacement. Thus both mechanisms will, for the present, exist in parallel. However, as the numeric_limits technique is more uniform and extensible, it should be expected that over time the older symbolic constants will become outmoded.

The template class numeric_limits provides a new and uniform way of representing this information for all numeric types. Instead of using a different symbolic name for each new data type, the class defines a single static function, named min(), which returns the appropriate values. Specializations of this class then provide the exact value for each supported type. The smallest character value is in this fashion yielded as the result of invoking the function numeric_limits<char>::min(), while the smallest floating point value is found by invoking numeric_limits<float>::min(), and so on.

Solving this problem by using a template class not only greatly reduces the number of symbolic names that need to be defined to describe the operating environment, but it also ensures consistency between the descriptions of the various types.

Fundamental data types

The standard library describes a specific type by providing a specialized implementation of the numeric_limits class for the type. Static functions and static constant data members then provide information specific to the type. The standard library includes descriptions of the following fundamental data types.

bool	char	int	float
	signed char	short	double
	unsigned char	long	long double
	wchar_t	unsigned short	
		unsigned int	
		unsigned long	

Certain implementations may also provide information on other data types. Whether or not an implementation is described can be discovered using the static data member field is_specialized. For example, the following is legal, and will indicate that the string data type is not described by this mechanism.

```
cout << "are strings described " <<
    numeric_limits<string>::is_specialized << endl;
```

For data types that do not have a specialization, the values yielded by the functions and data fields in numeric_limits are generally zero or false.

Numeric limit members

Since a number of the fields in the numeric_limits structure are meaningful only for floating point values, it is useful to separate the description of the members into common fields and floating-point specific fields.

Members common to all types

The following table summarizes the information available through the numeric_limits static member data fields and functions.

Type	Name	Meaning
bool	is_specialized	True if a specialization exists, false otherwise
T	min()	Smallest finite value
T	max()	Largest finite value
int	radix	The base of the representation
int	digits	Number of radix digits that can be represented without change
int	digits10	Number of base-10 digits that can be represented without change
bool	is_signed	True if the type is signed
bool	is_integer	True if the type is integer
bool	is_exact	True if the representation is exact
bool	is_bounded	True if representation is finite
bool	is_modulo	True if type is modulo
bool	traps	True if trapping is implemented for the type

Radix represents the internal base for the representation. For example, most machines use a base 2 radix for integer data values, however some may also support a representation, such as BCD, that uses a different base. The `digits` field then represents the number of such radix values that can be held in a value. For an integer type, this would be the number of non-sign bits in the representation.

All fundamental types are bounded. However, an implementation might choose to include, for example, an infinite precision integer package that would not be bounded.

A type is *modulo* if the value resulting from the addition of two values can wrap around, that is, be smaller than either argument. The fundamental unsigned integer types are all modulo.

Members specific to floating point values

The following members are either specific to floating point values, or have a meaning slightly different for floating point values than the one described earlier for non-floating data types.

Type	Name	Meaning
T	min()	The minimum positive normalized value
int	digits	The number of digits in the mantissa
int	radix	The base (or radix) of the exponent representation
T	epsilon()	The difference between 1 and the least representable value greater than 1
T	round_error()	A measurement of the rounding error
int	min_exponent	Minimum negative exponent
int	min_exponent10	Minimum value such that 10 raised to that power is in range
int	max_exponent	Maximum positive exponent
int	max_exponent10	Maximum value such that 10 raised to that power is in range
bool	has_infinity	True if the type has a representation of positive infinity
T	infinity()	Representation of infinity, if available
bool	has_quiet_NaN	True if there is a representation of a quiet "Not a Number"
T	quiet_NaN()	Representation of quiet NaN, if available
bool	has_signaling_NaN	True if there is a representation for a signaling NaN
T	signaling_NaN()	Representation of signaling NaN, if available
bool	has_denorm	True if the representation allows denormalized values
T	denorm_min()	Minimum positive denormalized value
bool	is_iec559	True if representation adheres to IEC 559 standard
bool	tinyness_before	True if tinyness is detected before rounding
	round_style	Rounding style for type

For the `float` data type, the value in field `radix`, which represents the base of the exponential representation, is equivalent to the symbolic constant `FLT_RADIX`.

For the types `float`, `double`, and `long double` the value of `epsilon` is also available as `FLT_EPSILON`, `DBL_EPSILON`, and `LDBL_EPSILON`.

A NaN is a "Not a Number." It is a representable value that nevertheless does not correspond to any numeric quantity. Many numeric algorithms manipulate such values.

The IEC 559 standard is a standard approved by the International Electrotechnical Commission. It is the same as the IEEE standard 754.

Value returned by the function `round_style()` is one of the following: `round_indeterminate`, `round_toward_zero`, `round_to_nearest`, `round_toward_infinity`, or `round_toward_neg_infinity`.

ObjectComponents programmer's guide

This part describes how to create different kinds of programs using ObjectComponents, a set of classes for creating OLE 2 applications in C++.

- **Chapter 36, "Overview of ObjectComponents,"** explains what ObjectComponents is.

- **Chapter 37, "Turning an application into an OCX or OLE container,"** describes how to make a container application whose compound documents can hold linked and embedded OLE objects.

- **Chapter 38, "Turning an application into an OLE server,"** describes how to make a server application that creates data objects for containers to link or embed.

- **Chapter 39, "Turning an application into an OLE automation server,"** describes what a program must do in order to let other programs control it through automation.

- **Chapter 40, "Turning an application into an OLE automation controller,"** describes the steps a program must take in order to manipulate automation objects.

36

Overview of ObjectComponents

Microsoft's OLE 2 operating system extensions require the programmer to implement a variety of interfaces depending on the tasks an application undertakes. Borland has developed an OLE engine, already used in several of its commercial applications, that simplifies the programmer's job by implementing a smaller set of high-level interfaces on top of OLE. The engine resides in a library called BOCOLE.DLL. The BOCOLE support library provides default implementations for many standard OLE interfaces.

C++ programmers can make use of the OLE support in BOCOLE.DLL through a set of new classes collectively called the ObjectComponents Framework (OCF). Instead of implementing OLE-style interfaces, you create objects from the ObjectComponents classes and call their methods. Your own classes can gain OLE capabilities simply by inheriting from the ObjectComponents classes. ObjectComponents translates between C++ and OLE.

Figure 36.1 shows how the layers of Borland's OLE support fit together.

The ObjectComponents classes implement OLE-style interfaces for talking to the BOCOLE support library. Your programs reach OLE by calling methods from ObjectComponents classes. When OLE sends information to you, ObjectComponents sends messages to your application using the standard Windows message mechanisms. The ObjectComponents classes also contain default implementations for all the OLE messages. You can override the default event handlers selectively to modify your application's responses.

ObjectComponents is not part of the ObjectWindows Library. That means C++ programs that don't use ObjectWindows can still take full advantage of ObjectComponents for linking, embedding, and automation. But ObjectWindows can simplify your work even more. ObjectWindows 2.5 introduces new classes such as *TOleWindow* and *TOleDocument* that inherit from ObjectComponents classes to bring OLE support into Borland's C++ application framework. An ObjectWindows application that uses the Doc/View model doesn't need to use ObjectComponents directly at all. A few simple changes to your Doc/View program will have you linking and embedding almost instantly. Programs that don't use the Doc/View model can do the same thing with just a little more work.

The chapters that follow explain step by step how to modify your code to create containers, servers, automation objects, and controllers.

Figure 36.1 How applications interact with OLE through ObjectComponents

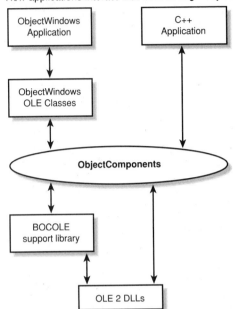

OLE 2 features supported by ObjectComponents

The following list summarizes the OLE 2 capabilities that ObjectComponents gives your applications. The descriptions assume you are using ObjectWindows, as well. All the same features are available through ObjectComponents without ObjectWindows, but then you have to code explicitly some things that ObjectWindows does by default.

- **Linking and embedding**: To embed data from one application in the document of another, ObjectComponents gives you classes to represent the data in the object and an image of the data for drawing on the screen. The data must be separable from its graphical representation because in OLE transactions they are sometimes handled by different programs. When the container asks the server for an object to embed, the server must provide data and a view of the data. The server can also be asked to edit the object even after it is embedded and to read or write the object to and from the container's document file. The ObjectComponents classes handle both sides of these negotiations for you.

- **Clipboard operations**: The default event handlers for the ObjectComponents messages handle cutting and pasting for you. If you add to your menus standard commands such as Insert Object and Paste Link, ObjectComponents will implement them for you.

- **Drag and drop operations**: The default event handlers for ObjectComponents messages help you here, too. If the user drops an OLE object on your container's window, ObjectComponents inserts it in your document. If the user double-clicks the embedded object, ObjectComponents activates it. If the user drags the object, ObjectComponents moves it.

- **Standard OLE 2 user interface**: OLE defines standard user interface features and asks OLE programmers to comply with them. Built into ObjectComponents are dialog boxes for commands like Insert Object, Paste Special, and Paste Link; a pop-up menu that appears whenever the user right-clicks an embedded object; and an item on the container's Edit menu that always shows the verbs (server commands) available for the active object. ObjectComponents even arranges to modify the container's window if the server takes over the container's tool bar, status bar, and menus for in-place editing.

- **Compound files**: A new ObjectComponents class (*TOcStorage*) encapsulates file input and output to compound files. If you convert an ObjectWindows Doc/View application into an ObjectComponents container, the document writes itself to compound files automatically, creating storages and substorages within the file as needed. (Instructions for the conversion appear in Chapter 37.)

- **EXE and DLL servers**: ObjectComponents lets you construct your OLE server as either a standalone executable program or as an in-process DLL server. DLL servers respond to clients more quickly because a DLL is not a separate process. OLE doesn't have to serialize calls or marshall parameters to communicate between a DLL server and its client. See "Creating a DLL server" in Chapter 38 for more information.

- **Automation**: ObjectComponents permits C++ classes to be automated without structural changes to the classes themselves. It accomplishes this with nested classes that have direct access to the existing class members. These nested classes instantiate small command objects that reach the members through standard C++ mechanisms, avoiding the use of restrictive, non-portable stack manipulations. The command objects support hooks for undoing, recording, and filtering automation commands. A program can even send itself automation commands using standard C++ code. Chapters 39 and 40 describe automation programming.

- **Type libraries**: A type library describes for OLE all the classes, methods, properties, and data members available for controlling an automated application. Once you create an automation server (following the steps in Chapter 39), you can ask ObjectComponents to build and register the type library for you.

- **Registration**: OLE requires applications to register themselves with the system by providing a unique identifier string. For servers, this string and much other information besides must be recorded in the system's registration database as part of the program's installation process. With ObjectComponents, all you have to do is list all the information in one place using macros. Every time your server starts up, ObjectComponents confirms that the database accurately reflects the server's status. When necessary, ObjectComponents records or updates registration entries automatically. For more about registration, see Chapter 37.

- **Localization**: OLE servers need to speak the language of their client programs. If an automation server is marketed in several countries, it needs to recognize commands sent in each different language. A linking and embedding server registers strings that describe its objects to the user, and those too should be available in multiple languages in order to accommodate whatever language the user might request. If you provide translations for your strings, ObjectComponents uses the right strings at the right time. Add your translations to the program's resources and mark the original strings as localized when you register them. At run time, ObjectComponents quickly and efficiently retrieves translations to match whatever language OLE requests. For more about localization, see Chapter 38.

How ObjectComponents works

The information in this section is not essential for using ObjectComponents, only for understanding what goes on behind the scenes when you create ObjectComponents connector objects.

The essential function of ObjectComponents is to connect you with OLE. ObjectComponents is an intermediate layer standing between OLE on one side and your C++ code on the other.

How ObjectComponents talks to OLE

Fundamentally, all OLE interaction of any sort requires the implementation of standard OLE interfaces, such as *IUnknown* and *IDispatch*, as defined by the Component Object Model (COM).

An *interface* is just a set of related function prototypes forming a pure base class. Every OLE object that implements the same interface can choose to implement the prescribed functions in its own way. All that matters is that the interface functions always accept the same parameters and always produce the same results. This makes it possible for any OLE object to call any standard function in any other OLE object that supports the interface.

Every OLE object must implement the *IUnknown* interface. One of the three functions in the *IUnknown* interface is *QueryInterface*. This common function implemented on all OLE objects lets you ask whether the object supports other interfaces that you want to use, such as automation interfaces or data transfer interfaces. This makes it possible for any OLE object to determine at run time what any other OLE object can do.

OLE defines a large number of standard interfaces that are notoriously tedious to implement. Borland's BOCOLE support library defines an alternate set of custom COM interfaces that collectively provide an alternative interface to OLE programming, one conceived at a higher level of abstraction. Client objects of the support library must still implement *IUnknown*, as all COM objects must, but instead of other standard OLE interfaces such as *IDataObject* and *IMoniker*, they implement interfaces defined by BOCOLE. The support library acts as an agent translating commands received through its custom interfaces into standard OLE. All the custom interfaces commands are carried out for you using standard OLE interfaces.

The custom interfaces in the BOCOLE support library have names like *IBContainer* and *IBDocument*. You'll see them used if you look in the ObjectComponents source code. Because the support library is an internal tool and subject to change, its interfaces are not documented. The complete library source code, however, comes with Borland C++, so you can refer to it if you need to track the OLE interactions minutely. You can also modify and rebuild the support library, just as you can the ObjectWindows Library, if that suits your purposes.

How ObjectComponents talks to you

Some of the ObjectComponents classes define COM objects. These objects derive from *TUnknown*, an ObjectComponents base class that implements the *IUnknown* interface and handles details of aggregation (a way of combining several objects into a single functional unit). They also mix in other base classes that implement interfaces from the BOCOLE support library.

The ObjectComponents objects that implement COM interfaces are called *connector objects*, because they connect your application to OLE. *TOcPart*, for example, is the connector object that implements the interfaces a container must support for each OLE object (part) that is placed in its document. To embed an object in your document, you take information ObjectComponents gets from the Clipboard, a drop message, or the Insert Object dialog box, and you pass the information to the *TOcPart* constructor. Among other things, the constructor (indirectly) calls a BOCOLE function to create an embedded OLE object. *TOcPart* holds the pointer to that object, queries it for interfaces, and stores the coordinates of the site where the part should be drawn. When you want the part to do something, you call *TOcPart* methods such as *Activate* and *Save*.

Linking and embedding connections

A linking and embedding application always creates a *TOcApp* object (usually it is created for you). *TOcApp* is a connector object that implements interfaces every linking and embedding application needs. Another connector object that all linking and embedding applications create is the view object, either *TOcView* for a container or *TOcRemView* for a server. You create one view object for each document you open. A view object is associated with the window where the document is drawn. The only other connector object used for linking and embedding is *TOcPart*, which containers create for each object deposited in their documents.

Of course communication through a connector object is not just one way. When you call methods on a connector object, the object calls through to OLE, but sometimes OLE needs to call you. For example, if when user chooses Insert Object and asks for an object from a server, OLE must invoke the server and ask it to create an object. The connector objects cannot, of course, call your functions the same way you can call theirs because they don't know anything about your code. When a connector object needs to communicate a request or a notification from OLE to you, it sends WM_OCEVENT message to one of your windows. *TOcApp* sends its messages to your frame window. The view and part objects send messages to the client window where you draw your document.

Communication from you to OLE happens through function calls to connector objects. Communication from OLE to you happens through messages from connector objects to your windows. Figure 36.2 diagrams these interactions.

Figure 36.2 How objects in your application interact with ObjectComponents

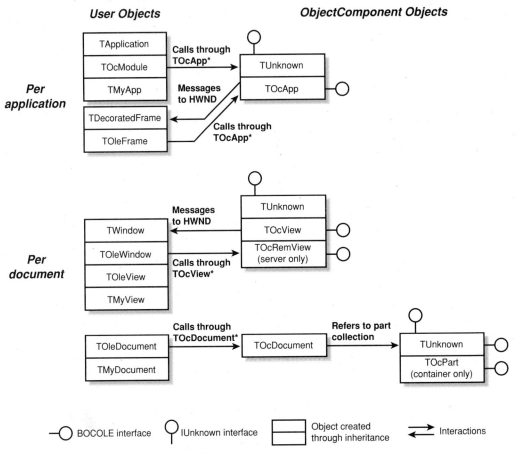

The objects on the left side are instances of the ObjectWindows classes you normally create: an application, a frame window, a document, and a view. In applications that do not use the Doc/View model or do not use ObjectWindows, different classes fulfill the same functions. You always have a frame window and a document window, for example. The flow of interaction is the same in every ObjectComponents application.

The objects on the right side are the helpers from ObjectComponents that connect corresponding parts of your application to OLE.

The initial wiring between you and ObjectComponents is established the first time the registrar object calls your factory callback function. The *TOcApp* object is bound to a window in *TOleFrame::SetupWindow*, or in the WM_CREATE handler of your main window.

Automation connections

Applications that support automation but not linking and embedding use a different set of objects. The central function of the automation layer in OLE is to pass arguments from the controller to the server, an operation with no user interface. The COM interfaces for automation are buried deeper in the implementation of ObjectComponents than the linking and embedding interfaces.

To support automation, ObjectComponents must identify exposed commands and arguments, attach type information to them, transfer values to and from the stack of VARIANT unions that OLE uses to pass values, and invoke your C++ functions when a controller sends a command. Once you set up the tables that describe what you want to expose, there is little in the automation process to customize or override. You never directly create or manipulate the connector objects for automation; ObjectComponents does it for you.

Advanced users who enjoy reading source code might like to know that *TServedObject* is the class that implements *IDispatch* and *ITypeInfo*, that *TTypeLibrary* implements *ITypeLib*, and that *TAutoIterator* implements *IEnumVARIANT*. Of these, only *TAutoIterator* is exposed as a public part of ObjectComponents. The others are considered internal implementation.

To automate a class, ObjectComponents asks you to build two descriptive tables from macros. A declaration table goes with the class declaration and declares which members are accessible to OLE. A definition table goes with the class implementation and assigns public names for controllers to use when invoking your functions. The automation macros also create nested classes within the automated parent, one for each exposed function or data member. The nested classes have an *Invoke* method that calls your function. Because the nested classes are friends of the surrounding class, they have direct access to it through normal C++ mechanisms.

TServedObject is the connector that receives *IDispatch* commands from OLE and translates them into the appropriate *Invoke* calls. *TServedObject* finds the information it needs to do this in an object of type *TAutoClass*, which holds the symbol information from the automation tables. *TServedObject* receives dispatch IDs, looks them up in *TAutoClass*, uses the information it finds to extract arguments from the stack of VARIANT unions passed by OLE. Finally it calls *Invoke* on the appropriate nested command object. Figure 36.3 diagrams the interaction of *TServedObject* with *TAutoClass* and your automated class.

Figure 36.3 How TServedObject connects an automated class to OLE

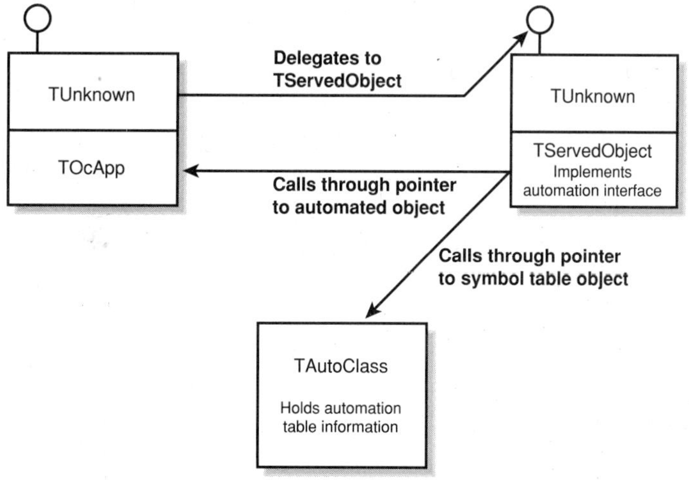

Building an ObjectComponents application

All ObjectComponents applications require exception handling and RTTI. Do not set any compiler options that disable these features.

Linking and embedding applications must use the large memory model. Automation applications can use the medium model as well (and they run faster in medium model).

The integrated development environment (IDE) sets the appropriate compiler and linker options for you automatically when you select OCF in the TargetExpert.

To build any ObjectComponents program from the command line, create a short makefile that includes the OWLOCFMK.GEN found in the EXAMPLES subdirectory. If your application does not use ObjectWindows, include the OCFMAKE.GEN instead. Here, for example, is the makefile that builds the AutoCalc sample program:

```
EXERES = MYPROGRAM
OBJEXE = winmain.obj autocalc.obj
HLP = MYPROGRAM
!include $(BCEXAMPLEDIR)\ocfmake.gen
```

EXERES and OBJRES hold the name of the file to build and the names of the object files to build it from. HLP is optional. Use it if your project includes an online Help file. Finally, your makefile should include OWLOCFMK.GEN or OCFMAKE.GEN.

Name your file MAKEFILE and type this at the command line prompt:

```
make MODEL=l
```

MAKE, using instructions in the included file, will build a new makefile tailored to your project. The new makefile is called WIN16L*xx*.MAK. The final two digits of the name tell whether the makefile uses diagnostic or debugging versions of the libraries. *01* indicates a debugging version, *10* a diagnostic version, and *11* means both kinds of information are included. The same command also then runs the new makefile and builds the program. If you change the command to define MODEL as *d*, the new makefile is WIN16D*xx*.MAK and it builds the program as a DLL.

For more information about how to use OCFMAKE.GEN and OWLOCFMK.GEN, read the instructions at the beginning of MAKEFILE.GEN, found in the same directory.

Table 18.1 shows the libraries an ObjectComponents program links with.

Table 36.1   Libraries for building ObjectComponents programs

Medium model	Large model	DLL libraries	Description
OCFWM.LIB	OCFWL.LIB	OCFWI.LIB	ObjectComponents
OWLWM.LIB	OWLWL.LIB	OWLWI.LIB	ObjectWindows
BIDSM.LIB	BIDSL.LIB	BIDSI.LIB	Class libraries
OLE2W16.LIB	OLE2W16.LIB	OLE2W16.LIB	OLE system DLLs
IMPORT.LIB	IMPORT.LIB	IMPORT.LIB	Windows system DLLs
MATHWM.LIB	MATHWL.LIB		Math support
CWM.LIB	CWL.LIB	CRTLDLL.LIB	C run-time libraries

The ObjectComponents library must be linked first, before the ObjectWindows library.

ObjectComponents Programming Tools

The most powerful tool in Borland C++ to help you with ObjectComponents programming is AppExpert. AppExpert generates a complete basic application according to your specification. It fully supports both linking and embedding and automation. Use it to create containers, servers, and automation servers. ClassExpert helps you modify the generated code to make it do what you need.

The TargetExpert in the integrated development environment (IDE) also supports ObjectComponents. Click the option for OCF and it automatically sets the right build options.

Utility programs

Borland C++ comes with some new utility programs that simplify common OLE programming chores. Some of them solve problems that other chapters explain in more detail.

AutoGen: Generates proxy classes for an automation controller. Scans the type library of an automated application and writes the source code for classes a controller uses to send commands automation commands.

DllRun: Launches a DLL server in executable mode. Any DLL server written with ObjectComponents can also run as a standalone application if you invoke it with DllRun. Running in executable mode sometimes makes it easier to debug the DLL. It also makes it possible to distribute a single program that your users can run either as an in-process server or as an independent application.

GuidGen: Generates globally unique identifiers for use in registering applications. Every server must have an absolutely unique ID. Containers need them in order to be link sources.

MacroGen: Generates automation macros for exposing functions with any number of arguments. The ObjectComponents headers declare versions of the macros for functions with up to four arguments. MacroGen saves you from having to revise the macros by hand to accommodate more arguments.

Register: Registers or unregisters any ObjectComponents EXE or DLL. Usually the applications register themselves if necessary when they run, or in response to command-line switches. Developers, however, sometimes need to register and unregister different versions of an application over and over. Register is especially useful for DLLs because you can't pass command-line switches to a DLL.

WinRun: A background program that makes it possible to launch Windows programs from the command line prompt in a DOS box. WinRun makes it possible to run GUI programs (such as Register) from a make file.

The source code for all the utilities but WINRUN is in the OCTOOLS directory.

You might find it helpful to install these tools in the integrated development environment (IDE). For more information, open the EXAMPLES\IDE\IDEHOOK\ IDEHOOK.IDE file and read the instructions in OLETOOLS.CPP.

37

Turning an application into an OCX or OLE container using ObjectComponents

Follow these steps to turn an application into an OCX container or an OLE container using ObjectComponents:

1 Include ObjectComponents header files.

2 Create an OLE memory allocator object.

3 Create OLE registration tables.

4 Connect an ObjectComponents application object to the main window.

5 Connect an ObjectComponents view object to the view window.

6 Handle OLE messages.

7 Handle OLE menu commands.

8 Create an ObjectComponents registrar object.

9 Compile and link the application.

Note If you're creating a new application, consider using AppExpert to save some work.

This chapter uses code from the examples in the EXAMPLES/OCF/CPPOCF directory:

Example	Description
CPPOCF0	A basic windows application.
CPPOCF1	The CPPOCF0 example turned into a basic OLE container that registers itself in the system's registration database, creates objects to initialize a new document, and allows standard OLE objects to be embedded.
CPPOCF2	The CPPOCF1 example turned into a basic OLE server.

Step 1: Including ObjectComponents header files

An OCX container must include the following ObjectComponents header files:

```
#include <ocf/ocapp.h>      // TOcRegistrar, TOcModule, TOcApp
#include <ocf/ocdoc.h>      // TOcDocument
#include <ocf/occtrl.h>     // TOcxView and TOcControl
#include <ocf/ocfevx.h>     // WM_OCEVENT message crackers
```

An OLE container must include the following ObjectComponents header files:

```
#include <ocf/ocapp.h>      // TOcRegistrar, TOcModule, TOcApp
#include <ocf/ocdoc.h>      // TOcDocument
#include <ocf/ocview.h>     // TOcView
#include <ocf/ocpart.h>     // TOcPart
#include <ocf/ocfevx.h>     // WM_OCEVENT message crackers
```

Step 2: Creating an OLE memory allocator object

An OLE application should create an OLE memory allocator (*TOleAllocator*) object to
initialize the OLE libraries. To create a *TOleAllocator* object, add this line to the
application's *WinMain* function.

```
TOleAllocator OleAlloc(0);
```

Step 3: Creating OLE registration tables

Like any other OLE application, a container must register information about itself in the
system's registration database. Registration is performed automatically by
ObjectComponents if you create a registration table for the application and each of its
document types, and then pass the resulting structures to a registrar object. (You will
learn more about the registrar object later.)

To create a registration table, use the registration macros.

This is the application registration table used in the CPPOCF1.CPP example:

```
BEGIN_REGISTRATION(AppReg)
   REGDATA(clsid,      "{8646DB80-94E5-101B-B01F-00608CC04F66}")
   REGDATA(appname,    "Container")
END_REGISTRATION
```

Note   For a container, you must specify the class id and appname keys in the application
registration table; and you must specify the progid, description, and format*n* keys in the
document registration tables.

Step 4: Connecting an ObjectComponents application object to the main window

In order for the application's main window to receive OLE messages, it must be connected to an ObjectComponents application (*TOcApp*) object.

To connect a *TOcApp* object to the main window,

1 Declare the *TOcApp* object.

For example, the following line declares a *TOcApp* object called *OcApp*:

```
TOcApp*      OcApp      = 0;
```

2 When the main window is created, call the SetupWindow method of the *TOcApp* object.

In the CPPOCF1.CPP example, the *SetupWindow* method is called from the *MainWnd_OnCreate* function:

```
bool
MainWnd_OnCreate(HWND hwnd, CREATESTRUCT FAR* /*lpCreateStruct*/)
{

HwndMain = hwnd;
  if (OcApp)

  OcApp->SetupWindow(hwnd);
  return true;
}
```

Note The actual *TOcApp* object is created by the registrar object in the *WinMain* function. (You'll learn more about the registrar object later.)

In an SDI application like CPPOCF1, the main window controls the view window. (Every ObjectComponents application needs an application window *and* a view window, as detailed in the next step.) When the main window receives a WM_SIZE message, it moves the view to keep it aligned with the client area of the main window. When the main window receives a WM_CLOSE message, it destroys both itself and the view window.

```
void
MainWnd_OnSize(HWND hwnd, UINT /*state*/, int /*cx*/, int /*cy*/)
{
  if (IsWindow(HwndView)) {
    TRect rect;
    GetClientRect(hwnd, &rect);
    MoveWindow(HwndView, rect.left, rect.top, rect.right, rect.bottom, true);
  }
}

void
MainWnd_OnClose(HWND hwnd)
```

```
{
  if (IsWindow(HwndView))
    DestroyWindow(HwndView);
  DestroyWindow(hwnd);
}
```

In an MDI application, each child window creates its own view window. The child window does what the main window does in an SDI application: it creates and manages a view for the information it displays.

When the main window is destroyed, it should release the *TOcApp* object.

You shouldn't call **delete** for a *TOcApp* object because the OLE system might still need more information before it allows the view to shut down. *ReleaseObject* tells the *TOcView* object that you don't need it any longer. The view subsequently destroys itself as soon as all other OLE clients finish with it. The *TOcApp* destructor is protected to prevent you from calling it directly.

Step 5: Connecting an ObjectComponents view object to the view window

A container must have a view window that is separate from its main window. Usually the view window has an invisible border and it exactly fills the client area of the main window. From the user's point of view, there is only one window in the application. But ObjectComponents expects to send some event messages to the main window and some to the view window.

In order for a view window to receive OLE messages, it must be connected to an ObjectComponents view object. (*TOcView* for an OLE container or *TOcxView* for an OCX container.)

And in order for a view object to keep track of the objects it contains, it must be connected to an ObjectComponents document (*TOcDocument*) object.

To connect a *TOcView* object to the view window,

1 Declare a *TOcView* object and a *TOcDocument* object:

```
TOcView*      OcView      = 0;
TOcDocument*  OcDoc       = 0;
```

2 Create the *TOcDocument* and *TOcView* objects, and then call the *SetupWindow* method of the *TOcView* object:

You should call the *SetupWindow* method when the view window is created, as shown in the CPPOCF1.CPP example.

```
bool
ViewWnd_OnCreate(HWND hwnd, CREATESTRUCT FAR* /*lpCreateStruct*/)
{
  OcDoc = new TOcDoc(*OcApp)
  OcView = new TocView(*OcDoc)
  if (OcView)
```

```
      OcView->SetupWindow(hwnd);
   return true;
   }
```

When the view window is destroyed, it should **delete** the *TOcDocument* object and release the *TOcView* object.

You shouldn't call **delete** for a *TOcView* object because the OLE system might still need more information before it allows the view to shut down. *ReleaseObject* tells the *TOcView* object that you don't need it any longer. The view subsequently destroys itself as soon as all other OLE clients finish with it. The *TOcView* destructor is protected to prevent you from calling it directly.

```
void
ViewWnd_OnDestroy(HWND /*hwnd*/)
{
:
   if (OcView)
     OcView->ReleaseObject();  // release the COM object.

}
```

Step 6: Handling OLE messages

To handle OLE messages, you must:

1 Handle the WM_OCEVENT message message in the main window and view window procedures. (Whenever an OLE event occurs, a WM_OCEVENT message is sent to the main window procedure and the view window procedure by the *TOcApp* and *TOcView* objects respectively.)

2 Create a function to handle specific OLE messages.

3 Create a function that corresponds to each OLE message that you handle in Step 2.

This is how OLE messages are handled in the CPPOCF.CPP example:

First, the WM_OCEVENT message is handled in the main window procedure and the view window procedure.

```
long CALLBACK _export
MainWndProc(HWND hwnd, uint message, WPARAM wParam, LPARAM lParam)
{
   switch (message) {
     // General message handlers:
     HANDLE_MSG(hwnd, WM_CREATE,  MainWnd_OnCreate);
     HANDLE_MSG(hwnd, WM_CLOSE,   MainWnd_OnClose);
     HANDLE_MSG(hwnd, WM_DESTROY, MainWnd_OnDestroy);
     HANDLE_MSG(hwnd, WM_COMMAND, MainWnd_OnCommand);
     HANDLE_MSG(hwnd, WM_SIZE,    MainWnd_OnSize);
     // The OLE message handler:
     HANDLE_MSG(hwnd, WM_OCEVENT, MainWnd_OnOcEvent);
   }
   return DefWindowProc(hwnd, message, wParam, lParam);
}
```

```
long CALLBACK _export
ViewWndProc(HWND hwnd, uint message, WPARAM wParam, LPARAM lParam)
{
  switch (message) {
    // General message handlers:
    HANDLE_MSG(hwnd, WM_CREATE,   ViewWnd_OnCreate);
    HANDLE_MSG(hwnd, WM_CLOSE,    ViewWnd_OnClose);
    HANDLE_MSG(hwnd, WM_DESTROY,  ViewWnd_OnDestroy);
    HANDLE_MSG(hwnd, WM_COMMAND,  ViewWnd_OnPaint);
    // The OLE message handler:
    HANDLE_MSG(hwnd, WM_OCEVENT, MainWnd_OnOcEvent);
  }
    return DefWindowProc(hwnd, message, wParam, lParam);
  }
```

Note   The HANDLE_MSG macro is defined in the ocf/ocfevx.h file.

Second, specific OLE messages are handled in the *MainWnd_OnOcEvent* and *ViewWnd_OnOcEvent* functions.

```
long
MainWnd_OnOcEvent(HWND hwnd, WPARAM wParam, LPARAM /*lParam*/)
{
  switch (wParam) {
    HANDLE_OCF(hwnd, OC_VIEWTITLE, MainWnd_OnOcViewTitle);
  }
  return true;
}
long
MainWnd_OnOcEvent(HWND hwnd, WPARAM wParam, LPARAM /*lParam*/)
{
  switch (wParam) {
    HANDLE_OCF(hwnd, OC_VIEWCLOSE, MainWnd_OnOcViewClose);
    HANDLE_OCF(hwnd, OC_VIEWTITLE, MainWnd_OnOcViewTitle);
  }
  return true;
}
```

Note   The HANDLE_OCF macro is defined in the ocf/ocfevx.h file.

Third, the *MainWnd_OnOcViewTitle*, *ViewWnd_OnViewTitle*, and *ViewWnd_OnOcViewClose* functions correspond to the OLE messages that are handled in the code shown above.

```
const char*
MainWnd_OnOcViewTitle(HWND /*hwnd*/)
{
  return APPSTRING;
}
const char*
ViewWnd_OnOcViewTitle(HWND /*hwnd*/)
{
  return APPSTRING;
}
```

```
const char*
MainWnd_OnOcViewClose(HWND /*hwnd*/)
{
  if (OcDoc)
    OcDoc->Close
  return true;
}
```

Therefore, the CPPOCF application returns the string defined in APPSTRING whenever the main window or the view window receives the OC_VIEWTITLE message.

And the view window closes itself when it receives the OC_VIEWCLOSE message.

Note   Most containers handle the OC_VIEWTITLE message in the view window only.

For a list of OLE messages that can be sent to the main window and view windows, see the OC_APPxxxx Messages and OC_VIEWxxxx Messages topics.

Using the new message-handling classes

You can also handle OLE messages by implementing the virtual functions of one of the new ObjectComponents event-handling classes: *TOcCtrlContainerHost* (OCX container) or *TOcContainerHost* (OLE container).

Step 7: Handling OLE menu commands

To specify how an application responds to OLE menu commands, you must:

1 Handle the WM_COMMAND message in the main window procedure.

2 Create a function to handle specific menu commands.

This is how OLE messages are handled in the CPPOCF1.CPP example:

First, the WM_COMMAND message is handled in the main window procedure:

```
long CALLBACK _export
MainWndProc(HWND hwnd, uint message, WPARAM wParam, LPARAM lParam)
{
  switch (message) {
    HANDLE_MSG(hwnd, WM_CREATE,   MainWnd_OnCreate);
    HANDLE_MSG(hwnd, WM_CLOSE,    MainWnd_OnClose);
    HANDLE_MSG(hwnd, WM_DESTROY,  MainWnd_OnDestroy);
    // The WM_COMMAND message handler:
    HANDLE_MSG(hwnd, WM_COMMAND,  MainWnd_OnCommand);
    HANDLE_MSG(hwnd, WM_SIZE,     MainWnd_OnSize);
    HANDLE_MSG(hwnd, WM_OCEVENT,  MainWnd_OnOcEvent);
  }
    return DefWindowProc(hwnd, message, wParam, lParam);
}
```

Note   The HANDLE_MSG macro is defined in the ocf/ocfevx.h file.

Second, specific menu commands are handled in the *MainWnd_OnCommand* function. (In this case, CM_INSERTOBJECT OLE is the only OLE command that is handled.)

```
void
MainWnd_OnCommand(HWND hwnd, int id, HWND /*hwndCtl*/, uint /*codeNotify*/)
{
  switch (id) {
    case CM_INSERTOBJECT: {
      try {
        TOcInitInfo initInfo(OcView);  // Initializing info structure
        if (OcApp->Browse(initInfo)) { // Show Insert Object dialog.
          TRect rect(30, 30, 100, 100);
          new TOcPart(*OcDoc, initInfo, rect);  // add object to doc.
        }
      }
      catch (TXBase& xbase) {
        MessageBox(GetFocus(), xbase.why().c_str(), "Exception caught", MB_OK);
      }
      break;
    }
    case CM_EXIT: {
      PostMessage(hwnd, WM_CLOSE, 0, 0);
      break;
    }
  }
}
```

Handling the InsertObject command

The code for inserting, dropping, or pasting an object into a document always begins with a *TOcInitInfo* structure. *TOcInitInfo* holds information describing the object about to be created: what container will receive it, whether to link or embed it, whether it already exists or will be newly created, and if it exists, where the data resides and in what format.

The constructor for *TOcInitInfo* receives a pointer to the view where you want the new object to appear. The next command, *OcApp->Browse*, invokes the standard Insert Object dialog box offering the user a choice of all the objects any server registered in the system can create. When the user chooses one, the *Browse* command places more information in *initInfo*.

The final step to insert a new OLE object is to create a *TOcPart* connector. *TOcPart* implements all the OLE services that a linked or embedded object is required to provide. It plugs into OLE, gets the data for the new object, adds itself to the list of parts in *OcDoc*, and draws itself on the screen in the position given by *TRect*.

Handling other OLE commands

For examples showing how to implement other OLE Edit menu commands, look at the source code for event handlers in OWL/OLEWINDO.CPP.

Step 8: Creating a registrar object

The registrar (*TOcRegistrar*) object records information about the application in the system registration database, processes any OLE switches on the application's command line, and notifies OLE that the application is running.

Before you create a *TOcRegistrar* object, you must declare it.

The following line declares a *TOcRegistrar* object called *OcRegister*:

```
TOcRegistrar* OcRegistrar = 0;
```

After you declare the *TOcRegistrar* object, create the object in *WinMain*. Then, instead of entering a message loop, call the *Run* method of the object.

When the *Run* method returns, the application is ready to shut down. Delete the registrar object before exiting the application.

The *WinMain* function of the CPPOCF1 example shows all the steps:

```
int PASCAL
WinMain(HINSTANCE hInstance, HINSTANCE hPrevInstance,
  char far* lpCmdLine, int nCmdShow)
{
  try {
  TOLEAllocator allocator(0);
  MSG msg;

    // Initialize OCF objects
    OcRegistrar = new TOcRegistrar(::AppReg, 0, string(lpCmdLine), 0);
    OcRegistrar->CreateOcApp(OcRegistrar->GetOptions(), OcApp);

      // per-instance and per-task initialization code goes here

    // Standard Windows message loop
    while (GetMessage(&msg, 0, 0, 0)) {
      TranslateMessage(&msg);
      DispatchMessage(&msg);
    }
  }
  catch (TXBase& xbase) {
    MessageBox(GetFocus(), xbase.why().c_str(), "Exception caught", MB_OK);
  }

  // free the registrar object
  delete OcRegistrar;
  return 0;
}
```

Step 9: Compiling and linking the application

Compile the container with the medium or large memory model.

Link the container to the OLE and ObjectComponents libraries.

For more information, see the section "Building an ObjectComponents application" in Chapter 36.

38

Turning an application into an OLE server using ObjectComponents

Follow these steps to turn an application into an OLE server using ObjectComponents:

1 Include ObjectComponents header files.

2 Create an OLE memory allocator object.

3 Create OLE registration tables and a document list object.

4 Connect an ObjectComponents application object to the main window.

5 Connect an ObjectComponents view object to the view window.

6 Handle OLE messages.

7 Create a factory callback function.

8 Create an ObjectComponents registrar object.

9 Compile and link the application.

Note If you're creating a new application, consider using AppExpert to save some work.

The topics that follow use code from the examples in the EXAMPLES/OCF/CPPOCF directory:

Example	Description
CPPOCF0	A basic windows application.
CPPOCF1	The CPPOCF0 example turned into a basic OLE container that registers itself in the system's registration database, creates objects to initialize a new document, and allows standard OLE objects to be embedded.
CPPOCF2	The CPPOCF1 example turned into a basic OLE server.

Step 1: Including ObjectComponents header files

An OLE server must include the following ObjectComponents header files:

```
#include <ocf/ocapp.h>    // TOcRegistrar, TOcModule, TOcApp
#include <ocf/ocreg.h>    // registration constants & app mode flags
#include <ocf/ocdoc.h>    // TOcDocument
#include <ocf/ocview.h>   // TOcView
#include <ocf/ocpart.h>   // TOcPart
#include <ocf/ocremvie.h> // TOcRemView
#include <ocf/ocfevx.h>   // WM_OCEVENT message crackers
```

Step 2: Creating an OLE memory allocator object

An OLE application should create an OLE memory allocator (*TOleAllocator*) object to initialize the OLE libraries. To create a *TOleAllocator* object, add this line to the application's *WinMain* function.

```
TOleAllocator OleAlloc(0);
```

Step 3: Creating registration tables and a document list object

Like any other OLE application, an OLE server must register information about itself in the system's registration database. Registration is performed automatically by ObjectComponents if you create a registration table for the application and each of its document types, and then pass the resulting structures to a registrar object. (You will learn more about the registrar object later.)

To create a registration table, use the registration macros.

This is the application registration table used in the CPPOCF2.CPP example:

```
BEGIN_REGISTRATION(AppReg)
  REGDATA(clsid,   "{BD5E4A81-A4EF-101B-B31B-0694B5E75735}")
  REGDATA(progid,  APSTRING".Application"
END_REGISTRATION
```

Note For an OLE server, you must specify the *class id* and *progid* keys in the application registration table. For more information, see the *ObjectWindows Reference*.

This is the document registration table used in the CPPOCF2.CPP example.

```
BEGIN_REGISTRATION(DocReg)
  REGDATA(description,  "Sample C Server Document")
  REGDATA(progid,       APPSTRING".Document.1")
  REGDATA(menuname,     "CServer")
  REGDATA(insertable,   "")
  REGDATA(verb0,        "&Edit")
  REGDATA(verb1,        "&Open")
  REGDATA(extension,    "scd")
  REGDATA(docfilter,    "*.scd")
```

```
    REGDOCFLAGS(dtAutoDelete | dtUpdateDir | dtCreatePrompt | dtRegisterExt)
    REGFORMAT(0, ocrEmbedSource,  ocrContent, ocrIStorage, ocrGet)
    REGFORMAT(1, ocrMetafilePict, ocrContent, ocrMfPict,   ocrGet)
  END_REGISTRATION
```

Note For an OLE server, you must specify the progid, description, menu name, insertable, extension, and format*n* keys in the document registration tables. For more information, see the *ObjectWindows Reference*.

To accommodate servers with many document types, the registrar accepts a pointer to a linked list of all the application's document registration structures. Each node in the list is a *TRegLink* object. Each node contains a pointer to one document registration structure and another pointer to the next node.

```
  TRegLink *RegLinkHead = 0;
  TRegLink  regDoc(DocReg, RegLinkHead);
```

RegLinkHead points to the first node of the linked list. *RegDoc* is a node in the linked list. The *TRegLink* constructor follows *RegLinkHead* to the end of the list and appends the new node. Each node contains a pointer to a document registration structure. In CPPOCF2, the list contains only one node because the server creates only one type of document. The node points to *DocReg*.

Step 4: Connecting an ObjectComponents application object to the main window

In order for the application's main window to receive OLE messages, it must be bound to an ObjectComponents application (*TOcApp*) object.

To bind a *TOcApp* object to the main window,

1 Declare the *TOcApp* object.

For example, the following line declares a *TOcApp* object called OcApp:

```
  TOcApp*       OcApp       = 0;
```

2 Bind the *TOcApp* object to the main window using the *SetupWindow* method.

You should call the *SetupWindow* method when the main window is created. For example, in the CPPOCF1.CPP file, the *MainWnd_OnCreate* function, which is called when the main window receives a *WM_CREATE* message, calls the *SetupWindow* method.

```
  bool
  MainWnd_OnCreate(HWND hwnd, CREATESTRUCT FAR* /*lpCreateStruct*/)
  {
    HwndMain = hwnd;
    if (OcApp)
      OcApp->SetupWindow(hwnd);
    return true;
  }
```

Note　The actual *TOcApp* object is created by the registrar object in the *WinMain* function. (You'll learn more about the registrar object later.)

In an SDI application like the CPPOCF2 sample program, the main window controls the view window. (Every ObjectComponents application needs an application window *and* a view window, as detailed in the next step.) When the main window receives a WM_SIZE message, it moves the view to keep it aligned with the client area of the main window. When the main window receives a WM_CLOSE message, it destroys both itself and the view window.

```
void
MainWnd_OnSize(HWND hwnd, UINT /*state*/, int /*cx*/, int /*cy*/)
{
  if (IsWindow(HwndView)) {
    TRect rect;
    GetClientRect(hwnd, &rect);
    MoveWindow(HwndView, rect.left, rect.top, rect.right, rect.bottom, true);
  }
}

void
MainWnd_OnClose(HWND hwnd)
{
  if (IsWindow(HwndView))
    DestroyWindow(HwndView);
  DestroyWindow(hwnd);
}
```

In an MDI application, each child window creates its own view window. The child window does what the main window does in an SDI application: it creates and manages a view for the information it displays.

When the main window is destroyed, it should release the *TOcApp* object.

You shouldn't call **delete** for a *TOcApp* object because the OLE system might still need more information before it allows the view to shut down. *ReleaseObject* tells the *TOcView* object that you don't need it any longer. The view subsequently destroys itself as soon as all other OLE clients finish with it. The *TOcApp* destructor is protected to prevent you from calling it directly.

Step 5: Connecting an ObjectComponents view object to the view window

A server must have a view window that is separate from its main window. Usually the view window has an invisible border and it exactly fills the client area of the main window. From the user's point of view, there is only one window in the application. But ObjectComponents expects to send some event messages to the main window and some to the view window.

In order for a view window to receive OLE messages, it must be connected to an ObjectComponents view (*TOcRemView*) object.

And in order for a view object to keep track of the objects it contains, it must be connected to an ObjectComponents document *(TOcDocument)* object.

To connect a *TOcRemView* object to the view window,

1 Declare a *TOcRemView* object and a *TOcDocument* object:

```
TOcRemView*    OcRemView    = 0;
TOcDocument*   OcDoc        = 0;
```

2 Create the *TOcDocument* and *TOcRemView* objects, and then call the *SetupWindow* method of the *TOcRemView* object:

You should call the *SetupWindow* method in the factory callback function, as shown in the CPPOCF2.CPP example. (The factory callback function is described later.)

```
HWndView   = CreateViewWindow(HwndMain);
OcDoc      = new TOcDoc(*OcApp);
OcRemView = new TocRemView(*OcDoc, &DocReg);
if (IsWindow(HWndView))
  OcRemView->SetupWindow(HWndView);
```

When the view window is destroyed, it should **delete** the *TOcDocument* object and release the *TOcRemView* object.

You shouldn't call **delete** for a *TOcRemView* object because the OLE system might still need more information before it allows the view to shut down. *ReleaseObject* tells the *TOcRemView* object that you don't need it any longer. The view subsequently destroys itself as soon as all other OLE clients finish with it. The *TOcRemView* destructor is protected to prevent you from calling it directly.

```
void
ViewWnd_OnDestroy(HWND /*hwnd*/)
{
  .
  .
  .
  if (OcRemView)
    OcRemView->ReleaseObject();  // release the COM object.
  OcDoc->Close(); // release the server for each embedded object
  delete OcDoc;    // delete the document object
}
```

Step 6: Handling OLE messages

Because the *TOcRemView::SetupWindow* method connected the *OcRemView* object to the view window, the object sends its event notification messages to the window. All ObjectComponents events are sent in the *WM_OCEVENT* message, so the view window procedure must respond to *WM_OCEVENT*.

```
long CALLBACK _export
ViewWndProc(HWND hwnd, uint message, WPARAM wParam, LPARAM lParam)
{
  switch (message) {
?
// other message crackers go here
```

```
      HANDLE_MSG(hwnd, WM_OCEVENT,  ViewWnd_OnOcEvent);
   }
   return DefWindowProc(hwnd, message, wParam, lParam);
}
```

The *HANDLE_MSG* message cracker macro for *WM_OCEVENT* is defined in the ocf/ocfevx.h header. The same header also defines another cracker for use in the *WM_OCEVENT* message handler.

```
// Subdispatch OC_VIEWxxxx messages
long
ViewWnd_OnOcEvent(HWND hwnd, WPARAM wParam, LPARAM /*lParam*/)
{
   switch (wParam) {
      // insert an event cracker for each OC_VIEWxxxx message you want to handle
      HANDLE_OCF(hwnd, OC_VIEWCLOSE, ViewWnd_OnOcViewClose);
   }
   return true;
}
```

Handling selected application events

The only ObjectComponents event that CPPOCF2 can handle in its main window is OC_APPSHUTDOWN. A server receives this message when the last linked or embedded object closes down. If the server was launched by OLE, it can terminate. If user launched the server directly, the server doesn't need to do anything.

```
const char*
MainWnd_OnOcAppShutDown(HWND hwnd)
{
   if (OcRegistrar->IsOptionSet(amEmbedding))
      DestroyWindow(hwnd);
}
```

The registrar sets the *amEmbedding* flag at startup if it finds the /Embedding switch on the application's command line. OLE pass the /Embedding switch when it launches a server to support a linked or embedded object.

Handling selected view events

Each HANDLE_OCF macro calls a different handler function. In the example, the handler function is called *ViewWnd_OnOcViewClose*.

```
bool
ViewWnd_OnOcViewClose(HWND hwnd)
{
   DestroyWindow(hwnd);
   return true;
}
```

A server receives this message when a container closes the document that contains the server's object. CPPOCF2 responds by closing the view window. The WM_DESTROY handler also deletes or releases the helper objects associated with the server document.

Painting the document

No special code is required in the server's paint procedure. It always paints its document the same way, whether or not it is painting an embedded object.

```
void
ViewWnd_OnPaint(HWND hwnd)
{
    PAINTSTRUCT ps;
    HDC dc = BeginPaint(hwnd, &ps);
    wsprintf(Buffer, "%u", Counter);
    TextOut(dc, 0, 0, Buffer, lstrlen(Buffer));
    EndPaint(hwnd, &ps);
}
```

When the view window is created, it starts off a timer. Every time the view receives a WM_TIMER message, it increments the value in the global variable *Counter* and calls *InvalidateRect* to make the view repaint itself. On each call, the paint procedure prints the value of *Counter*.

Using the new message-handling class

You can also handle OLE messages by implementing the virtual functions of *TOcServerHost*, a new ObjectComponents event-handling class.

Step 7: Creating a factory callback function

The factory callback is a function you implement and pass to the constructor of a registrar object. When it is time for the application to run, or when a container tries to insert one of the server's objects, ObjectComponents invokes the callback function.

The factory callback decides what to do by reading the parameters it receives and examining the running mode flags the registrar has set. The callback is called a factory because it creates OLE component objects on request.

The requirement that every ObjectComponents application must supply a factory callback function unifies the process of creating objects. Normally the process varies depending on whether the application is a container or a server, whether it is automated, whether it is running as a DLL or an executable program, and whether the application was invoked by the user directly or by OLE. The factory callback makes it possible to revise and run the application in a variety of ways without rewriting any code. For more information about factory callbacks, see the *ObjectWindows Reference*.

A set of factory templates such as *TOleFactory* and *TOleAutoFactory* make it easy to implement factories for ObjectWindows programs, but in a straight C++ program you have to write the factory yourself.

Factory callback procedures can have any name you like, but they must follow this prototype:

```
IUnknown* ComponentFactory(IUnknown* outer, uint32 options, uint32 id);
```

outer is used when aggregating OLE objects to make them function as a single unit. The factory's return value is also used for aggregation. Because containers don't aggregate, CPPOCF1 ignores *outer* and returns 0.

options contains the bit flags that indicate the application's running mode. The registrar object sets the flags when it processes the command line switches, before it calls the factory callback. The factory tests the flags to find out what it should do. The possible flags are defined by the *TOcAppMode* enumerated type, and they have names like *amRun* and *amShutdown*.

id is an identifier that tells the factory what kind of object to create.

The factory's parameters can direct the factory to perform one of three actions:

- Initialize the application. The first time it runs, the factory creates a *TOcModule* object. *TOcModule* connects the application to the OLE system by creating a *TOcApp* connector object. The factory also handles aggregation in this phase.

- Run the application. If the *amRun* flag is set, the factory enters the message loop. If the server is built as a DLL, then when OLE loads the server the registrar does not set the *amRun* flag and the server should not run its own message loop.

- Create an object. The *id* parameter tells the factory what kind of object to create. Because CPPOCF2 creates only one kind of object, it checks only whether *id* is greater than 0. In applications that register multiple document templates, *id* points to the template for the requested object.

The factory callback in CPPOCF2 refers to four global variables. One is *OcRegistrar*. Another is *OcApp*.

```
TOcRegistrar* OcRegistrar = 0;
TOcApp*       OcApp       = 0;
```

TOcApp is the connector object that implements OLE interfaces on behalf of the application. One of the factory's jobs is to create the connector object when the application starts and to destroy it when the application shuts down.

Here is the factory callback from CPPOCF2:

```
IUnknown*
ComponentFactory(IUnknown* outer, uint32 options, uint32 id)
{
  IUnknown* ifc = 0;

  // start the application or shut it down
  if (!OcApp) {
    if (options & amShutdown)  // no app to shutdown!
      return 0;
    OcRegistrar->CreateOcApp(options, OcApp);
  } else if (options & amShutdown) {
    DestroyWindow(HwndMain);
    return 0;
  }
```

```
    // aggregate if an outer pointer was passed
    if (id == 0)
      OcApp->SetOuter(outer);

    // enter message loop if the run flag is set
    if (options & amRun) {
      if ((options & amEmbedding) == 0) {
        HwndView = CreateViewWindow(HwndMain);
      }
      MSG msg;
      // Standard Windows message loop
      while (GetMessage(&msg, 0, 0, 0)) {
        TranslateMessage(&msg);
        DispatchMessage(&msg);
      }
    }

    // create a document if the id parameter is non-zero
    if (id) {
      OcDoc     = new TOcDocument(*OcApp);
      HwndView  = CreateViewWindow(HwndMain);
      OcRemView = new TOcRemView(*OcDoc, &DocReg);
      if (IsWindow(HwndView))
        OcRemView->SetupWindow(HwndView);
      ifc = OcRemView->SetOuter(outer);
    }
    return ifc;
  }
```

The factory's *outer* parameter is 0 unless some other object is aggregating with the newly created object. Aggregated objects are components that act together as a single unit. Objects can form aggregations at run time; you do not need access to an object's source code to aggregate with it. ObjectComponents supports aggregation by passing *outer* to the application factory. If *outer* is non-zero, it points to the *IUnknown* interface of anther object that wants the newly created object to subordinate itself. To allow aggregation, the factory calls the *SetOuter* method on the object it is creating, either *TOcApp* or *TOcRemView*. *SetOuter* returns a pointer to the object's own *IUnknown* interface. The factory should return the same pointer, too.

Note   *TOcApp::SetOuter* is only called when an application automates itself. CPPOCF2 includes the call anyway in case the application later becomes an automation server.

Step 8: Creating an ObjectComponents registrar object

The registrar (*TOcRegistrar*) object records information about the application in the system registration database, processes any OLE switches on the application's command line, and notifies OLE that the application is running.

Before you create a *TOcRegistrar* object, you must declare it.

The following line declares a *TOcRegistrar* object called *OcRegister*:

```
TOcRegistrar* OcRegistrar = 0;
```

After you declare the *TOcRegistrar* object, create the object in *WinMain*. Instead of entering a message loop, call the *Run* method of the object.

When the *Run* method returns, the application is ready to shut down. Delete the registrar object before exiting the application.

This excerpt from the CPPOCF1 *WinMain* function shows all the steps:

```
int PASCAL
WinMain(HINSTANCE hInstance, HINSTANCE hPrevInstance,
  char far* lpCmdLine, int nCmdShow)
{
  try {
  TOLEAllocator allocator(0);
  MSG msg;

    // Initialize ObjectComponents objects
    OcRegistrar = new TOcRegistrar(::AppReg, ComponentFactory,
                                   string(lpCmdLine), ::RegLinkHead,
                                   hInstance);

    if (OcRegistrar->IsOptionSet(amEmbedding))
      nCmdShow = SW_HIDE;

    // per-instance and per-task initialization code goes here

    OcRegistrar->Run();

    // free the registrar object
    delete OcRegistrar;
  }
  catch (xmsg& x) {
    MessageBox(GetFocus(), x.why().c_str(),"Exception caught", MB_OK);
  }
  return 0;
}
```

Step 9: Compiling and linking the application

Compile the server with the medium or large memory model.

Link the server to the OLE and ObjectComponents libraries.

For more information, see the section "Building an ObjectComponents application" in Chapter 36.

Creating a DLL OLE server

Typically, linking and embedding servers are stand-alone executables that can be launched directly by the user or invoked indirectly by an OLE container. You can also implement an OLE server in a DLL. A server built as a DLL is sometimes called an *in-process server* because DLL code runs in the same process as its client. The terms EXE *server* and *server application* refer specifically to a server implemented in an EXE.

ObjectComponents allows you to create both EXE and DLL servers. If you are using ObjectWindows, converting from one to the other requires only two simple changes.

Note   The discussion and instructions that follow apply to automation servers as well as linking and embedding servers.

Pros and cons of DLL servers

Advantages

The major advantage of DLL servers is performance. Because a DLL server lives in the address space of the container, it loads and responds very fast. An EXE server, on the other hand, is a separate process and requires some form of intertask communication to interact with a container. OLE serializes intertask calls and marshals the function calls with their parameters, packaging them into the proper format for the interprocess protocol. (The protocol it uses is called LRPC, for *Lightweight Remote Procedure Call*.) The process of serializing the drawing commands in a metafile is particularly slow, so DLL servers substantially increase the speed of creating presentation data for linked and embedded objects.

Disadvantages

There are a few disadvantages to using a DLL server, however. While OLE supports interaction between 16-bit and 32-bit executable applications, a 16-bit Windows application cannot use a 32-bit DLL server and a Win32 application cannot use a 16-bit DLL server. Also, DLLs do not have message queues. As a result, a DLL server cannot easily perform a task in the background. ObjectWindows overcomes this limitation by running a timer so that it can still call the *IdleAction* methods of objects derived from *TApplication* or *TOleFrame*. (ObjectWindows also uses the timer for internal processes such as command-enabling for tool bars, deleting condemned windows, and resuming thrown exceptions.)

Because a DLL server becomes part of the container's process, bugs in one can interfere with the other, making DLL servers sometimes harder to debug.

DLL servers also present user interface dilemmas. For example, when a container initiates an open edit session with a server, it doesn't matter to the user whether the server is an EXE or a DLL; the user interface for open editing is the same either way. But the lifetime of a DLL server is tied to the container that loads it. When the container quits, the server DLL is unloaded. That can cause problems if the server's user interface normally allows the user to edit serveral documents at once. If the user were to create a new document while editing an embedded object, the user might want to continue editing the new document even after the container quits, but then the server is no longer in memory. This is a particular problem for MDI servers because the MDI interface allows users to open multiple documents in a single session. Typically DLL servers do not allow multidocument editing.

Finally, DLL servers have one other disadvantage. While OLE 2 provides a compatibility layer to let OLE 2 servers interact with OLE 1 clients, the compatibility layer works only for EXE servers. A DLL server cannot support an OLE 1 client.

Debugging a DLL OLE server

The same general techniques used to debug DLLs apply to DLL servers. The steps that follow describe one approach, using Turbo Debugger for Windows to set breakpoints in a DLL server.

1 Build and register the DLL server.

   1 Build your server with debugging information.

   2 Register the server using the REGISTER.EXE utility.

   3 Verify that the registration was successful by running *RegEdit* and looking for your servers file types. (*RegEdit* is a registration editor included with Windows.)

2 Launch Turbo Debugger for Windows and load a container.

Select the File I Open menu option and enter the container's name in the Program Name field and click the OK button.

The debugger loads the container. If the container was built without debugging information, you may receive a warning. You can safely ignore it.

3 Load the server's debugging information.

   1 Select View I Module from the debugger's main menu. This activates the dialog titled "Load module source or DLL symbols." (You can also activate the module dialog by pressing *F3*.)

   2 Enter the full name of DLL server file in the DLL Name field.

   3 Select the Yes option in the Debug Startup field and click the Add DLL button. The name of your DLL server (followed by *!!*) appears as the selected entry in the DLLs & Programs list.

   4 Click the Symbol Load button.

If you receive an error message indicating that the DLL is not loaded , press the Escape key to return to the debugger's main menu and proceed to Step 4. Otherwise, proceed to Step 5.

Note   If you did not receive the error message that the DLL is not loaded, then your DLL server was already in memory before the container activated it. This happens if another container is currently running with one of your server's objects. More often, however, it indicates that your server crashed or was improperly terminated in an earlier session.

4 Run the container and insert one of your server's objects.

   1 Select the Run I Run menu option (or press *F9*) to start the container.

   2 Choose Insert Object from the container's Edit menu and insert your server's object.

The debugger pops up as soon as OLE loads your DLL server.

5 Display the DLL source modules and set breakpoints.

    1 Choose View I Module from the container's main menu to see the names of the source files used to build your server. The file names appear in Source Modules list.

    2 Select source files by double-clicking the file names.

    3 Set breakpoints in your server.

    4 Choose the Run I Run menu option (or press *F9*) to return control to the container application.

6 If you skipped Step 4, insert one of your server's objects into the container now.

The debugger stops at the breakpoints set in your source files and allows you to step through your server, inspect variables, and verify the logic of your code.

Tools for DLL OLE servers

Before running your DLL server, you must record its registration information in the system registration database. The *Register* tool does that for you. Another tool, *DllRun*, gives you the option of running your DLL server at any time as a standalone application, which is sometimes convenient for testing.

REGISTER.EXE

The REGISTER.EXE utility registers an ObjectComponents DLL server. On the command line, pass *Register* the name of your server followed by the **-RegServer** switch. Here is the command to register Tic Tac Toe:

```
register ttt.dll -RegServer
```

Even though the *Register* utility is a Windows application, not a DOS application, you can invoke it from a Windows DOS box. This ability is useful in makefiles. (To invoke other Windows programs from a DOS box command line, use the *WinRun* utility described in UTILS.TXT.)

Register can also unregister your server. Unregistering removes all entries related to your server from the registration database. It's good practice to unregister one version before you register the next. To unregister, use the **-UnregServer** switch. This command unregisters Tic Tac Toe:

```
register ttt.dll -UnregServer
```

DLLRUN.EXE

The DLLRUN.EXE utility lets you load and run an ObjectComponents DLL server as though it were a standalone executable program. The ability to run in executable mode is useful for debugging. It also lets you give customers the choice of running your server either way without having to distribute two versions of the same application.

On the command line, pass *DllRun* the *progid* of the server. This is the value assigned to the *progid* key in the server's registration table. This command runs the Tic Tac Toe server:

```
dllrun TicTacToeDll
```

DllRun launches the DLL server in the executable running mode. The running mode of an ObjectComponents application is represented by a set of bit flags that you can test by calling *TOcModule::IsOptionSet*. (Remember that the application object of a linking and embedding program derives from both *TApplication* and *TOcModule*.)

The running mode bit flags are defined in the *TOcAppMode* **enum**. *AmEmbedded* is set when the server is invoked by OLE, not by the user. *AmExeModule* is set in an application that was built as an EXE. *AmExeMode* is set in an application that is running as a standalone executable, even if it was built as a DLL.

This code tests the flags to determine the server's running mode.

```
void
TMyApp::TestMode()
{
  if (IsOptionSet(amExeMode))          // is server running as an EXE?
    if (!IsOptionsSet(amExeModule)) {  // if so, was it built as an EXE?
      // the server is a DLL running in EXE mode
    } else {
      // the server was built as an EXE
    } else {
      // the server is a DLL running in a client's process
    }
}
```

39

Turning an application into an OLE automation server

Follow these steps to turn an application into an OLE automation server using ObjectComponents :

1 Include ObjectComponents header files.

2 Create a registration table.

3 Create a registrar object.

4 Declare automatable methods and properties.

5 Define automatable methods and properties.

6 Compile and link the automation server.

Later, you can enhance your automation server by localizing symbol names, combining C++ objects, exposing collections, invalidating deleted objects, or creating a type library.

Note The AutoCalc example in the EXAMPLES/OCF/AUTOCALC directory illustrates many of the above steps. AutoCalc draws a calculator on the screen and lets the user click buttons to perform calculations. AutoCalc automates its classes so that an automation controller can send commands to do the same things a user does.

Step 1: Including ObjectComponents header files

An automation server must include the following header files:

```
#include <ocf/automacr.h>    // definition and declaration macros
#include <ocf/ocreg.h>       // TRegistrar class
```

The file list is short because an automation server does not need many of the ObjectComponents classes used for linking and embedding.

Step 2: Creating a registration table

An automation server must set five pieces of information in the application's registration table: its class ID, program ID, name, description, and command-line arguments for invoking the automation server.

To create a registration table, use the registration macros. The following code shows the registration table for AutoCalc (\OCF\EXAMPLES directory):

```
BEGIN_REGISTRATION(AppReg)
   REGDATA(clsid,       "{877B6200-7627-101B-B87C-0000C057CE4E}")
   REGDATA(progid,      "Calculator.Application")
   REGDATA(appname,     "AutoCalc")
   REGDATA(description, "Automated Calculator 1.2 Application")
   REGDATA(cmdline,     "/Automation")
END_REGISTRATION
```

Step 3: Creating a registrar object

An automation server needs a registrar object. Applications that support only automation without linking and embedding should create a *TRegistrar* object; objects the support automation with linking and embedding should create a *TOcRegistrar* object.

To create a registrar object, declare a static pointer to hold the *TRegistrar**. (Use the *TPointer<>* template to ensure that the registrar object is properly deleted when the program ends.)

```
TPointer<TRegistrar> Registrar;    // initialized at WinMain or LibMain
```

Then in the main procedure, you should create the registrar object and call its *Run* method. The following code shows the creation of the registrar object in the AutoCalc example (\OCF\EXAMPLES directory):

```
try {
   ::Registrar=new TRegistrar(AppReg,TOcAutoFactory<TCalc>(),
                              string(cmdLine), hInst);
   TAutoCommand::SetErrorMsgHook(ErrorLookup);
   if (!::Registrar->IsOptionSet(amAnyRegOption))
      ::Registrar->Run();
   ::Registrar = 0;  // deletes registrar by replacing pointer
   return 0;
}
catch (TXBase& x) {
   ::MessageBox(0, x.why().c_str(), "OLE Exception", MB_OK);
```

The first parameter of the *TRegistrar* constructor is the application registration structure, conventionally named *AppReg*. The second parameter is a factory callback function. The example uses a factory template to create the callback. For an automation server that doesn't use ObjectWindows, the appropriate template is *TOcAutoFactory*.

The call to *IsOptionSet* determines whether the application was passed a command-line switch asking the application to register itself in the system registration database and then quit. If not, the application calls *Run*. The registrar then calls the factory callback, where the message loop resides. When *Run* returns, the application has ended.

Step 4: Declaring automatable methods and properties

Automating a class requires building two tables, one in the class declaration and one in the class implementation. The first table is called the *automation declaration*, and it declares which members of the class a controller can reach. The second table is called the *automation definition*, and it defines public names that a controller uses to reach each exposed class member. This section tells how to build an automation declaration.

The automation declaration belongs inside the declaration of an automated class. It begins with the macro DECLARE_AUTOCLASS and includes one entry for each class member that you choose to expose. The macros add nested classes that ObjectComponents instantiates to process commands received from OLE. They do not alter the structure or size of the original class.

This sample automation declaration exposes functions and data members of a C++ class that mimics a calculator:

```
DECLARE_AUTOCLASS(TCalc)
    AUTODATA    (Accum,     Accum,      long,   )
    AUTODATA    (Opnd,      Opnd,       long,   )
    AUTODATA    (Op,        Op, short,  AUTOVALIDATE(Val>=OP_NONE && Val<=OP_CLEAR)  )
    AUTOFUNC0   (Eval,      Eval,       TBool, )
    AUTOFUNC0V(Clear,       Clear,              )
    AUTOFUNC0V(Display,     Display,            )
    AUTOFUNC0V(Quit,        Quit,               )
    AUTOFUNC1   (Button,    Button,     TBool, TAutoString,)
    AUTOFUNC0   (Window,    GetWindow, TAutoObject<TCalcWindow>,   )
    AUTOFUNC1   (LookAt,    LookAtWindow, long, TAutoObject<const TCalcWindow>,)
    AUTODATARO(MyArray,     Elem,       TAutoObjectByVal<TMyArray>,)
```

The automated class is called *TCalc*. Each AUTOFUNC or AUTODATA macro exposes one member of *TCalc*. Some of the *TCalc* member functions are *Eval, Clear, Display,* and *Quit*. Its data members include *Accum, Opnd, Op,* and *Elem. TCalc* also has other members that are not automated and are therefore excluded from the declaration table.

No termination macro is needed for an automation declaration. The END_AUTOCLASS macro that closes an automation definition is not used here. Also, each line of the declaration ends with a closing parenthesis, not with punctuation.

Note The automation declaration should appear at the end of a class declaration because the macros can modify the access specifier. If you put the declaration anywhere else, be sure to follow it immediately with an access specifier (**public, protected,** or **private**).

Writing declaration macros

Each of the macros within an automation declaration describes a single method or property that other programs can manipulate. The different macros expose different kinds of class members. AUTOFUNC1, for example, exposes a member function that takes one parameter. AUTOFUNC2V exposes a function that takes two parameters and returns nothing (**void**). AUTOPROP exposes a property through Set and Get functions that insert or retrieve a single value. AUTODATA exposes a data member that the controller can read and modify directly.

The general form of the automation macros is this:

```
MACRONAME( InternalName, FunctionName, ReturnType, ArgumentType, Options )
```

Some of the macros don't use all five parameters. AUTOFUNC1V, for example, doesn't have a *ReturnType* because the function has a **void** return. AUTOFUNC0 doesn't have any arguments, while AUTOFUNC2 has two different arguments. But whatever parameters are relevant appear in the order shown.

InternalName is an identifier you assign to each automatable property or function. It is used internally by ObjectComponents for keeping track of the members. The only other place you ever use the internal name is in the corresponding entry of the class's automation definition table. The internal name is a unique identifier for the member. (the names used in source code are not necessarily unique. They can be overloaded, for example.)

FunctionName is the name you use in your source code to refer to the same property or function. *FunctionName* can be any expression that evaluates to a function call. The expression must, however, be defined within the scope of the automated object. ObjectComponents attempts to reach the function through the **this** pointer.

The internal and function names should be the same unless the function name is overloaded or uses indirection. For example, suppose a class contains a data member that points to another object:

```
TObject* MyObject;
```

To expose a function call like *MyObject->MyFunction*, you should supply an internal name that does not use indirection. In this case, a good choice would be *MyFunction*.

```
AUTOFUNC0V( MyFunction, MyObject->MyFunction, )
```

If a function is overloaded, use the same function name for all versions but give each a different internal name. ObjectComponents can distinguish the overloaded functions by the return types and argument types in the parameters that follow.

The *ReturnType* and *ArgumentType* parameters can be any fundamental C type, such as **int** or **char**, or a pointer to any fundamental type. Some pointers, however, require special handling. If the data type is a string (type **char***), declare it to be a *TAutoString* instead. If the data type is a pointer or a reference to a C++ object, then declare it using the *TAutoObject<>* wrapper. The type substitutions help ObjectComponents convert between C++ data types and the VARIANT union type that OLE uses. Pointers and object references are hardest to convert because they refer to data that is not in the variable itself. The *TAutoString* and *TAutoObject* classes provide type information for the conversion so that ObjectComponents can pass the right information between server and controller applications.

The *TCalc* example shows how to use *TAutoObject*. One of the functions *TCalc* exposes is *GetFunction*, which returns a reference to a *TCalcWindow* object.

```
AUTOFUNC0 (Window, GetWindow, TAutoObject<TCalcWindow>, )
```

When it declares *TCalcWindow* as the return type, it makes use of the *TAutoObject* template to create a smart, self-describing pointer to a *TCalcWindow* object.

Providing optional hooks for validation and filtering

The final parameter of every automation macro names a hook function to be called whenever OLE calls the exposed class member. A *hook* is code that executes every time anyone uses a particular class member. ObjectComponents supports hooks to record commands, undo commands, validate command arguments, and override a command's implementation. Hooks are always optional.

To install a hook, use one of these macros as the last parameter to any automation declaration:

- AUTOINVOKE
- AUTORECORD
- AUTOUNDO
- AUTONOHOOK
- AUTOREPORT
- AUTOVALIDATE

Each macro receives a single parameter containing code to execute. The form of the required macro varies with its function.

To validate arguments, for example, the code should be a Boolean expression. The *Op* data member of *TCalc* holds an integer that identifies an operation to perform, such as addition or subtraction. The automation declaration installs a hook to be sure that *Op* is not assigned a value outside the legal range of operator identifiers.

```
AUTODATA(Op, Op, short, AUTOVALIDATE(Val>=OP_NONE && Val<=OP_CLEAR))
```

AUTOVALIDATE introduces the expression to execute for validation. Within the validation expression, use the name *Val* to represent the value received from the controller. When used to validate function arguments, AUTOVALIDATE uses the names *Arg1*, *Arg2*, *Arg3*, and so on.

Whenever any automation controller attempts to set a value in the *Op* data member, ObjectComponents verifies that the new value falls within the range OP_NONE to OP_CLEAR. If passed an illegal value, ObjectComponents cancels the command and sends OLE an error result.

The expression passed to AUTOVALIDATE can include function calls.

```
AUTODATA(Op, Op, short, AUTOVALIDATE(Val>=OP_NONE && NotTooBig(Val)))
```

Now ObjectComponents calls *NotTooBig* whenever a controller attempts to modify *Op*.

```
bool NotTooBig(int Val) {
  return (Val <= OP_CLEAR)
}
```

Step 5: Defining external methods and properties

In addition to declaring which of its members are automatable, an automated class must also create a second table of macros to assign public symbols for referring to the exposed methods and properties. The public symbols are what other applications see. They become the controller's interface to an automated OLE object.

Behind the scenes, ObjectComponents links the public names to the C++ object or objects that you create to implement the OLE object. The automation declaration table identifies which class members to expose, and the automation definition table assigns them names.

The automation definition belongs with the class implementation. It begins with the DEFINE_AUTOCLASS macro and ends with END_AUTOCLASS. Here's the automation definition for *TCalc*:

```
DEFINE_AUTOCLASS(TCalc)
    EXPOSE_PROPRW(Opnd,        TAutoLong,    "Operand",      "@Operand_",
            HC_TCALC_OPERAND)
    EXPOSE_PROPRW_ID(0,Accum,TAutoLong,   "!Accumulator", "@Accumulator_",
            HC_TCALC_ACCUMULATOR)
    EXPOSE_PROPRW(Op,          CalcOps,      "Op",           "@Op_", HC_TCALC_OPERATOR)
    EXPOSE_METHOD(Eval,        TAutoBool,    "!Evaluate",    "@Evaluate_",
            HC_TCALC_EVALU ATE)
    EXPOSE_METHOD(Clear,       TAutoVoid,    "!Clear",       "@Clear_", HC_TCALC_CLEAR)
    EXPOSE_METHOD(Display,     TAutoVoid,    "!Display",     "@Display_",
            HC_TCALC_DISPLA Y)
    EXPOSE_METHOD(Quit,        TAutoVoid,    "!Quit",        "@Quit_", HC_TCALC_QUIT)
    EXPOSE_METHOD(Button,      TAutoBool,    "!Button",      "@Button_",
            HC_TCALC_BUTTON )
    REQUIRED_ARG(              TAutoString, "!Key")
    EXPOSE_PROPRO(Window,      TCalcWindow,"!Window",        "@Window_",
            HC_TCALC_WINDOW)
    EXPOSE_METHOD(LookAt,      TAutoLong,   "!LookAtWindow","@LookAtWindow_",
            HC_TCALC_LOOKATWINDOW)
    REQUIRED_ARG(              TCalcWindow,"!Window")
    EXPOSE_PROPRO(MyArray,     TMyArray,    "!Array",        "@Array_",
            HC_TCALC_ARRAY)
    EXPOSE_APPLICATION(        TCalc,       "!Application", "@Application_",
            HC_TCALC_APPLICATION)
END_AUTOCLASS(TCalc, tfNormal, "TCalc", "@TCalc", HC_TCALC)
```

The EXPOSE_xxxx macros assign names to methods and properties. EXPOSE_PROPRW defines a property that controllers can both read and write. EXPOSE_PROPRO limits a controller's access so it can only read the property value. REQUIRED_ARG assigns a name to a function argument.

For example, a controller invokes the server's *LookAt* function by calling *LookAtWindow* and passing a *Window* parameter. The DEFINE_AUTOCLASS and END_AUTOCLASS macros assign "TCalc" as the public name for objects of type *TCalc*.

Most of the strings in this automation definition begin with a symbol, either ! or @. These symbols indicate that the AutoCalc application has in its resources translations for each public symbol. Each command from an automation controller comes with a locale ID indicating the language the controller is using. If the controller was written in

German, for example, it can pass the string "Auswerten" instead of "Evaluate," and ObjectComponents correctly invokes the *Eval* function.

Every item listed in the automation definition must already appear in the automation declaration. For example, every function name you define with EXPOSE_METHOD must have a corresponding AUTOFUNC declaration. Every EXPOSE_PROP must have a corresponding AUTOPROP, AUTOFUNC, AUTOFLAG, or AUTODATA, depending on how you implement the property.

The parts of a definition macro

The macros for exposing methods and properties have five parameters: the internal name, the type of value returned, the external name, and a documentation string. The optional fifth parameter allows you to associate a Help context ID with each member.

```
MACRONAME(InternalName, ReturnType, ExternalName, DocString, HelpContext )
```

- *InternalName* is the identifier string you assigned to the member in the automation declaration.

- *ReturnType* tells what automation data type the method returns or the property holds.

- *ExternalName* is what automation controllers see. A user sending commands from a controller refers to all properties and methods by their external names.

- *DocString* should explain to a user what the exposed property or method does. OLE displays this string if the user asks for help with a particular automation command. If you omit the document string, set the parameter to 0.

- *HelpContext*, the fifth parameter, is optional. It is a number that identifies a particular section of a Windows Help file (.HLP). You can create a Help file that describes the syntax and usage of all the members you expose. If you supply the context IDs for each member in the class's automation definition, then an automation controller can ask OLE to display the help screens for the user. A user writing an automation script, for example, can browse at run time for the list of members your application exposes, ask to see their document strings, and even ask to see a Help screen about each one.

    If you provide a Help file for automation, you should be sure to register its name with the *typehelp* key.

When exposing a method that takes arguments, you also need to add a macro describing each argument to the definition. Here is the prototype for a function that takes three arguments, along with the macros needed to define the method for automation:

```
// member function declaration
long TCalculator::AddNumbers(short Num1, short Num2 = 0, short Num3 = 0);

// later, this appears after DEFINE_AUTOCLASS(TCalculator)
EXPOSE_METHOD(AddNumbers, TAutoLong, "AddNumbers", "Sum up to 3 numbers",
              HC_ADDNUMBERS)
```

```
        REQUIRED_ARG(TAutoShort, "Num1")
    OPTIONAL_ARG(TAutoShort, "Num2", "0")
    OPTIONAL_ARG(TAutoShort, "Num3", "0")
```

The first argument, *Num1*, is required. The others are optional. All three are **short**
integers. When describing optional arguments, you need to supply a default value. In
the example, *0* is the default value for the two optional arguments.

OLE conventions suggest that each automation object should have a property
representing the application it belongs to. You can add this property to any automation
definition with the EXPOSE_APPLICATION macro.

```
EXPOSE_APPLICATION(TMyClass, "Application", "My Application",)
```

The class passed to EXPOSE_APPLICATION must be the same class passed to the
factory template.

Data type specifiers in an automation definition

Most of the macros in an automation definition ask for a data type of a function's return
value, of each function argument, or of a data member. The possible values for data
types within an automation definition are not fundamental C types. They can be any of
the following:

- An enumeration value previously defined for automation.

- The name of an automated class (such as *TCalc*).

- Any of the predefined classes that ObjectComponents provides to represent intrinsic
  C types.

The reason for exposing predefined classes rather than intrinsic C types is to make type
information available when browsing from the controller. For exposed classes,
ObjectComponents can extract type information using RTTI.

The automation data types are defined as structures that contain no data; they simply
retrieve a static value indicating a data type. The identifier values are the same
identifiers that OLE uses to distinguish the data types it supports. All the automation
data types derive from a base called *TAutoVal*, so they are polymorphic. In effect,
ObjectComponents can ask any value passed through automation to describe its own
data type.

Step 6: Compiling and linking an automation server

Automation servers and controllers can be compiled with any memory model except
Small. (They run fastest in medium model.) And automation servers must be linked
with the OLE and ObjectComponents libraries.

The IDE chooses the right build options for you when you ask for OLE support. To
build any ObjectComponents program from the command line, create a short makefile
that includes the OCFMAKE.GEN file found in the EXAMPLES subdirectory.

```
EXERES = MYPROGRAM
OBJEXE = winmain.obj myprogram.obj
!include $(BCEXAMPLEDIR)\ocfmake.gen
```

EXERES and OBJEXE hold the name of the file to build and the names of the object files to build it from. The last line includes the OCFMAKE.GEN file. Name your file MAKEFILE and type this at the command line prompt:

```
make MODEL=F, SYSTEM=WIN32
```

MAKE, using instructions in OCFMAKE.GEN, will build a new makefile tailored to your project. The new makefile is called WIN32F*xx*.MAK.

Note The first time the server runs, the registrar object records its information in the registration database. Be sure to run the server once before trying to use it with a controller.

For more information, see "Building an ObjectComponents application" in Chapter 36.

Exposing collections of objects

ObjectComponents lets an automated object expose collections of various types as object properties. The items in a collection can belong to an array, a linked list, or any other structure that organizes sets of similar items.

To expose a collection, you need to expose methods for manipulating it. These methods typically include a counter to show the size of the collection, an iterator to walk through the collection, and a random-access function to retrieve specific items in the collection.

A collection object is an object that returns on request individual items from a set of related items. It implements the methods that manipulate the items. In the AutoCalc sample program, the buttons on the face of the calculator are a set of related, similar objects. AutoCalc defines a new class, *TCalcButtons*, whose methods let a controller ask for individual button objects. The buttons themselves are automated objects, so once a controller receives a button it can send a push command or change the text the button displays.

Constructing and exposing a collection class

If you are automating an existing application, you may find that it does not already have a C++ class to act as a collection object. The items might be simple values, structures, or even system objects represented by handles. You have to create a new C++ class, and you have to expose the class in the parent's automation tables as a property of the parent class.

How you expose the collection in the parent's automation declaration table depends on what information the parent passes the collection object to construct it. This section considers several different possible constructors and shows the macros for adding the collection as a property of its parent.

Instances of the collection class are constructed only when a controller requests it. The collection object appears to the controller as a property of the parent class. In AutoCalc, for example, when a controller asks for what is in the *Buttons* property, ObjectComponents creates a *TCalcButtons* object on the fly. The constructor of a collection object must accept a single argument passed from the parent to initialize itself.

Because *TCalcButtons* manages a collection of child windows, its parent passes the handle of the parent window. The constructor looks like this:

```
TCalcButtons(HWND window) : HWnd(window) {}
```

For the handle to be passed to the constructor, the parent must add a line to its automation declaration:

```
// from the automation declaration of the parent class
DECLARE_AUTOCLASS(TCalcWindow)
  AUTODATARO(Buttons, hWnd, TAutoObjectByVal<TCalcButtons>,)
```

Buttons is assigned as the internal name of a read-only property whose value is *TCalcWindow::hWnd*. For the data type of this property, the table specifies a new class based on the collection class. *TAutoObjectByVal<T>* causes an instance of *T* to be constructed that persists until all external references to that instance are released (when the exposed object goes out of scope in the automation controller).

TCalcWindow must also expose the collection property in its automation definition:

```
// from the automation definition of the parent class
DEFINE_AUTOCLASS(TCalcWindow)
  EXPOSE_PROPRO(Buttons, TCalcButtons, "!Buttons", "@Buttons_",
            HC_TCALCWINDOW_BUTTONS)
```

When a controller asks for what is stored in the read-only property called *Buttons*, ObjectComponents creates a *TCalcButtons* object and passes *hWnd* to its constructor.

Other ways to expose a collection object

Here are three examples showing other ways a parent class might expose a collection object as one of its properties:

- **Case 1**: *TParent::DocList* points to the head of a linked list of *TDocument* objects. A new class, *TDocumentList*, is created as the collection object. The constructor of *TDocumentList* receives from its parent the head of the linked list:

  ```
  TDocumentList(TDocument*);
  ```

  The automation declaration of *TParent* exposes *DocList* as a read-only property, using the collection class to assign it a type.

  ```
  DECLARE_AUTOCLASS(TParent)
    AUTODATARO(Documents, DocList, TAutoObjectByVal<TDocumentList>,)
  ```

  The automation definition of *TParent* calls the collection *Documents* and says its type is *TDocumentList*.

  ```
  DEFINE_AUTOCLASS(TParent)
    EXPOSE_PROPRO(Documents, TDocumentList, "Documents", "Doc Collection", 270)
  ```

- **Case 2**: *TParent* contains a list. It passes **this** to the collection object, *TList*, which extracts list items by indirection through the parent's pointer. The constructor receives the pointer.

  ```
  TList(TParent* owner)
  ```

  The automation declaration of *TParent* exposes **this** as a read-only property, using the collection class to assign it a type.

```
DECLARE_AUTOCLASS(TParent)
    AUTOTHIS(List, TAutoObjectByVal<TList>,)
```

The automation definition of *TParent* calls the collection *List* and says its type is *TList*.

```
DEFINE_AUTOCLASS(TParent)
    EXPOSE_PROPRO(List, TList, "List", "List of items", 240)
```

- **Case 3**: *Elem* is an array of integers, defined as **short** *Elem[COUNT]*. The collection object is *TMyArray*, and the constructor receives from the parent a pointer to *Elem*.

```
TMyArray(short* array)
```

The automation declaration of *TParent* exposes *Elem* as a read-only property, using the collection class to assign it a type.

```
DECLARE_AUTOCLASS(TParent)
    AUTODATARO(MyArray, Elem, TAutoObjectByVal<TMyArray>,)
```

The automation definition of *TParent* calls the collection *Array* and says its type is *TMyArray*.

```
DEFINE_AUTOCLASS(TParent)
    EXPOSE_PROPRO(MyArray, TMyArray, "Array", "Array as collection", 110)
```

Implementing an iterator for the collection

The collection class performs whatever actions you want a controller to be able to perform with the collection. Common collection methods include *Count* and *GetObject*, which return the number of items in the collection or individual items specified by number. The only methods you need to implement, however, are the constructor and an iterator. You have already seen the constructor. An iterator function walks through the collection and returns successive items on each new call.

The easy way to define an iterator is with the AUTOITERATOR macro, which you add to the declaration table of the collection object.

```
DECLARE_AUTOCLASS(TCalcButtons)
    AUTOITERATOR(int Id, Id = IDC_FIRSTID+1, Id <= IDC_LASTID, Id++,
                 TAutoObjectByVal<TCalcButton>(::GetDlgItem(This->HWnd,Id)))
```

The parameters to AUTOITERATOR define the algorithm for enumerating objects in the collection. Each of the five macro arguments represents a code fragment, ordered as in a **for** loop.

1 Declare state variables for keeping track of loop iterations. For example,

```
int Index;
```

2 Assign initial values to the state variables. For example,

```
Index = 0;
```

3 Test a Boolean expression to decide whether to enter the loop. For example,

```
Index < This->Total
```

4 Modify state variables to prepare for the next iteration. For example,

```
Index++;
```

5 Retrieve one item from the collection. For example,

```
(This->Array)[Index];
```

Note that the server can return any data type for items—values or objects.

In the AUTOITERATOR parameters, only use commas inside parentheses. Semicolons can separate multiple statements, but cannot be used to end a macro argument. As in automated methods, *This* is defined to be the **this** pointer of the enclosing C++ class (here, the collection itself).

AUTOITERATOR puts an iterator in the automation declaration table, but the iterator member must still be exposed in the definition table. Use the EXPOSE_ITERATOR macro.

```
EXPOSE_ITERATOR(TAutoShort, "Array Iterator", HC_ARRAY_ITERATOR)
```

EXPOSE_ITERATOR takes fewer parameters than other EXPOSE_*xxxx* macros do. No internal or external names are supplied. A class can have only one iterator, and the external name is always *_NewEnum*. The first parameter describes the type of the items returned from the iterator.

The automation type describes the type of the items returned from the iterator, in the same manner as a function return. The previous example iterates an array of **short int** values, so its automation data type is *TAutoShort*. The second parameter is the documentation string describing the iterator property, and the third parameter, which is optional, identifies a context in an .HLP file for more information about the iterator.

From the external side, a script controller sees the enumerator as a property with the reserved name *_NewEnum* that returns an object supporting the standard OLE interface *IEnumVARIANT*. This interface contains methods to perform iteration. A controller makes use of an iterator in a loop like this one, which is written in Visual Basic for Applications:

```
For Each Thing in Owner.Bunch    ("Thing" is an arbitrary iterator name)
   Thing.Member......            (can access methods and properties)
   Next Thing                    (loops through all items in collection)
```

The AUTOITERATOR macro generates a nested class definition within the collection class. For complex iterators, you can choose to code the iterator explicitly in C++. Here is an example:

```
class TIterator : public TAutoIterator {
  public:
    ThisClass* This;
    /* declare state variables here as members */
    void Init() {/* loop initialization function body */}
    bool Test() {/* loop entry test function body */}
    void Step() {/* loop iteration function body;}
    void Return(TAutoVal& v) {/* current element return: v = expr */}
    TIterator* Copy() {return new TIterator(*this);}
    TIterator(ThisClass* obj, TServedObject& owner)
                : This(obj), TAutoIterator(owner) {}
    static TAutoIterator* Build(ObjectPtr obj, TServedObject& owner)
    { return new TIterator((ThisClass*)obj, owner); }
```

```
};
   friend class TIterator;     // make iterator a friend of the surrounding
                               // collection class
```

Adding other members to the collection class

In addition to exposing an iterator, a collection class by convention exposes a *Count*
method to return the number of items in the collection, an *Index* method for random
access to members of the collection, and optionally, methods such as *Add* and *Delete* to
manage the collection externally. Here, for example, is the complete code for the
TCalcButtons collection class in AutoCalc:

```
class TCalcButtons {     // class used only temporarily to expose collection
   public:
      TCalcButtons(HWND window) : HWnd(window) {}
      short GetCount() { return IDC_LASTID - IDC_FIRSTID; }
      HWND GetButton(short i) {return ::GetDlgItem(HWnd, i + IDC_FIRSTID+1);}
      HWND HWnd;
   DECLARE_AUTOCLASS(TCalcButtons)
      AUTOFUNC0 (Count, GetCount, short,)
      AUTOFUNC1 (Item,  GetButton, TAutoObjectByVal<TCalcButton>, short,
                 AUTOVALIDATE(Arg1 >= 0 && Arg1 < This->GetCount()) )
      AUTOITERATOR(int Id, Id = IDC_FIRSTID+1, Id <= IDC_LASTID, Id++,
                   TAutoObjectByVal<TCalcButton>(::GetDlgItem(This->HWnd,Id)))
};

DEFINE_AUTOCLASS(TCalcButtons)
   EXPOSE_PROPRO(Count, TAutoLong, "!Count", "@CountBu_", HC_TCALCBUTTONS_COUNT)
   EXPOSE_ITERATOR(TCalcButton, "Button Iterator", HC_TCALCBUTTONS_ITERATOR)
   EXPOSE_METHOD_ID(0, Item, TCalcButton,"!Item",  "@ItemBu_", 0)
      REQUIRED_ARG(TAutoShort, "!Index")
END_AUTOCLASS(TCalcButtons, tfNormal, "TButtonList", "@TCalcButtons",
              HC_TCALCBUTTONS)
```

Exposing data for enumeration

An automation server might also need to expose enumerated values. Use OLE
enumerations when you want to expose a set of internal data values and refer to them
with localizable strings. For example, AutoCalc defines the enumerated type operators
to represent different actions the calculator can perform with numbers.

```
enum operators {
   OP_NONE = 0,
   OP_PLUS,
   OP_MINUS,
   OP_MULT,
   OP_DIV,
   OP_EQUALS,
   OP_CLEAR,
};
```

As the calculator receives input, it stores the pending mathematical operation in a private data member called *Op*.

```
short Op;
```

Operations are identified by different OP_*xxxx* constants. The *Eval* method performs the pending operation using the number just entered and the total in the calculator's accumulator. AutoCalc exposes the *Op* data member to automation so that a controller can enter operators directly. Here's the automation declaration:

```
AUTODATA(Op, Op, short, AUTOVALIDATE(Val>=OP_NONE && Val<=OP_CLEAR))
```

The automation declaration shows that the *Op* data member holds a short value, but the symbols OP_PLUS and OP_MINUS are defined only within the server program. The controller can't use them when it passes commands. Ideally the controller should be able to use more readable strings such as "Add" and "Subtract" in scripts.

The place for declaring public symbols is the automation definition. Use the DEFINE_AUTOENUM macro to begin a table defining symbols for the enumerated values.

```
DEFINE_AUTOENUM(CalcOps, TAutoShort)
    AUTOENUM("Add",      OP_PLUS)
    AUTOENUM("Subtract", OP_MINUS)
    AUTOENUM("Multiply", OP_MULT)
    AUTOENUM("Divide",   OP_DIV)
    AUTOENUM("Equals",   OP_EQUALS)
    AUTOENUM("Clear",    OP_CLEAR)
END_AUTOENUM(CalcOps, TAutoShort)
```

The AUTOENUM macro takes two parameters: an enumeration string and a constant value. The enumeration string (which can be localized) is the external name exposed through OLE for use by controllers.

The macros that begin and end the enumeration table assign the name *CalcOps* to this enumerated type. They also associate the automated data type *TAutoShort* with this enumeration because the enumerated values are all **short int**s.

The following table lists the C++ types that can be enumerated and the corresponding automation types for exposing them.

C++ type	Enumeration type (for automation definitions)
bool	*TAutoBool*
double	*TAutoDoubl*
float	*TAutoFloat*
int	*TAutoInt*
long	*TAutoLong*
short	*TAutoShort*
const char*	*TAutoString*

Creating a table of enumerated values results in a new data type that you can use to describe arguments and return values in an automation definition. Now that ObjectComponents understands the *CalcOps* enumerated type, you can use the type to define the *Op* property.

```
EXPOSE_PROPRW(Op, CalcOps, "Op", "@Op_", HC_TCALC_OPERATOR)
```

This line says that *Op* is a read-write property holding a value of type *CalcOps*. When the controller tries to place "Multiply" or "Divide" in the *Ops* property, ObjectComponents correctly translates the string into the value defined as OP_MULT or OP_DIV.

Combining multiple C++ objects into a single OLE automation object

The complete set of member functions and properties that belong to a single automated OLE object can in fact be implemented by a combination of C++ objects. An automated calendar, for example, might begin with a *TCalendar* class. But the automated OLE calendar object might need to expose some methods and properties that don't happen to belong to the C++ *TCalendar* object.

For example, the background color might be inherited from *TCalendar*'s base class, and some of the input functions might belong to separate control windows in the calendar's client area. In that case, the automation declaration for *TCalendar* should delegate some tasks to other C++ classes.

To combine several C++ objects together into a single OLE object, add macros to the automation definition table.

```
// these lines belong in the definition block that begins
DEFINE_AUTOCLASS(TCalendar)
    EXPOSE_INHERIT(TCalendarWindow, "CalendarWindow")
    EXPOSE_DELEGATE(TWeekForwardButton, "WeekForward",
    GetWeekForwardButton(this))
```

Any exposed classes must also be automated. In other words, *TCalendarWindow* and *TWeekForwardButton* must also have their own AUTOCLASS tables. By exposing both of these classes in the *TCalendar* automation definition, you combine all the exposed members from all three classes into a single symbol table. When OLE sends an automation command to the calendar, ObjectComponents searches for the matching class member in *TCalendar*, then in *TCalendarWindow*, and finally in *TWeekForwardButton*.

The EXPOSE_DELEGATE macro takes as its third parameter a conversion function. To reach members in the delegation class, ObjectComponents needs a pointer to an object of that class. The conversion function has one parameter for receiving a **this** pointer to the object where the definition table appears. The function must return a pointer to the delegation object. Also, it must be a global function. For example, if *TCalendar* has a data member that points to the Week Forward button, this might be the conversion function.

```
TWeekForwardButton *GetWeekForwardButton ( TCalendar* this ) {
    return( this->m_ForwardButton );
}
```

You don't need to provide a conversion function when exposing an inherited function or property because in that case ObjectComponents can create its own templatized conversion function to reach the base class.

Another way to coordinate the actions of several automated objects within a single application is to give one object access functions that return the other objects.

For example, the sample program AutoCalc automates five different classes, but no class delegates to any other. When a controller asks for an object from the AutoCalc server, it receives only the automated *TCalc* object. *TCalc*, however, has a property called *Window* that holds a *TCalcWindow* object. *TCalcWindow*, in turn, has a property that holds the collection of buttons. The collection object returns individual button objects. Without properties or functions that return the other objects, the controller would never be able to reach them. Be sure to add access functions if necessary.

Telling OLE when the object goes away

If there is a chance that your program might delete its automated object while still connected to a controller, then you need to tell OLE when the object is destroyed. This precaution only matters if the logic of your program might cause the object to be destroyed through nonautomated means while an OLE session is still in progress. If OLE attempts to use an automation object whose underlying C++ object has been destroyed, it attempts to use an invalid pointer. A single function call prevents the error by sending OLE an obituary to announce that the object no longer exists.

```
// place this line in the destructor of your automated class
::GetAppDescriptor()->InvalidateObject(this);
```

GetAppDescriptor is a global function returning a pointer the application's *TAppDescriptor* object. *InvalidateObject* is a *TAppDescriptor* method. It tells OLE the object that was passed to the descriptor's InvalidateObject function is now invalid.

Although the object's destructor is a good place to call *InvalidateObject*, you can call it anywhere. If you do not own the class you are automating, it might not be possible to modify the destructor. This works, too:

```
TMyAutoClass* MyAutomatedObject = new TMyAutoClass;
?
::GetAppDescriptor()->InvalidateObject(MyAutomatedObject);
delete MyAutomatedObject;
```

The object pointer you pass to *InvalidateObject* must always represent the most derived form of the object. In other words, if the pointer is polymorphic, it must point to the class as it was created and not to any of its base classes. Calling *InvalidateObject* from the object's own destructor is safe because in that case **this** always points to the most derived class. If you call *InvalidateObject* from somewhere else, you might need the global function *MostDerived* to ensure that you are invalidating the correct object.

```
appDesc->InvalidateObject(::MostDerived(MyPolymorphObject,
                          typeid(MyPolymorphObject)));
```

In the example, *MyPolymorphObject* is a pointer to a polymorphic object, so it might point to a base class or to an object of any type derived from the base. *MostDerived* converts the pointer, making it point to an object of the type farthest down the hierarchy, the one furthest descended from the base.

Besides calling *InvalidateObject*, there are two other ways let OLE know when the object is destroyed. One way is to derive the object's class from *TAutoBase*. The only code in *TAutoBase* is a virtual destructor that calls *InvalidateObject* for you. This example declares a class called *TMyAutoClass*. OLE always knows when any object of type *TMyAutoClass* is destroyed.

```
class TMyAutoClass: public TAutoBase { /* declarations */ };
```

The other way is to put the AUTODETACH macro in the class's automation declaration table. This works without having to change the class derivation, but it does add one byte to the size of the class.

Localizing symbol names

The symbols that appear in an automation definition become visible to other OLE programs. Users writing scripts can see and use the symbols. The symbols become part of the program's user interface. Programs intended for international audiences need to translate the strings for different markets. For example, a property named "Color" in English should be called "Couleur" in a French script, "Farbe" in a German script, and "Colour" in a British one.

The external names in macros like EXPOSE_METHOD and EXPOSE_PROPRW are wrapped in objects of type *TLocaleString*, a localizable substitute for **char*** strings. A *TLocaleString* object contains code that searches a program's executable file for XLAT resources. All access to the XLAT resources is performed by *TLocaleString*.

The *TLocaleString* class is defined in winsys/lclstrng.h. You don't need to refer to *TLocaleString* directly. The macros and headers bring it in for you.

TLocaleString is very efficient. If the controller is working in the server's native language, then *TLocaleString* realizes the strings in the source code already match the locale and it doesn't waste any time reading resources.

Usually ObjectComponents determines the application's default language by reading the system's locale ID at compile time and storing it in the compiled program. You can override the default by including a line like this in your source code.

```
#include "winnls.h"  // include olenls.h for 16-bit applications
TLangId TLocaleString::NativeLangId=MAKELANGID(LANG_ENGLISH,SUBLANG_ENGLISH_US);
```

The olenls.h header holds national language support constants, including the MAKELANGID macro and the language and dialect symbols.

When it must resort to resources, *TLocaleString* does everything it can to minimize the time spent searching for translations. When it finds a string to match the current locale, it caches the string in memory and never has to load it again. That means only the first attempt to use each translated string incurs a performance hit. Subsequent requests are satisfied quickly. Once in memory, the strings are stored in a hash table so no space is wasted on duplicates. If *TLocaleString* fails to find a requested string, it remembers the failure as well and won't try to find the same string a second time.

The same localization mechanism works with strings your application registers. Some strings, such as the *progid*, should not be localized, but you can localize the following registration keys:

- *appname*

- *debugdesc*

- *description*

- *formatn*

- *menuname*

- *permname*

- *typehelp*

- *verbn*

The following excerpt from the AutoCalc registration tables shows where to put the localization prefixes. The *appname*, *description*, and *typehelp* keys are localized.

```
BEGIN_REGISTRATION(AppReg)
    REGDATA(clsid,      "{877B6200-7627-101B-B87C-0000C057CE4E}")
    REGDATA(progid,     APP_NAME ".Application")
    REGDATA(appname,    "@AppName")
    REGDATA(description,"@Desc")
    REGDATA(typehelp,   "@typehelp")
    REGDATA(version,    "1.2")
END_REGISTRATION
```

AutoCalc supplies translations for the *appname*, *description*, and *typehelp* strings in its resource script. Here are two of them.

```
Desc        XLAT "Automated Calculator 1.2 Application"
            GERMAN "Automatisierte Taschenrechner-Anwendung 1.2"
            XEND
Typehelp    XLAT "autocalc.hlp"
            GERMAN "acalcger.hlp"
            XEND
```

ObjectComponents determines the proper language for registration by examining the system settings at run time, but it is possible to override the system setting with the Language command-line switch.

OLE does its best to help you out by passing a number that indicates the user's language setting. This number is called a locale ID, or LCID. LCIDs are defined by OLE and the Win32 API. They consist of two numbers, one identifying a language and one identifying a subdialect within the language. When OLE passes an automation call into an automated application, it also passes an LCID. The automation controller might determine the LCID from the system settings at run time, or the person using the controller might choose a locale.

An automated program is expected to examine the LCID and respond with appropriately translated strings. ObjectComponents eases the burden by letting you build a resource table to supply localized versions of any strings you use. When handling automation calls, ObjectComponents automatically searches the table to find strings that match whatever language the controller requests.

ObjectComponents searches first for a string with the correct language and dialect IDs. Failing that, ObjectComponents searches for a match on primary language only, ignoring dialect. If still no match is found, ObjectComponents simply uses the original, untranslated string.

Putting translations in the resource script

To build a table of translations in your resource (.RC) file, use the XLAT resource type.

```
#include "owl/locale.rh"
Left    XLAT FRENCH "Gauche" GERMAN "Links" SPANISH "Izquierda" XEND
Right   XLAT FRENCH "Droit"  GERMAN DUTCH "Rechts"              XEND
Center  XLAT ENGLISH_UK FRENCH GERMAN "Centre" SPANISH "Centro" XEND
Help    XLAT FRENCH "Aide" GERMAN "Hilfe" SPANISH "Ayuda"       XEND
```

The locale.rh header file defines XLAT as a type of resource. XLAT and XEND are delimiters for all the translations of a single string. The same header also defines macros to represent various locale IDs. FRENCH, DUTCH, and ENGLISH_UK, for example, each represent a different LCID. UK is a subdialect of ENGLISH.

Each line in the localization table begins with a resource identifier. These examples use the original string itself to identify the resource that holds its translations.

A localization table is not obliged to provide the same set of translations for each string. For example, it is legal to provide FRENCH_FRANCE, FRENCH_BELGIUM, and SWEDISH for one string, but only FRENCH and ITALIAN for the next string. Also, if several languages use the same string, it is legal to write the string only once, as in this example:

```
Center XLAT ENGLISH_UK FRENCH GERMAN "Centre" SPANISH "Centro" XEND
```

In British English, French, and German, "Center" is translated as "Centre." in Spanish, it becomes "Centro." Writing "Centre" only once keeps the .EXE file smaller.

Marking translatable strings in the source code

Composing a resource table is the first step, but ObjectComponents still needs to be told when to use the table you have provided. In the automation definition, mark each translatable string by prefixing it with an exclamation point.

```
EXPOSE_METHOD(Clear, TAutoVoid, "!Clear", "Clear accumulator", HC_TCALC_CLEAR)
```

This line from *AutoCalc* exposes a class method named *Clear*. *Clear* returns **void**. The third parameter, *!Clear*, gives the external name that controllers see. The initial exclamation point tells ObjectComponents to look in the program's executable file for a localization resource whose identifier is the string *Clear*.

```
Clear XLAT GERMAN "AllesLöschen" XEND
```

The exclamation point prefix also marks *Clear* as the language-neutral form of the string. If an automation controller decides to use the locale ID GERMAN, then

ObjectComponents tells it that the exposed property is called *AllesLöschen*. If the controller sets any other locale ID, it receives the neutral form, *Clear*.

Argument names as well as properties and methods can be localized.

```
EXPOSE_METHOD(Button, TAutoBool, "!Button", "Button push sequence",
             HC_TCALC_BUTTON)
    REQUIRED_ARG( TAutoString, "!Key")
```

In determining what to call both the *Button* method and its one argument, ObjectComponents will search the program's localization resources for *Button* and *Key*.

```
Button      XLAT GERMAN "Schaltfläche" XEND
Key         XLAT GERMAN "Taste" XEND
```

The algorithm that searches for resources is not sensitive to case. Under 16-bit Windows, the algorithm does not allow the use of extended characters (such as characters with diacritical marks) in resource names. However, the strings stored in a resource can use any characters and do preserve their case.

A problem arises in naming your resource if the string contains spaces. Resource identifier strings cannot have spaces. Consider what happens if you try to localize the description string for this property:

```
// illegal: no spaces allowed in resource identifiers
EXPOSE_PROPRW(Caption, TAutoString, "!Caption", "!Window Title",
             HC_TCALCWINDOW_TITLE)
```

It's a good idea to localize descriptions as well as property names, but "Window title" is not a legal resource identifier. In cases like this, use @ instead of ! as the localization prefix, and follow it with any legal identifier.

```
EXPOSE_PROPRW(Caption, TAutoString, "!Caption", "@Caption_",HC_TCALCWINDOW_TITLE)
```

The @ prefix tells ObjectComponents that the string is *only* a resource identifier and should never be displayed no matter what locale the controller requests. To make the distinction even clearer for programmers reading the code, strings used only as identifiers conventionally end with an underscore, as in *Caption*.

To make "Window Title" the language-neutral string, do not assign it a locale ID in the localization resource.

```
Caption_ XLAT "Window Title" GERMAN "Fenster-Aufschrift" XEND
```

Now a controller that requests any locale setting other than GERMAN is given the string *Window Title*.

Besides ! and @, there is a third localization prefix: #. The # prefix must be followed by digits that identify a localization resource by number.

```
EXPOSE_PROPRW(Caption, TAutoString, "!Caption", "#10047",HC_TCALCWINDOW_TITLE)
```

This example tells ObjectComponents to look for a resource numbered 10047. This is how the resource should appear in the .RC file:

```
10047 XLAT "Window Title" GERMAN "Fenster-Aufschrift" XEND
```

Creating a type library

A type library is a binary file containing information about an automation server. The information describes the objects, properties, and methods the server supports. It is used by programming tools, such as automation controllers, that call the server. Controllers can query the type library for documentation and help with specific objects. The location of its type library is one of the pieces of information an automation server records in the system's registration database.

ObjectComponents can create a type library for you from information in the server's automation definitions. To make a type library, call the server and set the **-TypeLib** switch on the command line.

```
myapp -TypeLib
```

This command causes ObjectComponents to create a new file, MYAPP.OLB, in the same directory as MYAPP.EXE. ObjectComponents also records the library's location in the registration database.

The **-TypeLib** flag also accepts an optional path and file name.

```
myapp -TypeLib = data\mytyplib
```

ObjectComponents places MYTYPLIB.OLB in a subdirectory called DATA under the directory where MYAPP.EXE resides.

You can also make ObjectComponents generate multiple type libraries in different languages with the **-Language switch**. This command produces two type libraries, one in German and one in Italian.

```
myapp -Language=10 -TypeLib=italiano -Language=7 -TypeLib=deutsch
```

The number passed to **-Language** must be hexadecimal digits. The Win32 API defines *80C* as the locale ID for the Belgian dialect of the French language. For this command line to have the effect you want, *myapp* must supply Belgian French strings in its XLAT resources.

If you have a Help file, be sure to register it using the *typehelp* and *helpdir* registration keys. Use the final parameter of the EXPOSE_xxxx macros in the automation definition table to associate Help context IDs with each command. If the automation controller asks for help on a command, OLE launches the Help file automatically.

40

Turning an application into an OLE automation controller

Follow these steps to turn an application into an OLE automation controller using ObjectComponents:

1 Include ObjectComponents header files.

2 Create a memory allocator object.

3 Declare proxy classes.

4 Implement proxy classes.

5 Create and use proxy objects.

6 Compile and link the application.

Note In order to send commands to an OLE object, the automation controller must know the names of methods and properties the object's server exposes to OLE. Generally these names come from the server's type library. The controller uses the names in creating C++ proxy classes whose methods send commands to the server. It's possible to browse through available automation objects at run time and discover what commands they support, but to make use of commands discovered at run time usually requires a scripting language.

Step 1: Including ObjectComponents header files

An automation controller must include the following header files:

```
#include <ocf/autodefs.h>
#include <ocf/automacr.h>
```

The autodefs.h file defines automation classes such as *TAutoProxy*; the automacr.h file defines the macros a controller uses to implement proxy class methods.

Step 2: Creating a memory allocator object

Automation controllers must create a memory allocator (*TOleAllocator*) object to initialize the OLE libraries. To create a *TOleAllocator* object, add this line to your program.

```
TOleAllocator OleAlloc(0);
```

Note To initialize the OLE libraries under Win32, you must pass a zero argument to the *TOleAllocator* constructor. Under 16-bit Windows, you can also pass a pointer to a custom memory allocation function.

The constructor for *TOleAllocator* initializes the OLE libraries and its destructor releases them. Create an object of type *TOleAllocator* before you begin OLE operations and be sure the object is not destroyed until all OLE operations have ended. A good place to create the *TOleAllocator* is at the beginning of *WinMain* or *OwlMain*.

Step 3: Declaring proxy classes

A proxy class is a C++ stand-in for an automated OLE object. You create a proxy class whose interface corresponds to that of the OLE object. By deriving the proxy class from *TAutoProxy*, you connect it to ObjectComponents. When a *TAutoProxy* object is constructed, it calls an OLE API to request the *IDispatch* interface of the automated object that the proxy represents. When you call a function of the proxy class, the proxy sends the corresponding command to the automation server.

An automation controller declares one proxy class for every type of object it wants to control. In simple cases, a single proxy class might be enough. Controlling a complex application that creates several different kinds of automatable objects requires more proxies. To control a spreadsheet, for example, you might need a proxy application class, a proxy spreadsheet class, and a proxy cell class.

The easiest way to declare and implement proxy classes is with the AutoGen utility. AutoGen reads the server's type library and generates C++ source code for the proxy classes a controller needs to send any commands to the server. Simply compile the generated code into your application, construct proxy objects when you need them, and call their member functions to send commands.

As an example of a proxy class, here is the code that AutoGen generates for the automated class *TCalc* in the AutoCalc sample program. The opening comment shows descriptive information from AutoCalc's entries in the registration database including the value of AutoCalc's *version*, *clsid*, and *description* registration keys. The comments for individual members show the documentation strings that AutoCalc assigns to each member in its automation definition table, the dispatch ID that ObjectComponents assigned to identify each command, and whether the member is a function or a property.

```
// TKIND_DISPATCH: TCalc 1.2 {877B6207-7627-101B-B87C-0000C057CE4E}\409
// Automated Calculator Class
class TCalc : public TAutoProxy {
  public:
```

```
TCalc() : TAutoProxy(0x409) {}
// Pending operand
long GetOperand();        // [id(1), prop r/w]
void SetOperand(long);  // [id(1), prop r/w]
// Calculator accumulator
long GetAccumulator();      // [id(0), prop r/w]
void SetAccumulator(long);  // [id(0), prop r/w]
// Pending operation
TAutoString GetOp();       // [id(3), prop r/w]
void SetOp(TAutoString);  // [id(3), prop r/w]
// Evaluate operand, op
TBool Evaluate();  // [id(4), method]
// Clear accumulator
void Clear();  // [id(5), method]
// Update display
void Display();  // [id(6), method]
// Terminate calculator
void Quit();  // [id(7), method]
// Button push sequence
TBool Button(TAutoString Key);  // [id(8), method]
// Calculator window
void GetWindow(TCalcWindow&);  // [id(9), propget]
// Test of object as arg
long LookAtWindow(TCalcWindow& Window);  // [id(10), method]
// Array as collection
void GetArray(TCalcArray&);  // [id(11), propget]
// Application object
void GetApplication(TCalc&);  // [id(12), propget]
};
```

The constructor of an automation proxy class must pass to its base class, *TAutoProxy*, a number representing a locale setting. The locale tells what language the automation controller uses when it sends commands to objects. In the example, the number is 0x409, which is the locale ID for American English. AutoGen chooses this locale by reading the system settings when it runs, but you are free to change it to whatever locale you prefer.

The function members of class *TCalc* each send a different command to the calculator object. Read-write properties get two commands, one for getting the value and one for setting it. *GetOp* and *SetOp*, for example, write and read the value representing the next operation the calculator will perform. Other commands, such as *Display* and *Quit*, make the calculator perform some action.

Step 4: Implementing proxy classes

After declaring methods, you implement them. Each method must send a command through ObjectComponents to the automated object. Here is part of the implementation code that AutoGen generates for the *TCalc* proxy object. Every method simply calls the same three macros.

```
// TKIND_DISPATCH: TCalc 1.2 {877B6207-7627-101B-B87C-0000C057CE4E}/409
// Automated Calculator Class
```

```
TAutoString TCalc::GetOp()
{
  AUTONAMES0("Op")
  AUTOARGS0()
  AUTOCALL_PROP_GET
}
void TCalc::SetOp(TAutoString val)
{
  AUTONAMES0("Op")
  AUTOARGS0()
  AUTOCALL_PROP_SET(val)
}
TBool TCalc::Evaluate()
{
  AUTONAMES0("Evaluate")
  AUTOARGS0()
  AUTOCALL_METHOD_RET
}
void TCalc::Clear()
{
  AUTONAMES0("Clear")
  AUTOARGS0()
  AUTOCALL_METHOD_VOID
}
void TCalc::Display()
{
  AUTONAMES0("Display")
  AUTOARGS0()
  AUTOCALL_METHOD_VOID
}
void TCalc::Quit()
{
  AUTONAMES0("Quit")
  AUTOARGS0()
  AUTOCALL_METHOD_VOID
}
void TCalc::GetWindow(TCalcWindow& obj)
{
  AUTONAMES0("Window")
  AUTOARGS0()
  AUTOCALL_PROP_REF(obj)
}
```

The three macros supply all the code needed for each function. The first two macros, AUTONAMES and AUTOARGS, specify what arguments you want to pass. They are explained in the following table. None of the methods in the example takes any arguments. The AUTOCALL_*xxxx* macros tell whether the command is a function or a property and what kind of value it returns.

Macro	Description
AUTOCALL_METHODn(id, arg...)	Calls a method with n arguments that returns a value.
AUTOCALL_METHODnV(id, arg...)	Calls a method with n arguments that returns void.
AUTOCALL_METHODn_REF(id, prx, arg...)	Calls a method with n arguments that returns a proxy object.
AUTOCALL_PROPGET(id)	Retrieves the value of a property.
AUTOCALL_PROPSET(id, arg)	Assigns a value to a property.
AUTOCALL_PROPREF(id, obj)	Retrieves the value of a property that contains an object. (Objects must be passed by reference.)

Specifying arguments in a proxy method

The first two macros in the implementation of a proxy method indicate what arguments you intend to pass. The server can decide that some arguments to a method are optional. You must pass all required arguments, and you can choose to pass any of the optional arguments.

For example, a server might expose a method that takes ten arguments, of which five are optional. Optional arguments have default values. Your controller might only need one of the optional arguments, always using the default values for the other four. In that case, you can set up your proxy implementation so that you have to pass only six arguments instead of ten.

The AUTONAMES macro lists the optional arguments that you want to use. It lists them by the names the server assigns to them. (AutoGen reads the names from the server's type library for you.)

The first argument passed to an AUTONAMES macro always identifies the automation method that this proxy command invokes. The names of arguments come after. If the automation server uses ObjectComponents, then the names used in AUTONAMES come from the server's automation definition table. The function name is the external name in an EXPOSE_METHOD macro, and the argument names come from subsequent OPTIONAL_ARG macros.

The second parameter in a proxy method implementation, AUTOARGS, lists all the arguments that the controller chooses to pass for this command. It tells what will be pushed onto the command stack. AUTOARGS must always list all the required arguments in order first. At the end of the list are any optional arguments from the AUTONAMES macro. If five arguments are required and the controller wants to pass only one of five optional arguments, then the list in AUTOARGS includes six arguments, the optional one last.

The names used for required arguments are just dummy names. Their position in the list indicates which argument they represent. The names for optional arguments must be the same as the names used in AUTONAMES. For optional arguments, the name itself is what identifies a particular parameter.

Note   When an automation command passes an object as a parameter or a return value, be sure to pass by reference, not by value. For example, access functions for a property implemented as an object should follow this form:

```
GetObjectX( X& obj );
SetObjectX( X& obj );
```

Passing objects by assignment makes it impossible to provide C++ type safety.

Step 5: Creating and using proxy objects

Through a proxy class you can talk to an OLE object, but first the object has to exist. The *TAutoProxy* class defines a member function called *Bind* that asks OLE to create an object. The parameter passed to *Bind* determines the type of object to create. The most convenient identifier is usually a name the automation object has recorded in the registration database. (The object's unique *clsid* number also works but is harder to remember and write.) This is what an automation controller does to make OLE create a calculator object:

```
TCalc calc;                                 // create proxy object
calculator.Bind("Calc.Application");        // make OLE create real object
```

The string passed to *Bind* is what the automation server registered as its *progid*:

```
REGDATA(progid, "Calc.Application")      // from server's registration table
```

The destructor for *TAutoProxy* calls the *Unbind* method, so when *calculator* goes out of scope, the calculator object is destroyed.

While *calc* remains in scope, the controller program issues commands by calling methods on the proxy object. The commands in the following example add 1234 + 4321 and display the result in the calculator's window.

```
calc.SetOperand(1234);
calc.SetOp("Add");
calc.Evaluate();
calc.SetOperand(4321);
calc.Button("+");
calc.Evaluate();
calc.Display();
```

Step 6: Compiling and linking an automation controller

Automation servers and can be compiled with any memory model except Small. (They run faster in medium model.) And they must be linked with the OLE and ObjectComponents libraries.

The integrated development environment (IDE) chooses the right build options for you when you ask for OLE support. To build any ObjectComponents program from the command line, create a short makefile that includes the OCFMAKE.GEN file found in the EXAMPLES subdirectory.

```
EXERES = MYPROGRAM
OBJEXE = winmain.obj myprogram.obj
!include $(BCEXAMPLEDIR)\ocfmake.gen
```

EXERES and OBEXE hold the name of the file to build and the names of the object files to build it from. The last line includes the OCFMAKE.GEN file. Name your file MAKEFILE and type this at the command line prompt:

```
make MODEL=F, SYSTEM=WIN32
```

MAKE, using instructions in OCFMAKE.GEN, will build a new makefile tailored to your project. The new makefile is called WIN32F*xx*.MAK.

For more information, see "Building an ObjectComponents application" in Chapter 36.

Enumerating automated collections

Many automated objects have properties that represent a set of related items—for example, integers in an array, structures in a linked list, or a group of objects such as the buttons on the face of the calculator. To expose a collection, the automation server must implement a collection object with access functions. As OLE sees it, a collection object implements the standard *IEnumVARIANT* interface.

Here is what a controller must do to use a collection object and enumerate items in the server:

1 Declare a proxy collection class

2 Implement the proxy collection class

3 Declare a collection property

4 Send commands to the collection

Declaring a proxy collection class

A proxy collection class usually supplies member functions to find out how many items are in the collection, to retrieve individual items randomly by their position in the list, and to enumerate the items in the list sequentially. (On the server's side, ObjectComponents calls this *iterating*. The controller uses the server's iterator to enumerate the items.)

Here is the proxy class that AutoGen creates to enumerate the collection of calculator buttons in AutoCalc.

```
// TKIND_DISPATCH: TButtonList 1.2 {877B6204-7627-101B-B87C-0000C057CE4E}\409
// Button Collection
class TButtonList : public TAutoProxy {
  public:
    TButtonList() : TAutoProxy(0x409) {}
    // Button Count
    long GetCount(); // [id(1), propget]
    // Button Iterator
```

```
        void Enumerate(TAutoEnumerator<TCalcButton>&); // [id(-4), propget]
        // Button Collection Item
        void Item(TCalcButton&, short Index); // [id(0), method]
};
```

The only thing here that wasn't in the previous proxy classes is the use of the
TAutoEnumerator template. *TAutoEnumerator* encapsulates the code for manipulating
the *IEnumVARIANT* interface of a collection object. The type you pass to the template is
the type of value the collection contains. In the example, *TCalcButton* is another proxy
class representing an automated button object in the server.

Implementing the proxy collection class

This is the code that AutoGen writes to implement the proxy collection class. *Count* and
Item are straightforward. The *Enumerate* method does several new things, however.

```
// TKIND_DISPATCH: TButtonList 1.2 {877B6204-7627-101B-B87C-0000C057CE4E}\409
// Button Collection
long TButtonList::GetCount()
{
  AUTONAMES0("Count")
  AUTOARGS0()
  AUTOCALL_PROP_GET
}
void TButtonList::Enumerate(TAutoEnumerator<TCalcButton>& obj)
{
  AUTONAMES0(DISPID_NEWENUM)
  AUTOARGS0()
  AUTOCALL_PROP_REF(obj)
}
void TButtonList::Item(TCalcButton& obj, short Index)
{
  AUTONAMES0("Item")
  AUTOARGS1(Index)
  AUTOCALL_METHOD_REF(obj)
}
```

First, the parameter to the *Enumerate* method is a reference to an object of the type that
the collection contains. On successive calls, *Enumerate* returns collection items through
this parameter. The data type for the parameter must use the *TAutoEnumerator* template.

Second, the method is identified to AUTONAMES0 as DISPID_NEWENUM. This is a
predefined constant from oleauto.h representing the standard dispatch ID (which
happens to be –4) for an enumerating command. The AUTONAMES0 macro accepts a
dispatch ID instead of a function name. (The other AUTONAMES macros, those that
expect argument names as well, require a name string for the function.)

Finally, an enumerator is a property of its object and it passes an object by value; so the
enumerator implementation ends with the AUTOCALL_PROP_REF macro.

Declaring a collection property

TButtonsList is now fully defined as a proxy class for the server's collection object. What's needed now is a way to ask the controller for the collection. In AutoCalc, the collection of buttons is a property of the calculator's automated window object.

```
class TCalcWindow : public TAutoProxy {
  public:
    TCalcWindow() : TAutoProxy(0x409) {}
    // Button Collection
    void GetButtons(TButtonList&); // [id(5), propget]
```

The window class exposes the collection through a *GetButtons* command that returns the value of the collection property. *GetButtons* needs the *TButtonList* class to declare its parameter type.

Sending commands to the collection

This code from the sample program CallCalc sends the calculator commands that press its buttons. In the code, *window* is the automated window object. *TCalcButton* is the proxy class for individual buttons. *TButtonList* is the proxy object for the collection.

```
TButtonList buttons;               // declare a collection object
window.GetButtons(buttons);        // bind buttons to automated collection object
TAutoEnumerator<TCalcButton> list; // create an enumerator of TCalcButton objects
buttons.Enumerate(list);           // bind list to the server's iterator
TCalcButton button;                // declare a button object

for (i = IDC_FIRSTBUTTON;; i++) {
  list.Object(button);             // bind button to an automated button object
  button.SetActivate(true);        // press the calculator button
  list.Step()// list.Step advances to the next item in list
}
```

The *buttons*, *list*, and *button* variables are each created in one step and then bound to a server object in another. Each of them is a proxy object for something the server created; *buttons*, for example, is the proxy object for a collection of automated button objects. Simply declaring a proxy object, however, does not attach it to any particular automated object in the server.

To be able to send commands, a proxy object must be bound to something with an automation interface (*IDispatch* or *IEnumVARIANT*). Because the server defines the collection of buttons as a property of the calculator's window, this command retrieves the collection and connects it to the buttons proxy object:

```
window.GetButtons(buttons);  // bind buttons to automated collection object
```

The two other lines where the comments indicate binding takes place similarly connect *list* to the collection's iterator object and *button* to individual button objects in the collection.

A simple assignment statement might seem more intuitive than the binding step, but the only value that could be assigned in these cases is simply a pointer to an automation interface. A pointer carries no type information; a pointer to a collection's *IDispatch* looks just like the pointer to a button's *IDispatch*. Binding to an existing C++ object preserves information about what kind of automation object it represents.

VI

Visual Database Tools developer's guide

Visual Database Tools enables you, the C++ programmer, to create robust 16-bit or 32-bit database applications quickly and easily using database components. Your database applications can work directly with data created by desktop databases such as Paradox, dBASE, the Local InterBase Server, and ODBC data sources. You can also build database applications for remote database servers such as InterBase, Oracle, Sybase, Microsoft SQL Server, Informix, and ODBC data sources. Client applications can be scaled easily between mission-critical network-based client/server databases, and local databases on a single machine.

You use the Visual Database Tools components to design your database forms within the C++ Integrated Development Environment (IDE). You then write event handlers that respond to events that occur as your application runs.

This introduction to Part VI presents the various database tools that are available to you and the underlying architecture of Visual Database Tools. It also presents an overview of how to develop applications for either desktop or remote servers, and the methodology for developing database applications in general.

You should have a working knowledge of the Database Management System (DBMS) that your database applications will access, whether it is a desktop database such as dBASE or Paradox, or an SQL server.

This part assumes you have a basic understanding of relational databases, database design, and data management. There are many third-party books covering these topics if you need to learn more about them.

How this part is organized

After introducing you to Visual Database Tools, the following chapters provide the details:

Chapter 41, "Creating applications with Visual Database Tools," introduces you to the concept of components and gets you started creating your own database applications with Visual Database Tools.

Chapter 42, "Using data-access components and tools," provides an overview and general description of data-access components in the context of application development.

Chapter 43, "Using data-aware controls," describes basic features common to all data-aware controls, then describes how and when to use individual components.

Chapter 44, "Using SQL in applications," describes how to use SQL syntax directly by using the *TQuery* component.

Chapter 45, "Building a client/server application," describes how to develop applications that can access remote SQL servers such as Oracle, Sybase, Informix, and InterBase servers, as well as local Paradox and dBASE databases.

Chapter 46, "Programming with third-party VBX controls," discusses how to use third-part VBX controls in your applications.

Chapter 47, "Using local SQL," describes naming conventions, syntax enhancements, and syntax limitations for local SQL.

Visual Database Tool architecture

You build a Visual Database Tools application using data-access components, which let the applications you write access databases on either desktop or remote servers, and data-aware components, which lets users view and edit the data in the databases. A database application uses Visual Database Tools to communicate with the Borland Database Engine (BDE), which in turn communicates with the databases. The following figure illustrates the relationship of the Visual Database Tools and database applications to the BDE and data sources:

Figure VI.1   Visual Database Tools database architecture

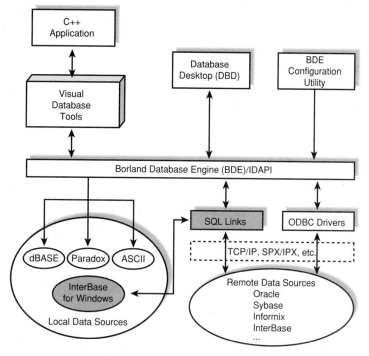

The following table summarizes the database features of the Visual Database Tools.

Table VI.1   Database features summary

Tool	Purpose
Data-access components	Access databases, tables, and stored procedures; run queries; and move data.
Data-aware components	Provide user interface to data in databases.
Borland Database Desktop	Create, index, and query Paradox and dBASE tables, and SQL databases. Access and edit data from all sources.
Borland Database Engine (BDE)	Access data from file-based Paradox and dBASE tables, and from local InterBase server databases.
Borland Database Engine Configuration Utility	Create and manage database connection aliases used by the BDE.
Borland Database Engine SDK online reference	Provide the online documentation for the Borland Database Engine Software Development Kit.

These features enable you to build database applications with live connections to Paradox and dBASE tables through the Borland Database Engine. In many cases, you can create simple database applications with these components without writing a line of code.

The Borland Database Engine is built into Visual Database Tools components so you can create database applications without needing to know anything about the Borland

Database Engine. Borland's Delphi, Visual dBASE, and Paradox use the Borland Database Engine also, as does Novell's Quattro Pro.

The Borland C++ installation program installs drivers and sets up configuration for Paradox and dBASE so you can begin working with tables native to these systems immediately. The BDE Configuration Utility lets you tailor database connections and manage database aliases.

Advanced BDE features are available to programmers who need more functionality. These features include local SQL, which is a subset of the industry-standard SQL that enables you to issue SQL statements against Paradox and dBASE tables; low-level API function calls for direct engine access; and ODBC support for communication with other ODBC-compliant databases, such as Microsoft Access and Btrieve.

The Borland Database Engine uses *aliases* as convenient shorthand names for often-used data sources, whether local or remote. The BDE Configuration Utility enables you to define and modify aliases that your database applications can use immediately. For more information about defining aliases, see the online Help for the BDE Configuration Utility.

Data sources

Visual Database Tools applications obtain their data through the Borland Database Engine. The different data sources that the Borland Database Engine can use are shown in Table VI.2.

Table VI.2   Database application data sources

Data source	Description	File extension
Paradox	Tables created with Paradox, dBASE, or Database Desktop (DBD). Each table is in a separate file.	.DB
dBASE	Tables created with Paradox, dBASE, or Database Desktop (DBD). Each table is in a separate file.	.DBF
ASCII files	Tables created with Paradox, dBASE, or Database Desktop (DBD). Each table is in a separate file.	.TXT
Local InterBase Server	Database created with InterBase Windows ISQL. Multiple tables in a single database file.	.GDB
SQL Database Server: Oracle, Sybase, Microsoft SQL Server, Informix, InterBase	Database created with server-specific tools, or the DBD, accessed across a network with SQL Links.	Depends on server
ODBC data sources	Databases such as Microsoft Access, Btrieve, FoxPro, etc.	Depends on data source

Visual Database Tools components

The Visual Database Tools components are divided into two categories: data-access components and data-aware controls. You will use both to create your database applications.

Data-access components

The data-access components are a set of components that encapsulate the Borland Database Engine and simplify database access. The architecture used to build these components is the Component Object Model (COM), the underlying architecture of OLE. Because all these components support the IDispatch interface, they can be used from an OLE Automation Controller such as Microsoft Excel. If you want to program using the COM interface, use the . . .INCLUDE\VDBT\bdtc.h header file.

You don't have to learn how to program with OLE or COM, however. If your application uses ObjectWindows or some other class library, you can program using ObjectWindows style classes in . . .INCLUDE\VDBT\bdto.h. If you use this interface to the data-access components, you can use a syntax that simplifies programming with components and their properties, methods, and events. This book and the online Help system explain how to program using the ObjectWindows style classes with the simplified syntax.

Although the data-access components are not visible while an application is running, you can see them in the C++ IDE. When Visual Database Tools is installed, the components appear as VBX components on the Data Access page of the Controls palette of the Dialog editor within the IDE. By placing a combination of data-access components and data-aware controls on a form you build in the Dialog editor, and setting property values with the Property Inspector, you can access "live" data in your database even as you continue to design your database form.

These are the data-access components:

Table VI.3   Data-access components

Icon	Component	Purpose
	TBatchMove	Copies a table structure or its data. Can be used to move entire tables from one database format to another.
	TDatabase	Sets up a persistent connection to a database, especially a remote database requiring a user login and password.
	TDataSource	Acts as a conduit between a dataset component (*TTable*, *TQuery*, or *TStoredProc*) and a data-aware component such as *TDBGrid*.
	TQuery	Uses SQL statements to retrieve data from one or more database tables via the BDE and supplies it to one or more data-aware components through a *TDataSource* component, or uses SQL statements to send data from a component to a database via the BDE. To query dBASE or Paradox tables, use local SQL.
	TStoredProc	Enables an application to access server stored procedures. Sends data received from a component to a database through a *TDataSource* component and the BDE.
	TTable	Retrieves data from a database table via the BDE and supplies it to one or more data-aware components through a *TDataSource* component. Sends data received from a component to a database via the BDE.

For more information about programming with data-access components, see Chapter 42, "Using data-access components and tools."

Data-aware controls

The data-aware controls are user-interface components that you can use to create forms-based database applications. Like data-access components, data-aware controls are VBX controls that are visible while you are designing forms. Unlike data-access components, they are also visible when your application runs.

Like the data-access components, you have programmatic access to them if your application uses the ObjectWindows libraries. At run time, you can set properties, call methods, and respond to events of the data-aware controls. VBX events become as easy to respond to as regular Windows events. Each data-aware control has its own header file, which is an extension to the ObjectWindows class libraries.

You can also use these VBX controls with any C or C++ application as standard VBX controls.

You use data-aware controls together with data-access components. While the data-access components give you access to your data, the data-aware controls provide a way to view and modify that data. They provide a user interface for database applications, whether the application accesses a local database file, or a remote database server.

The following table lists the data-aware controls.

Table VI.4   Data-aware components

Icon	Component	Purpose
	TDBCheckBox	Check box that displays a value from a column, or modifies a field value for the current record.
	TDBComboBox	Combo box that displays or edits values in a column of a table.
	TDBEdit	Edit control that displays and edits a value from a column of the current record.
	TDBGrid	Grid that enables the viewing and editing of data in a table.
	TDBImage	Image control that displays, cuts, or pastes graphical BLOB images to and from a table.
	TDBListBox	List box that presents a list of choices to the user. When the user selects one of them, that item becomes the value in a column of the current record.

Table VI.4   Data-aware components (continued)

Icon	Component	Purpose
	TDBLookupCombo	Combo box that displays values mapped through another table at run time.
	TDBLookupList	List box that displays values mapped through another table at run time.
	TDBMemo	Memo control that displays or edits text BLOB data from a column in a table.
	TDBNavigator	Navigation control with buttons that move a table's current record pointer forward or backward; start Insert or Edit mode; post new or modified records; cancel Edit mode; and refresh display to retrieve updated data.
	TDBRadioGroup	Radio group populated with radio buttons that display or set column values.
	TDBText	Text control that displays a value from a column of the current record.

To see how data-aware controls are used in an application, read Chapter 43, "Using data-aware controls."For a complete description of each Visual Database Tools component, see Part V of the *C++ Language Reference*.

Database Desktop

Database Desktop is a database maintenance and data definition tool. It enables programmers to query, create, restructure, index, modify, and copy database tables, including Paradox and dBASE files, and SQL tables. You do not have to own Paradox or dBASE to use Database Desktop with desktop files in these formats.

Database Desktop can copy data and data dictionary information from one format to another. For example, you can copy a Paradox table to an existing database on a remote SQL server. For a complete description of Database Desktop, see the online Help for Database Desktop.

Developing applications for desktop and remote servers

Visual Database Tools allows you to develop and deploy database client applications for both desktop and remote servers. You can adapt an application developed for the desktop to access data on a remote SQL server. The user interface can stay the same even if the source of the data changes. To an end user, the database application looks the same whether it accesses a local database file or a remote SQL database.

For simple applications that use *TQuery* components to access desktop data, the transition to a remote server might be as simple as changing the data source. For other applications, more significant changes may be needed. Some of these changes are the result of differing conventions and concurrency issues between desktop and SQL databases.

For example, desktop databases like Paradox and dBASE are record-oriented. They lock and access a single record at a time. Each time a user changes a record, the changes are written to the database immediately. Desktop database users can see a range of records, and can efficiently navigate forward and backward through that range.

In contrast, data in SQL databases is set-oriented, and designed for simultaneous multiuser access. Record ordering must be specified as part of an SQL query. To accommodate multiuser access to data, SQL relies on transactions to govern access. You can find more information about working with transactions in Chapter 45, "Building a client/server application."

Database application development methodology

Developing database applications with Visual Database Tools is similar to developing other types of software, but there are important distinctions and challenges that must be addressed. The methodology presented in this section should be used as a guideline that you can adapt to meet your specific business needs.

Development scenarios

Because an application's design usually depends on the structure of the database it will access, the database must be defined before the application can be developed.

Note Database development (also called *data definition*) is a part of the overall development process, but is beyond the scope of this manual. For more information, refer to the numerous books about relational database design.

There are four possible scenarios for database application development:

- The database does not yet exist or must be redefined.

  - Use the Database Desktop utility to define Paradox and dBASE tables. For more information, see the online Database Desktop help.

  - For SQL servers, use the tools provided with the server or the Database Desktop. For example, for an InterBase Workgroup Server, use Windows ISQL. For more information, see the InterBase *Data Definition Guide*.

- The database exists on a desktop or LAN data source (Paradox or dBASE) and the application accesses it there. If the Borland Database Engine and the data source are on the same machine as the application, then the application is a standalone (not client/server) application.

- The database exists on a desktop data source, and is being upsized to an SQL server. This scenario is discussed in Chapter 47, "Using local SQL."

- The database exists on an SQL server and the application will access it there. This is a standard client/server application. For information specific to developing a client/server application, see Chapter 45.

Database application development cycle

The goal of database application development is to build a product that meets end users' long-term needs. While this goal may seem obvious, it is important not to lose sight of it throughout the complexities and often conflicting demands of the development process. To create a successful application, it is critical to define the end users' needs in detail early in the development process.

The three primary stages of database application development are:

- Design and prototyping
- Implementation
- Deployment and maintenance

There are database and application tasks in each of these phases. Depending on the size and scope of the development project, the database and application tasks may be performed by different individuals or by the same individual. Often, one team or individual is responsible for the database tasks of the project, and another team or individual is responsible for the application tasks.

Figure VI.2   Development cycle

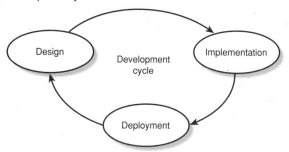

For client/server applications, the database and application tasks become more distinct, as they run on different platforms, often with different operating systems (for example, a Unix server and Windows 95 client).

When development responsibilities are divided this way, it is important to clearly delineate in the design phase which functions will be performed by the database server and which will be performed by the client application. Usually, the functional lines are clear cut. But database processes such as stored procedures can sometimes perform functions that can also be performed by the client application. Depending on the expected deployment configuration, application requirements, and other considerations, the design can allocate such functions to either client or server.

It is also important to realize that database application development is by its nature an iterative process. Users may not fully understand their own needs, or may define additional needs as development proceeds. User interface elements are always refined as they are used. Also, changing business needs will change requirements over time. Generally, a number of iterations through the development cycle will be required before an application can meet a significant portion of its requirements.

Design phase

The design phase begins with defining requirements. In consultation with knowledgeable end users, define the functional specifications for the database and applications. Determine which aspects of the functional requirements will be implemented in the database design, and which aspects will be implemented in the applications.

For client/server applications, often certain functions can be performed either by the server or by the application; for example, a complex mathematical transform function could be performed either by the client application or by a stored procedure on the server. The hardware deployment configuration will generally determine whether such functions are best performed on the server or client. For example, if the client platforms are expected to be low-end desktop PCs, and the server platform is expected to be a high-end workstation, it will probably be best to run computation-intensive functions on the server. If the hardware configuration changes, then it is possible to move the function between client and server in a later iteration.

Implementation phase

In the implementation phase, you use Visual Database Tools to build and test the application conceived in the design phase. During the implementation phase, you should use a duplicate data source, that is, a data source that has the same essential structure as the production database, but with a small subset of representative data. You should probably not develop an application against a production database, because the untested application might corrupt the data or otherwise interfere with normal database activities.

Note   It's possible you might have other applications running that use the Borland Database Engine. If so, you should close those applications before you begin testing or debugging your application to preserve the stability of your system.

If your application will ultimately use a desktop data source, make copies of the required tables with Database Desktop and populate them with representative "dummy" data.

If the application will ultimately use a remote data source (an SQL server), you can take two approaches during the implementation phase:

- Develop and test the application against a non-production database on the Local InterBase Server.

- Develop and test the application against a non-production database on the server.

The first approach has the advantage that it is isolated on the development platform(s), and so it will not interfere with other server activities. It will not consume server resources or increase network traffic. Its primary disadvantage is that only standard SQL server features can be used and tested during this phase, if you are using a server other than InterBase for the deployed application.

The second approach enables you to surface all server-specific features, but will consume network and server resources during testing. This approach can be dangerous, as it is conceivable that a programmer error could cause a server to crash during testing.

Deployment phase

In the deployment phase, the client/server application is put to the acid test: it is handed over to end users. To ensure that the application's basic functionality is error-free, deploy a prototype application before attempting to deploy a production application.

Because the ultimate judges of an application's usefulness are its users, developers must be prepared to incorporate changes to applications arising from their suggestions, changing business needs, and for general enhancement (for example, for usability). Sometimes application changes may require changes to the database, and conversely, changes to the database may require application changes. For this reason, application developers and database developers should work closely together during this phase. As features and enhancements are incorporated into the application, the application moves iteratively closer to completion.

Deploying a client/server application requires addressing a number of special issues including connectivity and multiuser access. These issues are discussed in Chapter 45.

Deploying an application

Deploying an application means giving it to the end users and providing the software they need to use the application in a production environment. Typically, when deploying a database application, you will create a package that includes all the files that end users need to run the application and access data sources.

Important   Before distributing any files, ensure that you have the proper redistribution rights. As described in the Borland C++ license agreement, you have distribution rights for the Borland Database Engine (including Paradox and dBASE support).

For information on deploying support for remote server access, see Chapter 45. For client/server applications, you also must ensure that the necessary communications software (for example, TCP/IP interface) is installed on the client platforms. This software is provided with databases servers. For more information, see your server documentation.

Deploying 16-bit applications

➤   To deploy a 16-bit application that uses COM classes only, you must provide:

- Your application .EXE file and .DLL files
- Required ancillary files (for example, a README file or .HLP files for online Help)
- Redistribution disks for Borland Database Engine (16-bit) support
- BDT50C.DLL, which contains the data-access COM classes

➤   If your application uses VBX controls (including Visual Database Tools components), your users need all files listed above and:

- BIVBX30.DLL, which is required for all applications that use VBX controls
- BDT50ACC.VBX, which contains all the data-access components
- BDT50CTL.VBX, which contains all the data-aware components
- BDT50EX.DLL, which converts the Visual Basic protocol to 16-bit Borland Database Engine
- Plus any third-party VBX controls your application uses

    If your application uses VBX controls, but not Visual Database Tools components, you need not distribute BDT50C.DLL, BDT50ACC.VBX, BDT50CTL.VBX, or BDT50EX.DLL.

➤ If your application uses OLE, you must provide the following:

- BDT50CF.DLL, which contains the 16-bit data-access COM classes
- BDT50.REG
- BDT50.TLB

Deploying 32-bit applications

➤ To deploy a 32-bit application that uses COM classes only, you must provide:

- Your application .EXE file and .DLL files
- Required ancillary files (for example, a README file or .HLP files for online Help)
- Redistribution disks for Borland Database Engine (32-bit) support
- BDT50CF.DLL, which contains the 32-bit data-access COM classes

➤ If your application uses VBX controls (including Visual Database Tools components), your users need all files listed above and:

- BIVBX30.DLL, which is required for all applications that use VBX controls
- BDT50ACC.VBX, which contains all the data-access components
- BDT50CTL.VBX, which contains all the data-aware components
- BDT50EXF.DLL, which converts the Visual Basic protocol to 32-bit Borland Database Engine
- Plus any third-party VBX controls your application uses

    If your application uses VBX controls, but not Visual Database Tools components or OLE, you need not distribute BDT50CF.DLL, BDT50ACC.VBX, BDT50CTL.VBX, or BDT50EXF.DLL.

➤ If your application uses OLE, you distribute the following:

- BDT50CF.DLL, which contains the 32-bit data-access COM classes
- BDT50.REG
- BDT5032.TLB

➤ For applications running under Windows 95 and using Visual Database Tools components, you need to include these two files:

- BIVBX30.32C
- BIVBX30C.DLL

➤ For applications running under Windows NT and using Visual Database Tools components, you need to include these two files:

- BIVBX30.32N
- BIVBX30N.EXE

Deploying BDE support

When you deploy a database application, you must ensure that the client platform has the correct version of the Borland Database Engine installed. Borland C++ includes the Redistributable Borland Database Engine, with its own installation utility, that you can redistribute with your applications. When you deploy an application, simply include a copy of the correct (16- or 32-bit) Redistributable Borland Database Engine disk.

Note The Borland license agreement requires you to make *all* the files in Redistributable Borland Database Engine available to your application users. This requirement enables users to install the new version of the BDE for Borland C++ without interfering with existing Paradox and dBASE applications. Therefore, to comply with the terms of the Borland license agreement, you *must* use either the Redistributable BDE disks to distribute BDE, or a third-party deployment tool that has been certified by Borland.

Language drivers

The Borland Database Engine provides the ability to localize applications with language drivers. The language driver DLL loads the drivers specified by Paradox or dBASE tables or in IDAPI.CFG for server databases. The language drivers are files with extension .LD installed in the LANGDRV subdirectory of the BDE directory.

Important For language drivers to load correctly, the WIN.INI file must have the following entry, assuming the default installation directory:

```
[Borland Languag  Drivers]
LDPath = C:\IDAPI\LANGDRV
```

ODBC Socket

The Borland Database Engine comes with an ODBC Socket. It has been certified with Microsoft's 2.0 ODBC Driver Manager. If you have a different version of the ODBC Driver Manager:

- Back up your existing ODBC.DLL and ODBCINST.DLL.

- Copy the version 2.0 files, ODBC.NEW and ODBCINST.NEW, from your BDE directory to your WINDOWS\SYSTEM directory.

- Rename these files to ODBC.DLL and ODBCINST.DLL.

Note The ODBC 2.0 Driver Manager does work with ODBC 1.x ODBC drivers.

Using third-party VBX controls

Many excellent third-party VBX controls are available for your applications. If you have invested in these VBX controls, or are thinking of doing so, Borland C++ includes a

Visual Basic emulator that can accommodate level 1, level 2, and level 3 VBX controls in both 16-bit and 32-bit applications.

For more information about programming with third-party VBX controls, see Chapter 46, "Programming with third-party VBX controls."

41

Creating applications with Visual Database Tools

When you are creating applications with Visual Database Tools, you are programming with components. This chapter introduces you to the notion of components and gets you started creating your own database applications with Visual Database Tools.

Programming with components

What is a component? How does a component differ from a C++ class?

A *component* is a functional entity that can be completely characterized by its inputs and outputs. A component can be used and tested as a unit, independent of the context in which the component is eventually used. The internal implementation of a component is completely hidden from the user.

Properties

A *property* is a value, or state, associated with the component. You might think of a property as a variable whose value can be directly read or written to, as you would in a C++ class.

Properties are more, however. Usually your application needs to have an action associated with the change in value of the property. For example, if your application changes the color of a visible object, the color should change visually onscreen. Properties, like methods, usually impart behavior to an object.

Visual Database Tools components have properties. Using a specific component, you can set the value of many properties before your application begins running so the characteristics of the component appear as you want them to. This is called setting the properties of a component at design time.

Through the code that you write, you can also change the value of properties while your application is running, and you'll see results of the change in value immediately onscreen. This is called setting the properties of a component at run time.

By changing property values, you are giving input to the component and changing its characteristics.

Methods

The methods of a component function just as they do for any C++ class. Methods impart behavior to a component in that they cause the component to perform some operation or action.

When your application calls a method, passing data to it through parameters, you are again giving input to the component.

Events

Components can output information to the users of the component. This output takes the form of event notification. The component informs other components that use the component that a particular type of event has occurred. An event might occur when a method of the component is called or a property value changed, or an event could occur when the user uses the component, such as selecting an element in a list box.

It is up to you, the programmer, to write an event handler, code that responds to the event when it occurs. It's not necessary to respond to every event in a component. You choose those events that are important to your application and write the code that handles those events, so that your application responds to the event in a manner that meets the needs of your application.

So far, this chapter has discussed the properties, methods, and events of components on a theoretical level. The next sections explain how to work with the properties, methods, and events of the Visual Database Tools components. The code examples are written using the ObjectWindows library.

Setting properties

You can set or change the values of the properties of Visual Database Tools components at design time or at run time.

Setting properties at design time

You can set the values of properties of a Visual Database Tools component when you are designing your dialog box, or form, in the Dialog editor of the C++ IDE.

Once the Visual Database Tools have been installed in the Dialog editor and you open it, you'll see the Visual Database Tools on the Data Access and Data Aware page of the Controls palette.

You must display the Property Inspector to set the value of properties.

➤ To display the Property Inspector in the Dialog editor, choose Dialog | Show | Property Inspector.

The Property Inspector appears. You are ready to set property values for components.

➤ To set the properties of a Visual Database Tools component:

1 Select the Visual Database Tools component from either the Data Access or Data Aware page of the Controls palette and place it on your form.

If the component you placed on the form is selected, the properties for the component appear in the Property Inspector.

2 In the Property Inspector, select a property and change its value.

If you must type a value, replace the existing value (to the right of the property name).

If an ellipsis button appears to the right of the property value, you can click it to display a special editor for the property, or simply double-click the current value for the property, and the editor appears. For example, double-clicking the value for the *BackColor* property of a component displays the Color dialog box.

If a down arrow appears to the right of the property value, you can use it to open a list of choices, or you can double-click the current value for the property and cycle through the choices.

When your application uses the dialog resource (or form) you designed, the property values you set with the Property Inspector will be set when the form first appears.

Setting properties at run time

You can write code to access property values at run time. When the code executes, the property value changes and the results are often reflected onscreen.

Assigning values to properties uses a very simple syntax. The left side of the assignment operator is the property name, fully qualified with the name of the component. On the right side of the assignment operator is the new value you are assigning to the property. For example, this code checks the database check box named *MyDBCheckBox*:

```
MyDBCheckBox.Checked = true;
```

Note You should rename components at design time by specifying a new value for the *Name* property, not by using code at run time.

Calling methods

You call a method of a Visual Database Tools component just as you would a method for any C++ class. Type the name of the method in your code, fully qualifying the method name with the name of the component. Pass any parameters within the parentheses following the method name.

For example, this code calls the *Append* method for a *TTable* component named *MyTable*:

```
MyTable.Append();
```

This code calls the *MoveBy* method for the same table, passing a parameter value of 5, indicating that the cursor should advance in the table by five records:

```
MyTable.MoveBy(5);
```

For a method that returns a value, assign the method to a variable or property. For example, this code returns a bookmark (the current location of the cursor in the dataset), storing it in the *MyBookmark* variable:

```
TBookmark MyBookmark;
MyBookmark = MyTable.GetBookmark();
```

Responding to events

Each component has a list of events that can occur. You can find the list of events for each component in the online Visual Database Tools reference.

Visual Database Tools components have default behavior, so for many database applications, you won't have to write any code at all. By simply linking database components together, you can create very useful database applications. To read more about linking database components together, see "Making the connections: linking database components" on page 619.

If you do need to write an event handler, the steps are relatively simple. Visual Database Tools uses event sources and event sinks (or handlers) to encapsulate everything necessary for responding to events. Here are the general steps:

1 Define the event source. By using Visual Database Tools components, you have already done this.

2 Define the event sink to handle the event. As you will see in the sections that follow, this is only a couple of lines of code.

3 Connect the event sink to the event handler method. This method is the actual code that you write.

4 Connect the event source to the event sink.

When the event occurs, the source calls the event sink. The sink calls the method identified as that event's handler, and your application performs the appropriate tasks.

It will be easier to understand this model by looking at an example event handler.

Defining the event source

Suppose you want your application to respond to events for a *TDBListBox* control. Looking up the list of events for a database list box, you see that it has these possible events:

Table 41.1 Events for a TDBListBox component

OnClick	*OnKeyUp*	*OnMouseMove*
OnDragOver	*OnKeyPress*	*OnMouseUp*
OnDragDrop	*OnEnter*	*OnMeasureItem*
OnEndDrag	*OnExit*	*OnDrawItem*
OnKeyDown	*OnMouseDown*	

This means that event sources are already defined for these events.

You decide that your application responds in some special way to the *OnEnter* event. You want something specific to happen when the database list box becomes the active control.

Defining the event sink

The event sink object responds to the event with the desired behavior. Because you included dblist.h, the typedefs and macros for the event sink are already in your code. Both the event sink statement and the actual event handler method go in your class definition for the event sink object:

```
class MyDialog : public TDialog, public TVbxEventHandler {
public:
  TDBListBoxEnterSink OnEnterSink;    \\here is the event sink declaration
  MyDialog( TWindow* parent, int ID );

// Declare the event handlers
  void EnterHandler( TDBListBoxNotifySink&, TDBListBox& );
};
```

Connecting the event sink to the handler method

One way to connect the event sink to the method that handles the event is to make the connection within the constructor. To help you do that, use the appropriate event sink macro that creates the event sink object for you.

To connect an event sink to the event handler:

1 Type the event sink followed by an open parenthesis. For example,

```
OnEnterSink(
```

2 Type the type of the event sink after the open parenthesis and add to it _MFUNCTOR. This calls the macro that connects the event sink to the event handler. Your code would look like this, so far:

```
OnEnterSink( TDBListBoxNotifySink_MFUNCTOR
```

3 Each MFUNCTOR macro takes at least two parameters: *this, and the event handler:

```
OnEnterSink( TDBListBoxNotifySink_MYFUNCTOR (*this, &MyDialog::EnterHandler)
```

Some events, such as mouse or key events, require more parameters.

4 Add the closing parenthesis:

```
OnEnterSink( TDBListBoxNotifySink_MYFUNCTOR (*this, &MyDialog::EnterHandler))
```

When this code executes as the dialog box is created, an event sink object is created and connected to the event handler that responds when the event occurs. Here is the constructor in which the event sink connection is made.

```
MyDialog::MyDialog()
:
   OnEnterSink( TDBListBoxNotifySinK_MFUNCTOR( *this, &MyDialog::EnterHandler ))
{
//the rest of the constructor
}
```

Connecting the event source to the event sink

Finally, connect the event source to the event sink, so that the correct method is called when the event occurs.

```
void OWLMain()
{
  TDBListBox Box( this, IDC_TDBLISTBOX1 );
  MyDialog DLG( this, IDD_MYDIALOG );
  Box.OnEnterSource += DLG.OnEnterSink;
  //the rest of the program
}
```

Event handling summary

This discussion has gone "under the hood" a little, to show you how Visual Database Tools handles events and to provide the information you might need to develop your own custom event handlers. Generally, you will be working only with the sink side of the equation. It will help to keep the following points in mind:

- Components that originate events must include sources for each event. These are in the class declaration. (Visual Database Tools does this part for you.)

- Components that respond to events must include sinks and handler methods for each event. Declare these in the class declaration for that component.

- For each event, connect the sink to the handler method in the constructor of the component.

- Connect the source object to the sink object in the main portion of your program.

An event-handling example

The example that follows uses a radio group control on a form. The radio group contains three buttons labeled Red, Green, and Blue. When the user selects one of these buttons, the background color of the form changes to match the color selected. The event that occurs when the value of the *Value* property of the radio group changes is the *OnChange* event.

Creating the container class

The class that contains the form with the radio group on it is derived from *TDialog*, but it also includes the event behavior from the *TVbxEventHandler* class. The declaration for the class is using multiple inheritance, inheriting and mixing behavior from both *TDialog* and *TVbxEventHandler*:

```
class EventDemoDlg : public TDialog, public TVbxEventHandler {
  private:
    TDBRadioGroup *DBRadio;
    TDBRadioGroupNotifySink OnChangeSink;

  public:
    EventDemoDlg();
    void OnRadioChangeHandler( TDBRadioGroupNotifySink&, TDBRadioGroup& );
    DECLARE_RESPONSE_TABLE( EventDemoDlg );
};
```

Note that the class includes a data member that holds a pointer to the radio group control on the form:

```
TDBRadioGroup *DBRadio;
```

The event sink for the *OnChange* event is declared within the class declaration:

```
TDBRadioGroupNotifySink OnChangeSink;
```

Also within the class declaration following the constructor, the event sink is connected to the *OnChange* event handler, which is named *OnRadioChangeHandler* in this example:

```
void OnRadioChangeHandler( TDBRadioGroupNotifySink&, TDBRadioGroup& );
```

The *EventDemoDlg* class includes a response table declaration for *EventDemoDlg*:

```
DECLARE_RESPONSE_TABLE( EventDemoDlg );
```

Therefore, outside of the class declaration a standard ObjectWindows response table is defined. Because *EventDemoDlg* is derived from two base classes, *TDialog* and *TVbxEventHandler*, the definition of the response table must include both classes:

```
DEFINE_RESPONSE_TABLE2( EventDemoDlg, TDialog, TVbxEventHandler )
END_RESPONSE_TABLE;
```

Connecting the event source to the event sink

The constructor for the *EventDemoDlg* class connects the form's *OnChangeSink* event sink object to the radio group's *OnChange* source object:

```
EventDemoDlg::EventDemoDlg()
  : TDialog( 0, AppName )
  , DBRadio( new TDBRadioGroup( this, IDC_TDBRADIOGROUP1 ) )
  , OnChangeSink( TDBRadioGroupNotify_MFUNCTOR( *this,
                  &EventDemoDlg::OnRadioChangeHandler ) )
{
  DBRadio->OnChangeSource += OnChangeSink;
}
```

Changing the form's color

The code within the *OnRadioChangeHandler*, which responds to the *OnChange* event, changes the background color of the form when it executes. This is the event handler:

```
void EventDemoDlg::OnRadioChangeHandler( TDBRadioGroupNotifySink&,
                                         TDBRadioGroup& rg )
{
  if( rg.Value == "Red" )
    SetBkgndColor( RGB( 255, 0, 0 ) );
  else if( rg.Value == "Green" )
    SetBkgndColor( RGB( 0, 255, 0 ) );
  else if( rg.Value == "Blue" )
    SetBkgndColor( RGB( 0, 0, 255 ) );
  Invalidate();
}
```

Here is the sample application in its entirety:

```
//-----------------------------------------------------------------------------
// ObjectWindows - (C) Copyright 1996 by Borland International
//                  All rights reserved.
//    Demo application - FuncDemo.cpp
//-----------------------------------------------------------------------------
#include <owl/owlpch.h>
#include <owl/applicat.h>
#include <owl/framewin.h>
#include <owl/dialog.h>
#include <owl/signatur.h>
#include <owl/eventhan.h>
#include <vdbt/bdto.h>
#include <vdbt/dbradio.h>
#include "evntdemo.h"

const char AppName[] = "EventDemo";

class EventDemoDlg : public TDialog, public TVbxEventHandler {
  private:
    TDBRadioGroup *DBRadio;
    TDBRadioGroupNotifySink OnChangeSink;

  public:
    EventDemoDlg();
    void OnRadioChangeHandler( TDBRadioGroupNotifySink&, TDBRadioGroup& );
    DECLARE_RESPONSE_TABLE( EventDemoDlg );
};

DEFINE_RESPONSE_TABLE2( EventDemoDlg, TDialog, TVbxEventHandler )
    END_RESPONSE_TABLE;

EventDemoDlg::EventDemoDlg()
  : TDialog( 0, AppName )
  , DBRadio( new TDBRadioGroup( this, IDC_TDBRADIOGROUP1 ) )
  , OnChangeSink( TDBRadioGroupNotify_MFUNCTOR( *this,
                  &EventDemoDlg::OnRadioChangeHandler ) )
{
  DBRadio->OnChangeSource += OnChangeSink;
}
```

```
void EventDemoDlg::OnRadioChangeHandler( TDBRadioGroupNotifySink&
                                       , TDBRadioGroup& rg )
{
  if( rg.Value == "Red" )
    SetBkgndColor( RGB( 255, 0, 0 ) );
  else if( rg.Value == "Green" )
    SetBkgndColor( RGB( 0, 255, 0 ) );
  else if( rg.Value == "Blue" )
    SetBkgndColor( RGB( 0, 0, 255 ) );

  Invalidate();
}
class EventDemoApp : public TApplication {
  public:
    EventDemoApp() : TApplication() {}
    void InitMainWindow()
    {
      SetMainWindow(new TFrameWindow(0, "DataAware Demo"
                                    , new EventDemoDlg, true));
    }
};
int OwlMain(int /*argc*/, char* /*argv*/ [])
{
  TBIVbxLibrary vbxLib;      // Loads & initializes the library
  return EventDemoApp().Run();
}
```

Note In the *OwlMain* function, the Visual Basic emulator is loaded and initialized. All Visual Database Tools applications must include this code.

You can find a similar, but more detailed version of this example in the online Help.

Component Object Model (COM) classes

So far this chapter has discussed programming database applications using the ObjectWindows style classes. For most C++ programmers, this is the simplest method.

Visual Database Tools also encapsulates the data-access components using the Component Object Model (COM), the underlying architecture of OLE. Because these components support the IDispatch interface, they can be used from an OLE Automation Controller, such as Microsoft Excel.

If you wish to use OLE or COM, you'll find the Borland Visual Database Tools COM interfaces in the ...\INCLUDE\VDBT\bdtc.h file. For OLE Automation, use the type library files BDT50.TLB and BDT5032.TLB.

Building database forms

Most Visual Database Tools applications require that you place at least three database components on the form you are building. This is the minimum number of components you need:

- One dataset component

  Dataset components, such as *TTable* and *TQuery*, communicate with the Borland Database Engine. Data received from a component is sent to the database through the BDE.

- One data-aware control

  Data-aware controls provide the user interface to the data in the dataset. Users can use data-aware controls to browse, edit, or enter data.

- One *TDataSource* component

  A *TDataSource* component acts as a conduit between a dataset component and a data-aware control. It links the data-aware control with the dataset component, and therefore, the data in the database. Without a *TDataSource* component, data-aware controls cannot access the data in a database.

The following figure illustrates how data-access and data-aware components relate to the data in a database, to one another, and to the user interface in a Visual Database Tools database application:

Figure 41.1 Database components architecture

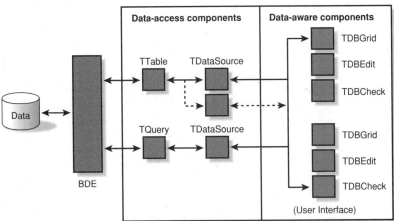

The figure shows two dataset components, *TTable* and *TQuery*. Each of these has at least one corresponding *TDataSource* component, although they can have more than one. Each *TDataSource* component identifies the source of the data for the data-aware controls. It also shows six data-aware controls; your application can include as many as it requires. Each data-aware control names the appropriate *TDataSource* component as the value of its *DataSource* property.

Making the connections: linking database components

This section describes how to connect database components. This allows you to create a single-table database application without writing a line of code. Follow the steps below to link a *TTable* component, a *TDataSource* component, and a data-aware component together:

1 Place a *TTable* component, a *TDataSource* component, and any data-aware control except the database navigator on a form.

Only the data-aware control will be visible when you run your application; therefore, it doesn't matter where you place the *TTable* and *TDataSource* components.

2 Set the *DatabaseName* property of *TTable* to the name of database you want to access.

While you are learning the technique of linking database components, try selecting the DBDEMOS alias that appears in list of database names available to *TTable*. DBDEMOS identifies a set of database tables that were installed as part of Visual Database Tools.

3 Set the *TableName* property of *TTable* to the name of the table in the database you want to access.

You will see a list of tables available from which you can choose.

4 Set the *Dataset* property of the *TDataSource* component to the name of the *TTable* component by choosing from the list of available dataset components.

If you have only one dataset component on the form, you will have only one choice.

5 Set the *DataSource* property of the data-aware control to the name of the *TDataSource* component by choosing from the list of available data source components.

If you have only one data source component on the form, you will have only one choice.

6 If the data-aware control has a *DataField* property, select the field you want the control to access by selecting it from the list of available fields.

All data-aware controls except the data grid (*TDBGrid*) and the database navigator (*TDBNavigator*) have a *DataField* property.

7 To display the data in the data-aware control, return to the *TTable* component and set its *Active* property to true.

Setting *Active* to true opens the table and the data displays in the data-aware control.

You might want to place one more data-aware control on your form. The database navigator (*TDBNavigator*) provides an easy way to move through the data in the dataset.

➤ To use a database navigator control:

1 Add the database navigator to the form.

2 Set its *DataSource* property to the name of the *TDataSource* component that links to the dataset you want to access.

To test the database navigator, select choose Dialog | Test Dialog. Your designed form is in test mode, and you can use the database navigator to move through the records in the dataset.

Creating a master-detail form

Many database applications require master-detail forms. In relational database terms, this can be a one to many relationship. This section describes building a simple master-detail form in which the user can scroll through customer records, and display all orders for the current customer. By working through the example, you will learn how to create your own master-detail forms.

➤ Follow these steps to create the master-detail form:

1 Place two *TTable*, two *TDataSource*, and two *TDBGrid* components on a form.

2 Set the properties of the first *TTable* component as follows:
   - *DatabaseName*: DBDEMOS
   - *TableName*: CUSTOMER.DB (the table containing customer records)
   - *CtlName*: CustTable (for ease-of-use)

3 Name the first *TDataSource* component "CustDataSource," and set its *Dataset* property to "CustTable."

4 Set the *DataSource* property of a data grid to "CustDataSource."

   When you open CustTable (by setting its *Active* property to true), the grid displays the data in the CUSTOMER table.

5 Set the properties of the second *TTable* component as follows:
   - *DatabaseName*: DBDEMOS
   - *TableName*: ORDERS.DB (the table containing order records)
   - *CtlName*: OrdTable (for ease-of-use)

6 Name the second *TDataSource* component "OrdDataSource," and set its *Dataset* property to "OrdTable."

7 Set the *DataSource* property of the second data grid to "OrdDataSource."

   When you open OrdTable (by setting its *Active* property to true), the grid displays the data in the ORDERS table.

   If you choose Dialog | Test Dialog at this time to test your form, you'll see that you have two tables that are not connected to one another.

8 Next link the CUSTOMER table (the master table) to the ORDERS table (the detail table) so that the form displays only the orders placed by the current customer. To do this, set the *MasterSource* property of OrdTable to CustDataSource.

9 In the Property Inspector, select the *MasterFields* property of OrdTable and click the ellipsis button to the right of the property value. The Field Link Designer dialog box opens.

- In the Available Indexes field, select "CustNo" to define the record order.
- Select "CustNo" in both the Detail Fields and Master Fields field lists.
- Click the Add button to add this join condition. In the Joined Fields list, "CustNo -> CustNo" appears.
- Choose OK to exit the Field Link Designer.

Choose Test Dialog on the Dialog menu. You will see that the tables are linked together, and that when you move to a new record in the CUSTOMER table, you see only those records in the ORDERS table that belong to the current customer.

The *MasterSource* property specifies the *TDataSource* from which *OrdTable* takes its master column values. This limits the records it retrieves, based on the current record in CustTable. To do this, you must specify for *OrdTable*:

- The name of the column that links the two tables.
- The index of the column in the ORDERS table that links to the CUSTOMER table.

You must also ensure that the ORDERS table has an index on the *CustNo* field. If it is a primary index, there is no need to specifically name it, and you can safely leave the *IndexName* field blank in both tables. If the table is linked through a secondary index, however, you must explicitly designate that index in the *IndexName* property.

In this example, the CUSTOMER table has a primary index on the *CustNo* column, so there is no need to specify the index name. The ORDERS table does not have a primary index on *CustNo*, however, so you must explicitly declare it in the *IndexName* property, in this case CusNo.

Note   You can also set the *IndexFieldNames* property to CustNo, and the correct index is supplied for you.

Sample database applications

Borland C++ is shipped with several demo applications. There are several applications that show you many practical uses for Visual Database Tools in the ...\EXAMPLES\ VDBT directory. You are encouraged to run the sample applications and examine the forms and code to see how they were put together.

42

Using data-access components and tools

This chapter describes how to use key Visual Database Tools when building database applications, including:

- The *TSession* component
- Dataset components (*TTable* and *TQuery*), their properties, methods, and events
- *TDataSource* components, their properties, methods, and events
- *TField* components, their properties, methods, and events
- The Fields editor to control *TField* components
- *TBatchMove* components, for batch move operations

This chapter provides an overview and general description of data-access components in the context of application development. For information about data-aware controls, see Chapter 43, "Using data-aware controls." For in-depth reference information on the database components, see the online Visual Database Tools reference.

Data-access components hierarchy

The data-access component hierarchy helps you understand that key components inherit the properties, methods, and events of their ancestors. These are the key data-access components:

- *TSession*, a global component created automatically at run time. It is not visible on dialogs or forms either when you are designing them in the IDE's Dialog editor (at design time) or when the application runs (at runtime).

- *TDatabase*, a component that provides an additional level of control over server logins, transaction control, and other database features. It appears on the Data Access page of the Controls palette of the IDE's Dialog editor.

- *TTable, TQuery,* and *TStoredProc,* known as dataset components because they descend from *TDataSet* and *TDBDataSet.* They appear on the Data Access page of the Controls palette of the IDE's Dialog editor.

- *TDataSource,* a conduit between dataset components and data-aware components. It appears on the Data Access page of the Controls palette of the IDE's Dialog editor.

- *TField* components, which correspond to columns within a database. They are created either dynamically at run time or at design time with the Fields editor. Data-aware controls use *TField* components internally to access data from a database. In addition, you can define calculated fields whose values are calculated based on the values of one or more database columns.

Figure 42.1   Visual Database Tools data-access components hierarchy

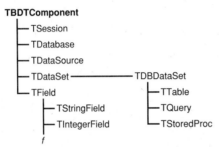

This chapter describes most of these components and the tools provided to work with them. The *TQuery* component is described in "Using the TQuery component" on page 85. The *TDatabase* and *TStoredProc* components are described in Chapter 45.

Using datasets

TTable and *TQuery* components descend from the *TDataSet* component through the *TDBDataSet* component. These components share a number of inherited properties, methods, and events. For this reason, it is convenient to refer to them together as datasets, when the discussion applies to both *TTable* and *TQuery*.

This section describes the features of datasets that are common to *TTable* and *TQuery*. A subsequent section discusses features unique to *TTable*. "Using the TQuery component" on page 85 describes features unique to *TQuery*.

Note   *TStoredProc* is also a dataset component as it descends from *TDBDataset* too. Therefore, much of this section also applies to *TStoredProc* if the stored procedure returns a result set rather than a singleton result. For more information on *TStoredProc*, see "Using stored procedures" on page 104.

Dataset states

A dataset can be in the following states, also referred to as *modes*:

Table 42.1   Dataset states

State	Description
Inactive	The dataset is closed.
Browse	The default state when a dataset is opened. Records can be viewed but not changed or inserted.
Edit	Enables the current row to be edited.
Insert	Enables a new row to be inserted. A call to *Post* inserts a new row.
SetKey	Enables *FindKey*, *GotoKey*, and *GotoNearest* to search for values in database tables. These methods only pertain to *TTable* components. For *TQuery*, searching is done with SQL syntax.
CalcFields	Mode when the *OnCalcFields* event is executed; prevents any changes to fields other than calculated fields. Rarely used explicitly.

An application can put a dataset into most states by calling the method corresponding to the state. For example, an application can put a *TTable* component named *MyTable* in Insert state by calling *MyTable.Insert* or Edit state by calling *MyTable.Edit*. A number of methods return a dataset to Browse state, depending on the result of the method call. A call to *Cancel* will always return a dataset to Browse state.

CalcFields mode is a special case. An application cannot explicitly put a dataset into CalcFields mode. A dataset automatically goes into CalcFields mode when its *OnCalcFields* event occurs. In *OnCalcFields*, an exception occurs if an application attempts to assign values to non-calculated fields. After the completion of the *OnCalcFields* event, the dataset returns to its previous mode.

Figure 42.2 illustrates the primary dataset states and the methods that cause a dataset to change from one mode to another.

The *State* property specifies the current state of a dataset. The possible values correspond to the states listed in Table 42.1 and are *dsInactive, dsBrowse, dsEdit, dsInsert, dsSetKey,* and *dsCalcFields*.

The *OnStateChange* event of *TDataSource* occurs whenever the state of a data source's dataset changes. For more information, see "Using TDataSource events" on page 645.

Figure 42.2 Dataset state diagram

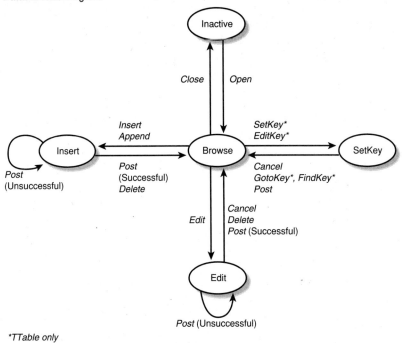

*TTable only

Opening and closing datasets

Before an application can access data through a dataset, the dataset must be open. You can open a dataset in two ways:

- Set the dataset's *Active* property to true, either at design time through the Property Inspector of the Dialog editor, or programmatically at run time. For example,

  ```
  MyTable.Active = true;
  ```

- Call the dataset's *Open* method at run time. For example,

  ```
  Query1.Open();
  ```

Both of these statements open the dataset and put it into Browse state.

Similarly, you can close a dataset in two ways:

- Set the dataset's *Active* property to false, either at design time through the Property Inspector of the Dialog editor, or programmatically at run time. For example,

  ```
  Query1.Active = false;
  ```

- Call the dataset's *Close* method. For example,

```
MyTable.Close();
```

Both of these statements return a dataset to Inactive state.

Navigating datasets

There are two important concepts essential for understanding how datasets are handled: *cursors* and *local buffers*. Each active dataset has a cursor, which is essentially a pointer to the *current row* in the dataset. A number of rows of data before and after the cursor are fetched into the local buffer. The number of rows fetched into the local buffer will always be sufficient to display the current row, plus additional rows to reduce the refresh time as the user scrolls up or down in the dataset:

Table 42.2   Navigational methods and properties

Method or property	Description
First method	Moves the cursor to the first row of a dataset.
Last method	Moves the cursor to the last row of the dataset.
Next method	Moves the cursor to the next row in the dataset.
Prior method	Moves the cursor to the prior row in the dataset.
AtBOF property	True when cursor is known to be at the beginning of the dataset, otherwise false.
AtEOF property	True when cursor is known to be at the end of the dataset, otherwise false.
MoveBy(n) method	Moves the cursor *n* rows in the dataset, where *n* is a positive or negative integer.

You can navigate within a dataset by calling these methods in the code you write, or you can let the user use a database navigator (*TDBNavigator*) to move to the desired record in the dataset. For more information on using navigator, see "Navigating and manipulating records with TDBNavigator" on page 75.

The Next and Prior methods

The *Next* method moves the cursor down (forward) by one row in the table. For example, to move to the next row in the table named *MyTable*, write this code:

```
MyTable.Next();
```

Similarly, the *Prior* method moves the cursor up (backward) by one row in the dataset. For example, to move to the previous row in the table, write this code:

```
MyTable.Prior();
```

The First and Last methods

As their names imply, the *First* and *Last* methods move to a dataset's first and last rows, respectively. For example, this code moves the cursor to the first row in the table named *MyTable*:

```
MyTable.First();
```

Similarly, the *Last* method moves to the last row in the dataset. To move to the last row in the table, the code would look like this:

```
MyTable.Last();
```

The AtBOF and AtEOF properties

AtBOF is a read-only Boolean property that indicates whether a dataset is known to be on its first row. The *AtBOF* property returns a value of true only after:

- An application first opens a table
- A call to the *First* method of a dataset
- A call to the *Prior* method of a dataset fails

Databases are dynamic; while one application is viewing data, another may be inserting rows before or after the first application's notion of the current row. For this reason, it's not safe to assume *AtBOF* is true for a table that isn't empty.

For example, consider the following code:

```
MyTable.Open();   // AtBOF == true
MyTable.Next();   // AtBOF == false
MyTable.Prior();  // AtBOF == false
```

After this code executes, *AtBOF* is false, even if there are no records before the current row. Once the table is open, the application can determine *AtBOF* only when an application explicitly calls *First* or a call to *Prior* fails. Similarly, an application can determine *AtEOF* only when an application explicitly calls *Last* or a call to *Next* fails.

The following code sample demonstrates a common technique for using the *AtBOF* property:

```
while ( ! MyTable.AtBOF ) {
  DoSomething();
  MyTable.Prior();
}
```

In this code sample, the hypothetical method *DoSomething* is called on the current record and then on all the records between the current record and the beginning of the dataset. The loop continues until a call to *Prior* fails to move the current record back. At that point, *AtBOF* returns a value of true and the program breaks out of the loop.

To improve performance during the iteration through the table, call the *DisableControls* method before beginning the loop. This prevents data controls from displaying the iteration through the table, and speeds up the loop. After the loop completes, call the *EnableControls* method. The same principles apply to the *AtEOF* property, which returns a value of true after:

- An application opens an empty dataset
- A call to the *Last* method of a dataset
- A call to the *Next* method of a dataset fails

The following code sample provides a simple means of iterating over all the records in a dataset:

```
MyTable.DisableControls();
MyTable.First();
```

```
while( ! MyTable.AtEOF )
  {
    DoSomething();
    MyTable.Next();
  }
MyTable.EnableControls();
```

In this case, the *Next* method and the *AtEOF* property are used together to reach the end of the dataset.

Caution   A common error in using such properties in navigating a dataset is to use a loop while forgetting to call *MyTable.Next,* as in the following example:

```
MyTable.First();
while( ! MyTable.AtEOF )
{
  MyTable.DoSomething();
  MyTable.DoSomethingElse();
}
```

If this code were executed, the application would appear to "freeze," because the same action would be endlessly performed on the first record of the dataset, and the *AtEOF* property would never return a value of true.

If you are navigating an empty table, both *AtBOF* and *AtEOF* return true.

The MoveBy method

The *MoveBy* method enables an application to move through a dataset backward or forward by a specified number of records. This method takes only one parameter, the number of records by which to move. Positive integers indicate a forward move, while negative integers indicate a backward move.

For example, to move two records forward in *MyTable,* use the following:

```
MyTable.MoveBy( 2 );
```

When using this method, keep in mind that datasets are fluid entities, and the record that was five records back a moment ago could now be only four records back, or six records, or it could have moved an unknown number of records, because multiple users may be simultaneously accessing the database and modifying its data.

Note   There is no functional difference between calling *MyTable.Next()* and calling *MyTable.MoveBy(1),* just as there is no functional difference between calling *MyTable.Prior()* or calling *MyTable.MoveBy(–1).*

Modifying data in datasets

The following methods enable an application to insert, update, and delete data in datasets:

Table 42.3   Methods to insert, update, and delete data in datasets

Method	Description
Edit	Puts the dataset into Edit state. If a dataset is already in Edit or Insert state, a call to *Edit* has no effect.
Append	Posts any pending data, moves current record to the end of the dataset, and puts the dataset in Insert state.
Insert	Posts any pending data, and puts the dataset in Insert state.
Post	Attempts to post the new or altered record to the database. If successful, the dataset is put in Browse state; if unsuccessful, the dataset remains in its current state.
Cancel	Cancels the current operation and puts the dataset into Browse state.
Delete	Deletes the current record and puts the dataset in Browse state.

The CanModify property

CanModify is a read-only property that specifies whether an application can modify the data in a dataset. When *CanModify* is false, the dataset is read-only, and it can't be put into Edit or Insert state. When *CanModify* is true, the dataset can enter Edit or Insert state. Even if *CanModify* is true, there is no guarantee a user can insert or update records in a table. Other factors may come in to play, such as SQL access privileges.

TTable has a *ReadOnly* property that requests write privileges when set to false. When *ReadOnly* is true, *CanModify* is automatically set to false. When *ReadOnly* is false, *CanModify* is true if the database allows read and write privileges for the dataset and the underlying table. For more information, see "Using TTable" on page 636.

Posting data to the database

The *Post* method is central to an application's interaction with a database table. *Post* behaves differently depending on a dataset's state.

- In Edit state, *Post* modifies the current record.
- In Insert state, *Post* inserts or appends a new record.
- In SetKey state, *Post* returns the dataset to Browse state.

Posting can be done explicitly, or implicitly as part of another procedure. When an application moves off the current record, the *Post* method is called implicitly. Calls to the *First*, *Next*, *Prior*, and *Last* methods automatically call the *Post* method if the table is in Edit or Insert state. The *Append* and *Insert* methods also post any pending data automatically.

Note   *Post* is not called automatically by the *Close* method. To post any pending edits at that time, write code within a *BeforeClose* event handler that explicitly posts the edits (calls the *Post* method).

Editing records

A dataset must be in Edit state before an application can modify records in the underlying table. The *Edit* method puts a dataset in Edit state. When in Edit state, the *Post* method changes the current record. If a dataset is already in Edit state, a call to *Edit* has no effect.

The *Edit* and *Post* methods are often used together. For example,

```
MyTable.Edit();
MyTable.FieldByName( "CustNo" )->AsString = "1234";
MyTable.Post();
```

The first line of code in this example places the dataset in Edit mode. The next line of code assigns the string "1234" to the CustNo field. Finally, the last line posts, or writes to the database, the data just modified.

Adding new records

To add a new record to a dataset, an application can call either the *Insert* method or the *Append* method. Both methods put a dataset into Insert state. *Insert* opens a new, empty record after the current record. *Append* moves the cursor to the end of the dataset and opens a new, empty record.

When an application calls *Post*, the new record is inserted in the dataset in a position based on its index, if defined. Therefore, for indexed tables, *Append* and *Insert* perform similarly. If no index is defined on the underlying table, then the record maintains its position—so *Append* adds the record to the end of the table, and *Insert* inserts it at the cursor position when the method was called. In either case, posting a new record in a data grid can cause all the rows before and after the new record to change as the dataset follows the new row to its indexed position and then fetches data to fill the grid around it.

Deleting records

The *Delete* method deletes the current record from a dataset and leaves the dataset in Browse mode. The cursor moves to the following record.

Canceling changes

An application can undo changes made to the current record at any time, if it has not yet directly or indirectly called *Post*. For example, if a table is in Edit state, and a user has changed the data in one or more fields, the application can return the record back to its original values by calling the table's *Cancel* method. A call to *Cancel* always returns a dataset to Browse state.

Working with entire records

The methods in Table 42.4 enable an application to work with an entire record in one statement.

Table 42.4   Methods used to work with entire records

Method	Description
AppendRecord(TVarRecs& values)	Appends a record with the column values specified as the values parameter of the method at the end of a table; analogous to *Append*. Calls the *Post* method automatically.
InsertRecord(TVarRecs& values)	Inserts the values specified as the values parameter of the method as a record after the current cursor position of a table; analogous to Insert. Calls the *Post* method automatically.
SetFields(TVarRecs& values)	Sets the values of the corresponding fields; analogous to assigning values to *TField* components. The application must then call the *Post* method.

Each of these methods takes a pointer to a *TVarRecs* structure as a parameter. This *TVarRecs* structure holds data of any type. You build the structure by adding to it the data you want to assign to column, or field, values. The first value you add to the structure will become the value for the first column of the current record. The second value you add will become the value for the second column of the current record, and so on. The values can be literals or variables.

For example, this code builds a *TVarRecs* structure:

```
TVarRecs values;
values.Add( "Japan" );
values.Add( "Tokyo" );
values.Add( "Asia" );
```

Once you have constructed the values variable, you can use it as the parameter for the *AppendRecord*, *InsertRecord*, or *SetFields* methods. Each value in the values parameter corresponds to a column in the underlying table. If the number of values in an argument is less than the number of columns in a dataset, then the remaining values are assumed to be blank.

For unindexed tables, *AppendRecord* adds a record to the end of the table and *InsertRecord* inserts a record after the current cursor position. For indexed tables, both methods place the record in the correct position in the table, based on the index. In both cases, the methods move the cursor to the record's position.

SetFields assigns the values specified in the *Values* parameter to fields in the dataset. The application must first call the *Edit* method to put the dataset in Edit state. To modify the current record, it must then call the *Post* method.

Because these methods depend explicitly on the structure of the underlying tables, an application should use them only if the table structure will not change.

For example, the COUNTRY table has columns for Name, Capital, Continent, Area, and Population. If MyTable were linked to the COUNTRY table, the following statements would insert a record into the COUNTRY table:

```
TVarRecs values;
values.Add( "Japan" );
values.Add( "Tokyo" );
values.Add( "Asia" );
MyTable.InsertRecord( values );
```

The statement doesn't specify values for Area and Population, so it inserts blank values for these columns. The table is indexed on Name, so the statement would insert the record based on the alphabetic collation of "Japan."

To update the record, an application could use the following code:

```
TVarRecs values;
MyTable.Edit();
values.Add( );                  //don't change the value "Japan"
values.Add( );                  //don't change the value "Tokyo"
values.Add( );                  //don't change the value "Asia"
values.Add( 344567 );           //change the Area value
values.Add( 164700000 );        //change the Population value
MyTable.SetFields( values );
MyTable.Post();
```

This code assumes that the cursor is positioned on the record just entered for Japan. It assigns values to the Area and Population fields and then posts them to the database. Notice the use of *Add( )*, with no arguments, to maintain the current value.

Setting the update mode

The *UpdateMode* property of a dataset determines how an application finds records being updated in a SQL database. This property is important in a multi-user environment when users may retrieve the same records and make conflicting changes to them.

When a user posts an update, the original values in the record are used to find the record in the database. This approach is similar to an optimistic locking scheme. *UpdateMode* specifies which columns an application uses to find the record. In SQL terms, *UpdateMode* specifies which columns are included in the WHERE clause of an UPDATE statement. If a record cannot be found with the original values in the columns specified (if another user has changed the values in the database), no update occurs and an exception is raised.

The *UpdateMode* property may have the following values:

- *WhereAll* (the default): Every column is used to find the record being updated. This is the most restrictive mode.

- *WhereKeyOnly*: Only the key columns are used to find the record being updated. This is the least restrictive mode and should be used only if other users will not be changing the records being updated.

- *WhereChanged*: Key columns and columns that have changed are used to find the record being updated.

For example, consider a COUNTRY table with columns for NAME (the key), CAPITAL, and CONTINENT. Suppose you and another user simultaneously retrieve a record with the following values:

- NAME = "Philippines"
- CAPITAL = "Nairobi"
- CONTINENT = "Africa"

Both you and the other user notice that the information in this record is incorrect and should be changed. Now, suppose the other user changes CONTINENT to "Asia,"

CAPITAL to "Manila," and posts the change to the database. A few seconds later, you change NAME to "Kenya" and post your change to the database.

If your application has *UpdateMode* set to *WhereKeyOnly* on the dataset, the original value of the key column (NAME = "Philippines") is compared to the current value in the database. Because the other user did not change NAME, your update occurs. You think the record is now ["Kenya," "Nairobi," "Africa"] and the other user thinks it is ["Philippines," "Asia," "Manila"]. Unfortunately, it is actually ["Kenya," "Asia," "Manila"], which is still incorrect, even though both you and the other user think you have corrected the mistake. This problem occurred because you had *UpdateMode* set to its least restrictive level, which doesn't protect against such occurrences.

If your application had *UpdateMode* set to *WhereAll*, all columns would be checked when you attempt to make your update. Because the other user changed CAPITAL and CONTINENT, you would not be allowed to make the update. When you retrieved the record again, you would see the new values entered by the other user and realize that the mistake had already been corrected.

Bookmarking data

It is often useful to mark a particular location in a table so that you can quickly return to it when desired. Bookmark methods provide this functionality. These methods enable you to put a bookmark in the dataset, and quickly return to it later.

These are the three bookmarking methods:

- *GetBookmark*
- *GotoBookmark*
- *FreeBookmark*

These methods are used together. The *GetBookmark* method returns a variable of type *TBookmark*. A *TBookmark* contains a pointer to a particular location in a dataset. When given a bookmark, the *GotoBookmark* method moves an application's cursor to that location in the dataset.

FreeBookmark frees memory allocated for the specified bookmark. A call to *GetBookmark* allocates memory for the bookmark, so an application should call *FreeBookmark* before exiting.

The following code illustrates a typical use of bookmarking:

```
void myFunction()
{
  TBookmark Bookmark;
  Bookmark = MyTable.GetBookmark();    // allocate bookmark
  MyTable.DisableControls();           // disable data-aware controls
  MyTable.First();
  while ( ! MyTable.AtEOF ) {
    // Do Something
    MyTable.Next();
  }
  MyTable.GotoBookmark( Bookmark );    // move cursor to bookmark location
```

```
    MyTable.EnableControls();           // enable data-aware controls
    MyTable.FreeBookmark( Bookmark );   // deallocate memory for bookmark
  }
```

Disabling, enabling, and refreshing data-aware controls

The *DisableControls* method disables all data-aware controls linked to a dataset. This method should be used to prevent "flickering" of the display as the cursor moves (for example, when iterating or searching through a dataset). As soon as the cursor is repositioned, an application should call the *EnableControls* method to re-enable data-aware controls. It is important to re-enable controls with *EnableControls* as soon as the application completes its iteration or searching, to keep the form synchronized with the underlying dataset.

The *Refresh* method flushes all local buffers and retrieves data from the specified dataset again. The dataset must be open. You can use this method to update a table if you think the table or the data it contains might have changed. Refreshing a table can sometimes lead to unexpected results. For example, if a user is viewing a record that has been deleted, then it will seem to disappear the moment the application calls *Refresh*. Similarly, data can appear to change while a user is viewing it if another user changes or deletes a record after the data was originally fetched and before a call to *Refresh*.

Using dataset events

Datasets have a number of events that enable an application to perform validation, compute totals, and perform other tasks, depending on the code written within the event handler. The events are listed in the following table.

Table 42.5   Dataset events

Event	Description
BeforeOpen, AfterOpen	Called before/after a dataset is opened.
BeforeClose, AfterClose	Called before/after a dataset is closed.
BeforeInsert, AfterInsert	Called before/after a dataset enters Insert state.
BeforeEdit, AfterEdit	Called before/after a dataset enters Edit state.
BeforePost, AfterPost	Called before/after changes to a table are posted.
BeforeCancel, AfterCancel	Called before/after the previous state is canceled.
BeforeDelete, AfterDelete	Called before/after a record is deleted.
OnNewRecord	Called when a new record is created; used to set default values.
OnCalcFields	Called when calculated fields are calculated.

For more information on the properties, methods, and events of the dataset components, refer to the online Visual Database Tools reference.

Using OnCalcFields

The *OnCalcFields* event is used to set the values of calculated fields. The *AutoCalcFields* property determines when *OnCalcFields* is called. If *AutoCalcFields* is true, then *OnCalcFields* is called when:

- The dataset is opened.
- A record is retrieved from the database.

OnCalcFields occurs whenever a non-calculated field's value changes, regardless of the setting of *AutoCalcFields*.

Typically, the *OnCalcFields* event occurs often, so it should be kept short. Also, if *AutoCalcFields* is true, the *OnCalcFields* event handler should not perform any actions that modify the dataset (or the linked dataset if it is part of a master-detail relationship), because this can lead to recursion. For example, if an *OnCalcFields* event handler calls the *Post* method, and *AutoCalcFields* is true, then the *OnCalcFields* event handler executes again, calling *Post* again, and so on.

If *AutoCalcFields* is false, then the *OnCalcFields* event occurs when the dataset's *Post* method is called (or any method that automatically calls *Post*, such as *Append* or *Insert*).

While the *OnCalcFields* event handler is executing, a dataset enters CalcFields mode. When a dataset is in CalcFields mode, the values of any fields other than calculated fields can't be set. After the *OnCalcFields* event handler finishes executing, the dataset returns to its previous mode.

Using TTable

TTable is one of the most important database component classes. It enables an application to access a database table.

Specifying the database table

TableName specifies the name of the database table to which the *TTable* component is linked. You can set this property at design time through the Property Inspector of the IDE's Dialog editor.

The *DatabaseName* property specifies where an application looks for the specified database table. It can be a Borland Database Engine alias, an explicit specification, or the *DatabaseName* defined by any *TDatabase* component in the application. For Paradox and dBASE tables, an explicit specification is a directory path; for SQL tables, it is a directory path and database name.

Instead of an actual directory path or database name, *DatabaseName* can also be a Borland Database Engine alias. The advantage of this is that you can change the data source for an entire application by simply changing the alias definition in the BDE Configuration Utility. For more information on using the BDE Configuration Utility, see the online help for the BDE Configuration Utility. For more information on the *DatabaseName* property, see the online Visual Database Tools reference.

Note   Neither of these properties can be changed when a table is open—that is, when the table's *Active* property is set to a value of true.

The TableType property

The *TableType* property specifies the type of the underlying database table. This property is not used for SQL tables.

If *TableType* is set to *Default*, the table's file-name extension determines the table type:

- Extension of .DB or no file-name extension: Paradox table
- Extension of .DBF : dBASE table
- Extension of .TXT : ASCII table

If the value of *TableType* is not *Default*, then the table is always of the specified *TableType*, regardless of file-name extension.

Searching a table

TTable has a number of methods that will search for values in a database table:

- Goto methods
- Find methods

The easiest way to search for values is with the Find methods, *FindKey* and *FindNearest*. These two methods combine the functionality of the basic Goto methods: *SetKey* combined with *GotoKey* or *GotoNearest*, which are described first.

In dBASE and Paradox tables, *Goto* and *Find* methods can search only on index fields. In SQL tables, they can search on any field, if the field name is specified in the *IndexFieldNames* property of the *TTable*. For more information, see "Indexes" on page 642.

To search a dBASE or Paradox table for a value in a non-index field, use SQL SELECT syntax with a *TQuery* component. For more information on using SQL and *TQuery* components, see "Using the TQuery component" on page 85.

Using Goto methods

The *GotoKey* and *GotoNearest* methods enable an application to search a database table using a key. *SetKey* puts a table in "search mode," more accurately referred to as SetKey state. In SetKey state, assignments indicate values for which to search in indexed fields. *GotoKey* then moves the cursor to the first row in the table that matches those field values.

Here is an example that searches for the key the user enters in a standard edit control; *Edit1* is an existing ObjectWindows *TEdit* control:

```
char str[50];

MyTable.SetKey();
Edit1.GetText( str, 50 );
MyTable.Fields[0]->AsString = str;          // First field is the key
MyTable.GotoKey();
```

The second line of code puts *MyTable* in SetKey state. This indicates that the following assignment to the table's *Fields* property specifies a search value. The first column in the table, corresponding to *Fields*[0], is the index. In this example, the value the application searches for is determined by the text the user types into the edit control, *Edit1*. Finally, *GotoKey* performs the search, moving the cursor to the record if it exists.

GotoKey is a Boolean function that moves the cursor and returns true if the search is successful. If the search is unsuccessful, it returns false and doesn't change the position of the cursor. For example,

```
MyTable.SetKey();
MyTable.Fields[0]->AsString = str;
if ( ! MyTable.GotoKey() ) {
  MessageBox( hwnd, "Record not found", "Search message box", MB_OK );
}
```

If a table has more than one key column, and you want to search for values in a subset of the keys, set *KeyFieldCount* to the number of columns on which you are searching. For example, if a table has three columns in its primary key, and you want to search for values in just the first, set *KeyFieldCount* to 1. For tables with multiple-column keys, you can search only for values in contiguous columns, beginning with the first. That is, you can search for values in the first column, or the first and second, or the first, second, and third, but not just the first and third.

GotoNearest is similar, except it finds the nearest match to a partial field value. It can be used only for columns of string data type. For example,

```
MyTable.SetKey();
MyTable.Fields[0]->AsString = "Sm";
MyTable.GotoNearest();
```

If a record exists with "Sm" as the first two characters, the cursor is positioned on that record. Otherwise, the position of the cursor doesn't change and *GotoNearest* returns false.

If it is not searching on the primary index of a local table, then an application must specify the column names to use in the *IndexFieldNames* property or the name of the index to use in the *IndexName* property of the table. For example, if the CUSTOMER table had a secondary index named "CityIndex" on which you wanted to search for a value, you would need to set the value of the table's *IndexName* property to "CityIndex." You could then use the following code when searching on this field:

```
char str[50];

MyTable.IndexName = "CityIndex";
MyTable.Open();
MyTable.SetKey();
Edit1.GetText( str, 50 );
MyTable.FieldByName( "City" )->AsString = str;
MyTable.GotoNearest();
```

Because indexes often have nonintuitive names, you can use the *IndexFieldNames* property instead to specify the names of indexed fields.

Each time an application calls *SetKey*, it must set all the field values for which it will search. That is, *SetKey* clears any existing values from previous searches. To keep previous values, use *EditKey*.

For example, to extend the above search to find a record with the specified city name in a specified country, an application could use the following code:

```
MyTable.EditKey();
Edit2.GetText( str, 50 );
MyTable.FieldByName( "Country" )->AsString = str;
MyTable.GotoNearest();
```

Using Find methods

The Find methods, *FindKey* and *FindNearest,* provide another way to search a table. They combine the functionality of *SetKey*, field assignment, and Goto methods into a single statement.

Each of these methods takes a pointer to a *TVarRecs* structure as a parameter. This *TVarRecs* structure holds data of any type. You build the structure by adding to it the data you want to assign to column, or field, values. For more information about building a *TVarRecs* structure, see "Working with entire records" on page 631.

FindKey is similar to *GotoKey*:

- It puts a table in search mode (SetKey state).

- It finds the record in the table that matches the specified values. If a matching record is found, it moves the cursor there, and returns true.

- If a matching record is not found, it doesn't move the cursor and returns false.

For example, if *MyTable* is indexed on its first column, then this code:

```
TVarRecs values;
char str[50];

Edit1.GetText( str, 50 );
values.Add( str );
MyTable.FindKey( values );
```

performs the same function as this code:

```
char str[50];

MyTable.SetKey();
Edit1.GetText( str, 50 );
MyTable.Fields[0]->AsString = str;   // First field is the key
MyTable1.GotoKey();
```

FindNearest is similar to *GotoNearest*, as it moves the cursor to the row with the nearest matching value. This can be used for columns of string data type only.

By default, both of these methods work on the primary index column. To search the table for values in other indexes, you must specify the field name in the table's *IndexFieldNames* property or the name of the index in the *IndexName* property.

Note   For Paradox or dBASE tables, these methods work only with indexed fields. For SQL databases, they can work with any columns specified in the *IndexFieldNames* property.

Using the KeyExclusive property in searches

The *KeyExclusive* property indicates whether a search positions the cursor on or after the specified record being searched for. If *KeyExclusive* is false (the default), then *GotoNearest* and *FindNearest* move the cursor to the record that matches the specified values. If true, then the search methods go to the record immediately following the specified key, if the key value is found.

Limiting records retrieved by an application

In the real world, tables can be huge, so applications often need to limit the number of rows they work with. The following methods of *TTable* enable an application to work with a subset of the data in a database table:

- *SetRangeStart* and *EditRangeStart*
- *SetRangeEnd* and *EditRangeEnd*
- *SetRange*
- *ApplyRange*
- *CancelRange*

The *SetRangeStart* method prepares the table to have the next assignments to key fields become the start value of a range.

To establish a range on a table, call the *SetRangeStart* method, and assign the values you want to begin the range to the key index fields. Next call the *SetRangeEnd* method and assign the values you want to end the range to the same key index fields. Finally, call the *ApplyRange* method to apply the range and filter the data visible to the application.

The corresponding *EditRangeStart* method keeps existing range values and updates with succeeding assignments. *SetRangeStart* differs from *EditRangeStart* in that it clears all the elements of the range filter to the default values (or blank). *EditRangeEnd* leaves the elements of the range filter with their current values.

ApplyRange applies the specified range. If *SetRangeStart* has not been called when *ApplyRange* is called, then the range begins with the beginning of the table; likewise, if *SetRangeEnd* has not been called, the range ends with the end of the table. *CancelRange* cancels the range filter, therefore making all the rows in the table accessible to the application.

The *SetRange* function combines *SetRangeStart*, *SetRangeEnd*, and field assignments into a single statement that takes an array of values as its argument.

Note   For Paradox or dBASE tables, these methods work only with indexed fields. For SQL databases, they can work with any columns specified in the *IndexFieldNames* property.

For example, suppose there is a form with a *TTable* component named Cust, linked to the CUSTOMER table. CUSTOMER is indexed on its first column (CustNo). The form has two edit controls named *StartVal* and *EndVal*, and you have used the Fields editor to create a *TField* component for the CustNo field. This code sets the start and end ranges using the values in the edit controls, and applies the new range to the table.

```
char str[50];

Cust.SetRangeStart();
StartVal.GetText( str, 50 );
CustNo.AsString = str;
Cust.SetRangeEnd();
EndVal.GetText( str, 50 );
if ( str[0] != '\0' )
```

```
    CustNo.AsString = str;
Cust.ApplyRange();
```

Notice that this code first checks that the text entered in *EndVal* is not blank before
assigning any value to a field. If the text entered for *StartVal* is blank, then all records
from the beginning of the table are included, because all values are greater than blank.
However, if the text entered for *EndVal* is blank, then no records are included, because
none are less than blank.

This code could be rewritten using the *SetRange* function as follows:

```
char startStr[50];
char endStr[50];
TVarRecs startValues;
TVarRecs endValues;

StartVal.GetText( startStr, 50 );
startValues.Add( startStr );
EndVal.GetText( endStr, 50 );
if (endStr[0] != '\0' )
  endValues.Add( endStr );
else
  endValues.Add( );
Cust.SetRange( startValues, endValues );
```

Using partial keys

If a key is composed of one or more string fields, these methods support partial keys.
For example, if an index is based on the LastName and FirstName columns, the
following range specifications are valid:

```
MyTable.SetRangeStart();
MyTable.FieldByName( "LastName" )->AsString = "Smith";
MyTable.SetRangeEnd();
MyTable.ApplyRange();
```

This example uses the *FieldByName* method, which lets you access the value of a field by
passing the name of the field or column as a parameter to the method. For more
information about using *FieldByName*, see "Using the FieldByName method" on
page 657.

The example includes all records where LastName is greater than or equal to "Smith."
The value specification could also be:

```
MyTable.FieldByName( "LastName" )->AsString = "Sm";
```

This would include records that have LastName greater than or equal to"Sm." The
following would include records with a LastName greater than or equal to "Smith" and
a FirstName greater than or equal to "J":

```
MyTable.FieldByName( "LastName" )->AsString = "Smith";
MyTable.FieldByName( "FirstName" )->AsString = "J";
```

The KeyExclusive property

The *KeyExclusive* property determines whether the filtered range excludes the range
boundaries. The default is false, which means rows are in the filtered range if they are

greater than or equal to the start range specified and less than or equal to the end range specified. If *KeyExclusive* is true, the methods filter out greater than and less than the specified values.

Indexes

An *index* determines how records are sorted when an application displays data. By default, data is displayed in ascending order, based on the values of the primary index column(s) of a table.

Visual Database Tools supports SQL indexes, maintained indexes for Paradox tables, and maintained .MDX (production) indexes for dBASE tables. Visual Database Tools doesn't support:

- Non-maintained indexes on Paradox tables.
- Non-maintained or .NDX indexes of dBASE tables.
- The *IndexFieldCount* property for a dBASE table opened on an expression index.

The *GetIndexNames* method returns a list of the names of available indexes on the underlying database table. For Paradox tables, the primary index is unnamed and therefore not returned by *GetIndexNames*.

IndexFields is an array of field names used in the index. *IndexFieldCount* is the number of fields in the index. *IndexFieldCount* and *IndexFields* are read-only properties that are available only during run time.

Use the *IndexName* property to sort or search a table on an index other than the primary index. In other words, to use the primary index of a table, you need do nothing with the *IndexName* property. To use a secondary index, however, you must specify it in *IndexName*. To change back to the primary index, set the corresponding *TTable*'s *IndexName* to a null string.

For tables in a SQL database, the *IndexFieldNames* property specifies the columns to use in the ORDER BY clause when retrieving data. The entry for this property is a semicolon-delimited list of field names. Records are sorted by the values in the specified fields. Sorting can be only in ascending order. Case-sensitivity depends on the server being used.

For example, to sort customer records in an SQL table by zip code and then by customer number, enter the following for the *IndexFieldNames* property:

```
ZipCode;CustNo
```

For Paradox and dBASE tables, an index is selected based on the columns specified in *IndexFieldNames*. An error occurs if you specify a column or columns that cannot be mapped to an existing index.

The *IndexName* and *IndexFieldNames* properties are mutually exclusive. Setting one property clears the value of the other.

The Exclusive property

The *Exclusive* property indicates whether to open the table with an exclusive lock. If true, no other user can access it at the same time. You can't open a table in Exclusive mode if another user is currently accessing the table.

If the underlying table is in a SQL database, an exclusive table-level lock may allow others to read data from the table but not modify it. Some servers may not support exclusive table-level locks, depending on the server. Refer to your server documentation for more information.

Other properties and methods

In addition to dataset properties shared with *TQuery*, *TTable* has a number of unique methods and properties. For example, the unique methods include

- *EmptyTable*, which deletes all records (rows) in the table.

- *DeleteTable*, which deletes the table.

- *BatchMove*, which copies data and table structures from one table to another, similar to the operation of *TBatchMove*.

A few of the more important properties and methods are discussed in this section. For a complete list and descriptions, see the online Visual Database Tools reference.

The ReadOnly and CanModify properties

If you want the user to be able to modify the data in the dataset, set the *ReadOnly* property for the table to false. This is the default value. If you want to prevent users from modifying data, but only allow them to view the data, set *ReadOnly* to true. Depending on the characteristics of the underlying table, the request for read and write privileges may or may not be granted by the database.

CanModify is a read-only property of datasets that reflects the actual rights granted for the dataset. When *ReadOnly* is true, *CanModify* is automatically set to false. When *ReadOnly* is false, *CanModify* is true if the database allows read and write privileges for the dataset and the underlying table.

When *CanModify* is false, the table is read-only, and the dataset can't be put into Edit or Insert state. When *CanModify* is true, the dataset can enter Edit or Insert state. Even if *CanModify* is true, it is not a guarantee that a user can insert or update records in a table. Other factors may come in to play. For example, the user might not have SQL access privileges.

The GotoCurrent method

GotoCurrent is a method that synchronizes two *TTable* components linked to the same database table and using the same index. This method takes a *TTable* component as its argument, and sets the cursor position of the *TTable* to the current cursor position of the argument. For example,

```
MyTable.GotoCurrent( AnotherTable );
```

Once this code executes, the cursor for *MyTable* points to the same record as the cursor for *AnotherTable*.

Creating master-detail forms

The *MasterSource* and *MasterFields* properties are used to define one-to-many relationships between two tables. The *MasterSource* property is used to specify a data source from which the table obtains data for the master table. For instance, if you link two tables in a master-detail relationship, then the detail table can track the events occurring in the master table by specifying the master table's *TDataSource* in this property.

To link tables based on values in multiple column names, use a semicolon-delimited list:

```
MyTable.MasterFields = "OrderNo;ItemNo";
```

The Field Link Designer

At design time, you click the button with the ellipses (...) for the *MasterFields* property in the Property Inspector of the Dialog editor to open the Field Link Designer dialog box.

Figure 42.3   Field Link designer

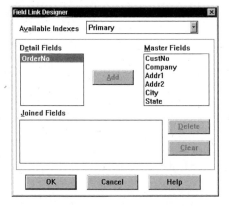

The Field Link Designer provides a visual way to link master and detail tables. The Available Indexes combo box shows the currently selected index by which to join the two tables. For Paradox tables, this is "Primary" by default, indicating that the primary index of the table will be used. Any other named indices defined in the table will be in the drop-down list.

Select the field you want to use to link the detail table in the Detail Fields list, the field to link the master table in the Master Fields list, and then choose Add. The selected fields are displayed in the Joined Fields list box. For example,

```
OrderNo -> OrderNo
```

For tables on a database server, the Available Indexes combo box doesn't appear, and you must select the detail and master fields to join them manually in the Detail Fields and Master Fields list boxes.

Using TDataSource

The *TDataSource* component acts as a conduit between datasets and data-aware controls. Often the only thing you must do with a *TDataSource* component is to set its *DataSet* property to an appropriate dataset component. Then you can set the *DataSource* property of data-aware controls to the specific *TDataSource* component. You also use *TDataSource* components to link datasets to reflect master-detail relationships.

Using TDataSource properties

TDataSource has only a few published properties in addition to the standard *Name* property.

The DataSet property

The *DataSet* property specifies the name of the dataset from which the *TDataSource* obtains its data. You can also set the *DataSet* property to a dataset on another form to synchronize the data-aware controls on the two forms. For example,

```
DataSource1.Dataset = Form1.MyTable;
```

The Enabled property

The *Enabled* property can temporarily disconnect a *TDataSource* from its dataset. When set to false, all data-aware controls attached to the data source go blank and become inactive until *Enabled* is set to true.

In general, it's recommended to use the datasets' *DisableControls* and *EnableControls* methods to perform this function, because they affect all attached data sources.

Using TDataSource events

TDataSource has three events associated with it:

- *OnDataChange*
- *OnStateChange*
- *OnUpdateData*

The OnDataChange event

The *OnDataChange* event occurs whenever the cursor moves to a new record. In other words, if an application calls *Next, Prior, Insert*, or any method that leads to a change in the cursor position, then an *OnDataChange* is triggered.

This event is useful if an application is keeping components synchronized manually.

The OnStateChange event

The *OnStateChange* event occurs whenever the mode (state) of a data source's dataset changes. A dataset's *State* property records its current state. This event is useful for performing actions as a *TDataSource*'s state changes, as the following examples illustrate.

During the course of a normal database session, a dataset's state will change frequently. To track these changes, you can use code in an *OnStateChange* event handler such as the following example that displays the current state in a *TStatic* control:

```
void MyTable::StateChangeHandler();
{
  string str;

  switch (MyTable.State) {
  case dsInactive:
    str = "Inactive";
    break;
  case dsBrowse:
    str = "Browse";
    break;
  case dsEdit:
    str = "Edit";
    break;
  case dsInsert:
    str = "Insert";
    break;
  case dsSetKey:
      str = "SetKey";
      break;
  }
  Static1.SetText( str.c_str() );
};
```

The OnUpdateData event

The *OnUpdateData* event occurs whenever the data in the current record is about to be updated. For instance, an *OnUpdateData* event occurs after *Post* is called but before the data is actually posted to the database.

This event is useful if an application uses a standard (non-data aware) control and needs to keep the text it displays synchronized with the value of a field in a dataset.

Using TField components and the Fields editor

TField components correspond to database columns. They are created

- At run time automatically whenever a dataset component is active. This creates a dynamic set of *TFields* that mirrors the columns in the table at that time.

- At design time through the Fields editor. This creates a persistent set of *TFields* that doesn't change, even if the structure of the underlying table changes.

There are *TField* components corresponding to all possible data types, including *TStringField*, *TSmallintField*, *TIntegerField*, *TWordField*, *TBooleanField*, *TFloatField*, *TCurrencyField*, *TBCDField*, *TDateField*, *TTimeField*, and *TDateTimeField*. This section discusses *TField* components in general, and the discussion applies to all the different subtypes. For information on the properties of a specific type, see the online Visual Database Tools reference.

What are TField components?

All data-aware components rely on an underlying component class, *TField*. Although not visible on forms, *TField* components are important because they provide an application a direct link to a database column. *TFields* contain properties specifying a column's data type, current value, display format, edit format, and other characteristics. *TField* components also provide events, such as *OnValidate*, that can be used to implement field-based validation rules.

Each column retrieved from a table has a corresponding *TField* component. By default, *TField* components are dynamically generated at design time when the *Active* property of a *TTable* or *TQuery* component is set to true. At run time, these components are also dynamically generated. Dynamic generation means *TField* components are built based on the underlying physical structure of a database table each time the connection to the table is activated. Thus, dynamically generated *TFields* always correspond to the columns in the underlying database tables.

To generate a persistent list of *TField* components for an application, use the Fields editor. Using the Fields editor to specify a persistent list of *TField* components is smart programming. It guarantees that each time your application runs, it uses and displays the same columns, in the same order, even if the physical structure of the underlying database has changed. Creating *TField* components at design time guarantees that data-aware components and program code that rely on specific fields always work as expected. If a column on which a persistent *TField* component is based is deleted or changed, an exception is generated rather than running the application against a non-existent column or mismatched data.

Using the Fields editor

When *TTable* and *TQuery* components are connected to a database and their *Active* properties are set to true, they dynamically generate a *TField* component for each column in a table or query. Each *TField* component stores display-related information about a field. The display information is used by data control components, such as *TDBEdit* and *TDBGrid*, to format data for display in a form. You can make *TField* components persistent and edit their display characteristics by starting the Fields editor.

The Fields editor enables you to:

* Create a static model of a table's columns, column order, and column type that doesn't change even if changes are made to the underlying physical table in the database.

* Specify the order in which fields are displayed and which fields to include.

- Specify all display characteristics of fields.

- Define calculated *TField* components that behave just like physical data columns, except that their values are calculated by the code you write in the *OnCalcFields* event handler.

Starting the Fields editor

➤ To start the Fields editor for a *TTable* or *TQuery* component, double-click the value column of the Edit property of *TTable* or *TQuery* in the Property Inspector. The Fields editor opens.

Figure 42.4   Fields editor

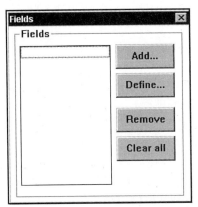

The Fields list box displays the names of persistent *TField* components associated with the data-access component. The first time you invoke the Fields editor on a particular *TTable* or *TQuery* component, the Fields list is empty because all *TFields* are dynamically created. If any *TField* components are listed in Fields, then data-aware components can only display data from those fields. You can drag and drop individual *TField* components within the Fields list box to change the order in which fields are displayed in controls, like *TDBGrid*, that display multiple columns.

The Add button enables you to see a list of column names in the physical dataset but not already included in the Fields list, and to create new *TField* components for them.

The Define button enables you to create calculated fields. Fields created this way are only for display purposes. The underlying physical structure of the table or data is not changed.

The Remove button deletes the selected *TFields*. The Clear All button deletes all the *TFields* shown in the Fields list.

Adding a TField component

The Add button of the Fields editor enables you to specify which *TField* components are included in a dataset.

To see a list of fields currently available to a *TTable* or *TQuery* component, click the Add button. The Add Fields dialog box appears.

Figure 42.5 Fields editor Add Fields dialog box

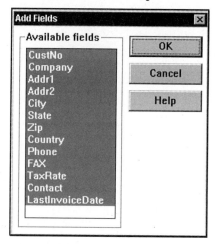

The *Available Fields* list box shows all database fields that do not have persistent *TFields* instantiated. Initially, all available fields are selected. Use the mouse to select specific fields and then choose OK. The selected fields move to the *Fields* list box in the main Fields editor window.

Fields moved from the *Available Fields* list become persistent. Each time the dataset is opened, the existence of each non-calculated field is verified or can be created from data in the database. If it cannot be verified to exist or can't be created, an exception is thrown, warning you that the field is not valid, and the dataset is not opened.

Deleting a TField component

Use the Remove button of the Fields editor to delete the selected *TField* components from the *Fields* list box. Fields removed from the Fields list box are no longer in the dataset and cannot be displayed by data-aware components. Removing a *TField* component is useful to display a subset of available fields within a table, or when you want to define your own field to replace an existing field.

Defining a calculated field

A calculated field is used to display values calculated at run time in the dataset's *OnCalcFields* event handler. For example, you might create a string field that displays concatenated values from two other fields. A calculated field is for display purposes only; the underlying physical structure of the table doesn't change. You can see a calculated field in a data grid, for example, but the number of fields in the actual database table doesn't change.

➤ To create a new calculated field:

1 Choose the Define button in the Fields editor.

2 Enter the name of the new field in the Field Name edit box, or select a field name from the drop-down list. A corresponding *TField* component name appears

automatically in the Component edit box as you type. This name is the identifier you use to access the field programmatically.

3 Select the data type for the field from the Field Type list box.

4 Check the Calculated check box if it isn't already checked.

5 Choose OK.

The newly defined calculated field is automatically added to the Fields list box.

➤ To edit the properties of the new *TField* component, select the component name in the Available Fields list box, and use the Property Inspector to set new values.

Programming a calculated field

Once you define one or more calculated fields, you write an *OnCalcFields* event handler that contains the code that actually calculates the value of these new fields.

➤ You begin by starting with the usual steps to respond to an event:

1 Declare the event sink for the table's *OnCalcFields* event within the form's class declaration.

2 Declare the *OnCalcFields* event handler in the form's class declaration.

3 Connect the event sink to the *OnCalcFields* event handler in the constructor for the form. Within the constructor, you must instantiate a new *TTable* component that attaches to the existing table component on the form.

4 Connect the table's *OnCalcFields* source object to the form's *OnCalcFieldsSink* object.

Now you are ready to write the *OnCalcFields* event handler code.

Writing an OnCalcFields event handler

➤ These are the steps to follow when you write an *OnCalcFields* event handler:

1 Instantiate existing field components whose values are used in the calculation.

Calculating the value of one or more new fields usually involves using the values of existing fields. For example, to calculate the total cost of an item, you would need to use the price of an item and add any applicable tax to it. Therefore, you need to instantiate a "Price" field, and maybe a "Tax Rate" field, depending on how you perform your calculation.

2 Instantiate the new field component(s) you defined as calculated in the Fields editor.

For example, if you defined a "Total Cost" field as a calculated field in the Fields editor, you must instantiate it in your code.

3 Write the code that calculates the value of the new field(s).

For example, you might write the code that calculates the value of the "Total Cost" field by multiplying the "Price" field by the "Tax Rate" field and adding the result to the "Price" field.

A calculated field example

This section describes a small application that uses calculated fields. After the steps are examined in detail, you will find the entire example listed with embedded comments.

This demo application assumes that the calculated fields "Calculated Profit" and "Calculated Profit Percent" were added to a *TTable* component using the Fields editor. The "Cost" and "Sale Price" fields already exist in the dataset the *TTable* component accesses. The name of the dialog, or form, is *CalcForm*.

Following the steps listed above, our first task is to declare the event sink for the table's *OnCalcFields* event within the form's class declaration. So our declaration would look like this:

```
TDataSetNotifySink OnCalcFieldsSink;
```

Now that the event sink exists, you can declare the *OnCalcFields* event handler within the form's class declaration:

```
void OnCalcFields( TDataSetNotifySink&, TDataSet& DataSet );
```

Within the form's constructor, connect the event sink to the form. This *CalcFieldDemo* constructor takes a HWND to the dialog that contains the *TTable* component:

```
CalcFieldDemo::CalcFieldDemo( HWND hDlg) :
  OnCalcFieldsSink( TDataSetNotify_MFUNCTOR( *this, &CalcFieldDemo::OnCalcFields ))
```

The constructor must instantiate a new *TTable* component that maps directly to the existing *TTable* component on the form. Once the instance exists, connect the form to it. So the entire constructor for *CalcFieldDemo* looks like this:

```
CalcFieldDemo::CalcFieldDemo( HWND hDlg) :
  OnCalcFieldsSink( TDataSetNotify_MFUNCTOR( *this, &CalcFieldDemo::OnCalcFields ))
  {
  table = new TTable(hDlg, IDC_TTABLE1);
  if (table)
  {
     table->OnCalcFieldsSource += OnCalcFieldsSink;
  }
}
```

Note that the constructor for the table instance takes the HWND to the form and the same ID of the existing *TTable* component. Any changes to either the *TTable* in the source code or to the table on the form are reflected in each other, as they share the same underlying pointers.

The actual *OnCalcFields* event handler begins by instatiating the field components for the two fields "Cost" and "Sale Price". These fields already exist in the data set:

```
void CalcFieldDemo::OnCalcFields( TDataSetNotifySink&, TDataSet& DataSet )
{
  TCurrencyField cost        = DataSet.FieldByName( string("Cost") );
  TCurrencyField salePrice   = DataSet.FieldByName( string("Sale Price") );
```

The two fields that are defined as calculated fields using the Fields editor are also instantiated:

```
TCurrencyField profit        = DataSet.FieldByName( string("Calculated Profit") );
TFloatField profitPercent    = DataSet.FieldByName( string("Calculated Profit
                               Percent") );
```

The values for *profit* and *profitPercent* are calculated using the values of *salePrice* and cost:

```
profit.Value = salePrice.Value - cost.Value;
profitPercent.Value = 100 * profit.Value / salePrice.Value;
```

This is the *OnCalcFields* event handler in its entirety:

```
void CalcFieldDemo::OnCalcFields( TDataSetNotifySink&, TDataSet& DataSet )
{
  TCurrencyField cost       = DataSet.FieldByName( string("Cost") );
  TCurrencyField salePrice  = DataSet.FieldByName( string("Sale Price") );
  TCurrencyField profit       = DataSet.FieldByName( string("Calculated Profit") );
  TFloatField profitPercent = DataSet.FieldByName( string("Calculated Profit
                               Percent") );
profit.Value = salePrice.Value - cost.Value;
profitPercent.Value = 100 * profit.Value / salePrice.Value;
}
```

The following is the example code with comments embedded:

```
#define IDC_TABLE1 42

class CalcFieldDemo
{
private:
  PTTable table;
public:
  CalcFieldDemo(HWND hDlg);
  ~CalcFieldDemo( void ) {if (table) delete table;}
  // Declare an event sink for the calculation event
  TDataSetNotifySink OnCalcFieldsSink;
protected:
  // This method handles the calculation of the values for the new fields.
  void OnCalcFields( TDataSetNotifySink&, TDataSet& DataSet );
};
// CalcFieldDemo constructor takes a HWND to the form containing the
// TTable component and the ID of the TTable component
CalcFieldDemo::CalcFieldDemo( HWND hDlg ) :
  // Connect the event sink to the OnCalcFields event handler
  OnCalcFieldsSink( TDataSetNotify_MFUNCTOR( *this, &CalcFieldDemo::OnCalcFields ))
{
  // Map a TTable object onto the existing TTable component
  // on the form. Changes made in either the source code or the table
  // component on the form are reflected in the other because they share
  // the same TTable underlying pointers.
  // The TTable constructor takes the HWND to the form containing
  // the existing TTable component and the ID of that TTable component.
  table = new TTable(hDlg, IDC_TABLE1);
  if (table)
  {
    // Connect the form with the table so that OnCalcFields event handler
    // whenever the field values need to be calculated.
    table->OnCalcFieldsSource += OnCalcFieldsSink;
  }
}
```

```
void CalcFieldDemo::OnCalcFields( TDataSetNotifySink&, TDataSet& DataSet )
{
  // Here's where the field values are actually calculated.
  // First field objects to access the existing fields "Cost" and
  // "Sale Price" are instantiated.
  TCurrencyField cost      = DataSet.FieldByName( string("Cost") );
  TCurrencyField salePrice = DataSet.FieldByName( string("Sale Price") );
  // Next the new field components added with the Fields editor are
  // instantiated.
  TCurrencyField profit      = DataSet.FieldByName( string("Calculated Profit") );
  TFloatField profitPercent = DataSet.FieldByName( string("Calculated Profit Percent"
) );
  // The two existing fields "Cost" and "Sale Price" are used
  // to calculate and assign the value to the "Profit" field
  profit.Value = salePrice.Value - cost.Value;
  // The existing field "Sale Price" and the calculated
  // field "Profit" are used to calculate and assign the value to the
  // "Profit Percent" field.
  profitPercent.Value = 100 * profit.Value / salePrice.Value;
}
// Assume CalcForm is a class derived from TDialog and it
// contains Visual Database Tools components.
CalcForm::EvInitDialog(HWND hFocusWnd)
{
  ...
  // Assuming CalcEm is a CalcFieldDemo property of CalcForm
  // then hook up the fields calculator
  CalcEm = CalcFieldDemo(*this, IDD_TABLE1);
  ...
}
```

Modifying a TField component

TField components have several properties that determine how the field is displayed by a data-awa re control. For example, such properties can determine whether the field can be modified at run time or whether the user is limited to entering a range of acceptable values in the field. You can modify the value of these properties at run time only.

The following table summarizes *TField* properties display.

Table 42.6   TField properties

Property	Purpose
Calculated	True: Field value can be calculated by a *CalcFields* method at run time.
	False: Field value is determined from the current record.
Currency	True: Numeric field displays monetary values.
	False: Numeric field does not display monetary values.
DisplayFormat	Specifies the format of data displayed in a data-aware component.
EditFormat	Specifies the edit format of data in a data-aware control.
EditMask	Limits data-entry in an editable field to specified type and ranges of characters, and specifies any special, non-editable characters that appear within the field (hyphens, parantheses, and so on).

Table 42.6 TField properties (continued)

Property	Purpose
FieldName	Specifies the actual name of column in the physical table from which the TField component derives its value and data type.
Index	Specifies the order of the field in a dataset.
MaxValue	Specifies the maximum numeric value that can be entered in an editable numeric field.
MinValue	Specifies the minimum numeric value that can be entered in an editable numeric field.
Name	Specifies the component name of the TField component.
ReadOnly	True: Field can be displayed in a component, but cannot be edited by a user.
	False: Field can be displayed and edited.
Size	Specifies the maximum number of characters that can be displayed or entered in a string-based field, or the size of byte fields.
Visible	True: Field is displayed by a TDBGrid component. User-defined components can also make display decisions based on this property.
	False: Field is not displayed by a TDBGrid component.

Not all properties are available to all *TField* components. For example, a component of type *TStringField* doesn't have *Currency*, *MaxValue*, or *DisplayFormat* properties. A component of type *TFloatField* doesn't have a *Size* property.

While the purpose of most properties is apparent, some properties, such as *Calculated*, require additional programming steps to be useful. Others, such as *DisplayFormat*, *EditFormat*, and *EditMask*, are interrelated; their settings must be coordinated. For more information about using the *Calculated* property, see "Programming a calculated field" on page 650. For more information about using *DisplayFormat*, see "Formatting Fields."

Formatting fields

Visual Database Tools provides built-in display and edit format routines and intelligent default formatting for *TField* components. These routines and formats require no action on the programmer's part. Default formatting conventions are based on settings in the Windows Control Panel. Only format properties appropriate to the data type of a *TField* component are available for a given component.

You can change the value of the *DisplayFormat* and *EditFormat* properties of a *TField* component to override the default display settings for a *TField*, or you can handle the *OnGetText* and *OnSetText* events for a *TField* to do custom programmatic formatting.

Handling TField events

The following table summarizes *TField* events:

Table 42.7 Published *TField* events

Event	Purpose
OnChange	Called when the value for a TField component changes.
OnGetText	Called when the value for a TField component is retrieved for display or editing.
OnSetText	Called when the value for a TField component is set.
OnValidate	Called to validate the value for a TField component whenever the value is changed because of an edit or insert operation.

OnGetText and *OnSetText* events are primarily useful to programmers who want to do custom formatting that goes beyond built-in formatting functions.

Using TField conversion functions

TFields have built-in functions for conversion among data types. Depending on the *TField* type, different conversion functions are available and do different things. The following table summarizes these functions.

Table 42.8   TField conversion functions

TField Type	AsString	AsInteger	AsFloat	AsDateTime	AsBoolean
TStringField	String type by definition	Convert to Integer if possible	Convert to Float if possible	Convert to Date if possible	Convert to Boolean if possible
TIntegerField TSmallIntField TWordField	Convert to String	Integer type by definition	Convert to Float	Not Allowed	Not Allowed
TFloatField TCurrencyField TBCDField	Convert to String	Round to nearest integer value	Float type by definition	Not Allowed	Not Allowed
TDateTimeField TDateField TTimeField	Convert to String. Content depends on DisplayFormat of Field	Not Allowed	Convert Date to number of days since 01/01/0001 Convert Time to fraction of 24 hours	DateTime type by definition Zero date or time if not specified	Not Allowed
TBooleanField	Convert to String "True" or "False"	Not Allowed	Not Allowed	Not Allowed	Boolean type by definition
TBytesField TVarBytesField TBlobField TMemoField TGraphicField	Convert to String (Generally only makes sense for TMemoField)	Not Allowed	Not Allowed	Not Allowed	Not Allowed

The conversion functions can be used in any expression involving a *TField* component, on either side of an assignment statement. For example, the following statements convert the value of the *TField* named *MyTableMyField* to a string and assigns it to the text of an edit control named *Edit1*:

```
string S;
S = MyTableMyField.AsString;
Edit1.SetText( s.c_str() );
```

or

```
Edit1.SetText( MyTableField.AsString -> c_str() );
```

Conversely, this statement assigns the text of the *Edit1* control to the *TField* as a string:

```
char str[50];
Edit1.GetText( str, 50 );
MyTableMyField.AsString = str;
```

An exception occurs if an unsupported conversion is attempted at run time.

Changing a field's value

An application can access the value of a database-column through a *TField* component's *Value* property. For example, the following statement assigns the value of the CustTableCountry *TField* to the text in the edit control named *Edit3*:

```
string str;
str = CustTableCountry.Value;
Edit3.SetText( str.c_str() );
```

Any properties of *TField* components that are available from the Property Inspector can also be accessed and adjusted programmatically as well. For example, this statement changes field ordering by setting the *Index* property of CustTableCountry to 3:

```
CustTableCountry.Index = 3;
```

Displaying data with standard controls

You can display database values at run time with standard components as well as data aware components. Besides accessing *TField* components created with the Fields editor, there are two ways to access column values at run time: the *Fields* property and the *FieldsByName* method. Each accesses the value of the current row of the specified column in the underlying database table at run time. Each requires a dataset component in the form, but not a *TDataSource* component.

In general, you should use the data-aware controls built in to Visual Database Tools in database applications. These components have properties and methods built in to them that enable them to be connected to database columns, display the current values in the columns, and make updates to the columns. If you use standard components, you must provide analogous code by hand.

Using the Fields property

You can access the value of a field with the *Fields* property of a dataset component, using as a parameter the ordinal number of the column in the table (starting at 0). To access or change the field's value, convert the result with the appropriate conversion function, such as *AsString* or *AsInteger*.

This method requires you to know the order and data types of the columns in the table. Use this method if you want to iterate over a number of columns or if your application works with tables that are not available at design time.

For example, the following statement assigns the current value of the seventh column (Country) in the *CustTable* table to the text of a standard edit control named *Edit1*:

```
Edit1.SetText( CustTable.Fields[6]->AsString->c_str() );
```

Conversely, you can assign a value the user enters in a standard control to a field. For example,

```
char str[50];

Edit1.GetText( str, 50 );
CustTable.Fields[6]->AsString = str;
```

Using the FieldByName method

You can access the value of a field with the *FieldByName* method by specifying the dataset component name, and then passing *FieldByName* the name of the field you want to access. To access or change the field's value, convert the result with the appropriate conversion function, such as *AsString* or *AsInteger*.

This method requires you to know the name of the field you want to access.

For example, the following statement assigns the value of the Country field in the CustTable table to the standard edit control named *Edit2*:

```
Edit2.SetText( CustTable.FieldByName( "Country" )->AsString->c_str();
```

Conversely, you can assign a value the user enters in a standard control to a field:

```
char str[50];

Edit2.GetText( str, 50 );
CustTable.FieldByName( "Country" )->AsString = str;
```

Using the TBatchMove component

The *TBatchMove* component enables you to perform operations on groups of records or entire tables. These are the primary uses for *TBatchMove*:

- Downloading data from a server to a local data source for analysis or other operations.

- Upsizing a database from a desktop data source to a server. For more information on upsizing, see Chapter 45, "Building a client/server application."

The *TBatchMove* component is powerful because it can create destination tables that correspond to the source tables, automatically mapping the column names and data types as appropriate.

Two *TBatchMove* properties specify the source and a destination for the batch move operation: *Source* specifies a dataset (a *TQuery* or *TTable* component) corresponding to an existing source table. *Destination* specifies a *TTable* component corresponding to a database table. The destination table may or may not already exist.

Batch move modes

The *Mode* property specifies what the batch move operation will do:

Table 42.9   Batch move modes

Property	Purpose
batAppend	Append records to the destination table. The destination table must already exist. This is the default mode.
batUpdate	Update records in the destination table with matching records from the source table. The destination table must exist and must have an index defined to match records.

Table 42.9   Batch move modes

Property	Purpose
batAppendUpdate	If a matching record exists in the destination table, update it. Otherwise, append records to the destination table. The destination table must exist and must have an index defined to match records.
batCopy	Create the destination table based on the structure of the source table. The destination table must not already exist—if it does, the operation will delete it.
batDelete	Delete records in the destination table that match records in the source table. The destination table must already exist and must have an index defined.

The *Transliterate* property controls whether character-by-character translations to another character set are made as the data is transferred from the source table to the destination datasets. If the source and destination datasets use different character sets, Transliterate should be true, so that the transliteration to the destination character set occurs during the batch move operation.

Data type mappings

In *Copy* mode, the batch move operation creates the destination table based on the column data types of the source table. In moving data between different table types, the batch move operation translates the data types as appropriate. The mappings from dBASE, Paradox, and InterBase data types are shown in the following tables.

Note   To batch move data to an SQL server database, you must have that database server with the appropriate SQL Link installed. For more information, see the *SQL Links for Windows User's Guide*:

Table 42.10   Physical data type translations from Paradox tables to tables of other driver types

From Paradox type	To dBASE type	To Oracle type	To Sybase type	To InterBase type	To Informix type
Alpha	Character	Character	VarChar	Varying	Character
Number	Float {20.4}	Number	Float	Double	Float
Money	Float {20.4}	Number	Money	Double	Money {16.2}
Date	Date	Date	DateTime	Date	Date
Short	Number {6.0}	Number	SmallInt	Short	SmallInt
Memo	Memo	Long	Text	Blob/1	Text
Binary	Memo	LongRaw	Image	Blob	Byte
Formatted memo	Memo	LongRaw	Image	Blob	Byte
OLE	OLE	LongRaw	Image	Blob	Byte
Graphic	Binary	LongRaw	Image	Blob	Byte
Long	Number {11.0}	Number	Int	Long	Integer
Time	Character {>8}	Character {>8}	Character {>8}	Character {>8}	Character {>8}
DateTime	Character {>8}	Date	DateTime	Date	DateTime
Bool	Bool	Character {1}	Bit	Character {1}	Character
AutoInc	Number{11.0}	Number	Int	Long	Integer
Bytes	Memo	LongRaw	Image	Blob	Byte
BCD	N/A	N/A	N/A	N/A	N/A

Table 42.11 Physical data type translations from dBASE tables to tables of other driver types

From dBASE type	To Paradox type	To Oracle type	To Sybase type	To InterBase type	To Informix type
Character	Alpha	Character	VarChar	Varying	Character
Number	Short	Number	SmallInt	Short	SmallInt
others	Number	Number	Float	Double	Float
Float	Number	Number	Float	Double	Float
Date	Date	Date	DateTime	Date	Date
Memo	Memo	Long	Text	Blob/1	Text
Bool	Bool	Character {1}	Bit	Character {1}	Character
Lock	Alpha {24}	Character {24}	Character {24}	Character {24}	Character
OLE	OLE	LongRaw	Image	Blob	Byte
Binary	Binary	LongRaw	Image	Blob	Byte
Bytes	Bytes	LongRaw	Image	Blob	Byte (only for temp tables)

Table 42.12 Physical data type translations from InterBase tables to tables of other driver types

From Interbase type	To Paradox type	To dBASE type	To Oracle type	To Sybase type	To Informix type
Short	Short	Number {6.0}	Number	Small Int	SmallInt
Long	Number	Number {11.0}	Number	Int	Integer
Float	Number	Float {20.4}	Number	Float	Float
Double	Number	Float {20.4}	Number	Float	Float
Char	Alpha	Character	Character	VarChar	Character
Varying	Alpha	Character	Character	VarChar	Character
Date	DateTime	Date	Date	DateTime	DateTime
Blob	Binary	Memo	LongRaw	Image	Byte
Blob/1	Memo	Memo	Long	Text	Text

By default the batch move operation matches columns based on their position in the source and destination tables. That is, the first column in the source is matched with the first column in the destination, and so on.

To override the default column mappings, use the *Mappings* property. This is a list of column mappings (one per line) in one of two forms. To map the column, ColName, in the source table to the column of the same name in the destination table, enter this as the value of *Mappings*:

```
ColName
```

Or, to map the column named SourceColName in the source table to the column named DestColName in the destination table, enter this as the value of *Mappings*:

```
DestColName = SourceColName
```

If source and destination column data types are not the same, the batch move operations performs a "best fit." It trims character data types, if necessary, and attempts to perform a limited amount of conversion if possible. For example, mapping a CHAR(10) column to a CHAR(5) column results in trimming the last five characters from the source column.

As an example of conversion, if a source column of character data type is mapped to a destination of integer type, the batch move converts a character value of '5' to the corresponding integer value. Values that can't be converted generate errors. See "Handling batch move errors" on page 660.

Executing a batch move

Use the *Execute* method to execute the batch operation at run time. For example, if BatchMoveAdd is the name of a *TBatchMove* component, the following statement executes it:

```
BatchMoveAdd.Execute();
```

Handling batch move errors

Basically, two types of errors can occur in a batch move operation: data type conversion errors and integrity violations. *TBatchMove* has a number of properties that specify how it handles errors. The *AbortOnProblem* property specifies whether to abort the operation when a data type conversion error occurs. The *AbortOnKeyViol* property indicates whether to abort the operation when an integrity (key) violation occurs.

The following properties enable a *TBatchMove* to create additional tables that document the batch move operation:

- *ChangedTableName* creates a local (Paradox) table containing all records in the destination table that changed as a result of the batch operation.

- *KeyViolTableName* creates a local (Paradox) table containing all records from the source table that caused an integrity violation (such as a key violation) as a result of the batch operation.

- *ProblemTableName* creates a local (Paradox) table containing all records that could not be posted in the destination table due to data type conversion errors. For example, the table could contain records from the source table whose data had to be trimmed to fit in the destination table.

Using TSession

The *TSession* component is rarely used, but can be useful for some specialized purposes. Each time a Visual Database Tools application runs, a *TSession* component named *Session* is created automatically. You can neither see nor explicitly create a *TSession* component, but you can use its methods and properties to globally affect an application.

Controlling database connections

TSession provides global control over database connections for an application. The value of the *Databases* property of *TSession* is all the active databases in the session. The

DatabaseCount property reports the number of active databases (*TDatabase* components) in the session. For more information on the *TDatabase* component, see "Using the TDatabase component" on page 99.

KeepConnections is a Boolean property that specifies whether to keep inactive database connections. A database connection becomes inactive when a *TDatabase* component has no active datasets. By default, *KeepConnections* is true, and an application maintains its connection to a database even if the connection is inactive. This is generally preferable if an application is repeatedly opening and closing tables in the database. If *KeepConnections* is false, a database connection is closed as soon as the connection is inactive. The *DropConnections* method drops all inactive database connections.

The *NetFileDir* property specifies the directory path of the Borland Database Engine network control directory. The *PrivateDir* property specifies the path of the directory in which to store temporary files (for example, files used to process local SQL statements). You should set this property if there will be more than one instance of the application running at a time. Otherwise, the temporary files from multiple application instances will interfere with each other.

Getting database information

TSession has a number of methods that enable an application to get database-related information. Each method has a parameter of type *TStrings* in which it returns multiple strings:

Table 42.13   TSession methods

Method	Returns
GetAliasNames	Defined BDE alias names.
GetAliasParams	Parameters for the specified BDE alias.
GetDatabaseNames	Database names and BDE aliases defined.
GetDriverNames	Names of BDE drivers installed.
GetDriverParams	Parameters for the specified BDE driver.
GetTableNames	All table names in the specified database.

For more information on these methods, see the online Visual Database Tools reference.

Accessing the Borland Database Engine directly

Visual Database Tools provides a wide range of built-in methods and properties that provide an interface to the Borland Database Engine, but applications are not limited to them. Some advanced applications might require direct access to BDE function calls, cursors, and so on. While direct BDE calls can provide additional functionality, they should be used with caution, as they bypass the built-in functionality that keeps data-aware components synchronized with datasets.

If your application requires direct access to the BDE, you should refer to the *Borland Database Engine User's Guide*. This documentation provides a complete reference and user's guide to the BDE.

The application must include the header file idapi.h. Then the code can make direct calls to the BDE application programming interface.

BDE function calls often require handles as parameters to specify the action to be performed. Your applications have access to these through the following properties of dataset components:

- *DBHandle* is the handle for the database to which they are connected.

- *Handle* is the handle for the underlying cursor on the database.

- *DBLocale* and *Locale* are used for ANSI/OEM conversion for localization of applications.

After performing a BDE call directly, it is a good idea to call *Refresh* or *UpdateCursorPos* to ensure that all data-aware components are synchronized with their datasets.

43

Using data-aware controls

Data-aware controls are used to display and edit data from a database. They include components such as *TDBGrid* for displaying and editing all specified records and fields in a table, and *TDBNavigator* for navigating among records, deleting records, and posting records when they change.

The following table summarizes the data-aware controls:

Table 43.1   Data-aware components

Icon	Component	Purpose
	TDBCheckBox	Check box that displays a value from a column, or modifies a field value for the current record.
	TDBComboBox	Combo box that displays or edits values in a column of a table.
	TDBEdit	Edit control that displays and edits a value from a column of the current record.
	TDBGrid	Grid that enables the viewing and editing of data in a table.
	TDBImage	Image control that displays, cuts, or pastes graphical BLOB images to and from a table.
	TDBListBox	List box that presents a list of choices to the user. When the user selects one of them, that item becomes the value in a column of the current record.

Table 43.1   Data-aware components (continued)

Icon	Component	Purpose
	TDBLookupCombo	Combo box that displays values mapped through another table at run time.
	TDBLookupList	List box that displays values mapped through another table at run time.
	TDBMemo	Memo control that displays or edits text BLOB data from a column in a table.
	TDBNavigator	Navigation control with buttons that move a table's current record pointer forward or backward; start Insert or Edit mode; post new or modified records; cancel Edit mode; and refresh display to retrieve updated data.
	TDBRadioGroup	Radio group populated with radio buttons that display or set column values.
	TDBText	Text control that displays a value from a column of the current record.

A data-aware control derives display data from a database source outside the application, and can also optionally post (or return) data changes to a data source. Data-aware controls are aware of data at design time, meaning that when you connect a component to an active data source while building an application, you can immediately see live data in the controls by switching the Dialog editor into test mode.

This chapter describes basic features common to all data-aware controls, then describes how and when to use individual components.

Data-aware component basics

Data-aware controls are linked to database tables through the *DataSource* property. The *DataSource* property specifies the name of the *TDataSource* component from which a control gets its data. The *TDataSource* component is linked to a dataset (for example, *TTable* or *TQuery*) that is, in turn, connected to a database table. For more information about *TDataSource*, *TTable*, *TQuery*, and the Fields editor, see Chapter 42, "Using data-access components and tools." For information about connecting data-access controls with other components, see "Making the connections: linking database components" on page 24.

Data-aware controls can only access columns in tables for which there are corresponding *TField* components. If the Fields editor is used to limit a dataset to a subset of columns in a table, then *TField* components exist only for those columns. Most data-aware controls provide a *DataField* property where you can specify the *TField* component with which it should be associated.

Placing data-aware controls on forms

When designing a form that accesses data, you must place at least one dataset component (for example, *TTable* or *TQuery*), at least one *TDataSource* component, and one or more data-aware controls on the form.

➤ To place a data-aware control on a form and link it to a dataset, follow these steps:

1 Select the control from the Data Aware page of the Controls palette in the Dialog editor and drop it on the form.

2 Set the *DataSource* property to the name of a *TDataSource* component already on the form. You can type the name or choose it from the drop-down list.

3 Set the *DataField* property to the name of a *TField* component in the dataset component named in the *DataSource* property. You can type the field name or choose it from the drop-down list.

Note Two data-aware controls, the data grid and the database navigator, access all available *TField* components within a dataset, and therefore do not have *DataField* properties. For these controls, omit step 3.

When a data-aware control is associated with a dataset, its *Enabled* property determines if its attached *TDataSource* component receives data from mouse or keyboard events. Controls are also disabled if the *Enabled* property of *TDataSource* is false, or if the *Active* property of the dataset is false.

Updating fields

Most data-aware controls can update fields by default. Update privileges depend on the status of the control's *ReadOnly* property *and* underlying *TField*'s and dataset's *CanModify* property. *ReadOnly* is set to false by default, meaning that data modifications can be made. In addition, the data source must be in Edit state if you want the user to be able to modify the data.

In all data-aware controls except *TDBGrid*, when you modify a field, the modification is copied to the underlying *TField* component when the user moves to another control. If the user presses the *Cancel* button on a database navigator before moving to another control, then any modifications are abandoned, and the value of the field reverts to the value it held before any modifications were made.

When a record is posted, all data-aware controls associated with the dataset are checked for a change in status. If there is a problem updating any fields that contain modified data, an exception is raised, and no modifications are made to the record.

Displaying data with TDBText

The database text control is a read-only data-aware control. *TDBText* gets the text it displays from a specified field in the current record of a dataset. Because *TDBText* gets its text from a dataset, the text it displays is dynamic—the text changes as the user navigates the database table. When *TDBText* is linked to a data field at design time, you can see the current value for that field when the Dialog editor is in test mode. A *TDBText* control is useful when you want to provide display-only data on a form that allows user input in other controls.

For example, suppose a form is created around the fields in a customer list table, and that once the user enters a street address, city, and state or province information in the form, you use a dynamic lookup to automatically determine the zip code field from a separate table. A *TDBText* component tied to the zip code table could be used to display the zip code field that matches the address entered by the user.

Note When you create a *TDBText* component on a form, make sure its *AutoSize* property is true (the default) to ensure that the control resizes itself as necessary to display data of varying widths. If *AutoSize* is set to false, and the control is too small, data display is truncated.

Displaying and editing fields with TDBEdit

A database edit control displays the current value of a data field to which it is linked. You can also modify values in this component.

For example, suppose DataSource1 is a *TDataSource* component that is active and linked to an open *TTable* called Customer. You can then add a *TDBEdit* control to a form, and set its properties as follows:

- *DataSource*: DataSource1
- *DataField*: CUSTNO

The database edit control immediately displays the value of the current row in the CUSTNO column of the CUSTOMER table, both in test mode at design time and at run time.

Editing a field

A user can modify a database field in a *TDBEdit* component if:

- The dataset is in Edit state.
- The *CanModify* property of the dataset is true.
- The *ReadOnly* property of the *TDBEdit* control is false.

Note Edits made to a field must be posted to the database by moving to a different record by using a navigation button on a database navigator control. Using the Post button posts edits without moving to a different record.

Viewing and modifying data with a data grid

 The data grid (*TDBGrid*) enables you to view and edit all records associated with a dataset in a spreadsheet-like format:

Figure 43.1 TDBGrid component

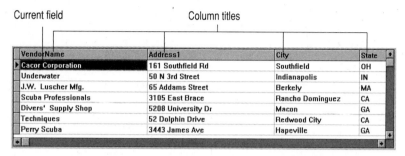

Which fields appear in the dataset displayed in the data grid depends on whether the *TField* components of the dataset are dynamically created at run time, or if you use the Fields editor to create a persistent set of *TField* components whose properties you can specify in the Property Inspector at design time.

If a dynamic dataset is generated at run time, all records are displayed using default record and field ordering, and default display and edit formats. In most cases, however, you will want to control field order and appearance. To do so, use the Fields editor to instantiate *TField* components and set their properties at design time.

When you use the Fields editor to instantiate *TField* components, you gain a great deal of flexibility over the appearance of records in a data grid. For example, the order in which fields appear from left to right in the data grid is determined by the way you order *TField* components in the Fields list box of the Fields editor. For more information about using the Fields editor to control *TField* properties, see "Using TField components and the Fields editor" on page 53.

To put a data grid on a form and link it to a dataset:

1 Select the *TDBGrid* control from the Data Aware page of the Controls palette of the Dialog editor, and place it on a form.

2 Resize the grid to the size you want.

3 Set the *DataSource* property to the name of a *TDataSource* component that specifies a *TTable* or *TQuery* component in its *Dataset* property.

Setting grid options

You can set properties at design time to control grid behavior and appearance at run time. The following table lists these properties:

Table 43.2 Important design-time properties for the data grid

Option	Purpose
AllowResize	True: Columns and rows can be resized by dragging the lines that separate the columns and rows in the title area.
	False: Columns and rows cannot be resized in the grid.
ShowGridLines	True: Displays grid lines between columns and rows.
	False: Does not display grid lines between columns and rows.
AllowTabs	True: Permits the *Tab* and *Shift+Tab* keys to move the cursor between cells in the selected range.
	False: Tabbing exits the data grid.
DataSetColumnNames	True: Displays field names as the headings of the columns in the data grid.
	False: Field-name display is turned off.

For more information about these options, see the online Visual Database Tools reference.

The data grid is a VBX control provided by a third party. It has many more properties available that make it very useful as a spreadsheet control. You can find more information about using the data grid as a spreadsheet control in the Formula One Spreadsheet VBX Control online help.

Editing in the data grid

At run time, users can use a data grid to modify existing data and enter new records, if the *ReadOnly* property of the *TTable* or *TQuery* dataset displayed in the grid is false. When the dataset's *ReadOnly* property is false, its *CanModify* property is true.

In data-aware controls, edits and insertions within a field are posted only when the user moves to a different record in the data grid or explicitly performs a *Post*. Even if the mouse is used to change focus to another control on a form, the data grid doesn't post changes until the cursor on the dataset moves to another row. When a record is posted, all data-aware components associated with the dataset are checked for a change in status. If there is a problem updating any fields that contain modified data, an exception is thrown, and the record is not modified.

The user can cancel all edits for a record by pressing the *Cancel* button on a database navigator in any field before moving to another record.

Navigating and manipulating records with TDBNavigator

 The database navigator (*TDBNavigator*) uses a simple control for navigating through records in a dataset, and for manipulating records. The navigator consists of a series of buttons that enable a user to scroll forward or backward through records one at a time, go to the first record, go to the last record, insert a new record, update an existing record, post data changes, cancel data changes, delete a record, and refresh record display.

Figure 43.2   TDBNavigator component

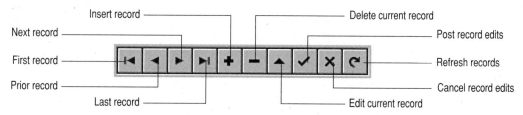

The following table describes the buttons on the navigator:

Table 43.3   TDBNavigator buttons

Button	Purpose
BtnFirst	Calls the dataset's *First* method to set the current record to the first record.
BtnPrevious	Calls the dataset's *Prior* method to set the current record to the previous record.
BtnNext	Calls the dataset's *Next* method to set the current record to the next record.
BtnLast	Calls the dataset's *Last* method to set the current record to the last record.
BtnInsert	Calls the dataset's *Insert* method to insert a new record before the current record, and set the dataset in Insert state.
BtnDelete	Deletes the current record. If the *ConfirmDelete* property is true, it prompts for confirmation before deleting.
BtnEdit	Puts the dataset in Edit state so that the current record can be modified.
BtnPost	Writes changes in the current record to the database.
BtnCancel	Cancels edits to the current record, and returns the dataset to Browse state.
BtnRefresh	Clears data-aware control display buffers, then refreshes its buffers from the physical table or query. Useful if the underlying data may have been changed by another application.

The database navigator has a property for each button. For example, the *BtnCancel* property gives you access to the button that cancels an edit on the navigator.

Hiding and disabling navigator buttons

When you first put a database navigator on a form, all its buttons are visible. You can choose to hide buttons you do not want to use on a form. For example, on a form that is intended for browsing rather than editing, you might want to hide the Edit, Insert, Delete, Post, and Cancel buttons.

Each button has three possible states as shown in this table:

Table 43.4   Navigator button states

Value	Meaning
btnOff	The button is not visible.
btnOn	The button is visible and enabled.
btnDisabled	The button is visible but disabled and appears grayed.

For example, to hide the BtnDelete button, set the property value for *BtnDelete* to *btnOff*.

Displaying and editing BLOB text with TDBMemo

The database memo control is a data-aware control that can display binary large object (BLOB) data. The *TDBMemo* control displays multi-line text, and permits a user to enter multi-line text as well. For example, you can use *TDBMemo* controls to display memo fields from dBASE and Paradox tables and text data contained in BLOB fields.

Figure 43.3   TDBMemo component

By default, *TDBMemo* permits a user to edit memo text. To limit the number of characters users can enter into the database memo, use the *MaxLength* property. To make a *TDBMemo* component read-only, set its *ReadOnly* property to true.

Several properties affect how the database memo appears and how text is entered. You can supply scroll bars in the memo with the *ScrollBars* property. To prevent word wrap, set the *WordWrap* property to false. To permit tabs in a memo, set the *WantTabs* property to true. The *Alignment* property determines how the text is aligned within the control. Possible choices are *taLeftJustify* (the default), *taCenter*, and *taRightJustify*.

At run time, users can cut, copy, and paste text to and from a database memo control. You can accomplish the same task programmatically by using the *CutToClipboard*, *CopyToClipboard*, and *PasteFromClipboard* methods.

Because the *TDBMemo* control can display large amounts of data, it can take time to populate the display at run time. To reduce the time it takes to scroll through data records, *TDBMemo* has an *AutoDisplay* property that controls whether the accessed data should be automatically displayed. If you set *AutoDisplay* to false, *TDBMemo* displays the field name rather than actual data. The user must double-click inside the control to view the actual data.

Displaying BLOB graphics with TDBImage

The database image control is a data-aware component that displays bitmapped graphics contained in BLOB data fields. It captures BLOB graphics images from a dataset, and stores them internally in the Windows .DIB format.

Figure 43.4   TDBImage component

By default, *TDBImage* permits a user to update the graphics image by cutting and pasting to and from the Clipboard. You can accomplish the same task programmatically by using the *CutToClipboard, CopyToClipboard,* and *PasteFromClipboard* methods. To make a *TDBImage* component read-only, set its *ReadOnly* property to true.

Because the *TDBImage* can display large amounts of data, it can take time to populate the display at run time. To reduce the time it takes to scroll through data records, *TDBImage* has an *AutoDisplay* property that controls whether the accessed data is automatically displayed. If *AutoDisplay* is set to false, *TDBImage* displays the field name rather than actual data. The user must double-click inside the control to view the actual data.

Using list and combo boxes

Four data-aware controls provide data-aware versions of standard list box and combo box controls. These useful controls provide the user with a set of default data values to choose from at run time.

The following table describes these controls:

Table 43.5   Data-aware list box and combo box controls

Data-aware control	Description
TDBListBox	Displays a list of items from which a user can update a specific column in the current data record.
TDBComboBox	Combines a *TDBEdit* control with an attached list. The application user can update a specific column in the current data record by typing a value or by choosing a value from the drop-down list.
TDBLookupList	Displays a list of items from which a user can update a column in the current data record. The list of items is looked up in a specific column in another dataset.
TDBLookupCombo	Combines a *TDBEdit* control with a drop-down version of *TDBLookupList*. The application user can update a field in the current database by typing a value or by choosing a value from the drop-down list that is looked up in a specific column in another dataset.

TDBListBox

A database list box is very similar to a database combo box, but instead of a drop-down list, it displays a scrollable list of available choices. When the user selects a value at run time, it becomes the new value for the field the database list box is linked to. Unlike *TDBComboBox*, the user can't type an entry that is not in the list.

Here is an example of how a *TDBListBox* control appears at run time.

Figure 43.5   TDBListBox component

While navigating through a dataset, a *TDBListBox* control displays values in the column by highlighting the corresponding entry in its list. If the current row's value is not defined in the *Items* property, no value is highlighted in the *TDBListBox*. Changing the selection changes the underlying value in the database column and is equivalent to typing a value in a *TDBEdit* component.

The *IntegralHeight* property controls the way the list box is displayed. If *IntegralHeight* is true (the default), the bottom of the list box moves up to the bottom of the last completely displayed item in the list. If *IntegralHeight* is false, the bottom of the list box is determined by the *ItemHeight* property, and the bottom item might not be completely displayed.

TDBComboBox

A database combo box is similar to a database edit control, except that at run time it has a drop-down list that enables a user to pick from a predefined set of values. Here is an example of what a *TDBComboBox* component looks like at run time:

Figure 43.6 TDBComboBox component

The *Items* property of the component specifies the items contained in the drop-down list. Use the String List editor to specify the values for the drop-down list. To display the String List editor, double-click the value column of the *Items* property. Each line you type in the String List editor becomes an item in the combo box.

At run time, the user can choose an item from the list or (depending on the value of the *Style* property) type a different entry. When the component is linked to a column through its *DataField* property, it displays the value in the current row, regardless of whether it appears in the *Items* list.

The following properties determine how the *Items* list is displayed at run time:

- *Style* determines the display style of the component:
  - *csDropDown* (default): Displays a drop-down list with an edit box in which the user can enter text. All items are strings and have the same height.
  - *csSimple*: Displays the *Items* list at all times instead of in a drop-down list. All items are strings and have the same height.
  - *csDropDownList*: Displays a drop-down list and edit box, but the user cannot enter or change values that are not in the drop-down list at run time.
  - *csOwnerDrawFixed* and *csOwnerDrawVariable*: Allows the *Items* list to display values other than strings (for example, bitmaps). For more information about owner-draw list and combo boxes, see the online Visual Database Tools reference.

- *DropDownCount*: the maximum number of items displayed in the list. If the number of *Items* is greater than *DropDownCount*, the user can scroll the list. If the number of *Items* is less than *DropDownCount*, the list will be just large enough to display all the items.

- *ItemHeight*: The height of each item when style is *csOwnerDrawFixed*.

- *Sorted*: If true, then the *Items* list is sorted and displayed in alphabetical order.

TDBLookupCombo

The *TDBLookupCombo* component is similar to *TDBComboBox*, except that it derives its list of values dynamically from a second dataset at run time, and it can display multiple columns in its drop-down list. With this control, you can ensure that users enter valid values into a dataset by providing an interface from which they can choose values. Here is an example of how a *TDBLookupCombo* control might appear at run time:

Figure 43.7   TDBLookupCombo component

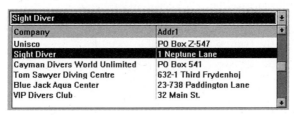

The lookup list for *TDBLookupCombo* must be derived from a second dataset. To display values from a column in the same table as the first dataset:

1 Drop a second data source and dataset component on the form.

2 Point them at the same data as the first data source and dataset.

Three properties establish the lookup list for *TDBLookupCombo* and determine how it is displayed:

- *LookupSource* specifies a second data source from where the control populates its list.

- *LookupField* specifies a field in the *LookupSource* dataset which links that dataset to the primary dataset. This must be a column in the dataset pointed to by *LookupSource*, and it must contain the same values as the column pointed to by the *DataField* property (although the column names do not have to match).

- *LookupDisplay*, if set, defines the columns that *TDBLookupCombo* displays. If you do not specify values in *LookupDisplay*, *TDBLookupCombo* displays the values found in the column specified by *LookupField*. Use this property to display a column other than that specified by *LookupField*, or to display multiple columns in the drop-down list. To specify multiple columns, separate the different column names with a semicolon.

You can also specify lines between columns or rows by setting the *ShowGridLines* property to true. Setting the *ShowColHeadings* property to true displays the field names as titles above the columns.

A TDBLookupCombo example

As a simple example, an order-entry form could have a *TDBLookupCombo* component to specify the customer number of the customer placing the order. The user placing the order can simply click on the drop down "pick list" instead of having to remember the customer number. The value displayed could be the customer name.

➤ To build this example,

1 Add a *TDataSource* component to the form, and set its *Name* property to OrdSource.

2 Add a *TTable* component to the form, and set the *Name* property to OrdTable, the *DatabaseName* property to DBDEMOS, the *TableName* property to ORDERS.DB, and the *Active* property to true.

3 Add a second *TDataSource* component on the form, and set its *Name* property to CustSource.

4 Add a second *TTable* component on the form, and set the *Name* property to CustTable, the *DatabaseName* property to DBDEMOS, the *TableName* property to CUSTOMER.DB, and the *Active* property to true.

5 Add a *TDBGrid* component and link it to OrdSource through its *DataSource* property so it displays the contents of the ORDERS table.

6 Add a *TDBLookupCombo* component, and set its *DataSource* property to CustNo. The database lookup combo box is now linked to the CustNo column of the ORDERS table.

7 Specify the lookup values of the *TDBLookupCombo* component:

- Set *LookupSource* to CustSource (so it looks up values in the CUSTOMER table).
- Set *LookupField* to CustNo (so it looks up and gets values from the CustNo column).
- In *LookupDisplay*, type `Company;Addr1`.

    This displays the corresponding company name and address in the drop-down list.

At run time, the *TDBLookupCombo* component displays a drop-down list of company names and addresses. If the user selects a new company from the list, the control is assigned the value of the corresponding customer number (CustNo). When the user moves to another order record in the data grid, the new customer number and information is posted to the row.

TDBLookupList

The database lookup list box is much the same as the database lookup combo box, but instead of a drop-down list, it displays a scrollable list of the available choices. These choices come from a second dataset, and are the values of the *LookupDisplay* column. When the user selects one at run time, the field in the first dataset is assigned the value of the *LookupField* of the current record in the second dataset. Like *TDBLookupCombo*, the user can't type in an entry that is not in the list. Here is an example of how a *TDBLookupList* component appears at run time:

Figure 43.8   TDBLookupList component

While you navigate through a dataset, a *TDBLookupList* component highlights the item in the list that corresponds to the value in the currently selected row. If the current row's value is not defined in the *Items* property, no value is highlighted in the *TDBLookupList* component. Changing the selection changes the underlying value in the database column and is equivalent to typing a value in a *TDBEdit* component.

TDBCheckBox

A database check box can be used to set the values of fields in a dataset. For example, a customer invoice form might have a database check box control that when checked, specifies that the customer is entitled to a special discount.

Figure 43.9   TDBCheckBox component

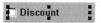

Like the other data-aware controls, *TDBCheckBox* is attached to a specific field in a dataset through its *DataSource* and *DataField* properties. Use the *Caption* property to display a label for the check box on your form.

Set the *ValueChecked* property to a value the control should post to the database if the control is checked when the user moves to another record. By default, this value is set to true, but you can make it any alphanumeric value appropriate to your needs. You can also enter a semicolon-delimited list of items as the value of *ValueChecked*. If any of the items matches the contents of that field in the current record, the check box is checked. For example, you can specify a *ValueChecked* string such as this:

```
MyDBCheckBox.ValueChecked = "True;Yes;On";
```

If&the field for the current record contains values of True, Yes, or On, then the check box is checked. Comparison of the field to *ValueChecked* strings is case-insensitive. If a user checks a box for which there are multiple *ValueChecked* strings, the first string is the value that is posted to the database.

Set the *ValueUnchecked* property to a value the control should post to the database if the control is not checked when the user moves to another record. By default, this value is set to false, but you can make it any alphanumeric value appropriate to your needs. You can also enter a semicolon-delimited list of items as the value of *ValueUnchecked*. If any of the items matches the contents of that field in the current record, the check box is unchecked.

A *TDBCheckBox* component is grayed out and disabled whenever the field for the current record does not contain one of the values listed in the *ValueChecked* or *ValueUnchecked* properties.

TDBRadioGroup

The database radio group lets you set the value of a data field with a radio button control where there is a limited number of possible values for the field. The radio group consists of one button for each value a field can accept.

TDBRadioGroup is attached to a specific field in a dataset through its *DataSource* and *DataField* properties. A radio button for each string value entered in the *Items* property is displayed on the form, and the string itself is displayed as a label to the right of the button.

Figure 43.10 A TDBRadioGroup component

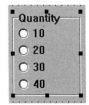

For the current record, if the field associated with a radio group matches one of the strings in the *Items* property, that radio button is selected. For example, if three strings, "Red," "Yellow," and "Blue," are listed for *Items*, and the field for the current record contains the value Blue, then the third button in the group is selected.

Note   If the field does not match any strings in *Items*, a radio button may still be selected if the field matches a string in the *Values* property. If the field for the current record does not match any strings in *Items* or *Values*, no radio button is selected.

The *Values* property can contain an optional list of strings that can be returned to the dataset when a user selects a radio button and posts a record. Strings are associated with buttons in numeric sequence. The first string is associated with the first button, the second string with the second button, and so on. For the three buttons labeled Red, Yellow, and Blue, if three strings, "Magenta," "Yellow," and "Cyan," are listed for *Values* and the user selects the first button (labeled Red), then "Magenta" is posted to the database.

If strings for *Values* are not provided, the label from a selected radio button (from *Items*) is returned to the database when a record is posted. Users can modify the value of a data field by clicking the appropriate radio button. When the user moves to another row, the value indicated by the radio button string is posted to the database.

44

Using SQL in applications

SQL (Structured Query Language) is an industry-standard language for database operations. Visual Database Tools enables your application to use SQL syntax directly through the *TQuery* component. Visual Database Tools applications can use SQL to access data from:

- Paradox or dBASE tables, using local SQL. The allowable syntax is a sub-set of ANSI-standard SQL and includes basic SELECT, INSERT, UPDATE, and DELETE statements. For more information on local SQL syntax, see Chapter 47, "Using local SQL."

- Databases on remote database servers. You must have installed the appropriate SQL Link. (SQL Links is available separately from Borland International.) Any standard statement in the server's SQL is allowed. For information on SQL syntax and limitations, see your server documentation.

Visual Database Tools also supports heterogeneous queries against more than one server or table type (for example, data from an Oracle table and a Paradox table). For more information, see "Creating heterogenous queries" on page 685.

Using the TQuery component

TQuery is a dataset component which shares many characteristics with *TTable*, as described in "Using datasets" on page 30. In addition, *TQuery* enables applications to issue SQL statements to a database engine (either the Borland Database Engine or a server SQL engine).

The SQL statements can be either static or dynamic; that is, they can be set at design time or include parameters whose values change at run time.

When to use TQuery

For simple database operations, *TTable* is often sufficient and provides portable database access through the BDE. However, *TQuery* provides additional capabilities that *TTable* does not. Use *TQuery* for:

- Multi-table queries (joins)
- Complex queries that require sub-SELECTs
- Operations that require explicit SQL syntax

TTable does not use SQL syntax; *TQuery* does use SQL, which provides powerful relational capabilities but may increase an application's overall complexity. Also, use of non-standard (server-specific) SQL syntax might decrease an application's portability among servers; for more information, see "Server portability" on page 96.

How to use TQuery

To access a database, set the *DatabaseName* property of a *TQuery* component to a defined BDE alias, a directory path for desktop database files, or a file name for a server database. If the application has a *TDatabase* component, *DatabaseName* can also be set to a local alias that it defines. For more information, see "Using the TDatabase component" on page 99.

To issue SQL statements with a *TQuery* component:

- Assign to the *TQuery* component's *SQL* property the text of the SQL statement. You can do this:

  - At design time, by editing the *TQuery*'s *SQL* property in the Property Inspector of the Dialog editor. Double-click the value column of the *SQL* property, and enter the SQL statements in the String List editor dialog box that appears.

  - At run time, by closing any current query with the *Close* method, clearing the *SQL* property with the *Clear* method, and then specifying the SQL text with the *Add* method.

- Execute the statement with the *TQuery* component's *Open* or *ExecSQL* method. Use *Open* for SELECT statements. Use *ExecSQL* for all other SQL statements. The differences between *Open* and *ExecSQL* are discussed in the section "Executing a query" on page 680.

- To use a dynamic SQL statement, call the *Prepare* method, provide the parameters, and then call *Open* or *ExecSQL*. It's not really necessary to call *Prepare*, but doing so improves the performance for dynamic queries executed multiple times.

The following diagram illustrates the lifetime of a *TQuery* component and the methods used to work with it:

Figure 44.1 TQuery methods and flow

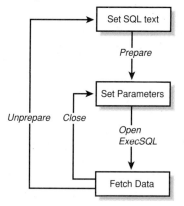

Note *Prepare* applies only to dynamic queries. It is not required, but is recommended in most cases. For more information, see "Dynamic SQL statements" on page 682.

The SQL property

The *SQL* property contains the text of the SQL statement to be executed by a *TQuery* component. This property is of type *TStrings*, which can hold a series of strings in a list. The list acts very much as if it were an array, but it is actually a special component with unique capabilities. For more information about *TStrings*, see the online Visual Database Tools reference.

A *TQuery* component can execute two kinds of SQL statements:

- Static SQL statements
- Dynamic SQL statements

A *static* SQL statement is fixed at design time and does not contain any parameters or variables. For example, this statement is a static SQL statement:

```
SELECT * FROM CUSTOMER WHERE CUST_NO = 1234
```

A *dynamic* SQL statement, also called a *parameterized* statement, includes parameters for column or table names. For example, this is a dynamic SQL statement:

```
SELECT * FROM CUSTOMER WHERE CUST_NO = :Number
```

The variable *Number*, indicated by the leading colon, is a parameter which must be provided at run time and may vary each time the statement is executed.

Creating the query text

You can enter the SQL text for a *TQuery* at design time by clicking the button with the ellipsis (...) for the *SQL* property in the Property Inspector. The SQL editor opens, so you can enter an SQL statement.

Figure 44.2   Editing SQL statements in the SQL editor

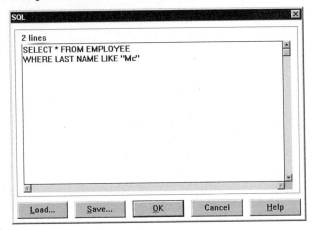

Choose OK to assign the text you enter to the *SQL* property of the query. Choose Load to include text from a file or Save to save the text to a file.

To specify SQL text at run time, an application should first close the query by calling the *Close* method and then clear the *SQL* property by calling the *Clear* method. For example,

```
Query1.Close();      // This closes the query
Query1.SQL->Clear(); // This clears the contents of the SQL property
```

It is always safe to call *Close*—if the query is already closed, the call has no effect. Use the *SQL* property's *Add* method to add the SQL statements to it. For example,

```
Query1.SQL->Add("SELECT * FROM COUNTRY");
Query1.SQL->Add("WHERE NAME = \"ARGENTINA\"");
```

Note   An application should always call *Clear* before specifying a new SQL statement. Otherwise, *Add* simply appends the statements to the existing one.

You can also use the *LoadFromFile* method to assign the text in an SQL script file to the *SQL* property. For example,

```
Query1.SQL->LoadFromFile("C:\\SCRIPTS\\MYQUERY.TXT");
```

Note   The *SQL* property can contain only one complete SQL statement at a time. In general, multiple statements are not allowed. Some servers support multiple statement "batch" syntax; if the server supports this, then such statements are allowed.

Executing a query

At design time, you can execute a query by changing its *Active* property in the Property Inspector to true. The results of the query are displayed in any data-aware controls connected to the *TQuery* component (through a *TDataSource* component).

At run time, an application can execute a query with either the *Open* or the *ExecSQL* methods. Call *Open* for SQL statements that return a result set (SELECT statements).

Call *ExecSQL* for all other SQL statements (INSERT, UPDATE, DELETE, and so on). For example,

```
Query1.Open(); // Returns a result set
```

If the SQL statement doesn't return a cursor and a result set from the database, call *ExecSQL* instead of *Open*. For example,

```
Query1.ExecSQL();  // Does not return a result set
```

The UniDirectional property

Use the *UniDirectional* property to optimize access to a database table through a *TQuery* component. If you set *UniDirectional* to true, you can iterate through a table more quickly, but you can only move in a forward direction. *UniDirectional* is false by default.

Getting a live result set

A *TTable* component always returns a live result set to an application. That is, the user sees the data "live" from the database, and can make changes to it directly through data-aware controls. A *TQuery* can return two kinds of result sets:

- "Live" result sets: As with *TTable* components, users can edit data in the result set with data controls. The changes are sent to the database when a *Post* occurs, or when the user tabs off a control, as described in "Using data-aware controls" on page 69.

- "Read-only" result sets: Users cannot edit data in the result set with data controls.

By default, a query always returns a read-only result set. To get a live result set, an application must request it by setting the *RequestLive* property of *TQuery* to true. For the BDE to be able to return a live result set, however, the SELECT syntax of the query must conform to the guidelines given below. If an application requests a live result set, but the syntax doesn't conform to the requirements, the BDE returns a read-only result set (for local SQL) or an error return code (for passthrough SQL). If a query returns a live result set, the *CanModify* property is set to true.

Table 44.1   Types of query result sets

RequestLive property	CanModify property	Type of result set
False	False	Read-only
True—SELECT syntax meets requirements	True	Live
True—SELECT syntax does not meet requirements	False	Read-only

If an application needs to update the data in a read-only result set, it must use a separate *TQuery* to construct an UPDATE statement. By setting the parameters of the update query based on the data retrieved in the first query, the application can perform the desired update operation.

Syntax requirements for live result sets

To return a live result set, a query must have *RequestLive* set to true. The SQL syntax must conform to that of Local SQL, as described in Chapter 47. Additionally, the syntax must meet these requirements:

A query of a Paradox or dBASE table can return a live result set if:

- It involves a single table.
- It doesn't have an ORDER BY clause.
- It doesn't use aggregates such as SUM or AVG.
- It doesn't use calculated fields in the SELECT list.
- The WHERE clause consists only of comparisons of column names to scalar constants. The comparison operators may be LIKE, >, <, >=, and <=. The clause may contain any number of such comparisons linked by AND or OR operators.

A query of a server table using passthrough SQL can return a live result set if:

- It involves a single table.
- It doesn't have an ORDER BY clause.
- It doesn't use aggregates such as SUM or AVG.

In addition, if the table is on a Sybase server, it must have a unique index.

Dynamic SQL statements

A dynamic SQL statement (also called a parameterized query) contains parameters that can vary at run time.

Supplying values to parameters

At design time, you can supply values to parameters with the Query Parameters editor.

1 Display the Query Parameters editor by clicking the button with the ellipsis (...) for the *Params* property of the *TQuery* in the Property Inspector. The Query Parameters editor opens.

Figure 44.3   Query Parameters editor

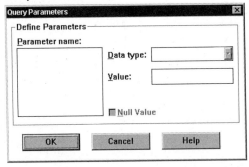

2 Select the desired data type for the parameter in the Data Type combo box.

3 Enter a value in the Value text field or select Null Value to set the parameter's value to NULL.

When you choose OK, the query is prepared and values are bound to the parameters. Then, when you set the query's *Active* property to true, the results of the SQL query with the specified parameter values show up in any data-aware controls connected to the query.

At run time, an application can supply values to parameters with the following *TQuery* properties:

- The *Params* property, using the order that the parameters appear in the SQL statement.

- The *ParamByName* method, using the parameter names specified in the SQL statement.

- The *DataSource* property to set values from another dataset for columns that match the names of parameters with no values.

Preparing a query

The *Prepare* method sends a parameterized query to the Borland Database Engine for parsing and optimization. A call to *Prepare* is not required to use a parameterized query. It is strongly recommended, however, because it will improve performance for dynamic queries that are executed more than once. If a query is not explicitly prepared, each time it is executed, it is automatically prepared.

Prepare is a Boolean property of *TQuery* that indicates if a query has been prepared. The Parameters editor automatically prepares a query when you use it to set parameter values at design time.

If a query has been executed, an application must call the *Close* method before calling *Prepare* again. Generally, an application should call *Prepare* once, then set parameters using the *Params* property, and finally call *Open* or *ExecSQL* to execute the query. Each time the query is to be executed with different parameter values, an application must call *Close*, set the parameter values, and then execute the query with *Open* or *ExecSQL*.

Preparing a query consumes some database resources, so it is good practice for an application to unprepare a query once it is done using it. The *UnPrepare* method unprepares a query. When you change the text of a query at run time, the query is automatically closed and unprepared.

Using the Params property

When you enter a query, a *Params* array is created for the parameters of a dynamic SQL statement. *Params* is a zero-based array of *TParam* components with an element for each parameter in the query; that is, the first parameter is *Params[0]*, the second *Params[1]*, and so on.

For example, suppose a *TQuery* component named *Query2* has the following statement for its *SQL* property:

```
INSERT
  INTO COUNTRY (NAME, CAPITAL, POPULATION)
  VALUES (:Name, :Capital, :Population)
```

An application could use *Params* to specify the values of the parameters as follows:

```
Query2.Params->Items[0]->AsString = "Lichtenstein";
Query2.Params->Items[1]->AsString = "Vaduz";
Query2.Params->Items[2]->AsInteger = 420000;
```

These statements would bind the value "Lichtenstein" to the *:Name* parameter, "Vaduz" to the *:Capital* parameter, and 420000 to the *:Population* parameter.

Using the ParamByName method

ParamByName is a method that enables an application to assign values to parameters based on their names. Instead of providing the ordinal location of the parameter, you must supply its name.

For example, an application could use *ParamByName* to specify values for the parameters in the preceding example as follows:

```
Query2.ParamByName("Name").AsString = "Lichtenstein";
Query2.ParamByName("Capital").AsString = "Vaduz";
Query2.ParamByName("Population").AsInteger = 420000;
```

These statements would have the same effect as the three previous statements that used the *Params* property directly.

Using the DataSource property

For parameters of a query not bound to values at design time, the value of the query's *DataSource* property is checked. This property specifies the name of a *TDataSource* component. If *DataSource* is set, and the unbound parameter names match any column names in the specified *DataSource*, Visual Database Tools binds the current values of those fields to the corresponding parameters. This capability enables applications to have linked queries.

The LINKQRY sample application illustrates the use of the *DataSource* property to link a query in a master-detail form. The form contains a *TQuery* component (named Orders) with the following in its *SQL* property:

```
SELECT Orders.CustNo, Orders.OrderNo, Orders.SaleDate
    FROM Orders
    WHERE Orders.CustNo = :CustNo
```

As illustrated below, the form also contains:

- A *TDataSource* named OrdersSource, linked to Orders by its *DataSet* property
- A *TTable* component (named Cust)
- A *TDataSource* named CustSource linked to Cust
- Two data grids; one linked to CustSource and the other to OrdersSource

Figure 44.4   Form with linked queries

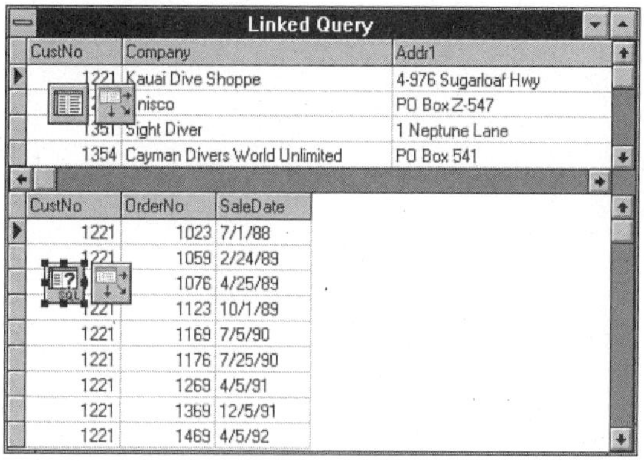

Orders' *DataSource* property is set to CustSource. Because the parameter :CustNo doesn't have any value assigned to it, at run time an attempt is made to match it with a column name in CustSource, which receives its data from the Customer table through Cust. Because there is a CustNo column in Cust, the current value of CustNo in the Cust table is assigned to the parameter, and the two data grids are linked in a master-detail relationship. Each time the Cust table moves to a different row, the Orders query automatically re-executes to retrieve all the orders for the current customer.

Creating heterogenous queries

Some applications may require queries of tables in more than one database. Such queries are called *heterogenous queries*, and are not supported by standard SQL. (SQL Links, available separately from Borland International, supports heterogenous queries.) A heterogenous query can join tables on different servers, and even different types of servers. For example, a heterogeneous query might involve a table in a Oracle database, a table in a Sybase database, and a local dBASE table.

Visual Database Tools supports heterogeneous queries, as long as the query syntax conforms to the requirements of local SQL, as described in Chapter 47.

To perform a heterogeneous query, you must define a BDE standard alias that refers to a local directory, and use the alias for the *DatabaseName* of the query component. You must also define BDE aliases for each of the databases being queried. In the query text, precede each table name with the alias for its database.

You can define BDE aliases with the BDE Configuration Utility, described in the online BDE Configuration Help. For example, suppose you define an alias called *Oracle1* for an Oracle database that has a CUSTOMER table, and *Sybase1* for a Sybase database that has an ORDERS table. A simple query against these two tables would be

```
SELECT CUSTOMER.CUSTNO, ORDERS.ORDERNO
FROM :Oracle1:CUSTOMER, :Sybase1:ORDERS
```

45

Building a client/server application

Visual Database Tools enables you to develop applications that can access remote SQL servers such as Oracle, Sybase, Informix, and InterBase servers, as well as local Paradox and dBASE databases. To use remote SQL servers, you also must have installed SQL Links (available separately from Borland International).

A *remote* server is one that is physically removed from the client machine on which the application runs. The server and client must be connected by a network.

A number of issues are particularly important when developing client/server applications:

Portability versus optimization: Will the application use any server-specific SQL syntax? To what degree will the database be optimized for a particular server?

Transactions: What kind of transaction control will the application require?

Server features: Will the application require the use of server features such as stored procedures? How will these be surfaced?

Connectivity: What communication protocol will the application use? Does the application need to be deployed to support multiple communication protocols?

Deployment: What executables, libraries, and other files does the application require and how are these delivered to the end user?

Portability versus optimization

In a client/server system, the database running on the server and the application running on the client define the overall system, referred to as the *database/application*. While these two elements are often designed separately and considered distinct, they must be integrated to build a successful client/server application. One of the important considerations is portability versus optimization.

Portability refers to the ease with which a database or an application can run on different servers. *Optimization* refers to the extent to which an application takes advantage of the special features of a particular system.

Client portability is not an issue, because Visual Database Tools applications will run on any 16-bit or 32-bit Windows platform. Server portability and communications portability can be considerations, however.

Because Visual Database Tools applications use the Borland Database Engine, they can be easily integrated with dBASE and Paradox applications (for desktop data sources) and other clients for server data sources.

Server portability

It may be desirable to design an application so that it can be easily ported to different types of servers, either because the end-users require multiple heterogeneous server support, or because the application will be used by different groups of end-users with different types of servers. In designing a client-server application, there is an inherent trade-off between portability and optimization, because making use of server-specific features results in increased application performance but decreased portability.

An application that uses only *TTable* components for data access will be fully portable among different server types. An application may benefit from improved performance by using *TQuery* components and passthrough SQL, and as long as the SQL syntax is ANSI standard, there will be little loss of portability.

As soon as SQL syntax departs from the ANSI standard, the application will no longer be fully portable. If server portability is a consideration, you must carefully weigh whether the gain in using server-specific syntax is worth the cost in portability. Maintainability of an application may be reduced by optimization for a specific server type, because each server-specific implementation may require separate maintenance.

An application can be further optimized by using server-specific features such as stored procedures. However, this usually requires server-specific implementation in the database, and perhaps the application, depending on how the features are surfaced.

It is also important to consider that servers' transaction processing can differ in subtle yet important ways. This and other distinctions among SQL servers may complicate portability. Before attempting to create a portable database/application, you should build an application that runs reliably against one type of server database. In some cases, it may be necessary to build the application separately against each of the target server types.

Client/server communication portability

Depending on the application requirements, it may be necessary to support multiple communication protocols, such as TCP/IP and Novell SPX. Providing for multiple communication protocols is simply a matter of ensuring that the client platforms have the proper communication software installed. This portability issue does not typically surface until the deployment phase, but it should be addressed in the implementation phase to ensure that the initial test deployment packages include the proper client communication software.

Connecting to a database server

Borland SQL Links for Windows enables a Visual Database Tools application to connect through the BDE to a remote database server. SQL Links drivers provide connections to Oracle, Sybase, Informix, Microsoft SQL Server, and InterBase databases.

Through the BDE Configuration Utility, you can set up an alias for each data source to which your application needs to connect. These aliases then become available to choose as the value of the *DatabaseName* property of *TTable* and *TQuery* components. For more information on the BDE Configuration Utility, see the online help for the BDE Configuration Utility.

Connectivity

Client applications can use any network protocol (such as TCP/IP or Novell SPX/IPX) supported by the server, as long as both the server and the client machines have the proper communication software installed. You must configure the SQL Link driver for the desired protocol. For more information, see the *SQL Links for Windows User's Guide*.

Establishing an initial connection between client and server can often be a problem, especially when using TCP/IP, because there are a number of critical factors that must all be in place before a connection can be established.

Using TCP/IP

TCP/IP is a widely used communication protocol that enables applications to connect to many different database servers. When using TCP/IP, you must ensure:

* The TCP/IP communication software and the proper WINSOCK driver are installed on the client.

* The server's IP address is registered in the client's HOSTS file or that Directory Network Services (DNS) is properly configured.

* The server's port number is entered in the client's SERVICES file.

* The application is searching the proper directory paths for the DLLs it needs. Check the PATH statement in AUTOEXEC.BAT.

For more information, see the *SQL Links for Windows User's Guide* and your server documentation.

Connection parameters

The *Params* property of a connected *TDatabase* object contains a *TStrings* list of all the SQL Link parameters required to connect to a server of the specified type. You can edit these parameters at design time by clicking the button with ellipsis (...) for the *Params* property in the Property Inspector. The Database Parameters editor opens with the parameters displayed. For example, here are the parameters for connection to an InterBase server:

Figure 45.1 InterBase parameters in the Database Parameters editor

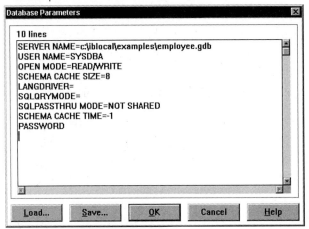

You can modify these parameters and add others as needed to customize the connection performed by the application. For more information, see the *SQL Links for Windows User's Guide*.

Using ODBC

A Visual Database Tools application can access ODBC data sources such as DB2, Btrieve, or Microsoft Access through the Borland Database Engine. To do this, you must set up an ODBC driver connection using the BDE Configuration Utility. An ODBC driver connection requires:

- A vendor-supplied ODBC driver
- The Microsoft ODBC Driver Manager
- A BDE alias, established with the BDE Configuration Utility

The BDE configuration setting AUTO ODBC (on the System page) enables an alias to automatically configure itself for use of ODBC. When AUTO ODBC is True, datasource and driver information are automatically imported from the ODBC.INI file.

For more information, see the online help for the BDE Configuration Utility.

Handling server security

Most database servers include security features to limit database access. Generally, the server requires a user name and password login before a user can access a database. If a server requires a login, then you are prompted at design time when you attempt to connect to a database on the server (for example, when you specify a *TableName* for a *TTable* component).

By default, a Visual Database Tools application opens the standard Login dialog box, whenever an application opens a connection to a database server. If a connection has already been established, the Login dialog box does not appear.

An application can handle server login several different ways:

- If the *LoginPrompt* property of a *TDatabase* component is true (the default), the standard Login dialog box opens when the application attempts to establish a database connection.

- By setting *LoginPrompt* to false, and including the USERNAME and PASSWORD parameters in the *Params* property of the *TDatabase* component. For example,

```
USERNAME = SYSDBA
PASSWORD = masterkey
```

This is generally not recommended as it compromises server security.

- Use the *OnLogin* event of *TDatabase* to set login parameters. The *OnLogin* event receives a copy of the *TDatabase*'s login parameters array. Use the *Values* property to change these parameters:

```
LoginParams.Values["SERVER NAME"] = "MYSERVERNAME";
LoginParams.Values["USER NAME"] = "MYUSERNAME";
LoginParams.Values["PASSWORD"] = "MYPASSWORD";
```

When control returns from your *DatabaseLogin* event handler, these parameters are used to establish a connection.

Using the TDatabase component

The *TDatabase* component is not required for database access, but it provides additional control over factors that are important for client/server applications, including the ability to:

- Create a persistent database connection
- Customize database server logins
- Create BDE aliases local to an application
- Control transactions and specify transaction isolation level

The *DataSets* property of *TDatabase* is an array of pointers to the active datasets in the *TDatabase*. The *DatasetsCount* property is an integer that specifies the number of active datasets.

Connecting to a database server

The *Connected* property indicates whether the *TDatabase* component has established a connection to a database. *Connected* is automatically set to true when an application opens a table in a database (logging in to a server, if required). Set *Connected* to true to establish a connection to a database without opening a table.

The *KeepConnection* property of a *TDatabase* component specifies whether an application remains connected to a database server even when no tables are open. If an application needs to open and close several tables in a single database, it is more efficient to set

KeepConnection to true. That way, the application remains connected to the database even when it does not have any tables open. It can then open and close tables repeatedly without incurring the overhead of connecting to the database each time.

The *TSession* component has an application-wide *KeepConnections* property. If *Session.KeepConnections* is false, a *TDatabase* component's *KeepConnection* property determines if database connections are maintained when no tables are open. If *Session.KeepConnections* is true (the default), database connections are always maintained. Specifically,

- Database connections are maintained until the application exits or until the Session's *DropConnections* method is called.

- Setting a *TDatabase* object's *Connected* property to false has no effect.

Creating application-specific aliases

The *TDatabase* component enables you to create BDE aliases specific to an application. To name the alias, enter a name in the *DatabaseName* property. Any dataset components can then use the local alias by using the specified *DatabaseName*.

To customize the parameters for a local alias, click the button with ellipses for the (Edit) property in the Property Inspector for the *TDatabase* component. The Database Properties editor opens:

Figure 45.2 Database Properties editor

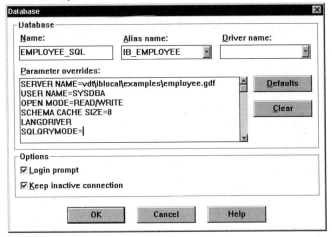

This tool enables you to customize application-specific aliases that are based locally on existing aliases.

The three text fields at the top of the dialog box correspond to the *DatabaseName*, *AliasName*, and *DriverName* properties.

- *DatabaseName* is the name of the database connection that can be used by dataset components instead of a BDE alias, directory path, or database name. In other words, this is the name of the local alias defined by the component that shows up in the *DatabaseName* list of dataset components.

- *AliasName* is the name of an existing BDE alias configured with the BDE Configuration Utility. The component obtains its default parameter settings from *AliasName*. This property clears if *DriverName* is set.

- *DriverName* is the name of a BDE driver, such as STANDARD (for dBASE and Paradox), ORACLE, SYBASE, INFORMIX or INTERBASE. This property clears if *AliasName* is set, because an *AliasName* specifies a driver type.

Choose the Defaults button to retrieve the default parameters for the selected alias. The values are in the Parameters list box. Any changes you make to the defaults are used instead of the default values for any database connection in the application that uses that *DatabaseName*.

The check boxes labeled "Login prompt" and "Keep inactive connection" correspond to the *LoginPrompt* and *KeepConnection* properties of the *TDatabase* component.

Understanding transaction control

SQL database servers handle requests in logical units of work called *transactions*. A transaction is a group of SQL statements that must all be performed successfully before the server finalizes (or *commit*) changes to the database. Either all the statements succeed, or all fail.

Transaction processing ensures database consistency even if there are hardware failures, and maintains the integrity of data while allowing concurrent multiuser access. For example, an application might update the ORDERS table to indicate that an order for a certain item was taken, and then update the INVENTORY table to reflect the reduction in inventory available. If there were a hardware failure after the first update but before the second, the database would be in an inconsistent state, because the inventory would not reflect the order entered. Under transaction control, both statements would be committed at the same time. Transaction control becomes even more important in a multiuser application.

In SQL, transactions end by a command to either accept or discard the actions performed. The COMMIT statement permanently commits the transaction, making changes visible to all users. The ROLLBACK statement reverses all changes made to the database in the transaction. Different database servers implement transaction processing differently. For the specifics of how your server handles transaction processing, refer to your server documentation.

Handling transactions in applications

Visual Database Tools applications can control transactions:

- **Implicitly:** Transactions are automatically started and committed as needed when an application calls the *Post* method (explicitly or implicitly in another method).

- **Explicitly:** Depending on the level of control the application requires, either with

  - The *StartTransaction*, *Commit*, and *Rollback* methods of *TDatabase*. This is the recommended approach.

- Passthrough SQL in a *TQuery* component. The application must use server-specific SQL transaction control statements. You must understand how your server performs transaction handling.

Transaction control statements are only meaningful when the database is on an SQL server. The *StartTrans*, *Commit*, and *Rollback* methods raise an exception if the underlying database is Paradox or dBASE.

Implicit transaction control

Visual Database Tools applications that use only the built-in methods can rely on implicit transaction control. Any operations on a server database that are not under explicit transaction control are under implicit control. Each individual write operation (*Post*, *AppendRecord*, and so on) is committed as a separate transaction, so database changes are committed on a row-by-row basis. This minimizes update conflicts, but can lead to heavy network traffic.

When using implicit transaction control, keep the SQLPASSTHRUMODE setting at SHARED AUTOCOMMIT, the default. For more information, see "Setting the SQL passthrough mode" on this page.

Implicit transaction control happens automatically, but doesn't provide much flexibility. If an application needs multi-row transactions or passthrough SQL, it should use explicit transaction control.

Explicit transaction control

The recommended approach for transaction control is to use the methods of *TDatabase*, because this results in clearer code and a more portable application. The methods for transaction control are

- *StartTransaction*: Begins a transaction at the isolation level specified by the *TransIsolation* property of *TDatabase*. If a transaction is currently active, an exception is raised.

- *Commit*: Commits the currently active transaction on the database. If no transaction is active, an exception is raised.

- *Rollback*: Rolls back the currently active transaction. All changes to the database since the last *Commit* are undone.

Some applications require additional server-specific transaction control features. In this case, use a *TQuery* component with passthrough SQL statements for transaction control. Ensure that SQLPASSTHRUMODE is set to NOT SHARED so that the passthrough SQL doesn't affect other transactions.

Setting the SQL passthrough mode

SQLPASSTHRUMODE in the BDE Configuration utility determines if passthrough SQL and standard BDE calls share the same database connection. For transactions, this translates to whether passthrough transactions and other transactions "know" about each other. Only applications that use passthrough SQL need be concerned with SQLPASSTHRUMODE.

SQLPASSTHRUMODE can have the following settings:

- SHARED AUTOCOMMIT (the default)
- SHARED NOAUTOCOMMIT
- NOT SHARED

With SHARED AUTOCOMMIT, each operation on a single row is committed. This mode most closely approximates desktop database behavior, but is inefficient on SQL servers because it starts and commits a new transaction for each row, resulting in a heavy load of network traffic.

With SHARED NOAUTOCOMMIT, the application must explicitly start and commit transactions. This setting can result in conflicts in busy, multiuser environments where many users are updating the same rows.

NOT SHARED means that passthrough SQL and the methods of the Visual Database Tools components use separate database connections.

Note   To control transactions with passthrough SQL, you must set SQLPASSTHRU MODE to NOT SHARED. Otherwise, passthrough SQL and the methods of the Visual Database Tools components might interfere with each other, leading to unpredictable results.

Transaction isolation levels

A transaction's *isolation level* determines how it interacts with other simultaneous transactions accessing the same tables. In particular, the isolation level affects what a transaction reads from the tables being accessed by other transactions.

Some servers enable you to set the transaction isolation level explicitly in passthrough SQL. If not specified, passthrough SQL operations will use a server's default isolation level. For more information, see your server documentation.

Transactions (both explicit and implicit) using the built-in methods of the components use the *TransIsolation* property of *TDatabase* to specify transaction isolation level. *TransIsolation* can have the following values:

- *tiDirtyRead*: The transaction can read uncommitted changes to the database by other transactions. This is the lowest isolation level.

- *tiReadCommitted*: The transaction can read only committed changes to the database by other transactions. This is the default isolation level.

- *tiRepeatableRead*: The transaction cannot read other transactions' changes to previously read data. This guarantees that once a transaction reads a record, it will not change if it reads it again. This the highest isolation level.

Database servers may support these isolation levels differently or not at all. If the requested isolation level is not supported by the server, then the next highest isolation level is used. The actual isolation level used by each type of server is shown in Table 45.1, "Server transaction isolation levels." For a detailed description of how each isolation level is implemented, see your server documentation.

Table 45.1   Server transaction isolation levels

TransIsolation setting	**Oracle**	**Sybase and Microsoft SQL servers**	**Informix**	**InterBase**
Dirty read	Read committed	Read committed	Dirty Read	Read committed
Read committed (Default)	Read committed	Read committed	Read committed	Read committed
Repeatable read	Repeatable read (READ ONLY)	Read committed	Repeatable Read	Repeatable Read

If an application is using ODBC to interface with a server, the ODBC driver must also support the isolation level. For more information, see your ODBC driver documentation.

Using stored procedures

A stored procedure is a server-based program that can take input parameters and return output parameters to an application. Stored procedures are associated with a database, and are actually part of metadata, like tables or domains. The *TStoredProc* component enables applications to execute server stored procedures.

The *DatabaseName* property of *TStoredProc* specifies the database in which the stored procedure is defined. This property is the same as for *TTable* and *TQuery*—it can be a BDE alias or an explicit directory path and database name. The *StoredProcName* specifies the name of the stored procedure. A drop-down list will display a list of all procedures defined in the specified database.

A *TStoredProc* can return either a singleton result or a result set with a cursor, if the server supports it.

Note   InterBase "select" procedures are called with the SELECT statement as if querying a table. To get output from such procedures, use a *TQuery* component with the appropriate SELECT syntax.

Input and output parameters

A stored procedure has a *Params* array for its input and output parameters similar to a *TQuery* component. The order of the parameters in the *Params* array is determined by the stored procedure definition. An application can set the values of input parameters and get the values of output parameters in the array similar to *TQuery* parameters. You can also use *ParamByName* to access the parameters by name. If you are not sure of the ordering of the input and output parameters for a stored procedure, use the Parameters editor.

To display the Parameters editor, click the button with the ellipses (...) for the *Params* property of the *TStoredProc* component in the Property Inspector. The following dialog box opens:

Figure 45.3 StoredProc Parameters editor

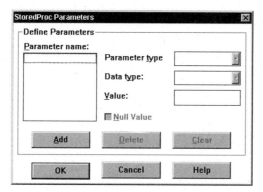

The Parameters editor displays the input and output parameters for the stored procedure. To prepare the procedure with the default parameter types and field types, simply choose OK. You can set values of input parameters at design time by choosing the parameter in the Parameters list and entering a value in the Value edit box. To specify NULL input parameter values, select the Null value check box. The Parameters editor is explained in more detail in Chapter 44, "Using SQL in applications."

Note   Visual Database Tools attempts to get information on input and output parameters from the server. For some servers (such as Sybase), this information might not be accessible. In such cases, you must enter the names and data types of the input and output parameters in the Parameters editor at design time.

Executing a stored procedure

Before an application can execute a stored procedure, you must prepare the stored procedure. You can do this

- At design time with the Parameters editor.
- At run time with the *Prepare* method of *TStoredProc*.

To prepare a stored procedure at run time, use the *Prepare* method before executing it. For example,

```
StoredProc1.Prepare();
```

To execute a prepared stored procedure, use the *ExecProc* method. Values can be assigned to and from a *TStoredProc* component just as for *TQuery* components, by using the *Params* array. For example,

```
char str[50];

Edit1.GetText( str, 50 );
StoredProc1.Params->Items[0]->AsString = str;
StoredProc1.ExecProc();
```

```
string s;
s = StoredProc1.Params->Items[1]->AsString;
Edit2.SetText( s.c_str() );
```

The first parameter, *Params*[0], is an input parameter. It is assigned the text entered by the user in *Edit1*. Then, assuming *StoredProc1* has been prepared at design time with the Parameters editor, calling the *ExecProc* method executes the procedure. Finally, the output parameter, *Params*[1], is displayed by *Edit2*.

On some servers, stored procedures can return a result set similar to a query. Applications can use data-aware controls to display the output of such stored procedures. You do this in the same way as you display output from *TQuery* components: use a *TDataSource* component and assign its name to a data grid's *DataSource* property.

Oracle overloaded stored procedures

Oracle servers allow overloading of stored procedures; that is, different procedures with the same name. The *Overload* property enables an application to specify the procedure to execute. If *Overload* is zero (the default), there is assumed to be no overloading. If *Overload* is one (1), then the first stored procedure with the overloaded name executes; if it is two (2), the second executes, and so on.

Upsizing

Migrating a desktop application to a client/server application is called *upsizing*. Upsizing is a complex topic and a full treatment of it is beyond the scope of this book. This section addresses some of the most important aspects of upsizing a Visual Database Tools application, however.

Upsizing has two major facets:

- Upsizing the database from the desktop to the server
- Upsizing the application to address client/server considerations

Upsizing requires a shift in perspective from the desktop world to the client/server world. Desktop databases and SQL server databases are different in many respects. Desktop databases are designed for one user at a time, while servers are designed for multiuser access. Desktop databases are conceptually record-oriented, while server databases are conceptually set-oriented. Desktop databases typically store each table in a separate file, while servers store all the tables in a database together.

Client/server applications must also address some entirely new issues, the most complex of which are connectivity, network usage, and transaction handling.

Upsizing the database

Upsizing a database includes the following steps:

- Defining metadata on the server, based on the existing desktop database structure.

- Migrating the data from the desktop to the server.

- Addressing issues such as:
  - Data type differences
  - Data Security and Integrity
  - Transaction control
  - Data Access Rights
  - Data Validation
  - Locking

There are two ways to upsize a database:

- Use the Database Desktop utility and choose Tools | Utilities | Copy to copy a table from desktop table to SQL format. For more information, see the online help for Database Desktop.

- Build an application that uses a *TBatchMove* component. For more information on *TBatchMove*, see Chapter 42.

Both of these options copy table structures and migrate data from the desktop source to the server destination. Depending on the database, it might be necessary to make changes to the tables created by these methods. For example, the datatype mappings might not be exactly as desired.

Additionally, you must add to the database any of the following features if required:

- Integrity constraints (primary and foreign keys)
- Indexes
- Check constraints
- Stored procedures and triggers
- Other server-specific features

Depending on the database, it might be most efficient to define the metadata first by using an SQL script and the server's data definition tools and then migrate the data using one of the two methods previously mentioned. If you define the table structure manually, then Database Desktop and *TBatchMove* copy only the data.

Upsizing the application

In principle, a Visual Database Tools application designed to access local data can access data on a remote server with few changes to the application itself. If a congruent data source has been defined on an SQL server, you can re-direct the application to access it rather than the local data source, simply by changing the *DatabaseName* property of *TTable* or *TQuery* components in the application.

In practice, however, there are a number of important differences between accessing local and remote data sources. Client/server applications must also address a number of issues that are not relevant to desktop applications.

Any Visual Database Tools application can use either *TTable* or *TQuery* for data access. Desktop applications generally use the *TTable* component. When upsizing to a SQL server, it might be more efficient to use *TQuery* objects instead in some instances. Depending on the specific application, *TQuery* might be preferable if the application will be retrieving a large number of records from database tables.

If the application uses mathematical or aggregate functions, it might be more efficient to perform these functions on the server with stored procedures. The use of stored procedures may be faster because servers are typically more powerful. This also reduces the amount of network traffic required, particularly for functions that process a large number of rows.

For example, an application might need to compute the standard deviation of values of a large number of records. If this function were performed on the client, all the values would have to be retrieved from the server to the client, resulting in a lot of network traffic. If the function were performed by a stored procedure, all the computation would be performed on the server, so the application would only retrieve the answer from the server.

Deploying support for remote server access

Deployment of a general database application is discussed in Chapter 1. In addition to the files required to deploy a desktop database application, deployment of a client/server application requires installation of the appropriate Borland SQL Links. These are not part of the Borland Database Engine, and must be installed separately. They are redistributable, according to the terms of the license agreement.

Each server type has a set of files for the SQL link. In addition, a file used by all the SQL Links is BLROM800.LD, the Roman8 language driver using binary collation sequence.

Oracle servers

This section provides information on connecting 16-bit applications to Oracle servers. For information on 32-bit applications, refer to the SQL Links online help.

The following files provide the SQL Links interface with Oracle servers. In addition, applications require Oracle client files for interface to low-level communication protocols such as TCP/IP. Refer to your server documentation.

Table 45.2 Oracle SQL Link files

File name	Description
SQLD_ORA.DLL	Borland SQL Link Oracle Driver
SQLD_ORA.HLP	Online help file
SQL_ORA.CNF	BDE Configuration File for Oracle Driver
ORA6WIN.DLL	Oracle Version 6.x client-side DLL
ORA7WIN.DLL	Oracle Version 7.x client-side DLL
SQL13WIN.DLL	Oracle client-side DLL
SQLWIN.DLL	Oracle client-side DLL
COREWIN.DLL	Oracle client-side DLL
ORAWE850.LD	Language driver based on DOS code page 850

Sybase and Microsoft SQL servers

This section provides information on connecting 16-bit applications to Sybase and Microsoft SQL servers. For information on 32-bit applications, refer to the SQL Links online help.

The following files provide the SQL Links interface with Sybase servers. In addition, applications require Sybase client files for interface to low-level communication protocols such as TCP/IP. Refer to your server documentation.

Table 45.3 Sybase SQL Link files

File name	Description
SQLD_SS.DLL	Borland SQL Link Sybase Driver
SQLD_SS.HLP	Borland SQL Link Sybase Driver Help
SQL_SS.CNF	BDE Configuration File for Sybase Driver
W3DBLIB.DLL	Sybase/Microsoft SQL Server client-side DLL
DBNMP3.DLL	Sybase/Microsoft SQL Server client-side DLL for Named Pipes
SYDC437.LD	Language driver based on DOS code page 850
SYDC850.LD	Language driver based on DOS code page 437

Informix servers

This section provides information on connecting 16-bit applications to Informix servers. For information on 32-bit applications, refer to the SQL Links online help.

The following files provide the SQL Links interface with Informix servers. In addition, applications require Informix client files for interface to low-level communication protocols such as TCP/IP. Refer to your server documentation.

Table 45.4 Informix SQL Link files

File name	Description
SQLD_INF.DLL	Borland SQL Link Informix Driver
SQLD_INF.HLP	Online help file
SQL_INF.CNF	BDE Configuration File for Informix Driver
LDLLSQLW.DLL	Informix client-side DLL
ISAM.IEM	Informix error message file
OS.IEM	Informix error message file
RDS.IEM	Informix error message file
SECURITY.IEM	Informix error message file
SQL.IEM	Informix error message file

16-bit InterBase clients

The following files provide the SQL Links interface to remote InterBase servers.

Table 45.5   16-bit InterBase SQL Link files

File name	Description
SQLD_IB.DLL	Borland SQL Link InterBase Driver
SQLD_IB.HLP	Borland SQL Link InterBase Driver Help
SQL_IB.CNF	BDE Configuration File for InterBase Driver
CONNECT.EXE or WSDIAG.EXE	InterBase connection diagnostic tool
CONNECT.HLP or COMDIAG.HLP	InterBase Windows connection diagnostic help file
GDS.DLL	InterBase API DLL
REMOTE.DLL	InterBase Networking interface DLL
INTERBAS.MSG	InterBase error message file

TCP/IP Interface

The following files provide InterBase client applications their interface to Winsock 1.1 compliant TCP/IP products.

Table 45.6   16-bit Winsock 1.1 client files

File name	Description
MVWASYNC.EXE	Asynchronous communication module
VSL.INI	TCP/IP transport initialization file
WINSOCK.DLL	Windows Socket DLL
MSOCKLIB.DLL	Maps Windows socket calls to VSL driver

For TCP/IP products that are not Winsock 1.1 compliant, InterBase client applications will require one of the following files. During installation, you are prompted to select the TCP/IP stack for which to install support. If the deployed application needs to support a different TCP/IP stack, you must copy the corresponding file from the installation disks.

Table 45.7   16-bit Non-Winsock compliant TCP support files

File name	TCP/IP Product
M3OPEN.EXE	3Com 3+Open TCP Microsoft LAN Manager Digital Pathworks for DOS
M3OPEN.DLL	3Com 3+Open TCP Version 2.0
MBW.EXE	Beame & Whiteside TCP/IP
MFTP.EXE	FTP PC/TCP
MHPARPA.DLL	HP ARPA Service for DOS
MNETONE.EXE	Ungermann-Bass Net/One
MNOVLWP.DLL	Novell LAN WorkPlace for DOS
MPATHWAY.DLL	Wollongong Pathway Access for DOS

Table 45.7 16-bit Non-Winsock compliant TCP support files (continued)

File name	TCP/IP Product
MPCNFS.EXE	Sun PC NFS
MPCNFS2.EXE	Sun PC NFS v3.5
MPCNFS4.DLL	Sun PC NFS v4.0
MWINTCP.EXE	Wollongong WIN TCP/IP for DOS

Other communication protocols

The InterBase workgroup server for NetWare supports Novell SPX/IPX protocol. Two client files are required: NWIPXSPX.DLL and NWCALLS.DLL.

The InterBase PC Client for Windows supports Microsoft Named Pipes protocol. No additional client files are required to support Named Pipes, but the client machine must have Microsoft LAN Manager, Windows for Workgroups 3.11, Windows NT, or Windows 95 installed.

32-bit InterBase clients

The following files provide the SQL Links interface to remote InterBase servers.

Table 45.8 32-bit InterBase SQL Link files

File name	Description
SQLINT32.DLL	Borland SQL Link InterBase Driver
SQL_INF.CNF	BDE Configuration File for InterBase Driver
WSDIAG.EXE	InterBase connection diagnostic tool
SQLLNK32.HLP	SQL Links online help file
COMDIAG.HLP	InterBase Windows connection diagnostic help file
GDS32.DLL	InterBase API DLL
INTERBAS.MSG	InterBase error message file
IB_LICEN.DAT	InterBase license file

TCP/IP Interface

TCP/IP connections for 32-bit InterBase client applications is provided by the standard WSOCK32.DLL installed with Windows NT or Windows 95.

Other communication protocols

The InterBase PC Client for Windows supports Microsoft Named Pipes protocol. No additional client files are required to support Named Pipes, but the client machine must have Microsoft LAN Manager, Windows for Workgroups 3.11, Windows NT, or Windows 95 installed.

46

Programming with third-party VBX controls

Visual Database Tools includes support for level 1, level 2, and level 3 VBX controls. If you have invested in third-party VBX controls, including those with multi-media and data-aware capabilities, you can include them in your C++ applications.

This chapter discusses how to use third-party VBX controls in your applications. These are the topics covered:

- Installing a VBX control in the Borland C++ IDE.
- The *TVbxControl* class
- Using the VbxGen utility
- Loading and initializing the VB emulator (BIVBX30.DLL)
- Using the BIVBX library functions

Installing a VBX control in the Borland C++ IDE

You can install a VBX control in the Dialog editor of the Borland C++ IDE and visually use the control to build a dialog box, form, or window that uses that control.

➤ To install a VBX control library,

1 In the Borland C++ IDE, choose Options | Environment | Control Libraries.

2 In the dialog box that appears, choose the Add button.

3 In the File Open dialog box that appears, navigate to your WINDOWS/SYSTEM directory and select the library you want to install, and choose OK.

The control(s) in your library are installed on the Custom page of the Controls palette of the Dialog editor.

Now you can select the control from the Custom page of the Controls palette and add it to the dialog, form, or window you are building. You can also use the Property Inspector to change the values of properties.

The TVbxControl class

The easiest way to program with VBX controls is to use ObjectWindows. It contains the *TVbxControl* class that is specifically designed to allow easy integration of VBX custom controls into Borland C++ applications.

Through *TVbxControl*, you can load a VBX control and read and set its properties. It also provides support for events and methods. In your application, each VBX control becomes a derived object from *TVbxControl*.

Using the VbxGen utility

The VbxGen utility provides an easy method of deriving a class from the Object Windows *TVbxControl* class, and defining member functions for getting and setting properties of the control. VbxGen also sets up stubs of response functions and places them in a response table.

The *TVbxControl* class is found in the VBXCTL.H file. Include this file with your application.

➤ To generate a VBX header file for your VBX control(s),

1 Start VBXGEN.EXE.

2 Select the name of the VBX library for your control(s).

3 Select the name of the header file to be generated and choose OK.

VbxGen generates the header file for you and displays a message box when it is finished.

The generated header file contains a section for each control in the VBX control library. Each section contains a set of symbolic property and event names, default property data, and a custom C++ class for use with Object Windows programs.

Include the generated header file in your application. Once the header file is included, create an instance of the class declared in the header file. You can then use the symbolic property and event names as you write the code for your application.

For more information about using the *TVbxControl* class, the symbolic property and event names, and default property data, look up VbxGen in the online Help.

Loading and initializing the Visual Basic emulator

Visual Database Tools includes a Visual Basic emulator in the BIVBX30.DLL. It enables you to use VBX controls that are compatible with versions 1.0, 2.0, and 3.0 of Visual Basic.

➤ To make the library available to your application,

1 Include VBXCTL.H in your application.

2 Instantiate an instance of the *TBIVbxLibrary* module in the *OwlMain* function before you call the *Run* function. Here is an example:

```
#include <OWL/VBXCTL.H>
int
OwlMain( int, char** )
{
  TBIVbxLibrary vbxLib;
  return TTestApp().Run();
}
```

Now Borland's Visual Basic emulator is loaded and initialized, ready to support your VBX controls.

Using the BIVBX library functions

There are a number of BIVBX library functions defined in the header file, BIVBX.H, located in your include directory. The functions initialize VBX support, return a VBX control handle, initialize a dialog window, handle events, and so on.

You can find complete information about using the BIVBX library functions in the online Help.

You can also find more information about programming with VBX controls in the online Help.

47

Using local SQL

The BDE enables limited access to database tables through local SQL (also called "client-based SQL"). Local SQL is a subset of ANSI-standard SQL enhanced to support Paradox and dBASE naming conventions for tables and fields (called "columns" in SQL). Two categories of SQL statements are supported:

- Data Manipulation Language (DML) for selecting, inserting, updating, and deleting table data.

- Data Definition Language (DDL) for creating, altering, and dropping tables, and for creating and dropping indexes.

This chapter describes naming conventions, syntax enhancements, and syntax limitations for local SQL. For a complete introduction to ANSI-standard SQL, see one of the many third-party books available at your local computer book store.

Naming conventions for tables

ANSI-standard SQL confines each table name to a single word comprised of alphanumeric characters and the underscore symbol (_). Local SQL is enhanced to support full file and path specifications for table names. Table names with path or file-name extensions must be enclosed in single or double quotes. For example,

```
SELECT * FROM 'PARTS.DBF'
SELECT * FROM "C:\SAMPLE\PARTS.DBF"
```

Local SQL also supports BDE aliases for table names. For example,

```
SELECT * FROM :PDOX:TABLE1
```

Finally, local SQL permits table names to duplicate SQL keywords as long as those table names are enclosed in single or double quotes. For example,

```
SELECT PASSID FROM "PASSWORD"
```

Naming conventions for columns

ANSI-standard SQL confines each column name to a single word of alphanumeric characters and the underscore symbol (_). Local SQL is enhanced to support Paradox and dBASE multi-word column names and column names that duplicate SQL keywords as long as those column name are

- Enclosed in single or double quotes.
- Prefaced with an SQL table name or table correlation name.

For example, the following column name is two words:

```
SELECT E."Emp Id" FROM EMPLOYEE E
```

In the next example, the column name duplicates the SQL **DATE** keyword:

```
SELECT DATELOG."DATE" FROM DATELOG
```

Data manipulation

With some restrictions, local SQL supports the following statements for data manipulation:

- SELECT, for retrieving existing data
- INSERT, for adding new data to a table
- UPDATE, for modifying existing data
- DELETE, for removing existing data from a table

The following sections describe parameter substitution, aggregate, string, and date functions, and operators available to DML statements in local SQL.

Parameter substitutions in DML statements

Variables or parameter markers (?) can be used in DML statements in place of values. Variables must always be preceded by a colon (:). For example,

```
SELECT LAST_NAME, FIRST_NAME
FROM "CUSTOMER.DB"
WHERE LAST_NAME > :var1 AND FIRST_NAME < :var2
```

Supported set (aggregate) functions

The following ANSI-standard SQL set (or "aggregate") functions are available to local SQL for use with data retrieval:

- *SUM()*, for totaling all numeric values in a column

- *AVG()*, for averaging all non-NULL numeric values in a column

- *MIN()*, for determining the minimum value in a column

- *MAX()*, for determining the maximum value in a column

- *COUNT()*, for counting the number of values in a column that match specified criteria

Note Expressions are not allowed in set functions.

Supported string functions

Local SQL supports the following ANSI-standard SQL string manipulation functions for retrieval, insertion, and updating:

- *UPPER()*, to force a string to uppercase

- *LOWER()*, to force a string to lowercase

- *SUBSTRING()*, to return a specified portion of a string

- *TRIM()*, to remove repetitions of a specified character from the left, right, or both sides of a string

Supported date function

Local SQL supports the *EXTRACT()* function for isolating a single numeric field from a date/time field on retrieval using the following syntax:

```
EXTRACT (extract_field FROM field_name)
```

For example, the following statement extracts the year value from a DATE field:

```
SELECT EXTRACT(YEAR FROM HIRE_DATE)
FROM EMPLOYEE
```

You can also extract MONTH, DAY, HOUR, MINUTE, and SECOND using this function.

Note *EXTRACT* does not support the TIMEZONE_HOUR or TIMEZONE_MINUTE clauses.

Supported operators

Local SQL supports the following arithmetic operators:

```
+, -, *, /
```

Local SQL supports the following comparison operators:

```
<, >, =, <>, IS NULL
```

Local SQL supports the following logical operators:

```
AND, OR, NOT
```

Local SQL supports the following string concatenation operator:

```
||
```

Using SELECT

The SELECT statement is used to retrieve data from one or more tables. A SELECT that retrieves data from multiple tables is called a "join." Local SQL supports the following form of the SELECT statement:

```
SELECT [DISTINCT] column_list
FROM table_reference
[WHERE search_condition]
[ORDER BY order_list]
[GROUP BY group_list]
[HAVING having_condition]
```

Except as noted below, all clauses are handled as in ANSI-standard SQL. Clauses in square brackets are optional.

The *column_list* indicates the columns from which to retrieve data. For example, the following statement retrieves data from two columns:

```
SELECT PART_NO, PART_NAME
FROM PARTS
```

Using the FROM clause

The FROM clause specifies the table or tables from which to retrieve data. *table_reference* can be a single table, a comma-delimited list of tables, or can be an inner or outer join as specified in the SQL-92 standard. For example, the following statement specifies a single table:

```
SELECT PART_NO
FROM "PARTS.DBF"
```

The next statement specifies a left outer join for *table_reference*:

```
SELECT * FROM PARTS LEFT OUTER JOIN INVENTORY
ON PARTS.PART_NO = INVENTORY.PART_NO
```

Using the WHERE clause

The optional WHERE clause reduces the number of rows returned by a query to those that match the criteria specified in *search_condition*. For example, the following statement retrieves only those rows with PART_NO greater than 543:

```
SELECT * FROM PARTS
WHERE PART_NO > 543
```

The WHERE clause can include the IN predicate, followed by a parenthesized list of values. For example, the next statement retrieves only those rows where a part number matches an item in the IN predicate list:

```
SELECT * FROM PARTS
WHERE PART_NO IN (543, 544, 546, 547)
```

Important   A *search_condition* cannot include subqueries.

Using the ORDER BY clause

The ORDER BY clause specifies the order of retrieved rows. For example, the following query retrieves a list of all parts listed in alphabetical order by part name:

```
SELECT * FROM PARTS
ORDER BY PART_NAME ASC
```

The next query retrieves all part information ordered in descending numeric order by part number:

```
SELECT * FROM PARTS
ORDER BY PART_NO DESC
```

Calculated fields can be ordered by correlation name or ordinal position. For example, the following query orders rows by FULL_NAME, a calculated field:

```
SELECT LAST_NAME || ', ' || FIRST_NAME AS FULL_NAME, PHONE
FROM CUSTOMERS
ORDER BY FULL_NAME
```

Using the GROUP BY clause

The GROUP BY clause specifies how retrieved rows are grouped for aggregate functions. In local SQL, any column names that appear in the GROUP BY clause must also appear in the SELECT clause.

Heterogeneous joins

Local SQL supports joins of tables in different database formats; such a join is called a "heterogeneous join." For example, it is possible to retrieve data from a Paradox table and a dBASE table as follows:

```
SELECT DISTINCT C.CUST_NO, C.STATE, O.ORDER_NO
FROM "CUSTOMER.DB" C, "ORDER.DBF" O
WHERE C.CUST_NO = O.CUST_NO
```

You can also use BDE aliases in place of table names.

Using INSERT

In local SQL, INSERT is restricted to a list of values:

```
INSERT INTO CUSTOMER (FIRST_NAME, LAST_NAME, PHONE)
VALUES(:fname, :lname, :phone_no)
```

Insertion from one table to another through a subquery is not allowed.

Using UPDATE

There are no restrictions on or extensions to the ANSI-standard UPDATE statement.

Using DELETE

There are no restrictions on or extensions to the ANSI-standard DELETE statement.

Data definition

Local SQL supports data definition language (DDL) for creating, altering, and dropping tables, and for creating and dropping indexes. All other ANSI-standard SQL DDL statements are not supported. In particular, views are not supported.

Local SQL does not permit the substitution of variables for values in DDL statements.

Using CREATE TABLE

CREATE TABLE is supported with the following limitations:

- Column definitions based on domains are not supported.

- Constraints are limited to PRIMARY KEY for Paradox. Constraints are unsupported in dBASE.

For example, the following statement creates a Paradox table with a PRIMARY KEY constraint on the LAST_NAME and FIRST_NAME columns:

```
CREATE TABLE "employee.db"
(
LAST_NAME CHAR(20),
FIRST_NAME CHAR(15),
SALARY NUMERIC(10,2)
DEPT_NO SMALLINT,
PRIMARY KEY(LAST_NAME, FIRST_NAME)
)
```

The same statement for a dBASE table should omit the PRIMARY KEY definition:

```
CREATE TABLE "employee.db"
(
LAST_NAME CHAR(20),
FIRST_NAME CHAR(15),
SALARY NUMERIC(10,2)
DEPT_NO SMALLINT
)
```

The following table lists SQL syntax for data types used with CREATE TABLE, and describes how those types are mapped to Paradox and dBASE types by the BDE:

Table 47.1 Data type mappings

SQL syntax	BDE logical	Paradox	dBASE
SMALLINT	fldINT16	fldPDXSHORT	fldDBNUM
INTEGER	fldINT32	fldPDXLONG	fldDBNUM
DECIMAL(x,y)	fldBCD	fldPDXBCD	N/A
NUMERIC(x,y)	fldFLOAT	fldPDXNUM	fldDBNUM(x,y)
FLOAT(x,y)	fldFLOAT	fldPDXNUM	fldDBFLOAT(x,y)
CHARACTER(n)	fldZSTRING	fldPDXALPHA	fldDBCHAR
x = precision (default: specific to driver); y = scale (default: 0); n = length in bytes (default: 0); s = BLOB subtype (default: 1)			

Table 47.1   Data type mappings (continued)

SQL syntax	BDE logical	Paradox	dBASE
VARCHAR(n)	fldZSTRING	fldPDXALPHA	fldDBCHAR
DATE	fldDATE	fldPDXDATE	fldDBDATE
BOOLEAN	fldBOOL	fldPDXBOOL	fldDBBOOL
BLOB(n,s)	See Subtypes below	See Subtypes below	See subtypes below
TIME	fldTIME	fldPDXTIME	N/A
TIMESTAMP	fldTIMESTAMP	fldPDXTIMESTAMP	N/A
MONEY	fldFLOAT, fldstMONEY	fldPDXMONEY	fldDBFLOAT(20,4)
AUTOINC	fldINT32, fldstAUTOINC	fldPDXAUTOINC	N/A
BYTES(n)	fldBYTES(n)	fldPDXBYTES	fldDBBYTES (in-memory tables only)

x = precision (default: specific to driver); y = scale (default: 0); n = length in bytes (default: 0); s = BLOB subtype (default: 1)

The following table specifies how BLOB subtypes translate from SQL to Paradox and dBASE through the BDE:

Table 47.2   BLOB subtype mappings

SQL subtype	BDE logical	Paradox	dBASE
1	fldstMEMO	fldPDXMEMO	fldDBMEMO
2	fldstBINARY	fldPDXBINARY	fldDBBINARY
3	fldstFMTMEMO	fldPDXFMTMEMO	N/A
4	fldstOLEOBJ	fldPDXOLEBLOB	fldDBOLEBLOB
5	fldstGRAPHIC	fldPDXGRAPHIC	N/A

Using ALTER TABLE

Local SQL supports the following subset of the ANSI-standard ALTER TABLE statement. You can add new columns to an existing table using this ALTER TABLE syntax:

```
ALTER TABLE table ADD column_name data_type [, ADD column_name data_type . . .]
```

For example, the following statement adds a column to a dBASE table:

```
ALTER TABLE "employee.dbf" ADD BUILDING_NO SMALLINT
```

You can delete existing columns from a table using the following ALTER TABLE syntax:

```
ALTER TABLE table DROP column_name [, DROP column_name . . .]
```

For example, the next statement drops two columns from a Paradox table:

```
ALTER TABLE "employee.db" DROP LAST_NAME, DROP FIRST_NAME
```

ADD and DROP operations can be combined in a single statement. For example, the following statement drops two columns and adds one:

```
ALTER TABLE "employee.dbf" DROP LAST_NAME, DROP FIRST_NAME, ADD FULL_NAME CHAR[30]
```

Using DROP TABLE

DROP TABLE deletes a Paradox or dBASE table. For example, the following statement drops a Paradox table:

```
DROP TABLE "employee.db"
```

Using CREATE INDEX

CREATE INDEX enables users to create indexes on tables using the following syntax:

```
CREATE INDEX index_name ON table_name (column [, column . . .])
```

Using CREATE INDEX is the only way to create indexes for dBASE tables. For example, the following statement creates an index on a dBASE table:

```
CREATE INDEX NAMEX ON "employee.dbf" (LAST_NAME)
```

Paradox users can only create secondary indexes with CREATE INDEX. Primary Paradox indexes can only be created by specifying a PRIMARY KEY constraint when creating a new table with CREATE TABLE.

Using DROP INDEX

Local SQL provides the following variation of the ANSI-standard DROP INDEX statement for deleting an index. It is modified to support dBASE and Paradox file names.

```
DROP INDEX table_name.index_name | PRIMARY
```

The PRIMARY keyword is used to delete a primary Paradox index. For example, the following statement drops the primary index on EMPLOYEE.DB:

```
DROP INDEX "employee.db".PRIMARY
```

To drop any dBASE index, or to drop secondary Paradox indexes, provide the index name. For example, the next statement drops a secondary index on a Paradox table:

```
DROP INDEX "employee.db".NAMEX
```

Borland Windows Custom Controls guide

This part discusses Borland Windows custom controls and is divided into the following chapters:

- **Chapter 48, "Using Borland Windows Custom Controls,"** explains how to use the custom dialog class and how to use the custom control drawing routines directly to optimize the drawing of dialog boxes.

- **Chapter 49, "Designing Borland Windows Custom Control dialog boxes,"** presents style considerations you can follow when designing Borland Windows Custom Control (BWCC) dialog boxes for your Windows-based software.

Chapter

48

Using Borland Windows
Custom Controls

The custom dialog class, BORDLG, works on both a visual and functional level:

- It changes the appearance of your dialog window by painting the background with a brush that varies according to the target display device. For screens of VGA and higher resolution, the background is a fine grid of perpendicular white lines, giving the effect of "chiseled steel." For EGA and monochrome screens, the background is white.

- It optimizes the drawing of dialog boxes by calling the custom control drawing routines directly instead of waiting for Windows to paint the controls. This eliminates the typical sluggish drawing of dialog boxes.

Using the Borland custom dialog class

To use the Borland custom dialog class:

1 Open the dialog resource you want to convert.

2 Double-click in an empty area of the dialog box to display the Dialog Property Inspector.

3 Select the Window Tab.

4 Enter `bordlg` as the Class and click OK.

Customizing existing applications for Borland Windows custom controls

Note   This procedure applies to 16-bit Windows applications only.

Resource Workshop allows you to customize existing Windows applications with Borland-style custom controls. There are two steps to this process:

1 Modify your WIN.INI file to load the Borland Windows Custom Control (BWCC) library each time you start Windows.

2 Edit the application in Resource Workshop to change user interface features such as dialog boxes, menus, icons, and so on.

Loading BWCC to enable Borland custom controls

The BWCC library, which provides support for Borland-style custom controls, must be loaded before an application can use BWCC's features.

Edit the WIN.INI file (located in the Windows main directory) so that Windows loads the file LOADBWCC.EXE into memory at start up. (The installation program should have put LOADBWCC.EXE in the language compiler directory and added this directory to your PATH.)

Add LOADBWCC.EXE to the beginning of the list of files that appear after the "LOAD=" statement. LOADBWCC.EXE must appear first in the statement to ensure that BWCC is loaded into memory before any modified applications are executed.

Borland custom controls

These Borland custom control styles available are:

Control Name	Control Description
3-State Checkbox	A Borland-style check box that has three states - on, off, and "indeterminate," which is displayed as a checkerboard pattern. The application determines what is meant by "indeterminate." The application must call the **CheckDlgButton** function to send a BM_SETCHECK message to check the selected box.
Auto 3-State Checkbox	A check box that's identical to a Borland-style 3-state check box, except that BWCC and Windows combine to handle checking the selection box.
Auto Checkbox	A check box that's identical to a Borland-style check box, except that BWCC and Windows combine to handle checking the selection box.
Auto Radiobutton	A radio button that's identical to a Borland-style radio button, except that BWCC and Windows combine to handle highlighting the selected button and deselect the other buttons.
Bitmap	A bitmap.
Checkbox	A Borland-style check box. The application must call the **CheckDlgButton** function to send a BM_SETCHECK message to check the selected box.
Default Pushbutton	A push button that's identical to a Borland-style push button, but includes a bold border indicating that it's the default response if the user presses Enter.

Horizontal Bump	A convex horizontal line.
Horizontal Dip	A concave horizontal line.
Pushbutton	A Borland-style push button. When the user clicks the button, a BN_CLICKED message is sent to the parent window.
Radiobutton	A Borland-style radio button. The application must call the **CheckRadioButton** function to send a BM_SETCHECK message to highlight the selected button and deselect other buttons
Raised Gray Group	A gray box that appears raised above the surface of the dialog box.
Recessed Gray Group	A gray box that appears recessed below the surface of the dialog box.
Static Text	A fixed text string used for labeling parts of the dialog box.
Vertical Bump	A convex vertical line.
Vertical Dip	A concave vertical line.

Borland button and check box enhancements

Borland push buttons, radio buttons, and check boxes have the following functional enhancements over standard Windows controls:

- An additional level of parent window notification and control over keyboard focus and tab movement. If you choose the Parent Notify option in the control's style dialog box, the control sends the appropriate message at run time:

  - BBN_SETFOCUS indicates to the parent window that the push button, radio button, or check box has gained keyboard focus through an action other than a mouse click.

  - BBN_SETFOCUSMOUSE indicates to the parent window that the push button, radio button, or check box has gained keyboard focus through a mouse click.

  - BBN_GOTATAB indicates to the parent window that the user has pressed the Tab key while the push button, radio button, or check box has keyboard focus. The parent can intervene in the processing of the keystroke by returning a nonzero value.

  - BBN_GOTABTAB indicates to the parent window that the user has pressed Shift-Tab (back-tab) while the push button, radio button, or check box has keyboard focus. The parent can intervene in the processing of the keystroke by returning a nonzero value.

- An owner-draw option that allows the parent window to draw the push button, radio button, or check box. Because your application handles drawing the control, it won't necessarily look like a Borland control, but it will have the standard behavior of that class of control.

49

Designing Borland Windows Custom Control dialog boxes

These topics present style considerations you can follow when designing Borland Windows Custom Control (BWCC) dialog boxes for your Windows-based software.

- Panels
- Fonts
- Group Boxes
- Push Buttons
- Examining Your Dialog Box

Panels

Each dialog box has two panels: a Main panel and an Action panel. The Main panel should contain all the required controls. The Action panel should contain the push buttons.

Your finished dialog box should be relatively square. If the Main panel is wider than it is tall, put the Action panel along the bottom of your dialog box. If the Main panel is taller than it is wide, put the Action panel on the right side.

Main panel

You can arrange the group boxes on the Main panel in either a single column or row, or in an array. Here are some guidelines for arranging group boxes on the Main panel. You should treat group titles as part of the group boxes.

- Space group boxes 8 dialog units apart, both vertically and horizontally.

- Leave a margin of 8 dialog units from all edges of the dialog to the nearest group box.

- In a column of group boxes, make all group boxes the same width. The width should accommodate the widest item or title. Widen the other group boxes to match.

- In a row of group boxes, vary the group box heights. Align the tops of the group boxes and let the bottoms of the group boxes vary.

- If some of the group boxes in a row have titles and some do not, align the top of the recessed group boxes with each other, not with the title rectangles. For these "mixed" groups of boxes, the margin above group boxes without titles should include the space for a title.

- If some of the group boxes you want to align in a row are taller than others, compute the bottom margin using the tallest group box.

Action panel

An Action panel can appear at the bottom or the right side of a dialog box. Here are the guidelines for Action panels:

- Make the Action panel tall or wide enough to contain the push buttons while leaving a margin of 8 dialog units above and below or to the sides of the push buttons.

- Distribute the push buttons evenly along the Action panel, leaving a minimum of 8 dialog units between the buttons and between the buttons and the edges of the dialog box. Try to use the same number of dialog units between each button and between the buttons and the edges of the dialog box. You can put more space between the buttons than between the buttons and the edges of the dialog box, if necessary, but the two margin spaces should be equal and the spaces between the buttons should be equal.

Fonts

Borland dialog boxes use 8-point Helvetica Bold. The Borland Windows custom dialog controls look best when you use this font. An 8-point font is small; using it prevents your dialog boxes from growing too big. Of course, you can use other fonts for other custom controls.

Group boxes

Collect all options that appear in the Main panel into Borland Windows custom group boxes. For example, place a group of related check boxes in a group box. You should place each single control, such as a file name text box or combo box, in a group box also. You will not have to do this with a Borland list box because a list box draws its own group box.

Group box title

A group box title identifies what a group box contains. By default, a group box title in a Borland dialog box has a gray background. Here are guidelines for using group box titles:

- If a group box contains multiple controls, place the group box title above and touching the top edge of the group box.
- If a group box contains a single check box, place the group box title above and touching the top edge of the group box.
- If a group box contains a single text box or combo box control, you can either put the title to the left of the control and 4 dialog units from the edge of the group box or you can put it above the control.
- If a group box contains two or more editable text fields or combo boxes or both, precede each with a short label.
- Align group box titles above the recessed group boxes.
- Make all group box titles 9 dialog units high.
- Make the titles the same width as the group boxes, including the beveled sides.

Group box elements

These suggestions help you arrange elements within a group box:

- Distribute controls within a group box vertically every 13 units from the bottom of one line of text to the bottom of the next.
- Left-justify the controls.
- The left and right margins between the edges of the group box and the widest control within it should be 4 dialog units wide.
- Make the margin between the top of the group box and the first control in the group 4 dialog units.
- Make the margin between the bottom of the group box and the last control in the group 4 dialog units.
- If a group box contains two or more editable text fields or combo boxes or both, make them the same width. Space them so that the bottom of one is 13 units from the bottom of the next one. Right-justify these controls in the group box 4 units from the right edge. Left-justify the titles, leaving a 4-unit margin. Make the group box wide enough to leave 4 units between the longest title and its control.

Push buttons

The following are style considerations for push buttons:

- The Borland custom push buttons use glyphs (small bitmapped images). For example, a question-mark glyph is used on the Help push button. Place the glyph inside the button on the left side.

- Use Helvetica (normal, not bold) for the text of a button text and right-justify it.

Action panel push buttons

The Action panel push buttons usually indicate the end of the user's work with a dialog box, but can also serve as a major departure from the function of the dialog box, such as bringing up Help with the Help button. The guidelines for these buttons are:

- Put the buttons on the Main panel rather than the Action panel.

- Do not put these push buttons in a group box. Place them directly on the surface of the Main panel.

- Make all push buttons in a group the same width. They should be just wide enough to accommodate the widest text string.

- Make the buttons 14 dialog units in height.

- Try to restrict text to 20 characters or less.

- Place the buttons in either a row or a column, depending on what looks best in your dialog box.

- Leave 8 dialog units to the left and right of a column of push buttons. The vertical space between the buttons and any other controls or borders above or below the buttons should be equal.

- Leave 8 dialog units above and below a row of push buttons. The horizontal space between the buttons and any other controls or borders to the left or right of them should be equal.

Examining your dialog box

When Windows calculates dialog units, it rounds the computation. Rounding errors can affect the appearance of your dialog box. Examine your dialog box carefully and look for these problems:

- A crack between the title text and the top of a gray group box

- Obvious uneven spacing in a vertical group of radio buttons or check boxes

- An inconsistent border width in exposed panel areas

Usually, making an adjustment of 1 dialog unit will fix these problems. Occasionally in a large group of repeating controls, two or more rounding errors can occur. You cannot tell how text in controls will appear when you are designing your dialog box. Editable text, large static text fields, and combo boxes fall into this category. You may have to modify your original design to be sure text appears correctly without being clipped at run time.

What is OLE?

OLE, which stands for Object Linking and Embedding, is an operating system extension that lets applications achieve a high degree of integration. OLE defines a set of standard interfaces so that any OLE program can interact with any other OLE program. No program needs to have any built-in knowledge of its possible partners.

Programmers implement OLE applications by creating objects that conform to the Component Object Model (COM). COM is the specification that defines what an OLE object is. COM objects support interfaces, composed of functions for other objects to call. OLE defines a number of standard interfaces. COM objects intended for public access expose their interfaces in a registration database. Interfaces have unique identifiers to distiguish them.

ObjectComponents encapsulates the COM specification for creating objects and provides default implementations of the interfaces used for two common OLE tasks: linking and embedding, and automation. *Linking* and *embedding* lets one application incorporate live data from other OLE applications in its documents. Automation lets one application issue commands to control another application.

Common uses for OLE

The following topics discuss common uses for OLE.

Linking and embedding

Linking and *embedding* refer to the transfer of data from one program to another. The first program, the server, sends its data to the second program, the *container*. For example, cells from a spreadsheet can be dropped into a word processing document. Of course you don't need OLE to pass data from one Windows program to another. You can do that much with just the Clipboard. The difference between OLE and the Clipboard is that in OLE the receiving program doesn't have to know anything at all about the format of the data in the object. Any OLE server application can give its data to any OLE container application. Thanks to OLE, the container doesn't care whether the object it receives is a metafile, a bitmap, or ASCII text. The server passes whatever data it uses internally and the container accepts it. Furthermore, the object remains dynamic even after being transplanted. When the container wants to display, modify, or save the object, it calls OLE to do it. OLE, working behind the scenes, calls the server to execute the user's command. The object belongs to the container's document, but OLE maintains a live connection back to the server. The user can continue to edit the object using all of the server's tools. As a result, the user can combine objects from different servers into a single document without losing the ability to update and modify any object as the document evolves.

Automation

Automation happens when one program issues commands to another. If you write a calculator program, for example, you might allow other programs to issue commands like these:

- Press the nine button.

- Press the plus button.

- Press the six button.

- Press the equals button.

- Tell me what's in the Total window.

These are commands a person might normally issue through the calculator's user interface. With automation, the calculator exposes its internal functions to other programs. The calculator becomes an *automation object*, and programs that send commands to it are automation controllers. OLE defines standard interfaces that let a controller ask any installed server to create one of its objects. OLE also makes it possible for the controller to browse through a list of automated commands the server supports and execute them.

What does OLE look like?

The linking and embedding features of OLE include a standard user interface for performing common operations such as placing OLE objects in container documents and activating them once they are linked or embedded. The OLE standards cover menu commands, dialog boxes, tool bars, drag and drop support, and painting conventions, so that the user interface for OLE operations is consistent across applications. Together, ObjectComponents and ObjectWindows execute most of the interface tasks for you.

Understanding OLE programming can be difficult without a clear grasp of the interface you are trying to create. The following sections present pictures of a container showing what happens onscreen at each step in a common sequence of OLE operations. The user runs a container, inserts objects from several OLE servers into the document, edits an object, and saves the document.

Inserting an object

The example program called SdiOle is an OLE container using the single-document interface (SDI) and written with ObjectWindows and ObjectComponents. The source code for SdiOle is in EXAMPLES/OWL/OCF/SDIOLE.

The SdiOle Edit menu contains five standard OLE commands that most containers possess: Paste Special, Paste Link, Insert Object, Links, and Object.

ObjectWindows implements all five of the standard commands for you if you like, but a container does not have to use them all.

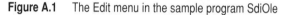

Figure A.1 The Edit menu in the sample program SdiOle

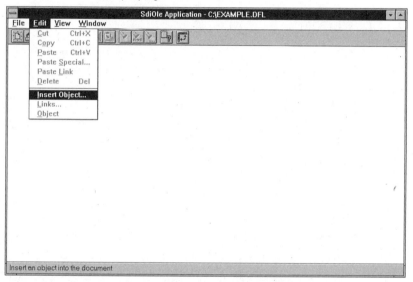

Like the common dialog boxes in Windows for opening files and choosing fonts, the Insert Object dialog box is a standard resource implemented by the system. For consistency, it is best to use the standard dialog boxes unless your application has some unusual requirement that the standard dialog box does not meet.

The box under Object Type lists all the kinds of objects available in the system. Whenever a server installs itself, it tells the system what objects it can create. The system keeps this information in its registration database. The Insert Object dialog box queries the database and shows all the types that OLE can create for you using the available server applications.

In the illustration, the user has chosen to insert a Quattro Pro spreadsheet. The Result box at the bottom of the dialog box explains what will happen if the user clicks OK now. Because the Create New button is selected, clicking OK will embed a new, empty spreadsheet object into the user's open document.

Figure A.2   The Insert Object dialog box

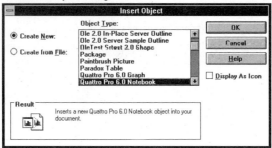

Editing an object in place

The example program called SdiOle is an OLE container using the single-document interface (SDI) and written with ObjectWindows and ObjectComponents. The source code for SdiOle is in EXAMPLES/OWL/OCF/SDIOLE.

The SdiOle Edit menu contains five standard OLE commands that most containers possess: Paste Special, Paste Link, Insert Object, Links, and Object.

If Quattro Pro is the server application that creates the active object, Quattro Pro will take over the SdiOle window and display its own menus and tool bars. All the Quattro Pro menu and tool bar commands can be executed right there in SdiOle. The feature of OLE that lets a server take over a container's main window is called *in-place editing*. It lets the user edit the object in its place, without switching back and forth between different windows. The programming task that makes this possible is called *menu merging*, combining menus from two programs in one menu bar.

Figure A.3   A newly inserted object being edited in place

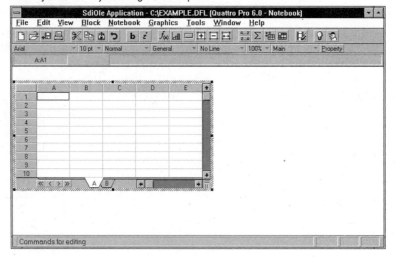

Although many programs let you paste data from other programs into your documents, without OLE you cannot continue to edit the objects after they are transferred.

SdiOle is a very simple application and knows nothing about columns and rows or fonts and shading. But, even though the Quattro Pro server created and formatted the object, that data in the object belongs to the container. When the user chooses File | Save from the SdiOle menu bar, what gets written is an SdiOle document, not a Quattro Pro document. With the help of ObjectComponents and the OLE system, SdiOle marks an area in its own file to store the data for the embedded object. When the user chooses File | Load to reload the same document, the spreadsheet cells will still be there. If the user tries to edit the object again, OLE invokes Quattro Pro to take over the SdiOle window once more. The object remains associated with the application that created it even though the object is stored in a foreign file.

When OLE places the data for an object directly into the container's document as it has the data for this spreadsheet, the object is said to be embedded. Besides embedding, OLE also links objects to container documents.

Activating, deactivating, and selecting an object

The example program called SdiOle is an OLE container using the single-document interface (SDI) and written with ObjectWindows and ObjectComponents. The source code for SdiOle is in EXAMPLES/OWL/OCF/SDIOLE.

The SdiOle Edit menu contains five standard OLE commands that most containers possess: Paste Special, Paste Link, Insert Object, Links, and Object.

An embedded object is outlined by a thick gray rectangle. The presence of this rectangle indicates that the object is active. The activation rectangle appears when you double-click the object. Usually activating an object initiates an editing session, but the server decides whether to follow that convention. For example, embedded sound objects might play when activated. In most cases, only one object can be active at a time.

When an activation rectangle has small black boxes spaced around it, they are called *grapples*. The user can resize the object by clicking a grapple and dragging the mouse. Also, the user can move the object by clicking anywhere else on the activation rectangle and dragging. ObjectWindows uses the *TUIHandle* class to draw rectangles and grapples around objects.

When the user clicks the mouse button outside the activated object, the activation rectangle goes away. The object is now *inactive*. Figure A.4 shows an inactive object. Deactivating an object tells OLE that you are through editing. The server relinquishes its place, and the container's window returns to normal. The only commands on the menu bar are the ones SdiOle put there. The tool bar and window caption are back to normal, as well.

Figure A.4 The container's restored user interface after the object becomes inactive

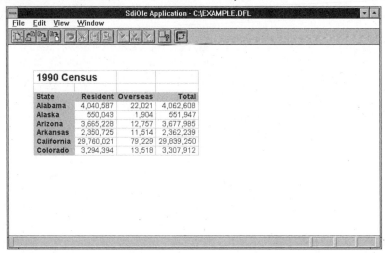

You can *select* an inactive object without activating it. When you press the mouse button over an inactive object, the container draws a thin black rectangle to show that you have selected it. Like the activation rectangle, it has grapples. The user can move and resize a selected object just like an active object.

Finding an object's verbs

The example program called SdiOle is an OLE container using the single-document interface (SDI) and written with ObjectWindows and ObjectComponents. The source code for SdiOle is in EXAMPLES/OWL/OCF/SDIOLE.

The SdiOle Edit menu contains five standard OLE commands that most containers possess: Paste Special, Paste Link, Insert Object, Links, and Object.

When an object is selected, the container modifies its menus to offer a choice of whatever actions the object's server can do with the object. OLE calls these actions verbs. Conventionally, the container displays available verbs in two places: on its Edit menu and on a SpeedMenu. For example, if a SpeedMenu pops up when the user right clicks, the first three commands on the SpeedMenu are always Cut, Copy, and Delete, as shown in Figure A.5. The fourth item, Notebook Object, changes depending on the object selected. When an object from Paradox is inserted, for example, the fourth item becomes Paradox 7 Object.

Figure A.5   The speed menu for a selected object

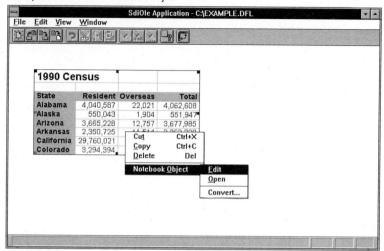

The smaller cascading menu lists the particular verbs that the server supports. Quattro Pro has only two verbs. It can edit an object or open an object. The Edit verb initiates an in-place editing session. The Open verb inititates an open editing session.

The final item, Convert, is the same for all objects. It invokes another standard OLE dialog box that lets the user convert an object from one server's data format to another. The Convert command is useful when, for example, you have Paradox installed on your machine, but someone gives you a compound document with an embedded object from some other database application. If Paradox knows how to convert data from the other database, then the Convert command binds the foreign database object to Paradox.

The speed menu for a selected object shows where verbs appear on the Edit menu. When no object is selected, the last command on the Edit menu is disabled and says simply Object. When an object is selected, the Object command changes to describe the selected object. In the example, Object changes to Notebook Object.

Linking an object

The example program called SdiOle is an OLE container using the single-document interface (SDI) and written with ObjectWindows and ObjectComponents. The source code for SdiOle is in EXAMPLES/OWL/OCF/SDIOLE.

The SdiOle Edit menu contains five standard OLE commands that most containers possess: Paste Special, Paste Link, Insert Object, Links, and Object.

By default, the Insert Object command creates a brand new empty object, and embeds it. Instead of embedding an object, you can choose to link it using the Insert Object dialog box as shown in Figure A.6.

Figure A.6   The Insert Object dialog box just before inserting a linked object

When OLE links an object, it does not store the object's data in the container's document. It stores only the name of the server file where the data is stored along with the location of the data within the file and a snapshot of the object as it appears onscreen. The snapshot is usually a metafile. The container doesn't receive a copy of the object; it receives a pointer to the object. OLE still draws the object in the container's document, just as though it was embedded, but the container doesn't own the data.

If the server document that holds the data for the linked object is deleted, then the user can no longer activate and edit the linked object. On the other hand, if the data in the server document is updated, then the updates appear automatically in all the container documents that have been linked to the same object. If several documents *embed* the same object, then they are creating copies, and changes made in one document have no effect on the copies in other documents.

What if you select the Create from File button in the Insert Object dialog box? Instead of creating a new empty object, you choose a file with existing data and OLE invokes the server that created the file. You can embed data from the file, but if the user has checked the Link box, when the user clicks OK, OLE does not copy data from CHECKS.DB into the server's document. It creates a link that refers back to the data stored in the original file.

The text in the Result box at the bottom of the dialog box explains what will happen when the user clicks OK. The EXAMPLE.DFL document now contains two OLE objects—the embedded Quattro Pro spreadsheet and the linked Paradox table.

Neither of the two objects is active. The spreadsheet is inactive and the database table is selected. Because the database table is linked, ObjectWindows draws the selection rectangle with a dashed line.

Opening an object to edit it

The example program called SdiOle is an OLE container using the single-document interface (SDI) and written with ObjectWindows and ObjectComponents. The source code for SdiOle is in EXAMPLES/OWL/OCF/SDIOLE.

The SdiOle Edit menu contains five standard OLE commands that most containers possess: Paste Special, Paste Link, Insert Object, Links, and Object.

The Edit and Open are the two most common verbs, and Quattro Pro and Paradox, for example, both use them. Choosing the Open verb makes the same table visible in two windows—the container window where it is linked and the server window where it is being edited. When finished editing in the server window, the user chooses File | Close and returns to the container. Any changes made during the editing session automatically appear in the container window afterward.

Figure A.7 An object opened for editing

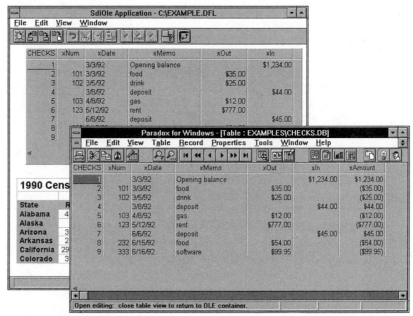

Contrast this editing session with another. In this session, the container window remains unchanged. The SdiOle window has only its own commands and its own tool bar. The editing takes place in a separate window that OLE opened just for this session. Returning to the server to edit is called open editing. Some servers support only open editing, not in-place editing.

These are common linking and embedding operations: the user links or embeds an object, selects it, activates it, edits it in place or open, and saves the compound document complete with its OLE object. The standard way is to link and embed objects with the Insert Object dialog box, but there are other ways as well. The Paste, Paste Special, and Paste Link commands can all create OLE objects from data on the Clipboard. You can also link or embed objects by dragging them from one applicaton and dropping them on another.

Glossary of OLE terms

The definitions in this section explain common terms in OLE programming. Read it for an introduction to important programming topics, or refer to it for clarification as you read other ObjectComponents chapters.

The definitions of advanced concepts assume you already know something about OLE and its standard interfaces. For more information about OLE, refer to the three OLE online Help files.

Activate

The user *activates* a linked or embedded object by double-clicking it. Activating an object causes the server to execute the object's primary verb. For document-style objects, the primary verb is generally initiates an editing session, either in-place or open. For other objects, such as movies and sounds, the primary verb is usually Play. Activating is not the same as selecting; see the entry for *Select*.

Aggregation

A way of combining several OLE objects to make them function as a single bigger object. Objects are aggregated at run time. You can aggregate with objects that you did not design. An object aggregates to delegate commands or to inherit and override the functionality of other objects.

Aggregation is an advanced programming technique. In order for aggregated objects to act as a unit, all the aggregated objects must delegate any *QueryInterface* call they receive to the primary object, usually called the outer object. The outer object begins an aggregation by passing its own *IUnknown* pointer. The second object remembers the outer *IUnknown* pointer and routes all requests for an interface to the outer object. If the outer object does not support a requested interface, it forwards the request to the first in what might be a chain of aggregated objects. A client can reach all the interfaces supported by any of the auxiliary objects through the *IUnknown* of the outer object.

Automated object

An OLE object that publishes commands other applications can send it. An automation server creates automated objects. The automated object can be the application itself or something that the application creates.

Automated application

An OLE object that publishes commands other applications can send it. An automation server creates automated objects. The automated object can be the application itself or something that the application creates.

Automation

The ability of an application to define a set of commands for other applications to invoke.

Automation controller

An application that invokes commands to control automated objects or applications. A controller is sometimes called an *automation client*.

Automation server

An application that exposes some of its own internal function calls as a set of commands that other programs can invoke. An *automation object* is what the server creates for other programs to control.

BOCOLE support library

A DLL of OLE implementation utility interfaces that ObjectComponents calls internally. The support library implements a number of custom OLE interfaces designed by Borland. The BOCOLE.DLL file should be distributed with any ObjectComponents program. Its custom interfaces are considered internal and so are not documented. The source code for the BOCOLE support library, however, is included with Borland C++.

COM object

An object whose architecture conforms to the Component Object Model, a Microsoft specification that forms the basis of the OLE system. Briefly stated, the characteristics of COM objects are

- They communicate through predefined interfaces.

- They all support the *IUnknown* interface, and *IUnknown* includes the *QueryInterface* method for getting other optional interfaces.

- They keep a reference count of their clients and delete themselves if the count reaches zero.

Only COM objects can communicate with OLE. Some of the classes in ObjectComponents are COM objects (see *Connector object*). ObjectComponents shields you from the details of interface methods, interface pointers, and reference counters. It connects you to OLE using familiar C++ and Windows programming models such as inheritance and messages.

Compound document

A document that contains OLE objects brought in from other applications. A compound document might contain pieces of information from a spreadsheet, a database, and a word processor, all in one document that the user loads or saves with a single command. The objects from other applications are either linked or embedded in the container's document.

Compound file

A single disk file that the operating system divides into independent compartments called *storages*. In effect, each storage has its own file I/O pointer so you can read, write, rewrite, and erase data in any one storage without needing to maintain offsets to other storages in the same file. Compound files are useful for storing compound documents because you can create a new storage for each linked or embedded object. OLE extends the file system by implementing interfaces to support compound files.

Connector object

An ObjectComponents class that communicates with OLE for you. Connector objects connect parts of your application to OLE. *TOcApp*, for example, performs OLE functions for the application. *TOcView* performs OLE functions for one view of a document. *TOcPart* performs OLE functions for a linked or embedded object. The connector objects are partners that work together with corresponding parts of your application. You call their methods and they send you messages. Connectors are Component Object Model objects and implement COM interfaces. (Not all ObjectComponents classes are connectors.)

Container

An application that permits OLE to embed or link objects from other applications into its own documents. Containers are also called *clients* of the servers that give them objects.

DLL server

A server whose code is in a dynamic-link library rather than an executable file. The advantage of a DLL server is speed. When OLE invokes an .EXE server to support an embedded object, it has to create a a separate process and marshall data to pass it between the two applications. A DLL, on the other hand, is part of the same system task as its client, so OLE calls from a container to a DLL server run much more quickly.

Document

This word has two different meanings for programmers. First, a document is a set of data that an application loads in response to File I Open. A document can be a spreadsheet, or a bitmap, or a letter, or any other set of data that an application treats as a whole.

Sometimes it is useful to distinguish between the data in a document and the appearance of the data onscreen. A spreadsheet, for example, might be able to display a single set of data as either a table of numbers or a chart. One document can be displayed different ways. In such cases, *document* refers only to the data, and each possible representation of the document is called a *view*.

ObjectWindows programmers are familiar with an application architecture called the *Doc/View model* that separates the code for managing document data from the code for displaying the data. ObjectComponents also has a document class and view classes, but they are not part of the ObjectWindows Doc/View model. The document class keeps track of the objects embedded in a document and the view classes draw the objects onscreen.

Embedded object

Data from a server application deposited by OLE in a container's document. OLE lets the user paste, drag, or insert objects into a container. If during these actions the user chooses to create an *embedded* object, then all the data in the object is copied to the container's document. When the user loads or saves the document, the data for the embedded object is written to the file along with the container's own native data.

Contrast embedded objects with *linked* objects, where the the data for the OLE object is stored in another application and the container receives only a reference to the object's file.

EXE server
A server application compiled and linked into an executable file. A server can also be built as a library; see *DLL server*.

GUID
Globally unique identifier, a 16-byte value. OLE uses GUIDs to identify applications, the objects they produce, and the interfaces that objects implement. For linking and embedding, OLE needs GUIDs to match embedded objects to their servers even after the user transfers a compound document from system to system. If two servers had the same ID, OLE might accidentally invoke the wrong one. Each server and object type must have an absolutely unique ID. Tools such as GUIDGEN create the ID for you. For more information, see the *clsid* entry in the *ObjectWindows Reference*.

IDispatch interface
The OLE interface that all automated objects implement. With the four methods of the *IDispatch* interface, you can ask any automated object for information about its automated commands, look up the identifiers for particular commands, or invoke any command. For more information, see the OLEAUTO.HLP Help file.

In-place editing
Editing an OLE object in the container's window. During in-place editing, the container lets the server display its own menus and tool bars in the container's window. The purpose of in-place editing is to let the user edit any object in a document without leaving the document's window. Contrast Open editing.

In-process server
A server whose code is in a dynamic-link library rather than an executable file. The advantage of a DLL server is speed. When OLE invokes an .EXE server to support an embedded object, it has to create a a separate process and marshall data to pass it between the two applications. A DLL, on the other hand, is part of the same system task as its client, so OLE calls from a container to a DLL server run much more quickly.

Interface
A set of function prototypes, usually declared as an abstract base class. OLE objects are able to communicate with each other because they implement standard interfaces, sets of functions that the system defines. The system defines only what functions an interface contains; it does not implement the functions. Each object implements the functions for itself. The interfaces are defined in the OLE system headers such as compobj.h and ole2.h. The OLE system communicates with applications and objects by calling the functions it assumes each one has implemented. For more about the OLE interface model, see the online help entry for *Component Object Model* (COM). For examples of standard OLE interfaces, see *IDispatch* and *IUnknown*.

Besides the standard interfaces, an object can define and implement its own custom interfaces. Of course the system can't call functions from custom interfaces because it doesn't know they exist, but other applications that know about the custom interface can use it. Internally, ObjectComponents works through a set of Borland custom interfaces. See the online Help entry for BOCOLE support library.

ObjectComponents shields you from having to understand or implement particular interfaces. Advanced users who want to manipulate interfaces directly or mix in their own custom interfaces are free to do so.

IUnknown interface

The root interface that all OLE objects and interfaces must implement. With the three methods of the *IUnknown* interface, you can ask any object for a pointer to another interface it might also support, and you can adjust the object's reference count. For more information, see the Help file, OLE.HLP.

Linked object

An object that appears in a container document but whose data really resides in another file. When dragging or pasting an object into a container, the user can choose to create a *link* to the object instead of embedding it. The container does not receive or store the linked object's data in its own document. Instead, it receives only a string identifying the location of the actual data, which can be in a file.

Several containers can link to the same object. In that case, all the containers receive the same string pointing to the same object. If the data in the original object changes, then the changes are reflected automatically in all the documents that link to it. If the user *embeds* one object in several containers, then each container has its own copy of the object's data and changes in one copy do not affect the other copies.

Link source

The document that a link refers to, the source for the data in a linked object. Usually the link source is a server document, but it is not uncommon for containers to export link source data so that other applications can link to objects embedded or linked in the container's document. For information on becoming a link source.

Localization

Adapting an application to display strings in the user's language, whatever that might be. OLE servers need to speak the language of their client programs. If an automation server is marketed in several countries, it needs to recognize commands sent in each different language. A linking and embedding server registers strings that describe its objects to the user, and those too should be available in multiple languages in order to accommodate whatever language the user might request. ObjectComponents lets you place translations for all your strings in your resource file as XLAT resources. ObjectComponents chooses the right string at the right time.

ObjectComponents framework

A set of C++ classes from Borland International that encapsulate linking and embedding functions as well as automation functions. Internally the ObjectComponents classes implement standard and custom OLE interfaces. With ObjectComponents you write for

OLE using familiar programming models such as inheritance and window messages instead of implementing COM interfaces.

ObjectWindows library

A set of C++ classes from Borland International that encapsulate standard Windows programming functions such as managing windows and dialog boxes. The current version of ObjectWindows introduces some new classes, such as *TOleWindow* and *TOleView*, that use ObjectComponents classes to acquire OLE capabilities. The new classes make it very easy to add OLE support to existing ObjectWindows applications.

OLE

Object linking and embedding, an extension to the Windows system. (In newer versions of Windows, OLE is an integral part of the system, not an extension.) the new commands that OLE implements and the interfaces it defines add many new features to the system, including linking and embedding, automation, and compound file I/O.

OLE interface

A set of function prototypes, usually declared as an abstract base class. OLE objects are able to communicate with each other because they implement standard interfaces, sets of functions that the system defines. The system defines only what functions an interface contains; it does not implement the functions. Each object implements the functions for itself. The interfaces are defined in the OLE system headers such as compobj.h and ole2.h. The OLE system communicates with applications and objects by calling the functions it assumes each one has implemented. For more about the OLE interface model, see the entry for *Component Object Model* (COM). For examples of standard OLE interfaces, see *IDispatch* and *IUnknown*.

Besides the standard interfaces, an object can define and implement its own custom interfaces. Of course the system can't call functions from custom interfaces because it doesn't know they exist, but other applications that know about the custom interface can use it. Internally, ObjectComponents works through a set of Borland custom interfaces. See the online help entry for BOCOLE support library.

ObjectComponents shields you from having to understand or implement particular interfaces. Advanced users who want to manipulate interfaces directly or mix in their own custom interfaces are free to do so.

Open editing

Editing an OLE object in the server's own window. Open editing happens when the user executes the Open verb. During open editing, the server's window opens up in front of the container's window. When the user finishes editing the object, the server window disappears and the modifications become visible back in the container window. Contrast In-place editing.

Part

An object linked or embedded in a compound document. An ObjectComponents container creates an object of class*TOcPart* to represent each object linked or embedded in its document.

Part is the container's word for an object created by a server. In the server's code, the same object is created as a normal server document. ObjectComponents presents the document to OLE as an OLE object. The container, when it receives the OLE object, creates a *TOcPart*. When the part needs to be painted, the part object communicates through OLE with the server's view object.

Reference counting

A way of remembering how many clients an object has. Every section of code that requires the object to exist calls the object's *AddRef* method to increment the reference count. When the client code is done, it calls the object's *Release* method to decrement the reference count. If a *Release* call causes the count to reach 0, then the object is allowed to destroy itself.

Every OLE object has *AddRef* and *Release* methods because they are part of the *IUnknown* interface. Knowing who is a client and when to call *AddRef* or *Release* is sometimes complicated. ObjectComponents manages reference counting for you. Only advanced users will find any need to call *AddRef* or *Release* directly.

Registrar object

An object of type *TRegistrar* or*TOcRegistrar*. Every ObjectComponents application needs a registrar object. The registrar processes the application's command line, sets running mode flags, verifies the application's entries in the system registration database, and calls the application's factory function to launch the application.

Registration: giving information about the application to the system. OLE programs perform two different kinds of registration. When an application is first installed, ObjectComponents writes information from the application's registration tables into the system registration database. This information is static and needs to be recorded only once. The registrar object performs this task.

Subsequently whenever the user launches the application, ObjectComponents tells OLE that the application is running and it registers a factory for each type of document the application can produce. When the application ends, ObjectComponents unregisters the factories. The *TOcApp* or *TRegistrar* object performs this task.

Registration database

A structured repository of information about applications installed on a particular computer. In 16-bit Windows, the database is kept in the REG.DAT file. In 32-bit Windows, the database is called the *system registry* and resides in private system files. Applications record their information during installation. The information includes identifiers for the application and its documents, descriptions of the application and its documents, the path to the application file, the default extension of the application's document files, and other details that help the OLE system associate servers with their objects.

Registration table

A table built with registration macros and containing information about an application or about the types of documents an application creates. The macros create a structure of type *TRegList*. The registrar object reads the registration structure and copies any necessary information to the system registration database.

Remote view

The view of its own object a server draws in a container's window. When an ObjectComponents server is launched to manage an object linked or embedded in a container's document, the server creates a *TOcRemView* object and a *TOcDocument* object. The view object draws in the container's window. The document object loads and saves the object's data.

Select

The user *selects* an object by clicking it once. The selected object does not become active and cannot be edited. Conventionally a container indicates that an object is selected by drawing a rectangle with grapples around the object. (*Grapples* are small handles for moving the rectangle.) the container might permit the user to select several objects at once to move or delete as a group, but usually only one object per child window can be active at a time.

Server

An application that creates objects for other applications to use. In this documentation, *server* usually refers to either a linking and embedding server or an automation server. A linking and embedding server creates data objects that containers can paste, drop, or insert into their own compound documents. An automation server creates objects that other applications can manipulate by sending commands for the object to execute. (A single application can choose to create both kinds of objects. It is even possible to link and embed automated objects.)

System registration database

A structured repository of information about applications installed on a particular computer. In 16-bit Windows, the database is kept in the REG.DAT file. In 32-bit Windows, the database is called the *system registry* and resides in private system files. Applications record their information during installation. The information includes identifiers for the application and its documents, descriptions of the application and its documents, the path to the application file, the default extension of the application's document files, and other details that help the OLE system associate servers with their objects.

Type library

A file describing the commands an automation controller supports. Creating a type library is the standard way for an automation server to publish the programming interface it implements. The type library tells what objects the server creates and describes the objects' properties and methods. Type information is read by compilers and interpreters that process automation commands. Some applications also allow the user to browse the type information.

Any ObjectComponents automation server generates a type library if you invoke it with the **-TypeLib** command line switch. Type libraries conventionally use the .TLB or.OLB extension. An automation server registers the location of its type library during installation.

Verb

A command that a linking and embedding server can execute with its objects. The server tells the container what verbs it supports and the container displays the verb strings on its own Edit menu. To execute a verb, the user selects an object and then chooses a verb from the menu. The container updates the verb menu each time the user selects a new object.

The server can support any verbs it chooses. Most servers support the Edit and Open verbs for in-place or open editing. Depending on the kind of data it owns, a server might choose to offer other verbs such as Play and Rewind.

View

The graphical representation of data. The term is used to distinguish between the way the data is painted and the data itself, usually called the *document*. A single word processor document, for example, might have three different views: a page layout view, a draft view without fancy fonts, and a print preview view.

In ObjectComponents, containers create views to draw their compound documents. Servers also create views to draw the objects they create. Both create a *TOcDocument* object to manage the data and a view object, either *TOcView* or *TOcRemView*, to draw the document.

In ObjectWindows, *Doc/View* refers to a particular application architecture supported by the framework that also treats data and its representation in separate classes.

Index

Symbols

Numerics

A

C

C comments 6
C language 210-211
C++
  comments 7
  defined 105
  scope 158
CalcFields mode (datasets)
  625, 636
calculated fields 625
  assigning values 635–636
  defining 653
  ordering 713
Calculated property 653
CALLBACK 196
callback functions 326-327
calling
  constructors 144
  destructors 148
  methods (Visual Database
    Tools) 611
Cancel method 631
canceling current operation 631,
  665, 669
CancelRange method 640
CanModify property 630,
  643, 681
Caption property (check
  boxes) 675
carriage returns, opening
  files 342
case
  conversions 711
  sensitivity 642
C-based structured excep-
  tions 180
ChangedTableName
  property 660
changing
  data 630–634, 665
    abandoning changes 631,
      665, 669
    committing changes 693-695
    rolling back changes 694
  datasets 646
  events 653-654
  property values 653–654
  tables 715
char (constant type) 15
character acccess strings 520
character constants 14

character sets 658
characters
  fills, setting 339-340
  null, inserting in strings 339
  padding 340
  screen cells 301
check boxes 675, 720
  enhancements 721
checking for null values 641
circles 306
Class (C++) scope 27
classes 128
  abstract classes 157
  access specifiers 128
  base classes 128
    virtual classes 138
  base-lists 128
  complex 513
  container classes 391
  DLLs
    importing and exporting 205
  friends 139
  hiding 159
  inheritance hierarchy 505
  initializing
    constructors 145
  member access operators,
    overloading 155
  member lists 130
  member-lists 128
  nested classes 135
  objects 129-130
  polymorphic classes 155
  proxy collection classes,
    declaring 591
  simulations 458
  templates 164
_clear87 function, floating point
  exceptions 258
Clear method 680
clearing
  data buffers 669
  screens 306
client platforms 615
client/server applications
  611-612
  deploying 700
  developing 687–689
  handling security 690–691
  transaction controls 693–696
client-based SQL 709
Clipboard 670-671
  EasyWin support 253

clipping 308
Close method
  datasets 627
  queries 680, 683
clreol manipulator 344
code 656
  hooks 567
  optimizing 628
  segment 266
collation sequence 700
collection class
  adding members 575
  iterators, implementing 573
collection property,
  declaring 593
  Object Components,
    exposing 571
colon (:; SQL statements) 22,
  679, 710
Color/Graphics Adapter (CGA)
  color palettes 310-311
  resolution 310
    high 311
columns
  combo boxes and multiple 673
  outlining 668
COM (Component Object
  Model) 727 classes (Visual
  Database Tools) 617
.COM files (memory models) 269
combo boxes 672–674
  assigning values 672
  multiple columns 673
  sorting items 673
comma operators (,) 22, 95
command-line compiler options
  code segment 275
  data segment 275
  far objects 275
  floating point
    code generation 256
    fast 256
  overlays 297
commands
  Options menu (Environ-
    ment) 705
  Run menu (Run) 560
  sending collection class 593
  View menu (Module) 561
comments 6
  nested comments 7
Commit method 702
COMMIT statements 693

discrete event-driven simulation 457
dispatch IDs 537
display attributes 653–654
DisplayFormat property 653
displaying data
current values 666
grids 667
run time 656
displaying large images 679
display-only data 654, 666
truncated 666
distributing applications 613–615
distribution rights 613
dlistimp.h 319
DllEntryPoint function
(DLLs) 202
DllRun utility 537
DLLRUN.EXE utility (DLL
servers) 561
DLL (Dynamic Link Libraries)
185, 201-202, 206
16-bit memory models 204
classes, importing and
exporting 205
creating 201
DllEntryPoint function 202
dynamic linking 202
functions
exporting 204
importing 204
LibMain function 202
servers 738
advantages 559
creating 558
debugging 560
disadvantages 559
DLLRUN.EXE utility 561
REGISTER.EXE utility 561
registering 537
tools 561
static data (16 bit) 206
static-link libraries 201
WEP (Windows Exit
Procedure) 203
DocString macros 569
document lists, creating 550
documents 738
painting 555
domains 696
DOS environment (87
variable) 257
dos.h 227

double quote ("; naming
conventions) 709-710
drawing functions 305
DriverName property 693
drivers
configuring 689
language 700-701
ODBC 690, 696
retrieving information 661
DROP INDEX keyword 716
DROP operations 715
DROP TABLE keyword 716
DropConnections method 661
DropDownCount constant 673
_ds keyword 273
DS register 266-267
dsBrowse constant 625
dsCalcFields constant 625
dsEdit constant 625
dsInactive constant 625
dsInsert constant 625
dsSetKey constant 625
duration 28
DX register 264
dynamic
duration objects 29
memory allocations (heaps) 190
SQL statements 682, 690
dynamic_cast operator
(typecasts) 112

E

EasyWin 249
Clipboard support 253
DOS applications, converting to
Windows 249
features 251
Print command 251
scrolling buffers 252
text, saving in output files 252
Windows program 250
edit boxes 666
Edit method 631
Edit mode 669
datasets 625, 631
CanModify property 630
editing
data 631, 653, 666
canceling current opera-
tions 631, 665, 669
grids 668

objects
OLE 730
opening 734
text 670
editors
Database Properties 692
Parameters 682-683, 697
String List 672, 679
ellipsis (...) 23
embedding 727
ObjectComponents 533
objects 738
EmptyTable method 643
emulation (floating-point) 214
EnableControls method 628, 635
Enabled property 645, 665
endl manipulator 339
ends manipulator 339
Enhanced Graphics Adapter
(EGA) 311
entering SQL statements 679-680
run time 680, 683
enumerating 69
automated objects 591
automation servers, exposing
data 575
constants 18
operators, overloading 70
environment (DOS; 87
variable) 257
Environment command
(Options menu) 705
EOF property 628
epilogs
compiling 186
exporting functions 189
equal sign (=) 23
equality operators 92
errno.h 230
errors 660
compilers 198
floating point, disabling 258
graphics, functions for
handling 312
logic errors 505
math, masking 258
out of memory 263
runtime errors 505
_es keyword 273
ES register 266
Esc key 665
escape sequences (constants) 16

huge memory model 267
  manipulating 267
  memory addresses 277
  memory models 267, 274
  modifiers 273
  near
    declaring 267–277
    function prototypes 277
    memory model size 276
    registers 267
  near memory model 267
  normalized 268
  objects 323-324
  overlays 298
  pointer constants 54
  pointer declarations 53
  segment 273-274
  stack 265
  storing 458
  streams 336, 338
  templates, eliminating 166
polymorphic classes 155
  virtual functions 155
porting data 687–689
positive offsets 265
Post method 630-631
  Edit method 631
  OnCalcFields event 636
postfix expressions 79-83
posting records 630-631, 666
  automatically 669
  data grids 668
pound sign (#) 23
#pragma directives 213, 275
precedence (overloaded
  operators) 337
precompiled header files 220-221
  limitations 221
  optimizing 222
  rules 221
predefined values 671
predicates 386
prefix expressions (opcodes;
  inline assembly) 215
Prepare method 678, 683, 697
primary expressions 78
primary indexes 642, 716
Print command (EasyWin) 251
printing data 330
Prior method 627
priority queues 455-456, 461
  containers, initializing 456
  event-driven simulations 457

ice cream store example
  program 459
private access specifiers 136
PrivateDir property 661
ProblemTableName
  property 660
procedures (stored) 607, 624,
  696–698
  executing 697
  overloading 698
process.h 237
producer (streams) 335
profilers 298
programming components 609
programs
  large, overlaying 293
  Windows, 183
project files 613
  graphics library listed 303
prologs
  compiling 186
  exporting functions 189
properties 653
  accessing 656
  automation servers, declaring
    automatable 565
  changing 653–654
  components 609
  data-aware controls 664
  macros, declaring external 568
  run time (Visual Database
    Tools) 611
  Visual Database Tools
    design time 610
    run time 611
    setting 610
protected access specifiers 136
protocol (communications)
  688-689
prototypes
  far and near pointers 277
  functions 58
  mixing modules 277
proxy
  classes
    declaring 586
    generating 537
    implementing 587
  collection classes
    declaring 591
    implementing 592
  methods (arguments,
    specifying) 589
  objects, creating 590

public access specifiers 136
punctuators 21
  asterisks (*) 23
  braces ({ }) 22
  brackets ([ ]) 21
  colons (:) 22
  commas (,) 22
  ellipsis (…) 23
  equal sign (=) 23
  parentheses 21
  pound signs (#) 23
  semicolons (;) 22
push buttons 721
  dialog boxes 725
  enhancements 721
put to operator (<<; stream
  outputs) 337

Q

queries (multi-table) 685, 712
  heterogeneous joins 713
Query component 677, 679
QueryInterface, IUnknown 532
question mark (?) SQL
  statements 710
queues
  adaptors 447
  containers, initializing 456
  data abstraction 450
  FIFO structure 447
queues.h 319
quotation mark ("; naming
  conventions) 709-710

R

radio buttons 676, 721
  enhancements 721
radix sort algorithm 421
Raised Gray Groups 721
RAM (Random Access
  Memory) 263
random access iterators 379
ranges
  containers 373
  iterators 374
RDS.IEM 701
Read function (streams;
  compatibility) 354
ReadBaseObject member
  function 350
read-only controls 666, 670
  graphics 671

X-Y-Z